BEGINNING
OBJECT-ORIENTED PROGRAMMING WITH C#

Continues

BEGINNING

Object-Oriented Programming with C#

BEGINNING

Object-Oriented Programming with C#

Jack Purdum

John Wiley & Sons, Inc.

Beginning Object-Oriented Programming with C#

Published by
John Wiley & Sons, Inc.
10475 Crosspoint Boulevard
Indianapolis, IN 46256
www.wiley.com

ISBN: 978-1-118-33692-2
ISBN: 978-1-118-38794-8 (ebk)
ISBN: 978-1-118-41647-1 (ebk)
ISBN: 978-1-118-54075-6 (ebk)

Manufactured in the United States of America

10 9 8 7 6 5 4 3 2 1

For general information on our other products and services please contact our Customer Care Department within the United States at (877) 762-2974, outside the United States at (317) 572-3993 or fax (317) 572-4002.

Wiley publishes in a variety of print and electronic formats and by print-on-demand. Some material included with standard print versions of this book may not be included in e-books or in print-on-demand. If this book refers to media such as a CD or DVD that is not included in the version you purchased, you may download this material at http://booksupport.wiley.com. For more information about Wiley products, visit www.wiley.com.

Library of Congress Control Number: 2012948651

To Jane

ABOUT THE AUTHOR

 **DR. JACK PURDUM** started his programming career on an IBM 360 mainframe as a graduate student in the 1960s. In the mid-1970s, he became interested in software development for microcomputers, and he founded his own software development company (Ecosoft, Inc.) in 1977. The company's main product was a statistics package (Microstat) that he wanted to rewrite in a new language called C. Lacking a suitable C compiler, Dr. Purdum's company developed its own MS-DOS-based C compiler and other programming tools. He has been involved with language instruction ever since. Dr. Purdum has authored 17 texts and numerous programming articles and has received several teaching awards. He retired from Purdue University's College of Technology and is currently involved with on-site training and embedded systems programming.

CREDITS

Executive Editor
Robert Elliott

Project Editor
Tom Dinse

Technical Editor
Rod Stephens

Production Editor
Rebecca Anderson

Copy Editor
Apostrophe Editing Services

Editorial Manager
Mary Beth Wakefield

Freelancer Editorial Manager
Rosemarie Graham

Associate Director of Marketing
David Mayhew

Marketing Manager
Ashley Zurcher

Business Manager
Amy Knies

Production Manager
Tim Tate

Vice President and Executive Group Publisher
Richard Swadley

Vice President and Executive Publisher
Neil Edde

Associate Publisher
Jim Minatel

Project Coordinator, Cover
Katie Crocker

Proofreader
Sarah Kaikini, Word One

Indexer
Johnna VanHoose

Cover Designer
LeAndra Young

Cover Image
© Vladislav Lebedinski / iStockPhoto

ACKNOWLEDGMENTS

NO BOOK IS WRITTEN without massive effort by others. Tom Dinse and the editorial staff at Wrox have all made this a better book.

A large group of people also contributed to this book in a variety of different ways, providing everything from encouragement to ideas for examples. First, thanks to my students who served as guinea pigs for virtually everything used in this text. Others who contributed include Jerry and Barb Forro, Bill Gromer, Joe Kack, Katie Mohr, John Purdum, and John Strack. A special vote of appreciation to Jane Holcer for her unwavering support and encouragement throughout the process of writing this book.

CONTENTS

INTRODUCTION

OVER THE PAST 30 YEARS I'VE WRITTEN 18 BOOKS on various programming topics. You might wonder, why so many...? Didn't I get it right the first time? Well, no, I didn't...not really. When I wrote my first book more than 30 years ago, object-oriented programming (OOP) was obscure at best and unknown to most. Like so many others, I had to go through the OOP learning process before I could appreciate what OOP was all about. I have a feeling that there are a lot of people out there who still feel that way.

Each time I teach a programming class, I learn new and better ways to explain things. When I look out across a classroom filled with students and it looks like a still-life painting, it's time to back off, retool, and try a different approach to whatever concept it is I'm trying to teach. Every class I've taught has offered new perspectives on how I teach and how students learn. I've had the opportunity to teach both in a university setting and on site at various companies both here and in Europe. Each experience presented different teaching challenges. Changing my examples and the techniques I use to teach programming concepts is one of the reasons I came back to teaching after so many years away.... I missed the learning experience.

A number of the books I wrote were concerned with languages other than C#, but that too provides for an enriching experience for me as an instructor. The strengths and weaknesses of a language can be appreciated only if you've grappled with some other less-than-perfect languages. The fact that programming languages continue to evolve supports the conclusion that I'm not the only one who is still learning. After all this time, the one thing that I have learned with absolute certainty is that whatever I know today will likely be out of date tomorrow.

Perhaps the question you should ask yourself is, "Why should I buy this book instead of someone else's book?" A number of factors come into play, but only one actually makes a difference: This book provides the techniques, examples, and approach to teaching the various programming concepts I've honed through working with literally thousands of students. I've learned what works and what doesn't. So many authors today are, no doubt, brilliant coders, but they haven't had to stumble through the bad examples and teaching methods that simply don't work. Writing good code does not necessarily equate to writing good books.

I think you will find this book informative, clear in its examples, and perhaps even entertaining in its narrative. I hope you'll give it a chance.... I think you'll enjoy the book. Even more important, however, is that you will come to appreciate all that object-oriented programming and C# can do for you.

WHO THIS BOOK IS FOR

The book assumes no prior programming experience. That does not mean, however, that the book is "dumbed down" in any way. I build slowly, placing you on solid ground before the next topic is introduced. I encourage you to write your own programs and do the exercises at the end of each chapter. If you try to take shortcuts, you're actually shortchanging yourself. You should type in every line of code in this book and experiment with it. Do so and you will pick up the language twice as fast and with greater understanding than if you don't do the examples. (You can download the code from the Wrox website. Details are provided later.) You can learn programming only by writing programs and I encourage you to do so at every possible opportunity.

If you have some programming experience, that's fine, too. This book will likely be an easy read for you. However, you will learn some things along the way. If you have never programmed before... perfect! You don't have the bad programming baggage so many bring to the experience when they learn a new language.

This is the perfect book for someone who knows a programming language but learned that language before object-oriented programming techniques came into existence. There are a lot of "old-timers" like myself who would like to retrain themselves in OOP techniques and gain a full appreciation of what OOP brings to the table. This book suits that need perfectly.

Unlike other books, I don't recommend skipping chapters if you already know a programming language or have some other prior programming experience. If you're familiar with symbol tables, lvalues, and rvalues, and the Bucket Analogy, good—but it won't hurt you to read about them again from a different perspective. No shortcuts, remember.

WHAT THIS BOOK COVERS

This text begins with a nonprogramming-language introduction to object-oriented programming. The goal of that chapter is to present the concept of objects first and then ease into how objects may be viewed in C#. Virtually all of the *concepts* presented in this book are portable to other languages. The program design skills, coding style and techniques, and debugging methods are applicable to almost any programming language. C# and Visual Studio are simply the vehicle for teaching these skills.

Throughout the book common, easily understood examples introduce new programming concepts. Most of the C# programming language is covered; although, there are a few less-common topics not covered. These omissions aren't important to the task at hand, which is to teach you OOP using C#. When you have completed this book, you should feel comfortable designing, writing, testing, and debugging complex OOP programs of your own design.

HOW THIS BOOK IS STRUCTURED

The sequencing of the chapters was dictated by what I use when I taught this class to freshmen students. The chapter count is no accident and is geared to a college programming course of one semester in length. If you use the book as a self-study guide, great, but don't feel that you need to speed through the book. Understand each chapter before moving onto the next. Take the time to let things "sink in."

The sequence makes logical sense, and each chapter builds upon the information contained in the previous chapters. Although you could skip around, this would detract from the learning experience. I have my own way to explain things and some are unusual...but they work.

Each chapter has several questions and exercises at the end of it. You are encouraged to work through those examples before you progress to the next chapter. As said previously, you can learn programming only by writing programs. It's easy to get lulled into a false sense of security by reading code and saying, "Yeah, I got that." Perhaps...perhaps not. Writing your own programs is the *only* way to know for sure.

WHAT YOU NEED TO USE THIS BOOK

All the examples in this book were written using Visual Studio 2012 and C#. As I write this material, C# Express is available only for Windows 8. However, Visual Studio Professional is available for other versions of Windows. Although Visual Studio Professional has a limited trial period, that time slice is more than long enough to work through this book. By the time you finish this book, you will likely want to purchase Visual Studio, anyway.

Instructions in Chapter 1, "Introducing C#," tell you how to download and install Visual Studio Professional and C# from Microsoft at no charge. If you use Windows 8, you may want to download the Express version of Visual Studio. It is an incredible piece of software and has most of the functionality of the full Visual Studio. There are some nice tools missing from the Express edition, but there is enough there for you to experience most of what Visual Studio and C# have to offer.

You should use a Pentium-based system (although emulators also exist for the Mac and Linux, and they appear to work well) with at least 4G of memory and 11G of disk space. As mentioned, the version of Windows you use may affect which flavor of Visual Studio you want to download. The examples in this book work with either the Professional or Express versions of C#. After those requirements, the system you use is a matter of taste.

The source code for the samples is available for download from the Wrox website at:

    www.wrox.com/remtitle.cgi?isbn=1118336925

CONVENTIONS

To help you get the most from the text and keep track of what's happening, this book uses a number of style conventions throughout the book. What follows is a list of the book's style conventions. (You will also see a number of programming conventions, which are introduced as needed throughout the text.)

TRY IT OUT

The Try it Out is an exercise you should work through, following the text in the book.

1. They usually consist of a set of steps.

2. Each step has a number.

3. Follow the steps through with your copy of the code.

How it Works

After each *Try It Out*, the code you've typed will be explained in detail.

> **NOTE** *Notes, tips, hints, tricks, and asides to the current discussion are offset and placed in italics like this.*

As for styles in the text:

➤ We *italicize* new terms and important words when we introduce them.

➤ We show keyboard strokes like this: Ctrl+A.

➤ We show filenames, URLs, and code within the text like so: persistence.properties.

Code snippets and listings are presented in this way:

```
We use a monofont type with no highlighting for most code examples.
Code snippets and listings are almost always more than one line long.
```

SOURCE CODE

As you work through the examples in this book, you may choose either to type in all the code manually or to use the source code files that accompany the book. All the source code used in this book is available for download at www.wrox.com.

You can also search for the book at www.wrox.com by ISBN (the ISBN for this book is 978-1-118-33692-2 to find the code. And a complete list of code downloads for all current Wrox books is available at www.wrox.com/dynamic/books/download.aspx.

At the beginning of each chapter, we've provided the folder name for the code in the chapter. Throughout each chapter, you can also find references to the names of the individual code files as needed in listing titles and text.

Most of the code on www.wrox.com is compressed in .ZIP, .RAR, or a similar archive format appropriate to the platform. After you download the code, just decompress it with an appropriate compression tool.

ERRATA

We make every effort to ensure that there are no errors in the text or in the code. However, no one is perfect, and mistakes do occur. If you find an error in one of our books, like a spelling mistake or faulty piece of code, we would be grateful for your feedback. By sending in errata you may save another reader hours of frustration, and at the same time you can help us provide even higher-quality information.

To find the errata page for this book, go to:

```
www.wrox.com/remtitle.cgi?isbn=1118336925
```

and click the Errata link. On this page you can view all errata that has been submitted for this book and posted by Wrox editors.

If you don't spot "your" error on the Book Errata page, go to www.wrox.com/contact/ techsupport.shtml and complete the form there to send us the error you have found. We'll check the information and, if appropriate, post a message to the book's errata page and fix the problem in subsequent editions of the book.

P2P.WROX.COM

For author and peer discussion, join the P2P forums at http://p2p.wrox.com. The forums are a web-based system for you to post messages relating to Wrox books and related technologies and to interact with other readers and technology users. The forums offer a subscription feature to e-mail you topics of interest of your choosing when new posts are made to the forums. Wrox authors, editors, other industry experts, and your fellow readers are present on these forums. I try to check the forum on a regular basis, visiting at least several times each week.

At http://p2p.wrox.com you can find a number of different forums that to help you not only as you read this book, but also as you develop your own applications. To join the forums, just follow these steps:

1. Go to http://p2p.wrox.com and click the Register link.
2. Read the terms of use and click Agree.
3. Complete the required information to join, as well as any optional information you want to provide, and click Submit.

4. You will receive an e-mail with information describing how to verify your account and complete the joining process.

> **WARNING** You can read messages in the forums without joining P2P, but to post your own messages, you must join. After you join, you can post new messages and respond to messages other users post. You can read messages at any time on the web. If you want to have new messages from a particular forum e-mailed to you, click the Subscribe to This Forum icon by the forum name in the forum listing.

For more information about how to use the Wrox P2P forum, be sure to read the P2P FAQs for answers to questions about how the forum software works as well as many common questions specific to P2P and Wrox books. To read the FAQs, click the FAQ link on any P2P page.

BEGINNING

Object-Oriented Programming with C#

PART I
Getting Started

1

Introducing C#

WHAT YOU WILL LEARN IN THIS CHAPTER:

➤ How to download Visual Studio

➤ How to install Visual Studio Professional

➤ How to create a simple project

➤ How to develop a small program in Visual Studio

➤ Some features found in the Visual Studio IDE

➤ Running a Visual Studio program

Welcome to the world of object-oriented programming and C#! The primary goal of this book is to use the C# programming language from Microsoft to teach you object-oriented programming, or OOP. This book assumes that you have no prior programming experience in any language and that you know nothing about OOP. As such, this book must be viewed as a "beginning" text.

If you do have programming experience and some familiarity with OOP, that's fine. Having that experience makes things easier for you. However, I still encourage you to read the book from start to finish for a number of reasons. First, this book represents the distillation of 25 years of programming and teaching experience. I have a good idea of what works and what doesn't work to explaining complex topics so that they're easy to understand. Reading each chapter gives you the tools to understand the next chapter. Second, I may introduce topics in one chapter and then rely heavily on those topics in a much later chapter. In other words, the process used to learn OOP and C# is one that introduces new topics based upon ones that were introduced earlier. Obviously, you must master the earlier content before tackling the later content. Finally, the programming examples I use also build on concepts presented in earlier program examples. It will be easier for you to understand the later program examples if you've experimented with those programs introduced earlier in the book.

One more thing: You cannot learn programming by just reading about it. You have to dig in and start programming. For that reason, there are exercises at the end of each chapter designed to help you hone your programming skills. The learning process is even more interesting if you try to create your own programs based upon some real problems you'd like to solve. Don't worry if things don't fall together instantly on the first try. You should plan to make a ton of "flat-forehead" mistakes...you know, the kind of mistake in which, upon discovering it, you pound the heel of your hand into your forehead and say, "How could I make such a stupid mistake!" Not to worry...we've all been there. Such mistakes are just part of the process to become a programmer, and you should expect to make your fair share. However, stick with it, read the book, and you'll be surprised at how fast things can come together. Indeed, I think you'll find programming to be a truly enjoyable pastime.

A SHORT HISTORY OF OBJECT-ORIENTED PROGRAMMING (OOP)

Many people believe that OOP is a product of the 1980s and the work done by Bjarne Stroustrup in moving the C language into the object-oriented world by creating the C++ language. Actually, SIMULA 1 (1962) and Simula 67 (1967) are the two earliest object-oriented languages. The work on the Simula languages was done by Ole-John Dahl and Kristen Nygaard at the Norwegian Computing Center in Oslo, Norway. Although most of the advantages of OOP were available in the earlier Simula languages, it wasn't until C++ became entrenched in the 1990s that OOP began to flourish.

C was the parent language of C++ and it was often said that C was powerful enough to shoot yourself in the foot multiple times. C++, on the other hand, not only was powerful enough to shoot yourself in the foot, but also you could blow your entire leg off without too much difficulty. Most programmers admit that C++ is a powerful language and it is still in widespread use today. However, with that power comes a lot of complexity. Language developers wanted a simpler and perhaps less complex language for OOP development.

The next step in the development of OOP started in January 1991 when James Gosling, Bill Joy, Patrick Naughton, Mike Sheradin, and several others met in Aspen, Colorado, to discuss ideas for the Stealth Project. The group wanted to develop intelligent electronic devices capable of being centrally controlled and programmed from a handheld device. They decided that OOP was the right direction to go with the development language but felt that C++ was not up to the job. The result was the Oak programming language (named after an oak tree outside Gosling's window), which eventually morphed into the Java programming language. (Oak had to be renamed because the team discovered that a language by that name already existed.)

Java quickly grew in popularity, spurred by the growth of the World Wide Web. In both cases this rapid growth was in part because the "guts" necessary to run Java programs on the web quickly became an integral part of various web browsers. With the improved web functionality augmented by Java, the web hit light speed.

To many programmers, C# is Microsoft's answer to Java. Some would even say that C# is the result of Microsoft's stubbornness to refuse to promote a language it did not develop. That sentiment is a bit too harsh. Microsoft had good reasons for developing C#, not the least of which was that it wanted *type-safe programs* that run in a managed environment. You may not appreciate exactly what that means right now, but it will become clear as you learn C#.

C# provides you with a robust object-oriented programming language and an impressive set of tools to tackle almost any programming task. Whether you want to develop desktop, distributed, web, or mobile applications, C# can handle the task.

As you become familiar with C#, you can appreciate its relatively few keywords, its crisp syntax, and its easy-to-use development environment. You'll discover that pieces of programs you write in C# can be reused in other programs. Finally, you might appreciate that there are many job opportunities for programmers who know C#.

INSTALLING C#

If you have already purchased and installed Visual Studio 2012 and C#, you can skip this section. If you haven't installed C#, this section tells you how to download and install the Visual Studio version of Visual Studio. Visual Studio is a modified version of C# that is available from Microsoft at no charge. Although the Express version of C# is missing some features found in the commercial version of Visual Studio, you should compile and run all the sample programs in this book using Visual Studio.

At the present time, the Express version of Visual Studio requires the use of Windows 8. If you do not have Windows 8, you can download a trial version of Visual Studio Professional. By registering the trial version, you can use Visual Studio Professional for a period of 90 days. After you are convinced that you should do all your development work in C# (and you will be), you can purchase the full version of Visual Studio. Of course, if you later purchase Windows 8, you can always download the Express version of Visual Studio.

Due to the newness of Windows 8, you probably are not using Windows 8 and, hence, must use the trial version of Visual Studio Professional. The next section discusses how to download the trial version of Visual Studio Professional.

Downloading Visual Studio Professional

At the time that this book is written, you can go to `http://www.microsoft.com/visualstudio/11/en-us/downloads#professional` to download the Professional version of Visual Studio. The download page should look similar to what is shown in Figure 1-1. As you can see if you look closely at the figure, the download is for the 90-day trial version of Visual Studio Professional. Click the Install Now button to begin the installation process.

FIGURE 1-1: Download page for Visual Studio Professional

Depending upon the speed of your system and Internet connection, it can take more than 1 hour to download and install the 6+ gigabytes of files used during the installation process. You must first agree to the licensing terms, as shown in Figure 1-2.

After you agree to the licensing terms, the program displays a dialog box that tells you the items that are about to be installed. Unless you are constrained by disk space, you should leave all the options checked so that they are all installed. Otherwise, you can uncheck those options that you do not want installed. See Figure 1-3.

Having made your selections, click the Install button to initiate the installation process. Your display will look similar to Figure 1-4...for a *long* time.

FIGURE 1-2: License terms dialog

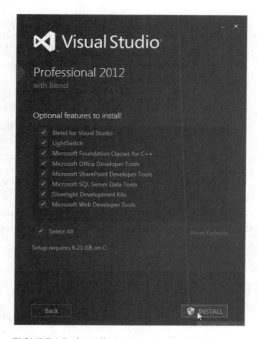

FIGURE 1-3: Installation items checklist

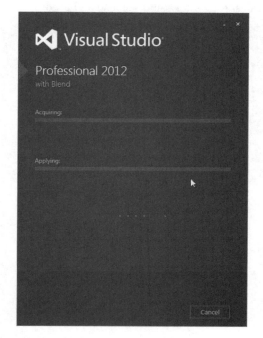

FIGURE 1-4: Installation process

> **NOTE** *While I was working through the installation process, the install software sensed that some of the Windows software on my system was outdated. I was asked if I wanted to install the updates and patches that had come out since I last updated my system. Because the list also included several patches to Visual Studio, I said yes. It took almost 2 hours to download and update my software. However, when the updates were finished, the Visual Studio installer picked up right where it had left off and the installation continued without a hitch. Although it does take some time, you should update your software if the installer offers you that option.*

Eventually, the installation process ends…honest! If you updated your system software as part of the installation process, the installer asks you at some point if you want to restart your computer. Answer yes if you are asked. After the system restarts and the software has been installed, you should see a new icon on your desktop labeled Visual Studio. You should double-click the new icon and launch Visual Studio.

A TEST PROGRAM USING C#

Although things may appear to have been installed properly, you can't be certain until you actually write a program and try to run it. That's the purpose of this section of the chapter. The program is about as simple as you can make a program while remaining confident that the installation was successful.

After you double-click the Visual Studio icon on your desktop, you should see a Visual Studio startup screen similar to the one shown in Figure 1-5.

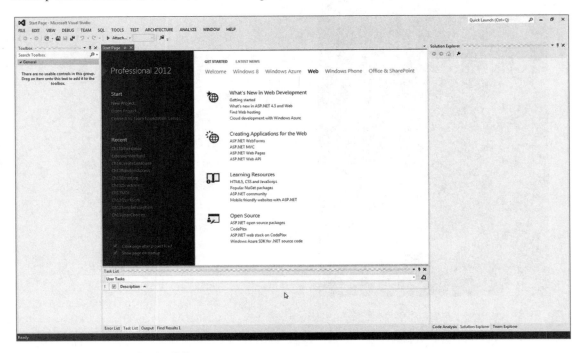

FIGURE 1-5: The Visual Studio IDE

Creating a Project

Move the cursor to the upper-left side of the screen, and select the File ⇨ New ⇨ Project menu option from the main program menu bar, as shown in Figure 1-6.

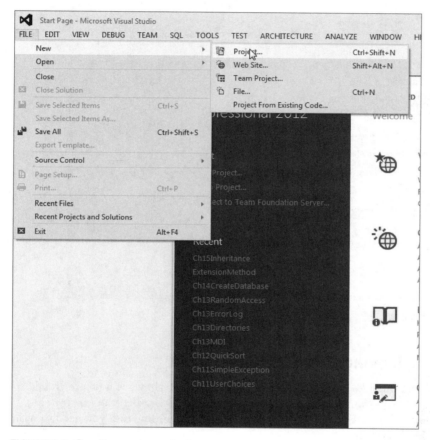

FIGURE 1-6: Creating a new project

Select New Project from the menu. Your program screen changes, as shown in Figure 1-7.

Figure 1-7 shows a number of predefined project templates from which to choose. Make sure you have selected the Templates Visual C# Windows menu option that appears on the left side of the screen. These templates define the types of programs that you can develop with C#. For your purposes, you want to select the Windows Forms Application template.

When you select one of the templates, Visual Studio creates that type of project for you as well as writing some stub code for you. *Stub codes* are predefined pieces of code that Visual Studio writes for you as a background process. From the templates shown in Figure 1-7, select the Windows Forms Application template. You should also type in the name you want the program to have. I have typed in TemplateProgram for the example and designated the project to be placed in the C:\Temp\ directory. You can use the Browse button to select some other directory, or you can check the Create

Directory for solution and let Visual Studio create a directory for you. Click OK after you enter the program name you want to use.

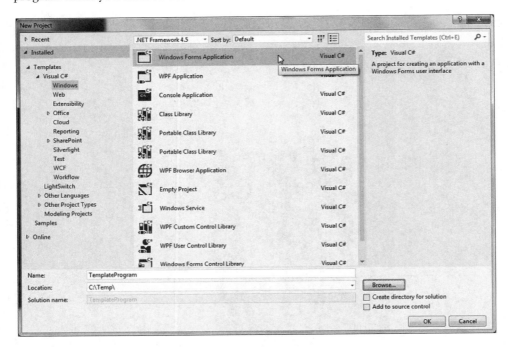

FIGURE 1-7: New Project dialog

The C# Integrated Development Environment

You should now see something like Figure 1-8 on your screen, which shows you where you'll be spending a lot of your programming time as you read this book. It's called the *Integrated Development Environment*, or IDE, because virtually every programming tool you need to write C# programs is available to you there.

Back in the Dark Ages of programming, you had to load and run a programming editor to write the program's source code. Next, you had to close the editor and load the language compiler program to check the program's statements for errors. Then you had to load an assembler program to convert the source code to assembly language. Finally, you had to load and run a linker program to combine all the elements of your program into an executable program. The Visual Studio IDE provides all these functions within a single program. This makes it much easier to write and test the programs you create.

The Major IDE Windows

The IDE shown in Figure 1-8 divides the screen into three *windows*. The left window shows the Visual Studio Toolbox, which, by default, shows some of the objects Visual Studio makes available to you. If you look closely you can see that the Toolbox presents a smorgasbord of objects you can use in your programs, including textboxes, labels, buttons, and other controls you will find useful as you develop your programs.

The middle window is referred to as the Source window and currently shows an unadorned Visual Studio form object. (Microsoft refers to the window as the Forms Designer window.) As presented in Figure 1-8, the form has no other objects placed on it...yet. That is, you haven't added any other objects (such as textboxes or buttons) from the Toolbox onto the form. You change this in the section "Adding a Toolbox Object to a Windows Form" later in this chapter.

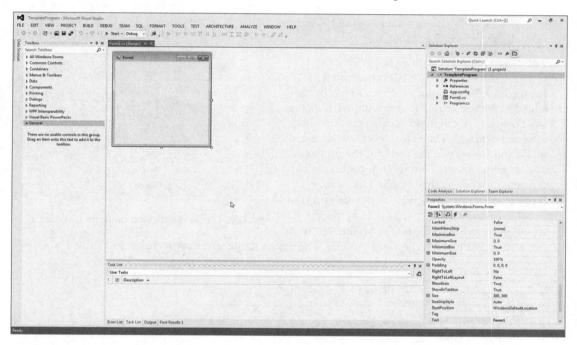

FIGURE 1-8: The Visual Studio IDE

The right side of the IDE currently shows two subwindows. The subwindow on top shows the Solution Explorer. Simply stated, the Solution Explorer shows the current development state of your project. It shows the forms the program has and its references, plus other information that is discussed in later chapters.

Below the Solution Explorer window is the Properties window. The purpose of the Properties window is to show you the properties associated with the object currently in focus in the Source window. If you look closely at the form in the Source window in Figure 1-8, you'll notice that it has a couple of small white boxes along its edge. These are called *sizing boxes* and their purpose is to enable you to alter the size of the objects to which they are attached. However, the sizing boxes also show which object in the Source window currently has the attention, or *focus*, of Visual Studio. Whatever object has the focus in the Source window is also the object that the Properties window displays. In Figure 1-8 the properties shown in the Properties window apply to the form shown in the Source window. Visual Studio always maintains this relationship between the object in focus in the Source window and the information displayed in the Properties window.

Using the Source Code Window

If you right-click `Form1.cs` in the Solution Explorer window, a small menu opens up from which you can select to view the source code for the file you just right-clicked. You can move to the Solution Explorer menu bar and click the source code icon to view the code that Visual Studio has written for you thus far. As you can see in Figure 1-9, you can also use the F7 key to view the source code for the file.

The code associated with right-clicking the filename shown in Figure 1-9 is presented in Figure 1-10. Notice that another tab has been added at the top of the Source window. One tab has Form1.cs [Design] on it, whereas the other tab has Form1.cs. The first tab is the source code mode and shows you the code for the program under development. Even though you haven't written any code, Visual Studio has already written some program code for you behind your back! You can see the `TemplateProgram` C# source code in Figure 1-10. The second tab is for

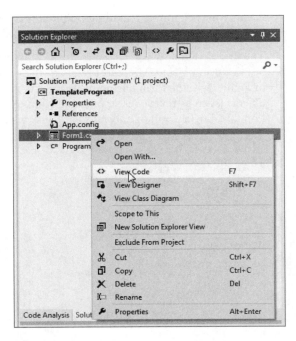

FIGURE 1-9: Right-clicking the form filename

the view of the form in the design mode. (The design mode was shown earlier in Figure 1-8.)

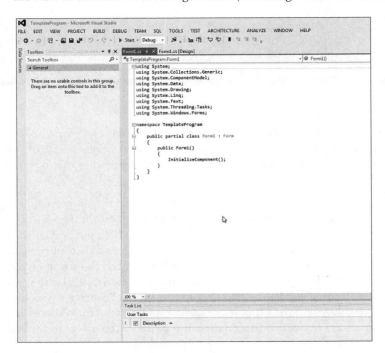

FIGURE 1-10: Source code for file

It's not necessary that you understand the code shown in Figure 1-10 at this time. All you're trying to do at this point is to write a short program to see if the installation was done correctly. However, you will be spending a lot of time in the source code window as you write your own programs.

Adding a Toolbox Object to a Windows Form

A form with nothing on it isn't interesting. Now change the form so that, when the program runs, it displays the message, My First Program. You need to add a label to the form object shown in the Source window in Figure 1-8 to hold your program message. There are two ways to add a label object to a form. First, as shown in Figure 1-11, you can click the label object in the Toolbox, and while holding the left mouse button down, drag the label over to the form and release the mouse button. Second, you can simply double-click the label object in the Toolbox. The mouse double-click causes Visual Studio to place a label object near the upper-left corner of the form shown in the Source window.

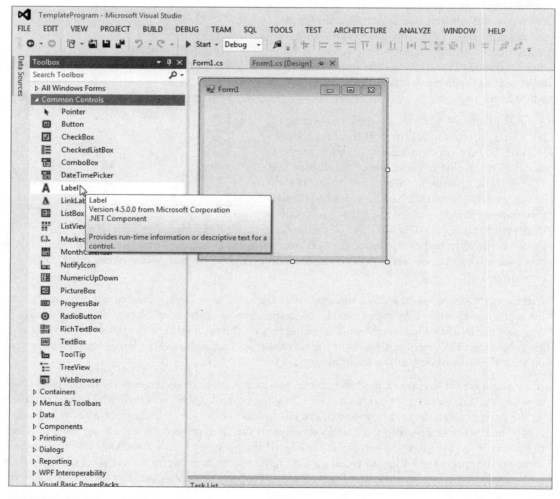

FIGURE 1-11: Adding a label object to a form

You should try both methods to place a label on the form. After you see that both actions do place a label on the form, click one of the labels to move Visual Studio's focus to the label you just clicked. You know this is true because you see the sizing boxes on the label you just clicked. Because you need only one label in this test program, press the Delete key on your keyboard. The label is then removed from the form.

You can click the label in the Source window while holding the left mouse button down and drag the label to wherever you want it to appear on the form object. When you have positioned the label object where you want it on the form, simply release the mouse button.

Changing the Text of a Label Object

After you position the label object on the form, you can set the text for the label. One of the things that Visual Studio does automatically is size the label to be just big enough to accommodate the label's text. Given the default font size used by Visual Studio, the default height for a label is 13 pixels. (A *pixel* is one dot, or point of light, on the screen of your display device.) If you change the font size of the label object, the height of the label is automatically adjusted for you.

Actually, I am not a big fan of automatic sizing of labels. For that reason, I turn off the auto-sizing feature. To turn off auto-sizing, go to the Properties Window on the lower-right side of the display and change the AutoSize property from True, as shown in Figure 1-12, to False. You may need to scroll the Property window to see the AutoSize property displayed in the Properties window. Click the down

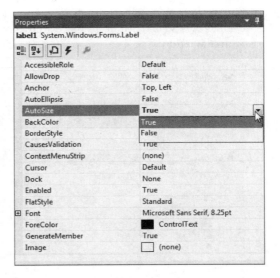

FIGURE 1-12: Changing the AutoSize property

arrow at the right end of the AutoSize textbox to display the choices you have for the property. In this case you can choose only True or False. Select False. The auto-sizing of the label object is now turned off.

After you set AutoSize to False, you can resize the label object in the Source window by clicking the white sizing boxes that appear on the ends and corners of the label object. You can increase the width of the label by clicking the middle sizing box on the right edge of the label object and dragging the edge to the right until you get the wanted size. Then released the left mouse button to end up with the label object, as shown in Figure 1-13.

After you have set the size of the label object, you can change the text property of the label object to whatever you want to appear in the label. In your example, you want the text **My first program**. At the present time, the text property of the label object is label1, which is not what you want. Scroll the contents of the Property window down to the Text property for the label object, change it to My first program, and press the Enter key. (If the property window should ever "disappear" for some reason, press the F4 key to recall it.) Changing the Text property for the label object is shown in Figure 1-14. Notice how the first line below the Property window's title bar shows the name of the object currently in focus in the Source window (label1 in Figure 1-13).

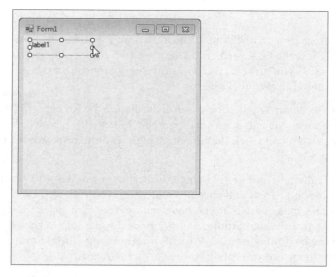

FIGURE 1-13: Resizing the label object

By default, the text of a label object is positioned so that it appears in the upper-left corner of the label. If `AutoSize` is set to `True`, you can't position the text with the label object; it's set for you automatically. However, because you turned off auto-sizing, you can position the text within the label wherever you want. Figure 1-15 shows how to do this using the `TextAlign` property in the Properties window. If you look closely at Figure 1-15, you can see that `TextAlign` is currently set to `TopLeft`. There are nine positions where you can place the text in a label that you can resize. You want to right-justify your text in the center of the label object. If you look where the cursor is positioned in Figure 1-15, clicking that box right-justifies the text in the label object.

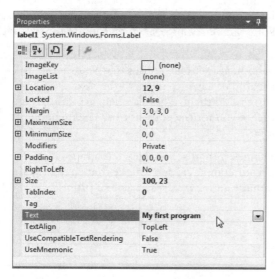

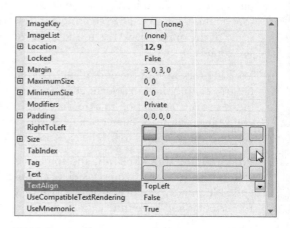

FIGURE 1-15: Changing the TextAlign property for the label object

FIGURE 1-14: Changing the Text property of the label object

Running the Program

This is all that you want to do at the present time to test your C# installation. If you can run the program at this point, you have probably installed C# correctly. There are two simple ways to run a program. The easiest is to press the F5 key. If you do that, the program should appear on the screen in a few moments with your message centered in the label object.

The second way is to click the Run Program icon. If you look carefully at Figure 1-11, below the DEBUG menu option near the top of the form you can see a small triangle followed by the word Start. (On your screen, the triangle appears green.) Click that green triangle and the program begins execution.

If your program does not run correctly and you're not getting an error message from within Visual Studio, go back to the start of the installation process and check to make sure you followed each step correctly. Before you start the reinstall, make sure that you have enough free disk space to hold Visual Studio. If you get an error message from Visual Studio, you performed some step in the coding process incorrectly. Just go back to the beginning of the "A Test Program Using Visual Studio" section of this chapter to check each step to ensure you followed the correct sequence.

SUMMARY

In this chapter you learned how object-oriented programming started more than four decades ago. This chapter also showed you how to download and install Visual Studio's Professional edition. Finally, you wrote a simple program to test the installation to make sure it was done correctly. So, now what?

You could immediately proceed to the next chapter and start reading. Not a good idea. Now that you have a simple program up and running, this is the perfect time to experiment a little. For example, your program doesn't have any text in the program's title bar. Surely C# provides a property that enables you to change the title bar. (Hint: It does provide such a property!) Play around with some of the other properties to see what they do. For example, change the foreground property and see what happens.

Looking forward, at the end of each chapter in this book are set of exercises that you should do before reading the subsequent chapter. You will probably be eager to move to the next chapter, but resist the temptation to skip the exercises—be sure to do them. They can help crystallize what you've learned in the current chapter and better prepare you for the content of the next chapter. You can find the solutions to all the exercises in Appendix A.

Programming should be fun, and some of that fun comes from discovering what happens if you change this to that. If you see smoke coming out of your computer, don't make that change again. (Just kidding...you can't hurt your computer if you make an incorrect change to a property.) Experiment and have fun!

▶ WHAT YOU LEARNED IN THIS CHAPTER

TOPIC	KEY POINTS
Short history of OOP	How OOP actually started with Simula in the 1960s but gained strength in the 1980s with C++, Java, and C#.
Download and install C#	The process of downloading and installing Visual Studio.
A sample program	Although very simple, the program does test your installation of Visual Studio.

2

Understanding Objects

WHAT YOU WILL LEARN IN THIS CHAPTER:

- ➤ What an object is
- ➤ What the term *state* means to objects
- ➤ What a class is
- ➤ What it means to instantiate an object
- ➤ What properties are
- ➤ What methods are
- ➤ How to use objects provided by Visual Studio .NET

WROX.COM CODE DOWNLOADS FOR THIS CHAPTER

You can find the wrox.com code downloads for this chapter at www.wrox.com/remtitle .cgi?isbn=9781118336922 on the Download Code tab. The code in the Chapter02 folder is individually named as shown in this chapter.

The concepts introduced in this chapter lay the ground work for understanding object-oriented programming (OOP). Before you move on to Chapter 3 you should feel comfortable with the concepts introduced here. You should end this chapter feeling that you understand what objects, properties, and methods are and how they are used in an OOP program. If any of these concepts seem fuzzy after your first reading of this material, read the chapter again.

If any topic presented in this book still seems unclear after two or more passes through the chapter, you should log on to the Wrox website for this book and ask a question about the subject that is giving you trouble. If it's unclear to you, chances are it may be unclear to others. Wrox expends a lot of effort to make that web resource available to you, so use it whenever you feel unclear on some issue or topic.

UNDERSTANDING OBJECTS

As you learned in Chapter 1, programming with objects has been around for more than four decades. However, it's only in the last 20 years that object-oriented programming has become the norm rather than the exception. This chapter presents a simple example of how you can use objects in an everyday situation. You then expand on the concepts presented in that example to an actual program you build using Visual Studio .NET and the objects it provides.

Suppose you are the personnel manager for a company and you need to hire someone to fill an important position. After sifting through dozens of résumés, you select one candidate to call to arrange for a face-to-face interview at your company offices. You call her (let's say her name is Jane) on the phone and chat for a few minutes to confirm that she appears to be the right person for the job. You (pretend your name is Jack) make arrangements for Jane to fly to your location, stating that you will meet her at the airport, as shown in Figure 2-1.

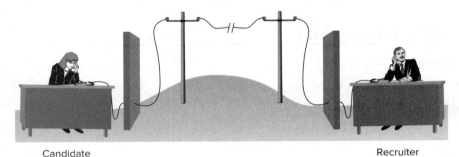

Candidate   Recruiter

FIGURE 2-1: Arranging a job interview

However, because the two of you have never met before, you start asking a few questions so that you can recognize each other at the airport. Jane says she's medium height with blonde hair and that she will be wearing a black business suit and carrying a tan leather briefcase. You then describe yourself as 6 feet tall with sandy hair and say that you'll be wearing a gray suit. You then set a date and time for the flight, and everything's ready for the interview.

Everyday Use of Objects

Perhaps without realizing it, both of you used objects in the course of your conversation. First, without thinking about it, you implicitly created a person class during the phone call. A *class* is a template used to describe an object. As such, a class is an abstraction, or simplification, of some object you observe in the real world. You can break a class down into two basic components:

➤   Properties that describe the object

➤   Methods, or actions, that you want to associate with the object

Class Properties

The *class properties* are the data that you want to associate and record with an object. If you want to create a class person object (referred to as `clsPerson`), a list of properties might include those shown in Table 2-1.

TABLE 2-1: clsPerson Properties

PROPERTIES
name
height
hairColor
eyeColor
build
glasses
clothing
shoes
accessories
gender

Although not a rule, many programmers use variable names for properties that start with a lowercase letter but use uppercase letters at the start of any words contained within the property name. Because you may want to follow this convention, too, the property names in Table 2-1 follow this convention.

Prior to the phone conversation, the list of properties for the clsPerson named Jane is virtually empty. All you could fill in from her résumé were her name and gender. However, after the phone conversation you filled in almost all the properties for the clsPerson object named Jane. (You might scare her away if you tried to fill in the Build and eyeColor properties over the phone or face a lawsuit.)

While you were filling in a clsPerson object named Jane, she was doing the same thing for a clsPerson object named Jack. Prior to the phone call, the clsPerson object Jane created to be associated with the name Jack may have been totally empty because Jane had no idea who might be calling her about a job interview. However, the dialog on the phone enabled each party to fill in at least some of the property values for the other person. From Jane's point of view, her clsPerson object went from a totally nondescript object to (at least) a partially identifiable object after the phone call was completed.

By changing the values of the class properties, you can change the state of the object. The *state of an object* is determined by the values of the properties used to describe the object. In the example, the properties used to describe the state of a clsPerson object are those shown in Table 2-1. Prior to the phone call, there are no meaningful values for the properties shown in Table 2-1.

Although people don't change their names often, it happens occasionally. Likewise, people do gain and lose weight, dye their hair, wear tinted contacts, change clothes, and alter their accessories. If any of these property values change, the state of the object also changes. Just keep in mind that *anytime the value of a property changes, the state of the object—by definition—also changes.*

It should also be obvious that it is the value of the properties that enable someone to distinguish a Jane clsPerson object from a Jack clsPerson object. That is, different objects usually have different values for their properties. It also follows, therefore, that different objects have different states.

Class Methods

Just as there are property values that define the state of an object, there are usually class methods that act on the properties. For a `clsPerson` object, you would want that object to talk, wave her arms, walk, change clothes, and so forth. In short, the *class methods* determine the behaviors or actions the object can perform. Methods are used to describe whatever actions you want to associate with the object. Class methods often are used to manipulate the data contained within the object.

You can depict the phone conversation between Jane and Jack as objects of the person class, as shown in Figure 2-2.

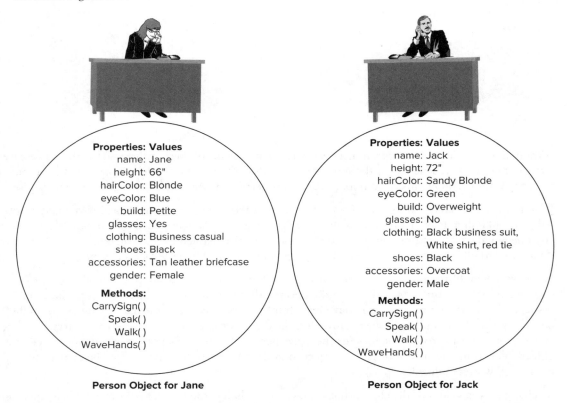

Properties: Values
name: Jane
height: 66"
hairColor: Blonde
eyeColor: Blue
build: Petite
glasses: Yes
clothing: Business casual
shoes: Black
accessories: Tan leather briefcase
gender: Female

Methods:
CarrySign( )
Speak( )
Walk( )
WaveHands( )

Person Object for Jane

Properties: Values
name: Jack
height: 72"
hairColor: Sandy Blonde
eyeColor: Green
build: Overweight
glasses: No
clothing: Black business suit,
White shirt, red tie
shoes: Black
accessories: Overcoat
gender: Male

Methods:
CarrySign( )
Speak( )
Walk( )
WaveHands( )

Person Object for Jack

FIGURE 2-2: Filling in property values during the phone conversation

Often, class methods are used to take one or more property values, process the data those properties contain, and create a new piece of data as a by-product of the method's process. For example, you might develop a business application and need to create an invoice object that has `priceEach` and `quantityOrdered` (among others) as properties of an `clsInvoice` class. You might then create a method named `salesTaxDue()` as a class method that computes the sales tax due for the invoice. You might have another `clsInvoice` property named `salesTax` that is filled in automatically as part of the code contained in the method named `salesTaxDue()`.

If you think about it, a class property may be viewed as a noun: a person, place, or thing used to describe an object. Class methods, on the other hand, often behave like verbs, denoting some kind of action to be taken on the class properties (that is, the data in the class) or an action the object can perform.

How Many Properties, How Many Methods?

One question that you must grapple with as a programmer is how many properties and methods you should have in a class. For example, in the clsPerson object, you could also include a photograph of the person, fingerprints, a retinal scan, blood type, a DNA sample, dental records, shoe size, plus hundreds of other things that may be part and parcel of a person object. Likewise, you can create methods to simulate talking, running, writing, walking, digestion, elimination, sleeping, dreaming, and a bunch of other actions humans can do. So where do you stop? What is the proper number of properties and methods?

Classes Are Simplifications of Objects

Keep in mind that for every property and method you add to a class, you must write program code to implement that property or method. As a general rule, the less code a program has, the fewer things there are to go wrong. From a programmer's perspective, writing less code is a good thing, provided the code accomplishes the task at hand. In other words, when you design a class, you need to strike a balance between minimizing the code you write and fulfilling the design goals for the class.

> **NOTE** *The proper number of properties and methods in a class is the minimal number of properties and methods that gets the job done.*

The number of properties and methods in a person class the FBI needs to find criminals is going to be vastly different from the number of properties and methods in a person class you might create to write an address book to keep track of your friends.

You'll also find that if you omit unnecessary details in a class, there's a greater likelihood that you can reuse that same class code in some other project. The concept of *code reuse* is one of the main advantages of object-oriented programming. The more generic the class is, the easier it is to reuse the class. In a sense, therefore, you might want to define your classes as the minimal abstraction necessary to describe an object in a way that fulfills your needs.

Always keep in mind that if there is a simple way and a complex way to accomplish the same goal, simple is almost always the best choice. Some programmers get a kick out of writing clever code that no one else can understand. That's probably okay, as long as no one else has to work with their code. In a commercial setting, however, clever, obfuscated code is rarely a good thing. Given alternatives, stick with the code that is easily understood.

What Do I Do After I've Defined a Class?

As mentioned earlier, a class is a template for an object. In that sense, a class is like a cookie cutter that enables you to shape specific cookie objects. By this release of Visual Studio, Microsoft has buried within the .NET Framework approximately 4,000 available classes. This means you have approximately 4,000 cookie cutters already hanging on the wall ready for you to use. (You'll use some of these cookie cutters later in this chapter.) Part of your job as a fledgling programmer is to learn about those classes that already exist. After all, there's no reason for you to reinvent the wheel.

There will be times when you will use one of these 4,000 objects but will say to yourself: "If only this object had such-and-such property or had a method that could do such-and-such." OOP provides a mechanism called *inheritance* to do just that. However, that topic is deferred to Chapter 16. For the moment, you should concentrate on using those objects built into Visual Studio.

VISUAL STUDIO AS AN IDE

As pointed out in Chapter 1, Visual Studio is an IDE that incorporates numerous programming tools. Prior to the advent of IDEs, programmers had separate programs for writing the course code (an editor), compiling the program (a compiler), assembling the program (an assembler), and combining the program into an executable program (a linker). With an IDE, all these disparate functions are combined into a single package.

A huge part of the functionality of Visual Studio comes from the .NET Framework, including all those cookie cutters. As you write your code, components within the IDE combine your code with elements from the .NET Framework and produce Microsoft Intermediate Language (MSIL) code. It is this MSIL code, passed through the Common Language Runtime (CLR) component of Visual Studio that actually gets your program to run.

Rather than make the distinction between each of the "pieces" that comprise Visual Studio when some specific function is performed, you simply say something like: "Visual Studio takes your code and does whatever is necessary to produce an executable program." If a situation arises in which the distinction is important, we will use the proper nomenclature. For now, just remember that, as an IDE, Visual Studio is composed of a lot of different components acting in concert to make your life easier.

Most of the time you must write some of your own classes in addition to those provided for you by Visual Studio. This means that, after you finish writing your class, you now have 4,001 cookie cutters hanging on the wall, each one of which can create an object of that class's type. But note: Just because you have defined a class (or a cookie cutter) does not necessarily mean you have an object (or a cookie). Just because the cookie cutter your Mom gave you is sitting in the kitchen drawer, in and of itself, doesn't put any cookies on the table.

As stated before, a class is just a template for the object. Just as a cookie cutter works to cut specific shapes out of cookie dough, a class is used to carve out chunks of memory used to hold objects of that class. Until you've used the class template to actually carve out an object, that object does not yet exist.

Figure 2-3 shows the relationship between a class and the objects you can instantiate from that class. The class is shown as a diamond-shaped cookie cutter. The class is named `clsDiamond`. You can think of the properties of `clsDiamond` as holding the values that determine the exact shape of the cookie cutter. In other words, the state of the properties makes the class look like a diamond rather than some other shape (for example, a heart). To get an object of the class, you must press the cookie cutter (class template) into the cookie dough (computer memory) to get an actual cookie (object).

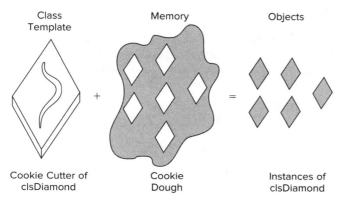

Class Template	Memory	Objects
Cookie Cutter of clsDiamond	Cookie Dough	Instances of clsDiamond

FIGURE 2-3: Class template versus an object of the class

An object is also called an *instance of a class*. The act to use a class to define an object is called *instantiation*.

An object, therefore, is something that you can actually use in a program. Just as you can't eat a cookie cutter, you can't directly use a class. You must use the class to instantiate an object of the class in memory before you can use it in your program.

NAMING OBJECTS

Throughout this text, I have adopted a convention under which you prefix the name of certain objects with a specific combination of letters. For example, I use `cls` before class names, `txt` before the names of text box objects, `btn` before button objects, and so on. You can discover other examples as you read this text. This convention is a modified form of what is called Hungarian notation but not its "pure" form. At the extreme, Hungarian notation prefixed every data item with its data type, such as `iHatSize` for an integer variable, `cLetter` for a character variable, `fWage` for a floating-point variable, `objMyData` for a data object, plus many other similar variations. At the extreme, some programmers also include a scope identifier, as in `igHatSize`, which means: "an integer variable with global scope named HatSize." This notation has lost followers simply because what it brought to the table in terms of code clarity wasn't worth the effort. So why do I continue to use a modified version of Hungarian notation?

One reason is that I feel our version is definitely worth the effort. The major reason is that the prefixes reinforce the object type used in the program. That is, at a glance you can see that `txtName` is a textbox object and that it's different from `lblName`, which is a label object.

continues

(continued)

A second reason is the way Visual Studio looks at your program data as you type in program code. For example, if you have three textboxes in your program, all pre-fixed with txt, Visual Studio knows about these objects and can open up a small "look-ahead" window the instant it sees you type in the prefix **txt**. You can then select the appropriate textbox object in the window, press the Tab key, and Visual Studio fills in the rest of the object's name for you. If you didn't prefix the textbox names with txt and you couldn't recall anything about the object (even its name) other than it's a textbox object, the names would be scattered throughout the look-ahead window, thus making the look-ahead feature less useful.

Because this look-ahead feature is a real time-saver, prefixes are used for objects in the program examples. If you don't feel it's worth the effort, you can use your own style.

Instantiating an Object of a Class

Consider the following statement:

```
clsPerson myFriend;
```

To help explain what is taking place with this statement, consider the simplified memory map of your computer system, as shown in Figure 2-4.

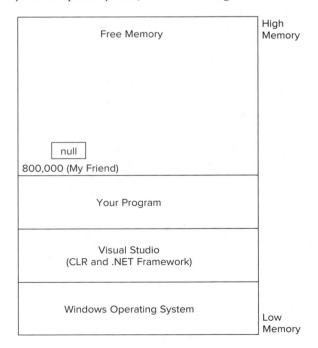

FIGURE 2-4: Simplified Windows memory map

Simply stated, the program statement statement says: "Go to the cookie cutter wall and look for a cookie cutter named clsPerson. When you find it, take it down from the wall, carve out a chunk of memory for it and label that chunk myFriend." The end result is that .NET asks the Windows operating system for 4 bytes of memory where it can store a *reference*, or *memory address*, for the variable named myFriend.

Assume that the Windows Memory Manager finds 4 bytes of free storage at memory address 800,000. For the moment, you haven't done anything with the memory at this address, so its current value is *null*. (The word *null* means the variable has nothing useful currently stored in it.)

What you have at this point is a cookie cutter named myFriend just waiting around at memory address 800,000 for something useful to happen. Things start to happen with the next program statement:

```
myFriend = new clsPerson();
```

Words that have special meaning in a programming language are called *keywords*. The *new* keyword in C# means that you want to set aside enough memory to hold a new clsPerson object. Further assume that it takes 2,000 bytes of memory to hold all the data associated with a clsPerson object. (.NET figures out how many bytes it needs for an object by examining the program code of the class.) If you verbalize what is happening on the right side of this programming statement, you might say, "Hey, Windows! It's me...Visual Studio. My programmer wants to create a new clsPerson object. Do you have 2,000 bytes of free memory available for such an object?" The Windows Memory Manager then looks through its table of available memory and probably finds 2,000 bytes of free memory somewhere in the system. Assume the 2,000-byte memory block starts at address 900,000. The Windows Memory Manager then sends a message back to Visual Studio and says, "Hey, VS! It's me...the Windows Memory Manager. I found 2,000 bytes of free memory starting at address 900,000." Visual Studio says, "Thanks," and proceeds to set up things to use the clsPerson object named myFriend, which now exists at memory location 900,000.

When Visual studio finishes with the statement, the memory map now looks like the one shown in Figure 2-5.

Notice what happened. The value associated with the variable myFriend at memory address 800,000 has changed from *null* to the memory address where the data associated with the newly created myFriend object is stored. You have now carved out a clsPerson object that you can access via the variable named myFriend. The purpose of the myFriend variable is to tell you where to find the data associated with the myFriend object.

Again, the correct programming term is that you have *instantiated* a clsPerson object referenced by the variable myFriend. An instantiated object is an object that you can use in your program. It should also be clear that myFriend is a reference that enables you to "find" the object's data (that is, the values of its properties).

Repeating the two programming statements (Chapter 4 explains the purpose of the slashes in the following statements):

```
clsPerson myFriend;        // Grab a specific cookie cutter from the wall
                           // and name it myFriend
myFriend = new clsPerson();// Use the cookie cutter to make a clsPerson
                           // cookie and refer to it as myFriend
```

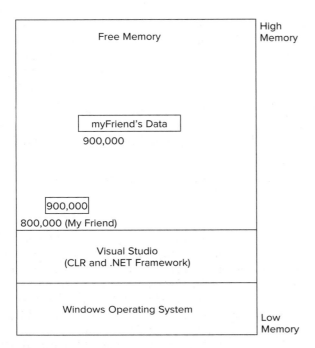

FIGURE 2-5: Memory map after object instantiation

The first statement means that you intend to create an object of clsPerson and refer to that object using the variable named myFriend. The second statement says you carried through with your intent and instantiated a new object of a clsPerson type and associated it with the object variable named myFriend. You reference the object's data for the remainder of the program using the variable named myFriend. Using the cookie cutter analogy, the cookie cutter (that is, the reference) is found at memory address 800,000, but the cookie itself (that is, the object's data) is found at memory address 900,000.

You can combine the two statements into a single statement if you want:

```
clsPerson myFriend = new clsPerson();
```

The interpretation is exactly as before. You have simply collapsed the two statements into one. Because programmers prefer less code to more code, you will see the abbreviated form used more often.

You must understand the difference between a class and an object of the class. When you write the code for a class, you are actually acting like an architect designing a house. The plans you craft might be used to build one house or hundreds of houses. The point is that the class code is the design to be used at some later date. Later, carpenters, plumbers, and other craftsmen actually construct the house. The craftsmen grab the blueprints (that is, the class) from the wall, read them, and then instantiate the house. The "usefulness" of a class (that is, a house) actually comes into being after an object of the class is instantiated (that is, the house is actually built). Although Santa indirectly appreciates what a cookie cutter does, he'd much rather see a pile of (instantiated) cookies on a plate than a stack of rusting cookie cutters.

I Have an Object...Now What?

You now have instantiated an object of the clsPerson type. The obvious question is, "So what?" At the present time, the object named myFriend is fairly nondescript. Indeed, every property in the object is instantiated with the value of zero, false, or *null* by default, depending upon the data type of the property. None of the information previously presented in Table 2-1 has been filled in for the myFriend object. You need to change the faceless myFriend object into one that has some meaningful information in it.

You can change the object by changing the information contained in the properties defined within it. From Table 2-1, you might do the following:

```
myFriend.name = "Jane";
myFriend.gender = "F";
myFriend.height = 66;
myFriend.build = "Petite";
myFriend.hairColor = "Blonde";
myFriend.eyeColor = "Blue";
myFriend.clothing = "Business casual";
myFriend.accessories = "Tan leather briefcase";
```

Notice what these statements do. They change the faceless myFriend object into one that gives you some impression of what this particular clsPerson object looks like. In these statements, the equals sign (=) is called the *assignment operator*. The assignment operator takes the information in the expression on the right side of the assignment operator and copies that information into the expression on the left side of the assignment operator. This means that somewhere near memory address 900,000, the name property has been changed from *null* to Jane. Similar changes have occurred for the other myFriend properties. In programming terms, the assignment statements change the *state* of the object from a faceless, nondescript person to an attractive female named Jane.

Object Syntax

It is important to note the syntax associated with changing the state of an object. The *syntax* of a programming language refers to the rules governing the use of the language. The general syntax for using the property of an object is as follows:

```
objectName.Property
```

Note the period, or dot, between objectName and Property. The period that appears between the object name and the property (or method) name is called the *dot operator* in C#. If you think of an object as a steel box surrounding the properties and methods of the object, the dot operator is the key that unlocks the object's door and lets you inside the object to gain access to the object's properties and methods.

In the statement

```
myFriend.Name = "Jane";
```

the computer processes the statement from right to left. You might verbalize the process implied by the statement as the following sequence of steps:

1. Place the word Jane in a wheelbarrow.

2. Go to the object named myFriend.

3. Insert your key (the dot operator) into the door of the box.

4. Open the door of the box.

5. Guide your wheelbarrow over to the `name` property.

6. Dump the letters `Jane` into the `name` property.

You can visualize these steps, as shown in Figure 2-6.

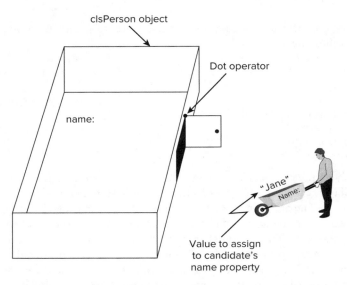

clsPerson object

Dot operator

name:

"Jane"
Name:

Value to assign
to candidate's
name property

FIGURE 2-6: Changing the value of the Name property

Now that you've followed these steps, the object associated with the `myFriend` variable has a name assigned to it. This also means that the state of the `myFriend` object has changed from an object with no name to one with the name `Jane`.

The object may be used "in the opposite direction," too. For example, suppose you have assigned Jane's name to the `myFriend` object. Later in the program you want to display her name in a textbox object on a form. If the textbox object is named `txtName`, you could write

```
txtName.Text = myFriend.Name;
```

Again, because an assignment statement is processed from right to left, the code causes the program to do the following:

1. Go to the `myFriend` object.

2. Insert the key (the dot operator) into the steel box's lock.

3. Open the door of the `myFriend` object.

4. Push an empty wheelbarrow over to the `name` property of `myFriend`.

5. Make a copy of the bytes stored in the `name` property (that is, `Jane`).

6. Place the copy into the wheelbarrow.

7. Come out of the object's box. (The door closes automatically!)

8. Push the wheelbarrow over to the textbox object named `txtName`.

9. Insert the key (the dot operator) into the lock for the `txtName`'s box.

10. Open `txtName`'s door in its box.

11. Push the wheelbarrow over to the `Text` property of the `txtName` object.

12. Dump `Jane` into the `Text` property.

You can visualize these steps, as shown in Figure 2-7.

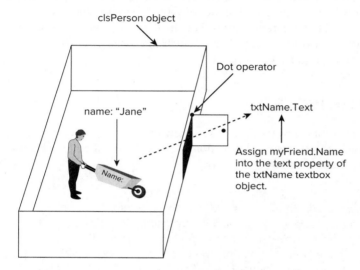

clsPerson object

Dot operator

name: "Jane"

txtName.Text

Name:

Assign myFriend.Name into the text property of the txtName textbox object.

FIGURE 2-7: Copying a property value into another variable

This sequence of steps illustrates two important concepts to remember:

➤ You *did not change* the state of the object associated with `myFriend` in this last sequence. You simply went inside the object, copied its contents, and left. Because the code didn't alter the contents of any of the properties (data) of `myFriend`, its state remains unchanged.

➤ You *did change* the state of the `txtName` object. This is true because you went into the `txtName` object and assigned the copy of `Jane`'s name to the `Text` property of the `txtName` object. Because the `Text` property's data changed, the state of the `txtName` object was changed.

You can make two important generalizations from these observations:

➤ If an object's property appears on the right side of the assignment operator (equals sign, =), you are simply reading the property of the object, not changing its state.

➤ If an object's property appears on the left side of the assignment operator, you *are* changing the data of one of its properties and, therefore, changing that object's state.

Although there are a few exceptions, these generalizations can serve you well most of the time.

Why Hide the Data Inside an Object?

In an oversimplified way, the discussion in this section describes how objects work and how properties, or the object's data, should be hidden inside an object. Why hide the properties inside an object? You hide them for the same reason that kings used to hide their daughters in the castle tower...to keep other people from messing around with them.

By encasing the properties (data) of the object inside a steel box, you can restrict access to those properties by forcing everyone to have a proper key (the object's dot operator) to gain access to the properties. Stated differently, you bury the data inside an object in an attempt to protect the data from accidental changes by other parts of the program. The process to hide data within an object is called *encapsulation*. Encapsulation is one of the cornerstones of OOP. You learn more about encapsulation and the other elements of OOP in later chapters. For the moment, however, just keep in mind that you want to encapsulate (hide) your objects' data as much as possible, yet still make that data available to those parts of your program that need it.

GETTING STARTED WITH OBJECTS

In the following Try It Out you write a simple program that uses a few of the many objects that Visual Studio provides for you. Follow the same general directions you used to create the program to test your installation of Visual Studio in Chapter 1.

> **NOTE** *Virtually every program in this book starts with the C# template described here, using the same sequence of steps described next. Therefore, you should make note of this page number (perhaps writing the page number on the back cover) and refer to it whenever you are asked to start a new project. After a while, you will know the sequence by heart.*
>
> *If the following sequence does not apply to a particular project, you will be told so and a different set of instructions will be presented. With the exception of the project name, the steps are the same for all future projects.*

TRY IT OUT   Create New Project

Create a new program project using the following steps:

1. From the File menu, select New ⇨ Project.

2. Select C# Windows Empty Project.

3. Name the program Chapter02Program01.

4. Uncheck the Create Directory for Solution if you don't want to add a separate folder. (I usually uncheck it but you don't have to. See Figure 2-8.)

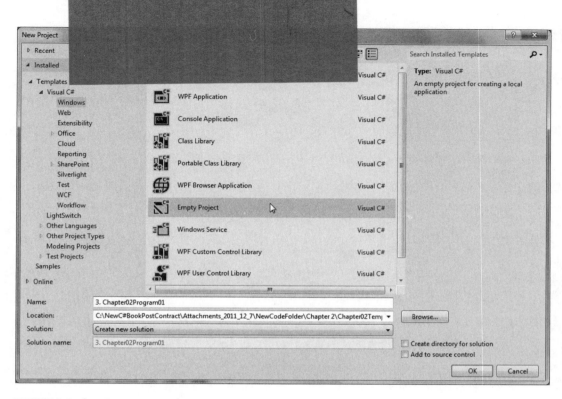

FIGURE 2-8: Creating a new project

5. Add a form to the project using the Project ⇨ Add Windows Form ⇨ Windows Form; give it the name **frmMain.cs** and click Add.

Type your program name into the Name textbox (near the bottom of the dialog box in Figure 2-8) for the project name, and click the OK button. Visual Studio creates the project for you, using the default file location for the project (such as `C:\Documents and Settings\`*yourUserName*`\Local Settings\Application Data\Temporary Projects\`*ProgramName*).

You should now see the project listed in the Solution Explorer window. If you don't see the Solution Explorer window, use the View ⇨ Solution Explorer menu sequence. (You can also use the keyboard shortcut to display the Solution Explorer window by pressing the Control (Ctrl) and W keys at the same time and then pressing the S key.)

6. Now use the Project ⇨ Add Windows Form menu sequence to invoke the dialog, as shown in Figure 2-9. The starting point for all C# programs is with a method named Main(). For consistency, therefore, this text always names the starting form as frmMain.cs. Although this is not a C# requirement, this convention is used throughout the text. When you click the Add button, an empty form appears where the Source Code window was. This new window is called the Form Designer Window.

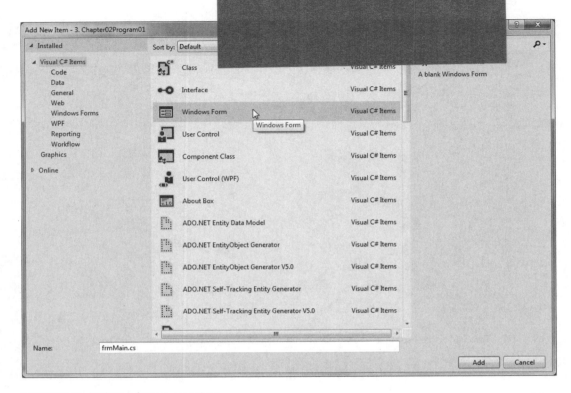

FIGURE 2-9: Adding a form to a project

7. In the Form Designer window, double-click the empty form, and then delete all the code currently on the form. (The fastest way to delete the code is to press Ctrl and then the A key (Ctrl-A) at the same time. Or, you can place the cursor at the top of the code, left-click and hold the button down, and drag the cursor down to highlight all the code. Then press the Delete button.)

8. Type the code from Listing 2-1 into the Source Code window for frmMain. You should save a copy of this code as virtually every program in this book begins with this code. In subsequent programs, the source code files are available from the Wrox website. However, in this case, you need to type the code in yourself. Use the File ⇨ Save As menu option, and save the file to the Desktop as C#Template.cs. Later in this chapter you learn how to use the template in a new program. When you saved the frmMain.cs file, Visual Studio also saved files frmMain.Designer.cs and frm-Main.resx. You should delete these from the Desktop by right-clicking each file and pressing the Delete menu option.

LISTING 2-1: The C# frmMain Template Code

```
using System;
using System.Windows.Forms;

public class frmMain:Form
{
#region Windows Code
```

```
        private void InitializeComponent()
        {
        }
#endregion
        public frmMain()
        {
                InitializeComponent();
        }
         [STAThread]
        public static void Main()
        {
                frmMain main = new frmMain();
                Application.Run(main);
        }
    }
```

9. Delete the `frmMain.Designer.cs` file from the project. You can see this file by clicking the small triangle immediately in front of `frmMain.cs` in the Solutions Explorer window near the top right of your display.

10. Select the Project ⇨ Chapter02Program01 Properties menu option, and set the Startup Object to frmMain and the Output Type to Windows Application. (The option appears at the bottom of the menu and always uses the program's name in the menu option.) Your dialog should look similar to Figure 2-10.

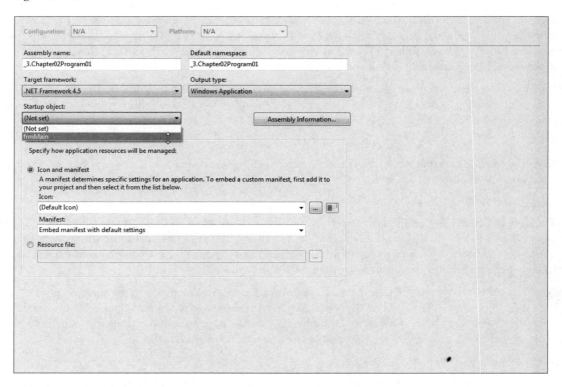

FIGURE 2-10: Setting project properties

At this point, you can actually run this program, but all it does is show an empty form. Still, you have a functioning Windows application that runs with relatively little coding on your part. Now, add some more objects to the form.

Double click the `frmMain.cs` object in the Solution Explorer window. This causes the empty form to reappear in the Source Code window. Now click the empty `frmMain` form to make the Toolbox window appear on the left side of the screen. Double-click the Label object in the Toolbox window. Visual Studio places a label object on your form in the upper-left corner of the form. If you want, you can move the cursor over the label, which causes an "arrow cross" to appear. If you press the left mouse button and hold it down, you can drag the label to wherever you want on the form.

How It Works

If you look carefully at Figure 2-8, you can see that you should *not* select the Windows Forms Application template (that is, the first option in the list) as you did in Chapter 1. Instead, you should click the Visual C# ⇨ Windows sequence and then select the Empty Project template. You do this because using the Empty Project template causes Visual Studio to generate less code "behind your back" than does the Windows Application template. That's the good news. The bad news is that using the Empty Project template does require you to do a little more work up front than you might otherwise have to do.

Although it may seem stupid to ask you to write code that Visual Studio can write for you, using the Empty Project template serves your purpose better. The goal in this (and subsequent) chapters is to teach *you* how to write object-oriented programs. Visual Studio already knows how to do that and I assume you don't! In other words, using the Empty Project template enables me to better teach you how to write your own programs. My philosophy is that you learn more if you have to do it yourself. (Also, if you're using this book to learn OOP but with a different language, such as Java, this approach can make using that language a little easier.)

If you double-click an empty space on the form, Visual Studio shifts you from the Design View to the Code View. If you look closely, you can expand the `#region` Windows section by clicking on the plus sign (+) and see code like:

```
this.label1 = new System.Windows.Forms.Label();
```

This line of code is responsible for creating a new label object named `label1` using syntax similar to what you saw before:

```
clsPerson myFriend = new clsPerson();
```

The only difference is that the keyword *this* is a form of shorthand for the fully qualified name for the label object of `System.Windows.Forms.Label`. In other words, the statement line simply creates a label object on your form. Some of the other lines you can see determine where you placed the label and some other overhead information associated with label objects.

Now click the frmMain.cs [Design] tab of the Source Code window to make the form reappear. Click the label object and note that the Properties Window appears on the lower-right side of the display. Go to the `Text` property in the Properties Window, double-click `label1`, and change it to `Name:`. If you now click the frmMain.cs tab, you see that one of the lines of code has changed to:

```
this.label1.Text = "Name:";
```

What does this mean? Because you changed the `Text` property of the label object, you changed the state of the label object. Because you placed the label on a form object, you also changed the form object as well. Therefore, dropping objects on a form changes the state of the form object. Likewise, changing any of the properties of those objects also changes the state of both the object itself as well as the form that holds those objects.

Now go to the textbox object and drag the textbox so that it aligns with the label object. Now double-click the button object. Visual Studio automatically switches you to the Source Code window, and you can see this code:

```
private void button1_Click(object sender, EventArgs e)
{
}
```

This is *stub code* for the button object. Now add the following line of code between the two parentheses of the stub code:

```
frmMain.ActiveForm.Text = textBox1.Text;
```

What does this line do? Because the assignment operator (=) takes the data on the right side of the operator and assigns it to the object on the left side of the operator, this statement simply moves whatever you typed into the textbox object and makes it the title of the form object, `frmMain`. The dot operator gets you into the object so that you can access the property in which you are interested.

WHY MORE THAN ONE DOT OPERATOR?

Why are there two dot operators in the expression `frmMain.ActiveForm.Text`? Well, the first operator (moving from left to right) gets you "inside" the `frmMain` object. However, inside the `frmMain` object is another "black box object" that represents the `ActiveForm` object. To get inside that object, you need another key (that is, another dot operator) to open its door. When inside the `ActiveForm` object, you can see the `Text` property that you can then access as you need.

It may seem confusing at first, but you can have objects-within-objects-within-objects as deep as is necessary. A long time ago, I had to use a (poorly designed) database library that required me to use 12 dot operators to get to the property I actually needed. That's an extreme case, but you should expect to see two-level deep dot operators fairly often.

Run the program using the F5 key or click the "triangle" near the top of the Source Code window, type something into the textbox, and then click the button and observe the change to the form's title.

This simple program is actually doing quite a bit of work "behind the scenes." If you look at the `InitializeComponent()` method in the Source Code window, you can see that Visual Studio has written quite a bit of code behind your back while you weren't looking. Take some time to study that code to get a feel for what is going on when you add objects to a form. You might even try changing some of the numbers you see there, switch back to the Design window, and see the impact the change had on the form. Clearly, making such changes does change the state of the object, including the `frmMain` object.

Experimenting like this is a great way to see how changes to the various properties affect the program. If you're like most beginning programmers, you might be a little afraid that you'll "break" something. Not to worry. You might get an ugly looking form or something else weird may happen, but it's nothing you can't fix by simply resetting the property to its original value. For that reason, it's best if you make changes to a property "one at a time" so that you are sure of that change's impact, plus being able to return the property to its original state if you want to do so. Please... experiment and have fun with this simple program.

Although you did just write a complete Windows program, it's a simple program that was kind of thrown together off the top of my head. In real life, programming tasks are rarely this simple.

DEVELOPING A PROGRAM PLAN

Now put what you've learned thus far to use designing a program. Of necessity, you can leave out some code that would make your little program more bulletproof simply because you haven't learned how to do that yet. (You will learn how to make programs more bulletproof soon enough.) The goal here is to show you how to start writing a program to solve a specific task.

Where to Start? The Five Program Steps

Without a doubt, one of the hardest things for beginning programmers to figure out is where to begin writing a program. As a general rule, when I assign an in-class programming assignment, most students start solving the program problem by dragging and dropping controls from the toolbox onto a form as their first step in writing a program.

Wrong!

Don't confuse movement with problem solving. If you start dragging and dropping objects all over the place without a coherent plan, you're in for some unexpected disappointments. Inevitably, you'll end up backtracking and developing a plan of attack for the task at hand, so you may as well start out with a plan in the first place.

Indeed, to write good programs you must have a plan. Central to a programming plan is an algorithm. An *algorithm* is simply a step-by-step recipe, or plan, for how you want to solve the programming task at hand. A good place to start a program plan is with the Five Program Steps.

The Five Program Steps

As a broad generalization, you can describe all programming problems in terms of five steps.

Step 1: Initialization

The Initialization step involves those things that are done before the user sees anything displayed on the screen. For example, some programs "remember" the last four or five files that you worked on with the program and tack those file names on to the end of the File menu. Microsoft Word, Excel, PowerPoint, Visual Studio, and other programs do this in one way or another. Clearly, those programs must read that information from somewhere before the program can display the File menu on the screen.

Likewise, a program might establish a network connection, initialize a printer, connect to a database, read a sensor, or do all kinds of other activities before the user sees anything on the screen. All these activities are lumped under the Initialization step.

Simply stated:

The Initialization step is responsible for establishing the environment in which the program is to be run.

The activities of the Initialization step take place before the user sees anything appear on the screen.

Step 2: Input

If you think about it, all programs take some kind of input into the program, process it in some way, and then display some variation of the data that was derived from the original inputs. The Input step, therefore, is concerned with getting those inputs into the program.

Most of the time you tend to think of program input as coming from the keyboard or mouse. However, input can come from many other input sources, too. Some examples are an engine sensor, bar-code reader, retinal scanner, network connection, fire or smoke alarm sensor, information from a database, or a host of other input devices. The important aspect of the Input step, however, is that data in some form is collected by the program.

It's always a good practice to validate the input data. Users do make mistakes when entering data, network connections sometimes do weird things, data sources can be locked, and other unexpected occurrences can corrupt the data. You will learn more about data validation in later chapters. For now, I have assumed a really bright user who never makes a typing mistake and all the hardware is working perfectly! (This assumption enables you to concentrate on the essence of the objects being used in the program.)

Step 3: Process

This is the step in which you take the program inputs and process them in some way. You might perform some kind of mathematical operation on them, or perhaps the inputs are the name and account number of a customer, and this step reads a database to calculate a bill to be sent to the customer. In a jet aircraft, the inputs might be the current airspeed and GPS coordinates to calculate when the plane will touch down at a specific airport. In all cases, the Process step involves taking the inputs, acting upon them, and producing some form of result or answer.

What is meant by "taking the inputs and acting upon them"? That sentence fragment should make something itch in the back of your mind. What do you call those thingies that take an object's data and act upon them? Right...methods! Quite often, therefore, the Process step uses class methods to transform the data provided by the Input step. Hmmm? Could it be that the data used in the Process step might be provided by the properties of the class?

You must remember that often a variety of methods can be used to take the same inputs, process them, and produce the same answer. Just as you can find a variety of ways to fly from New York to Los Angeles (such as nonstop, or through Chicago, or Denver, or Houston), the result's the same: You end up in L.A. Likewise, you can use different algorithms to take the same inputs into a program, process them differently, but generate the same results. For example, there are dozens of different algorithms available to sort data using a computer. However, as you shall see in subsequent chapters, some algorithms are more efficient than others. Always keep your mind open to new ways to accomplish old tasks.

Step 4: Display

The Display step is responsible for displaying the results produced in the Process step. Usually, this means showing the results on the display screen, but other options exist. Perhaps it means skipping the display screen and simply printing a bill and mailing it to a customer. Or perhaps the program is responsible for updating a customer record in a database. There are many programs that run themselves (called *batch programs*) and don't display anything on the screen or ask for any inputs from the user as they run. Instead, batch programs often start automatically at a predetermined time (perhaps at 1 a.m. when no one else is using the system), read the input information from some input source (like a database), and generate reports based on the input information.

The Display step doesn't always result in your "seeing" a result displayed on a screen. Sometimes the result of the program is passed on to another process, or a database, a website, or even automatically sending an email. The key is that you have used the inputs to produce something new and you want to "see," "use," or "save" that new result. However, for most of the programs you write while using this book, the Display step does show some information to the user via the display device.

Step 5: Termination

The Termination step doesn't necessarily mean that you simply end the program. It also means "cleaning up" after the program has finished. For example, if the Initialization step reads the four latest files used in the program and appends them to the File menu, then this step needs to update those filenames to reflect what the user has done during the current session of the program. If the Initialization step sets up a printer or database connection, this step should close that connection.

Quite often, whatever is done in the Initialization step is "undone" in the Termination step. Finally, the Termination step should provide a graceful exit from the program, even if an error occurred while the program was running. (You learn more about how to plan for error conditions in Chapter 11.)

CREATING A SIMPLE APPLICATION USING OBJECTS

Now use the Five Program Steps you just learned to design and write a simple program. The goal of the program is to gather address information about the user and then simply redisplay that information as if it were a mailing label. For now you won't actually do anything with the information, but after you get a little more C# programming under your belt, you could use this program as an input process for some larger programming task, such as creating a customer account or writing your own personal mailing list. The primary objective here, however, is to get you additional experience using a few of the objects provided to you as part of Visual Studio and .NET.

Using the Program Steps to Create a Program Plan

Your first task is to develop a plan to solving the task at hand. A good place to start the plan is with the Five Program Steps presented earlier.

1: Initialization

This is a simple program, and you don't actually have any fancy initialization to do. Any necessary initialization tasks are done automatically for you by Visual Studio. You take a look at Visual Studio's background handiwork a little later.

2: Input

This is the step where you must ask yourself, "What information do I need to solve the programming task at hand?" Because you want to arrange user information the way a mailing label does, you need to know the user's:

➤ Name

➤ Street address

➤ City

➤ State

➤ ZIP (or postal) code

You could write the program and hard-code values in for each piece of data into the program. When you *hard-code* a value into a program, it means that you make that value a permanent part of the program itself. If you hard-code the data for this program, you write program code that embeds the user's name and address as data directly into the program. However, hard-coding values directly into a program makes the program less flexible than it might otherwise be. For example, each time you wanted a mailing label for a new user, you'd need to write new data values into the program's code before you could display the information. Not good.

A more flexible approach is to ask the user to enter the necessary information while the program runs and to display the information as a mailing label when they finish. After they enter the information, you can arrange the data for display on the screen. The easiest way to code this approach to the solution is to use label and textbox objects for each piece of information, or input, you want to collect. When the user is satisfied that he has entered the requested information, he can click a button to display the information as a mailing label.

Designing a Program's User Interface for the Input Step

In this program, you decide to use labels and textboxes to collect the information from the user. The labels help to inform the user about the data you are requesting, and the textboxes provide a means for him to type in his responses. These labels and textboxes become part of the user interface of your program. A program's *user interface* simply refers to how the program interacts with the user running the program. In this program the user interface consists of labels, textboxes, and buttons arranged on a form.

Entire books have been written about how to design a good user interface. Although this chapter can't possibly do justice to the subject of user interface design, consider the following guidelines:

➤ **Follow the KISS (Keep It Simple Stupid) principle.** What this means is that you should make the user interface as simple as possible yet still acquire the information you need with minimal chance for input error. Resist the urge to add objects to a form if they don't contribute to the functionality of the program.

➤ **Use familiar interfaces.** For example, in this program you ask the user for address information. Chances are good that the user has filled in a tear-out magazine subscription form or filled in a driver's license form that asks for address information. Try to model your interface in a way that the user might already be familiar with, or do your best to make an unfamiliar user interface easy to understand.

➤ **The user interface should have a natural flow to it.** In a Windows program, the *Tab key* is used to advance from one input field to the next. It wouldn't make much sense to have the user type in his name and, after he presses the Tab key, to jump to the ZIP Code field, have him enter its value, and then jump back to the Address field. The flow would make more sense to the user if the program went from the Name field to the Address field to the City field to the State field, and so forth. Likewise, English-speaking users read from top left to bottom right, whereas Chinese readers progress from top right to bottom left. Therefore, even language and cultural factors can influence the flow of the user interface. Simply stated, the flow of a user interface should be intuitive and make sense to the user.

➤ **Don't use any GWF in the program.** The *Gee-Whiz Factor* refers to any user interface change you might make that doesn't serve any purpose other than to get the user to say, "Gee whiz!" Beginning programmers often change the background color for labels and textboxes, change the font color from black to purple, and make other changes that add nothing useful to the user interface other than to show that they know how to make such changes. The fact remains, however, that Microsoft has probably spent more money on research that tests the colors, shapes, and other default property values for objects than you will make in a lifetime. As a result, there are not many good reasons not to accept the results of that research.

Always keep in mind that the goal of a user interface is to make it easy for the user to run your program. Try to make the user interface intuitive and simple from the user's point of view.

3: Process

This is the step where you devise the algorithm that produces the wanted result of the program. The wanted result of this program simply is to display the user information in a mailing-label format. The Input step provides you with the information you need via the user interface you designed. Therefore, to actually begin the Process step, you need to have a button (such as a Display button) so that the program knows when all the input data has been entered and it can begin to address the task at hand.

Event-driven Programs

Microsoft Windows programs are event-driven. An *event-driven program* means that some agent (such as the user) must generate an event of some type for the program to perform the next program task. For example, in this program, if the user does not interact with the program in some way, the program will obediently sit there and wait until she does. In your program, the user must click the Display button to trigger the event associated with the Process step.

Human action is not the only way to trigger a Windows event. For example, the time of day might be constantly monitored by a program, and when a certain time is reached, the program triggers an event that causes that program to perform some type of action. A fire sensor might sit there for years monitoring the fire sensors and never trigger an event. But when the fire sensor does trigger an event, alarms go off, sprinklers turn on, and automated phone calls are sent out. For most of the programs you will write in this book, however, the user provides the activity (for example, a mouse click or a keystroke) that fires a Windows event.

The Process step for this program is simply to arrange the information entered by the user in the form of an address label. A button-click event triggers the Process step and is used to inform the program that all the necessary data has been entered and is ready for use. (Assume the user does not trigger the event before all the data is entered. This is a bright user, remember?)

4: Display

In this program, you simply display the user's name and address information as a mailing label.

5: Termination

Because you didn't write any code to do anything tricky in the Initialization step, you don't need to do anything in the Termination step to clean up and gracefully end the program. Instead, you can simply have a button object (such as an Exit button) that the user can click to end the program.

Now you have a plan based upon the Five Program Steps. Planning does not require you to do any programming. However, skipping this planning process is a common mistake *all* programmers make, including seasoned programmers.

Still, many of you will be like most of my students: You'll plunge ahead without formulating any kind of plan...and that's okay. However, eventually, you have to formulate a program plan, and it's always quicker to do it at the outset.

Now, all you need to do is implement your plan.

USING C# TO IMPLEMENT YOUR PROGRAM PLAN

Now that you have a plan, you need to write the program code to solve the task at hand. You're going to do this by using the objects provided by Visual Studio and .NET in concert with your own program logic using C#. It won't be difficult for you to do this because...you have a plan! Because you started with a plan rather than by just dragging and dropping objects onto a form puts you light years ahead of most beginning programmers.

True, you too will be dragging and dropping objects onto a form soon enough, but your approach to the problem is different. There's a method to your dragging and dropping...it is guided by "the plan." Too often beginning programmers start dragging labels and textboxes onto a form without a plan. However, movement without a plan generates more heat than light. Therefore, the lesson to learn is:

Never start coding a program without a plan.

Although you performed in Chapter 1 some of the steps presented in the next few sections, you didn't learn why you were doing those steps. Also, you do things a little differently now that you have some understanding of OOP. In the following Try It Out you begin.

> **NOTE** *Earlier in this chapter you learned that .NET has approximately 4,000 classes available that you can use in your programs. Although all these classes are available to you, you don't actually need to use all 4,000 in a single project. For that reason, Visual Studio enables you to specify the categories of reference classes that you do want to use in your program. In this section you see how to select those groups of classes that you want to include in your current project.*

Creating a New C# Project (Chapter02Program01.zip)

Your first task is to create a new C# project for the mailing label program.

1. Use the same File ⇨ New Project ⇨ Visual C# ⇨ Windows menu sequence discussed earlier in this chapter (refer to Figure 2-8).

2. Add program references to your project. Use the Project ⇨ Add Reference menu sequence to show the Add Reference dialog box. Now click on the Assemblies ⇨ Framework options to get a list of the assemblies that are available to you. Figure 2-11 shows you what the Add Reference dialog box looks like. In that figure, the System assembly is selected, which is the base for all Windows system references, which brings into your program all the classes that deal with Windows Forms objects. Click the Add button to add the assembly to your program.

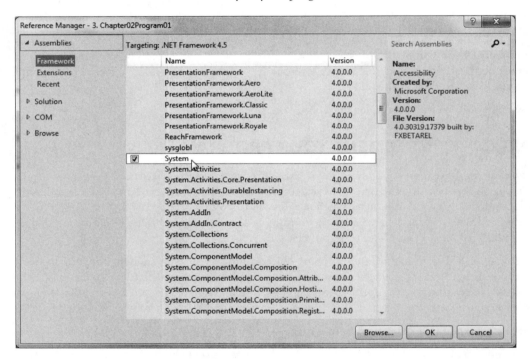

FIGURE 2-11: Selecting program references

You can select additional references from the list by simply clicking the check box for each reference you want to include in the project. The references you need are:

➤ `System`

➤ `System.Drawing`

➤ `System.Windows.Forms`

Almost every program you write add these three references.

After you select these three references, click the OK button. You should see the references you selected under the References heading in the Solution Explorer window. If you don't see all three references, go back to the Add Reference dialog box and select the missing reference(s).

3. Add a new item to the project. Now you need to create a form object that is going to hold the (label, textbox, and other) objects that you want to use in your program. Use Project ⇨ Add New Item to display the Add New Item dialog box. (You need to scroll the dialog list to get to the Code File option.) Figure 2-12 shows this dialog box.

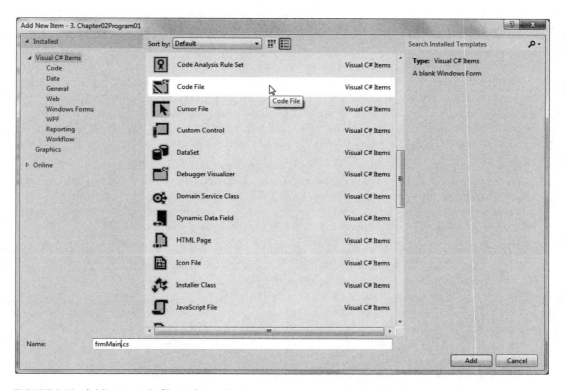

FIGURE 2-12: Adding a code file to the project

Scroll down the list of template objects until you see Code File from the list of available templates, and enter **frmMain.cs** in the Name textbox at the bottom of the dialog box, as shown in Figure 2-12. Click the Add button. (The "cs" secondary filename identifies the file to Visual Studio as a C# source code file.) You should now see frmMain shown in the Solution Explorer. Also the Source Window now has a new tab labeled frmMain.cs [Design] at the top of the Source Windows. The Source Window displays an empty form at this point.

If you double-click the empty form, a new tab named frmMain.cs is created, and you can see some code that Visual Studio created for you. Highlight all the code you see, and press the Delete key to remove the code from the form. (The fastest way to highlight the code is Ctrl-A, as mentioned earlier.)

4. Add program code to the `frmMain` object. Virtually every program you create while reading this book begins with exactly the same program statements. These program statements are exactly the same as shown earlier in the chapter in Listing 2-1. If you saved those statements in a C# template file as suggested, just cut-and-paste those lines of code into the Source window for frmMain.cs.

5. Set the project properties. You should now set the properties that govern the environment in which the program will execute. Select the Project ➪ Chapter02Program01 menu sequence. The dialog is the same one you saw in Figure 2-10.

Because you want your program to run as a Windows application, select Windows Application from the Output Type choices. Next, set the Startup Object to be the object that contains the `Main()` method for the application. As mentioned in Chapter 1, *every C# program must have a Main() method* because it is the `Main()` method that tells Visual Studio where to begin executing the program. As you can see in Figure 2-11, it is the `frmMain` object that contains the `Main()` method. Select `frmMain` from the list of startup objects.

6. Delete the design code. Because you control the program code rather than relying on Visual Studio, you can delete the `frmMain.Designer.cs` source code file. You can find this file by moving the cursor to the Solution Explorer window and clicking the small triangle you see in front of the `frmMain.cs` file. Right-click the `frmMain.Designer.cs` filename, and select the Delete option. You will be prompted if you want to delete the file from the project. Click OK.

In the Solution Explorer window, right-click the `frmMain.cs` file, and you are presented with a list of options, as shown in Figure 2-13. Click the View Designer option. This causes a blank form to reappear in the Source Window, as shown in Figure 2-14.

FIGURE 2-13: Selecting the View Designer from the Solutions window

FIGURE 2-14: The Designer view

You are now ready to start adding objects to the form.

7. Add objects to the `frmMain` object. If you have followed the directions correctly, your screen should look similar to Figure 2-14. You can now add the various program objects to the form.

Table 2-2 presents the object and property values for each of the objects you should place on the form. (You need to scroll the Properties Window to find some of the properties.)

TABLE 2-2: Objects and Their Property Values

OBJECT NAME	PROPERTY NAME	PROPERTY VALUE
frmMain	Text	Mailing Label Program
	StartPosition	CenterScreen
label1	Text	Name:
	AutoSize	False
	BorderStyle	Fixed3D
	Size	75, 20
label2	Text	Address:
	AutoSize	False
	BorderStyle	Fixed3D
	Size	75, 20
label3	Text	City
	AutoSize	False
	BorderStyle	Fixed3D
	Size	75, 20
label4	Text	State
	AutoSize	False
	BorderStyle	Fixed3D
	Size	40, 20
label5	Text	ZIP
	AutoSize	False
	BorderStyle	Fixed3D
	Size	40, 20
txtName		Default values for all properties
txtAddress		Default values for all properties

continues

TABLE 2-2 *(continued)*

OBJECT NAME	PROPERTY NAME	PROPERTY VALUE
txtCity		Default values for all properties
txtState		Default values for all properties
txtZip		Default values for all properties
txtDisplayOutput	MultiLine	True
	ReadOnly	True
btnDisplayOutput	Text	&Display
btnExit	Text	E&xit

Because the program does not manipulate the property values of the label object in the program, you can leave their names unchanged from the default names supplied for labels by Visual Studio. However, because you do want to manipulate and use the information contained in the textboxes, you should give them meaningful names, as suggested in Table 2-2.

Thus far, you have not specified the size of the objects (for example, buttons, textboxes, and labels) used on the form. However, when you finish adding the objects to the form and setting their property values, your form should look similar to the form object shown in Figure 2-15. You can adjust the sizes of the objects by using their sizing boxes. (The sizing boxes appear when you click an object and that object is capable of being resized.)

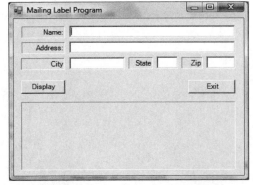

FIGURE 2-15: The program's user interface

8. Add program code for the Process step. When the user runs your program, she is expected to fill in the various textboxes and click the Display button. A button-click generates an event message that causes the code tied to the btnDisplayOutput click event to be executed. With the form visible in the Source Window, double-click the Display button. Recall that a double-click on the button object causes Visual Studio to generate the stub code for the button's click event. In this case, the stub code looks like:

```
private void btnDisplayOutput_Click(object sender, EventArgs e)
{
}
```

Your task is to fill in the necessary code between the opening and closing parentheses that causes the program to accomplish its task. Now add the following program code to the btnDisplayOutput click event stub so that it looks like:

```
private void btnDisplayOutput_Click(object sender, EventArgs e)
{
        String buffer;

        buffer = "Mailing Label:" + Environment.NewLine +
                        Environment.NewLine;
        buffer = buffer + "    Name: " + txtName.Text +
                    Environment.NewLine;
        buffer = buffer + "Address: " + txtAddress.Text +
                        Environment.NewLine;
        buffer = buffer + "    City: " + txtCity.Text +
                " State: " + txtState.Text +"  Zip: " + txtZip.Text;
        txtDisplayOutput.Text = buffer;
}
```

In the code some of the string elements are "padded" with blanks spaces before them (that is,
" Name:"). This is an attempt to make things line up nicely when they display. Now run the program and fill in the textboxes with the appropriate information. Figure 2-16 shows a sample run
of the program.

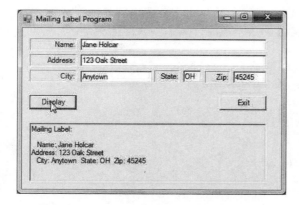

FIGURE 2-16: Sample run of the program

How It Works

The program begins by building the form in memory, placing the various objects on the form where
you told them to be placed when you constructed the user interface described in Table 2-2. Anytime
you move an object on the form, Visual Studio automatically adjusts the code to reflect the new position. If you change a property of an object using the Property Window, Visual Studio makes the
appropriate changes to the code for you. Recall that changing a property is, after all, changing the
state of the object.

You can examine the code Visual Studio wrote for the user interface by looking at the statements in the
InitializeComponent() method. Because the code is fairly lengthy and repetitive, only the first few
statement lines are shown here.

```
private void InitializeComponent()
{
    this.label1 = new System.Windows.Forms.Label();
```

```
       this.txtName = new System.Windows.Forms.TextBox();
       this.txtAddress = new System.Windows.Forms.TextBox();
       this.label2 = new System.Windows.Forms.Label();
       this.txtCity = new System.Windows.Forms.TextBox();
       this.label3 = new System.Windows.Forms.Label();
       this.label4 = new System.Windows.Forms.Label();
       this.txtZip = new System.Windows.Forms.TextBox();
       this.label5 = new System.Windows.Forms.Label();
       this.btnDisplayOutput = new System.Windows.Forms.Button();
       this.btnExit = new System.Windows.Forms.Button();
       this.txtDisplayOutput = new System.Windows.Forms.TextBox();
       this.txtState = new System.Windows.Forms.TextBox();
       this.SuspendLayout();
       //
       // label1
       //
       this.label1.BorderStyle = System.Windows.Forms.BorderStyle.Fixed3D;
       this.label1.Location = new System.Drawing.Point(12, 18);
       this.label1.Name = "label1";
       this.label1.Size = new System.Drawing.Size(75, 20);
       this.label1.TabIndex = 0;
       this.label1.Text = "Name:";
       this.label1.TextAlign =  System.Drawing.ContentAlignment.MiddleRight;
       //
       // txtName
       //
       this.txtName.Location = new System.Drawing.Point(93, 18);
       this.txtName.Name = "txtName";
       this.txtName.Size = new System.Drawing.Size(297, 20);
       this.txtName.TabIndex = 1;

        // More statements follow
   }    // End of the InitializeComponent() method
```

Consider the first program line:

```
this.label1 = new System.Windows.Forms.Label();
```

Previously this chapter discussed what this statement does. Keeping in mind that the keyword *this* refers to the current object, or frmMain in this case, a label object is one of the cookie cutters you can use to instantiate an object. In this case you can create a cookie named label1, and a few lines later Visual Studio wrote the following code:

```
this.label1.BorderStyle = System.Windows.Forms.BorderStyle.Fixed3D;
this.label1.Location = new System.Drawing.Point(12, 18);
this.label1.Name = "label1";
this.label1.Size = new System.Drawing.Size(75, 20);
this.label1.TabIndex = 0;
this.label1.Text = "Name:";
this.label1.TextAlign = System.Drawing.ContentAlignment.MiddleRight;
```

This code changes a number of properties (like BorderStyle, Location, Name, Size, TabIndex, Text, and TextAlign) for the label1 object. Because the object's properties appear on the left side of the assignment operator, the code changes the values for each of the properties shown. This also means that the state of the label1 object has been changed.

Code similar to that shown here is generated for the other objects you placed on the form. In each case, the state of the object is changed according to the properties you changed while constructing the user interface.

If you look closely at Figure 2-15, you can see the 3-D border effect created using the `Fixed3D` `BorderStyle` property with the label objects. You should also change their `TextAlign` property so they are right justified. Strictly speaking, Windows programs do not use borders on label objects. Given that borders are nonstandard, why are they used in this example? There are two reasons.

First, the use of borders reinforces the purpose of an object's properties. Changing an object's property values changes the state of the object. In this case, changing the state of the `BorderStyle` property changes the way the label looks on the screen. The second reason to use borders on the labels is that they look kind of cool. If you want to follow the strict Windows style or don't like the way label borders look, don't use them. After all...it's your program.

Now examine program code found in the `btnDisplayOutput` click event method. The first statement in the method is:

```
String buffer;
```

This line simply creates a program variable named `buffer`. As you will learn in the next chapter, a *variable* is nothing more than a name for an area of computer memory used to hold a piece of program data. The keyword `String` denotes a specific type of variable that is capable of storing textual data. (You will learn more about variables and data types in Chapter 3.) As you are using it here, `buffer` is used to hold some textual characters you've hard-coded into the program (such as Mailing Label) plus some textual characters that the user has supplied via the textbox objects.

The next program line takes the characters `Mailing Label:` and adds two newline characters (as stored in the `Environment.NewLine` property of the `Environment` object) to the end of the sequence of characters:

```
buffer = "Mailing Label:" + Environment.NewLine +
      Environment.NewLine;
```

A *newline character* causes subsequent characters to print on the next line. Because you have used two newline characters, this has the effect to display a blank line in the output. Refer to Figure 2-16 to see the blank line.

The next line of program code takes the current value of `buffer` and adds the characters `Name:` to it:

```
buffer = buffer + "   Name: " + txtName.Text +
      Environment.NewLine;
```

The statement then accesses the `txtName` object and uses the dot operator to access the data stored in the `Text` property of the `txtName` object. Using the data shown in Figure 2-16, the `Text` property of the `txtName` object currently holds the name `Jane Holcar` in it. This data is then added on to the end of `buffer` to produce the following:

```
Mailing Label:
Jane Holcar
```

This is the sequence of characters currently stored in `buffer`. This sequence of actions on the `txtName` object is similar to what is depicted in Figure 2-7. Lastly, a newline character is added to `buffer` so that any additional characters added to `buffer` appear on a new line in the display.

You can summarize the statement as a series of steps, with the step number appearing in parentheses below its associated action:

```
buffer = buffer + "   Name: " + txtName.Text + Environment.NewLine;
(5)      (1)              (2)        (3)              (4)
```

This may be read as the following sequence of steps. (Recall that statements on the right side of the assignment operator (=) are processed first.)

1. Take the original content of `buffer` (that is, `Mailing label:`) that existed prior to the execution of this statement.

2. Add the characters `Name:` after the characters `Mailing label:` and the two newline characters.

3. Use the dot operator to fetch the characters stored in the `Text` property of the `txtName` object.

4. Add a newline character at the end of the characters.

5. Assign this new sequence of characters back into `buffer` so `buffer` contains the old plus the new characters.

After the statement has been processed, `buffer` now contains the first three lines displayed in Figure 2-16.

The remaining program code statements add the address, city, state, and ZIP code entered by the user, and work the same way the first two program lines did. The end result of the program statements that assign data into `buffer` is what you see displayed in the textbox at the bottom of the form.

The following program statement simply moves the characters stored in `buffer` into the `Text` property of the `txtDisplayOutput` object:

```
txtDisplayOutput.Text = buffer;
```

Because this changes the value of the `Text` property of `txtDisplayOutput`, the state of the `txtDisplayOutput` object is changed, which causes the display to change and look like what is shown in Figure 2-16.

The `btnExit` click event code does nothing more than call the `Close()` method, which causes the program to terminate. The `btnExit` text property has an ampersand (&) imbedded in it after the `E`. This enables the user to use the Alt+X keystroke sequence in lieu of using the mouse to click the Exit button. In this example, the letter X is the "hot key" (or accelerator) alternative to clicking the Exit button. *Hot keys* enable the user to run the program using just the keyboard in the absence of a mouse device. The same interpretation applies to the letter `D` in the `btnDisplayOutput` button. That is, the user can press Alt+D instead of clicking the Display button.

As mentioned earlier, a programming style convention is to start object names with specific prefixes. For example, textbox names begin with `txt` and button names start with `btn`. Such a prefix is followed by a name that describes the object, such as `txtName` for the user's name, `txtAddress` for the address, and so on. The object name used after the prefix is capitalized. The practice to use an uppercase letter for the subnames within object and variable names is called *Camel Notation*. You can see the use of camel notation in the object names shown in Table 2-2 (such as `btnDisplayOutput`). Camel notation makes it easier to read and understand object and variable names. You learn more about object and variable names in Chapter 3.

Critique of the btnDisplayOutput Click Event Code

The program code found in the `btnDisplayOutput` click event is an example of what I call *RDC...Really Dumb Code*. This is true for a number of reasons. First, there is no validation of the contents that have been typed into the various textboxes by the user. To make the program code smarter, you should add code to verify that something was typed into the textbox and that the data is appropriate for the information wanted. For example, if you want to validate the content of the `Text` property for the ZIP code textbox object, perhaps you should check to see if only digit characters are entered. Or if there is a mixture of alpha and digit characters, perhaps you should check to make sure exactly six characters were entered. This way you could allow Canadian postal codes, too, because those codes use both alpha and digit characters.

A second improvement would make the output a little easier to read. If you look closely at the output in Figure 2-16, you can notice that the fields don't line up properly. This is true even though you made an effort to align the Name, Address, and City fields in the program statements by using an appropriate number of spaces before each field. Why didn't this work?

The reason is that label objects have their default `Font` property set to the Microsoft Sans Serif font. This is what is called a TrueType font. A TrueType font is a variable-spaced font. What that means is that each character in a *TrueType variable font* takes up only as much screen space as it needs to be seen on the display device. The letter *I*, for example, takes up less space on the screen than does the letter *W*. Therefore, because different letters take up different amounts of space, it is difficult to get letters on different lines to align with each other.

You can solve this alignment problem by changing the font to a fixed font. With a *fixed font*, each letter takes up exactly the same amount of space. If you change the `Font` property of the `txtDisplayOutput` object to the Courier New font, which is a fixed font, the letters align perfectly. You can see the result of the font change by comparing the display output in Figure 2-16 with that in Figure 2-17.

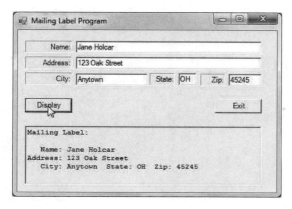

FIGURE 2-17: Sample run after changing the font

SUMMARY

You covered quite a bit of ground in this chapter. The remainder of this book builds upon the basic concepts presented in this chapter. You should spend enough time with the material presented here to be comfortable with all the terms introduced in this chapter (such as class, object, property, method, dot operator, instantiate, and so on). A little time spent now learning these concepts can generate huge rewards in later chapters. Take your time, experiment, and have fun.

EXERCISES

You can find the answers to the following exercises in Appendix A.

1. What is a class? What is an object? How are the two related? How are they different?

2. In one sentence each, describe the Five Program Steps.

3. Explain what each of the following two statements do:
   ```
   clsThingie myThingie;
   myThingie = new clsThingie();
   ```

4. Design a class for a kitchen oven object.

5. What constitutes a "good" user interface?

6. Why are you making the effort to learn OOP?

7. Using the mailing label program, pick six or seven properties for the label and textbox objects and change their values. What is the impact on the program? (You might use the list of properties shown in Table 2-2 as a starting place.)

▶ **WHAT YOU LEARNED IN THIS CHAPTER**

TOPIC	KEY POINTS
Class	A simplification of something
Property	A piece of data that is used to describe an object and its state
Method	An action, or ability, you want the object capable of doing
Object	A piece of memory that implements the design of the class. If a class is the architectural drawings of a house, object is the house.
Dot operator (.)	Used to gain access to an object's properties or methods
User interface	How the end user interacts with a program
Five Program Steps	A methodology for designing a program

PART II
Understanding C# Syntax

3

Understanding Data Types

WHAT YOU WILL LEARN IN THIS CHAPTER:

➤ Integer data types

➤ The range of values for different data types

➤ Floating-point data types

➤ Which data type should be used to represent financial data

➤ The boolean data type

➤ When to use one data type versus anotherIntelliSense

WROX.COM CODE DOWNLOADS FOR THIS CHAPTER

You can find the wrox.com code downloads for this chapter at `www.wrox.com/remtitle` `.cgi?isbn=9781118336922` on the Download Code tab. The code in the `Chapter03` folder is individually named according to the names throughout this chapter.

As you learned in Chapter 2, most computer programs are centered on solving problems by taking data in one form, transforming it in some manner, and then presenting that new data to the user. The data the computer manipulates can be stored in many different shapes and sizes. When you finish this chapter you will have a good understanding of why C# offers you such flexibility to select a data type.

COMPUTER DATA

Computer programs usually input data in one form, process it, and then show the new data on the computer screen. This can invite the question: What is data? Simply stated, *data* is information. Computer data is information stored in a variable for use in a program. In a broad sense, there are two basic kinds of computer data: numeric data and textual data.

Numeric data is any kind of data that can have arithmetic operations performed on it. You can add, subtract, multiply, and divide numeric data. You can perform other operations on numeric data, such as finding a square root, a sine, or a cosine of a numeric quantity, and so on. You will also see numeric data types referred to as *value types*. The precise meaning of this term is discussed in Chapter 5. For now, however, you can think of them as those data types whose variables can have data stored directly into them.

Textual data are character representations of data. Your name is a piece of data that can be represented in a program in a textual fashion. Some students become confused when you ask them whether a ZIP code is numeric or textual information. Because ZIP codes are usually not manipulated in mathematical expressions (for example, you wouldn't need to multiply or divide a ZIP code), they are usually treated as textual information.

Integer Data Types

An *integer data type* is any numeric value expressed as a whole number. Integer values cannot have a fractional component associated with them. If you try to assign a fractional value to an integer variable, C# truncates the value. For example, if val is an integer data type, the statement

```
val = 6.9999;
```

assigns the value of 6 to val. This means that integer operations on fractional values do not round those values; they truncate them. That is, if an integer data type has a fractional value, C# simply throws away the fractional component.

Table 3-1 lists the various integer data types that you can use in your programs.

TABLE 3-1: Integer Data Types

TYPE SPECIFIER	BITS	RANGE	DATA SUFFIX
byte	8	0 through 255	
sbyte	8	−128 through 127	
short	16	−32,768 through 32,767	
ushort	16	0 through 65,535	
int	32	−2,147,483,648 through 2,147,483,647	
uint	32	0 through 4,294,967,295	U, u
long	64	−9,223,372,036,854,775,808 through 9,223,372,036,854,775,807	L, l
ulong	64	0 through 18,446,744,073,709,551,615	UL, ul

As you can see in Table 3-1, some data types are prefixed with the letter "s" (sbyte) while others are prefixed with the letter "u". The "s" means the data are signed quantities, while the "u" means they are unsigned quantities. (The next section explains why these are important distinctions.)

Data suffixes are used to tell the compiler the data type being used in an expression. For example,

```
long bigNum;
// some code...
bigNum = 15L;
```

tells the compiler unequivocally that the numeric constant is 15 expressed as a `long` data type. If the suffix is not used, the compiler may complain that an `int` is being assigned into a `long`. Also, although lower case suffixes are recognized by the compiler, you should use only upper case suffixes. They are easier to see, plus the lower case "el" looks a lot like the digit "1" and may make debugging harder than it should be.

Range of Integer Data Types

Each of the integer data types has a range of values that it can accommodate. Consider the `byte` data type, which uses 8 bits. A *binary digit*, or *bit*, is the smallest unit of computer storage and may assume the value of on (1) or off (0). This means that the most basic unit of information in a computer—the bit—has only two possible states: on and off. Because there are only two possible states, information is stored in a computer in a binary, or base-2, format. Although you perform mathematical operations using a base-10 numbering system, the computer prefers base-2 numbers.

From an engineering standpoint, it is more convenient to group the bits into a larger unit called a byte. A *byte* is a collection of 8 bits. Because each bit has two possible values, a byte can have 2^8, or 256, unique combinations. If you refer to Table 3-1, you can see that a `byte` data type can represent the values 0 through 255.

Understanding Binary Numbers

Wait a minute! Eight bits can be used to represent 256 values, not 255? So why is the range of a byte limited to 255? The reason is that 8 bits can represent 256 unique values, and one of those values is zero. Therefore, if all bits are turned off, the byte has a value of 0. If all bits are turned on, the byte has the value 255. Table 3-2 further illustrates the relationship between bits and their associated numeric values.

TABLE 3-2: Bit Positions and Their Binary Equivalents

Bit Position	7	6	5	4	3	2	1	0
Base 2 Representation	2^7	2^6	2^5	2^4	2^3	2^2	2^1	2^0
Value	128	64	32	16	8	4	2	1
10 =	0	0	0	0	1	0	1	0
73 =	0	1	0	0	1	0	0	1
132 =	1	0	0	0	0	1	0	0
255 =	1	1	1	1	1	1	1	1

Referring to Table 3-2, you can see the numeric value of a byte depends upon which bits are turned on. For example, for the value 73, you see

```
01001001
```

which is interpreted as

```
0 + 64 + 0 + 0 + 8 + 0 + 0 + 1
```

If you sum up the values, the total is 73. If all the bits are turned on, the byte appears as this:

```
11111111
```

which becomes this:

```
128 + 64 + 32 +16 + 8 + 4 + 2 + 1
```

and totals 255.

Signed Integer Values

Given this information, why is the sbyte data type limited to a maximum value of 128? The reason is that the sbyte data type is a *signed byte*. Because it is signed, sbyte data may assume positive or negative values. The highest bit of the byte (bit position 7) is used to store the sign of the number. For signed numbers, the high bit is called the *sign bit*. If the sign bit is turned on, it is a negative number. If the sign bit is turned off, it is a positive number. Because of the sign bit, only seven bits (2^7 combinations) are available instead of eight bits (2^8 combinations). Because 2^7 is 128, only 128 unique values are possible, and because 0 is one of those values, the maximum positive value is 127. If the sign bit is turned on, you still have 128 unique values available, all of which can be negative. This is true because you have already accounted for the value 0 in the positive range of values. This means the negative range extends from −1 to −128. Referring to Table 3-1, you can see that if the range of permissible values begins with 0, that integer data type does not use a sign bit. If the range includes negative values, it does use a sign bit. You can also see that integer data types that do use a sign bit have a maximum value that is approximately one-half that of their corresponding unsigned data types. The reason, of course, is that the highest bit is reserved for the sign of the number.

Which Integer Should You Use?

One problem beginning programmers face is deciding which integer data type to use. There is no single correct answer. There are, however, several factors to keep in mind:

➤ **Range of values:** If you are interested only in counting the number of healthy teeth in a person's mouth, the byte data type works. On the other hand, if you measure the day's high temperature, even an sbyte may not have enough range if your sample site includes both Death Valley and Juneau, Alaska. Always err on the high side so that you have sufficient range to accommodate your needs.

➤ **Memory limitations:** For most of the applications you write, you probably have at least half a gigabyte of memory available to you. If you select a long data type instead of an int, chances are the 4 extra bytes used per integer value aren't going to gobble up much additional memory. However, if you write programs for a toaster or an engine sensor, it could be that memory limitations for the device are restrictive. In such cases you would want to select the smallest data type with sufficient range to do the job.

➤ **Processor considerations:** Each computer has a central processing unit, which is the heart of a computer. Back in the late 1970s, CPUs had internal storage units, called *registers*, which could process data in 1-byte (8-bit) chunks. Later, the CPU registers had 16-bit registers, then 32-bit registers, and finally 64-bit registers. Integer data types that can snuggle neatly into a register without adding or losing bits may have a slight speed advantage for some of the operations a CPU performs on the data. What this means is that a 32-bit CPU may actually process a 32-bit integer faster than a 16-bit integer even though the 16-bit integer is smaller. Although the performance hit on a single mismatch is small, this could make a difference when millions of calculations are performed repeatedly.

➤ **Library considerations:** You already know that the .NET Framework provides thousands of classes for you. Some of these classes have methods you might use often. For example, the math class includes a square root method. You send a data value to the method, and it sends that value's square root back to you. Most of the math methods (such as `Sqrt()`, `Cos()`, and `Pow()`) ask that you send a `double` data type (discussed later in the section on floating point data types) to it, and the method returns the answer as a `double`. If that's the case, it would make sense to have all the data types be `double` if they interact with the math classes. If you don't supply a data type that matches what a method expects, the compiler must generate code to do the conversion before the data even get to the method. Although the time to process this additional "conversion code" is small, in a large program loop that involves many such conversions, the time penalty can be noticeable.

➤ **Convention:** Sometimes convention (a nicer word for "habit") determines the data type used with certain programming constructs. For example, in Chapter 8 you learn about program loops that use a variable to control the loop. Convention finds that an `int` data type is most often used to control program loops. Although there may be other reasons to use an `int` to control the loop (such as processor considerations and native register sizes), most programmers simply define an `int` to control the loop without a whole lot of thought. Convention doesn't necessarily make a choice of data type right, but it may explain why so many programmers tend to use certain data types with certain programming constructs.

In the final analysis, the range of values is probably the most important factor to consider when selecting an integer data type. With a little experience, you develop a knack to select the proper data types for the task at hand.

Variable Naming Rules and Conventions

Before you create your first program, you need to understand program variables. A *variable* is simply a name you give to a specific piece of data. Back in the dark ages of programming, you might store an integer value at memory address 900,000. In those days there were no variable names. You simply typed in `900000` anytime you wanted to reference that integer value. It didn't take long before programmers started writing programming tools that let them use symbolic names (such as `operand1`) for memory addresses, which made the act of writing programs much easier and less error-prone, hence the advent of variable names.

A variable name, also called an *identifier*, has several syntax rules you must follow to keep the Visual Studio compiler happy. These syntax rules are as follows:

➤ Variable names may begin only with an alpha character (a through z, A through Z) or an underscore character (_).

> ➤ Punctuation characters and operators are not allowed.

> ➤ The variable name cannot be a C# keyword.

> ➤ Digit characters are allowed after the first character (for example, `Apollo5`, but not `5Apollo`).

Although it is not a rule, you should always try to use variable names that make sense in the context in which they are used. In the preceding code, `operand1` is a better name than `o1` even though Visual Studio accepts either name. A second convention, called *camel notation*, is that long variable names start with lowercase letters and that each following word in the name is capitalized, as in `myHatSize`. Camel notation makes it easier to read the variable names. The code in the `btnCalc_Click()` event adheres these rules and conventions for naming the `flag`, `operand1`, `operand2`, and `result` variables.

Let's put what you've learned about data types to work in a simple program that uses integer data.

TRY IT OUT A Program Using Integer Data (Chapter03.zip)

Now write a simple program that accepts two values from the keyboard and performs a mathematical operation on the two values. As always, you need a plan to guide you as you write the program. The basis for the plan is always the Five Program Steps.

1. Formulate a program plan. Because this is a simple program, it doesn't need any special Initialization step code beyond what Visual Studio does for you automatically. The Input step suggests that you want to collect two integer values from the user. The Process step states that you want to perform some math operation on the data values entered by the user. Assume you want to divide the two numbers. Because Windows programs are event-driven, you need to add a Calculate button to begin the processing of the data. The Output step assumes that you want to show the user the end result of the math operation division in your program. There's nothing special for you to do in the Termination step, so you can just provide an Exit button to end the program.

2. Select New ➪ Project from the main menu.

3. Select Empty Project from the Template Window. (Make sure it's for C# if you have the full Visual Studio.)

4. Type in the name and location for the new project. This can be any folder name and location you want. However, you might consider making a new folder on your C drive. Call it something such as **BookExamples** and then create subfolders for each chapter of this book and place the code in those subfolders.

5. Select Project ➪ Add References, selecting `System.dll`, `System.Drawing.dll`, and `System.Windows.Forms.dll`. (Or click the Recent Tab, and select from there.)

6. Select Project ➪ Add New Item; select Code File, and name the file **frmMain.cs**.

7. Place the cursor in the Source window, and copy the C# template code you saved in a file from Chapter 2 (Listing 2-1) into `frmMain.cs`.

8. Select Project ➪ Properties ➪ Application. Set Output Type to Windows Application, and set Startup Object to `frmMain`.

9. Highlight the `frmMain.cs` file in the Solution Explorer window, and click the View Designer icon.

10. Add the controls presented in Table 3-3 to `frmMain`.

TABLE 3-3: Controls for Integer Program

CONTROL ID	DESCRIPTION
label1	Label with text for first input. Set properties to: AutoSize = False BorderStyle = Fixed3D Text = Enter first integer value TextAlign = MiddleRight
label2	Label with text for first input. Set properties to: AutoSize = False BorderStyle = Fixed3D Text = Enter second integer value TextAlign = MiddleRight
txtOperand1	Textbox
txtOperand2	Textbox
txtResult	Textbox with properties set to: ReadOnly = True
btnCalc	Button with Text set property set to: &Calculate
btnExit	Button with Text set property set to: E&xit
frmMain	Text = "Interger Division" StartPosition = CenterScreen

When you finish, your form should look similar to Figure 3-1.

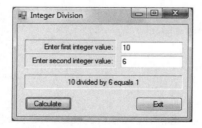

FIGURE 3-1: User interface for integer data program

11. In the Design View, double-click on the btnCalc button, which causes Visual Studio to add the stub code for the button click event. The double-click event automatically switches you to the Source Window. Now add the button click code shown in Listing 3-1 to the stub code. The code is part of the Chapter03.ZIP file.

LISTING 3-1: Button Click Event Code

```
private void btnCalc_Click(object sender, EventArgs e)
{
  bool flag;
  int operand1;
  int operand2;
  int answer;

      //                        Input Step
      // Check first input...
  flag = int.TryParse(txtOperand1.Text, out operand1);
  if (flag == false)
  {
    MessageBox.Show("Enter a whole number", "Input Error");
    txtOperand1.Focus();
    return;
  }

      // Check second input...
  flag = int.TryParse(txtOperand2.Text, out operand2);
  if (flag == false)
  {
    MessageBox.Show("Enter a whole number", "Input Error");
    txtOperand2.Focus();
    return;
  }

      //                     Process Step
  answer = operand1 / operand2;

      //                     Display Step
  txtResult.Text = operand1.ToString() + " divided by " +
                   operand2.ToString() +
                 " equals " +answer.ToString();
  txtResult.Visible = true;

}

private void btnExit_Click(object sender, EventArgs e)
{
  Close();
}
```

How It Works

When you run the program, you can find that the action is done in the Process step, which you have tied to the button click event for btnCalc. You begin the code for the btnCalc() click event by defining a boolean variable named flag, followed by the definitions for three integer variables of type int. (boolean variables can only have the values associated with logic true or logic false. These are covered at the end of the chapter.)

Using the TryParse( ) Method

The next statement in the program is this:

```
flag = int.TryParse(txtOperand1.Text, out operand1);
```

The statement may seem rather formidable, but it actually isn't.

The purpose of the int.TryParse() method is to examine what the user entered from the keyboard to see if that input can be converted into an integer data type. You know it's attempting an integer conversion from textual data to an integer because of the keyword int before TryParse().

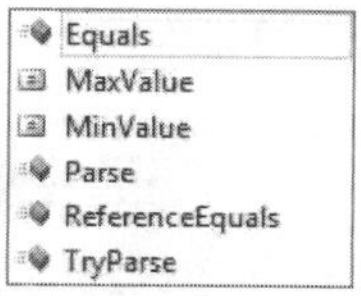

Wait a minute! What's the dot operator doing between the int and TryParse()? C# provides you with a class for every data type. In this example, when you type in the keyword int and then the dot operator, you can see Visual Studio pop up a small window that looks like Figure 3-2.

If you look closely at Figure 3-2, you can see four lines begin with a 3-D cube and two lines begin with a square. The *cubes* represent class methods, whereas the *squares* are for class properties. As you can see in the figure, the int class has several methods, including TryParse(). Therefore, in the code statement, the dot operator is used because you want to call the TryParse()class method found in the int class. Sometimes, you will see the term *wrapper class*, which often means that some piece of data is "wrapped" inside a class. The int class shown here is an example of a wrapper class because the basic data type provides you with specific properties and methods to make it a little more flexible.

FIGURE 3-2: The int class properties and methods

Keep in mind that anything the user types into a textbox is entered as textual data. However, your program wants to manipulate numeric data in the form of integers. Simply stated, the purpose of TryParse() is to convert apples (textual data) into oranges (numeric data).

Sometimes, users do make typing errors and the conversion doesn't go smoothly. If you look at your keyboard, you can see it's not too hard to accidentally hit the o (oh) key when you meant to hit the 0 (zero) key. They're only about one-half an inch apart. What TryParse() does is examine each character the user typed into the txtOperand1 textbox to make sure it was a digit character. Now simplify what comprises the TryParse() statement:

```
flag = int.TryParse(txtOperand1.Text, out operand1);
```

This is actually nothing more than what you've seen before:

```
flag = Object . MethodName(argument1, argument2);
```

You have an assignment operator (=) with two operands. The operand on the left is a boolean variable named flag, and the operand on the right is an object named int. You use the dot operator to get inside the object and use the TryParse() method buried inside the int object. TryParse() needs two pieces of information, called *arguments*, sent to it to perform its job. In this example, the TryParse() method wants the Text property of the txtOperand1 object and an integer variable you defined as operand1 sent to it. Why does TryParse() need this information? Simply stated, argument1 supplies the property with the textual data to be examined, and argument2 gives the method a place to store the numeric result of the conversion if everything goes well. The flag variable simply holds the value that TryParse() returns when it's done doing its thing. If the conversion were completed successfully,

`TryParse()` returns true. If things didn't go so well, `TryParse()` returns false. You can then test the value of `flag` to see how the conversion faired with an `if` statement, as was done here. (You learn about the C# `if` statement in detail in Chapter 6.)

Now refer to the original code you typed in for the `TryParse()` statement. If `TryParse()` finds that the user did type in all digit characters, it converts those digit characters (which are textual data) into numeric data of type `int`. It takes that new numeric value and places it into `operand1`. Because the conversion of the textual data in the `Text` property of the `txtOperand1` object was successful, it returns the boolean value `true`. This value (`true`) then gets assigned into `flag`. Therefore, a successful call to the `TryParse()` method converts the textual data of the `Text` property of the `txtOperand1` object and places that integer number into the second argument of the call to `TryParse()`. Because you use the `TryParse()` method found inside the `int` object, the data is converted to an `int` data type and copied into the `int` variable named `operand1`.

CALLING A METHOD

The term *calling a method* refers to the process of directing program control to a method to perform some particular task. You might also see the term *caller* used with calling a method. A caller is a point of execution in a program, not a person or thing. In the `btnCalc_Click()` code presented earlier, the first line after the data definitions of `operand1`, `operand2`, and `result` is a call to the `TryParse()` method of an `int` object. To refer to the process to call the `TryParse()` method, a programmer might say, "`btnCalc` calls `TryParse()`." Another programmer might say, "`flag` calls `TryParse()`." Either phrase simply means that program control jumps away from the current sequence to execute the program statements in the `btnCalc_Click()` method to execute those statements found in the `TryParse()` method.

When the program finishes executing the statements in `TryParse()`, program control is sent back to the point at which `TryParse()` was called. This process to send control back to the point at which the method was called is associated with the phrase *return to the caller*.

If the method returns some form of data, such as the boolean value `true` or `false`, as part of its task, you might hear the phrase, "The method returns `true` (or `false`) to the caller." In the example, `TryParse()` is designed to return the boolean value of either `true` or `false` to the caller. The way to visualize what happens is to look at the state of the information just before the `TryParse()` method is called:

```
flag = int.TryParse(txtOperand1.Text, out operand1);
```

This shows the information that is about to be sent to `TryParse()`. When `TryParse()` finishes its job to examine the contents of `txtOperand1.Text`, it returns `true` or `false` to the caller. Assuming the user typed in only digit characters, `operand1` contains the numeric value of the user's input, and `true` is returned to the caller. Therefore, when program control returns to the caller, the statement appears to be the following:

```
flag = true;
```

This means that `TryParse()` has done its job and converted the user's textual input into a numeric value now stored in `operand1` and returned `true` to the caller.

The terms and phrases introduced here are used throughout the text.

If the user typed in something other than digit characters into the textbox, `TryParse()` cannot successfully convert the textual characters into a numeric value. In that case, `TryParse()` sets operand1 to 0 and returns the value `false`. The return value (`false`) is then assigned into the boolean variable named `flag`.

You might wonder, "Why mess around with returning `true` or `false` to the caller? Why not just set the second argument to zero if the conversion fails and be done with it?" The problem is that zero is a legitimate integer value, and the `TryParse()` method must cope gracefully if the value is 0. If you return 0 regardless of what the user types in, how would you know if the value is good or bad? If the user wants the value to be zero but accidentally hits the "o" key, it appears that the conversion was successful when it shouldn't be. By returning a boolean value from the call, you can test to see if the conversion failed.

An example might help reinforce what's being done. Suppose the user enters **1234** for the input into the txtOperand1 textbox object. The statement line looks like this:

```
flag = int.TryParse(txtOperand1.Text, out operand1);
```

It becomes this:

```
?  = int.TryParse("1234", out ?);
```

The `flag` and operand1 values are shown as question marks because, at the moment, they could contain unknown garbage values. After `TryParse()` examines the string of input data from the txtOperand1 textbox object (1234), it decides that it can successfully convert those digit characters into a numeric value of type `int`. Because the conversion is successful, `TryParse()` sets operand1 to the new value (1234) and returns `true` to the caller. In this case, the caller is the assignment operator that takes the return value (`true`) and assigns it into the `flag` variable. The end result is as follows:

```
true = int.TryParse("1234", out 1234);
```

The keyword `out` in the second argument to `TryParse()` is required and tells Visual Studio it's okay to use operand1 as an argument even though it hasn't yet been initialized to a meaningful value.

The code that follows the `TryParse()` method call tests the `flag` variable to see if the conversion were successful . If the conversion failed, the `if` statement sees that `flag` is `false`, and the program executes the code controlled by the `if` statement. (Chapter 6 discusses `if` statements in detail.) The statements following the `if` keyword are executed only if the `flag` variable is `false`:

```
if (flag == false)
{
  MessageBox.Show("Enter a whole number", "Input Error");
  txtOperand1.Focus();
  return;
}
```

The program then creates a `MessageBox` object and uses its `Show()` method to display an error message on the screen. After the user reads and dismisses the error message, the program calls the `Focus()` method of the txtOperand1 object. A call to the `Focus()` method causes the program to place the cursor back into its textbox. The `return` keyword causes the program to leave the btnCalc click event code and redisplay the frmMain form object. The cursor sits in the txtOperand1 textbox waiting for the user to enter a proper integer value.

The same sequence of checks is performed on the contents of the txtOperand2 textbox object. The `TryParse()` method performs the same checks on the textual data held in the `Text` property of txtOperand2.

Processing and Displaying the Result

After both operands are assigned values from their associated textboxes, you are ready to perform the division operation. The forward slash (/) is the C# operator for division. The code to perform the calculation and display the results is shown here.

```
answer = operand1 / operand2;
txtResult.Text = operand1.ToString() + " divided by " +
                 operand2.ToString() +
                 " equals " +answer.ToString();
txtResult.Visible = true;
```

Because you want to use the division operator, the first statement divides the integer `operand1` value by the `operand2` value. The assignment operator then assigns the result of that division expression into the variable named `answer`.

All you need to do now is display the answer for the user to see. However, again you have the "apples and oranges" problem. That is, `operand1`, `operand2`, and `answer` are all numeric data, but you need to display them in a textbox that expects the data to be in textual form. As mentioned earlier, each variable of a given value type has a wrapper class associated with it, which provides certain properties and methods. One of those available methods is `ToString()`. The purpose of the `ToString()` method is to take the current numeric value of the integer object and convert it into textual data. You can think of `ToString()` as a reversal of the `TryParse()` method. In this example, `ToString()` simply takes the numeric value of the variable `operand1` and converts it into the appropriate sequence of digit characters.

After all three values have been converted into text, each text representation of the value is concatenated to the next piece of text by means of the concatenation operator (the + operator). After all the text is concatenated together, the combined text is assigned into the `Text` property of the `txtResult` object. (*Concatenation* is a fifty-cent word that means to "append to.")

The last thing the program does is set the `Visible` property of the `txtResult` object to `true`. You do this because when you designed the user interface, you set the `Visible` property to `false`. Therefore, when the user first runs the program, he cannot see the textbox that ultimately displays the results. Although this program is simple and doesn't have a lot of "clutter" on the form, this technique to hide the display step objects until they contain something useful may help to declutter the user interface while the user performs the input step. Hiding the textbox also prevents the user from attempting to type something into this textbox.

You might want to experiment with your program a bit. Try changing the math operator from division to addition (+), subtraction (-), multiplication (*), and modulo divide (%) in the program statement line just after the Process step comment. (*Modulo divide*, %, gives you the remainder of division operation.)

Another interesting thing to do is enter input data that "breaks" the code. For example, what happens if you enter a zero as the second operand in the current program? What happens if you enter huge values that you know exceed the range of the data type (refer to Table 3-1) you selected? Breaking your code is a great way to discover the limitations of the data and the kinds of problems you run into out there in the "real world." Even more important, you can see how Visual Studio complains to you when that type of error creeps into your programs. This can help you when you try to debug programs in later chapters.

FLOATING-POINT DATA TYPES

A floating-point data type is a numeric data type, but it can represent fractional values. Table 3-4 shows the floating-point data types and their associated ranges.

TABLE 3-4: Floating-Point Data Types

TYPE SPECIFIER	BITS	RANGE	DATA SUFFIX
Float	32	$\pm 1.5 \times 10^{-45}$ to $\pm 3.4 \times 10^{38}$	F, f
Double	64	$\pm 5.0 \times 10^{-324}$ to $\pm 1.7 \times 10^{308}$	D, d

The range of values for either type of floating-point number is quite large (refer to Table 3-4). Usually you select floating-point values when you need the data to reflect fractional values, or you need to use small or large numbers in your program.

In the following Try It Out sections, you create a program that uses floating point numbers in place of the integer numbers used in the previous program.

TRY IT OUT A Program Using Floating-Point Numbers (Chapter03.zip)

You can modify your program that used integer numbers to work with floating-point numbers fairly easily. Assuming you still have the code from the previous Try It Out loaded into Visual Studio:

1. Change the statement lines in the `btnCalc` click event code from

```
int operand1;
int operand2;
int answer;
```

to this:

```
float operand1;
float operand2;
float answer;
```

2. Now try to run the program.

How It Works

After you make the changes, run the program. You get the following error message:

```
The best overloaded method match for 'int.TryParse(string, out int)' has some
invalid arguments.
```

What this error message tells you is that `TryParse()` is confused because it expects the second argument to be an integer, but you've passed `operand1` as a `float` data type. This isn't a serious problem because each of the data types has its own version of `TryParse()`. Change the `TryParse()` method calls in the program to the following:

```
flag = float.TryParse(txtOperand1.Text, out operand1);
```

This change uses the `float` wrapper class for the conversion process.

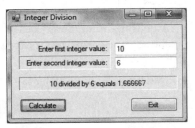

Now compile and run the program. When you ran the integer version of the program and supplied the two input values as 10 and 6, the answer was 1. The reason for this is that integer math doesn't allow a fractional component. The integer version of the program simply truncated the result to 1. If you use those same inputs in the float version of the program, the result becomes 1.666667, as shown in Figure 3-3. (You didn't change the labels, so those still show the prompt for integer data. You can easily change these if you want.)

FIGURE 3-3: Program using float data type

The result of the `float` division presents a fractional value, which was not possible when the `int` data type was used.

TRY IT OUT **A Program That Tests Floating-Point Precision (Chapter03.zip)**

Using the same program you just wrote in the previous Try It Out, make the following change to that program. Note how we change the data type from the previous version to use the `double` data type here:

1. Change

```
float operand1;
float operand2;
float answer;
```

to

```
double operand1;
double operand2;
double answer;
```

Do you need to change the data type for the call to the `TryParse()` method? (Hint: Only if you want the program to run.)

2. Now recompile, and rerun the program with the same inputs.

> ### SEARCH AND REPLACE IN VISUAL STUDIO
>
> In the `float` version of the program under discussion, you were directed to change all instances of the keyword `float` to `double`. You could search through the program code looking for each occurrence of the `float` keyword and change it to `double`. However, this is exactly the type of no-brainer task perfectly suited for the computer to do for you.

If you want to search the entire program for a specific word or phrase, place the cursor at the top of the program in the Source window and press Ctrl+F. You should quickly see the Find and Replace dialog box. There are two options immediately below the title bar. Select the Quick Replace option. Now type in what you are looking for (such as `float`) and then enter what you want to replace it with (such as `double`). The Find and Replace dialog box should look like what is shown in Figure 3-4.

FIGURE 3-4: Using Find and Replace

You should now click the Find Next button to find the next occurrence of the word `float` in the program source code. If you want to change that occurrence of the word `float` to `double`, click the Replace button. The word `float` is then replaced with `double`, and the program proceeds to the next `float` keyword it finds in the program.

There is a tremendous temptation to click the Replace All button, which goes through the entire source code file and automatically makes the replacements without asking you to click the Replace button. Don't cave in to this temptation! Search and Replace has the innate intelligence of a box of rocks. Suppose you want to change from an `int` to a `double`. You type those inputs into the dialog box and press Replace All. Now, when you look at your source code, you find the old program line,

```
int interestRate;
```

has been changed to:

```
double doubleerestRate;
```

This is probably not what you wanted to do. The sad thing is that your code will still execute correctly because all instances of `interestRate` were faithfully changed to `doubleerestRate`. However, your effort to pick a meaningful variable name has been tossed out the window. Suggestion: Never *ever* use Replace All. Use the Find Next and Replace buttons only. A safer way to rename a variable is to right click the variable name at its point of definition and select the Refactor ⇨ Rename menu options. You are then given a dialog that allows you to change the variable name.

How It Works

Now the result is 1.66666666666667. Notice there are more digit characters in the answer using the `double` data type version than when you used the `float` version. This is because the precision of a `float` is limited to 7 digits, whereas the precision of a `double` is 15 digits.

The *precision* of a number refers to the number of significant digits that a data type can represent. Referring Table 3-4, you can see that a `float` can represent a number with a value as large as 1.0 e38. That's a number with up to 38 digits. However, because the precision of a `float` is limited to only 7 digits, only the first 7 digits of that number are significant. The remaining 31 digits are simply the computer's best guess as to the rest of the digits in the number. When you changed the data type to `double`, you increased the precision to 15 digits. Although the answer could go on for up to 308 digits for a `double`, the computer gave up after 15 digits and said, "The heck with it; 1.66666666666667 is as good as it gets."

Which Floating-Point Data Type Should You Use?

It's probably obvious from Table 3-4 that the increased precision for a `double` is possible because C# uses twice as much memory to store a `double` as a `float`. This invites the question...again, "Which floating-point data type should you use?" Once again, the answer is, "It depends." The same factors that influence your choice of integer data types (memory limitations, processor and library considerations, convention, and so on) play a part to make the right data type choice. The processor and library considerations, however, are especially important when you deal with floating-point data.

First, Intel's Pentium-class CPU has a math coprocessor built into it. The math coprocessor is specifically designed to make floating-point math operations as fast as possible. Using the math coprocessor involves no special coding work on your part. Floating-point data is automatically routed to the math coprocessor when your program performs math operations on floating-point data.

Second, almost all the methods in the `Math` class (`Sqrt()`, `Pow()`, `Log()`, `Cos()`, and so on) expect to use the `double` data type. Again, if you pass a `float` data type to the `Sqrt()` method of the `Math` class, code must be executed to expand the data value from 32 bits to 64 bits. The process to expand a data value from a smaller to a larger number of bits is called *data widening*. After `Sqrt()` has done its job, code must be executed to shrink the result back to the 32 bits your `float` data type demands. The process to shrink a data value from a larger to smaller number of bits is called *data narrowing*. The code associated with data narrowing and data widening can be avoided if you use a `double` data type when using the methods found in the `Math` class.

Finally, the two floating-point data types give you different levels of precision. The `double` data type has more than twice the number of significant digits of a `float` data type. Unless there are severe memory limitations and given the other advantages to use a `double` data type, most of the time you should use the `double` data type for floating-point operations.

MONETARY VALUES: THE DECIMAL DATA TYPE

It might seem that the `double` data type would also be a good choice for monetary values. The only problem is that even 15 digits of precision may not be enough to represent important monetary values. To overcome the problems associated with limited precision in financial calculations, C# created the `decimal` data type. Table 3-5 shows the details of the `decimal` data type.

TABLE 3-5: Range for Decimal Data Type

TYPE SPECIFIER	BITS	RANGE	DATA SUFFIX
Decimal	128	±1.0 × 10–28 to ±7.9 × 1028	M, m

The greatest advantage of the `decimal` data type is that is has 28 digits of precision—almost twice the precision of a `double`. This means that even in financial calculations involving large amounts you can keep track of the pennies. The disadvantage of the `decimal` data type is that each variable takes 16 bytes of memory to store its value. Also, because the math coprocessor is not set up to handle 16 bytes, math operations on the `decimal` data type are much slower than they are on the `double` data type.

The program in the next Try It Out is used to see the impact that changing the data type has on the precision of the numbers.

TRY IT OUT   A Program That Tests decimal Precision (Chapter03.zip)

You can modify the program you've been using to test the various data types by simply changing the `int` keywords in the code listing presented for the `btnCalc_Click()` method with the `decimal` keyword.

1.   Change

```
double operand1;
double operand2;
double answer;
```

to

```
decimal operand1;
decimal operand2;
decimal answer;
```

2.   Now run the program, using the same input values of `10` and `6` for the two operands. What happened? Did you change the `TryParse()` call? (The devil is in the details.)

How It Works

Figure 3-5 shows the output for the program. (The input prompts for the two label objects or the text for the `frmMain` object are not changed, so the word "integer" is a little misleading in the figure. Change them if you want.)

The program runs exactly as the earlier versions of this program with one major exception: The result has significantly more digits in the answers in Figure 3-5; the enhanced precision of the `decimal` data type is so large the answer doesn't fit in the text-box space allocated for it. Because nobody likes to throw money away, the expanded precision of the `decimal` data type is a good thing in financial calculations.

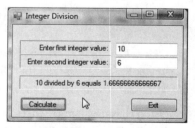

FIGURE 3-5: Program run using decimal data type

USING INTELLISENSE TO LOCATE PROGRAM ERRORS

After you change the variable's data types to the `decimal` data type, try inserting the following program statement into the program just after the definition of `answer` but before the call to the `TryParse()` method:

```
operand1 = .5;
```

When you compile the program, a squiggly blue line appears under `.5` in the statement. The *blue squiggly line* points out that Visual Studio sensed an error in the statement line where the squiggly blue line appears.

Syntax Rules and Error Messages

IntelliSense is the name Microsoft has given to the part of Visual Studio responsible for checking your statements to make sure they obey the syntax rules of C#. A *syntax rule* simply refers to the language rules C# expects you to follow to form a valid C# program statement. (You can find more details on language rules in Chapter 4.) Just as the English language expects a sentence to have a noun and a verb, C# has rules it expects you to follow when you write program statements.

If you break (or bend) the syntax rules of C#, IntelliSense draws a blue squiggly line under the offending part of the statement. If you move the cursor over the blue line, IntelliSense provides you with some information about the error. This information about the nature of the error is presented in the form of an *error message*. In the preceding statement, the error message is as follows:

```
Literal of type double cannot be implicitly converted to type 'decimal';
use an 'M' suffix to create a literal of this type
```

In other words, Visual Studio is confused about what `.5` is. You have defined `operand1` as a decimal data type, but you are trying to assign the value `.5` into it. Unless told otherwise, whenever IntelliSense sees a fractional value like `.5` in the source code, it assumes you want to use a `double` data type. (A pure number such as `.5` in a program's source code is called a numeric *literal* because a variable is not used to store the value. Instead, the numeric value is "literally" part of the program's source code.) Therefore, IntelliSense sees your program statement attempting to take a `double` data value (`.5`) and put it into a `decimal` data type (`operand1`). This is like trying to make a person who wears a size-4 shoe walk around in a size 8…. It just doesn't fit right. The error message is saying the same thing, only a little more formally. In its own way, the IntelliSense error message says this:

```
The literal .5 looks like a double to me and I cannot convert it to type 'decimal'
for you; use an 'M' suffix to create a literal of this type
```

Okay…that makes sense. Now, follow its recommendation and correct the statement to see what happens. The corrected line should be

```
operand1 = .5M;
```

Using the information in Table 3-5, you can make the meaning of the literal `.5` crystal-clear to IntelliSense by placing the `decimal` data type's suffix, `M`, after the literal. After you make this change, *voila!*…the squiggly blue line disappears.

As a general rule, whenever you see the dreaded squiggly blue line, move the cursor over the blue line and read the error message IntelliSense gives you. Sometimes the message may appear a bit cryptic, but with a little experience you can begin to interpret the error messages correctly.

THE DISAPPEARING SQUIGGLY BLUE LINE

When IntelliSense finds an error, it does its best to pinpoint what it thinks is the exact line number of the program error and draw the squiggly blue line there. Most of the time IntelliSense does a great job identifying the exact statement in which the error occurred. Other times, however, the nature of the error is such that IntelliSense doesn't realize an error has occurred until it has examined several more lines. In situations in which the line with the squiggly blue line appears to be syntactically correct, look at the lines immediately above it for a statement that is amiss.

Note that the squiggly blue line does not always disappear when you correct the error in the statement line. The best way to determine if a program change does fix an error is to recompile the program to see if the error message and dreaded squiggly blue line disappear.

Finally, the squiggly line may also appear red. The *red squiggly line* is often associated with a missing statement element. For example, if you type in the following:

```
int i
```

a red squiggly line would appear at the end of the line to inform you that you forgot to add a semicolon at the end of the line. Chapter 11 has a lot more detail about program bugs and debugging.

THE BOOLEAN DATA TYPE

Of the two fundamental types of data, numeric and textual, thus far you have studied only numeric data types. (You can read more about textual data types in Chapter 6.) The boolean data type is one of those gray areas that doesn't exactly fit into either a numeric or textual data type. Although it is not a precise fit, you learn about the `bool` data type with the numeric data types because it is used to reflect the state of a piece of data, rather than some textual representation of that data.

One of the elemental features of a computer is that it can make decisions based upon the data it processes. You have seen this decision-making ability in the sample programs. For example, in the integer-division program you wrote earlier, you had the following program statements:

```
flag = int.TryParse(txtOperand1.Text, out operand1);
if (flag == false)
{
  MessageBox.Show("Enter a whole number", "Input Error");
  txtOperand1.Focus();
  return;
}
```

The variable named `flag` that was set by the call to `TryParse()` was used to decide whether the user had typed in a valid integer number into the `Text` property of the `txtOperand1` textbox object. If the user input could be converted successfully into an integer value, `flag` was set to `true`, and the value of `operand1` was set to the value entered by the user. If the user entered text that could not be converted to an integer (such as the letter o instead of the zero digit character, 0), `flag` was set to `false` and `operand1` was set to `0`. In that case, an error message displays and the user is given another chance to enter the data.

In the preceding code snippet, `flag` is a boolean variable. Boolean variables are defined by the `bool` keyword. (You can see the definition of `flag` in the `btnCalc_Click()` method shown earlier in this chapter.) Table 3-6 shows the relevant information for a `bool` data type.

TABLE 3-6: The Boolean Data Type

TYPE SPECIFIER	BITS	VALUES	DATA SUFFIX
bool	8	true, false	None

Referring to Table 3-6, there is no "range" for a boolean variable. A `bool` data type can hold only two possible values: `true` or `false`. Therefore, a boolean variable is used to hold the state of the variable, not a specific value.

If you've ever had a logic course, you've been exposed to truth tables where conditions are stated as either `true` or `false`. Quite often those conditions are presented with `1` representing true and `0` representing false. You cannot, however, use `1` and `0` to represent `true` and `false` in a C# program. First, `true` and `false` in C# are keywords, and IntelliSense knows that these are the only two values you can store in a `bool` variable. If you type in the statement

```
flag = 0;
```

IntelliSense issues an error message stating

```
Constant value '0' cannot be converted to a 'bool'
```

This message tells you that Visual Studio is unhappy with your attempt to assign a zero (an integer literal) into the boolean variable named `flag`. If you change the zero to `false` and recompile the program, the error message goes away because `flag` now is assigned the proper type of data.

> **DON'T USE A BOOL DATA TYPE FOR THE WRONG PURPOSE**
>
> Because a `bool` data type can reflect only the states `true` or `false`, it cannot be used to count data. A `bool` variable should be used only when the information associated with the variable truly can have only two states. For example, a programmer was hired to write a program to track information about the members of a club. One of the variables, named `Status`, was implemented as a `bool` with the interpretation that `true` meant the person was an active member of the club and `false` meant the person was not an active member. After the program was written, the club noticed that the program didn't properly handle a member who had been granted a temporary leave of absence. This little change by the club caused the program to fail because the boolean `Status` variable was now asked to record three states: 1) active member, 2) inactive member, and 3) member on leave of absence. The programmer had to go back into the code and change `Status` from a `bool` to an `int`.
>
> The lesson is simple: use a `bool` only when you are absolutely certain that the only possible states for the variable are `true` and `false`.

SUMMARY

The discussion in this chapter concentrated on the various value types of data that you can use in your C# programs. More specifically, you learned about the various numeric data types you can use. Any time you want to manipulate data in a mathematical way, you will likely use one of the numeric data types discussed in this chapter. You also read about the bool data type in this chapter because it is a value type; although, it is not manipulated in a mathematical sense. (The char value type is excluded from this chapter even though it is a value type. Because its use is associated with textual data, its discussion is postponed until Chapter 6.)

In the next chapter you expand on your understanding of the basic value types and how they are used in a program. Make sure you understand what the different value types are and how they may be used in a program before advancing to Chapter 4.

EXERCISES

You can find the answers to the following exercises in Appendix A.

1. Why does C# support unsigned data types?

2. Identify each of the following variable names as legal or illegal.

```
SetPort        9WaysToSunday    myCar

_system        Windows7         Ms.Mini

extern         your_car         My#Eye

for_2_Nut
```

3. Explain the following statement:

```
int len = txtInput.Text.Length;
```

4. What are the major differences between the float and double data types?

5. Suppose you want to generate a series of values that simulate throwing a pair of dice. Write a method named ThrowDice() that returns a value that is the sum of the two dice.

6. Gold can be used in financial transactions. With gold priced approximately $1,600 per ounce, what data type would you use to process financial transactions that use gold as the medium of exchange and why?

▶ **WHAT YOU LEARNED IN THIS CHAPTER**

TOPIC	KEY POINTS
Integer data	Numeric values that cannot have a fractional value, each with a specific range of values
`bool`	A data type that can only have the values associated with logic true or logic false
Floating-point data	Data that can assume fractional values, as in `float` or `double`
`decimal`	A data type that has greater precision than floating-point data types, used most often for money data.
Precision	Refers to the number of significant digits for a given data type
Data selection	Factors you should consider when selecting a specific data type
IntelliSense	How intelliSense can make debugging easier

Understanding C# Statements

WHAT YOU WILL LEARN IN THIS CHAPTER:

- ➤ Operators and operands
- ➤ Expressions
- ➤ Statements
- ➤ lvalues and rvalues
- ➤ What a symbol table is and how Visual Studio uses it
- ➤ How Visual Studio interacts with Windows
- ➤ The Bucket Analogy
- ➤ Using the Visual Studio debugger
- ➤ Magic numbers and why to avoid them

WROX.COM CODE DOWNLOADS FOR THIS CHAPTER

You can find the wrox.com code downloads for this chapter at `www.wrox.com/remtitle .cgi?isbn=9781118336922` on the Download Code tab. The code is in the `Chapter04` folder and is individually named according to the names throughout this chapter.

Most beginning books do not discuss many of the topics presented in this chapter. This may cause you to wonder why you need to understand them. There are several reasons. First, after you master these topics, many of the other elements of C# (and other programming languages in general) become clearer and more intuitive. Memorizing certain rules is one approach to learning a language: After you memorized (and obey) a rule, you can avoid some of the error messages that Visual Studio might throw at you. However, truly understanding why a rule exists in the first place is a vastly superior way to learn. It is this higher level of understanding that you should seek. If you understand the material presented in this chapter, finding and correcting program errors becomes easier. Error detection becomes easier because you have a deeper understanding of what C# does "under the hood." Finally, your knowledge of the material presented here is portable. That is, the concepts and techniques discussed in this chapter apply to all programming languages, not just C#. If you decide to learn another programming language later, these concepts can help you learn that new language.

BASIC BUILDING BLOCKS OF A PROGRAMMING LANGUAGE

Although the specific rules of a programming language differ from one language to another, the underlying foundation upon which all programming languages are built is similar. There is a hierarchy that all languages follow:

Programs ⇨ Statements ⇨ Expressions ⇨ Operands and Operators

You can verbalize this hierarchy like this: "Programs consist of one or more statements. Statements consist of one or more expressions. Expressions consist of one or more operands with one or more operators." Therefore, at its lowest level, to write a program you must understand operands and operators. You begin your journey into the innards of C# by learning about operands and operators.

Operands and Operators

In Chapter 3 you wrote a program that used two variables to store the information that was entered by the user. The program was designed to divide the first number by the second number. In the examples for the program in Chapter 3, the user typed in **10** for the first number and **6** for the second. You've been doing this kind of math since you were in grade school. You can write the process of dividing 10 by 6 as:

```
10 / 6
```

This simple math process involves taking the value 10 and dividing it by 6. In this example, 10 and 6 are called operands. An *operand* is simply a piece of information or data. The information associated with an operand might be stored in a variable, or it may be one literal value divided by a second literal value, as previously shown.

To make the program in Chapter 3 more flexible, however, you created variables to store the values entered by the user in the program. In that program, you defined two variables named operand1 and operand2. If operand1 has a value of 10 and operand2 has a value of 6, you can write the same process like this:

```
operand1 / operand2
```

The essence of the division process remains the same. All that has been changed is to replace the literal values 10 and 6 with the variables operand1 and operand2.

Sandwiched between the two operands is the division sign (/) that tells you what to do with the two operands. The division sign is the operator. An *operator* specifies what action should be done with the operand(s). In this example you simply want to divide operand1 by operand2. This leads to the following generalization for a math process:

```
operandOne operator operandTwo
```

For all math operations (add, subtract, multiply, divide, and modulo), the math operator (+, -, *, /, and %) requires two operands to perform its function. Because these math operators require two operands, they are called *binary operators*. Indeed, any operator that requires two operands to perform its task is a binary operator. If an operator requires only one operand, it's a *unary operator*. The negation operator (!) is a unary math operator. Finally, if an operator requires three operands, it is a *ternary operator*. Most of the C# operators are binary operators.

Expressions

An *expression* is simply one or more operands and their associated operator treated as a single entity. For example, in the integer division program in Chapter 3, you wrote the following line:

```
answer = operand1 / operand2;
```

This line uses the two operands and the division operator to calculate the result of dividing operand1 by operand2. Because an expression is simply one or more operands and operators treated as a unit, you can visualize this program statement as

```
answer = expression1;
```

with the understanding that expression1 consists of operand1 divided by operand2. But, if you generalize the statement

```
answer = expression1;
```

it can be rewritten as this:

```
operand4 = operand3;
```

where answer is replaced with operand4 and expression1 is replaced with operand3. The only thing that's different is that the operator has changed to the assignment operator (=). From this, you can also conclude that the assignment operator is a binary operator.

Suppose operand1 equals 10 and operand2 equals 5. Notice the sequence followed in processing the program line:

```
answer = operand1 / operand2;
answer = 10 / 5;
operand4 = 10 / 5;
operand4 = 2;
2;
```

The process to calculate the result of the division involves little more than using each operator and its operands to generate the proper result. When the chain of events finishes, operand4 holds the result of the division.

Statements

In C#, a *program statement* is one or more expressions terminated by a semicolon. However, because expressions are composed of operands and operators, it follows that the following is a program statement:

```
answer = operand1 / operand2;
```

This program statement actually contains two operators (the division operator and the assignment operator) and three operands (`answer`, `operand1`, and `operand2`) terminated by a semicolon.

You can make program statements as complex as you want, as long as they end with a semicolon. For example, you could take the following program lines:

```
part1 = v + w;
part2 = x + y;
solution = part1 * part2;
```

and write them as a single statement:

```
solution = v + w * x + y;
```

Now apply some values to the variables in the preceding statement. Assume $v = 2$, $w = 3$, $x = 4$, and $y = 5$. You can view the program statement as the following:

```
solution = 2 + 3 * 4 + 5;
```

The question is, "What does `solution` equal?" Is the answer 25 or is the answer 19? If you look back at the original set of three program statements, `part1` equals 5 after its statement is processed, while `part2` resolves to 9. The third statement multiplied `part1` by `part2` and assigned the result into `solution`. Because `part1` resolves to 5 and `part2` resolves to 9, `solution` is 45, not 25 or 19. What happened? Why did your collapsed statement version produce the wrong answer?

Operator Precedence

Any time a program statement involves multiple operators, like the one you just saw, there must be a set of rules that enables you to properly process the operators and operands in the expressions. Table 4-1 presents the precedence, or order, in which operators are processed.

TABLE 4-1: Operator Precedence

ORDER	TYPE	SYMBOL
1	Negation	!
2	Multiply, divide, modulus	*, /, %
3	Add, subtract	+, −
4	Assignment	=

Table 4-1 shows that the multiply, divide, and modulus operations should be performed before you perform any addition or subtraction operations. Given the information in Table 4-1, the order of processing in the program statement

```
solution = 2 + 3 * 4 + 5;
```

is performed in the following order:

```
        (4)    (2) (1) (3)
 solution = 2 + 3 * 4 + 5;
```

This means that C# expects the multiplication operation (3 * 4) to be performed first, followed by the addition of 2 to the result, followed by the addition of 5 to that result and, finally, the values assigned into `solution`. You can show the operator precedence in action in the following steps:

```
solution = 2 + 3 * 4 + 5;
solution = 2 + 12 + 5;
solution = 14 + 5;
solution = 19;
```

How can you know to add 2 and 12 together first and then add 5? Any time two math operators have the same precedence level, you process them from left to right. You resolve the order of execution of operators of equal precedence by the operators' *associativity rules*. When ties are resolved by processing from left to right, the operators are called *left-associative*. If ties are broken by the rightmost operators being processed, the operators are said to be *right-associative*.

Math operators are left-associative. The assignment operator, however, is right-associative. Because the assignment operator is right-associative, everything on the right side of the assignment operator is resolved before anything is assigned into the operand on the left side of the assignment operator. In the preceding statements, these precedence and associativity rules ensure that the answer assigned into `solution` is 19.

Overriding the Default Precedence Order

Suppose you actually do want the correct `solution` value to be 45 instead of 19. This would be the same as writing the following:

```
part1 = 2 + 3;
part2 = 4 + 5;
solution = part1 * part2;
```

What you actually want, therefore, is the final statement to resolve to this:

```
solution = 5 * 9;
```

The preceding code assigns a value of 45 into `solution`. However, you saw earlier that

```
solution = 2 + 3 * 4 + 5;
```

resolves to a `solution` value of 19, not 45. How can you get the wanted result?

You can *override the default precedence order* by using parentheses. If you change the statement to

```
solution = (2 + 3) * (4 + 5);
```

the *parentheses* tell C# to perform the operations inside the parentheses before any other operations. The parentheses cause the following sequence to be performed:

```
solution = (2 + 3) * (4 + 5);
solution = 5 * 9;
solution = 45;
```

The end result is that `solution` equals 45. Parentheses are left-associative.

You now know the basic rules necessary to writing program statements in C#. Writing even the most complex program simply boils down to stringing the right sequence of operands and operators together to form expressions that are then used to form program statements. Now you need a thorough understanding of how variables are defined so that you can use them as operands in an expression.

The following program and its modifications will help you better understand how the precedence of operators affects the result of an expression.

TRY IT OUT | **Understanding Operator Precedence (Chapter03Program01.zip)**

To make things easier, you can reuse the integer math program from Chapter 3:

1. Load the Integer math program from Chapter 3 (Chapter03Program01.zip).

2. In the button click event code, change the statement

```
answer = operand1 / operand2;
```
to
```
answer = 2 + operand1 * operand2 + 5;
```

3. Recompile and run the program, entering the value 3 for operand1 and 4 for operand2. If you run the program, the result displayed is 19.

4. Now change the program statement to

```
answer = (2 + operand1) * (operand2 + 5);
```

When you run the program a second time, you can see the answer is changed.

How It Works

Running the program after the first modification that adds the multiplication operator and entering the appropriate values yields the answer of 19. The reason is because the multiplication operator (*) has higher precedence than does the addition operator (+). Therefore, the first test of the program using the statement

```
answer = 2 + operand1 * operand2 + 5;
```
resolves to
```
answer = 2 + 3 * 4 + 5;
answer = 2 + 12 + 5;
answer = 19;
```

Now change the statement to the second statement variation that uses parentheses to force a different sequence of expression evaluations. Now the statement resolves to

```
answer = (2 + operand1) * (operand2 + 5);
answer = (2 + 3) * (4 + 5);
answer = 5 * 9;
answer = 45;
```

Because any expressions surrounded by parentheses are evaluated before those with lower precedence, the use of parentheses alters the evaluation of the expressions that prevailed before the parentheses were added. The end result is that you get a totally different result even though the same values are used in the statement.

DEFINING VARIABLES

Some programmers see a statement like

```
int val;
```

and think that the program is defining or declaring a variable named `val`. Many programmers use the terms *define* and *declare* interchangeably. Defining a variable is different from declaring a variable. The two terms are actually quite different.

Defining a Variable from the Compiler's Point of View

Suppose you write the statement

```
int i;
```

in a program. In your mind, you are simply telling the program that you want to create an integer variable named `i` for use in your program. To Visual Studio, however, things aren't quite that simple. Consider what Visual Studio has to do just to process this simple statement.

Step 1: Preliminary Syntax Checking

First, Visual Studio must check the statement for syntax errors. A *syntax error* occurs anytime you write a program statement that does not obey C# syntax rules. For example, you know that a variable name cannot begin with a digit character or contain punctuation characters. If you try to create a variable with either of these conditions, Visual Studio issues an error message. You learned in Chapter 3 that if you make a syntax error in a program statement, IntelliSense places a squiggly line under the offending statement. Because you know the syntax of your program statement is correct, there is no squiggly line, and Visual Studio moves to the next step.

Step 2: Symbol Table Checking

Just because you have the syntax for the statement right doesn't mean there can't be other problems. Therefore, the next thing Visual Studio does is examine its symbol table to see if you have already defined a variable named `i`. A *symbol table* is a table internal to Visual Studio that it uses to keep track of the data you want to use in your program. Table 4-2 shows a hypothetical symbol table. (Although a "real" table might have dozens of columns in it, the simplified symbol table shown in Table 4-2 serves your purpose nicely.)

TABLE 4-2: Hypothetical Symbol Table

ID	DATA TYPE	SCOPE	LVALUE	...
hatSize	double	0	650,000	
k	int	0	630,480	

In Table 4-2, assume that column one (ID) shows the names of the variables that have already been defined. (Variable names are often referred to as *identifiers*, hence the column header name, ID.) The second column of the symbol table tells Visual Studio the data type of the variable. You learn the meaning of the third column, Scope, shortly. The fourth column, lvalue, is where in memory each variable is located. In other words, the lvalue for hatSize is 650,000. Simply stated, if Visual Studio needs to use the value associated with hatSize, it must access memory address 650,000 to find its value.

In this step, Visual Studio scans the ID column to see if you have already defined a variable named i. Because there is no variable in the symbol table with an ID of i, Visual Studio proceeds to step 3. If you had already defined a variable named i (at the same scope level), you would get an error message like this:

```
A local variable named 'i' is already defined in this scope
```

If Visual Studio enabled you to define another variable named i at the same scope level, it would not know which i to use when you try to use the variable in some other expression. This particular error message is called a *duplicate definition error* message and tells you that it is illegal to have two variables with the same name at the same scope level.

However, because you know you can't have two variables with the same name, i does not appear in the symbol table. Therefore, Visual Studio knows it's okay to add i to the symbol table. Table 4-3 shows the state of the symbol table after you add the variable named i.

TABLE 4-3: Adding New Variable to Symbol Table

ID	DATA TYPE	SCOPE	LVALUE	...
hatSize	double	0	650,000	
k	int	0	630,480	
i	int	0	?	

Notice that the lvalue column for variable i does not have a value in it. (Technically, the lvalue is automatically set to null by Visual Studio. However, because *null* cannot be a valid memory address, you can think of the value as unknown.) You can also represent the current state of variable I, as shown in Figure 4-1.

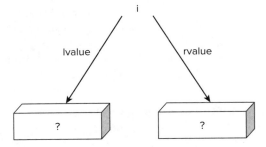

FIGURE 4-1: lvalues and rvalues

lvalues and rvalues

Figure 4-1 shows variable i with two "legs" extending from it, labeled lvalue and rvalue. The *lvalue* of a variable refers to the memory address where the variable is stored. The lvalue for a variable is always interpreted as a memory address. (The term lvalue was coined decades ago when programmers used assembly language to write their programs. The lvalue of a variable was an abbreviation for its "location value," or memory address. Note also that lvalues are the "left leg" when diagrammed as it is in Figure 4-1. This has caused some interpretations of lvalue to mean "left value.") The lvalue appears as a question mark for the moment, because you do not presently know variable i's memory address.

The *rvalue* of a variable refers to the actual data value currently stored in the variable. (The rvalue term also had its roots in assembly language programming and stood for "register value." Again, some interpretations have this associated as the "right value" because is it the right leg in the figure.) Normally, you use the assignment operator to set the rvalue of a variable. For example, the statement

```
i = 10;
```

assigns the value of 10 into the rvalue of variable i. However, because you are still checking the symbol table entries at this point, nothing is presently associated with the rvalue of variable i. Therefore, you also can see the rvalue for i in Figure 4-1 as an unknown value as represented by a question mark.

> **NOTE** *In some languages such as C and C++, you can observe the lvalue of a variable by using the ampersand (address of) operator with an identifier, as in* &myHatSize. *You can observe the rvalue using the indirection operator (*), as in* *myHatSize. *However, C# enables only these operations in code blocks defined using the* unsafe *keyword. Because Microsoft uses the* unsafe *keyword for a reason, these operators are not discussed in this book.*

Step 3: Defining a Variable

Because Table 4-2 does not have another variable named i in it, IntelliSense gives the syntax for the statement a clean bill of health. Visual Studio is now ready to associate a memory address with variable i in the symbol table.

However, assigning memory addresses to specific variables is not Visual Studio's job. It is the responsibility of the operating system to find enough memory for a variable. Therefore, Visual Studio sends a message to the operating system (assume it's the Windows operating system) and says, "Hey, Windows! It's me...Visual Studio. My programmer wants to define an integer variable for use in a program. Can you find 4 bytes of free memory for me?"

Recall from Chapter 3 that each integer variable requires 4 bytes (32 bits) of storage. Upon receiving the message from Visual Studio, Windows routes the message to the Windows Memory Manager because the Memory Manager is responsible for fulfilling memory requests.

You might ask, "Why can't Visual Studio allocate the memory itself?" "The reason is because Windows enables more than one program to execute at a time. Because Visual Studio doesn't bother tracking what other applications are doing, if it allocated the memory, it runs the risk to trample the data of some other application. The Windows Memory Manager, however, is responsible for tracking memory use for every application currently running on the computer.

The Windows Memory Manager scans its list of free memory and probably does find the requested 4 bytes. You can assume that the Windows Memory Manager finds the 4 bytes for the integer starting at memory address 900,000. Having found the requested memory, the Windows Memory Manager sends a message back to Visual Studio, "Hey, Visual Studio! It's me…the Windows Memory Manager. I found you 4 bytes of free memory for variable i starting at memory address 900,000." Visual Studio gets the message and immediately puts that memory address into the symbol table for variable i. The symbol table now looks like Table 4-4.

TABLE 4-4: Symbol Table After New Memory Allocation

ID	DATA TYPE	SCOPE	LVALUE	...
hatSize	double	0	650,000	
K	int	0	630,480	
I	int	0	900,000	

Notice how the lvalue in the symbol table records the memory address of where the variable named i resides in memory. You can reflect this change in Figure 4-2.

The rvalue remains unchanged, but the lvalue reflects that variable i is stored starting at memory address 900,000.

You can now state that you have defined variable i. (You see examples of data declarations later in the book.) Whenever you say that a variable is defined, it means that variable appears in the symbol table and has a valid memory address (lvalue) associated with it.

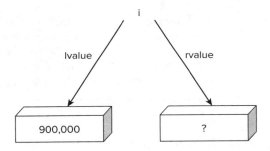

FIGURE 4-2: lvalue after memory allocation

> **NOTE** *A variable is defined if, and only if, the lvalue column for that variable in the symbol table has a memory address assigned to it. When you declare a variable, the lvalue column in the symbol table for that variable does not contain a valid memory address. The value* `null` *is the lvalue for a declared variable in the symbol table because* `null` *is not a valid memory address. The necessary and sufficient conditions to define a variable require that the symbol table contain a valid (that is, non-*`null`*) memory address for the variable. If a variable appears in the symbol table with a* `null` *lvalue, the variable is declared, not defined.*

USING A VARIABLE IN A PROGRAM

Now that you understand what a symbol table is and the information it contains, examine how Visual Studio processes something as simple as an assignment statement. Assuming that you have defined an integer variable named i, suppose you write the following statement:

```
i = 10;
```

The program statement seems simple enough, but now examine the steps Visual Studio must perform to process the statement.

1. **Syntax checking:** As before, Visual Studio must first make sure that the program statement obeys the syntax rules of the C# language. Because IntelliSense doesn't find anything wrong with the statement's syntax, Visual Studio progresses to the next step.

2. **Symbol table checking:** Because the statement wants to assign the value 10 into a variable named i, Visual Studio needs to verify that variable i has been previously defined. Two things could go wrong in this step. First, the programmer may have forgotten to define a variable named i. If you forgot to define variable i, Visual Studio issues the following error message:

```
The name 'i' does not exist in the current context
```

The second possible problem is that a variable named i was defined, but at a scope level that the current context cannot reach. Without going into details at this moment, the *scope* of a variable refers to its visibility at each point in a program. As mentioned in Chapter 3, hiding data is a basic principle of encapsulation and a cornerstone of object-oriented programming. Because a variable may not be in scope is a good thing in many cases because it means that you can't inadvertently change that variable's value. A variable must be in scope for you to alter its value. If variable i is not in scope, you get the same error message that was issued when the variable was not defined.

Because your variable is defined at the current scope level, IntelliSense is happy and no squiggly line appears.

3. **Get the lvalue of variable i:** Because the statement wants to assign the value of 10 into variable i, Visual Studio needs to know where to store the value 10. (Remember, the expression on the right side of the assignment operator is copied into the expression on the left side of the operator. This also means you are changing the state of the variable.) You already know that the lvalue of variable i, as found in the symbol table, tells you where the value 10 should be stored in memory. Visual Studio dutifully creates a binary representation of the value for 10 (that is, 000000000000 00000000000001010) and moves the value to the 4 bytes of memory starting at memory address 900,000. Figure 4-3 shows the change in the value for variable i.

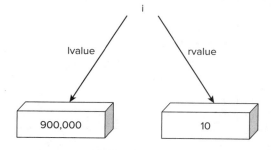

FIGURE 4-3: rvalue for variables

The rvalue of variable i has been changed from the question mark shown in Figure 4-2 to the value 10. Because the rvalue has changed, you can also say the state of variable i is changed by the assignment statement.

THE BUCKET ANALOGY

The Bucket Analogy can help you remember what lvalues and rvalues are all about and reinforce your understanding of what a data definition is. Suppose you write the statement

```
int val;
```

Recall that Visual Studio checks the syntax of this statement and then searches the symbol table to make sure val has not already been defined at the current scope. Assuming those checks are passed and IntelliSense is happy, Visual Studio sends a message to the Windows Memory Manager asking for 4 bytes of free memory for the int you want to define. Assuming all goes well, the Windows Memory Manager sends back the memory address at which val will be stored. Now assume that the memory address for val is 750,000. That memory address is then entered into the lvalue column in the symbol table.

The Bucket Analogy assumes that you have a pile of empty buckets lying around. The buckets come in different sizes. Some are big enough to hold 1 byte of data, some can hold 2 bytes of data, and some buckets are big enough to hold 16 bytes of data. Because you want to define an int data type, you select a bucket big enough to hold an int data type. As you learned in Chapter 3, an int takes 4 bytes of memory, so you grab a 4-byte bucket.

Now, paint the variable's name, val in this example, on the side of the bucket so that you can distinguish it from other buckets that might be stored in memory. Now, pretend you can physically take the bucket inside your computer and place it at memory address 750,000. When you finish, you might see something like what is shown in Figure 4-4.

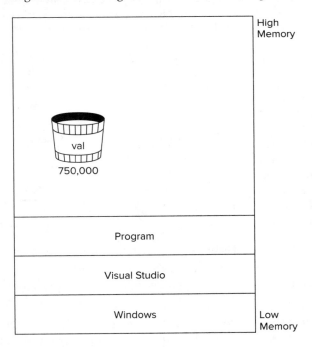

FIGURE 4-4: Memory map with bucket

The Bucket Analogy relates to a data definition in the following way:

1. The lvalue of a bucket tells you where to find the bucket in memory.

2. The rvalue of a bucket tells you what is stored inside the bucket.

3. The data type of the item (such as int) tells you how big a bucket is (in this case 4 bytes).

The Bucket Analogy is used again in Chapter 5, to help explain some additional concepts associated with data definitions and how the data is used in a program. For now, simply remember the three major points of the Bucket Analogy. Those points should help you understand the content in later chapters and make it easier to detect, isolate, and fix program errors.

TYPES OF PROGRAM ERRORS

There are three basic types of program errors. Obviously, your objective is to write programs totally free of program errors. Program errors are also referred to as program *bugs*. (The term "bug" was created because one of the earliest program errors ever detected involved a moth flying into the computer and short-circuiting the electronics. The process to remove program errors is called *debugging*.)

The easiest way to remove program bugs is to write perfect code so there are no bugs in the first place. Although that goal is laudable, every programmer, no matter how seasoned, writes programs that contain errors. A skilled programmer, however, can detect, isolate, and correct program errors more quickly than a less skilled programmer. Also, experienced programmers do make fewer programming errors simply because of their experience. The lesson here is that you should expect to make a lot of program errors in the beginning...every novice programmer does.

In the beginning you start with the "flat-forehead" type of programming error. Those are the kind of errors that, when you do find them, you slam the heel of your hand into your forehead while mumbling, "How could I make such a silly mistake?" Relax. We've all made those mistakes... and still do! The key is not to get discouraged. View each program error as a challenge and learn from the experience. Alas, as your programming skills advance, so will the type of errors you make. Although there will be fewer errors as you gain experience, those errors you do make tend to become more sophisticated and harder to isolate and fix. Now take a quick overview of the three types of program errors. You learn a lot more about errors and debugging in later chapters. For now, however, just categorize the types of program errors.

Syntax Errors

The first type of error is a syntax error. You already know that *syntax errors* are caused when you don't obey the syntax rules of the programming language used. A common syntax rule you might make in the beginning is forgetting to terminate each program statement with a semicolon.

IntelliSense does an excellent job of catching syntax errors. Although you may hate the squiggly line that IntelliSense displays, it's a lot easier for IntelliSense to detect and isolate syntax errors than it is for you to do it.

Semantic Errors

A *semantic error* occurs when you obey the syntax rules of the language but use the statement out of context. For example, a sentence in English is expected to have a noun and a verb. Consider the sentence, "The dog meowed." This sentence does obey the syntax rules of having a noun and a verb, but the context of the sentence is out of whack. Dogs don't meow; therefore the context of the statement is incorrect.

The error message you saw earlier,

```
The name 'i' does not exist in the current context
```

refers to a type of semantic error. There may well be a variable named i defined somewhere in the program, but it is not currently in scope. That is, you are trying to use i when it is out of scope. IntelliSense does a good job to detect semantic errors. Semantic errors are, however, a little more sophisticated than simple syntax errors.

Logic Errors

Logic errors are those errors that remain after all the semantic and syntax errors have been removed. Usually, logic errors manifest themselves when the result the program produces doesn't match the result your test data suggest it should produce. Most of the time, logic errors are found in the Process step you studied in Chapter 3. However, it is also quite possible that the Input step has captured a faulty value and fed it to the Process step. (This is a GIGO problem: Garbage In, Garbage Out.) Logic errors often occur when you implement the algorithm to solve the problem incorrectly.

The key to fixing logic errors is to reproduce the error consistently. A repeatable logic error is much easier to track down and fix than an error that appears to be occurring randomly. (In Chapter 5 you learn the details to use some of the tools Visual Studio provides to help you detect and isolate program bugs.)

THE VISUAL STUDIO DEBUGGER

Visual Studio provides a number of tools to help you detect errors in your programs. IntelliSense is one of those tools that sits in the background carefully examining your program code as you type it into the Source window. IntelliSense does a great job of finding syntax and semantic errors but is less helpful to find logic errors. Because the computer has no intelligence of its own, it blindly follows whatever instructions you give it even if those instructions are wrong. After you have the syntax and semantics of your program stated correctly, you need a different set of tools to help you if the program produces incorrect results. The next line of defense in fixing program errors is the Visual Studio debugger.

The Debugging Process

A *debugger* is a programming tool designed to help you locate, isolate, and fix program errors. Visual Studio has a powerful program debugger built into its IDE. The process to remove program errors is called *debugging*. Following are four steps in the debugging process:

1. **Detection:** Obviously, to correct a program error you must know the program contains an error. Detection requires that you have a set of data you can use to test whether the program works properly. Often the test data set is generated by hand or is an input data set known to produce a correct result. My company produced a statistics package, and for years the Stepwise Multiple Regression test performed flawlessly for tens of thousands of users. Then one day a user passed U.S. Gross National Product data, in dollars, to the test. Because the algorithm uses the sums of squares of the values in the data set, that particular variable eventually got too large for a double to hold, and the program died an ugly death for the user.

Moral of the story: Just because a program runs for years without error doesn't necessarily mean it's bug free.

2. **Stabilize:** When you suspect that there is a program error, the next task is to stabilize the error. Stabilizing an error means that you can repeat the error consistently. A *stabilized error* occurs when a consistent set of input data yields a consistent incorrect result. The worst kind of program error is one that acts randomly—that is, one for which some program runs yield correct results, whereas other runs show an error.

3. **Isolation:** When the program bug first makes itself known, you may feel that you have no idea where in the program to begin looking for it. If you use the Five Program Steps to design the program, test each step starting with the Initialization step. Most of the time you will discover the bug in the Input and Process steps. Obviously, you need to examine the data to make sure it's correct and then watch how that data transforms during the Process step. The Visual Studio debugger makes this step much easier than it would be otherwise.

4. **Correction:** After you isolate the bug and know what caused it, it usually takes only a few minutes to make the correction. Make sure you understand the bug before you correct it. Too many students take the attitude, "Let's change this statement and hope that fixes the bug." This is the *shotgun approach to debugging* and is rarely successful and may actually introduce new bugs. Stumbling onto the exact program line that causes the bug and then blindly typing in the precise form for the statement to fix the bug is about as likely as winning the lottery. Study the bug and understand why it gives you incorrect results. Only then can you truly fix it.

Making Repetitious Debugging Easier

If your program has a particularly nasty bug, chances are that you must rerun the program many times. Frequently, this repetition also requires you to type in the same data set each time the program is rerun. Retyping the data into the textboxes each time you run the program gets tedious in a hurry. If you feel that correcting the bug is going to take several repeated runs of the program, you may want to consider using the Properties window to set the Text property of each of the input textbox objects to its associated test value. This can save you from retyping the input data each time you rerun the program. After you fix the bug, be sure to remove the test data from the Text property of each textbox object.

Let's exercise the debugger a bit in the following Try It Out using a program that you wrote earlier.

TRY IT OUT Using the Debugger (Chapter03IntegerDivision.zip)

The Visual Studio debugger becomes active whenever you run a program within the IDE. To learn how to use the debugger:

1. Load in the integer division program you wrote in Chapter 3.

2. In the button click event code, place a comment symbol (//, which is explained in a later section of this chapter) in front of the definition of operand1 and run the program. What error message did you receive?

3. Somewhere in the program, remove a semicolon (;) from a statement and note the error message you receive.

4. In the button click event code, remove the `.ToString()` code from one of the statements and note the error message you receive.

5. Place a digit character in front of the definition of `operand1` (that is, `int 3operand1`) and note the error message.

Although that program is so simple there's not much that can go wrong, you can use it to illustrate some of the features of the Visual Studio debugger. After you load the program, open the Source Code Window so that you can inspect the source code and use the debugger.

How It Works

When you comment out a data definition using the comment characters (//), in essence you remove that variable from the program. When the program tries to access that variable, it sees that the variable in not in the symbol table, so it must issue an error message telling you the variable is undefined. (Visual Studio usually says something like, "The name operand1 does not exist in the current context." This is Visual Studio's way to tell you that the variable is undefined.

If you leave a semicolon out of a statement, IntelliSense draws a red squiggly line at the point where it expects to see the semicolon. If you try to run the program (perhaps you didn't see the red line), the error message is usually "; Expected." Because forgetting a semicolon is a syntax error, the debugger usually nails the spot in the source code where the semicolon needs to be placed.

If you forget to use the `ToString()` method, you may not receive an error message. Sometimes Visual Studio is smart enough to generate the correct code even though your source code isn't completely correct. In this program, the program executes without issuing an error message. However, a different context may result in an error message from the debugger if Visual Studio cannot figure out the correct context.

If you place a digit character at the start of `operand1` (that is, `3operand1`), IntelliSense shows a red squiggly line but gives the error message: "; Expected." Odd. Why would it give that message? The reason is because Visual Studio tried to make sense of what you wrote and assumes you want to assign the value 3 into a `decimal` data type, but forgot the name of the variable.

It is useful to force errors into the program one at a time and note the error message that displays. Doing this gives you a feel for the types and nature of the Visual Studio error messages. Forcing the errors yourself in a controlled environment simply makes it easier to understand the nature of the message and what caused it.

There's no visual sign that the debugger is active while a program is running. The debugger just sits in the background waiting for you to do something to make it a useful tool. One of the basic debugging functions is setting a breakpoint in the source code.

USING THE VISUAL STUDIO DEBUGGER

A number of features are available to you in the Visual Studio debugger. The point of this section is not to present an exhaustive list of those features but to show you some of the more useful features that you can use again and again.

Setting a Breakpoint

A basic feature of any debugger is the capability to set a breakpoint in the program. A *breakpoint* is simply a point in the program at which you would like to pause the execution of the program. Because program execution pauses at the breakpoint, you can use the debugger to inspect the state of various program variables as they exist at that point.

If the values of the variables aren't what you expected at that breakpoint, the error most likely occurred at some earlier point in the program's execution. In that case, set another breakpoint at some earlier point in the program. If the values are correct at the current breakpoint, remove that breakpoint, and move it to a later execution point in the program.

There are two ways to set a breakpoint. First, you can place the cursor on the program line at which you want to pause the program and press the F9 key. This causes the debugger to highlight that line in red and place a red dot in the extreme left margin of the Source window, as shown in Figure 4-5.

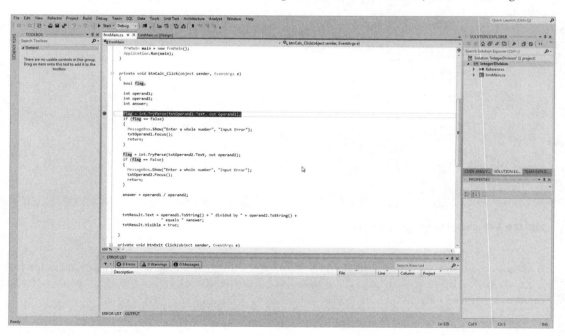

FIGURE 4-5: Setting a breakpoint

A second way to set a breakpoint is to click the mouse while it's located in the extreme left margin of the Source Window and even with the program line at which you want to pause the program. (The extreme left margin is where the red dot appears in Figure 4-5.)

To remove a breakpoint, move the cursor to the red line of the breakpoint to be removed, and press the F9 key again. You can use the F9 key to toggle a breakpoint on and off for a particular line. Likewise, you can click the extreme left margin a second time to remove a breakpoint.

Using a Breakpoint to Examine Variables

After you have set a breakpoint, run the program until it stops there. When the breakpoint is reached, Visual Studio switches to the Source Window and displays the line where the breakpoint was set. Figure 4-6 shows the state of Visual Studio at the point where the breakpoint was set.

FIGURE 4-6: Opening the Locals window

Although it doesn't show in Figure 4-6, the breakpoint line has changed its background color from red to yellow. Also note that the red dot now has an arrow inside of it, pointing to the line at which the breakpoint was set.

To examine the variables at that point in the program, use the Debug Windows Locals menu sequence to activate the Locals window. Visual Studio should look similar to Figure 4-7.

FIGURE 4-7: Using the Locals window

The Locals window appears near the bottom of Figure 4-7 and shows you those variables with local scope. Variables that have local scope are those variables that are visible within the current statement block. In Figure 4-7 the program is paused in the `btnCalc_Click()` method. Therefore, the Locals window enables you to examine those variables with local scope relative to the `btnCalc_Click()` method.

Figure 4-8 presents an enlarged view of the Locals window for the breakpoint shown in Figure 4-7.

Name	Value	Type
⊞ 🔵 this	{frmMain, Text: Integer Division}	frmMain
⊞ ● sender	{Text = "&Calculate"}	object {System.Windows.Forms.Button}
⊞ ● e	{X = 51 Y = 13 Button = Left}	System.EventArgs {System.Windows.Forms.MouseE
● flag	false	bool
● operand1	0	int
● operand2	0	int
● answer	0	int

FIGURE 4-8: Locals window

In Figure 4-8, the C# keyword `this` refers to the currently active object. In the current program, `frmMain` is the currently active object. If you click the plus sign shown in the left margin of the

Locals window of the `this` entry, you can see the other objects associated with `frmMain`. When you click the plus sign, the window displays details about the entry, and a minus sign is shown where the plus sign used to be. If you click the minus sign, the image reverts back to its previous state. Therefore, clicking a plus sign in the Locals window expands the window to present additional information, whereas clicking a minus sign restores the previous (collapsed) state of the window.

The next two lines in Figure 4-8 display information about the `sender` and `e` parameters, respectively. These two variables provide information about the event that caused the program to execute the `btnCalc_Click()` method. (Recall that Windows is an event-driven operating system, so the event information is shared with Windows.) Finally, the last four lines provide information about the `flag`, `operand1`, `operand2`, and `answer` variables, respectively.

You can also observe the value of a variable by moving the cursor over the variable in the Source window. This action causes Visual Studio to display the current value of the variable. This is the fastest way to view the value of a given variable. Use the Locals window when you need to view more than one variable at a time.

Single-Stepping the Program

In Figure 4-7 the breakpoint line has changed from red to yellow. The fact that the line is yellow is the debugger's way to tell you that it is about to execute the breakpoint line. This means that the debugger has stopped the program *before* executing the breakpoint line. This is exactly what you want. Because you set a breakpoint at a place in the program where you think a particular statement is causing a problem, the yellow line means that you can examine the state of the variables just before the line is executed.

Now, press the F10 key. Notice how the yellow line advances to the next program line and the original breakpoint line reverts to its red background color. The arrow drawn in the margin has moved down to the line that is about to be executed, and the red dot has reverted to its original state. You can see the changes produced by the F10 key in Figure 4-9.

The process to advance the program one line at a time is called *single-stepping* the program. Because the program has advanced to the next line, you can now examine the values of the variables to see if executing the statement in which the breakpoint was set changed these values in the wanted way. If not, something in the breakpoint line caused a problem. If the values of the variables are as expected, you can continue to press the F10 key to execute additional lines or set another breakpoint at some other place in the program and run the program to that breakpoint.

To restart the program so it runs "at full speed," simply press the F5 key or click the Start icon (see Figure 1-8). If you have set another breakpoint that is executed at a later point in the program, the F5 key causes the program to execute normally until the new breakpoint is reached. You can continue to set additional breakpoints until you find the statement line that is causing the error. After you locate the source of the error, correcting it is usually fairly simple.

As you can see, the debugger is a powerful tool when you try to perform the Isolation step of the debugging process. You use many other debugger features in later chapters. However, simply setting a breakpoint, examining the values of variables, and single-stepping the program can go a long way toward correcting program errors.

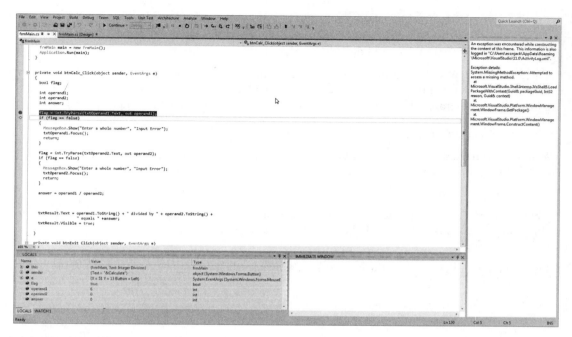

FIGURE 4-9: Reaching a breakpoint

DEFENSIVE CODING

As stated earlier, the best way to avoid program errors is to write perfect code. Because that's not going to happen anytime soon, the next best thing is to write your code with the expectation that something may go wrong. The primary step in this defensive strategy is simple: Write your code so that others can read and understand it.

Write Your Code So That Someone Else Can Easily Understand It

Consider the following list of things you can do in your program source code to make it easier to understand.

Use Program Comments

A *program comment* is simply a message you leave in the program to help the reader understand the code. There is an art to using comments. Too few comments force the reader to take more time to understand what the program is doing. Too many comments can actually get in the way of understanding the code by adding unnecessary clutter. Commenting every line in a program is almost never necessary. At the other extreme, the code might be so complex that it is easier to put in the name and page numbers of a reference book than to explain it.

Try to use comments for those statements that do something unusual or are critical to processing the data. Simply stated, a comment should make it easier for the reader to understand your code and not get in the way of that understanding.

There are two types of program comments: single-line comments and multiline comments. Always keep in mind that comments are ignored by the compiler, so they have no impact on the performance of the program. (There goes one excuse for not having comments in a program!)

Single-Line Comments

You have seen single-line comments before. These are comments introduced with a pair of slashes (//) followed by the comment. The comment must fit on one line, for example:

```
answer = operand1 / operand2;      // This is the Process step
```

This line uses a comment to identify that this statement performs the Process step in the program. (In real life, such a comment probably adds little to the understanding of the program and could just as well be left out.)

One issue is whether to place the comment as shown in the preceding example or to have the comment precede the line, as here:

```
// This is the Process step
answer = operand1 / operand2;
```

If you work for a company writing commercial code, there may be a company policy that dictates the style of comments used. Otherwise, which one you select is a matter of personal preference.

> **NOTE** My choice is dictated by the comment itself. If the comment can fit at the end of a line without the reader having to scroll the Source window to read it, I prefer to place the comment at the end of a program statement. Doing this means that I can see one more line of source code in the Source window over the alternative style.
>
> If the comment is fairly long and would require scrolling to read it, I place the comment above the program statement. If the comment is still too long to fit on a single line without scrolling, I'll split the comment and place the remainder on a new line immediately below the first comment line. If it's still too long, I'll use a multiline comment. Either way, remember that everything on the line after the double-slash character pair (//) is ignored by the compiler.

Multiline Comments

Multiline comments are introduced with a backslash-asterisk combination of characters and terminated with an asterisk-backslash, for example:

```
/* Purpose: The btnCalc-Click() event method is used to
 * calculate the result of dividing two integer values.
 */
private void btnCalc_Click(object sender, EventArgs e)
```

Anything that appears between the comment pairs /* and */ is treated as a comment and ignored by the compiler. The asterisk at the start of the second line of the comment was automatically supplied by Visual Studio. The asterisks help make the comment lines stand out in the code. The most obvious use for the multiline comment is when you need to place a long comment in the code. As a rule, you should make each line short enough so that it doesn't require horizontal scrolling to read it.

Using Multiline Comments as a Debugging Aid

However, you can do more with multiline comments than add lengthy comments to a program. There will be times when you have a section of code giving you a problem and you'd like to try an alternative algorithm. Because you're not sure the new algorithm will work and you don't want to retype the original code if the change fails, the easiest way to remove the code from the program yet still have it available is to surround it with a multiline comment, for example:

```
/*     This is the original code
 * x = y * .33  (m * g);
 * z = x % 2 + sigma;
 */
// Start new code...
x = y * .45  (m * g);
z = x % 3.2 + sigma;
// End new code
```

In this example the multiline comment has the effect of removing the original two lines of code by surrounding them with the multiline comment pairs. My style is to precede the trial code with a single-line comment marking the start of the new code, followed by the new trial code, followed by a second single-line comment marking the end of the trial code. If the trial code doesn't work properly, it's easy to restore the program to its original state by removing the trial code and uncommenting the original code.

Program comments are useful in documenting what the code is doing and also for trying alternative code. Because comments have no impact on the performance of the program and make it easier for others to read and understand your code, you should use them often.

Use Meaningful Variable Names

Just because you've followed the C# rules to create variable names does not mean you've implemented a good variable name. A good variable name has two characteristics:

➤ The variable name reflects the purpose or use of the data in the program. If you write a program that converts Fahrenheit to Celsius temperatures, the variable names t1 and t2 aren't actually helpful to the reader of your code. Select variable names that help the reader understand the code.

➤ The variable name must be long enough to indicate its use, but short enough that you don't get tired of typing it. Although t1 and t2 are too short to be helpful, changing them to currentFahrenheitTemperature and convertedCelsiusTemperature is probably overkill. (You'd get tired of typing in such long variable names even though IntelliSense helps fill in the variable name after you begin typing the name.)

Try to strike a balance between names that are long enough to be helpful and names that are tedious to type. In this case, perhaps `tempCelsius` and `tempFahrenheit` would work.

Avoid Magic Numbers

Beginning programmers often use literal values in a program, which I call *magic numbers* because they are often used without any clue as to their purpose. Suppose you read the following line in a program:

```
f = 125 + (sl) * 10;
```

It might take a bit of head-scratching to figure out what the statement means without additional information. Now contrast that statement with this:

```
speedingFine = MINIMUMSPEEDINGFINE + (postedSpeedLimit) *
               DOLLARSPERMILEOVERLIMIT;
```

Symbolic Constants

The new statement makes more sense because you have used better variable names and replaced the magic numbers with symbolic constants. A *constant* is simply a variable whose value cannot be changed while the program runs. A *symbolic constant* is a constant that has a name that reflects the constant's function in the program. Convention finds symbolic constants rendered entirely in upper-case; although, that is not a language requirement.

Symbolic constants are usually defined near the top of the class in which they appear, for example:

```
public class frmMain : Form
{
  const decimal MINIMUMSPEEDINGFINE = 125M;
  const decimal DOLLARSPERMILEOVERLIMIT = 10M;
  // Rest of the class code appears below...
```

The C# keyword `const` in front of a data type means that you are defining a constant of that data type. Because it is a constant, you must initialize the constant at the point where you define it in the program, as shown in the preceding code. After these values are initialized, they cannot be changed while the program is running.

You gain another advantage from using symbolic constants. Suppose you didn't use `MINIMUMSPEEDINGFINE` for the minimum fine. Instead, suppose you used the magic number 125 throughout the program. Further assume that that same value is also the minimum fine for over-weight trucks and motorcyclists who don't wear a helmet. Finally, assume that these three amounts are scattered several dozen times throughout the program. Now some politician decides to raise the minimum speeding fine to $150 for cars. The truck and helmet fines stay the same. Your boss now hands you the program and says, "Fix it!"

You can't just do a global search-and-replace for 125 in the program. That would change the truck and helmet fines, too. You are forced to find each program occurrence of 125, decipher the code to see whether the 125 relates to a speeding fine, and then either make the change or leave the line alone. This is a slow process just waiting for a train wreck to happen.

Suppose instead you had originally written the program like this:

```
const decimal MINIMUMSPEEDINGFINE = 125M;
```

```
const decimal TRUCKOVERWEIGHTFINE = 125M;
const decimal NOHELMETFINE = 125M;
```

This way, you avoid the use of magic numbers in the code. Not only is your code easier to read, simply changing one line in the program to

```
const decimal MINIMUMSPEEDINGFINE = 150M;
```

and recompiling the program makes all the necessary changes to the program automatically. Using a symbolic constant permits you to make the necessary program change in seconds and still be absolutely certain that the correct values are used the next time the program is run.

Symbolic constants make your programs easier to read and change when necessary. Avoid magic numbers in your code and use symbolic constants often. They can save you time in the long run.

Use a Consistent Coding Style

If you are writing code just for yourself, eventually you will develop your own coding style. That is, you will place statement block braces in the same place for each C# keyword. You will define variables in the same place within a method. You will create object (for example, clsPort, txtName, btnExit, lblResult, and so on) and variable names (for example, myHat, yourAddress, herName, and so on) in a consistent manner. Such style consistencies make it easier for you to read and debug your code.

If you work in a commercial development environment, someone else (perhaps company policy guidelines) may set the coding style. Clearly, you must follow that style unless you have enough clout to change it. Although you may be unhappy that you must follow a company style that you don't think is as "good" as your own style, be thankful that your company *has* a coding style policy. You'd be surprised how development can get bogged down when 30 programmers use 30 different coding styles.

Regardless of your coding environment, pick a coding style and stick with it. It can save you time in the long run.

Take a Break

If you have a particularly nasty bug that has caused you to chase it for several hours, it's time to get up and go some place else for a few minutes. Long sessions without a break tend to make you see what you want to see rather than what's actually going on. Just leaving your desk to get a cup of coffee can help give you a fresh view of the code.

Use a Second Set of Eyes

Looking at the same page of code for hours also causes you to see what you expect to see, not what's actually there. You will have times when you tell yourself that the code cannot be doing what it's doing. Well, it *is* doing what the code says it's doing, but you're suffering from the Forest-for-the-Trees syndrome.

Many times it's useful to get a colleague to look at the code. More often that I'd like to admit, a colleague will see the error in a few seconds even though I've stared at it for an hour. Just like guys who hate to ask for directions, programmers hate to ask for debugging help. Such an attitude is counterproductive. If help's available, use it.

SUMMARY

In this chapter you learned what you need to do to define a variable for use in a program. Although the approach taken here may seem like using an H-bomb to kill an ant, understanding what Visual Studio is doing with something as simple as a data definition can ultimately make you a better programmer.

Make sure you understand completely what lvalues and rvalues are and how they relate to data definitions. Those terms are used often in subsequent chapters.

EXERCISES

You can find the answers to the following exercises in Appendix A.

1. Using a program that you've previously written, set several breakpoints in the program, and single-step through the program. Are there any points in the source code where you cannot set a breakpoint?

2. Rewrite the program from the exercise at the end of Chapter 3 that converts Fahrenheit temperatures to Celsius. Use symbolic constants to make the program easier to understand.

3. What is an lvalue and what is an rvalue? How can they be used to explain the difference between a data definition and a data declaration?

4. When you use the Bucket Analogy to explain lvalues and rvalues at your next cocktail party (hey… it could happen), what determines the size of the bucket? What are the key elements of the Bucket Analogy?

5. Write a program that asks for the price of an item and how many are purchased, and then add the sales tax due based on your state's sales tax rate. Would it make sense to use any symbolic constants in your program?

6. Write a program that figures the monthly car payment using this formula:

payment = (rate + rate / (1 + rate)^months − 1) * amount where rate is the annual rate divided by 1,200 (that is, 6 % has rate = .005) and the carat character means "raised to the power of." The syntax to use the power function is

Math.Pow(val, power)

▶ **WHAT YOU LEARNED IN THIS CHAPTER**

TOPIC	KEY POINTS
Operators and operands	The most basic building blocks in a program
Expression	How operators and operands combine to make an expression
lvalues and rvalues	Conceptual views of where a variable is stored in memory and what value is stored at that location
Symbol table	How data items are tracked by the compiler
Bucket Analogy	An easy way to remember lvalues and rvalues
Debugging	How a debugger can help you locate errors in your program
Magic numbers	Why you should avoid them

5

Understanding Reference Data Types

WHAT YOU WILL LEARN IN THIS CHAPTER:

➤ Reference data types

➤ How reference data types differ from value data types

➤ How the Bucket Analogy can be applied to reference data types

➤ String variables

➤ Verbatim string literals

➤ DateTime variables

➤ Constructor methods

➤ Overloaded methods

➤ Method signatures

WROX.COM CODE DOWNLOADS FOR THIS CHAPTER

You can find the wrox.com code downloads for this chapter at `www.wrox.com/remtitle .cgi?isbn=9781118336922` on the Download Code tab. The code in the `Chapter05` folder is individually named as shown in this chapter.

In Chapter 3, you learned about the different value data types that C# makes available for use in your programs. This chapter concentrates on the other major type of data in C#: reference data types. Object-oriented programming owes much of its popularity to the power that reference data types bring to the programming table. Reference types are fundamental to object-oriented programming, and you will use them a lot.

STRING VARIABLES

You already know that data used in a computer program falls into two broad categories: numeric data and textual data. Chapter 3 presented the value types that are used to store numeric data in a program. *String variables* are used to store textual data.

Data entered by a user into a program's textbox object is textual data. However, if you want to manipulate the user's input, you must first convert the textual data to numeric data by using the data type's `TryParse()` method. For example, if you want to convert the content of the `txtOperand1` textbox object into an `int` data type, use the following statement:

```
flag = int.TryParse(txtOperand1.Text, out val);
```

This statement converts the textual data typed into the `txtOperand1` textbox object into an `int` data type, storing the integer result in variable `val`. What you may not realize is that the `Text` property of the textbox object is actually a string variable. The purpose of the `TryParse()` method is to convert the string data into a numeric data type.

In this chapter, you learn that string variables are simply places in memory to store textual data. Textual data, as a general rule, are not meant to be manipulated mathematically. Instead, you want to keep the data in a text format by storing it in a string variable. It's common to use textual data for storing names, addresses, phone numbers, ZIP codes, customer IDs, and so on. Some textual data actually is pure numbers, such as a ZIP code. How do you decide when to store something as a string or as a numeric data type? The rule is simple: If you are not going to manipulate the data in some mathematical way, store the data as a string.

Defining a String Reference Variable

Suppose you want to store the name `"Hailey"` in a program. Placing the double quotation marks around a sequence of text marks everything between the quotes as a *string literal*. Stated differently, you "literally" want to assign the word `"Hailey"` into the `name` variable. The double quotation marks that surround the string literal are not part of the literal. The quotation marks simply serve to tell Visual Studio the starting and ending points for the textual data.

You can assign the string literal `"Hailey"` into `name` with the following two lines of code:

```
string name;
name = "Hailey";
```

IntelliSense parses each of these two lines and finds the syntax to be correct. There is no dreaded squiggly line. So far, so good. Now consider the details of what Visual Studio is doing with the first statement line. Because there are no syntax errors in the first line, Visual Studio inspects the symbol table in the manner discussed in Chapter 4. Table 5-1 shows a simplified symbol table similar to what you saw in Chapter 4.

TABLE 5-1: Simplified Symbol Table

ID	DATA TYPE	SCOPE	LVALUE	...
hatSize	double	0	650,000	
k	int	0	630,480	

Because the variable `name` is not in the symbol table, Visual Studio sends a message to Windows requesting enough memory for a reference variable. All *reference variables* use the same amount of storage: 4 bytes. Provided the Windows Memory Manager can find 4 bytes of free memory, Windows returns the memory address for the reference variable `name`. You can assume that the memory address for `name` is 670,000. Visual Studio makes an entry into the symbol table, as shown in Table 5-2.

TABLE 5-2: The Reference Variable Added Symbol Table

ID	DATA TYPE	SCOPE	LVALUE	...
hatSize	double	0	650,000	
k	int	0	630,480	
name	string	0	670,000	

Using the diagrams you studied in Chapter 4, you can show the lvalue and rvalue values for `name` as shown in Figure 5-1.

The interpretation of the lvalue of `name` in Figure 5-1 is exactly as in Chapter 4. That is, the lvalue is the memory address where the string reference variable `name` is stored in memory.

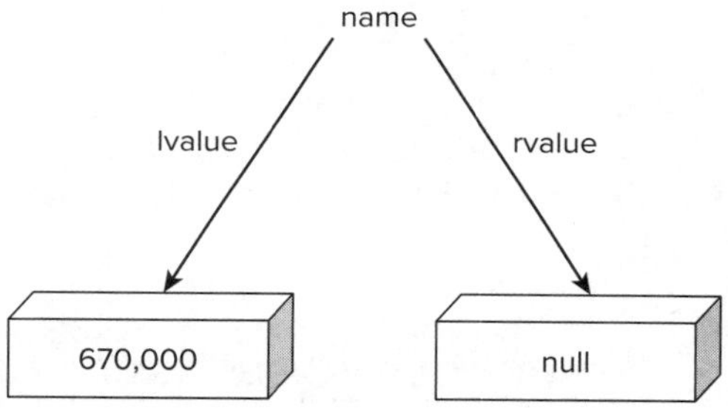

The Meaning of null

After Visual Studio has received the reference variable's lvalue from the Windows Memory Manager, it immediately assigns `null` into the rvalue of `name`. Recall that `null` is a keyword in C# that signifies that no useable data is currently associated with the variable. Anytime a variable has an rvalue equal to `null`, Visual Studio knows there is nothing useful associated with that variable. Figure 5-2 shows a memory map for the current state of the `name` reference variable.

FIGURE 5-1: New lvalue and rvalue

Using the Bucket Analogy from Chapter 4, you can verbalize the information in Figure 5-2 like this: The bucket for the `name` reference variable is stored at memory location 670,000 (its lvalue) and the content (rvalue) of its 4-byte bucket is `null`.

Now consider what happens when the second line is executed:

```
name = "Hailey";
```

Each textual letter in the name Hailey takes 2 bytes of storage. (See the sidebar "Unicode Versus ASCII.") This means that the string literal `Hailey` actually requires 12 bytes of storage. However, you just read that the Windows Memory Manager returned only 4 bytes of storage for the rvalue of `name`. You are probably saying to yourself, "Wait a minute! How do you hold 12 bytes of data in a 4-byte bucket?" Answer: You don't!

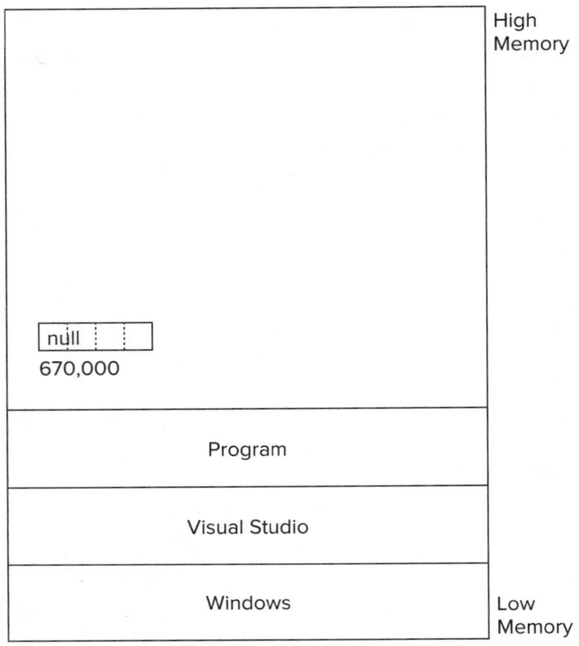

FIGURE 5-2: Memory map for string variable

UNICODE VERSUS ASCII

The need for a standard way to code computer information was recognized as early as the 1960s. The result was the American Standard Code for Information Interchange, or ASCII character set. The codes spanned 128 characters and included alpha and digit characters and punctuation, plus some nonprinting codes. Because there were only 128 characters, the entire ASCII set could be represented in one byte (that is, $256 = 2^8$) with room to spare.

Problems began to arise as computing took on a more international flavor. Many languages and systems, such as the Kanji system for writing Japanese, have thousands of characters. The World Wide Web also pushed the need for a universal character set to the forefront. The result is the Unicode character set. The Unicode character set uses two bytes per character and permits more than 65,000 individual characters to be represented. C# uses the Unicode character set by default. This means that the actual storage requirement for a string variable is about twice as large as the number of characters in the string. (Many languages use a structure called a string descriptor block that is tied to the actual storage requirements. For your purposes, however, just think of each character as requiring 2 bytes of storage.)

Why Reference Types Are Different from Value Types

This is the cool part about reference variables: Reference variables can be associated with as much or as little data as necessary. The value data types you studied in Chapter 3 all have fixed storage requirements. For example, a `byte` data type requires 1 byte of storage but a `long` data type requires 8 bytes of storage. However, if you simply wanted to store the value 1 in a `long`, you still need to use 8 bytes of storage even though a single byte could store that value. For value data types, the number of bytes required to hold the rvalue is etched in stone for each one. Although using a fixed number of bytes for value types works fine, it won't work for things like string data. After all, the string might be used to hold a name like Hailey, but some other string variable in the program might be used to store the Declaration of Independence. Clearly, reference data types have to work differently to accommodate the varying lengths of data that can be associated with them. The way C# (and other programming languages) manages this is elegantly simple.

With a reference variable, the second line of code

```
name = "Hailey";
```

causes Visual Studio to send a *second* message to Windows. In essence, the message is, "Hey, Windows! It's me, Visual Studio...again. I need 12 bytes of free memory to store some data. Can you help me out?" Notice that Visual Studio doesn't say anything about the nature of the data other than how many bytes it needs for storage. When the value types are discussed in Chapter 3, you assume that Windows knows how many bytes are associated with the various value types. With reference types, Visual Studio can't assume Windows knows anything about the number of bytes needed because the storage requirements can be fairly short (`"Hailey"`) or long (the Declaration of Independence).

Assuming there's some free memory available in the system, the Windows Memory Manager sends a message back saying: "Hey, Visual Studio! I found the storage you need starting at memory location 725,000. Now leave me alone for a while...I'm busy." Memory Managers get cranky from time to time because they have other programs making similar requests, too. After all, there could be other programs running at the same time that you're running Visual Studio. Because you just asked it for a place to store `name`, it's not happy to hear from you again so soon for this 12-byte storage request. (Not to worry...the Memory Manager will get over it.)

When Windows returns the memory address 725,000 to Visual Studio, Visual Studio immediately takes the name `"Hailey"` and moves it into memory starting at address 725,000. The state of the memory map for `name` now appears as shown in Figure 5-3.

Reference Variable Rules

Compare Figures 5-2 and 5-3. First, note how the rvalue of `name` has changed from its previous value of `null` to the memory address where the data is stored. Second, you can see that the 12 bytes starting at memory location 725,000 now hold the string literal `"Hailey"`. These observations illustrate the following rules for reference variables:

➤ The rvalue of a reference variable can have only one of two values: `null` or a memory address.

➤ If the rvalue of a reference variable is `null`, the reference variable contains no useful data.

➤ If the rvalue of a reference variable is not `null`, it contains the memory address where the data associated with the reference variable is stored.

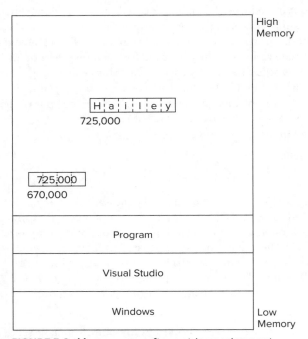

FIGURE 5-3: Memory map after a string assignment

The first rule confirms several things about reference variables. First, unlike a value type, which has an rvalue that holds the data you're interested in, a reference variable does not hold the actual data you want to use in a program. Second, because the rvalue of a reference can hold only `null` or a memory address, the size of a reference variable is *always* 4 bytes on 32 bit systems. This means that the size of a reference variable's bucket is always the same regardless of the actual data that might be associated with it—4 bytes. When this topic comes up at your next party, you can look smart by saying, "The state of a reference variable is either `null` or a valid memory address."

The second rule affects the way IntelliSense enforces the syntax of C# statements that use reference variables. If you try to perform some type of string operation on a reference variable whose rvalue is `null`, IntelliSense complains and issues an error message. For example, if you try to pass `name` to a method when it contains a `null` rvalue, IntelliSense will say something like this:

```
Use of unassigned local variable 'name'.
```

IntelliSense does this because it knows the `null` rvalue means the program has no useful data associated with the variable.

The third rule is the most important. If a reference variable contains a non-null value, that value is the memory address where the actual data is stored. Indeed, this is why they are called reference variables. The *non-null rvalue* of a reference variable refers you to the memory location at which the data is stored.

Reference Type Variables Versus Value Type Variables

Consider the interpretation of the Bucket Analogy as it relates to the two types of variables. With value type variables, you look in the bucket, and you immediately find the data you are interested in stored in the variable's rvalue. Also, with value types, the size of the bucket varies according to the type of data stored in the bucket. That is, the bucket size for an int data type is 4 bytes, whereas the bucket size for a decimal data type is 16 bytes. Therefore, you are interested in the size of a value type's bucket because it gives you a clue as to the type of data stored there.

With a reference type variable, you look into the bucket and find either null or a memory address. If you find a null in the bucket, the variable has nothing interesting associated with it. On the other hand, if you look into the bucket and see something other than null, you must jump to that memory address to inspect the data.

The conclusion is simple: Value types have an rvalue that *is* the data. Reference types have an rvalue that either refers you to the data (a memory address) or does not reference any data (null).

Why Do Reference Variables Work the Way They Do?

Why did the people who designed C# make reference variables work the way they do? Consider the way value types work. Suppose you write a method that squares the number entered into the program by the user. After you convert the user's input into a value type, like an int, you now want to pass that value to a method you plan to write named SquareIt(). The purpose of the SquareIt() method is to take that value, square it, and return that squared value to the caller. To do this, Visual Studio makes a *temporary copy* of the value of the number, calls your SquareIt() method, and tells it where that temporary copy of the number is located. Because an int uses only 4 bytes of storage, the process to make a copy of the int is fast and doesn't use up much additional memory for the temporary copy.

Now suppose you have a program with a string variable that refers to the text of three chapters of a book. (Perhaps you read the data from a disk file into the program.) This means that the string variable might point to a block of memory with hundreds of thousands of bytes in it. Now suppose that you write a method whose purpose is to search those hundreds of thousands of bytes looking for a specific word. If the method call works as it does for value types, Visual Studio must copy those hundreds of thousands of bytes into a temporary memory location. Copying hundreds of thousands of bytes has two disadvantages. First, it's fairly slow relative to copying just a few bytes as with a value type. Second, the temporary copy of the chapters would take up another huge chunk of memory, possibly causing the program to run out of memory.

C# solves these performance and memory-limitation problems by simply passing the *address* of the memory location where the data is stored. Because the rvalue of a reference variable tells Visual Studio where to find the data, the 4-byte rvalue of a reference variable is all the method needs to find the data. Visual Studio doesn't need to copy the data. The method can find the data by just jumping to the memory location it receives from the reference variable's rvalue. This approach saves both time and memory.

That's the good news.

Pass by Value Versus Pass by Reference

The bad news is that the method that uses a reference variable has direct access to the data. Recall that a method that uses a value type receives a *copy* of the variable's value, not the lvalue of the variable itself. This means that the method cannot permanently change the user's value. With value types there are two buckets in memory: the original bucket and the bucket containing the copy. The method can alter the copy's rvalue but has no clue where the original bucket is stored. Therefore, this *pass by value* way to send data to a method protects the original data because only a copy of the data is seen by the method.

With a reference variable, you send the actual memory location of where the data is stored. Passing the actual memory location is called *pass by reference*. This means that the method has direct access to the original data, not to a copy of it. It also means that, if the method wants to, it can permanently affect the data associated with the reference variable.

The old saying, "There's no such thing as a free lunch," applies to programming, too. You can use reference variables when writing a method to improve its performance and conserve memory. However, the price you pay is that you expose the data to the possibility of contamination because the method has direct access to it. This is sort of like a medieval king who takes the time to hide his daughter away in the castle tower, but then turns around and hands out her room key to every knight in the kingdom...probably not a good idea. Similarly, making the effort to hide data isn't terribly worthwhile if you tell everyone where it's hidden. Chapter 10 revisits these (encapsulation) issues and offers ways to cope with them.

A Little Efficiency Gain

As discussed earlier, the following statements caused Visual Studio to send *two* memory requests to the Windows Memory Manager:

```
string name;
name = "Hailey";
```

The first was to find storage for `name` and the second was to find storage for `"Hailey"`. Anything you can do to lessen the number of messages sent between Windows and Visual Studio is probably a good thing. This is because exchanging messages between Visual Studio and Windows takes time. You can accomplish the same thing and save some time by collapsing the two statements into one:

```
string name = "Hailey";
```

In this case, only one message needs to be sent to the Windows Memory Manager. That message might be stated as, "Windows...wake up! I need a reference variable capable of storing 12 bytes of data." Windows knows a reference variable requires 4 bytes of storage. Assuming it responds with the information shown in Figure 5-3, the message sent back might be, "Hey, Visual Studio! I've stored your reference variable at memory address 670,000 and set its rvalue to 725,000. You're welcome." Visual Studio then proceeds to store `"Hailey"` starting at memory address 725,000 (refer to Figure 5-3).

The end result is exactly the same regardless of whether you use the one- or two-line version for assigning the string literal. The one-line version, however, accomplishes the same task with one less message sent to Windows. True, doing away with one Windows message isn't going to make much of a performance difference. However, if your program repeats a message thousands of times, the user might notice the difference. Obviously, either way works just fine. However, you are likely to see experienced programmers use the second form more often. If you do see the shorter version, it could well be that program speed has nothing to do with it. The programmer may have chosen it simply because it requires less typing!

USING STRING VARIABLES

String variables are reference variables that enable you to store and manipulate textual data. Although most people associate computers with number crunching, a large part of the work done by computers involves manipulating textual data, not numbers. Indeed, database programs are often pushing around huge amounts of textual data, often even more than numeric data.

String Concatenation

You used string concatenation in an earlier program, but nothing much was said about it. Simply stated, *string concatenation* is the process of taking one string and adding it to another to form a new string, for example:

```
string name = "Hailey";
name = name + " Mohr";
```

In the preceding statements, `name` is assigned `"Hailey"`, as explained earlier. The second line concatenates the string literal `" Mohr"` (there is a space before `Mohr"`) to form the new string `"Hailey Mohr"`. This new string is then assigned into `name`. As you can see, string concatenation is little more than adding one string onto another string. In this example, the string concatenation takes the first and last names and concatenates them into a full name.

Shorthand Assignment Operators

Taking one value and adding a second value to it is such a common task in programming that C# provides a number of shorthand assignment operators for the basic math and string concatenation operators. For example, suppose the variable `name` currently holds the string `"Hailey"` as you saw just now. You can take the original line shown earlier:

```
name = name + " Mohr";
```

and rewrite it, using a shorthand concatenation operator, as

```
name += " Mohr";
```

The result is exactly as before: `"Hailey Mohr"`. In the statements

```
int i = 10;
i += 5;
```

the value of i is now 15. Therefore, the "+=" assignment operator serves a dual purpose: It performs string concatenation when string variables are used, or it can be used for addition when value type variables are used. Table 5-3 presents a list of the shorthand assignment operators.

TABLE 5-3: Shorthand Operators

OPERATOR	EXAMPLE	INTERPRETATION
+=	val += days;	val = val + days;
-=	val -= days;	val = val - days;
*=	val *= days;	val = val *days;
/=	val /= days;	val = val / days;
%=	val %= days;	val = val % days;

Of the operators shown in Table 5-3, only the concatenation operator (+) makes sense when you work with string data. All the operators in the table, however, may be used with value types. Obviously, the shorthand operators don't give you anything you didn't already have. However, programmers usually don't like to type more than they have to, so experienced C# programmers use the shorthand operators often.

String Manipulation

You already know that a string is a reference data type. You also know that reference types and value types are different. The rvalue of a value type variable is the data value of the variable. For reference type variables, however, the rvalue is either null or the memory addresses where the data reside. All reference types in C# behave as objects of a class. As such, reference types can have properties and methods just as textboxes, labels, buttons, and other objects do. This section introduces you to some of the more common properties and methods in the string class.

String Length

One common task when working with string data is to verify that the string contains the proper data. For example, if you ask a user to enter a ZIP code, you may want to verify that the user typed exactly five characters into the textbox object used to collect the ZIP code string. (Yeah, I know there can be 9-digit zip codes, but ignore that for the moment.) For example, suppose you've written a program that uses txtZipCode to collect the ZIP code from the user. Your next task might be to determine if the user typed five characters into the textbox. One of the properties provided by the string class is the Length property:

```
int length;
string zip = "45245";
length = zip.Length;
```

In the code fragment above, zip is assigned the literal value "45245". The integer variable length is then assigned the value of the Length property of the zip string object. In the example, the zip .Length property has a value of 5. Therefore, the length variable has an rvalue of 5 after the assignment statement in the last line of the preceding code is executed.

Letting IntelliSense Show You Properties and Methods

You might ask, "Are there other properties or methods in the string class?" Yes, there are a bunch of them. Any time you want to find the properties or method of an object (string or otherwise), let IntelliSense give you the list. For example, Figure 5-4 defines a string variable named temp. A few lines later you want to find out what property you might use to determine the length of the string. To do this, type in the name of the string variable followed by the dot operator. IntelliSense immediately presents you with a listbox containing all the properties and methods for the current object, a string named temp in this case. (Refer to Figure 5-4.)

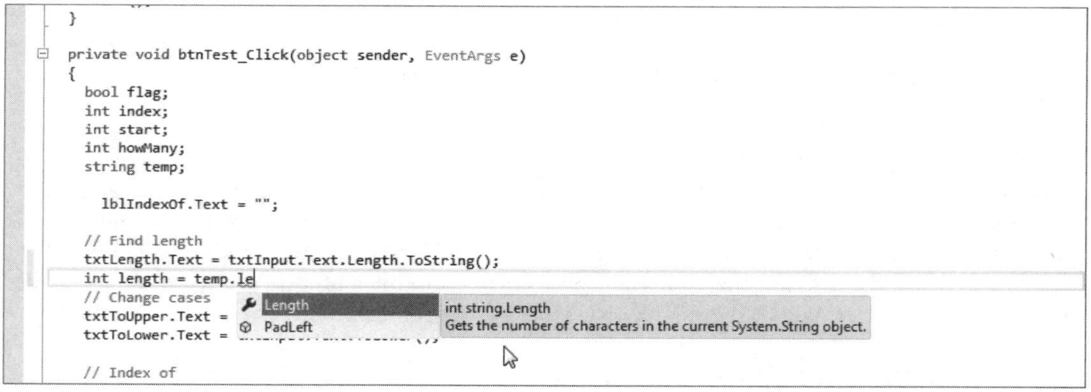

```
    }

    private void btnTest_Click(object sender, EventArgs e)
    {
        bool flag;
        int index;
        int start;
        int howMany;
        string temp;

            lblIndexOf.Text = "";

        // Find length
        txtLength.Text = txtInput.Text.Length.ToString();
        int length = temp.le
        // Change cases          🔧 Length              int string.Length
        txtToUpper.Text =        ⚙ PadLeft              Gets the number of characters in the current System.String object.
        txtToLower.Text =

        // Index of
```

FIGURE 5-4: Using IntelliSense to find a string property

If you look closely at Figure 5-4 (or better yet, write some test code of your own), you can see the Length property in the listbox object. If your eyes are good, you can see that the icon to the left of the word Length in the listbox object is a hand pointing to a page of code. The *hand icon* denotes an object property. If you look to the right of the listbox object, you can see that IntelliSense also gives you a brief description:

```
int string.Length
Gets the current number of characters in the current System.String object.
```

The first word (int) of the first line tells you that string.Length is an int data type. (This is why you make length an int data type in the preceding code fragment). The second line simply provides a brief description about the property (or method).

Finally, if you look at the last item in the listbox object shown in Figure 5-4, you can see a 3-D purple box next to the word Remove. Because Remove has a 3-D box icon next to it, it is a method. If you had selected Remove from the list, the screen would show something like Figure 5-5.

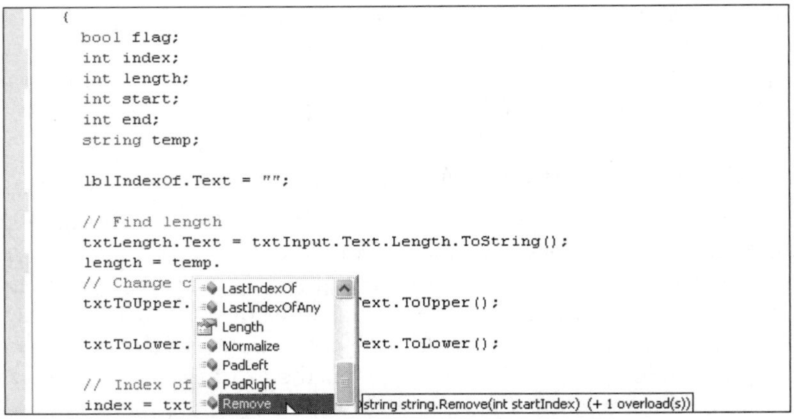

```
{
    bool flag;
    int index;
    int length;
    int start;
    int end;
    string temp;

    lblIndexOf.Text = "";

    // Find length
    txtLength.Text = txtInput.Text.Length.ToString();
    length = temp.
    // Change c  ╔══════════════════╗
    txtToUpper.  ║ ◆ LastIndexOf    ║ ext.ToUpper();
                 ║ ◆ LastIndexOfAny ║
                 ║ 🔧 Length        ║
    txtToLower.  ║ ◆ Normalize      ║ ext.ToLower();
                 ║ ◆ PadLeft        ║
                 ║ ◆ PadRight       ║
    // Index of  ║ ◆ Remove         ║
    index = txt  ╚══════════════════╝ string string.Remove(int startIndex) (+ 1 overload(s))
```

FIGURE 5-5: Using IntelliSense to find a string method

Note that the nature of the message from IntelliSense has changed. It now says this:

```
string string.Remove(int startIndex) (+ 1 overload(s))
```

The first word (`string`) says that the method returns a `string` data type. The phrase `string .Remove(int startIndex)` says that the `Remove()` method is part of the string class and that it expects an integer value to be supplied with it. (A complete example of how to use `Remove()` is given later in the Try It Out section, "Using String Class Properties and Methods.") Finally, `(+1 overload(s))` indicates that there are multiple "flavors" of this method. You're not ready to discuss what that means…yet, but you will be a little later in the section titled "Overloaded Methods."

Using an IntelliSense Option

IntelliSense wouldn't present you with all the options in a listbox if you couldn't use the listbox. For example, Figure 5-4 shows the `Length` property highlighted. If you now press the Tab key, IntelliSense automatically fills in the word `Length` in your source code. You can use the same technique for object methods, too. The bad news is that if you select a method rather than a property, IntelliSense does *not* automatically supply the parentheses for the method. You must type the parentheses in.

An Important Distinction Between Properties and Methods

Properties are variables associated with an object. As such, they do not require parentheses to follow their names. On the other hand, all methods *must* have parentheses following the method name. Violating these rules evokes a squiggly line nastygram from IntelliSense.

Thinking About Object Properties and Methods

You have just seen that the string data type offers you a host of properties and methods from which to choose. You must think about string data as an object. Drawing on the discussion from Chapter 2, a string variable is actually an object with a box that you can open up using the dot operator. The dot operator then makes that object's properties and methods available to you. This can greatly simplify using reference type data because Visual Studio has already written the code for many properties and methods for you.

When you see IntelliSense open up a listbox with that object's properties and methods listed, take a moment to scroll through the list, highlighting each property and method. As you highlight each option in the listbox, IntelliSense gives you a brief description of the purpose of that property or method. In the process of doing this, you may discover that the task you need to accomplish has already been done for you.

In the following Try It Out section you will use a number of the String class method and properties. While not all of the String class methods and properties are used, the program does exercise those methods and properties you are most likely to use in your own programs.

TRY IT OUT Using String Class Methods and Properties (Chapter05StringMethods.zip)

Figure 5-4 shows that numerous properties and methods are associated with strings. In this section, you write a program that exercises some of those properties and methods. Figure 5-6 shows the user interface for the program.

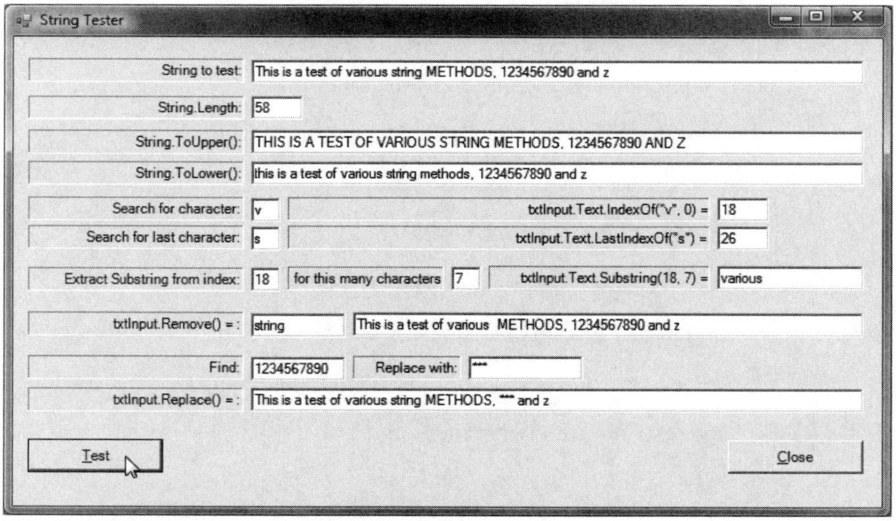

FIGURE 5-6: User interface for a string program

To create the program, use the following steps:

1. Create a new project using the sequence of steps you have used before when creating a new project, including inserting the C# template code presented in Listing 2-1 (in Chapter 2).

2. Add the label and textbox objects using the variable names shown in Table 5-4. (The table is organized such that the names of the textboxes shown in Figure 5-6 are presented from top to bottom and left to right.)

3. Also add two button objects for the Test and Close buttons.

4. Download the code found in the `Chapter05StringMethods` folder and copy it to the current project.

TABLE 5-4: Program Objects and their Description

TEXTBOX NAME	DESCRIPTION
txtInput	The textual data to be used.
txtLength	The length of the input data.
txtToUpper	The result of converting the data to uppercase.
txtToLower	The result of converting the data to lowercase.
txtSearchChar	A character in the data to search for.
txtSearchIndex	The position where the character was found.
txtLastChar	Find the last occurrence of this letter.
txtLastIndexOf	The position where the last occurrence was found.
txtStartIndex	Start from this position within the string.
txtEndIndex	Copy this many characters from the string.
txtSubstringResult	The substring that is copied.
txtRemove	The text to remove from the string.
txtRemoveResult	The string after the text has been removed.
txtReplaceChars	Find this sequence of characters within the string.
txtReplaceWith	Replace the preceding sequence with this sequence of characters.
txtReplaceResult	The resultant string after the replacement.

You can arrange the textboxes in a different order if you want. Because there are so many string methods used in this program, the How It Works section that follows is longer than most. However, understanding how the string data type works is extremely important.

How It Works

You can see in Figure 5-6 that the program asks the user to enter a line of text into the top textbox (`txtInput`). After the text is entered, the user clicks the Test button to exercise some of the many string methods provided by Visual Studio. The code for the Test button click event is shown in Listing 5-1. Each of the features shown in Figure 5-6 is explained in the following sections.

LISTING 5-1: btnTest Click Event Code (frmMain.cs)

```csharp
private void btnTest_Click(object sender, EventArgs e)
{
  bool flag;
  int index;
  int start;
  int howMany;
  string temp;

  lblIndexOf.Text = "";
  // Find length
  txtLength.Text = txtInput.Text.Length.ToString();
  // Change cases
  txtToUpper.Text = txtInput.Text.ToUpper();
  txtToLower.Text = txtInput.Text.ToLower();

  // Index of
  index = txtInput.Text.IndexOf(txtSearchChar.Text, 0);
  lblIndexOf.Text = "txtInput.Text.IndexOf(\"" + txtSearchChar.Text +
                "\",0) = ";
  txtSearchIndex.Text = index.ToString();

  //LastIndexOf
  index = txtInput.Text.LastIndexOf(txtLastChar.Text);
  lblLastIndexOf.Text = "txtInput.Text.LastIndexOf(\"" + txtLastChar.Text + "\")
                 = ";
  txtLastIndexOf.Text = index.ToString();

  // Substring
  flag = int.TryParse(txtStartIndex.Text, out start);
  if (flag == false)
  {
    MessageBox.Show("Improper numeric input. Re-enter.");
    txtStartIndex.Focus();
    return;
  }
  flag = int.TryParse(txtEndIndex.Text, out howMany);
  if (flag == false)
  {
    MessageBox.Show("Improper numeric input. Re-enter.");
    txtEndIndex.Focus();
    return;
  }
  lblSubstring.Text = "txtInput.Text.Substring(" +     start.ToString() + ", " +
                    howMany.ToString()+ ") = ";
  txtSubstringResult.Text = txtInput.Text.Substring(start, howMany);

  // Remove
  temp = txtInput.Text;
  index = temp.IndexOf(txtRemove.Text);
  if (index > 0)
  {
    txtRemoveResult.Text = temp.Remove(index, txtRemove.Text.Length);
```

continues

LISTING 5-1 *(continued)*

```
    }
    // Replace
    temp = txtInput.Text;
    txtReplaceResult.Text = temp.Replace(txtReplaceChars.Text, txtReplaceWith.
Text);
    }
```

For the sample test run shown in Figure 5-6, you can type in the following string:

```
This is a test of various string METHODS, 1234567890 and z
```

For the sections that follow, repeat specific lines of code relative to the method or property under discussion.

The Length of a String: Length

The `Length` property stores the number of characters of a string. This count includes everything in the string, including blank spaces, punctuation, and digit characters. The code shown in Listing 5-1 for the `Length` property is:

```
    // Find length
    txtLength.Text = txtInput.Text.Length.ToString();
```

You're probably saying, "Hold on a minute! Why so many dot operators in the statement?" Good question. Now break apart the right side of the expression first. Suppose you type in the following in the Source window of Visual Studio:

```
    txtLength.Text = txtInput.
```

In Chapter 2 you learned that the dot operator is used to separate an object (the `txtInput` textbox object in this example) from the properties and methods available to that object. In other words, the dot operator "opens the box" of the object to give you access to the properties and methods of that object. (Refer to Figure 2-7 in Chapter 2.) The instant you type in the period after the name of the `txtInput` textbox object, Visual Studio displays the listbox, as shown in Figure 5-7.

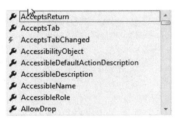

FIGURE 5-7: A textbox list of properties and methods

The listbox shown in Figure 5-7 actually contains more than 200 properties and methods associated with a textbox object. In this particular case, you are interested in the `Text` property of the `txtInput` textbox object. So you type in `Te` and the listbox automatically scrolls down to the `Text` property of the `txtInput` textbox object. Press the Tab key and Visual Studio fills in the rest of the word `Text` for you. So far, so good.

Now ask yourself this question: What kind of data type is the `Text` property? Well, if the `Text` property is storing textual data, the data must be stored in a string data type. Because the `Text` property of a textbox object is a string variable, it also means the `Text` property is a string *object*. Therefore, you should type in another dot operator to see what's available in that string object. So you type in the dot operator:

```
txtLength.Text = txtInput.Text.
```

After you do that, Visual Studio presents you with a listbox containing the properties and methods associated with a string object. This new list is shown in Figure 5-8.

If you scroll through this list, you find there are a lot of methods for string objects, but only one property: Length. You can either scroll down to the Length property or type in the first few letters and let Visual Studio scroll you to the Length property. If you press the Tab key, Visual Studio fills in the property name for you. Your statement now looks like this:

FIGURE 5-8: The properties and methods for a Text object

```
txtLength.Text = txtInput.Text.Length
```

Now you have a problem. The length of a string is stored as an int data type. The problem is that you want to assign a numeric integer value (txtInput.Text.Length) into a textual property that is a string data type (txtLength.Text). The bad news is that you have an apple on one side of the assignment operator and an orange on the other side. The good news is that C# can treat value types as objects when it needs to...like right now. (See the "Data Wrappers" sidebar.) Therefore, because Length is an int value type that can be treated as an object when necessary, you add another dot operator to the expression:

```
txtLength.Text = txtInput.Text.Length.
```

Visual Studio immediately senses that you want to treat Length as an object, so it presents you with a list of properties and methods associated with value data types. The list of methods for value data types is shown in Figure 5-9.

FIGURE 5-9: List of methods for value types

As illustrated in Figure 5-9, Visual Studio provides only six methods for value types. However, one of those six is the ToString() method, which is exactly what you need. You now complete the statement:

```
txtLength.Text = txtInput.Text.Length.ToString();
```

Now your problem has disappeared. You have a string data type property (Text) on the left side of the assignment operator and a string data type on the right side because you use the ToString() method to convert the integer value of Length into a string. Ta-da! You can now see the input string's length properly displayed in the txtLength textbox object. (Refer to Figure 5-6.)

This rather lengthy explanation may seem like using an H-bomb to kill an ant, but you must understand that one object (such as a textbox) can have another object (such as a string) stored as a property inside it. Further, that string object (Text) can also have a property (such as Length) that may be treated as an object, too. All value types have the six methods shown in Figure 5-9 available should you need them. In this example, you needed to use the ToString() method of the Length property so that you could convert the integer value of Length into a string for display in the txtLength textbox.

DATA WRAPPERS

In non-OOP languages, value types and reference types suffer the old oil-and-water problem...they don't mix well. C#, on the other hand, was designed to be an object-oriented programming language from the start. The designers knew, therefore, that there would be times when the programmer would like to treat the value type data as though it were an object. For that reason, C# has a wrapper class that envelops the value type. (You already read some information about wrapper classes in Chapter 3.) Although it's a bit of a simplification, you can think of a value type wrapper class as having one property (its value) and six methods (see Figure 5-9). Of the six methods, the ToString() method is used most often and enables you to convert the value of the data type to a string.

Changing the Case of a String: ToUpper( ) and ToLower( )

Sometimes certain tasks can be simplified if the textual data is all in the same case. For example, one person may write her last name as "Van d'Camp" whereas another person writes it as "van d'Camp." If you were searching a list of strings that contain people's names, you might miss the person you were looking for because you didn't enter the name using exactly the same case the user did. To avoid problems like this, you can change the string to a single case and use that case during the search process. The following statements change the input string shown in Figure 5-6 to all uppercase letters using the ToUpper() method:

```
txtToUpper.Text = txtInput.Text.ToUpper();

txtToLower.Text = txtInput.Text.ToLower();
```

The resulting changes are shown in their respective textbox objects. The second statement changes the string to all lowercase letters. The right side of the preceding assignment statements may be verbalized as, "Find the txtInput textbox object, locate its Text property, and because it's a string variable, use its ToUpper() or ToLower() methods to change the Text property to upper- or lowercase, respectively." You can find both of these methods by scrolling the listbox shown in Figure 5-8.

Finding a Specific Character: IndexOf( )

Suppose you want to find a specific character in a string. In Figure 5-6, you typed in the character v and used the IndexOf() method to find the first occurrence of that character. The next textbox (txtSearchIndex) on the same line has the number 18 displayed in it. This means that the IndexOf() method found the letter v at index number 18 in the string. If you count the number of letters and spaces up to the letter v, you discover that the v is the 19th character.

What?

The reason the value is 19 is that programming languages start counting characters in a string referencing the first position as position zero, not position one. If you count the number of characters and spaces beginning with zero, you can find that the v is, indeed, at position 18. Programmers use the word *index* to refer to the zero-based position of a character in a string.

The code that accomplished the search is found in the following statements:

```
// Index of
index = txtInput.Text.IndexOf(txtSearchChar.Text, 0);
lblIndexOf.Text = "txtInput.Text.IndexOf(\"" + txtSearchChar.Text
                + "\",0) = ";
txtSearchIndex.Text = index.ToString();
```

Now examine the first statement. The right side of the assignment operator says, "Get the Text property of the txtInput textbox object and use the Text's method named IndexOf()." Unfortunately, IndexOf() can't do its job without two additional pieces of information. First, IndexOf() needs to know what character you want to find. The character to find is the letter the user typed into the txt-SearchChar textbox object. (It's the textbox with the v in it in Figure 5-6.) You retrieve that character using the txtSearchChar.Text property. Second, IndexOf() wants to know the index where you want to begin the search. In your case, you want the search to start at the beginning of the string, so you use the index value 0. (The first character in a string is at position zero, remember?) These two pieces of information are called the arguments of the IndexOf() method. Simply stated, *method arguments* are information that you pass to a method so the method can perform its task. Method arguments can be in the form of variables, like txtSearchChar.Text, or literal values, like the second argument, 0. (Actually, there are two "flavors" of the IndexOf() method. If you only pass in a single argument, the IndexOf() method assumes the search starts with position 0 in the string. The "Overloaded Methods" section later in this chapter explains how this works.) After you enter the proper method arguments for IndexOf(), the program transfers program control to the program code for the IndexOf() method. Simply stated, the IndexOf() code starts examining itself (after all, IndexOf() is part of the Text property, so it knows what the string is) starting at the index you passed to it. Because you passed a zero to the IndexOf() method, it begins its search with the first character in the string, which is at position 0. The code examines the first character and compares it to the character you passed to it, the v. Because there is no match, it looks at the second position. It continues this process until it finds a match, which it finds at position 18. Okay...now what?

The IndexOf() method was successful in finding a match at index 18, but it needs a way to convey that information back to the point in the program where we invoked the IndexOf() method. Although the technical details of how the value 18 is passed back to the point in the program that needs it is covered in Chapter 10, for now, simply think of the right side of the assignment expression,

```
index = txtInput.Text.IndexOf(txtSearchChar.Text, 0);
```

as being replaced with this:

```
index = 18;
```

The reason to use the txtInput object was to get to the Text property so you could use its IndexOf() method to locate a specific character. Because the object (txtInput) and its property (Text) and method (IndexOf()) have all done their jobs, the code could determine the exact location of the v character in the string. In formal language you would say, "The IndexOf() method returned the integer value of 18." When the statement is complete, the variable index now has an rvalue of 18 assigned into it.

"Calling" a Method

You read about calling a method in Chapter 3, but it's worth repeating here but with a slight twist. It's common to refer to the variable on the left side of an assignment statement as the *caller* when a method is used to resolve an expression. That is, index is invoking, or "calling," the IndexOf() method so that it can have a proper position value assigned into itself. Likewise, you often hear something like, "IndexOf() returns the value 18 to the caller." The interpretation is that the value determined by the IndexOf() method is assigned into the caller—index in this example.

What happens if the string doesn't contain the character you're looking for? In that case, IndexOf() returns the value −1 to the caller. If IndexOf() returns a negative value, you know the search failed. One more thing: Although the example presented here illustrates IndexOf() as searching for a single character, the first argument to IndexOf() can also be a string with more than a single character. In that case, IndexOf() returns the index of the first character in the string where the match occurred. If IndexOf() cannot find an exact match for the character sequence of the string passed to it, it returns a −1.

Searching for the Last Occurrence of a Character: LastIndexOf( )

The IndexOf() method enables you to search for the first occurrence of a particular character in a string. Now suppose that there are one-half-dozen occurrences of that character, but you're interested in the position of the last one. You could call IndexOf() five times, having the method return an index for each (unwanted) position. That is, you could then call IndexOf() again, using the index plus one as the second argument in the method call. (Think about what that means.) However, it's more efficient to use the LastIndexOf() string method instead.

The code for the LastIndexOf() method is this:

```
index = txtInput.Text.LastIndexOf(txtLastChar.Text);
lblLastIndexOf.Text = "txtInput.Text.LastIndexOf(\"" +
                      txtLastChar.Text + "\")
                      = ";
txtLastIndexOf.Text = index.ToString();
```

There is only one argument to LastIndexOf() and it is the character for which you are searching. It doesn't need a second argument for the starting position for the search because LastIndexOf() automatically starts the search at the end of the string, searching backward toward the start. The method returns the (zero-based) index of the character if the search is successful and −1 if no match is found. The remaining two lines of code have virtually the same interpretation as the IndexOf() code fragment. (Refer to Figure 5-6 to see what the contents of the label look like.)

Searching for a Substring

If you have ever used a word processor and searched a document for a specific word, chances are the word processor was using a method similar to the Substring() method to copy the substring that appears at the specified point in the string. The code that uses the Substring() method is shown here:

```
lblSubstring.Text = "txtInput.Text.Substring(" +
                    start.ToString() + ", " +
                    howMany.ToString()+ ") = ";
txtSubstringResult.Text = txtInput.Text.Substring(start, howMany);
```

You already know how to use the `TryParse()` method calls. Suffice it to say that the two `TryParse()` method calls in Listing 5-1 simply convert the digit characters entered by the user in the two textbox objects into integer variables named `start` and `howMany`.

In Figure 5-6, the `start` position is set to position `18` (`start = 18`). Again, because string positions are always referenced from position `0`, you are actually going to start the substring with the 19th character in the string. If you count 19 characters (including spaces and punctuation) in the string, you find that the 19th character is the v in the word `various`.

The `howMany` variable might have a different meaning than you think. The value of `howMany` tells the `Substring()` method how many characters to copy, beginning with position `start`. The variable `howMany` does *not* set the ending index value for `Substring()`. In Figure 5-6 you can see that the value for `howMany` is set to `7`. Therefore, the statement

```
txtSubstringResult.Text = txtInput.Text.Substring(start,
howMany);
```

becomes

```
txtSubstringResult.Text = txtInput.Text.Substring(18, 7);
```

that functionally results in

```
txtSubstringResult.Text = "various";
```

This means that the substring you want to copy from the string is the word `various`. You can see the result in Figure 5-6. You should experiment with the program and try different start and end values to see the impact it has on the substring.

Removing a Substring

Suppose you have a string that is actually a memo to a colleague who has botched a job you asked him to do. You find that your memo uses the word "idiot" several times, and your assistant suggests that it might not be politically correct to call him an "idiot" because he's your boss's son. You decide to remove the word "idiot" from the memo. The editor you use to remove the word "idiot" probably works like the `Remove()` string method.

The statements to use `Remove()` from Listing 5-1 are as follows:

```
// Remove
temp = txtInput.Text;
index = temp.IndexOf(txtRemove.Text);
if (index > 0)
{
   txtRemoveResult.Text = temp.Remove(index,
                       txtRemove.Text.Length);
}
```

First, the code copies the original string entered by the user, so it doesn't permanently change the string as it appears in the first textbox. Next, the code uses the `IndexOf()` method to find the position where the "target string" is located. In the preceding discussion, the target string would be the word "idiot." In Figure 5-6, the target string is the word "string." In the code, the target string is whatever the user types into the txtRemove textbox object as stored in the Text property. The code then calls IndexOf() to locate the target string. Note that IndexOf() is capable of searching for a string with a single character, as you saw in the IndexOf() discussion section earlier, or it can locate a string with multiple characters in it.

If the search is successful, variable index is assigned the starting position of the string. If the search fails to find a match, index is assigned −1 (as explained earlier). The if statement prevents an unsuccessful search from calling the Remove() method.

Figure 5-6 shows that you searched for the word string when exercising the Remove() method. The target string starts at an index position of 26. This value becomes the first argument in the call to the Remove() method. The second argument is the number of characters you want to remove. You know that string has six characters in it, so you could "hard-code" the literal value 6 into the second argument. However, that's not flexible. Anytime you want to find a different string, you likely need to adjust the second Remove() method argument. Because the txtRemove textbox object holds the string you want to remove, you can always use the Length property to adjust the second argument to the proper value. Therefore, the statement

```
txtRemoveResult.Text = temp.Remove(index,
                        txtRemove.Text.Length);
```

becomes

```
txtRemoveResult.Text = temp.Remove(26, 6);
```

which resolves to

```
txtRemoveResult.Text = "This is a test of various  METHODS,
                1234567890 and z";
```

The new string then displays in the txtRemoveResult textbox object by assigning the new string to its Text property. (Note: There is a little hiccup in this code. Because the code removed only the word string from the original string, there are now two blank spaces between the words various and METHODS where there should only be one space. How would you fix this problem?)

Replacing a Substring

Sometimes you need to change one word in a larger string with a replacement word. For example, suppose your boss tells you to send the program specifications to Gene, which you obediently do, only to find out that Gene is actually Jean. In this case, you need to replace the word Gene with Jean. This task is exactly what the Replace() string method is designed to do.

Figure 5-6 suggests that you want to replace the substring 1234567890 with ***. The statements that accomplish this task are the following:

```
// Replace
temp = txtInput.Text;
txtReplaceResult.Text = temp.Replace(txtReplaceChars.Text,
                    txtReplaceWith.Text);
```

The first line simply copies the input string so you don't permanently change the Text property of the txtInput textbox object. The Replace() method requires two arguments. The first argument is the string you want to replace. The second argument is the string you want to substitute for the first argument. In the example shown in Figure 5-6, the method calls resolves to

```
txtReplaceResult.Text = temp.Replace("1234567890", "***");
```

that means you want to replace the digit characters with three asterisks. After the replacement takes place, the statement appears as this:

```
txtReplaceResult.Text = "This is a test of various string METHODS,
                         *** and z";
```

The new string is assigned into the Text property of the txtReplaceResult textbox object. If the target string does not exist in the original string, the original string is left unchanged.

The listbox in Figure 5-4 shows a partial listing of literally hundreds of string methods available to you. Obviously, it's not practical to show all the string methods here. However, you may want to spend a few moments scrolling through the list of possible string methods from which you can choose. Chances are good that anything you ever want to do to manipulate string data is already in the list.

Strings and Escape Sequences

You've already seen how a string variable can be assigned a literal value, as in

```
string name = "Katie";
```

However, sometimes certain string literals can pose problems. For example, suppose you want to display the following message:

```
John said: "Reach for the sky!"
```

If you try to write this as a normal string literal:

```
string message = "John said: "Reach for the sky!"";
```

Visual Studio gets confused because the double quotation marks are used to delimit the start and end of a string literal, not as part of the string itself.

To solve this problem, C# uses a special *escape character* within the string to signify that what follows is to be treated differently. The special escape character is the backslash character (\). In essence, the escape character says to treat whatever follows it as though it were part of the string literal. For example, suppose you rewrite the string literal like this:

```
string message = "John said: \"Reach for the sky!\"";
```

The double quotation mark before the word Reach and the double quotation mark at the end of the sentence are now treated as part of an escape sequence and, therefore, are printed out as part of the string literal. The end result is that the statement displays this:

```
John said: "Reach for the sky!"
```

Table 5-5 presents a list of the special escape sequences.

TABLE 5-5: Escape Sequences

ESCAPE SEQUENCE	INTERPRETATION
\"	Display a double quotation mark.
\'	Display a single quotation mark.
\\	Display a backslash.
\0	Null (nonprinting).
\a	Alarm (beep terminal alarm).
\b	Backspace. (Back up one character position.)
\f	Form feed. (Advance to next page.)
\n	Newline. (Advance to next line.)
\r	Carriage return. (Move to left margin.)
\t	Tab. (Advance one tab space, often eight characters.)
\v	Vertical tab.

There are other instances in which escape sequences come in handy. For example, suppose you want to set the directory path to the C# folder on the C drive. You would need to use the following command:

```
string path = "C:\\C#";
```

With longer path names, the `path` string starts to look rather messy. C#, however, it has a way to make it less so.

Verbatim String Literals

Suppose you want to issue a message stating the following:

```
Go to the C:\Programs\Source directory and send a \n character.
```

You would have to write the message as:

```
string message = "Go to the C:\\Programs\\Source directory and send a \\n
                   character.";
```

This looks ugly; C# provides a way to make such literals prettier. You can use the *verbatim string literal character* (@) to tell Visual Studio to build the string exactly as it appears within the double quotation marks. Therefore,

```
string message = @"Go to the C:\Programs\Source directory and send a \n
                   character.";
```

displays the message exactly as you have written it without you worrying about using escape sequences in the proper places. The verbatim string literal character is not needed often, but it comes in handy when you need to pass directory information around in a program.

DATETIME REFERENCE OBJECTS

Many business applications need to manipulate dates and times. Banks need to calculate interest payments on loans based on dates. Producing certain products, like bread, requires that specific ingredients be added after so many minutes or hours have passed. Visual Studio provides a `DateTime` data type to enable you to work with dates and time easily.

The way Visual Studio tracks time is interesting. The Windows operating system maintains a system clock as part of its duties. Most of you can observe the current local time in the lower right corner of your display. Visual Studio uses the system clock to track the number of ticks on the system clock. A *tick* is a unit of time measured in 100-nanosecond blocks. A nanosecond is one-billionth of a second. That's a fairly small time slice. In fact, light travels approximately only 18 inches in a nanosecond.

The `DateTime` object maintains a count of the number of ticks since midnight, January 1, 0001 A.D. using the Gregorian calendar. That's a whole bunch of ticks to the present! However, by manipulating the tick count, the `DataTime` object can determine all kinds of things relative to times and dates.

Figure 5-10 shows a sample run of a program that uses some of the `DateTime` methods and properties.

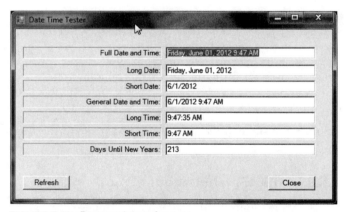

FIGURE 5-10: Date and time formats

DateTime and ToString( ) Conversions

As mentioned earlier, all C# data types provide a `ToString()` wrapper conversion method that enables you to express the data as a string. However, some data types enable you to pass an argument to the `ToString()` method, so the data can be formatted a specific way. Table 5-6 presents the most common formatting characters for use with a `DateTime` data type. In each case, the letter shown in column one of Table 5-6 becomes the argument to `ToString()`. For example, `myDate .ToString("F")` displays the full date and time for the `myDate` variable. The table example assumes the date is Oct. 25, 2007.

TABLE 5-6: Commonly Used Date and Time Conversion Characters

CONVERSION CHARACTER	DESCRIPTION	SAMPLE OUTPUT
`"F"`	Full date and time, including seconds	Thursday, October 25, 2007 12:00:59 PM
`"f"`	Full date and time, without seconds	Thursday, October 25, 2007 12:02 PM
`"D"`	Full date	Thursday, October 25, 2007
`"d"`	Short date	10/25/2007
`"G"`	General date, including seconds*	10/25/2007 12:04:54 PM
`"g"`	General date, without seconds	10/25/2007 12:05 PM
`"T"`	Full time, including seconds	12:05:48 PM
`"t"`	Full time, without seconds	12:05 PM

* The "G" conversion character is the default format if no conversion character is used with ToString().

The first column in Table 5-6 shows the conversion character you may use as an argument to the `ToString()` method when using a `DateTime` variable. The third column of the table presents an example of what the resulting output looks like. As a general rule, an uppercase conversion character presents more detailed information than does its lowercase counterpart. Note that many of the date conversions are locale-aware. That is, the data are formatted in a stlye common to the locality where the program is run. In Europe, for example, May 19, 2013 would be written as: 19\05\2013 with the day coming before the month.

The following Try It Out shows you the impact of some of the commonly used string formatting options.

TRY IT OUT | **String Formatting (Chapter0501StringMethods.zip)**

The program code that produced the output shown in Figure 5-10 is shown in Listing 5-2.

1. Create a new project in the normal manner.

2. Download the `Chapter05DateTimeMethods.zip` file and copy it into the current project.

Unlike in previous programs, here is all the program code less the code automatically generated by Windows.

LISTING 5-2: The frmMain class definition. (frmMain.cs)

```
using System;
using System.Windows.Forms;

public class frmMain : Form
{
    private Label label1;
```

```
private TextBox txtLongDate;
private Label label2;
private TextBox txtShortDate;
private Label label3;
private TextBox txtGeneralDateAndTime;
private Label label4;
private TextBox txtLongTime;
private Label label5;
private TextBox txtShortTime;
private Label label6;
private TextBox txtDaysToNewYears;
private Label label7;
private Button btnClose;
private Button btnRefresh;
private TextBox txtCompleteDateAndTime;

#region Windows code
#endregion

public frmMain()
{
    InitializeComponent();
    UpdateTimeInfo();        // Update textboxes
}

public static void Main()
{
    frmMain main = new frmMain();
    Application.Run(main);
}

private void UpdateTimeInfo()
{
    int days;
    DateTime myTime = new DateTime();
    myTime = DateTime.Now;
    DateTime newYears = new DateTime(myTime.Year, 12, 31);

    txtCompleteDateAndTime.Text = myTime.ToString("f");
    txtLongDate.Text = myTime.ToString("D");
    txtShortDate.Text = myTime.ToString("d");
    txtGeneralDateAndTime.Text = myTime.ToString("g");
    txtLongTime.Text = myTime.ToString("T");
    txtShortTime.Text = myTime.ToString("t");

    days = newYears.DayOfYear  myTime.DayOfYear;
    txtDaysToNewYears.Text = days.ToString();
}

private void btnRefresh_Click(object sender, EventArgs e)
{
    UpdateTimeInfo();
}

private void btnClose_Click(object sender, EventArgs e)
{
```

continues

LISTING 5-2 *(continued)*

```
            Close();
        }
    }
}
```

How It Works

Listing 5-2 presents the body of code that illustrates a number of different date and time format options. The program begins by informing Visual Studio of the references it plans to use via the `using` keywords. Then the code begins the definition for the class you are writing, named `frmMain`. The `:` `Form` at the end of the statement simply tells Visual Studio that you are going to use the Windows `Form` class as a starting point but add your own objects to that class and reference them with the name `frm-Main`. Next, the program defines the control objects (such as labels, textboxes, and buttons) that you are adding to a generic Windows form (`Form`) to make the new class (`frmMain`) suit your needs. Now things start to get interesting.

As part of this sample program, a number of topics common to all C# programs as well as the program itself are discussed.

#region and #endregion

Toward the top of Listing 5-2 are the following lines:

```
#region Windows code
#endregion
```

`#region` and `#endregion` are C# program directives that tell Visual Studio to either hide or show a block of code. Assuming you use the C# template presented in Chapter 2 as the starting point for all programs, and then add the control objects to the form, Visual Studio generates a ton of code for you automatically. When you look at your program, the `#region` directive line has a small plus sign (+) in the left margin of the Source window. If you click that plus sign, Visual Studio expands the program listing to reveal the code it generated behind your back while you weren't looking! The code looks similar to that shown in Figure 5-11.

Note how the first several lines after the `#region` Windows code appear similar to this:

```
private void InitializeComponent()
{
    this.label1 = new System.Windows.Forms.Label();
    this.txtCompleteDateAndTime = new
                        System.Windows.Forms.TextBox();
    this.txtLongDate = new System.Windows.Forms.TextBox();
    this.label2 = new System.Windows.Forms.Label();
    this.txtShortDate = new System.Windows.Forms.TextBox();
    this.label3 = new System.Windows.Forms.Label();
```

This is the code that Visual Studio sneaked into the program for you. Now look at the first line inside the `InitializeComponent()` method:

```
this.label1 = new System.Windows.Forms.Label();
```

```
        private Button btnClose;
        private Button btnRefresh;
        private TextBox txtCompleteDateAndTime;

        #region Windows code
        private void InitializeComponent()
        {
            this.label1 = new System.Windows.Forms.Label();
            this.txtCompleteDateAndTime = new System.Windows.Forms.TextBox();
            this.txtLongDate = new System.Windows.Forms.TextBox();
            this.label2 = new System.Windows.Forms.Label();
            this.txtShortDate = new System.Windows.Forms.TextBox();
            this.label3 = new System.Windows.Forms.Label();
            this.txtGeneralDateAndTime = new System.Windows.Forms.TextBox();
            this.label4 = new System.Windows.Forms.Label();
            this.txtLongTime = new System.Windows.Forms.TextBox();
            this.label5 = new System.Windows.Forms.Label();
            this.txtShortTime = new System.Windows.Forms.TextBox();
            this.label6 = new System.Windows.Forms.Label();
            this.txtDaysToNewYears = new System.Windows.Forms.TextBox();
            this.label7 = new System.Windows.Forms.Label();
            this.btnClose = new System.Windows.Forms.Button();
            this.btnRefresh = new System.Windows.Forms.Button();
            this.SuspendLayout();
```

FIGURE 5-11: Using #region and #endregion

This statement tells Visual Studio to grab a label cookie cutter and carve out a piece of memory and reference that chunk of memory as `label1`. The keyword `this` is a kind of shorthand Visual Studio uses to refer to the current object used. Because you dragged a label object onto the form named `frmMain`, the keyword `this` is actually referring to the current instance of the object `frmMain`. The end result is that Visual Studio creates a new `Label` object named `label1` and places it inside `frmMain`.

Sliding Down the Object Chain

You should also decipher the meaning of the right side of the statement:

```
this.label1 = new System.Windows.Forms.Label();
```

As you learned in Chapter 2, the `new` keyword means you want to create a new object of some kind. So you go to the `System` object and use the dot operator to look inside it. Inside the `System` object you see a bunch of stuff, including a `Windows` object. Because that looks promising, you use another dot operator to look inside the `Windows` object. Inside the `Windows` object you see some more properties and methods, including one that is a `Forms` object. Now you're getting close, so you use another dot operator to gain access to the `Forms` object. Inside the `Forms` object you find the `Label()` method that you can call to instantiate a new label object. Perfect! Because that's precisely what you want to do. You call the `Label()` method to instantiate a new label object named `label1`.

Don't let multiple dot operators scare you. Just keep in mind that the dot operator always separates an object (to the left of the dot operator) from a property or method inside that object (to the right of the dot operator). However, because one object can contain another object, you might need to use another dot operator to peek inside *that* object. In the preceding statement the `System` object evidently has a `Windows` object inside it. So you use another dot operator to go inside the `Windows` object, and you find a `Forms` object is defined inside the `Windows` object. Undaunted, you go inside the `Forms` object and find there is a `Label` object. Finally you call the `Label()` method to instantiate a label object for you in memory. Visual Studio then enters the information about that label object into the symbol table using the ID `label1`. No matter how complex the statement, if you bump over enough dot operators, you'll eventually end up looking at the property or method you're interested in. Even though you had to plow through three objects to get there, eventually you found the method that constructs a new label object for you named `label`. Piece of cake!

Always remember: Each time you do use a dot operator, Visual Studio displays a listbox of the properties and methods available in the object. You saw this in Figure 5-4. (Some of the properties actually represent classes that can be used to instantiate a new object, but you can still think of them as properties.)

Visual Studio wrote the next line in the `InitializeComponent()` method for you:

```
this.txtCompleteDateAndTime = new System.Windows.Forms.TextBox();
```

This creates a new textbox object, gives it the name `txtCompleteDateAndTime`, and adds it to `frmMain`. This process repeats itself until all the form objects (labels, textboxes, and buttons) have been added. If you look further down the code listing in the `InitializeComponent()` method, you can see the property values you set when you created your user interface. That is, you can see the text you placed in the labels, the locations of each label, textbox, and button after you dragged them onto the form, and any associated properties you may have changed (such as border style, size, AutoSize, and so on).

How a Program Begins Execution

You learned in Chapter 1 that every C# program begins its execution with a special method named `Main()`. Consider the following statements from Listing 5-2:

```
public static void Main()
{
    frmMain main = new frmMain();
    Application.Run(main);
}
```

These statements define the `Main()` method and marks the spot where the program starts executing. The first line says you want to create a new object of the `frmMain` class and give it the name `main`. (Remember that C# is case-sensitive, so `Main` is not the same as `main`.) If you look at the top of Listing 5-2, you can see that the name of the class you define is `frmMain`. Therefore, this statement tells Visual Studio you want to create an object of type `frmMain`.

Class Constructors

Because the right side of the assignment operator is processed first, the first thing that happens is that the `new` keyword sends a message to Windows asking for enough memory to hold a `frmMain` object. Assuming Windows can find enough memory, the program then calls the `frmMain()` method. The method called shares the same name as the object you try to instantiate. A method that has the same name as its class is called a *class constructor*. The purpose of a constructor is to perform any initialization tasks that need to be done before you use the object of the class. From Listing 5-2, you can see that the constructor looks like this:

```
public frmMain()
{
    InitializeComponent();
    UpdateTimeInfo();        // Update textboxes
}
```

There are several things you need to remember about constructors:

➤ Constructors always have the same names as the classes in which they appear.

➤ Constructors always use the `public` keyword before their names if you want to instantiate objects of that class.

➤ Constructors can never return a value to their callers.

Inside the constructor for the `frmMain` class, the first thing that happens is that the code calls the `InitializeComponent()` method. However, as you saw in Figure 5-11, all `InitializeComponent()` does is place all the label, textbox, and button objects in the correct positions on the form and set their properties to whatever values you specified by dragging and dropping the objects on the form when you were creating the user interface.

When the `frmMain()` constructor finishes, your `frmMain` object sits in memory exactly the way you wanted it to look while you designed it. Now what?

Well, the next thing that happens is that the program calls the `UpdateTimeInfo()` method that you wrote (we will discuss this in a few moments). In essence, all the `UpdateTimeInfo()` method does is fill in the textboxes with date and time information using a variety of format options.

Invoking the Application

Having initialized the object, the program hits the closing curly brace for the `frmMain()` constructor method and knows it's time to return to the caller. Returning to the caller means that program control reverts back to the statement

```
frmMain main = new frmMain();
```

Your code has now created an image of your `frmMain` object in memory and associated it with an object named `main`. The next line says, "Okay, everything's set up and ready to go. Begin executing the program by calling the `Run()` method using the object named `main`":

```
Application.Run(main);
```

At this point...shazam! Your `frmMain` object named `main` appears on the display screen, and the user actually sees what all your work has accomplished. The output should look similar to what is shown in Figure 5-10.

You should prove these actions to yourself. To do that, place the cursor on the following line and press F9:

```
frmMain main = new frmMain();
```

This sets a breakpoint at that point in the program. (The program line now has a red background.) Now run the program.

Shortly, Visual Studio halts the program on the line where the breakpoint is set, setting the background color to yellow. Think of yellow as a caution, informing you that Visual Studio is ready to execute that line. Now press F11. You see the yellow line jump to the frmMain() constructor. You can continue to press the F11 key to advance to the InitializeComponent() method. If you continue pressing the F11 key, Visual Studio continues to single-step through each line in the program. If you get bored, press Shift+F11, and Visual Studio sends you back to the caller, the frmMain() method. Using the debugger to march through the program code is a great way to see what's going on. It's even more informative if, when the first breakpoint is reached, you invoke the Debug Windows Locals menu sequence. This opens up a debugging window that enables you to observe program variables as you single-step through the code. Good stuff.

The UpdateTimeInfo( ) Method

The code for the UpdateTimeInfo() method is reproduced here for convenience:

```
private void UpdateTimeInfo()
{
    int days;
    DateTime myTime = new DateTime();
    myTime = DateTime.Now;
    DateTime newYears = new DateTime(myTime.Year, 12, 31);

    txtCompleteDateAndTime.Text = myTime.ToString("f");
    txtLongDate.Text = myTime.ToString("D");
    txtShortDate.Text = myTime.ToString("d");
    txtGeneralDateAndTime.Text = myTime.ToString("g");
    txtLongTime.Text = myTime.ToString("T");
    txtShortTime.Text = myTime.ToString("t");

    days = newYears.DayOfYear  myTime.DayOfYear;
    txtDaysToNewYears.Text = days.ToString();
}
```

The method begins by defining an integer variable named days followed by a DateTime object named myTime. The right side of the statement calls a method named DateTime():

```
DateTime myTime = new DateTime();
```

However, because that method shares the same name as the class, you know that the DateTime() method is the constructor for the DateTime class. Therefore, after the statement executes, an object named myTime of type DateTime exists in memory and is ready to be used in the program.

The next statement creates another DateTime object named newYears by calling the DateTime() constructor:

```
DateTime newYears = new DateTime(myTime.Year, 12, 31);
```

Wait a minute! This time it appears that the DateTime() constructor has arguments supplied to it, but there were no arguments when you called the constructor for myTime. What's going on here?

Overloaded Methods

Earlier in this chapter you read that a constructor is used to perform any initialization tasks that need to be performed before you use the object. Usually, "performing initialization tasks" means setting the state of the object's properties to some nondefault value. When you created the `myTime` object, you didn't use any arguments to the constructor. That's because you were satisfied with the default values for the `DateTime` properties (that is, 0 or `null`). Figure 5-12 uses the same old dot operator technique to get a list of the properties and methods available for a `DateTime` object.

FIGURE 5-12: DateTime Object properties and methods

As you can see in the listbox, one of the properties is named `Day`. Evidently you were happy assigning the value of 0 to `Day` when `myTime` was instantiated. If you scroll the listbox shown in Figure 5-12, you find properties for `Month` and `Year`, too. These properties are also initialized to their default values of 0 for the `myTime` object. If you don't initialize any of the properties for a `DateTime` object, it displays the date and time of Monday, January 01, 0001, 12:00 AM, which is the starting date when the number of ticks is zero!

Suppose you backtrack and type in the statement

```
DateTime newYears = new DateTime(
```

to observe what you see on the screen. You should see something similar to Figure 5-13.

```
        }

    public static void Main()
    {
        frmMain main = new frmMain();
        Application.Run(main);
    }

    private void UpdateTimeInfo()
    {
        int days;
        DateTime myTime = new DateTime(
        DateTime newYears   4 of 12   DateTime.DateTime (int year, int month, int day)
                            year: The year (1 through 9999).

        myTime = DateTime.Now;

        txtCompleteDateAndTime.Text = myTime.ToString("f");
        txtLongDate.Text = myTime.ToString("D");
        txtShortDate.Text = myTime.ToString("d");
        txtGeneralDateAndTime.Text = myTime.ToString("g");
        txtLongTime.Text = myTime.ToString("T");
        txtShortTime.Text = myTime.ToString("t");

        days = newYears.DayOfYear - myTime.DayOfYear;
```

FIGURE 5-13: DateTime methods

Your screen actually shows a small box stating `1 of 12 DateTime.DateTime()` with up and down arrows surrounding the `1 of 12` part of the message. What IntelliSense is telling you is that there are 12 "flavors" of the `DateTime()` constructor method available to you. Figure 5-13 shows that you want to use the fourth flavor that passes the year, month, and day to the constructor. It also tells you that each of these arguments should be an integer value. In your code you used the constructor with three integer arguments:

```
DateTime newYears = new DateTime(myTime.Year, 12, 31);
```

You are telling Visual Studio you're not happy initializing the newYears DateTime object with its default values. Instead, you want to initialize the state of the newYears DateTime object with the values that correspond to December 31, 2012. (This book is written in 2012.) This works properly because the statement before the instantiation of the newYears DateTime object is

```
myTime = DateTime.Now;
```

That sets the Year property of the myTime object to 2012. (Now is a property of the DateTime class that holds the current tick value as measured by the Windows system clock. The current tick value also determines the values for the Month and Day properties.)

The end result is that the program now has two DateTime objects it can use. The first object, myTime, holds the current date and time because you used the Now property to assign its state. You initialized the second object, newYears, to December 31, 2012, by using the fourth DateTime constructor and supplying the proper arguments to that constructor.

Given how the two DateTime objects have been initialized, the following two statements use the DayOfYear property to calculate the number of days until New Year's:

```
days = newYears.DayOfYear - myTime.DayOfYear;
txtDaysToNewYears.Text = days.ToString();
```

The rest of the code in the UpdateTimeInfo() method simply illustrates several of the different formatting options available through the ToString() characters presented in Table 5-6.

Method Signatures

When an overloaded method is called, which flavor of the method ends up being called? After all, if a method is overloaded, it means that multiple methods use the same method name. How does Visual Studio know which one to call? Visual Studio makes the decision based upon the signature of the method.

A *method signature* is everything from the method name through the closing parenthesis of the method. For example, you already know that the DateTime() constructor method has 12 different forms. You have seen 2 of these. The 2 forms you have used are these:

```
public DateTime()
public DateTime(int year, int month, int day)
```

The signature for the first constructor is DateTime(). The signature for the second is DateTime(int year, int month, int day). The signatures are different because the parameter lists for the two methods are different. That is, the first version of the constructor does not have any arguments passed to it. The second signature, however, expects three integer arguments to be passed to it. Therefore, the three statements from Listing 5-2 are as follows:

```
DateTime myTime = new DateTime();
myTime = DateTime.Now;
DateTime newYears = new DateTime(myTime.Year, 12, 31);
```

The first statement causes Visual Studio to call the constructor that has no arguments being passed to it. The third statement causes Visual Studio to call the constructor that expects three integer variables to be passed to it. This leads to an important rule about overloaded methods: *Methods* may be overloaded provided no two overloaded methods have the same signature. What this means is that only one overloaded method can have zero arguments passed to it. Likewise, only one overloaded method can have three integers passed to it. An overloaded method can have three other variables passed to it, but they cannot all be integers. For example, you could have an overloaded method named countThis() with the following signatures:

```
public int countThis(int val);
public int countThis(long val);
```

These are perfectly acceptable because their signatures are different. True, both flavors accept one argument, but the data type for that argument is different; therefore, the signatures are different. If you scroll through the 12 constructors for the DateTime data type, you discover that all 12 have different arguments passed to them.

Overloaded methods are great when you need to write methods that behave differently when different information is passed to them. You see other examples of overloaded methods in later chapters.

The Refresh Button

In the last Try It Out section, the purpose of the refresh button is to update the time aspects of any strings using the time component. The code is simple:

```
private void btnRefresh_Click(object sender, EventArgs e)
{
    UpdateTimeInfo();
}
```

When the user clicks the refresh button (btnRefresh), the code calls the UpdateTimeInfo() method to update the information in the textboxes. Note that you call the UpdateTimeInfo() method in two different places in the program: once in the frmMain() constructor and again in the btnRefresh_Click() method.

Because you can call a method illustrates another important feature of methods: They enable you to avoid writing duplicate code. You could, after all, take the following code and shove it into both the frmMain() constructor and the btnRefresh_Click() methods:

```
int days;
DateTime myTime = new DateTime();
myTime = DateTime.Now;
DateTime newYears = new DateTime(myTime.Year, 12, 31);

txtCompleteDateAndTime.Text = myTime.ToString("f");
txtLongDate.Text = myTime.ToString("D");
txtShortDate.Text = myTime.ToString("d");
txtGeneralDateAndTime.Text = myTime.ToString("g");
txtLongTime.Text = myTime.ToString("T");
txtShortTime.Text = myTime.ToString("t");

days = newYears.DayOfYear  myTime.DayOfYear;
txtDaysToNewYears.Text = days.ToString();
```

But if you did that you'd have twice as much code to write and maintain. By placing the code in a method, you write, test, and debug the code only once, but you can call it from anywhere in the program as many times as you want. Methods make programming much easier! Chapters 9 and 10 get into writing your own methods in greater detail.

SUMMARY

You've covered a lot of ground in this chapter. The information is important because so much of program writing deals with manipulating string data in one form or another. You must understand the difference between reference types and value types before you move to the next chapter. A little time spent now to understand the concepts presented in this chapter can yield huge benefits later.

EXERCISES

You can find the answers to the following exercises in Appendix A.

1. Explain the difference between a reference variable and a value type variable.

2. Suppose you have a long message that you wrote and stored in a string named `message`. You have this nagging feeling that you misspelled `Friday` as `Frday` somewhere in the string. Write the statement(s) that would find and correct the misspelling.

3. There is an error in the program that uses the `Remove()` method. The problem is that after the word is removed there are two spaces between the remaining words. How would you fix this bug?

4. What is a constructor and when should it be used?

5. Suppose the user typed her birthday into a textbox named `txtBirthday` in the form MM/DD/YY and you want to show how old she is in a textbox named `txtAge`. What would the code look like?

6. Suppose you are writing a program that inputs names and addresses of people who belong to a club in your city. Could you use a constructor to make the data entry person's life easier? (Hint: 99% of the members live in your city and your state.)

► **WHAT YOU LEARNED IN THIS CHAPTER**

TOPIC	KEY POINTS
Reference data type	Different than value types because rvalue is a memory address, not data.
Reference versus value types	rvalue for value type is the data.
Bucket analogy	Used to explain rvalue and lvalues.
String variables	Used to represent textual data.
Verbatim string literals	How to use the @ operator in strings.
DateTime variables	How to use the methods and properties of this data type.
Constructors	How to instantiate an object.
Overloaded methods	When and why to use them.
Method signatures	Rules when overloading a method.

Making Decisions in Code

WHAT YOU WILL LEARN IN THIS CHAPTER:

➤ Relational operators

➤ Comparing value types

➤ Comparing reference types

➤ The `if` and `else` keywords

➤ Cascading `if` statements

➤ Logical operators

➤ The `switch`, `case`, `break`, and `default` keywords

➤ Data validation

WROX.COM CODE DOWNLOADS FOR THIS CHAPTER

You can find the wrox.com code downloads for this chapter at `www.wrox.com/remtitle .cgi?isbn=9781118336922` on the Download Code tab. The code in the `Chapter06` folder is individually named according to the names throughout the chapter.

If computers could not use data to make decisions, they would be little more than expensive boat anchors. Because it is hard to write a nontrivial program without some form of decision-making ability in it, some decision-making keywords were used in previous programs. However, what those keywords actually do was never explained. That changes by the end of this chapter.

This chapter also presents some thoughts on coding style. *Coding style* simply refers to the way you write program code. There are a myriad of coding styles. Because C# is not form-specific, you are free to use just about any coding style you wish. I have known brilliant programmers whose code is almost impossible to read or decipher. On the other hand, I've had mediocre students who write code that is a joy to read. True, beauty is in the eye of the beholder. However, experience has taught me that 80 percent of a program's development time is spent in testing, debugging, and maintaining the code, and only 20 percent in writing it. For that reason, anything you can do to make your code clearer and more easily understood is a good idea.

RELATIONAL OPERATORS

Making a decision about anything involves comparing one thing against another. It's no different in a computer program. You learned in Chapter 3 that statements are built up from operators and operands. You used the math operators to illustrate how program statements are constructed from those basic building blocks. In this section you learn another set of operators that you have at your disposal: the relational operators. The relational operators are presented in Table 6-1.

TABLE 6-1: Relational Operators

RELATIONAL OPERATOR	RELATIONAL TESTS	EXAMPLE	RESULT
==	Equal	15 == 20	false
!=	Not equal	15 != 20	true
<	Less than	15 < 20	true
<=	Less than or equal to	15 <= 20	true
>	Greater than	15 > 20	false
>=	Greater than or equal to	15 >= 20	false

Referring to Table 6-1, every example has one operand on the left side of the relational operator (15) and a second operand on the right side of the operator (20). Again, two operands are associated with the use of a relational operator, so all relational operators are binary operators. Therefore, combining two operands with a relational operator results in a *relational expression.*

Each relational expression ultimately resolves to a logic True or logic False state. In C#, logic True and logic False are expressed as boolean values. The result of a boolean expression resolves to the C# keywords true or false. Referring to Table 6-1, each example shown in the third column resolves to the state shown in the fourth column. In the table, literal values are used simply to make the relational expression more concrete. In programming situations, however, the operands in a relational expression are usually variables rather than literals.

Using Relational Operators—The if Statement

Now consider what you've learned about relational operators and put them to work in a C# if statement. Although you have seen several examples of the if statement in earlier chapters, how they work hasn't been explained. That's the purpose of this section.

The syntax form for an if statement is as follows:

```
if (expression1)
{
```

```
     // Logic true: if statement block
}
```

expression1 appears between the opening and closing parentheses following the `if` keyword. Usually, `expression1` represents a relational test to be performed. Referring to Table 6-1, the outcome of a relational expression is either logic True or logic False. The code that appears between the two curly braces is called the *if statement block*. If `expression1` evaluates to logic True, then the `if` statement block is executed. If `expression1` evaluates to logic False, program control skips over the `if` statement block and resumes program execution at the next statement following the closing curly brace of the `if` statement block. You can see how the program flows based on the outcome of `expression1` in Figure 6-1.

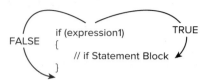

FIGURE 6-1: The if statement block

Let's test your understanding of how an `if` statement works using a simple program that determines whether a number entered by the user is an odd or even number.

TRY IT OUT Testing for Odd or Even (Chapter06ProgramOddEven.zip)

To illustrate a simple use of an `if` statement, consider the program shown in Figure 6-2.

1. Create a new project as shown in Chapter 2 using the C# template.

2. Add two label objects, one textbox object and two buttons.

3. Set the objects' properties as you want. Figure 6-2 is one user interface that you might use.

4. Add the button click event code, as shown in Listing 6-1.

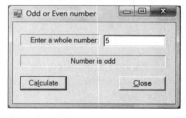

FIGURE 6-2: The if program for odd or even Numbers

The user enters a number, and based upon its value, the program tells whether the number is odd or even. The program should also check that the user entered a valid sequence of digit characters for the number. The letter O is just below the zero digit character (0) and sometimes people in a hurry press the wrong key.

LISTING 6-1: The btn_Click event code (frmMain.cs)

```csharp
private void btnCalc_Click(object sender, EventArgs e)
{
  bool flag;
  int val;
  string output = "Number is even";

  // Convert from text to number
  flag = int.TryParse(txtNumber.Text, out val);
  if (flag == false)
  {
    MessageBox.Show("Not a number. Re-enter.");
    txtNumber.Clear();
    txtNumber.Focus();
```

continues

LISTING 6-1 *(continued)*

```
        return;
    }

    // See if odd or even
    if (val % 2 == 1)
    {
      output = "Number is odd";
    }
    // Show result
    lblOutput.Text = output;

}
```

How It Works

The code that does all the work is found in the button click event method (refer to Listing 6-1).

The `btnCalc_Click()` method begins by defining several working variables. Note how you initialized the string variable named `output` with the string literal `Number is even`. You then used the `TryParse()` method to convert the text entered by the user into a numeric value.

How the TryParse( ) Method Works

You have briefly studied the `TryParse()` method in earlier chapters. However, because it is such a useful method, a more complete discussion using some of the terms you learned in the last chapter is presented here.

The `TryParse()` method is normally used to convert data from a string format to a numeric format. In this example, the `TryParse()` method is part of the `int` object type, as shown by the `int.TryParse()` method call in Listing 6-1. The `TryParse()` method requires two arguments: 1) the string to be converted, and 2) the variable that will hold the numeric value if the data conversion is successful.

The keyword `out` in the second argument is necessary and must precede the numeric variable name. The data type of the variable (such as `val`) must match the flavor of `TryParse()` you use (such as `int.TryParse()` in this example). You can think of the `out` keyword as serving two purposes.

First, the `out` keyword tells C# that it's okay to use this variable even though it has not been initialized to any known value. (You should always assume that an uninitialized C# variable contains random junk. You will write better code making this assumption.)

Second, the `out` keyword also tells C# that it is the lvalue being passed to the method, not the rvalue. Recall that, by default, arguments are passed by making a copy of the rvalue of the data item. With `TryParse()`, it is the lvalue that gets passed. Using the Bucket Analogy, this means that the `TryParse()` method knows where the bucket for `val` is located in memory. Because this flavor of `TryParse()` is a method for the `int` object type, it also knows the size of the bucket. Given that `TryPrase()` knows where the data resides in memory and its type, `TryPrase()` has everything it needs to permanently change the value of the variable being passed to it in its second argument.

`TryParse()` takes the string of characters from the first argument and tries to format those characters into a numeric data value. If one of the characters is inconsistent with a numeric digit character, the conversion fails. `TryParse()` returns `false` to the caller and moves the value `0` into the rvalue for the variable. `TryParse()` has no problems setting `val` to `0` because it knows where `val` resides in memory and how many bytes it takes.

If the `TryParse()` method fails (for example, because the user entered a nondigit character), the variable `flag` is logic False. The `if` statement,

```
if (flag == false)
```

checks the state of `flag` using the equality relational operator (`==`). If `flag` is `false` because `TryParse()` failed to convert the user's input into an integer value, the expression in the `if` statement is logic True. That is, it is true that `flag` is `false`. (Think about it.) The code then executes the `if` statement block code, which displays a message about the error, sets the program focus back into the textbox object, and then returns program control back to the caller.

To Clear() or Not to Clear()

The `Clear()` method simply removes any characters that currently exist in the `Text` property of a textbox object. The program statement in the `if` statement block is controversial:

```
txtNumber.Clear();
```

This is because some people think you should allow the user to see his mistake after he has viewed the message you displayed by the call to `MessageBox.Show()`, whereas the other school of thought says that you should clear out the error in preparation for the entry of the new, hopefully correct, value. There is no "right" answer here. You can choose either approach, as long as you use it consistently. Users like consistency, so pick a style and stick with it.

Assuming the user entered a proper numeric value, that number is assigned into `val` by the `TryParse()` method. The next `if` statement uses the modulus operator to find the remainder of the user's number:

```
if (val % 2 == 1)
{
output = "Number is odd";
}
```

Obviously, if you divided a number by two and there is a remainder, the number must be odd. Therefore if

```
val % 2
```

yields a result of `1`, then the `if` test appears as if it were written like this:

```
if (1 == 1)
```

The result of this test is obviously logic True. Therefore, if the number is odd, its remainder is `1` and the `if` test expression is `true`. That means that the code for the `if` statement block is executed and `output` is assigned the string literal `Number is odd`.

You can cause the program to ignore or execute the statements in the `if` statement block based upon the state of the `if` expression. Whenever the expression is `true`, the statement block is executed. Whenever the expression is `false`, the statement block is skipped. As simple as it is to understand, the `if` statement is the major building block that enables computers to have the processing capabilities they do.

The absolute *best* way to understand how an `if` statement alters the flow of a program is to single-step through the code using different values for `val`. To do this, place your cursor on the statement that reads

```
flag = int.TryParse(txtNumber.Text, out val);
```

and press the F9 key to set a debugging breakpoint. Now run the program. When the program reaches the breakpoint, single-step the program by repeatedly pressing the F10 key. (You can also use the F11 key, which is even better because it causes the program to single-step through any methods that you wrote as well.)

"use of unassigned local variable"

Sometimes, when you use the `if` statement, you may get the following error message:

```
use of unassigned local variable i
```

You can illustrate this error with the following code snippet:

```
int i;
// Some additional lines of code
if (x == MAX)
{
    i = 10;
}
i *= i;
```

Visual Studio issues the error message for the last program line, stating that you are trying to use variable `i` before a value has been assigned to it. The reason Visual Studio acts this way is that it does not know at compile time whether the `if` statement resolves to logic True to assign the value 10 into `i`. If the `if` expression is logic False, variable `i` is uninitialized and has no known value assigned to it. You can fix this problem by simply initializing variable `i` with a default value. Most of the time, you do this when the variable is defined. Simply change the definition of `i` to this:

```
int i = 0;
```

This sets the rvalue of `i` to 0 and Visual Studio is happy because `i` now has a known value regardless of the outcome of the `if` test expression.

The if-else Statement

If you look closely at the code in Listing 6-1, you can notice that the `output` string is set to the literal `Number is even` at the moment the string is defined. Therefore, the string is changed only when the number is odd. If you think about it, what you actually want to do is set the output string based upon whether the number is odd or even. The program works, but it doesn't reflect what you want to do.

The `if-else` statement is the perfect solution to clarify your code. The syntax for the `if-else` statement is the following:

```
if (expression1)
{
```

```
      // Logic true: if statement block
    }
    else
    {
      // Logic false: else statement block
    }
```

With the `if-else` statement, if `(expression1)` evaluates to logic True, the `if` statement block is executed. If `expression1` is logic `false`, the statements within the curly braces following the `else` keyword are executed. The group of statements within the curly braces following the `else` keyword is called the *else statement block*. The program flow for the `if-else` statement is shown in Figure 6-3.

As you can see in Figure 6-3, the `if-else` statement creates a "this-or-that" kind of decision. That is, the

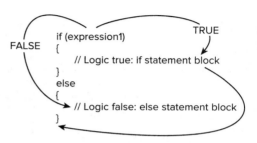

FIGURE 6-3: if-else statement block

decision produces one of two mutually exclusive outcomes. In the following Try It Out you revise the program shown in Listing 6-1 to use an `if-else` construct.

TRY IT OUT   if-else Statement (Chapter06ProgramOddEven.zip)

To illustrate a simple use of an `if-else` statement block, revise the program shown in Figure 6-2.

1. Load the program for the simple `if` test you wrote earlier in this chapter.

2. Change the definition of `output` to

```
string output;
```

3. Replace the second `if` statement with this:

```
// See if odd or even
if (val % 2 == 1)
{
output = "Number is odd";
}
else
{
output = "Number is even";
}
```

How It Works

Most programmers would agree that this form is easier to understand because the outcomes are clearly stated in one place. With the first form of the program, you had to look at a different section of the program (the definition and initialization of `output`) to see what the string was when the number was even.

What if you were writing this logic test for a toaster where memory limitations restrict you to a few kilobytes of code space? Could you rewrite the code to save a few bytes? What if you initialize the string as follows:

```
string output = "Number is ";
```

and then recode the `if-else` block as

```
// See if odd or even
if (val % 2 == 1)
{
  output += "odd";
}
else
{
  output += "even";
}
```

In the `if` statement test expression, if the result is logic `true`, then the word `"odd"` is appended to `"Number is "` for output. If the test evaluates to logic `false`, then `"even"` is appended to output. The rest of the code behaves the same as it did earlier.

Don't even think about reading further until you are convinced that the program still behaves as before, but you can understand how a few bytes might be saved.

Shorthand for Simple if-else: The Ternary Operator

Because `if-else` statements are so common in programs, C# has a special operator designed specifically to replace a simple (that is, one statement) `if-else` statement block. C# uses the ternary operator to replace simple `if-else` statements. The syntax for the ternary operator is

```
(expression1) ? trueExpression : falseExpression
```

The statement works by first evaluating expression1. If expression1 evaluates to logic True, then trueExpression is evaluated. If expression1 is logic False, then falseExpression is evaluated. The logic flow can be seen in Figure 6-4.

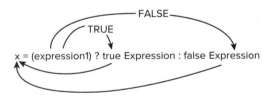

In the following Try It Out you rewrite the *if-else* version of the odd-even program, replacing the if-else statement blocks with the ternary operator.

FIGURE 6-3: if-else statement block

Ternary Operator: (Chapter06ProgramOddEven.zip)

To illustrate a simple use of the ternary operator, revise the program shown in Figure 6-2 as follows:

1. Load the program for the simple `if-else` test that uses the code from Figure 6-2.

2. Replace the second `if-else` statement block with this:

```
// See if odd or even
output = (val % 2 == 0) ? "Number is even" : "Number is odd";
```

Now run the program to see if it behaves as it did before.

How It Works

Using the modified code, the variable `output` is assigned the string literal `Number is even` if `val % 2` resolved to `0`. Otherwise, if the modulus operator yields a value of `1`, `output` is assigned `Number is odd`. You should set a breakpoint on the line and single-step through the code to see that it behaves as expected.

Although the ternary operator is a shorthand form of a simple `if-else` statement, I'm not a big fan of its use. There are three reasons why. First, it takes most programmers more time to understand a ternary expression than a simple `if-else` statement block. If you return to a piece of code during a debugging session a month after you originally wrote it and it uses a ternary operator, it will take you longer to understand its intent than it should. Second, I just have this nagging feeling that programmers who use it do so to show they can use it. I come away after reading a ternary statement feeling like the programmer is saying: "Watch this, Billy-Bob." Third, if either of the test statement blocks need multiple statements to provide the correct results, you have to write some fairly ugly code to get the correct results. Given these reasons, if the code is clearer with a simple `if-else` statement, why use the ternary operator?

Style Considerations for if and if-else Statements

C# is a format-insensitive language. This means that you could write the `if-else` statement as a single line, like this:

```
if (val % 2 == 1){output = "Number is odd";}else{output = "Number is even";}
```

Visual Studio would process the statements just fine. However, most programmers would find the preceding line much more difficult to read without the line breaks and indentation. Such formatting issues are factors in the style you use to write your code. You do have some choices.

For example, when an `if` or an `else` statement block consists of a single statement, you don't need the curly braces. That is, you could write this code:

```
if (val % 2 == 1)
{
  output = "Number is odd";
}
else
{
  output = "Number is even";
}
```

as this:

```
if (val % 2 == 1)
  output = "Number is odd";
else
  output = "Number is even";
```

The program would execute exactly as before. However, when the `if` statement block contains multiple statements, you *must* use the curly braces. For example, suppose you wrote the following code:

```
if (val % 2 == 1)
  {
```

```
        output = "Number is odd";
        oddCounter++;
    }
```

Your intent is to count the number of odd numbers using `oddCounter`. If you write the same code without curly braces:

```
if (val % 2 == 1)
    output = "Number is odd";
    oddCounter++;
```

your intent may be the same, but without the curly braces what you actually have is this:

```
if (val % 2 == 1)
{
  output = "Number is odd";
}
        oddCounter++;
```

The reason the code functions differently is that without the curly braces, the `if` statement controls only a single statement. The result of this error is that `oddCounter` is always incremented regardless of the value of the number `val`—probably not what you wanted to do.

So the style question becomes, "Should you use curly braces when the `if` statement block contains only one statement?" The answer is yes. Always use curly braces. First, always using curly braces promotes consistency in your coding. Anytime you use an `if` statement, curly braces follow. Second, often what starts out as a single statement in the `if` statement block ends up with multiple statements after testing and debugging. You'll have to add the braces anyway, so you might as well add them from the get-go. Third, most programmers think the curly braces make the statement blocks stand out more and make them easier to read. The lesson learned here is always to use curly braces, even when the `if` statement block only contains one statement.

Another style consideration is where to place the curly braces. For example, because C# doesn't care about statement formatting, you could write the previous code as follows:

```
if (val % 2 == 1){
  output = "Number is odd";
} else {
  output = "Number is even";
}
```

Note that the required curly braces are still where they need to be, but that their location is different. This *K&R style* was made popular by the C programming book written by Brian Kernighan and Dennis Ritchie in the 1970s (*The C Programming Language*, Prentice Hall, 1978). One reason this style is popular is that it uses two fewer screen lines, meaning that you can make better use of your display's nano-acres. Seeing more source code without scrolling is usually a good thing.

So which style should you use? Well, obviously C# doesn't care; although Visual Studio places the braces on separate lines by default. If you work on a programming team, such style considerations should be a team (or company) decision. If you just write code for yourself, it's your choice. Personally, I really like the K&R style mainly because C was the first language I enjoyed using, and most C programmers used the K&R style. Also, fewer students do something silly like

```
if (x == 2);
    x++;
```

when they use braces and the K&R style. What this little snippet actually is becomes more obvious when braces are added:

```
if (x == 2){
    ;
}
x++;
```

This is probably not what the programmer meant to do. Always using braces helps reduce this type of silliness.

> **NOTE** By default, Visual Studio prefers placing the braces on a separate line. That is, if you try to put the brace on the same line as the `if` expression, it automatically reformats the statement with the curly brace moved to the next line. However, after the reformatting, if you move the brace back to the previous line, Visual Studio enables you to keep it there.
>
> You can change the default behavior of the editor to enable you to keep the brace on the same line by using the Tools ⇨ Customize ⇨ Text Editor ⇨ C# ⇨ Formatting ⇨ New Lines menu sequence and removing the check mark from the Place Open Brace on New Line for Control Blocks option. You can scroll down and do the same thing for the `else` part of the statement block. (Make sure you have a check mark in the Show All Settings check box.)

There is no "correct" style. However, whatever style you select, use it consistently.

Nested if Statements

You can have `if` statements within `if` statements. For example, suppose you own a bar and ladies get drinks at half price on Tuesdays. You might have code like this:

```
decimal price = FULLPRICE;
if (age >= 21)
{
    if (gender == "Female")
    {
        price *= .5M;
    }
} else {
    MessageBox.Show("Illegal minor.");
}
```

In this example, you take the drink price (why is the symbolic constant FULLPRICE used here?) and multiply it by .5 if the customer is a female age 21 or older. If the gender is male, the full price prevails. Because you have an `if` statement contained within the `if` statement block, this is called a *nested if statement*. The `else` statement block may also contain nested `if` statements.

You may ask, "What's with the letter M after the .5?" Recall from the discussion of data types that several value types have suffixes that can be appended to them to make it clear what the data type is. In this case, because you deal with the price of a drink (that is, with money), you want to use the decimal data type. If you don't place the M after the .5, C# assumes the literal .5 is a double data type by default. C# views this as an error because you try to assign a `double` into a `decimal` data type and issues an appropriate error message. Also, the `decimal` data type is smart enough to keep track of only the pennies on a price, whereas a double may have many more than two decimal places.

Finally, you might ask why multiply by `.5` instead of dividing by 2. After all, the results are the same, so why not use the conventional divide-by-2 approach? There are two reasons. First, multiplying by `.5` is a fairly common programming idiom for dividing a number in half. Also, the `.5` does convey the "half price" concept of the discount. (Although a comment on the line wouldn't hurt.) Second, division is the slowest of the four basic math operations. Multiplication is slightly faster than division. Although the speed improvement in this example would be unnoticeable, such would not be the case if the operation were performed in a tight loop doing tens of thousands of iterations. Also, you needed to see an example of this idiom in case you run across it while looking at someone else's code.

RDC

You probably noticed that the code does work on forming a discounted price for ladies, but it does not consider that the discount is only to apply on Tuesdays. How would you fix that problem?

Sometimes you need to do a search that involves multiple values, any of which might be correct depending upon some variable. For example, suppose you have a variable that tells what day of the week it is and you want to perform various tasks based on that value. You might write the following code:

```
if (day == 1)
{
    doMondayStuff();
}
if (day == 2)
{
    doTuesdayStuff();
}
if (day == 3)
{
    doWednesdayStuff();
}
if (day == 4)
{
    doThursdayStuff();
}
if (day == 5)
{
    doFridayStuff();
}
if (day == 6)
{
    doSaturdayStuff();
}
if (day == 7)
{
    doSundayStuff();
}
```

Perhaps the method doTuesdayStuff() adjusts the price for ladies' drinks.

Regardless, the code depicted is another example of *RDC* (Really Dumb Code). The reason is that the structure shown here often causes unnecessary code to be executed. For example, suppose you want to do Monday's tasks (day == 1). The first if test is logic True, so the code executes doMondayStuff(). That's the good news. The bad news is that when program control returns after executing the doMondayStuff() method, it then performs six unnecessary if tests on variable day. The tests are unnecessary because you already know that day's value is 1. Therefore, the code executes six unnecessary if tests even though you know they can't be logic true.

When you realize what makes your code RDC, you usually perform a flat-forehead slap and ask yourself why you didn't see it in the first place. Not to worry...most good programmers have well-earned flat foreheads! The important thing in becoming a good programmer is to move to more complex bugs and not repeat the same old ones over and over.

Believe it or not, I actually saw this kind of RDC code in a production environment, but was even worse because it was written to handle 31 days of the month issues. The code meant that if it were the first day of the month, there would be 30 unnecessary if tests executed.

The next section shows you how to get rid of this kind of RDC. Next, let's see how to improve the code and avoid all the potentially unnecessary if tests.

TRY IT OUT   **Getting Rid of RDC: (Chapter06ProgramOddEven.zip)**

Again you can reuse the code you wrote for the odd-even program shown in Listing 6-1 for this example.

1. Load the program code.

2. Delete the code in the button click event after the comment line:

```
// See if odd or even
```

and replace it with the following code. (In more realistic code, each if block would likely call a method to do something useful.)

```
int day;
day = val;
if (day == 1)
{
    day += 1; // Simulate doing Monday's stuff
} else
    if (day == 2)
    {
        day += 2;  // Simulate doing Tuesday's stuff
    } else
        if (day == 3)
        {
            day += 3;  // Simulate doing Wednesday's stuff
        } else
            if (day == 4)
            {
             day += 4;  // Simulate doing Thursday's stuff
```

```
        } else
          if (day == 5)
          {
          day += 5;  // Simulate doing Friday's stuff
          } else
            if (day == 6)
            {
             day += 6;  // Now Saturday's stuff
            } else
              if (day == 7)
              {
              day += 7;  // Lastly Sunday's stuff
      }
```

Now compile and run the program.

How It Works

Code like the preceding code is called a *cascading if statement*. As a general rule, cascading `if` statements perform different tasks based upon the state of a particular variable. In this code snippet, it appears that different methods are called based up on the value of the variable `day`. If you follow the logic carefully, you see that the six unnecessary `if` tests are no longer executed when the first test is logic True. (Use the debugger to prove this is the case.) The reason the unnecessary code is now skipped is that when an `if` statement becomes logic True there is no reason to evaluate any subsequent `if` expressions.

Quite often cascading `if` statements are a bit clumsy and difficult to read, simply because there are so many `if` statements and curly braces that things can appear a little confusing. (Imagine how ugly this code would look for 31 days in a month!) The other problem is that if you use proper indentation with each `if` expression, your code gets pushed farther and farther to the right of the display screen. Eventually, this can force you to use horizontal scrolling, which most programmers dislike. You see a more effective way to write cascading `if` statements in the section that discusses the `switch` keyword.

LOGICAL OPERATORS

Sometimes it is necessary to make complex decisions based upon the state of two or more variables. For example, to determine if a year is a leap year, you apply the following test:

If the year can be evenly divided by 4, but not by 100, it is a leap year. The exception occurs if the year is evenly divisible by 400. If so, it is a leap year.

If you try to code this as a series of simple `if` statements, the code gets messy. It's actually easier to code the algorithm if you can use a combination of logical operators in a single statement block. The C# conditional logical operators are shown in Table 6-2.

TABLE 6-2: Conditional Logic Operators

ITEM	MEANING	EXAMPLE	
Logical &&	Logical AND	x && y	
Logical ||	Logical OR	x || y	
Logical !	Logical NOT	!x	

Because these are logical operators, each one resolves to a `true` or `false` expression. You can see these relationships by using truth tables. Table 6-3 shows the truth table for the logical AND operator.

TABLE 6-3: Logical AND Truth Table

Expression1	Expression2	Expression1 && Expression2	
True	True	True	
True	False	False	
False	True	False	
False	False	False	

The last column in Table 6-2 shows that the logical AND truth table is constructed using two expressions with the && operator. Table 6-3 shows the outcome for all possible values for those two expressions and the impact on the logical AND result. For example, if `Expression1` resolves to logic `true` and `Expression2` resolves to logic `false`, the result is logic `false`. This is because a logical AND requires both expressions to be `True` for the result to be `True`. All other combinations yield a result that is logic `False`.

Table 6-4 shows the truth table for the logical OR operator. As you can see in the table, the result of a logical OR statement is `True` if either or both expressions is logic `true`. Only when both expressions are `false` is the result `false`.

TABLE 6-4: Logical OR Truth Table

Expression1	Expression2	Expression1 || Expression2	
True	True	True	
True	False	True	
False	True	True	
False	False	False	

Finally, Table 6-5 shows the truth table for the logical NOT operator. Unlike the other operators, logical NOT is a unary operator, which means it uses only a single expression. Therefore, Table 6-5 is rather simple.

TABLE 6-5: Logical NOT Truth Table

Expression1	!Expression
True	False
False	True

As you can see from Table 6-5, the logical NOT operator simply "flips" the current logic state of the expression.

Using the Logical Operators

Now revisit the algorithm to determine if a year is a leap year. The algorithm is, "If the year can be evenly divided by 4, but not by 100, it is a leap year. The exception occurs if the year is evenly divisible by 400. If so, it is a leap year."

You might code the algorithm like this:

```
if (year % 4 == 0 && year % 100 != 0 || year % 400 == 0)
{
  return 1;      // It is a leap year
}
else
{
  return 0;      // Nope
}
```

If you examine the algorithm and then the code, you should convince yourself that the single if statement does implement the algorithm correctly.

Note that this leap year code returns either one or zero, where most leap year methods (that is, both .NET and Java) return a boolean of true or false. Why is it coded differently? With this version, you can do something like

```
days = DAYSINFEBRUARY + isLeapYear(myYear);
```

where DAYSINFEBRUARY is a constant that assumes the value of 28. If the method returns a *bool*, you have no choice but to use an if statement like

```
if (isLeapYear(myYear))
{
    days = DAYSINFEBRUARY + 1;
}
```

The version that returns an integer is more flexible. Clearly, there's some bright people who disagree. There is almost always more than one way to solve a given programming problem.

However, things are not always as simple as a leap-year calculation. You might get something like this:

```
if (x + y < b && z - y == c || z * 5 - b == d)
{
    answer = x * y * z;
}
```

The preceding `if` statement mixes logical, conditional, and math operators together. So how do you know what to do to resolve such a complex `if` statement? (The first thing you do is fire the idiot who wrote the code. Program statements rarely need to be this complex, and debugging it would be a nightmare.) As you learned in Chapter 4, the precedence order determines the order in which operators are evaluated. However, because you have added new operators in this chapter, you need to expand the precedence table to include the new operators. The expanded precedence table is presented in Table 6-6. (Although you haven't studied all the operators shown in Table 6-6, they are presented here for completeness.)

TABLE 6-6: Operator Precedence

OPERATOR	TYPE	
. ++ -- new	Primary	
!	Unary	
* / %	Math	
+ -	Math	
< > <= >=	Relational	
== !=	Relational	
&& ||	Logical	
? :	Ternary	
= *= /= %= += -=	Assignment	
,	Comma	

If you're not happy with the order in which a group of expressions are evaluated, you can always force something to be evaluated out of its natural precedence by containing the expression within parentheses. (You may want to write this page number on the inside of the back cover page of this book because you will likely need to refer to this table at some later time.)

Associativity

How is precedence resolved when an expression contains two operators with the same precedence level? Precedence-level ties are broken by the associativity rules for operators. As a general rule operators are *left-associative*, which means the expressions are evaluated from left to right in the statement. Again, if you need to override the precedence and associativity rules, you can use parentheses to force your preferred order. Consider the following code:

```
x = 5 + 6 * 10;
```

The answer is 65. This is because multiplication has higher precedence than addition, so the sequence becomes:

```
x = 5 + 6 * 10;
x = 5 + 60;
x = 65;
```

If you actually need the answer to be 110, then you would use parentheses:

```
x = (5 + 6) * 10;
x = 11 * 10;
x = 110;
```

THE SWITCH STATEMENT

You learned earlier that you could replace the RDC with a cascading if statement when you want to test for a specific day, as in the days-of-the-week example:

```
if (day == 1)
{
     doMondayStuff();
} else
     if (day == 2)
     {
          doTuesdayStuff();
     } else
          if (day == 3)
          {
               do WednesdayStuff();
          }
// The rest of the days are similar to above
```

Although this code works just fine, it's often difficult to read cascading if statements. That's because you still must match up the proper if statement with its associated day value. Secondly, if the cascade is fairly long, the code starts to scroll off to the right. Programmers hate horizontal scrolling because it wastes time. They would rather read all the code without scrolling. Third, code like this may also force you to do vertical scrolling. The switch statement offers one way to resolve some of these drawbacks.

The syntax for the switch statement is as follows:

```
switch (expression1)
{
     case 1:
        // Statements for case 1
           break;
     case 1:
       // Statements for case 2
```

```
            break;
    case 2:
      // Statements for case 3
            break;
    default:
     // Statements for default
            break;
    }
```

With a `switch` statement, the value of `expression1` determines which `case` statement block is executed. You can think of each `case` statement block as starting with the colon (:) following the `case` keyword and extending to the end of the associated `break` keyword.

If `expression1` does not match any `case` statement, the `default` expression is evaluated. Unlike an `if` statement block, no parentheses are necessary for a `case` statement block. The `break` statements are necessary to prevent program control from "falling through" to the next `case` statement. The `break` statement causes program execution to resume with the first statement after the `switch` statement block's closing curly brace.

Next let's write a simple program that uses a `switch` statement block to make complex decisions instead of a bunch of nested `if-else` blocks. You will find the `switch` version much easier to read and it is slightly more efficient.

TRY IT OUT   Using a switch Statement: (Chapter06ProgramSwitch.zip)

Load the code from the `Chapter06ProgramSwitch.zip` file or use the code shown in Listing 6-2. Only the btnCalc click event code is shown in the listing because the remaining code is virtually the same as all the other programs you've written.

LISTING 6-2: The btn_Click event code (frmMain.cs)

```csharp
private void btnCalc_Click(object sender, EventArgs e)
{
    bool flag;
    int myDay;
    string msg = "Today is ";   // Don't duplicate it 7 times
// Make text into int
    flag = int.TryParse(txtDay.Text, out myDay);
    if (flag == false)
    {
        MessageBox.Show("Numeric only, 1 thru 7");
        txtDay.Focus();    // Send 'em back to try again
        return;
    }

    switch (myDay)
    {
        case 1:
            lblResult.Text = msg + "Monday";
            break;
        case 2:
```

continues

LISTING 6-2 *(continued)*

```
                lblResult.Text = msg + "Tuesday";
                break;
            case 3:
                lblResult.Text = msg + "Wednesday";
                break;
            case 4:
                lblResult.Text = msg + "Thursday";
                break;
            case 5:
                lblResult.Text = msg + "Friday";
                break;
            case 6:
                lblResult.Text = msg + "Saturday";
                break;
            case 7:
                lblResult.Text = msg + "Sunday";
                break;
            default:
                lblResult.Text = "You should never get here";
                break;

        }
    }
```

In a more realistic situation, each of the case statements would do something a little more interesting. However, this simple code can service your purpose nicely.

How It Works

If you study this code fragment, you can discover that it works like a cascading if statement; only it's quite a bit easier to read. Also, you don't need to do horizontal scrolling to see all the code at once.

It is the value of day that determines which case statement block is executed. The break statement in each case block sends program control to the first statement following the closing curly brace of the switch statement block. Therefore, it is the break statement that enables the switch to perform like a cascading if statement, thus avoiding unnecessary if tests.

If variable day does not have a value between 1 and 7, the default case is executed. (You are not required to use a default case, but it's a good idea to include one in each switch statement.) This situation displays a simple error message. It's fairly common to have the default case call a logging method that records the nature of the error. Often, the error log file is just a simple text file that can be read with any word processing program. Perhaps the ErrorLog() method records the value of day in the error log file so that the person in charge to support the program can ask the user over the phone to read the last line in the error log file. The support person would, therefore, have some idea of the value for day that produced the error.

SUMMARY

This chapter presented the basics to make decisions in a program. The basic building block of computer decision making is the simple `if` statement. From that, you learned about the `if-else` and `switch` statements and showed when it may be appropriate to use them. You also read some thoughts on programming style and the issues involved in deciding which coding style to use. Even though C# doesn't care about your coding style, other people who may read your code do. In all cases, try to make your code as easy to read as possible.

EXERCISES

You can find the answers to the following exercises in Appendix A.

1. Suppose a movie theater charges half price for children 12 or under or adults age 65 or older. Write an `if` statement that accounts for this pricing policy.

2. What are the important style considerations when you're writing `if-else` statements?

3. When is it appropriate to use a cascading `if` statement?

4. What errors do you see in the following code snippet?

```
if  (x = y);
{
    price =* .06;
}
```

5. Suppose a small pizza sells for $6, a medium is a dollar more, and a large is a dollar more than a medium. Assuming that the variable `size` stores the customer's selection, how would you write the code to determine the final price?

6. Write a program that accepts a year as input and then calls a method named `IsLeapYear(int year)` to then display the proper number of days in February for the year entered by the user.

▶ WHAT YOU HAVE LEARNED IN THIS CHAPTER

TOPIC	KEY POINTS
`if`	How to use the `if` statement.
`TryParse()`	Greater detail on how to use this conversion method.
`if-else`	Use of the `if-else` statement block.
Cascading `if`'s	How to use cascading `if` statements while avoiding redundant if tests.
`?:`	The ternary operator.
Logical operators	What are the logical operators and their truth tables.
`switch`	How to use the switch, case, break, and default statements.

Statement Repetition Using Loops

WHAT YOU WILL LEARN IN THIS CHAPTER:

➤ What a loop is and when it should be used

➤ What constitutes a well-behaved program loop

➤ What happens when loops are ill-behaved

➤ What a `for` loop is

➤ What a `while` loop is

➤ What a `do-while` loop is

➤ When to use the `break` and `continue` statements

WROX.COM CODE DOWNLOADS FOR THIS CHAPTER

You can find the wrox.com code downloads for this chapter at `www.wrox.com/remtitle .cgi?isbn=9781118336922` on the Download Code tab. The code in the `Chapter07` folder is individually named according to the names throughout the chapter.

Computer programs are good doing repetitive tasks…much better than humans because computers don't get bored. In this chapter, you learn about *program loops*. These are simply a means by which a program can repeat the execution of a given set of program statements.

Most nontrivial programs use some form of program loop. Loops are so useful that C# makes several different types available. Now see what loops can do for you.

PROGRAM LOOPS

If you're sitting in a public building right now, look at the ceiling; chances are you can see sprinklers embedded there. In most modern office buildings, each room has one or more sprinklers in it. Modern sprinklers are monitored by software that tests each one to see if it senses a fire. If a building has 500 sprinklers, the program samples the current state of sprinkler number 1 and, assuming everything's okay, goes on to test sprinkler number 2. This process continues until sprinkler 500 is tested. Assuming all 500 passed the test and no fire is sensed, the program goes back to the start and tests sprinkler 1 again. The program then moves on to sprinkler 2 and the entire process repeats itself. It's fairly quick, probably taking less than a few seconds to test all 500 sprinklers.

The process of repeated testing is performed by a program loop within the fire system software. If one of the sprinkler system tests failed, the software would likely branch out of the loop and process code that would sound the alarm, make sure there is water pressure to feed the sprinkler system, turn on the sprinkler system, and place a call to the fire department. Loops are everywhere around us, in everything from fire alarms to elevators to circuits in your car's engine and safety equipment. Indeed, people who find their lives boring are perhaps caught in endless loops wherein they do the same things over and over again!

Good Loops, Bad Loops

Not all loops are created equal. As you see in a moment, there are good loops and bad loops. To understand the difference, consider the conditions of a well-behaved loop.

The Three Conditions of a Well-Behaved Loop

In general, well-behaved loops:

> Always initialize the starting state of the loop.

> Provide a test expression to decide whether another iteration of the loop is needed.

> Alter the current state of a variable that controls the loop.

The first condition means that your code should always start executing a program loop in a known state. Usually this means that you assign the variable that controls the loop some initial value. Failure to initialize a loop variable almost always means that the loop executes an unexpected number of times—not good!

The second condition means that you must have some form of test that decides whether another pass through the loop is needed. Usually this means testing the variable that you initialized as part of the first condition against some termination criteria. This condition often means that a relational operator is part of the condition.

The third condition means that some variable must change its value during the execution of the loop. If the state of the loop does not change during execution, there is no condition that can terminate the loop. This produces an *infinite loop*, which is one that continues to execute forever. Most of the time, an infinite loop is the result of an error in the logic of the program.

INFINITE LOOPS

Infinite loops are often unintentional and can "hang" the program. Therefore, any time you write code that involves program loops, it's a good idea to save your code before running it. By default, Visual Studio saves your code when you run the program (F5). You can save the project's code explicitly by using either the File ⇨ Save All menu sequence or the Ctrl+Shift+S key combination. By saving your code before a trial run, you can pick up where you left off if the code enters an infinite loop. Usually you can regain control by clicking the small blue square icon or pressing Shift+F5. Sometimes these don't work, and you may need to use the dreaded Ctrl+Alt+Delete to regain control of the system when an infinite loop is executed.

To illustrate the three conditions of a well-behaved loop, consider the C# `for` loop.

The for Loop

The syntax for a `for` loop is as follows:

```
for (expression1; expression2; expression3)
{
     // for loop statement block
}
```

`expression1` is normally used to initialize the starting value of a variable that controls the loop. `expression2` is usually a relational test that determines if another iteration of the loop is needed. Finally, `expression3` is often a statement that increments or decrements the variable controlling the loop. A concrete example should help identify these expressions. Suppose you want to generate a table of squares for values from 0 through 100. The `for` loop controlling the processing might look like this:

```
for (i = 0; i <= 100; i++)
{
     // statements to calculate the values
}
```

`expression1` is the statement that immediately follows the opening parenthesis of the `for` loop:

```
i = 0;
```

This expression sets, or initializes, the initial state of the variable that controls the loop. In this case you start the table-of-squares calculations with the value 0. Because the variable `i` appears in all three expressions, it is the variable that controls the `for` loop. If you want to initialize the state of the loop with the value 1, you would change `expression1` to be

```
i = 1;
```

The second expression,

```
i <= 100;
```

checks the current value of variable i against the wanted ending value of 100. If this expression resolves to logic True, another pass through the loop code is made. That is, the for loop's statement block is executed again.

The third expression,

```
i++;
```

is responsible for changing the state of the loop during each pass. In this case the code simply increments the value of variable i. Note that you can place any expression statement here, including a decrement if you want.

Increment and Decrement Operators

expression3 uses the expression i++. This is an example of a post-increment operator. The interpretation of the *post-increment operator* (i++) is:

```
i = i + 1;
```

That is, the *post-increment operator* takes the current value of variable i and adds 1 to it.

You can also use a *post-decrement operator*, which has the syntax form of i--. The interpretation of the post-decrement operator is:

```
i = i - 1;
```

The post-decrement operator, therefore, takes the current value of variable i and subtracts 1 from it.

When a increment or decrement operator "stands by itself" as it does in the for loop, only the single variable is affected. Now consider the following statement:

```
k = i++;
```

If the value of i just before this statement is 5, what's the value of k? Is k equal to 5 or 6? In other words, at what point does the increment take place? In this example, because you use the post-increment operator, the value of k is 5, but the value of i when the statement finishes executing is 6. This is why it is called a post-increment operator. You use the value first (using the assignment operator in this example) and *then* you perform the increment operation.

As you probably suspected, there is also a *pre-increment operator*. A pre-increment operation places the two plus signs *before* the variable name. With pre-increment operations, the increment is performed before the value is used. Therefore, if i is 5 before the following statement:

```
k = ++i;
```

the value of k is 6, as is the value of i.

C# also enables you to use pre- and post-decrement operations. If the value of i is 5 before the following statement:

```
k = i--;
```

the value of k is 5, but the value of i is 4. Again, the reasoning is the same: The decrement operation is done after the assignment is performed. If a pre-decrement operator were used,

```
k = --i;
```

the value of both k and i are 4 because the decrement is performed before the assignment takes place.

You should convince yourself that a standalone increment or decrement expression behaves exactly the same from the program's point of view. It's only when the increment or decrement operation is used as part of some other expression (like an assignment operation) that it matters whether the pre- or post-operator is used. In the `for` loop, `expression3` is not used with any other subexpression, so you can use either a pre- or post-increment operator.

Sequencing in a for Loop

There is a well-defined sequence for the order of statement execution in a `for` loop. This sequencing is illustrated in Figure 7-1.

In the figure, step 1 is usually the initialization of the variable that controls the loop. After step 1 is accomplished, program control is transferred to step 2. Note that `expression1` in step 1 is never revisited. The sole purpose of `expression1` is to initialize the loop; after that is done, that expression is not executed again.

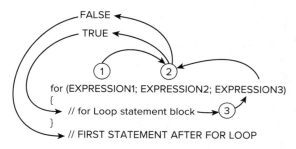

FIGURE 7-1: Execution sequence of a for loop

Step 2 is the relational expression. Often this means the code compares two variables to decide what to do next. As shown in Figure 7-1, if the outcome of the relational test in `expression2` is logic `true`, program control is sent to the statements in the `for` loop statement block. If `expression2` evaluates to logic `false`, program control is sent to the first statement following the closing curly brace of the `for` loop statement block, and the loop body is skipped.

Assuming step 2 is logic `True`, the code between the opening and closing curly braces is executed. When the last statement of the `for` loop statement block is executed, step 3 sends program control to `expression3`. Normally, `expression3` is responsible to change the state of the `for` loop. Perhaps the most common statement for `expression3` is an increment operation of the variable that was initialized in step 1.

After `expression3` is executed, program control is immediately sent back to `expression2`. Again, the code in `expression2` is tested to see if another pass through the loop statement block is needed. If the test is logic `True`, another pass through the `for` loop statement block is made. This repeated sequence continues until `expression2` evaluates to logic `False`, at which time the `for` loop terminates.

Just like the `if` statement block you studied in the last chapter, when the `for` loop controls only a single program statement, the curly braces can be left out and the C# compiler won't complain. However, just like you should always use braces with the `if` statement, you should always use curly braces with `for` loops for the same reasons: The braces make loops easier to read, and quite often you need to add more statements later.

Now that you understand what each of the three expressions in a `for` loop does, compare their tasks with the three conditions required of a well-behaved loop. See any relationship? The three expressions needed to use a `for` loop *are* the three required conditions of a well-behaved loop!

In the following Try It Out you write a program that uses a `for` loop to generate a table of squares for a sequence of numbers. Note how all of the conditions for a well-behaved loop are stated on a single line of the program.

TRY IT OUT **Table of Squares (Chapter07ProgramTableOfSquares.zip)**

In this example you write a program that produces a table of squares for a series of numbers. Figure 7-2 shows what the user interface looks like for your program.

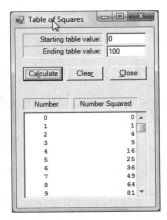

FIGURE 7-2: Table of squares program using a for loop

1. Create a new project, and add in the C# template using the procedure explained in Chapter 2.

2. Add four label objects, two textbox objects, and three button objects following the general layout shown in Figure 7-2. Obviously, you can use a different user interface if you want.

3. Add a listbox object, set the ScrollAlwaysVisible property to True, and name the listbox lstOutput.

The code behind the interface is shown in Listing 7-1. In this example, all the code is shown, including the template C# code from Listing 2-1 in Chapter 2. (See Chapter07ProgramTableOfSquares.zip)

LISTING 7-1: Table of squares program (frmMain.cs)

```
using System;
using System.Windows.Forms;

public class frmMain : Form
{
    private Label label2;
    private TextBox txtStart;
    private TextBox txtEnd;
    private Button btnCalculate;
    private Button btnClear;
    private Button btnClose;
    private ListBox lstOutput;
    private Label label3;
    private Label label4;
    private Label label1;
```

```csharp
#region Windows code       // This code is hidden...

public frmMain()
{
  InitializeComponent();
}

public static void Main()
{
  frmMain main = new frmMain();
  Application.Run(main);
}

private void btnCalculate_Click(object sender, EventArgs e)
{
  bool flag;
  int i;
  int start;
  int end;
  string buff;

  //================ Gather inputs =====================

  // Convert start from text to int
  flag = int.TryParse(txtStart.Text, out start);
  if (flag == false)
  {
    MessageBox.Show("Numeric data only", "Input Error");
    txtStart.Focus();
    return;
  }

  // Convert end from text to int
  flag = int.TryParse(txtEnd.Text, out end);
  if (flag == false)
  {
    MessageBox.Show("Numeric data only", "Input Error");
    txtEnd.Focus();
    return;
  }
      if (start >= end)                        // Reasonable values?
      {
        MessageBox.Show("Start greater than end.", "Input Error");
        txtStart.Focus();
        return;
      }

  //================ Process and Display ==============

  for (i = start; i <= end; i++)
  {
    buff = string.Format("{0, 5}{1, 20}", i, i * i);
    lstOutput.Items.Add(buff);
  }
```

continues

LISTING 7-1 *(continued)*

```
    }

    private void btnClose_Click(object sender, EventArgs e)
    {
        Close();
    }

    private void btnClear_Click(object sender, EventArgs e)

    {
        txtStart.Clear();
        txtEnd.Clear();
        lstOutput.Items.Clear();
    }
}
```

If you label the button and textbox objects with names other than those shown in Listing 7-1, you will need to adjust the code accordingly.

How It Works

All of the real work is done, as usual, in the click event code for the Calculate button. Several working variables are defined, and then the code works on securing the input data from the user interface objects. In this example, the user has typed the starting and ending values into the txtStart and txtEnd textbox objects, respectively. (The TryParse() method was discussed in detail in Chapter 6, so there is no need to repeat that discussion here.) If both TryParse() methods perform without error, the user typed in valid digit characters that can be converted into the variables start and end. This also means that you have completed the Input step of the Five Program Steps discussed in Chapter 2.

Now review the code in the for loop:

```
    for (i = start; i <= end; i++)
    {
        buff = string.Format("{0, 5}{1, 20}", i, i * i);
        lstOutput.Items.Add(buff);
    }
```

The first condition of a well-behaved loop is that you must set the initial state of the loop. In this example, expression1 of the for loop (i = start) sets the starting state of the variable controlling the loop (i) to its initial value (start). (This corresponds to step 1 in Figure 7-1.) Having done that, the program then moves to expression2 of the for loop, i <= end. Suppose the user typed in 0 for the starting value and 100 for the ending value. Because i has been initialized to 0, the expression

```
    i <= end;
```

may be viewed as

```
    0 <= 100;
```

Because 0 is less than 100, the expression evaluates to logic True, which means that the statements in the loop body are executed next.

Formatting String Data

The statement

```
buff = string.Format("{0, 5}{1, 20}", i, i * i);
```

is a special formatting method provided for you by the string class. The arguments to the method are the key to its usefulness. The first argument of the `Format()` method is always a quoted string literal. Within that string is a list of options about how you want the data formatted. The first option shown is `{0, 5}`. This option says to take the first argument (that is, argument 0) and right-justify it in a field of five characters. (Programmers reference almost everything from zero, so the first argument is actually argument zero.) The second option is `{1, 20}`, which says to format the second argument (that is, argument number 1) as right-justified in a field of 20 characters. This is why the output lines up in nice columns in Figure 7-2.

Okay, so you know how to format the arguments, but — where *are* the arguments? After the closing double quote in the quoted format string (`"{0, 5}{1, 20}"`) is a comma followed by a list of the arguments. The option string indicates there are two arguments. Following the option string are two arguments: `i` and `i * i`. Therefore, the first argument is the value of variable `i`, and the second argument is the value of `i * i`, or the square of `i`. These two pieces of data are then formatted by the `Format()` method and placed in the string variable `buff`.

Some additional `Format()` method options are shown in Table 7-1. You can use Visual Studio's online help to see other formatting options. The vertical lines in the third column of Table 7-1 show the width of the field being requested in the options string. It is permissible to not specify a field width. Note how the use of a minus sign left-justifies the data. The absence of a minus sign produces the default right-justification of the data.

TABLE 7-1: Format Strings

FORMAT OPTION STRING	ARGUMENT	OUTPUT	
{0}	"Katie"	|Katie|	
{0, 15}	"John"	|	John|
{0, -15}	"Tammy"	|Tammy	|
{0,15:C}	5.10	|	$5.10|
{0,-15:C}	5.10	|$5.10	|
{0, mm}	9:15	|15|	
{0, 5:hh}	12:15	| 12|	
{0, 15:hh mm}	12:15	|	12:15|
{0, dddd MMMM}	1/1/2008	|Tuesday January|	

If you want to format columns in a listbox, even when using the `Format()` method of the string class, there are still problems to overcome. If you try the code in Listing 7-1 as it is, the column output in your listbox looks good, but not perfect. Why isn't your output perfectly aligned as in Figure 7-2?

Fonts and Column Alignment

The reason the columns in your program aren't straight is that the default font for a listbox is Microsoft Sans Serif. This is a *TrueType font*. This means that each character gets only as many screen pixels as are necessary to display the character. Therefore, the digit character 1 may take only 3 pixels to display, whereas the digit 8 might take 7 pixels to display. The result is that the digit characters won't line up right because each digit character in the listbox uses a different amount of pixel real estate.

If you switch from a TrueType font to a *fixed font*, such as Courier New, the columns line up perfectly. This is because each character in the Courier New font character set takes exactly the same number of pixels regardless of how wide (or skinny) the character is. Therefore, all you need to do to fix this alignment problem is go to the listbox's font property and change it to Courier New. (Are you changing the state of the listbox?) You can do this by clicking the listbox in the Design window, selecting the Font property, and clicking the ellipsis operator (...). Then scroll through the list of fonts in the listbox shown in the font dialog until you come to the Courier New font. You can see the Font window in Figure 7-3. You can alter the style (for example, bold, italics) and the size of the font, too. The Sample (read-only) textbox shows you what your style selections will look like.

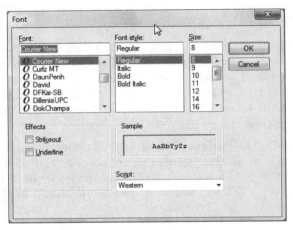

FIGURE 7-3: Font Property option

After the value of i and i * i have been formatted into `buff` by means of the `Format()` method, the code places the string into the listbox object. The statement to add a string to a listbox is simply:

```
lstOutput.Items.Add(buff);
```

You should figure out why there are two dot operators in this statement. The listbox object `lstOutput` has a property named `Items` that is an object. (Technically, `Items` is a collection object; you learn about these in Chapter 8. For now, you can just think of `Items` as a group of object thingies that can store string data.) The code calls the `Add()` method of the `Items` object, which results in one line of output being added to the listbox.

After the string data in `buff` has been added to `lstOutput`, program control jumps to the third expression of the `for` loop, a post-increment operation, `i++`, (refer to Figure 7-1). This increment expression is the third step in a well-behaved loop: It changes the state of the loop. If you didn't change the state of the loop counter variable, `i`, you would have an infinite loop because the second expression in the `for` loop would always be true. In this case, an infinite loop would not be a good thing.

After `i` has been incremented by means of the `++` increment operator, program control is transferred to `expression2`. For your `for` loop, this expression is

```
i <= end;
```

The second expression, therefore, compares the newly incremented value of i to the variable end to decide whether another pass through the for loop's statement body is warranted. As long as the current value of i is less than or equal to the value of the variable end, another pass through the loop is made. Eventually, after 101 passes through the loop, expression2 becomes logic False and the for loop statement block is skipped. Program execution then resumes with whatever statement follows the closing curly brace of the for loop statement block. You can see in Listing 7-1 that the next statement is actually the closing brace for the btnCalc click event. Therefore, your table of squares is now complete.

When to Use a for Loop

The most common use of for loops is to count something or perform a sequence of instructions a specific number of times. That is, the terminating condition as stated in expression2 of the for loop is usually known when the loop is entered. In the preceding program, for example, you knew that the variable end determines how many passes should be made through the for loop statement block.

You will discover hundreds of situations in which the for loop offers the perfect way to solve a given problem. Of the various looping structures C# makes available to you, it is probably the one used most often. A bonus feature of the for loop is that all three requirements for a well-behaved loop are specified in the three expressions used in a for statement. Having all three requirements for a well-behaved loop in one place makes it difficult to forget any of them.

NESTED FOR LOOPS

Sometimes you need to solve problems that require a loop within a loop. When one loop appears inside another loop, it is called a *nested loop*. Now modify your table-of-squares program by putting a new twist on it. Many years ago the author discovered, quite by accident, that you can square a number in a different way from simple multiplication. The algorithm is:

The square of a number N is equal to the sum of N positive odd integers, starting with 1.

Reread the algorithm again and think about it. For example, suppose you want to find the square of the number 3. You already know the answer is 9, but use the new algorithm to calculate the answer:

```
N2 = 1 + 3 + 5
N2 = 9
```

Note how you simply added up three positive odd integers, starting with 1, to arrive at the square of 3, which is 9. Suppose you want to find the square of 5:

```
N2 = 1 + 3 + 5 + 7 + 9
N2 = 25
```

Although this is an RDC way to square a number, it is an interesting test to see if you can figure out how to implement the algorithm in code.

Next let's take the table of squares program discussed earlier in this chapter and improve it slightly with a few modifications. The result should look a little better when viewed on the display.

TRY IT OUT   Table of Squares, Version 2 (Chapter07ProgramTableOfSquaresVersion2.zip)

For this example, you could reuse the code from Listing 7-1 as a starting point. (After all, one of the key advantages of object-oriented programming is code reuse! Or you could make things easy for yourself and download the program code.) You still want to generate a table of squares, so the user interface doesn't need to change. However, instead of the simple i * i means of squaring the number, you want to implement the new squaring algorithm.

1.   Load the original table of squares program (that is, your program that used Listing 7-1).

2.   Replace the `for` loop code following the Process and Display comment with the following code:

```
for (i = start; i <= end; i++)
{
    nextOddInteger = 1;      // Set first odd integer
    square = 0;              // Always start with square = 0

    for (j = 0; j < i; j++)    // Nested j loop
    {
        square += nextOddInteger; // Sum the odd integer
        nextOddInteger += 2;      // Set the next odd integer
    }
    buff = string.Format("{0, 5}{1, 20}", i, square);
    lstOutput.Items.Add(buff);
}
```

You should take a piece of paper and hand write the code that implements the new algorithm. It's far too easy to read on to see how to write the code. You learn more by trying to write the code yourself.

You need to add a few new variables to the original version of the program. The new variables that you need to add to the `btnCalculate` click event code are the following:

```
int j;
int square;
int nextOddInteger;
```

These new variables should be added to the `btnCalculate` click event code.

How It Works

Of the newly-defined variables, `j` is used to control a new `for` loop, `square` is used to hold the squared value, and `nextOddInteger` is used to create the series of odd integers in the loop. In the revised `for` loop code:

```
for (i = start; i <= end; i++)
{
    nextOddInteger = 1;      // Set first odd integer
    square = 0;              // Always start with square = 0

    for (j = 0; j < i; j++)    // Nested j loop
    {
        square += nextOddInteger; // Sum the odd integer
```

```
            nextOddInteger += 2;        // Set the next odd integer
        }
        buff = string.Format("{0, 5}{1, 20}", i, square);
        lstOutput.Items.Add(buff);
    }
```

The `for` loop controlled by variable `i` is called the *outer loop*. The `for` loop controlled by variable `j` is called the *inner loop*.

Together, these loops are the *nested loops* mentioned earlier. The outer loop still cycles through all the values you want to display in the table of squares. Both loops are constructed using your three requirements for a well-behaved loop. Now examine the code in the inner loop.

Suppose variable `i` from the outer loop has a value of 3. This means you want to calculate the square of 3. The code sets `nextOddInteger` to 1 and clears variable `square` to 0. Replacing variable `i` with its current value in `expression2` of the loop, the `j for` loop looks as though it is written like this:

```
for (j = 0; j < 3; j++)        // Nested j loop
{
    square += nextOddInteger;  // Sum the odd integer
    nextOddInteger += 2;       // Set the next odd integer
}
```

Because `expression2` is `j < 3`, the code makes three passes through the loop (0, 1, and 2 because `expression2` becomes logic `False` when `j = 3`). If you need to refresh your memory bank, Table 5-3 in Chapter 5 explains what the `+=` operator does. On the first pass, the loop looks like this:

```
for (j = 0; j < 3; j++)     // Nested j loop
{
    square = 1;             // Sum the odd integer
    nextOddInteger = 3;     // Set the next odd integer
}
```

Therefore, after the first pass, `square` equals 1 and `nextOddInteger` is increased to 3. The partial result therefore is

```
square = 1
nextOddInteger = 1 + 2 = 3
On the second pass through the loop, you find:
        for (j = 0; j < 3; j++)    // Nested j loop
        {
            square = 4;            // Sum the odd integer
            nextOddInteger = 5;    // Set the next odd integer
        }
```

from the processing of the following code:

```
square = 1 + 3 = 4
nextOddInteger = 3 + 2 = 5
```

On the third and final pass through the loop, you find:

```
square = 1 + 3 + 5 = 9
nextOddInteger = 5 + 2 = 7
```

No additional passes through the inner loop are needed because expression2 (j < 3) is now logic False. Therefore, the next two statements display the output in the listbox as before:

```
buff = string.Format("{0, 5}{1, 20}", i, square);
lstOutput.Items.Add(buff);
```

The only difference is that you replaced i * i with the variable square. To the user running the program, the output in the listbox looks exactly the same as before. The only difference is that you used a weird algorithm and a nested for loop to generate the squares of the numbers.

Use the Debugger as a Learning Tool

The best way for you to see how loops work is to single-step through the program. For example, place the cursor on the following for statement:

```
for (i = start; i <= end; i++)
```

Press the F9 key to set a breakpoint at that statement. (The text background changes to red for that statement line.) Now press the F5 key to run the program. Eventually, you'll get to the breakpoint statement. (You may have to click in the Source window to see the breakpoint, which now has the statement displayed with a yellow text background.)

Now start pressing the F10 key to single-step through the program code. Make sure you have the Locals debugger window visible (Debug Windows ⇨ Locals or Ctrl+D, L) so that you can see the values of the variables change as you go. Using the debugger is a great way to understand how the flow of the program changes based upon the values of the variables.

WHILE LOOPS

Another type of program loop is the while loop. The general syntax for a while loop is as follows:

```
while (expression2)
{
    // while loop statement block
}
```

For a while loop to be well behaved, it must follow the same three rules you applied to a for loop. However, unlike the for loop, the while loop does not make all three conditions part of the syntax of the loop structure. Only the second condition (expression2) is part of a while loop's syntax.

The first expression (expression1) of a well-behaved while loop that initializes the loop control variable is set before you enter the loop structure. The third expression (expression3) is set within the while loop statement block.

You can modify the earlier table of squares program to use a *while* loop, too. That's the topic of the next Try It Out.

Table of Squares, while Loop Version (Chapter07ProgramWhileLoopVersion.zip)

Because `while` loop structures are different from `for` loops, use the table of squares program again so you can see how the two loop structures differ.

1. Load the original table of squares program (using Listing 7-1).

2. Replace the `btnCalculate()` code with the code shown in Listing 7-2.

LISTING 7-2: Table of Squares, while loop variation. (frmMain.cs)

```
private void btnCalculate_Click(object sender, EventArgs e)
{
    bool flag;
    int i;
    int start;
    int end;
    string buff;

    //============ Gather inputs =====================
    // Convert start from text to int
    flag = int.TryParse(txtStart.Text, out start);
    if (flag == false)
    {
        MessageBox.Show("Numeric data only", "Input Error");
        txtStart.Focus();
        return;
    }

    // Convert end from text to int

    flag = int.TryParse(txtEnd.Text, out end);
    if (flag == false)
    {
        MessageBox.Show("Numeric data only", "Input Error");
        txtEnd.Focus();
        return;
    }

    if (start >= end)          // Reasonable values?
    {
        MessageBox.Show("Start less than end.", "Input Error");
        txtStart.Focus();
        return;
    }
    //============ Process and Display ==============

    i = start;    // Initialize loop counter: condition 1
    while (i <= end)   // Another iteration:  condition 2
    {
```

continues

LISTING 7-2 *(continued)*

```
            buff = string.Format("{0, 5}{1, 20}", i, i * i);
            lstOutput.Items.Add(buff);
            i++;        // Change state of loop:  condition 3
        }
    }
```

How It Works

You can see in Listing 7-2 that the first condition for a well-behaved loop is set prior to the `while` loop's being entered. That is, variable `i` is initialized to the value of variable `start` just *before* the `while` statement. The exact position of the initializing statement (that is, `expression1`) does not need to be the statement before the `while` loop block begins. Indeed, you could stick the statement anywhere before the `while` statement block. However, solid coding practices strongly suggest it's a good idea to place the code that initializes the loop control variable near the start of the `while` statement block. That placement makes it easier to see the initial condition should debugging be necessary. (What? You're not writing perfect code for every program yet?)

The interpretation of the conditional expression controlling the `while` loop is exactly the same as `expression2` in the `for` loop (`i <= end`) in Listing 7-1. This is the second condition of a well-behaved loop.

The `while` loop body extends from the opening curly brace following `expression2` to the closing curly brace. The loop body is exactly the same as the `for` loop body in Listing 7-1, except that you must place the third expression within the `while` loop body (`i++`). Note that all three conditions for a well-behaved loop are still present, but the `while` loop scatters them around a bit, whereas the `for` loop had them all in one place. The output from the program is exactly the same as before. This invites the question, "Why use a `while` loop?"

Why Have More Than One Type of Loop?

Any code that uses a `for` loop structure can be rewritten as a `while` loop, so why does C# bother with two kinds? Simply stated, C# gives you a choice of loop types because the nuances of different programming tasks may suit one loop type better than another. For example, there will be many times where you look for a specific piece of data in a list, such as a specific customer name in a list of customers, and you don't know exactly where it appears. Most programmers would code such a task as a `while` loop because they can't be sure of exactly how many iterations it's going to take to find the name. On the other hand, if you need to read 14 sensors on a machine and react to those sensors, you would likely use a `for` loop because the number of required passes through the loop is known. (Would it be a good idea to code the second expression of the loop using a symbolic constant? Hint: Yes. That would make it easier to read and change the code if the need arises.)

The ability to choose different loop structures simply makes certain programming tasks easier. Although you might contort all your code to fit into a single loop structure, having choices means you don't need to. Multiple loop structures means you have multiple tools at your disposal to attack different programming problems. After all, if the only tool you have is a hammer, it's not surprising that all your problems start to look like a nail. Multiple tools make for more elegant solutions to different programming problems.

DO-WHILE PROGRAM LOOPS

C# provides a third loop variation that you can add to your loop toolkit called a do-while loop. The syntax for a do-while loop is as follows:

```
do
{
    // do-while statement block
} while (expression2);
```

The do-while loop variant is similar to the while loop with one major exception: A do-while loop *always* makes at least one pass through the loop statement block. If you look at the other two loop variations, the test of expression2 takes place *before* the loop statement block is ever executed. With the for and while loop statements, it is quite possible for expression2 to evaluate to logic False at the start of the loop. If expression2 is false for either the for or while loop, no pass is made through the statements in the loop body.

This is not true for a do-while loop. A do-while loop always makes at least one pass through its statement block. This is because the expression that evaluates whether another pass should be made through the loop is made at the *bottom* of the loop and is arrived at after the statements in the loop body have been executed at least once. In other words, program control must pass through the do-while statement block at least one time.

While you could use the table of squares program again to use the do-while statement, in the following Try It Out you shake things up a bit and generate a series of random numbers instead. Note that the conditions for a well-behaved loop still exist, the conditions simply are not in one place in the code.

TRY IT OUT **Generate Random Numbers**
(Chapter07ProgramDoWhileRandomNumbers.zip)

C# provides a class capable of generating a series of random numbers. Now write a program that tests whether that class generates a series of random numbers wherein two identical random numbers are produced back-to-back.

1. Create a new project using the procedures and C# template presented in Chapter 2.

2. Add two label and button objects to the form plus one textbox object.

3. Arrange the objects as you see fit, although Figure 7-4 presents a sample run of the program and may be used as a model for the user interface.

Listing 7-3 shows the code for the program.

LISTING 7-3: Random numbers program. (frmMain.cs)

```csharp
using System;
using System.Windows.Forms;

public class frmMain : Form
{
    const int MAXITERATIONS = 200000;  // Limit loop passes

    private Button btnClose;
    private Label lblAnswer;
    private Label label1;
    private TextBox txtMax;
    private Button btnStart;
    #region Windows code

    public frmMain()
    {
        //========== Program Initialize Step ==============

        InitializeComponent();
    }

    public static void Main()
    {
        frmMain main = new frmMain();
        Application.Run(main);
    }

    private void btnStart_Click(object sender, EventArgs e)
    {
        bool flag;
        int counter;     // Pass counter
        int max;         // Max value for random number
        int last;
        int current;
        Random randomNumber = new Random();

        //========= Program Input Step =================
        flag = int.TryParse(txtMax.Text, out max);
        if (flag == false)
        {
            MessageBox.Show("Digit characters only.", "Input Error",
              MessageBoxButtons.OK, MessageBoxIcon.Stop);
            txtMax.Focus();
            return;
        }
        //======= Program Process Step ==============
        counter = 0;
        last = (int) randomNumber.Next(max);
        do
        {
            current = randomNumber.Next(max);
            if (last == current)
```

```
                {
                    break;
                }
                last = current;
                counter++;
            } while (counter < MAXITERATIONS);

            //========= Program Output Step ==============
            if (counter < MAXITERATIONS)
            {
                lblAnswer.Text = "It took " + counter.ToString() + " passes to
    match";
            } else {

                lblAnswer.Text = "No back-to-back match";
            }
        }

        //=========== Program Termination Step ========
        private void btnClose_Click(object sender, EventArgs e)
        {
            Close();
        }
    }
```

How It Works

A sample run of the program is shown in Figure 7-4.

The value of `1000` in the textbox object says the program should generate random numbers between 0 and 1000, exclusively. (That is, the random values vary between `0` and `999`.) Figure 7-4 shows that it took 5017 passes through the loop before the random number generator produced the same value back to back. Now take a closer look at the code.

The program begins by using the C# template discussed in Chapter 2. Near the top of Listing 7-3 is this statement:

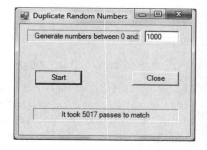

FIGURE 7-4: Identical random numbers program

```
    const int MAXITERATIONS = 200000;     // Limit on loop passes
```

This statement is used to constrain the maximum iterations of the `do-while` loop. This is done because it might be possible to make several billion passes through the loop without having two identical values generated in sequence. Using the symbolic constant `MAXITERATIONS`, you can easily change the limits on the loop without having to change code in the loop. True, you could hard-code the value `200000` in the `while` loop, but then you'd have a "magic number" in the code that doesn't tell you what its purpose is. Using the symbolic constant `MAXITERATIONS` helps document what the number does. Also, if you decide to change `MAXITERATIONS` to some other value, simply change it at the top of the program, and the new value is used automatically in the rest of the program.

The statement,

```
    Random randomNumber = new Random();
```

is used to create a `Random` object named `randomNumber`. The program then uses the `TryParse()` method to construct the range within which the user wants the random numbers to fall. The `Random` class method `Next()` is called to produce a random value between `0` and `max` minus 1. The following code fragment does most of the work in the program:

```
counter = 0;
last = randomNumber.Next(max);
do
{
    current = randomNumber.Next(max);
    if (last == current)
    {
        break;
    }
    last = current;
    counter++;
} while (counter < MAXITERATIONS);
```

The variable named `counter` is initialized to `0` prior to entering the loop. (This statement serves the purpose of `expression1` in a `for` loop.) This is the variable used to control the loop. The program then uses the `Next()` method of the `Random` class to generate a random number and assign it into the variable `last`. However, because the goal of the program is to compare two random values, you know you must generate another random value before you can test to see if the two are the same. This is why you use the `do-while` loop: You need to execute the loop body at least once to produce the two random values for the comparison. The second random value is assigned into the variable named `current`. You now have two random numbers to compare.

The break Keyword in Loops

The `if` statement compares the values of `last` and `current` to see if they are the same. If they are, the `if` statement is logic `True` and the `break` statement is executed. Anytime a `break` statement is executed within a loop statement block, the `break` sends program control to the first statement following the closing curly brace of the loop statement block. In this program, control is sent to the

```
if (counter < MAXITERATIONS)
```

statement shown in Listing 7-3.

If the values for the variables `current` and `last` are not the same, the `break` statement is not executed, and the program evaluates the `expression2` element of the `do-while` block:

```
while (counter < MAXITERATIONS);
```

The evaluation of this statement determines whether another pass through the loop should be made. At the moment, the symbolic constant `MAXITERATIONS` is set to `200000`, but you could alter the constant if you want. (Notice how this symbolic constant is used again in subsequent lines to determine the message displayed to the user.) Assuming that `counter` does not exceed `MAXITERATIONS`, the `while` test results in another pass through the loop statement block.

The number of passes made through the loop is limited using the test against `MAXITERATIONS` for two reasons. First, an integer variable can hold values in excess of 2 billion, and the user may not want to sit there waiting for the loop to plow through 2 billion passes. Second, and more important, it might take *more* than 2 billion passes through the loop to produce matching values for `last` and `current`. This means that the program might produce a value for `counter` that is too large for an integer variable to store. This could produce what is called a *numeric overflow exception* and your program would die an ungraceful death! (You learn how to prevent such ugliness in Chapter 11.)

Eventually, either a match for the two variables occurs or `counter` equals `MAXITERATIONS` and the do-while loop is terminated. At that point, the final `if` statement is evaluated, and the appropriate message displays in the `lblAnswer` label object.

As you might expect, the number of passes required to produce a match increases as the value of `max` is increased by the user. Indeed, if the user enters a large value (such as `200000`), the program frequently produces a no-match condition.

THE CONTINUE STATEMENT

Sometimes situations arise in which you need to do something special within a loop before you continue processing it. For example, you might have a loop polling the fire sprinkler sensors mentioned at the beginning of this chapter. However, instead of breaking out of the loop when a sensor is tripped, perhaps you want to continue reading the rest of the sensors to see how fast the fire is spreading. The code might look like this:

```
while (true)
{
    id++;
    state  = readSensor(id);
    if (state == true)
    {
        soundAlarm();
        callFireDepartment();
        continue;
    }
    if (id == MAXSENSORS)
    {
        id = 0;     // 0 so increment operator sets it to 1
    }
}
```

In this code fragment, you establish an infinite `while` loop by design by stating that the test expression (`expression2`) is always logic `True`, as shown in the first program statement. The code increments a sensor identification number (id) and then reads the appropriate sensor. If the sensor does not return `true`, the program makes another pass through the loop. If there is a fire and the sensor returns `true`, the alarm is sounded, the fire department is called, and then the code continues execution at `expression2` of the `while` loop because of the `continue` statement. Because `expression2` is always logic `True`, the loop continues to execute the code.

When a `while` or `do-while` loop is used, the `continue` statement always sends control to the expression that determines whether another pass through the loop is necessary (that is, `expression2`).

The same type of code using a `for` loop would be the following:

```
for (id = 0; true; id++)
{
    state  = readSensor(id);
    if (state == true)
    {
        soundAlarm();
        callFireDepartment();
        continue;
    }
    if (id == MAXSENSORS)
    {
        id = 0;      // 0 so increment operator sets it to 1
    }
}
```

In this situation, if there is a fire, variable state is `true`, and the alarm and fire department methods are executed; then continue is executed. (Look at `expression2` of the `for` loop.) The continue statement sends program control to `expression3` (id++) of the `for` statement, which increments the sensor `id`. Program control is then sent to `expression2` to determine if another pass through the loop is needed. Because `expression2` is always logic True, the code makes another pass through the loop. You should convince yourself that this is an infinite loop.

Unlike the `break` statement that transfers program control out of the loop, a `continue` statement keeps program control in the loop to decide if another pass is warranted. As an experiment, you might write dummy methods for the `soundAlarm()` and `callFireDepartment()` methods and then use the debugger to single-step through the code. Again, using the debugger is a great way to gain a more complete understanding of what the code is doing.

For the sake of completeness, you should know that C# supports the `goto` keyword, which can be used with a label to create a loop structure. However, because `goto`'s are such an ugly coding structure (that is, a coding hack), you aren't shown how to write such a loop. If you actually want to know, you can probably find an example online. (Warning: Rumor is that you can get warts by just looking at `goto` statements.)

SUMMARY

Loop structures are one of the fundamental elements in most programs. You should study the concepts presented in this chapter until you are confident how and when to use each loop type. You should also make sure you do these exercises and perhaps make up a few examples of your own.

EXERCISES

You can find the answers to the following exercises in Appendix A.

1. Write the loop code necessary to calculate the factorial of a number. For example, 5 factorial is written like this:

```
5! = 5 * 4 * 3 * 2 * 1

5! = 120
```

You may assume that a variable named `num` is defined to hold the number used for the factorial and that a variable named `i` is used to control the loop.

2. Even though the solution shown in Appendix A for Exercise 1 produces correct answers, it has two hiccups in it. Can you determine what they are?

3. Given that 1 ounce equals 28.3495231 grams, write a loop that produces a table in a listbox that shows the conversion into grams for weights from 1 ounce through 4 pounds.

4. Look at the solution code for Exercise 3. Can you find a minor change that improves the code?

5. Assuming that a monetary asset grows by *x* percent each year, calculate how much the asset is worth at the end of *n* years (using simple interest).

▶ WHAT YOU'VE LEARNED IN THIS CHAPTER

TOPIC	KEY POINTS
Well-behaved loops	The necessary and sufficient conditions for writing a well-behaved program loop.
`for, while, do-while loops`	The three types of program loops used in C#.
Which loop to use	How to decide which loops structure provides the best way to iterate over a set of program statements.
`break, continue`	How to use these keywords in program loops.

8

Understanding Arrays and Collections

WHAT YOU WILL LEARN IN THIS CHAPTER:

➤ Arrays

➤ Array indexes and elements

➤ How to set the size of an array

➤ Some of the array class methods commonly used

➤ Multidimensional arrays

➤ Array lists

➤ Collections

➤ Jagged arrays

WROX.COM CODE DOWNLOADS FOR THIS CHAPTER

You can find the wrox.com code downloads for this chapter at www.wrox.com/remtitle .cgi?isbn=9781118336922 on the Download Code tab. The code in the Chapter08 folder is individually named according to the names throughout the chapter.

In this chapter you learn about arrays, array lists, and collections. These data structures are useful to solve many types of programming problems. When you finish this chapter, you'll have an appreciation of how arrays can make certain programming problems much easier to solve.

WHAT IS AN ARRAY?

An *array* is a group of identical data types that share a common name. The syntax to define an array is as follows:

```
typeSpecifier[] arrayName = new typeSpecifier[numberOfElements];
```

where:

➤   *typeSpecifier* is the data type you want to use.

➤   *arrayName* is the name you want to use for the array.

➤   *numberOfElements* is the number of array elements you want.

Each of these parts is explained in a moment using the following example.

Suppose you have an address book with 100 names in it. Because you want to manipulate those names in some way in your program, each unique name must be stored in a unique variable. Because names are textual data, you could use something like this:

```
string name00;
string name01;
string name02;
string name03;
//...Many more variables...
string name98;
string name99;
```

Although this would work, it suffers two serious drawbacks. First, you would get tired of typing in all those variable names. Even worse, think what would happen if the address book had a million names in it! Second, how would you perform the common task to search the names in the list for a specific person? You'd be forced to plow through 100 `if` statements looking for a particular name:

```
if (name00.Equals(targetName))
{
        index = 0;
}
else
{
    if (name01.Equals(targetName))
    {
        index = 1;
    }
    else   //...and so on...
```

Remember that when you compare objects like strings, you don't compare rvalue-to-rvalue. Instead, you want to compare what is stored at the memory address contained in the object's rvalue. Therefore, when comparing strings, you should use the `Equals()` method, which is available for all string objects. Such a programming solution is not practical, which is precisely why arrays were created.

Instead of using 100 different variables, one for each name, you would define a single string array to hold the names using the syntax you saw earlier:

```
string[] names = new string[100];
```

The program now has a string array variable named names that can store 100 names. You can use what you learned about loops in the previous chapter to simplify the code:

```
for (i = 0; i < names.Length; i++)
{
    if (names[i].Equals(targetName))
    {
        index = i;
        break;
    }
}
```

If you read the code carefully, you can see that on the first pass through the loop, the if test compares the first name in the list (names[0]) to the name stored in targetName, the name you want to find. If the test fails, the loop counter variable i is incremented by the third expression of the for loop (i++) and the code makes the next comparison test (if names[1].Equals(targetName)). The loop continues until a match is found. At that time, the index is assigned the value of i (so you can reference that person later) and the break statement sends program control to the first statement following the for loop. If no match is found, index is unchanged and the search fails. (Setting index to -1 before entering the loop is a good way to tell if the search failed because -1 cannot be used as an index into an array.)

As you can see, there is a symbiotic relationship between arrays and loops, and they are used together often to solve a myriad of programming problems. Also note that names.Length is used for the expression2 in the for loop above since it returns the number of elements in the array. This is much preferred to hard coding a value for the number of elements in the array.

Some Array Details

To justify the use of arrays, a number of important details about them were ignored. You cover those details in the next few paragraphs.

Array Element Versus Array Index

An *array element* is a single unit of an array. Consider the following array definition:

```
int[] myData = new int[10];
```

The statement says that you want 10 integers arranged back to back in memory and that you want to refer to them as myData. You can see how this might look in memory in Figure 8-1.

Each of those 10 integers is referred to as one element in the array. When you define the size of the array, you always specify the number of elements you want. That number appears between the last set of brackets at the end of the definition statement ([10] in this example).

An *array index* refers to the position of a specific element in the array. In the example you requested 10 elements, but the position of the first element is index 0. Like almost everything else, C# counts array indexes starting with 0. Therefore, in

```
val = myData[0];
```

val would equal the content of the first element of the myData array. This also means that an index of 0 accesses the first element of the array. (In Figure 8-1, val is assigned the value stored at the 4 bytes beginning at memory location 900,000.)

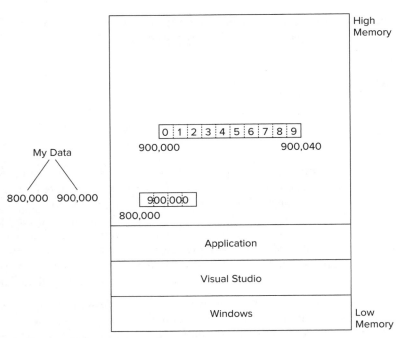

FIGURE 8-1: Memory image of an array

N – 1 Rule

Your definition of the myData array requested 10 elements for the array size. This means that the valid indexes for the array run from 0 through 9. This gives you the N – 1 Rule:

> The highest index permitted for an array is one less than the number of array elements.

This is a frequent stumbling block for beginning programmers. Because you asked for 10 elements, it would seem reasonable to use an index of 10 to access the last array element. Not so. Visual Studio issues an out-of-bounds error if you attempt to reference an element using something like this:

```
val = myData[10];
```

The reason for the error message is that the statement tried to access an element that doesn't exist within the boundaries of the array. Only elements 0 through 9 are valid array index values. If you get an out-of-bounds error, remember the N – 1 Rule to see if you're trying to index outside the limits of the array.

If you are uncertain about how large the array is, you can always use the following code:

```
size = myData.Length;
```

The Length property of the array object returns the number of elements in the array. (It does *not* return the number of bytes in memory occupied by the array.) In this example, size would equal 10 after the statement is executed. (Note the Length property used in the sample for loop at the beginning of this chapter.)

In the following Try It Out, you write a simple program that counts the number of occurrences of letters in a section of text. You will use arrays to keep track of things as the code executes.

TRY IT OUT Letter Count (Chapter08ProgramLetterCount.zip)

Now write a short program that has the user enter a couple of sentences in a multiline textbox and then count how many times each letter occurs in that text. You are not interested in punctuation, spaces, digit characters, or the distinction between upper- and lowercase letters—just alpha characters.

Given the program design stated in this section, how would you attack the problem? Again, start thinking about solving a programming problem using the Five Program Steps you learned about in Chapter 2. The Initialization step is done for you by Visual Studio. The Input step is simply the text entered by the user. The Process step involves examining each letter typed into the textbox object and counting how many times each alpha character occurs. The Output step simply involves copying the letter counts to a listbox for display. The Termination step is simple in this program. You simply end the program with the `Close()` method. Clearly, the actual work is done in the Process step.

To create this program, use the following steps:

1. Create a new project in the usual manner and add the C# code as shown in Listing 8-1.

2. Add three label objects, a multiline textbox for the input letters, a listbox to show the letter counts, and two button objects. You can arrange these objects as you want, but Figure 8.2 shows a sample run using one possible user interface.

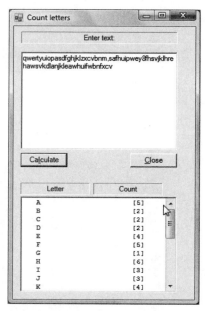

FIGURE 8-2: Program to count letters in text

As you can see in Listing 8-1, the actual work is done in the Process step, as shown in the button click event code.

LISTING 8-1: Letter count program (frmMain.cs)

```csharp
using System;
using System.Windows.Forms;

public class frmMain : Form
{
  private const int MAXLETTERS = 26;            // Symbolic constants
  private const int MAXCHARS = MAXLETTERS  1;
  private const int LETTERA = 65;

  private TextBox txtInput;
  private Button btnCalc;
  private Button btnClose;
  private ListBox lstOutput;
  private Label label2;
  private Label label3;
  private Label label1;

  #region Windows code

  public frmMain()
  {
    InitializeComponent();
  }

  public static void Main()
  {
    frmMain main = new frmMain();
    Application.Run(main);
  }

  private void btnCalc_Click(object sender, EventArgs e)
  {
    char oneLetter;
    int index;
    int i;
    int length;
    int[] count = new int[MAXLETTERS];
    string input;
    string buff;

    length = txtInput.Text.Length;
    if (length == 0)     // Anything to count??
    {
      MessageBox.Show("You need to enter some text.", "Missing Input");
      txtInput.Focus();
      return;
    }
    input = txtInput.Text;
    input = input.ToUpper();

    for (i = 0; i < input.Length; i++)    // Examine all letters.
    {
```

```
      oneLetter = input[i];              // Get a character
      index = oneLetter - LETTERA;       // Make into an index
      if (index < 0 || index > MAXCHARS) // A letter??
        continue;                        // Nope.
      count[index]++;                    // Yep.
    }

    for (i = 0; i < MAXLETTERS; i++)
    {
      buff = string.Format("{0, 4} {1,20}[{2}]", (char)(i + LETTERA),
             " ",count[i]);
      lstOutput.Items.Add(buff);
    }
  }

  private void btnClose_Click(object sender, EventArgs e)
  {
    Close();
  }
}
```

How It Works

The solution for the programming task is shown in Listing 8-1. The program begins by defining a series of symbolic constants.

```
private const int MAXLETTERS = 26;            // Symbolic constants
private const int MAXCHARS = MAXLETTERS - 1;
private const int LETTERA = 65;
```

You already know why using symbolic constants in a program is a good thing. If nothing else, it prevents you from using magic numbers in the program.

The LETTERA constant needs some explanation. When you press a letter on your keyboard, it completes an electrical circuit in the keyboard matrix, which is decoded and sent to the computer as a single-byte numeric value. (Some keyboards can send 2-byte Unicode characters, but assume that's not the case here.) The code sent to the computer uses the ASCII character set as explained in Chapter 5. The ASCII value for the letter A is 65. The ASCII value for Z is 90, which means the codes are in alphabetical order. That is, B is 66, C is 67, and so on. Therefore, if you convert the text the user typed into the textbox object to uppercase letters, it's a simple matter to create the proper index into the array that holds the letter counts. The array that holds the counts is defined as follows:

```
int[] count = new int[MAXLETTERS];
```

Because the symbolic constant MAXLETTERS is 26, you define an array with 26 elements in it, which means the indexes can have values from 0 through 25. (The N – 1 Rule, remember?) Plan to use count[0] to store the count for the A's, count[1] for the B's, count[2] for the C's, and so on.

Now suppose the user typed in the word Abe. Because lower- and uppercase letters do have different ASCII values, the first thing you need to do is convert everything to uppercase letters. (Your program design said you don't care about the case of the letters.) The following statements from Listing 8-1 take the input typed in by the user and assign it into the string variable named input:

```
input = txtInput.Text;
```

```
input = input.ToUpper();
```

The code then uses the `ToUpper()` method to convert all the letters to uppercase. The text is now ABE. Having made the case conversion, you are now ready to count the letters.

The statement

```
oneLetter = input[i];          // Get a character
```

makes use of the fact that you can treat a character string as though it is an array. Therefore, in the `for` loop, when i is 0, `input[i]` is the A in ABE. Here's the next statement:

```
index = oneLetter - LETTERA;   // Make into an index
```

resolves to this:

```
index = 'A' - 65;       // Make into an index
```

However, A is actually 65 when it is viewed as an ASCII character. So the expression becomes this:

```
index = 65 - 65;        // Make into an index
index = 0;
```

The next three lines first check to make sure the index that was just calculated falls between 0 and 25. If it doesn't, the character is not an alpha letter, and you don't want to count it:

```
if (index < 0 || index > MAXCHARS)  // A letter??
   continue;                         // Nope.
count[index]++;                      // Yep.
```

Because your index is 0, you execute the following statement:

```
count[0]++;
```

This increments the contents of the first integer in the array. (All value-type array elements are initialized to 0 at the moment they are defined in C#. Arrays of objects are initialized to null. (You read more about these details in the section "Initializer Lists for String Objects" and in Table 8-1, for example.) If you think about it, `count[0]` corresponds to the letter A—which is exactly the element you want! `count[0]` now equals 1 because the code counted the letter A in ABE.

The processing for the next letters is as follows:

```
index = 'B' - 65;
index = 66 - 65;
index = 1;
```

This means the code increments `count[1]` to 1 because you counted the B in ABE. Finally:

```
index = 'E'  65;
index = 69 - 65;
index = 4;
```

Here `count[4]` is incremented to 1, which counts the letter E. This process continues as long as there are characters in the string left to process. (Note expression2 in the `for` loop: i < input.Length, which limits the number of passes through the loop.)

You should convince yourself that the final `for` loop,

```
for (i = 0; i < MAXLETTERS; i++)
```

```
    {
      buff = string.Format("{0, 4} {1,10}[{2}]", (char)(i + LETTERA),
            " ",count[i]);
      lstOutput.Items.Add(buff);
    }
```

increments through the `count []` array and displays the characters in the `ListBox` object (refer to Figure 8-2).

Casts

Notice how the format string uses an empty string for the second argument and has brackets surrounding the third argument. The expression

```
(char)(i + LETTERA)
```

uses a form of C# syntax called a *cast*. The syntax for a cast is

```
(dataTypeDesired) dataTypeYouHave
```

The cast uses parentheses to surround the wanted data type. Simply stated, you should use a cast anytime you want to assign one data type into a different data type. Most often you see a cast used in a code sequence like

```
char c;
int val;
// some code...
c = (char) val;            // You are casting an int into a char
```

Technically, casts are necessary only when moving from a data type with a larger byte count for storage than the target data type. However, it's good coding practice to always use a cast when different data types are used because it helps document what your intentions are.

In the program example, it is necessary to use a cast in the `Format()` method because you take the sum of the numeric values `i` and `LETTERA`, which are `int` data types of 4 bytes each, but want to display them as a `char` data type of 2 bytes each. Because you want to pour 4 bytes of data into a 2-byte bucket, you must cast the sum of `i` and `LETTERA` to a `char` data type before you can display it as an alphabetic character. Again, use the formatting capabilities of `string.Format()` to make the columns line up in the listbox (using a fixed font).

When the program finishes executing, the output looks similar to that shown in Figure 8-2. (Just to get a good distribution of letters, simply drag your finger over all three rows of letters on the keyboard and add a few more letters after doing that.) The two labels above the listbox identify what displays in the listbox.

THE LISTVIEW OBJECT

Formatting columns of data in a listbox is such a common practice that Visual Studio provides a special control dedicated to that specific purpose. It's called the `ListView` object.

In the next Try It Out you use a `ListView` object instead of an ordinary listbox to display the results of the program. You will find that the `ListView` object offers several nice features not found in the `ListBox` object.

Using a ListView Object (Chapter08ProgramLettersVersion02.zip)

The easiest way to code this exercise is to simply use the code available for download for this chapter. You could also use the code presented in Listing 8-1 and simply change the `ListBox` object to a `ListView` object following these instructions:

1. Select the `ListView` object from the Toolbox and drag (or double-click) it onto the form as you would any other control. Indeed, at this juncture, it looks the same as a `ListBox` object. Now the neat stuff begins.

2. With the focus set to the `ListView` object in the Source window, scroll to the `View` property in the Properties window, and set it to `Details` from the list of choices. This enables you to see the impact of property changes for the object as you make them. Now scroll to the `Columns` property in the Properties window. (If the Properties window is hidden, press the F4 key.) Click the ellipsis button of the `Columns` property. You should see a dialog box similar to that shown in Figure 8-3.

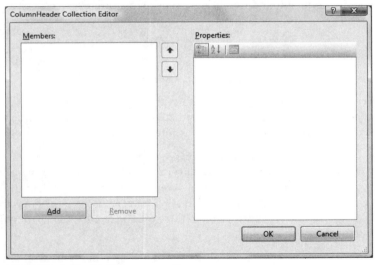

FIGURE 8-3: The ListView properties

Now click the Add button, and the display changes to that shown in Figure 8-4.

3. On the left side of the dialog box is a box area labeled Members. This area contains the columns you want to define for the `ListView` object. (Because you haven't added any members yet, the box has filled in the default name of `columnHeader1`.) On the right side of the dialog form is a box that presents the properties you can use for each column, arranged by function (in this example Behavior, Data, Design, and Misc). Personally, I don't like this arrangement of ordering by function.) At the top of the box is an icon showing the letters A and Z with a downward-pointing arrow next to them. If you click this icon, the list in the box changes to show the properties arranged in alphabetical order. The dialog box now looks like that shown in Figure 8-5.

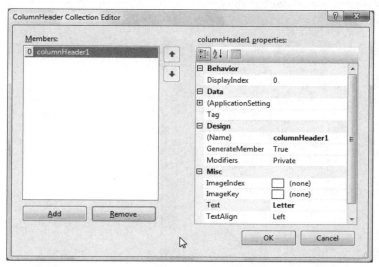

FIGURE 8-4: ListView after clicking the Add button

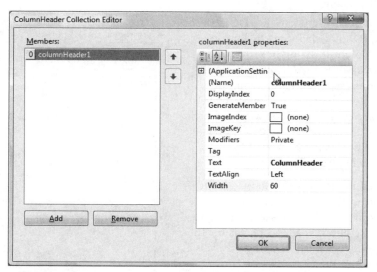

FIGURE 8-5: Listing properties alphabetically for a ListView object

The contents of the properties box appears less cluttered than before because the functional area titles have been removed. If you prefer it the other way (as shown in Figure 8-4), simply click the categorized icon next to the alphabetical icon you just clicked. The rest of the discussion assumes that you, too, prefer the "decluttered" version of the properties list.

4. Change the `Text` property for `columnHeader1` in the right box to `Letter` and its `Width` property to `110`, as shown in Figure 8-6.

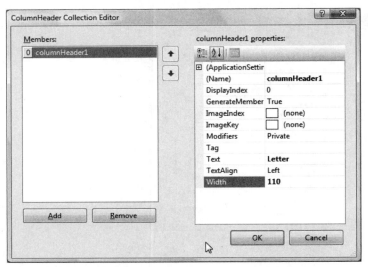

FIGURE 8-6: Setting the width property

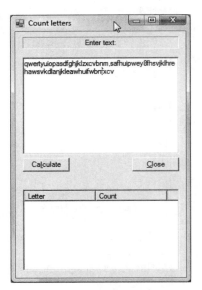

FIGURE 8-7: The ListView object after setting the properties

Now click the Add button. (Do not click the OK button because that dismisses the Columns dialog box and you're not through with it yet.) If you drag the Columns dialog box out of the way, you should see the changes you just made reflected in the `ListView` object in the Source window. The dialog box now shows a second column header in the Members box. Set its `Text` property to `Count` and its `Width` property to `115`. Now click OK. Your `ListView` object should look similar to Figure 8-7.

The `Width` property is stated in pixels, and you may want to experiment with its value until the `ListView` object looks "good" to you. In Figure 8-7 you can see a small gap to the right of the `ListView` column headers. This is for the scroll bar control that appears automatically when there is more data than can be shown in the `ListView` object.

Guesstimating Column Widths

So how can you determine that each column should be 115 pixels wide? Well, after setting the `View` property to `Details`, you can see that the `ListView` object had its `Size` property set to `251, 133`. This means that the width of the `ListView` object is 251 pixels. Because a scroll bar object takes approximately 20 pixels of display real estate, simply divide the remaining 231 pixels in half to get approximately 115 pixels for each column.

Although this approach isn't exact, especially with an odd number of columns, it's close enough for government work.

With the `ListView` object's properties set, you need to modify the code that places the data in the `ListView` object. To do this, remove the following lines from Listing 8-1:

```
for (i = 0; i < MAXLETTERS; i++)
{
  buff = string.Format("{0, 4} {1,10}[{2}]", (char)(i + LETTERA),
       " ",count[i]);
  lstOutput.Items.Add(buff);
}
```

Replace them with this:

```
ListViewItem which;
for (i = 0; i < MAXLETTERS; i++)
{
    oneLetter = (char)(i + LETTERA);
    which = new ListViewItem(oneLetter.ToString());
    which.SubItems.Add(count[i].ToString());
    lsvOutput.Items.Add(which);
}
```

The first statement creates a `ListViewItem` reference object variable named `which`. You can think of a `ListViewItem` object as a group of data that defines one row of the `ListView` object. The `for` loop remains unchanged from the previous version. The third statement simply constructs the cast you used in the first version and assigns the character that's constructed from the sum of variable `i` and `LETTERA` into the variable `oneLetter`. When `i` is `0`, the sum is `65`, which is then cast to a `char`, which becomes the character `A` in the Unicode character set and is assigned into `oneLetter`.

A `ListViewItem`, however, prefers to work with `string` data rather than `char` data. Therefore, you use the `ToString()` method for `char` objects to convert `oneLetter` to a string when the code creates the `ListViewItem` object in statement four using its constructor method. This statement has the effect of creating a `ListViewItem` named `which` with its first column initialized to the current letter (in this example `A`).

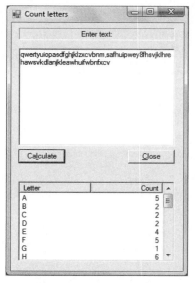

The fifth statement takes the count for the current letter as stored in the `count[]` array and adds it to the `ListViewItem` named `which`. Notice that `which` contains an object named `SubItems` and uses its `Add()` method to add this column data to the first column's data. The last statement is virtually the same as the `ListBox` object's `Add()` method, except that you pass it the `ListViewItem` object named `which` instead of a formatted string.

How It Works

After you have the objects on the form and the properties set for the `ListView` object, you can run the program. The result of these code changes is shown in Figure 8-8.

FIGURE 8-8: Sample program output with ListView object

Although you did have to add a few new lines of code and tinker around with the `Columns` property of the `ListView` object, the results do look a little better than the output in Figure 8-2. The biggest visual improvement is that the column headers are more closely tied to the data. (Try modifying the code in the second version to surround the counts with brackets, as the first version does.)

The actual behavior of the `ListView` object is similar to that of the `ListBox` object, However, although it is a more complex to set up a `ListView` object, the end results are usually worth it.

ARRAYS ARE OBJECTS

Unlike in some other programming languages, arrays in C# are objects. This means each array object has a set of properties and methods that you can use with it. The code in Listing 8-1 makes use of the `Length` array property to control the number of iterations made through the loop. What is less obvious is that all array objects are derived from the `System.Array` class. Table 8-1 presents a partial list of some of the properties and methods available through the `System.Array` class.

TABLE 8-1: Partial List of Array Class Properties and Methods

EXAMPLE	DESCRIPTION
`System.Array.BinarySearch(count, target)`	Performs a binary search on a sorted, one-dimensional array named `count` looking for `target`.
`System.Array.Clear(count, start, count.Length)`	Clears value type arrays from element `start` through element `Length` to `0`. Reference arrays are cleared to `null`.
`System.Array.Copy(Source, Dest, Length);`	Copies `Length` elements from the `Source` array to the `Dest` array.
`System.Array.IndexOf(count, val)`	Returns the index in the `count` array where the first occurrence of `val` is found.
`System.Array.LastIndexOf(count, val)`	Returns the index in the `count` array where the last occurrence of `val` is found.
`System.Array.Sort(count)`	Sorts a one-dimensional array named `count` into ascending order.
`System.Array.Reverse(count)`	Reverses the current values of a one-dimensional array named `count`. Note: If you call `Sort()` and then `Reverse()`, it puts the array into descending order.

EXAMPLE	DESCRIPTION
`count.Rank`	Returns the number of dimensions for the array named `count`.

`count.GetUpperBound(val)`	Returns the highest index number for dimension `val` for the `count` array. For example, if the definition for an array named `test` is as follows:
	
	`int[,] test = new int[5,10];`
	
	the statement
	
	`max = test.GetUpperBound(1);`
	
	sets `max` to `9`. Remember that a two-dimensional array uses dimensions `0` and `1`, and the N − 1 Rule applies! Getting the `Rank` property first would enable you to call this method with valid dimensions if they are unknown.

`count.Initialize()`	Calls the default constructor to set each element. For value data types the value is `0`; for reference data types the value is `null`.

Many of the methods presented in Table 8-1 are overloaded. You can use IntelliSense to see the overloaded parameter lists for the various array methods.

After you define an array, you can use the properties and methods presented in Table 8-1. For example, if an array named `val` has 100 random values in it and you want them sorted into ascending order, the statement

```
System.Array.Sort(val);
```

reorganizes the values into sorted order. If you then call

```
System.Array.Reverse(val);
```

the values in the `val` array are now in descending order. As you can see, manipulating array data is greatly simplified by the properties and methods in Table 8-1 compared to you writing the code.

MULTIDIMENSIONAL ARRAYS

So far you have read only about one-dimensional arrays, which are great for describing lists of data. However, data is often organized in tables of rows and columns. For example, you might want to see the distribution of grades in a class where the columns represent the student's class and the rows represent the grades, as shown in Table 8-2.

TABLE 8-2: Grade Distribution by Class

GRADES	FRESHMEN	SOPHOMORES	JUNIORS	SENIORS
A	1	4	6	5
B	4	7	11	4
C	11	13	11	3
D	3	4	3	1
F	2	1	0	0

If you want to define an array to store the data shown in Table 8-2, you might use the following code:

```
int[,] grades = new int[5, 4];
```

This definition states that you want to define a table, or matrix, with five rows and four columns. Note the comma within the brackets at the beginning of the definition statement. The first comma in the brackets on the left side of the assignment expression simply tells C# that you are about to define a two-dimensional array. The second set of brackets on the right side of the assignment expression specifies exactly how many elements there are in the table. Because there are two dimensions, you say the `grades` array has a rank of two. That is, the term *rank* refers to the number of dimensions associated with the array.

You can use more than two dimensions if you need them. For example, 3-D graphics are drawn using X, Y, and Z coordinates. To define an array with three dimensions, you might use this code:

```
int[,,] images = new int[20, 20, 20];
```

This defines a data cube rather than a table or list. If you want N dimensions (such as three), there are always N – 1 commas (in this case two commas) within the brackets.

You may even need more than three dimensions. If you write game software, for example, you might need three dimensions for the placement of the 3-D images in the game and a fourth dimension to keep track of the time at which each image should appear. (I tried to think of an example using five dimensions and all I got was a headache.) C# appears to support more ranks than you can ever reasonably be assumed to need.

In the next Try It Out you apply some of the array concepts we've been discussing, but applies them to a two-dimensional array. Although the processing is similar, there are small differences that you need to handle.

TRY IT OUT   **Using a Two-Dimensional Array**
(Chaper08ProgramTwoDimensionalArray.zip)

Now assume you want to write a program that lets the user enter the number of rows she wants in a table that shows the number, the square of the number, and the cube of the number. The program requires a two-dimensional array with a user-supplied number of rows and three columns. For this

project, you can download the code in the
`Chaper08ProgramTwoDimensionalArray.zip` file or use the
following steps:

1. Create a new project, and insert the C# template as
usual.

2. Add a label object, two button objects, a textbox object,
and a `ListView` object.

3. Arrange the objects as you see fit, but a sample arrangement and run is shown in Figure 8-9. (Don't forget to
set the `ListView`'s `View` property to `Details` before
you start working with the `ListView` object. This
makes it easier to see the impact of changing the properties as you go.)

4. Add the code presented in Listing 8-2.

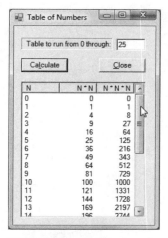

FIGURE 8-9: User interface for multidimensional array program

---

LISTING 8-2: A two-dimensional array program (frmMain.cs)

```csharp
using System;
using System.Windows.Forms;

public class frmMain : Form
{
    private TextBox txtMax;
    private Button btnCalc;
    private Button btnClose;
    private ListView lsvTable;
    private ColumnHeader columnHeader1;
    private ColumnHeader columnHeader2;
    private ColumnHeader columnHeader3;
    private Label label1;
    #region Windows code

    public frmMain()
    {
        InitializeComponent();
    }

    public static void Main()
    {
        frmMain main = new frmMain();
        Application.Run(main);
    }

    private void btnCalc_Click(object sender, EventArgs e)
    {
        bool flag;
        int number;
        int i;
```

continues

LISTING 8-2 *(continued)*

```
        ListViewItem which;

        flag = int.TryParse(txtMax.Text, out number); // check input
        if (flag == false)
        {
            MessageBox.Show("Numeric data only.", "Input Error");
            txtMax.Focus();
            return;
        }
        if (number < 0)            // Make sure it's positive
        {
            number = number * 1;
        }
        number++;    // Do this because of N - 1 Rule

        int[,] myData = new int[number, 3];      // Define array

        for (i = 0; i < number; i++)
        {
            myData[i, 0] = i;           // first column of table
            myData[i, 1] = i * i;       // second column of table
            myData[i, 2] = i * i * i;   // third column of table
        }

        for (i = 0; i < number; i++)    // Now show it
        {
            which = new ListViewItem(myData[i, 0].ToString());
            which.SubItems.Add(myData[i, 1].ToString());
            which.SubItems.Add(myData[i, 2].ToString());
            lsvTable.Items.Add(which);
        }
    }

    private void btnClose_Click(object sender, EventArgs e)
    {
        Close();
    }
}
```

How It Works

The code for the program is presented in Listing 8-2. As usual, things get interesting in the btnCalc_
Click() event code. First, several working variables are defined, including a ListViewItem object
named which. The code draws upon the TryParse() method to validate that the user entered numeric
data. If she entered a negative number, you force it to be positive. When these checks are complete,
the variable number holds the number of rows you want to display in the ListView object. That value
is incremented because you want to display the data through the number the user entered, inclusively.
That is, if the user types in 100, you actually want to display 101 values, 0 through 100—it's that pesky
N – 1 Rule again.

The statement

```
int[,] myData = new int[number, 3];      // Define array
```

defines the array that holds the data. The loop simply assigns the values needed for each column of the array:

```
for (i = 0; i < number; i++)
{
    myData[i, 0] = i;            // first column of table
    myData[i, 1] = i * i;        // second column of table
    myData[i, 2] = i * i * i;    // third column of table
}
```

As you can see, variable i controls the loop but also dictates the number of rows in the table. Therefore, variable i is used to set the first dimension of the array in the loop, or its row value. The second dimension (values 0, 1, 2) determines the values for the three columns in the table.

The next for loop formats the data into the ListView object named lsvTable:

```
for (i = 0; i < number; i++)      // Now show it
{
    which = new ListViewItem(myData[i, 0].ToString());
    which.SubItems.Add(myData[i, 1].ToString());
    which.SubItems.Add(myData[i, 2].ToString());
    lsvTable.Items.Add(which);
}
```

This code is similar to the code you saw earlier in the discussion of the ListView object. The only contextual difference is that there are now three columns instead of the two shown in Figure 8-8.

If you've looked at the code closely you're probably saying, "Hey, doofus! The three expressions controlling the two for loops are identical, so why not collapse them into a single for loop?" This piece of RDC was done purposely to minimize the "busyness" of the code. You can easily move the four statements from the second for loop and place them after the three statements in the first for loop. You can then do away with the second for loop altogether. (Of course, if you do that, you can do away with the array completely and the whole purpose of the program disappears!)

INITIALIZING ARRAYS

Often you know that certain arrays have specific values and you want to initialize the array elements to those values. For example, you might have an array named days that holds a count of the number of days in each month. You could use the following code:

```
days[0] = 31;      // January
days[1] = 28;      // February
days[2] = 31;      // March
```

and so on. As you can see, this is a repetitive task that requires 12 statements that are almost identical. C# provides you with an easier, more direct way to set the values of an array. The syntax is shown here:

```
typeSpecifier [] arrayID = new typeSpecifier [elementCount] { val1, val2, val3,. . .};
```

Using the example of the days in each month, you might use this:

```
int[] days = new int[12] {31,28,31,30,31,30,31,31,30,31,31};
```

This statement sets all 12 monthly values in a single statement. Setting the values of an array as part of the definition of the array is called *initializing* the array. The list of values that appears between the curly braces is often referred to as the *initializer list*.

Variations for Initializing an Array

What's interesting is that C# provides two additional syntax variations for initializing an array. These variations for the same array shown in the previous section are

```
int[] days = new int[] {31,28,31,30,31,30,31,31,30,31,31};
```
or

```
int[] days = {31,28,31,30,31,30,31,31,30,31,31};
```

The first variation does not fill in the element count for the array. The compiler does that automatically by counting the number of values in the initializer list. The second variation does away with the new keyword and the type specifier with brackets.

Which Array Definition/Initialization Syntax Is Best?

Given that you have three ways to accomplish the same task, which should you use? As always, whenever you have options for the way to code a specific task, the important thing is that you are consistent in the option you use. You (or your programming team) should pick one and always use that variation. It makes no difference to C# which one you use.

That said, I would opt for the following definition:

```
int[] days = new int[] {0, 31,28,31,30,31,30,31,31,30,31,31};
```

There are several reasons to choose this variation. First, the use of the new keyword in the definition reinforces that arrays are objects. Second, there is no good reason for you to fill in the element count for the initializer list. The compiler is good at counting, so you should let it do its thing. Finally, if you need to add or delete elements from the initializer list, the compiler automatically adjusts for the new size when you don't specify the element count. (If you do supply the element count and it doesn't match the initializer list, Visual Studio gets cranky and issues an error message complaining about the rank of the array. This message is a little misleading because the problem is that the number of elements supplied doesn't match the elements specified.)

Code Like a User

Did you notice that the preferred definition for the days array has 13 elements in it? An extra element is added because of the way users think about this type of data. After all, if you ask someone, "What is the first month of the year?" most won't answer, "February!" Yet, element 1 in the array, days[1], has the value 28. True, you as the programmer can always make the mental adjustment when using zero-based arrays; however, programs work with familiar data sizes (such as days in the month, days of the week, number of holes in a round of golf, and so on) often have fewer bugs when the first value in the array is initialized to 0 to make the data align with a ones-based counting system.

If you do use a ones-based data set, it doesn't hurt to call attention to that fact with a comment:

```
// CAUTION: Human thinking ones-based array follows:
int[] days = new int[] {0, 31,28,31,30,31,30,31,31,30,31,31};
```

Again, whatever choice you make about initializing arrays, make that choice and stick with it consistently in your code. Consistency helps to make the code easier to read and understand, which in turn makes debugging easier.

Initializing Multidimensional Arrays

You may also use initializer lists with multidimensional arrays. For example, suppose you want to initialize a two-by-three array (an array with two rows and three columns). You could use this code:

```
int [,] myData = new int[ , ] { {1,2,3}, {4,5,6} };
```

The syntax rule for initializing multidimensional arrays is that the values for each row are enclosed in their own set of curly braces. If you want to supply the element counts, as in

```
int [,] myData = new int[2 ,3 ] { {1,2,3}, {4,5,6} };
```

you may do so. However, again, the compiler is good at doing this for you. Because you already have enough on your plate, why not let the compiler perform those tasks for which it has a comparative advantage?

Some programmers find it useful to use a different style to present multidimensional array initializer lists:

```
int [] myData = new int[,] {
                            {1,2,3},
                            {4,5,6}
                          };
```

Although this style does reinforce the idea that the data definition establishes a matrix of data values, it also takes up three extra rows of display real estate that you may be reluctant to give up. Still, if you think it makes it easier to understand the data, select this style and apply it consistently in your code.

Initializer Lists for String Objects

You can use initializer lists for string objects, too. For example:

```
string[] weekDays = new string[] { "Monday", "Tuesday",
                    "Wednesday", "Thursday", "Friday",
                    "Saturday", "Sunday" };
```

The syntax is the same as for value-type data. However, the way in which arrays of objects (that is, an array of reference-type data) work is not exactly the same as it is for value-type data. Figure 8-1 showed how the memory map for an array of integer value types appears in memory. Although the author has taken a few liberties with the details, you should visualize the memory map for the weekDays array as something like that shown in Figure 8-10.

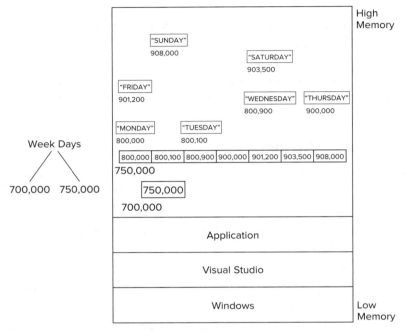

FIGURE 8-10: Memory map for string objects

The memory map in Figure 8-1 for integer data shows that the actual integer data values are in a contiguous set of bytes starting at memory address 900,000. (The rvalue of myData in that figure is 900,000.) Now compare Figure 8-1 with Figure 8-10.

In Figure 8-10, you can see that the lvalue for weekDays is 700,000 and its rvalue is 750,000. This means that there is an array of memory addresses that begins at memory address 750,000. Because the initializer list contains seven strings, there is enough memory allocated for the weekDays array to hold seven contiguous *memory addresses*, not the strings themselves, starting at address 750,000. Each element of the array contains a memory address that points to the memory location where its string data is stored. For example, the first string object in the array is stored at memory location 800,000. Go to that address, and you find Monday stored starting at that memory location. Look at the other values in the array, and you can find they are stored in the same manner.

What would the weekDays array look like if you didn't have the initializer list? In Figure 8-10, instead of finding seven memory addresses starting at memory location 750,000, you would find that each element in the array contains the value null. When each element of the weekDays array is assigned a piece of string data to store, the Windows operating system hands Visual Studio a memory address, based upon where the Windows Memory Manager found enough memory for the string data item, to replace the null value for that element in the array.

Why doesn't C# just store the data back to back as it does the integer data shown in Figure 8-1? The reason is that the memory requirements (based on its length) for each object in the string array can vary. Although each integer always takes 4 bytes, each object in an array of string objects can require differing amounts of memory. That is, the memory needed to store Friday is different from the amount of memory needed to store Wednesday. Because you cannot assume the memory requirements for elements of an object array are symmetrical, C# must store an array of memory addresses (which *are* symmetrical), each element of which points to the memory location of the actual data for that element in the array.

Ragged Arrays

It is this lack of symmetry in object arrays that gives rise to the term *ragged array* (or *jagged array*). That is, if you were to stack an array of integer elements one on top of the other, they would form a smooth vertical column with a width of 4 bytes per element. If you take the days-of-the-week array and stack the elements on top of each other, the column would probably be ragged, because each element may have a differing width.

Arrays of value data types are guaranteed always to be symmetrical. That is, you can always think of arrays of value types as being stored in the manner presented in Figure 8-1. Arrays of objects, however, cannot make that guarantee and use the storage mechanism depicted in Figure 8-10.

Defining Ragged Arrays at Runtime

You can illustrate how to define a ragged array at run time with another example. Suppose you have three people who agree to provide blood samples. The first person hates needles but agrees to give 3 samples. The second person isn't bothered by needles and agrees to give 10 samples. The third person simply agrees to give 5 samples. Suppose these sample counts are inputted by the user and maintained in variables count1, count2, and count3, respectively. If you keep in mind that a two-dimensional array is an array of arrays, understanding the following code snippet should be easy.

```
int[][] samples = new int[3][];  // Note last spec empty

// Some code that sets the element counts for each person
samples[0] = new int[count1];   // Person 1
samples[1] = new int[count2];   // Person 2
samples[2] = new int[count3];   // Person 3

for (i = 0; i < 3; i++)         // Set 1st three values to equal i
{
    samples[0][i] = i;
    samples[1][i] = i;
    samples[2][i] = i;
}
```

This code snippet also shows another syntax style for declaring multidimensional arrays. Note how the first statement starts with [] [] after the type specifier and ends with the second dimension unspecified in the second set of brackets ([3] []). If you want to leave the second dimension unspecified, you must use the syntax presented here. (Using a comma to separate dimensions does not work.)

The next three definition statements fill in the missing dimensions according to the subjects' desire to provide samples. (The keyword `new` in the three statements is a tipoff that Visual Studio is having conversations with the Windows Memory Manager.) Finally, the `for` loop demonstrates how you can assign values into the new array elements. Therefore, the syntax presented here enables you to define ragged arrays at run time. Always keep in mind, however, that only the last dimension of a multidimensional array can be unspecified.

COLLECTIONS

A *collection* is a set of objects that shares the same characteristics. You can have a collection of strings, as you do with the `weekDays` array, or you can have collections of complex objects, such as a `ListView` or similar control object.

In the next Try It Out you use collections to create a table of squares and cubes. While you could easily write the program without using collections, it can be used to illustrate how collections can be used.

TRY IT OUT   Squares and Cubes (Chapter08ProgramCollections.zip)

Suppose you want to iterate through the `days` and `weekDays` arrays. Because arrays are objects, you can treat them as a collection. Create a new project using the following steps:

1. Create a new project in the usual manner, and add the code shown in Listing 8-3.

2. Add two button objects and a `ListBox` object.

Figure 8-11 shows a sample user interface and program run.

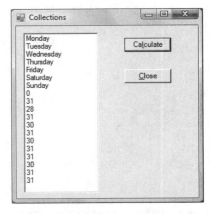

FIGURE 8-11: A program to demonstrate collections

Notice how you can place either collection in the `ListBox` object.

LISTING 8-3: Sample collections program (frmMain.cs)

```
using System;
using System.Windows.Forms;

public class frmMain : Form
{
    private Button btnCalc;
    private Button btnClose;
    private ListBox lstTest;
    #region Windows code

    public frmMain()
    {
        InitializeComponent();
    }

    public static void Main()
    {
        frmMain main = new frmMain();
        Application.Run(main);
    }

    private void btnClose_Click(object sender, EventArgs e)
    {
        Close();
    }

    private void btnCalc_Click(object sender, EventArgs e)
    {
        int[] days = new int[] { 0, 31, 28, 31, 30, 31, 30, 31, 31, 30,
                    31, 31 };
        string[] weekDays = new string[] { "Monday", "Tuesday",
                        "Wednesday", "Thursday", "Friday", "Saturday",
                        "Sunday"};

        foreach (string str in weekDays)
        {
            lstTest.Items.Add(str);
        }
        foreach (int val in days)
        {
            lstTest.Items.Add(val.ToString());
        }
    }
}
```

How It Works

The code for the program is shown in Listing 8-3.

The two arrays are defined in the button-click event method. Notice the use of the keyword `foreach` in the loops that iterate through the collections:

```
foreach (string str in weekDays)
{
    lstTest.Items.Add(str);
}
foreach (int val in days)
{
    lstTest.Items.Add(val.ToString());
}
```

A `foreach` loop is designed specifically to iterate through a collection of objects. It is similar to a standard `for` loop, except that the first expression (`expression1` in a standard `for` loop) is always set to the first object in the collection, and the loop iterates through all elements of the array one by one (`expression3` in a standard `for` loop). The data type used in the loop must match the data type in the collection. This is why `str` is a `string` in the first loop, and `val` is an `int` in the second loop.

You should think of the `foreach` loop as a read-only loop. That is, you should not use a `foreach` loop to change the value of any of the objects in the collection. Collections provide a convenient way to view objects by iterating through them, but you should not try to change those objects within a `foreach` loop.

ARRAYLIST OBJECTS

The arrays discussed thus far are called *static arrays*. This is because when you set their element sizes, they cannot be changed. Indeed, you cannot use a static array until its dimension or dimensions have been determined. However, life isn't always that simple. Quite often you have a situation in which you know you need to store the data in an array but don't have a clue how many elements you might need. For example, you might write a program that records the names and addresses of friends in an object called `Friends`. When you run the program, you might need 50 array elements, but another person might need only 20 elements. The issue is, "How do you decide how many elements to allocate for the array?"

With static arrays, the usual solution is to settle for a worst-case design. A *worst-case design* is one in which you try to guess the largest reasonable value you will ever need for the size of the array and then set the dimension for the array to that size. This can be inefficient because you will likely overestimate the required size for the array most of the time. The `ArrayList` object overcomes this limitation of static arrays. `ArrayList` objects have the effect to create dynamic arrays for which you don't have to specify a size. Now see how this works.

`ArrayList` objects offer some features that are not available with simple array. This is especially true for those arrays where you don't know the size of the array at compile time. The following Try It Out shows you how you can use `ArrayLists` in your programs.

TRY IT OUT   **ArrayList Example (Chapter08ProgramArrayList.zip)**

Write a simple program that enables you to add a person's name to a list. Because you have no idea how many names will be added by the user, you decide to use an `ArrayList` object.

1.   Create a new project in the usual manner.

2. Add a textbox object, three button objects, a label object, and a `ListBox` object. A sample interface is shown in Figure 8-12.

3. Add the code shown in Listing 8-4.

FIGURE 8-12: Sample program using an ArrayList object

The program has the user type in a name after which he clicks the Add button. This process can continue as long at the user wants. When he finishes, he can click the Show button to review the list of names he has entered.

LISTING 8-4: Using ArrayLists (frmMain.cs)

```
using System;
using System.Windows.Forms;
using System.Collections;

public class frmMain : Form
{
    ArrayList names = new ArrayList();

    private TextBox txtName;
    private Button btnAdd;
    private Button btnShow;
    private Button btnClose;
    private ListBox lstNames;
    private Label label1;

    #region Windows code

    public frmMain()
    {
        InitializeComponent();
    }

    public static void Main()
    {
```

continues

LISTING 8-4 *(continued)*

```
        frmMain main = new frmMain();
        Application.Run(main);
    }

    private void btnAdd_Click(object sender, EventArgs e)
    {
        if (txtName.Text.Length != 0)
        {
            names.Add(txtName.Text);      // Add new name
            txtName.Clear();              // Clear it out
            txtName.Focus();              // Get ready for another name
        }
        else
        {
            MessageBox.Show("Please enter a name.", "Input Error");
            return;
        }
    }

    private void btnShow_Click(object sender, EventArgs e)
    {
        foreach (string str in names)
        {
            lstNames.Items.Add(str);
        }
    }

    private void btnClose_Click(object sender, EventArgs e)
    {
        Close();
    }
}
```

How It Works

The first thing to notice in Listing 8-4 is that you must add a new `using` statement:

```
using System.Collections;
```

This new `using` statement is required because it is part of the `Collections` class and is not included in a program by default.

Inside the `frmMain` class, you find the statement

```
ArrayList names = new ArrayList();
```

This statement defines the `ArrayList` object used to hold the names entered by the user. I defined `names` outside any method so it has class scope. This means that `names` is visible at all points in the `frmMain` class. Even though the `ArrayList` is used like an array, no dimension size is associated with its definition.

All the work is done in the click event for the Add button:

```
private void btnAdd_Click(object sender, EventArgs e)
{
    if (txtName.Text.Length != 0)
    {
        names.Add(txtName.Text);    // Add new name
        txtName.Clear();            // Clear it out
        txtName.Focus();            // Get ready for another name
    }
    else
    {
        MessageBox.Show("Please enter a name.", "Input Error");
        return;
    }
}
```

The code simply checks to make sure the user typed in a name and then uses the Add() method of the ArrayList object to add the new name to the array list. The program then clears out the name that was just entered from the txtName textbox object and sets the focus back into the textbox object in preparation for another name. The user may continue this process until all names have been entered.

When the user finishes entering the names, he can click the Show button to view the list of names he just entered. The code in the Show() click event uses a foreach loop to iterate through the ArrayList object and add each name to the ListBox object. ArrayList objects make it easy to use dynamic arrays in a program.

Also note that ArrayList objects have most of the methods and properties shown in Table 8-1 available for you to use. For example, if you want to present the names in sorted order before displaying them in the listbox, just add the statement

```
names.Sort();
```

before the foreach loop, and the names display in ascending order.

If ArrayList objects enable you to create dynamic arrays, why would you ever use a static array? It's just like the old saying: "There's no such thing as a free lunch." The same holds true in programming. The dynamic behavior of ArrayList objects adds a fair amount of overhead to them, so they tend to consume more memory than static arrays for the same objects. This additional overhead also means there is a slight performance hit during processing for ArrayList objects compared to static arrays. Still, the ability to use an "undimensioned" array in a program adds sufficient flexibility that the ArrayList is a valuable tool to add to your toolkit.

SUMMARY

Arrays are a fundamental data structure in any programming language, and you should be comfortable with the concepts presented in this chapter before moving to Chapter 9.

You can find the answers to the following exercises in Appendix A.

1. A recent research study suggests that a person's ideal weight is related to his height in inches. It said that a person's ideal weight can be calculated from the following equations:

   ```
   Female = 3.5 * height (in inches) - 108
   
   Male = 4.0 * height (in inches) - 128
   ```

   Write a program that has the user enter a starting and ending height, calculates a table of ideal weights for males and females, and stores the results in an array. The program should then display the table in either a listbox or `ListView` object.

2. In what way are arrays of objects different from arrays of value types?

3. Write a program that stores 100 random values in an `int` array and then displays those values in a listbox. Have a Sort button that, when clicked, sorts the values and redisplays them in the listbox.

4. Modify the program you wrote for Exercise 3 so that it displays a bar graph for the data, as shown in Figure 8-13.

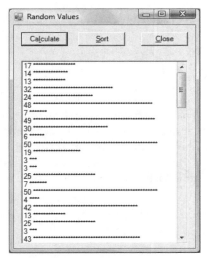

FIGURE 8-13: Textual bar graph

5. Given the following statements

```
string [] str1 = new string[100];
string[] temp;

str1[0] = "Hailey";
// Some more code
temp = str1;
```

What does the rvalue of `temp` equal?

▶ **WHAT YOU LEARNED IN THIS CHAPTER**

TOPIC	KEY POINTS
Array	What an array is and how they are different for value type versus reference types.
Array index versus array element	Why these two items are different and why that difference is important.
Array rank	How many dimensions an array has.
Jagged arrays	Not all arrays are symmetrical.
Array initialization	The different ways that arrays can be initialized.
Array class	What properties and methods are available.
Collections	How collections behave like arrays of objects.

PART III
Writing Your Own Classes

Designing Classes

WHAT YOU WILL LEARN IN THIS CHAPTER:

➤ What elements constitute good class design

➤ Scope

➤ The static storage class

➤ Access specifiers

➤ Class properties and methods

➤ Class components and writing style

➤ UML Light

➤ General versus helper methods

➤ User interfaces

WROX.COM CODE DOWNLOADS FOR THIS CHAPTER

You can find the wrox.com code downloads for this chapter at www.wrox.com/remtitle .cgi?isbn=9781118336922 on the Download Code tab. The code in the Chapter09 folder is individually named according to the names throughout the chapter.

Chapter 2 stated that classes are like cookie cutters, and that Visual Studio provides you with a room full of cookie cutters hanging on the wall that you can use. You have used many of those cookie cutters in the sample programs, including labels, textboxes, buttons, listboxes, and listview objects, all of which are extensions of the basic Windows Forms class. Up to this point, you've been writing code that uses those objects in a single class consistently named frmMain. It used this name because all the programs used a single class containing the Main() method that marks the starting point for all C# programs.

Well, it's time to cut the apron strings.

In this chapter, you learn how to make your own cookie cutters to hang on the wall. This chapter concentrates on the design considerations you need to think about to write "good" code for your own classes. A well-designed class becomes another cookie cutter that you can hang on the wall and use over and over in other programs. Poorly designed classes tend to become use-once-and-throw-away cookie cutters. Given that one of the major advantages of OOP is code reuse, you need to think about class design anytime the opportunity presents itself.

The next two chapters are probably the two most important chapters in this book because these two chapters reveal two of the major benefits to be derived from OOP: data encapsulation and code reuse.

CLASS DESIGN

This chapter creates a `clsDates` class as a reference point for learning about class design. You can add two methods to this class: a leap year method that's a little different from the method offered by the `DateTime` class and a `getEaster()` method to determine the date on which Easter falls. (Easter falls on a Sunday in either March or April, depending on the state of the lunar calendar.)

FIGURE 9-1: User interface for clsDates example

The first thing you need to do is create a project that serves as a test platform for the discussion of class design. As always, you begin by following the steps outlined in Chapter 2. This initial class is still called `frmMain` because it contains the `Main()` method that marks where program execution begins. The project name is `ClassDesign`. Figure 9-1 shows the user interface for the project.

The user enters the year of interest, and your program informs the user if it is a leap year and the date on which Easter falls. There are two labels below the buttons to display the output, `lblLeapYearResult` and `lblEasterResult`.

Next, let's walk through the steps necessary to add a class to a program. Although similar to adding a new form to a project, adding a class does not have a design element to it, which does make it a little different. Also, while I tend to treat a new class like any other object (i.e., lowercase for the first three letters), many programmers prefer to use an uppercase letter for the first letter of a class name. It's your choice, but again, use your choice consistently.

TRY IT OUT   Adding a Class to a Project (Chapter09ProgramClassDesign.zip)

Now create a project that uses a new class.

1.   Create a new project called ClassDesign in the usual manner.

2.   Use the Project ⇨ Add Class menu sequence (or Shift+Alt+C) and name the new class `clsDates`. (Visual Studio adds `.cs` for the second part of the filename.) See Figure 9-2.

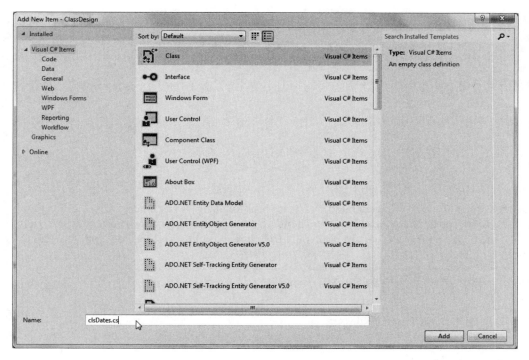

FIGURE 9-2: Adding a class to a project

Note how the Class template is selected and the new class name is filled in at the bottom of the form. Now click the Add button to add this new class to your project. Your Solution Explorer window should look like Figure 9-3.

There are several things to notice in Figure 9-3. First, the icon to the left of clsDates in the Solution Explorer window is different. Although class frmMain has a Windows form icon, clsDates uses an icon that looks like the C# logo. This is to reinforce that you just added a class to the project, *not* a new Windows form. Second, you can see that Visual Studio added two new references (System.XML and System.Data) to the project while you weren't looking. Although you won't explicitly use these references, you can simply ignore them for now.

How It Works

The project can be run at it stands, but it doesn't do anything. Although you could blindly add the code at this point and then consider how the program works, you need to take an important detour before moving to a discussion of how the program works. Although this detour is a deviation from normal sequencing, it makes sense to do so.

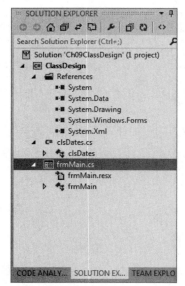

FIGURE 9-3: Solution Explorer window with new class

Scope

If you look in the Source window, you can see the following code for the new class:

```
using System;
using System.Collections.Generic;
using System.Text;

namespace ClassDesign
{
    class clsDates
    {
    }
}
```

This code stub was automatically generated by Visual Studio when you created clsDates. For purposes of discussion, the code for clsDates is expanded. *Do not make the code changes shown in Listing 9-1*. The code changes shown are done only to help you understand the concept of scope.

LISTING 9-1: Hypothetical clsDates source

```
using System;
using System.Collections.Generic;
using System.Text;

namespace ClassDesign
{

    class clsDates                                    // Namespace scope
    {
        int scopeClass;                               // Class scope

        public int MyFunction()
        {
            int scopeLocal;                           // Local scope

                                                      // Block scope
            for (int scopeBlock = 0; scopeBlock < 20; scopeBlock++)
            {
                // for statement block

            }       // End block scope

        }           // End local scope

    }               // End class scope

}                   // End namespace scope
```

The code in Listing 9-1 is not "real" code you are going to use. However, you can use Listing 9-1 to understand an important concept called scope. Earlier chapters mentioned scope a few times, but scope was never fully explained. That's about to change.

Simply stated, *scope* refers to the visibility and lifetime of a variable. As long as a variable is *in scope*, you have access to it and can use it in your code. If a variable is *out of scope*, it's as though the variable doesn't exist; you cannot use it in your program. Now investigate the concept of scope in greater detail starting from the "inside" of Listing 9-1.

Block Scope

Consider the definition of the variable `scopeBlock` in the following code:

```
                                        // Block scope
for (int scopeBlock = 0; scopeBlock < 20; scopeBlock++)
{
        // for statement block

}     // End block scope
```

When program control reaches the `for` loop shown in the preceding code, `expression1` of the `for` loop defines a variable named `scopeBlock`. At the moment of its definition, `scopeBlock` becomes available for use in the program. This means that `scopeBlock` is now in scope and can be used in your code. Stated another way, `scopeBlock` has begun its lifetime.

Now assume that the `for` loop has made 20 passes through the `for` loop statement block and program control is ready to execute whatever statement follows the closing brace of the `for` loop. Now here's the interesting part: When program control reaches the closing curly brace of the `for` loop, the variable `scopeBlock` ceases to exist in the program. Because the closing curly brace marks the end of the `for` loop and `scopeBlock` is defined within that `for` loop, `scopeBlock` is no longer available for use in the program. When the closing curly brace of the `for` loop is reached, `scopeBlock` goes out of scope and cannot be used.

> **NOTE** *The scope of a variable extends from its point of definition to the closing curly brace of the code block in which it is defined.*
>
> *It follows, then, that block scope extends from the point of definition of the variable to the closing curly brace of the statement block in which the variable is defined. If you'd like to prove the concept of block scope, make the following code changes in the* Main() *method in* frmMain *of your* ClassDates *program. The code changes are shown in Listing 9-2.*

LISTING 9-2: Code fragment illustrating block scope

```
public static void Main()
{
    int j = 1;

    frmMain main = new frmMain();
    Application.Run(main);
```

continues

LISTING 9-2 *(continued)*

```
        if (j == 1)
        {
            int i;      // defined with block scope
            i = 10;
            // pretend more code here manipulates i in some way...
        }               // End of if statement block
        j = i;          // Error will occur here
    }
```

Now try to compile the program. You can see the following error message:

```
The name 'i' does not exist in the current context
```

The code fails at the statement wherein the code attempts to assign variable i into j. The reason is that variable i has `block scope`. Variable i is defined within the `if` statement block, so its scope and lifetime extend from its point of definition within the `if` statement block to the closing brace of the `if` statement block. Because the assignment statement is outside the `if` statement block, variable i is no longer in scope and cannot be used, so Visual Studio must issue an error message.

Local Scope

Now move up the food chain and examine *local scope*. Local scope variables are defined within a method block, but outside a statement block. (Some programmers may refer to local scope as *method scope*.) Therefore, local scope extends from the variable's point of definition to the closing curly brace of the method in which the variable is defined. Variable j in Listing 9-2 is an example of a local scope variable. Variable j comes into scope at its point of definition within the method named Main(). Variable j goes out of scope and ceases to exist when program control reaches the closing brace for the Main() method in Listing 9-2.

You should see that variable scopeLocal in Listing 9-1 has local scope. When program control reaches the closing brace in Listing 9-1, variable scopeLocal is no longer in scope and can no longer be used in the program:

```
    }       // End local scope
```

Local scope variables can be used within a statement block, but the reverse is not true. That is, block scope variables cannot be used outside of the statement block in which they are defined, but local scope variables can be used within any statement blocks that are within the same method.

Class Scope

You have probably figured this out already, but plow through it anyway. Variables with *class scope* are those that are defined within a class, but outside of a method. (Some programmers refer to class scope as *module scope*.) Class scope makes the variable accessible at all points in the class. Variable scopeClass in Listing 9-1 is an example of a class scope variable. Class scope subsumes both method and statement block scope. This means that a variable with class scope can be used at both the method and statement block levels of scope. If you think about it, variables with class scope are the properties of the class. Methods in the class always have class scope.

Namespace Scope

Namespace scope applies to any variable defined within the current namespace. Near the top of Listing 9-1 you can find the following statement:

```
namespace ClassDesign
{
```

You can tell from this statement that the current project under development is named `ClassDesign`. Because the project is named `ClassDesign`, it also means that, if you want to do so, you can reference the program's entry point as the following:

```
ClassDesign.frmMain.Main();
```

Every program you have written thus far has a `frmMain.Main()` method. Think how confusing it would be to invoke the correct `frmMain.Main()` method if you didn't know which project you were referencing. One of the primary reasons for namespace scope is to prevent name collisions for classes and methods that exist within multiple namespaces. If two programs both have a `clsDatabase` class in them, you can apply the correct namespace to use the correct class from the project you want to use. That means you can have `JonesProject.clsDatabase.ReadOneRecord()` and `SmithsProject.clsDatabase.ReadOneRecord()`, and the two `ReadOneRecord()` methods will remain distinct from one another even though they share the same class name. Namespace scope subsumes all program elements (such as variables, classes, and methods) within the current project and makes it possible to distinguish program elements that may share a common name.

Visualizing Scope

If you're into imagery, try to imagine a tall ladder that spans several platforms, like the one shown in Figure 9-4. Place yourself and several friends on the ground at the bottom of the ladder. The only weird thing is that none of you can look up higher than eye level. This is block scope. You can see and interact with your friends provided you are all defined within the same statement block. In the figure, data items with block scope have a field of vision (FOV) that includes only those items with block scope.

Now, climb up the ladder to the second platform. You look around to see some more of your friends on the local scope platform. You can go to the edge of the platform, look down, and see your friends below you as well as those on the same platform. The only difference is that your friends below you can no longer see or interact with you because they can't look up. Because you are now at a higher scope level, you can interact with them only if you climb down the ladder to join them at their *statement block scope level*. That is, any statement that involves you and has local scope must occur within the statement block that defines the statement block variable. For example, if you are variable x with local scope and you have a friend named i with block scope, the statement

```
x = i;
```

can occur only if you climb back down the ladder to interact with variable i in his statement block. This means the statement must occur within the statement block where i lives. Otherwise, the statement cannot occur because i can exist only within its own statement block. In terms of Listing 9-2, you can interact with variable i only if you place the assignment statement within the if statement block. Therefore, variables with local scope have a field of vision that includes data items with both local and block scope but can interact with block scope items only within those items' statement block.

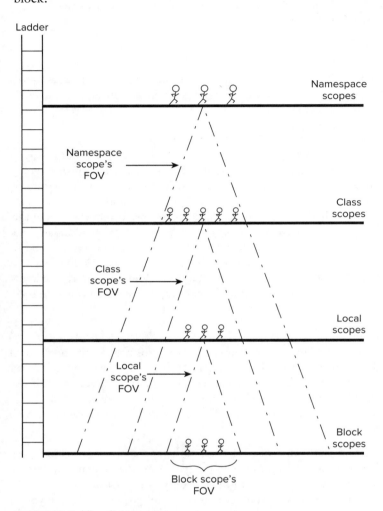

FIGURE 9-4: Visualizing scope

Now climb even higher to the class scope platform. Again, you have friends at this scope level with whom you can interact directly. Looking below you, you can see both your local and statement block friends, but to interact with them, you must climb down the ladder to their levels. That is, for you to interact with local variables, any statement involving you must take place within the method in which your local block friend is defined, or the statement block within which your block scope friend is defined. Notice how the FOV for class scope includes data items defined with both local and block scope.

Finally, climb up to the highest platform. Again you can see some new friends at this level (such as global data items), but looking down you can see everything! All data items in the program are visible to you. To interact with them, however, still means you must climb down to their levels because they cannot look up and see you. Suppose you are a variable with namespace scope. To interact with variable i in Listing 9-2, you must climb all the way down the ladder to make yourself present within the if statement block where variable i exists.

Why Does C# Support Scope?

Most modern (and all OOP) languages support the concept of scope. This support is an attempt to minimize the unwanted interaction effects that can occur among data items in a program. Consider what might happen if you were using a language that didn't support scope. In such languages, all variables behave like namespace variables. Suppose a variable named x starts behaving badly and has a value it shouldn't have. Without scope, where do you start looking for the cause of the weird value for x? The entire program is the playing field because x is visible everywhere throughout the program. Any element of the program could be messing around with x, and you don't have a clue where it is being contaminated. Debugging such a problem becomes a hit-or-miss proposition, and it's only by chance that you finally locate the bug. Systematic debugging under such circumstances goes out the window and finding and correcting the bug becomes more an issue of luck, incantations, and eye of newt.

With data items that are scoped, the magnitude of the problem shrinks immensely. If x is a variable defined with block scope, clearly something is messing around with x in the statement block where it is defined. After all, x cannot live outside the block in which it's defined when it has block scope. In a large program with 3,000 lines of code, you can immediately eliminate almost all 3,000 lines and concentrate on the relatively few lines of code that form x's statement block.

If x is defined with local scope, you can still eliminate thousands of lines of code because only the code within the method in which x is defined comes into play. Although a local scope variable is likely in scope for a larger number of code lines than a block scope variable, it's still a lot better than no scope at all.

As you climb the scope ladder in Figure 9-4, more lines of code come into play, offering more places for x to get messed up. (This is because of the widening FOV.) Because more lines must be considered as a variable's scope widens, debugging becomes more difficult. For that reason, your program design should try to work with data at the narrowest scope level possible that still makes sense for the task at hand. The process to isolate the data in a program is called *encapsulation*, one of the cornerstones of object-oriented programming. Although it may be easier to slap a program design together with little or no thought about scope or encapsulation, you'll pay for it in the long run with more debugging and maintenance time.

Think Before You Write

The lesson to learn: Take the time to *think* about program design before you start writing. I cannot begin to tell you how many times he's given an in-class programming assignment only to have the students immediately start banging on the keyboards and dragging-and-dropping objects onto a form. As I watch the students, there's usually one or two who sit in their seats either doodling something on a piece of scratch paper, or perhaps they just stare at the ceiling. In a few minutes, they eventually start writing their programs. The great thing is that these doodlers and ceiling-watchers almost always finish their programs before the rest of the class and generally have better program solutions. The reason? The time they spend doodling or ceiling-watching is actually spent creating a program design.

Many students confuse simple movement with problem solving. That is, they think that because they are dragging and dropping textbox and label objects onto a form that they are working toward the program solution. However, as they get into the problem, it's not uncommon to see them remove the objects they originally thought they needed and replace them with something else—lots of movement, but no useful work. Such students would be miles ahead if they had just taken a few minutes to think through the problem and come up with a design first, *before* they did anything else.

So...how *do* you design a program? This is exactly what you want to examine in the rest of this chapter.

DESIGNING A PROGRAM

Perhaps the most difficult task a new programmer faces is knowing where to start when designing a program. Every program is a little different, so each design must be a little different. Given that, where's the best place to start?

Although it is true that programs are different, you already know that all programs have at least one thing in common: the Five Program Steps. With that in mind, return to the clsDates program that you started at the beginning of the chapter. The goal of the program is to write a class that can determine the date of Easter and tell you whether the year in question is a leap year. Now see how you can use the Five Program Steps as a starting point for your design.

The Five Program Steps

Assume that the user interface shown in Figure 9-1 is good enough for the program. Under that assumption, examine the Five Program Steps from a design-perspective.

Initialization Step

For this program, about the only thing the Initialization step needs to do is properly initialize the objects you've placed on the frmMain form and display that form on the screen. Listing 9-3 shows the frmMain code as it currently exists after you've followed the instructions at the beginning of the chapter.

LISTING 9-3: The clsDates test code. (frmMain.cs)

```
using System;
using System.Windows.Forms;

public class frmMain : Form
{
    private TextBox txtYear;
    private Button btnCalc;
    private Button btnClose;
```

```
private Label lblLeapYearResult;
private Label lblEasterResult;
private Label label1;
#region Windows code

private void InitializeComponent()
{
    // Windows initialization code for frmMain form
}

#endregion

public frmMain()                    // Constructor
{
    InitializeComponent();
}

public static void Main()
{
    frmMain main = new frmMain();   // Programs starts here
    Application.Run(main);
}
}
```

When the program starts executing, you already know that the origin for its execution is with the method named Main(). Within Main(), the statement

```
frmMain main = new frmMain();   // Programs starts here
```

says that the first thing the program does is create an instance of an object of the frmMain class and name it main. To create the object named main, the program must first call the method named frmMain(). As you learned in Chapter 5, any method that shares the same name as the class in which it is defined is the constructor for that class. If you look at the frmMain() constructor in Listing 9-3, you can see that it calls a method named InitializeComponent(). Actually, you have been using these exact code lines for every program you've written, beginning with your first program in Chapter 1.

The purpose of the InitializeComponent() method is to enable Windows to re-create the form that you built while you were dragging and dropping objects onto the empty form. The only difference is that Windows is now rebuilding that form in memory so that it can launch your program. If you look at the code that hides between the #region and #endregion directives, you can see the details about how your form is rebuilt each time you run the program.

After that form is built in memory, control eventually returns to Main() and executes the following statement:

```
Application.Run(main);
```

When the Run() method is executed, Windows displays the form image for the frmMain class as it is currently stored in memory, and the screen now looks like Figure 9-1. At this point the Initialization step is complete, and the program waits for the user to do something.

Input Step

Only two inputs are needed from the user running the program: The year and a click of the Calculate button. Assume that the user types in 2012 for the year and clicks the Calculate button. At that point, program control enters the btnCalc_Click() event method. After program control enters that method, the program needs to convert the textual data for the year into a numeric data type and assign its value into a variable. Because the program needs only the year entered by the user and a click of the Calculate button, the Input step is simple.

Process Step

If all goes well, the program now needs to call another method that takes the value for the year entered by the user and determines the date for Easter. Having done that, the program needs to call yet another method to determine if that year is a leap year. You can assume that the date for Easter is returned to you as a string and that the leap year value is returned as an int.

Display Step

The display requirements are simple: Fill in the Text property of the two label objects on the form with the information from the Process step.

Termination Step

Because the program hasn't done anything tricky or used any special resources that you need to clean up after, you can simply call the Close() method to end the program.

You can diagram the state of your current design, as shown in Figure 9-5.

If you examine Figure 9-5, it should be clear that everything you've done can be placed within the confines of the frmMain class. That is, the Initialization step sets up the way you want the form to look, the Input step uses the form to collect the input(s) from the user, the Process step converts the data into the wanted answers, the Display step shows the results to the user, and the Termination step simply ends the program. Now, think about the steps shown in Figure 9-5 and how they work.

```
Initialization Step
    Main( ) → frmMain( ) → InitializeComponent( )
    Run (Main)
Input Step
    bfnCalc_Click( )
    Convert text to year
Process Step
    String Easterday = getEaster(Year);
    int Leap = getLeapYear(Year);
Display Step
    lblEasterResult.Text = easterDay;
    lblLeapYearResult.Text = Leap;
Termination Step
    Close( ):
```

FIGURE 9-5: Current program design

Look at the Forest, Not Just the Trees

In a sense, all the steps are tied to the frmMain class, except the Processing step. That is, all the steps except the Processing step interact with visual components represented on the form frmMain. Only the Processing step has nothing that relates directly to the visual representation or objects of the frmMain form. This means that, if you want to, you can totally isolate the Process step from the visual state of the form. All the Process step needs to function properly is a variable that stores the year. Given that fact, you should ask yourself, "Will I ever, in my programming lifetime, need to reuse a method that can figure out the date for Easter in a given year or whether that year is a leap year?" If you think this answer might be yes, you should consider writing the code for the Process step as a method in a separate class. Why?

One of the driving forces behind OOP is code reuse. If you can write the code once and use it many times in the future, why reinvent the wheel each time you need to accomplish the same task? Although it may take a tiny bit more effort in the short run, the benefits can be huge in the long run. You need to view writing a new class as an investment in the future. Invest a little work time now to get more free time down the road. A side benefit is that debugging programs that are class-based is often easier than if all the code is crammed into `frmMain`.

Think about how some of those 4,000 cookie cutters that Microsoft wrote have simplified things for you so far. How much more difficult would the programming examples in this book have been if you had to personally rewrite the code that creates a textbox, a label, and button objects for every program? You'd still be back in Chapter 2! Having the ability to use those objects without writing their code has saved you countless hours of typing and debugging time.

Because you just may want to reuse the Easter and leap year methods at some point in the future, you implement those methods as part of a new class named `clsDates`.

UML LIGHT

The Unified Modeling Language (UML) is a standardized specification language for modeling objects. It evolved from a joint effort by James Rumbaugh, Grady Booch, and Ivar Jacobson in the 1990s. Entire volumes have been written on UML, and there is no way that to do justice to it here. Still, you can make use of a small subset of UML called a *UML class diagram*. This is a visual representation of the parts that comprise a class. Rather than use all the features of UML class diagrams, you use only a small subset, hence the term *UML Light*. (Don't bother Googling "UML Light"...the author made up the term a long time ago.)

Figure 9-6 shows the general format for a UML class diagram.

A UML class diagram may be viewed as three stacked boxes. The top box holds the name of the class (in this case `clsDates`). This is the name you see on the cookie cutter when it's hanging on the wall. Below the class name box is a box that describes the properties of the class. (Other OOP languages might refer to these properties as *class members* or *class attributes*.) The third box describes the methods that this particular class supports. (The latest version of UML supports a fourth box that describes how the class is *persisted*, or permanently stored, in a disk data file or a database. The light version ignores this fourth box.)

Access Specifiers

The first line in the properties box contains the following line:

```
- year : int
```

The minus sign at the beginning of the line is used as a symbol to represent the access specifier for this particular property. Only two possible access specifiers are discussed here: `private` and `public`. Both of these access specifiers are keywords in C#. The keyword `private` means that this property can be accessed only from outside the class by using its property methods. (The discussion of an object's property methods is deferred until Chapter 10.) The minus sign in Figure 9-6 is a UML symbol for the keyword `private` in C#.

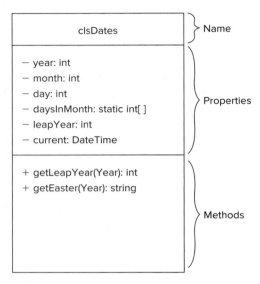

FIGURE 9-6: Using UML Light

You can also define a property using the `public` keyword. The keyword `public` means that the property is directly accessible without the need to use the object's property methods. The UML symbol for the `public` keyword is the plus sign.

The minus sign appears at the beginning of the line before the word `year`. The word `year` is the name you want to give to this particular class property. Following the property name is a colon (:). The colon simply serves to separate the property name from the type specifier for the property. In this case, the type specifier is `int`. This means that `year` is an `int` data type. The entire line tells you quite a bit about the property. That is, `year` is an integer property of the `clsDates` class and uses the `private` access specifier.

In Figure 9-6, you can see that all the properties use the `private` access specifier. There are good reasons for using this specifier, as you see shortly. For now, simply think of the `private` access specifier as affording more protection for the properties than does the `public` access specifier. In a sense, the `private` access specifier encapsulates a variable within its class and protects it from contamination by the outside world.

Access Specifiers and Scope

The properties of a class have class scope by default. This means that the class property variables are visible at all points within the class from their points of definition to the closing brace of the class code. The *default access specifier* for class properties is `private`. Class scope also means that class property variables do *not* have namespace scope. For example, if you define the property year according to the specification shown in Figure 9-6, it appears in `clsDates` as the following statement:

```
int year;
```

Because the `private` access specifier is the default storage class, what you are writing is

```
private int year;
```

Now suppose you create an object named `myDate` of `clsDates` in `frmMain`. As things currently stand, you might try this statement:

```
myDate.year = 2008;
```

Visual Studio gets upset and tells you:

```
ClassDesign.clsDates.year' is inaccessible due to its protection level
```

This is Visual Studio's way to tell you that `year` is not in scope. In other words, the `private` access specifier you gave to `year` in the `clsDates` class affords it some level of protection from the evil forces that lurk in the outside world. Again, the `private` access specifier means the variable `year` is only visible in `clsDates`, not `frmMain`.

Now change the definition of `year` in `clsDates` to

```
public int year;
```

and try to compile the program. Visual Studio no longer gets upset. The reason is that you have done away with the data protection afforded by the `private` keyword. Now anyone with a `clsDates` object is free to change `year` to any value she wants, and there's nothing you can do about it. Not good.

By defining the class property data with the `private` access specifier, you are acting like the smart medieval king who locks his valuable possessions (data) in the castle keep. Because you have the key to the tower, you control who has access to the possessions and they must play by your rules. On the other hand, if you define class properties with the `public` access specifier, you might as well make a thousand copies of the key and leave them hanging on the gate next to the moat. Outsiders no longer have to play by your rules and can change things as they see fit...also not good.

In summary, the `private` access specifier reinforces the OOP design goal to encapsulate data. Although there may be some technical reasons to argue for using the `public` access specifier, those reasons are few and far between. As a general rule, use the `private` access specifier for all property data.

The static Keyword

What does the line

```
- daysInMonth : static int[]
```

mean? The word `static` is a C# keyword that conveys information about how something is stored in computer memory. In this case, you can verbalize the line like this: "`daysInMonth` is a `private` integer array that uses the `static` storage class." The brackets after the `int` keyword tell you that `daysInMonth` is an integer array. The keyword `static` means several things, but the most important is that, regardless of how many instances of this class you create in a program, storage is reserved by the Windows Memory Manager for only one array named `daysInMonth`.

For example, suppose you write a program that, for some reason, needs a million objects of the `clsDates` type. Each one of those objects gets its own copy of the `year`, `month`, `day`, `leapYear`, and `current` properties shown in Figure 9-6. However, all the million objects share a single instance of the `daysInMonth` array. Why only one copy? Well...are you *really* going to redefine how many days there are in a month? I don't think so. Because there is no good reason to have more than one instance of the array, you can save several million bytes of storage by defining it only once and letting all the other instances share its data.

As you see later in the chapter, the `daysInMonth` array stores a count of how many days each month has in it, as in 31, 28, 31, 30, and so on. Because these monthly counts aren't likely to change anytime soon, there's no reason to create multiple copies of the array. Such an array is just a read-only array because there is no conceivable reason to change these values. Therefore, because no object ever has a need to change the content of the array, there's no reason to duplicate it. The needs of the program for the content of the array are such that each class object can share this data.

Another thing about `static` data items: They are created the moment the program is loaded. You may not have noticed that the method `Main()` uses the `static` storage class. This means that a copy of that method exists the moment the program is loaded into memory. If you think about it, this makes sense. After all, if the program didn't immediately create a copy of the `Main()` method when it loaded, how would you ever get the program to start executing? You need the `Main()` method to get the program running.

As a general design rule, you should use the `static` keyword with any data that can safely be shared between instances of the class, or any data that must be present the moment the program is ready to start executing. You can apply the `static` access specifier to methods with the same effect.

UML Methods

The interpretation of the UML class method entries is similar to that of its properties. Consider this entry:

```
+ getLeapYear(year) : int
```

It states that the `getLeapYear()` method is a `public` method (+) that is passed one argument named `year` and that returns an `int` data type value. The interpretation for `getEaster()` is similar, except that it returns a `string` value to the caller.

Design Intent and Access Specifiers for Methods

Like class properties, class methods may use either `public` (+) or `private` (-) access specifiers. The interpretation of `public` methods is similar to that for `public` properties. However, the *intent* of a `public` access specifier for a method is different from that for a class property. Class properties are data and, as a general rule, you want to hide the class data as much as possible. Again, data hiding is the basis for encapsulation and one of the real benefits of OOP. Class methods, however, are different.

public Methods

Most class methods are designed to perform one specific task on one or more pieces of data. (A common fault of beginning students is to write methods that are the equivalent of a Swiss Army knife. Methods are not multitaskers. They should be designed to perform one task and do that task well.) Quite often, those pieces of data come from the class properties. Given that class methods are used to manipulate the class data, it seems reasonable to assume that the programmer using the class wants access to that newly transformed data. For example, in a few moments you are going to write a class method that returns the value 1 if a year is a leap year or 0 if it is not. You are writing the method so that whoever calls that method knows whether the year he passed to the method is a leap year. Clearly, you want to make that result known outside the class. Therefore, you would write the `getLeapYear()` method using the `public` access specifier.

All elements of a class that you give the `public` access specifier become part of the *user (or public) interface* for the class. That is, you purposely are designing properties and methods using the `public` access specifier specifically because you want the outside world to have access to them. As mentioned earlier, I take a dim view of `public` properties. However, I am thrilled about `public` methods. The reason for the disparity is that you want to hide the data (that is, the properties) but make the class useful via the `public` class methods and the functionality those class methods bring to the party.

Sometimes you hear the term *class API*. This refers to the class Application Programming Interface. Therefore, a class API refers to all the elements of the class that use the `public` access specifier. This makes sense if you think about it because the only way the outside world can interact with a class is through its `public` properties and methods.

private (Helper) Methods

Just as a class can have `public` methods, it can also use `private` class methods. By definition, `private` class methods cannot be part of the class API. If the method is `private`, it has class scope and is not visible outside the class in which it is defined.

You're probably asking, "If `private` class methods cannot be accessed outside the class itself, what use are they?" Good question, and it's best answered with an example.

Suppose you collect personal data about people for use in an electronic phone book application you're writing. You decide to collect each person's home phone number as well as his cell and work phone numbers. You know that people often make mistakes when entering numbers, so you want to verify that the numbers they entered for each phone number uses a valid format. Now you have a design choice. You can duplicate your validation code three times, once for each phone number type, or you can write a single method named `validatePhoneNumber()` and call it when it is needed. Hmmm…which is a better decision? Write three times as much code and then test and debug it three times, or write the code once and test and debug just that version once? Seems like a no-brainer.

The `validatePhoneNumber()` method exists in the class to make your job of verifying phone numbers easier. Any class method that simply makes your job easier and that you do not want to make part of the class API should be defined using the `private` access specifier. Quite often, such `private` class methods are called *Helper methods* because they are in the class to make your work as a programmer easier and *do not* form part of the class API that you expose to the outside world.

Class Property and Method Names

When you design a class, you have a lot of freedom for what you name your properties and methods. Obviously, you cannot use C# keywords for names, but just about everything else is fair game. (The rules for naming classes are the same as for naming variables.) Given that freedom, does it matter what names you give to your properties and methods? Obviously, the names you use within a class do matter or you wouldn't need this section of the chapter. Consider the following class-naming conventions as you design your classes.

Use Lowercase Letters for Property Names

First, start the names of your properties with lowercase letters. The full explanation for this decision is deferred until Chapter 10. The brief explanation is that using lowercase letters enables you to implement a naming convention that is common to many C# programmers.

> **NOTE** Microsoft has naming conventions and style that are different than that presented here. While I have my reasons for the style presented here, you can review Microsoft's conventions at http://msdn.microsoft.com/en-us /library/x2dbyw72%28v=vs.71%29.aspx.

Hint as to Their Functions

Second, select names for your API methods that give a hint as to what their functions are. For example, the method name SortData() seems like a good choice, until you realize that the class contains more than one piece of data. A better name might be SortZipCodes() because that name gives a better idea of what's about to happen. If you need to sort all the class data based upon the ZIP codes, you might name that method SortAllDataByZip(). Using functional names makes it easier to recall what each method does when IntelliSense presents you with a list of the method names available in a class.

Use Action Names for API Methods

Third, because most API class methods interact with the class data, method names often imply an action of some kind and hence are verb-based. For example, SortZipCodes() implies an active change in the ZIP code data from its current state to a sorted state. CalculateSaleTaxDue() might be a method in a company sales package that changes the salesTaxDue property of the class. By contrast, an API method Name() doesn't provide any clue about what the method does, only that it likely has something to do with the names data. A better choice would be getClientName() because that suggests what the method does.

API Method Names Should Be Implementation-Neutral

Fourth, the API class methods should *not* reflect how the functionality of the methods is implemented. I have seen code in which two API methods were named SearchLeftTreeNode() and SearchRightTreeNode(). It doesn't take much imagination to figure out that the programmer who wrote the class is probably using a binary tree to search for something. Now suppose that some bright propeller-head somewhere develops a new, superfast searching algorithm and you want to implement it in your code. Do you change the API class names to reflect the new algorithm, or do you leave them as they are? If you change the API method names, older versions of the code will break because those methods are no longer in the class. If you don't change the names, you're sort of lying about what the methods do to anyone who uses your class. This is a dilemma: two choices, both bad. The solution is to never use an implementation-based name.

Programmers search binary trees because they want to find something, and the API method name should reflect that fact. For example, if the binary tree search is performed using the client's ID number to find the client's demographic data, a better API method name would be getClientData(). This API method name says nothing about *how* you accomplish a task. To the outside world, your API class methods should appear to be black boxes: The user doesn't need to know the specific type of magic that produces a result, only that the magic works. Implementation-neutral method names enable you to change the *way* you accomplish a task without making you feel guilty the next morning. This lack of guilt is the result of the method name being implementation-neutral and making no promises about how things are done within the method.

Think Like a User

One more aspect of class design is to think like the user who ultimately uses the properties and methods of your class. (The user in this sense is a programmer, not someone who runs the program.) For example, in a few moments you see the code for the clsDates class. One of the properties in that class is defined as follows:

```
private static int[] daysInMonth = { 0, 31, 28, 31, 30, 31, 30, 31,
                                     31, 30, 31, 30, 31};
```

If you look at the initialization data for the daysInMonth array, it's obvious that the values reflect the number of days in each month. However, closer inspection shows that the first element of the array is 0. Why?

The reason is the way people think, as was mentioned in Chapter 8. If you ask people how many days there are in month one (that is, January) of a year, few are going to say 28. That is the answer you get, however, if the user of the class passes you the value 1 in a method that is supposed to return the number of days in a given month. True, you can always recall the N – 1 Rule and adjust the value users pass to you when you index into the array. But you too are a "people," and you probably think the same way your user thinks. Debugging a method is easier if the data is organized to match the way you think about the data. Yes … you wasted 4 bytes. Big deal. When each computer now comes with a mega-munch of memory, frittering away 4 bytes is not going to make or break the application. Also, the time you save working with logically organized data pays for itself in reduced testing and debugging time.

The lesson is simple: Organize your data in a way that makes sense to you (and to any others who may have to support your code).

THE CLSDATES DESIGN

Now use some of your design ideas to implement the design for clsDates. The code for clsDates is shown in Listing 9-4.

LISTING 9-4: clsDates source code (clsDates.cs)

```csharp
using System;
using System.Collections.Generic;
using System.Text;

public class clsDates
{
    // =============== symbolic constants ==================

    // =============== static members =====================
    private static int[] daysInMonth = { 0, 31, 28, 31, 30, 31, 30, 31,
                                          31, 30, 31, 30, 31};

    // =============== instance members (Properties) =====================
    private int day;
    private int month;
    private int year;
    private int leapYear;

    private DateTime current;

    // =============== constructor(s) =====================

    public clsDates()
    {
        current = DateTime.Now; // Sets DateTime to right now
    }
    // =============== property methods =====================

    // =============== helper methods =====================

    // =============== general methods =====================

    /*****
     * Purpose: To determine if the year is a leap year. Algorithm
     *          taken from C Programmer's Toolkit, Purdum, Que Corp.,
     *          1993, p. 258.
     *
     * Parameter list:
     *    int year       the year under consideration
     *
     * Return value:
     *    int            1 if a leap year, 0 otherwise
     *****/

    public int getLeapYear(int year)
    {
        if (year % 4 == 0 && year % 100 != 0 || year % 400 == 0)
            return 1;    // It is a leap year
        else
            return 0;    // Nope.
    }
```

```
/*****
 * Purpose: To determine the date for Easter given a year. Algorithm
 *          taken from C Programmer's Toolkit, Purdum, Que Corp.,
 *          1993, p. 267.
 *
 * Parameter list:
 *    int year       the year under consideration
 *
 * Return value:
 *    string         the date in MM/DD/YYYY format
 *****/
public string getEaster(int year)
{
    int offset;
    int leap;
    int day;
    int temp1;
    int temp2;
    int total;

    offset = year % 19;
    leap = year % 4;
    day = year % 7;
    temp1 = (19 * offset + 24) % 30;
    temp2 = (2 * leap + 4 * day + 6 * temp1 + 5) % 7;
    total = (22 + temp1 + temp2);
    if (total > 31)
    {
        month = 4;              // Easter is in April...
        day = total - 31;    // ...on this day
    }
    else
    {
        month = 3;              // Easter is in March...
        day = total;          // ...on this day
    }
    DateTime myDT = new DateTime(year, month, day);
    return myDT.ToLongDateString();
}
}
```

namespace Modifier

If you look closely at Listing 9-4, you'll notice that I removed the following (default) statements from the clsDates code:

```
namespace ClassDesign
    {
    }
```

Why? The reason is that you want your clsDates class to be usable in other programs you might develop, without your having to use the project's namespace as part of the class hierarchy.

For example, if you leave the namespace lines in and you want to create an object named `myDate`, you must define it with the following statement if the class is from a different namespace:

```
ClassDesign.clsDates myDate = new ClassDesign.clsDates();
```

This syntax seems a little cumbersome. By removing the namespace statements in `clsDates`, you can define the object with this statement:

```
clsDates myDate = new clsDates();
```

This syntax structure is more commonly employed even though there might be a small risk of namespace collision with another class that might use `clsDates` as a class name. If you want to leave the namespace in as part of the class definition, that's fine. Just remember to supply the complete hierarchy when you define an object of the class.

Class Organization

In Listing 9-4 you can see how I've added comments to section off various parts of the class. Those parts are (from top to bottom):

➤ Symbolic constants

➤ `static` members of the class

➤ Instance members

➤ Constructors

➤ Property methods

➤ Helper methods

➤ General methods

There is nothing etched in stone about this organization for a class. It is, however, an organizational structure that has worked for me in my writing of commercial applications over the years. A few comments about the organization are warranted.

static Data Versus Instance Members

Notice the division of the properties into those that are `static` and those that are not. As mentioned earlier in this chapter, `static` data are created at program load time. This means that, even if the program never gets to a point in which it defines a `clsDates` object, the `daysInMonth` array always exists in memory. Also recall that no matter how many objects of `clsDates` are created, they all share the same `daysInMonth` array. For those two reasons, place `static` data in its own category.

Instance members is the common term for all the non-`static` properties of the class. Instance members are those class properties that are created for each object instantiated from the class. Simply stated, each instance of the class gets its own set of the (non-`static`) class properties, hence the term *instance members*.

Property and Helper Methods

Set these methods off by themselves for reasons explained more completely in Chapter 10. Also, keep the code in the current example simple.

General Methods

The general methods are those methods that become part of your API for the class. As such, all general methods are written using the `public` access specifier.

General Method Headers

For nontrivial general methods, usually supply a header for the method using the following style, as was shown in Listing 9-4:

```
/*****
 * Purpose: To determine if the year is a leap year. Algorithm
 *          taken from C Programmer's Toolkit, Purdum, Que Corp.,
 *          1993, p. 258.
 *
 * Parameter list:
 *    int year      the year under consideration
 *
 * Return value:
 *    int           1 if a leap year, 0 otherwise
 *****/
public string getEaster(int year)
{
```

The header for a method simply states the purpose of the method, the parameter list of data that is passed to it (if any), and the return data type (if any). If the method uses code based on some special algorithm and you think you may want to refer back to it, place that reference in the method header. Note that I use multiple-line comment characters to block off the header.

If you enforce this structure in your programming team's code, you can use it to create class documentation on-the-fly. That is, you can write a program that examines the source code files looking for the sequence /*****. You can then copy the text that follows that sequence into a disk data file, ending the copy process when you read one additional line after the sequence *****/. The additional line is copied to get the signature for the method. When you finish reading all the program source code, you end up with a file that you can print, documenting each method in the source code. In the following Try It Out you see how all the parts fit together by writing a program that exercises the clsDates code.

TRY IT OUT   The clsDates Programs

Now that you've written the code for the clsDates class, write the code for a form that can test the class. A sample run was shown earlier in Figure 9-1. Also, you have already created the project and added the necessary class file to the project. So all that you need at this point is a more detailed explanation of how the code works.

How It Works

The code for the frmMain class is shown in Listing 9-5.

LISTING 9-5: Test program for clsDates. (frmMain.cs)

```csharp
using System;
using System.Windows.Forms;

public class frmMain : Form
{
    private TextBox txtYear;
    private Button btnCalc;
    private Button btnClose;
    private Label lblLeapYearResult;
    private Label lblEasterResult;
    private Label label1;
    #region Windows code

    public frmMain()
    {
        InitializeComponent();
    }

    public static void Main()
    {
        frmMain main = new frmMain();
        Application.Run(main);
    }

    private void btnCalc_Click(object sender, EventArgs e)
    {
        bool flag;
        int year;
        int leap;
        clsDates myDate = new clsDates();

        // Convert validate integer
        flag = int.TryParse(txtYear.Text, out year);
        if (flag == false)
        {
            MessageBox.Show("Digit characters only in YYYY format.",
                            "Input Error");
            txtYear.Focus();
            return;
        }
        leap = myDate.getLeapYear(year);
        lblLeapYearResult.Text = year.ToString() + " is " +
                ((leap == 1)? "":"not ") + "a leap year";
        lblEasterResult.Text = myDate.getEaster(year);
    }

    private void btnClose_Click(object sender, EventArgs e)
```

```
    {
        Close();
    }
}
```

There isn't much in Listing 9-5 that you haven't seen before. Notice the definition of `myDate`:

```
clsDates myDate = new clsDates();
```

Because you removed the namespace attribute from the `clsDates` code, you can instantiate the `myDate` object by simply using the class name. The `TryParse()` and `if` statement block converts the text stored in the `Text` property of the `txtYear` object into an integer and assigns it into a variable named `year`. The statement

```
leap = myDate.getLeapYear(year);
```

calls the general method named `getLeapYear()` in the `clsDates` class, returns either 1 (a leap year) or 0 (not a leap year), and assigns this value into `leap`.

Why didn't I write `getLeapYear()` to return a `bool` that returns `true` for a leap year and `false` otherwise? After all, that's the way Microsoft wrote the code and those guys are smart. So, why the difference? As mentioned before, the reason is that programmers frequently use a leap year calculation to determine the number of days in February for a given year. This enables you to write code like this:

```
int februaryDays = 28;
// Some code. . .
februaryDays += myDate.getLeapYear(year);
```

If you make the code return a `bool`, you cannot use this kind of statement. Returning 1 or 0 better suits the way programmers frequently use leap year calculations. (The nice thing about writing the class yourself is that you can change the code if you want.) If you type in

```
leap = myDate.
```

IntelliSense is smart enough to present you with a list of methods defined in the `clsDates` class. (Note the trailing dot operator. In the next chapter, you learn how to have the properties appear in the list as well.)

The next statement is used to build a message string stating whether the year is a leap year:

```
lblLeapYearResult.Text = year.ToString() + " is " +
          ((leap == 1)? "":"not ") + "a leap year";
```

That message string is then assigned into the `Text` property of the `lblLeapYearResult` label object. Quite honestly, this statement is an example of SOC, or *Show-Off Code*. It uses the ternary operator to determine how the message string is built. If you study the code for a moment, you should figure out how it works. However, you could also use an `if` statement and accomplish the same thing. (You didn't study the code, did you? If not, go back and study it...now!)

The last statement in the click event simply calls `getEaster()` and writes the string that is returned from the call into the `Text` property of the `lblEasterResult` object. Note how easy it was to create this string in the `getEaster()` code in `clsDates`:

```
DateTime myDT = new DateTime(year, month, day);
return myDT.ToLongDateString();
```

Just two lines of code and you have a perfectly formatted date string for Easter. The reason this works the way it does is that you used an overloaded constructor to pass in the month and day as calculated by the Easter algorithm, along with the year supplied by the user. The `DateTime` method named `ToLongDateString()` builds the date string shown in Figure 9-7. The lesson to be learned here is that life is often easier when you take the time to explore the properties and methods of the class you are using.

USER INTERFACES VERSUS USER INTERFACES

You need to be a little careful when you talk about user interfaces. Care is needed because the terms can be used in multiple contexts. First, most people think of a user interface as being that part of a program with which the end user interacts. This type of user interface has visual objects presented on a form, such as `frmMain` has always used. The user then interacts with textbox, button, listbox, and a host of other types of objects on the form. The user interface, in this instance, serves as the primary means to get input from and display results to the end user.

The second type of user interface does not require a visual representation. For example, all the properties and methods that have the `public` access specifier comprise the *user interface for a class*. In this case, the user is actually a programmer. The `public` properties and methods of the class form the API for that class and thus define how the programmer interfaces with it. For these reasons, this type of user interface is also referred to as the *public interface* whereby the programmer interfaces with the class.

When you speak about the user interface in the context of a class, the "user" is a programmer working through the API to interact with the class. When you speak about the user interface in the context of a Windows form that has visual objects on it (such as textboxes and buttons), the "user" is the end user who actually runs the program. If you try to make a concerted effort not to confuse the two, casual conversations with other people will be less confusing. The rule of thumb to follow: If you're unclear which user interface is under discussion, ask.

SUMMARY

This chapter discussed the fundamental design factors you need to consider when you start to create your own classes. Hopefully, you understand the benefits of doing a program design before you start and have an idea of when you might consider writing your own class from a program.

Additional details about writing and using classes continue in the next chapter.

EXERCISES

You can find the answers to the following exercises in Appendix A.

1. Suppose you are adding the following data items as properties to a class. How would you write them in the class?

    a. A person's last name

    b. A ZIP code

    c. The days of the week

2. Suppose you want to add a general method to the `clsDates` class that returns the number of days in a given month. How would you write the code?

3. Give a good example of where you would use the `public` access specifier to define a class property.

4. Modify the following SOC code to use an `if` statement instead:

```
lblLeapYearResult.Text = year.ToString() + " is " +
            ((leap == 1)? "":"not ") + "a leap year";
```

Which form would you use in your own code and why?

5. Suppose you overload the `clsDates` constructor so that the following constructor is available. Would you modify your `getLeapYear()` method and, if so, how?

```
public clsDates(int yr)
{
    year = yr;
}
```

► WHAT YOU LEARNED IN THIS CHAPTER

TOPIC	KEY POINTS
Class design	When you should use a class in a program
Scope	How different scope levels affect the way data may be used in a program
Access specifiers	How public and private access specifiers are used
Class properties	What class properties are and how they should be used
Class methods	What class methods are and how they can be used to form a user interface for the class
UML Light	How to visualize the elements of a class
User interfaces	How the user of the class uses the API for the class
static storage class	How static data differs from other storage classes

10

Designing and Writing Custom Classes

WHAT YOU WILL LEARN IN THIS CHAPTER:

- ➤ Constructor details
- ➤ Method overloading
- ➤ Cohesion
- ➤ Coupling
- ➤ Property methods
- ➤ Getters and setters
- ➤ Changing the state of an object
- ➤ Sensing an error in a class method

WROX.COM CODE DOWNLOADS FOR THIS CHAPTER

You can find the wrox.com code downloads for this chapter at www.wrox.com/remtitle .cgi?isbn=9781118336922 on the Download Code tab. The code in the Chapter10 folder is individually named according to the names throughout the chapter.

Chapter 9 was an introduction about designing your own classes. That chapter ended by designing and writing a simple class named clsDates that added two methods: getLeapYear() and getEaster(). This chapter continues the theme of class design but discusses additional details about writing classes.

When you finish this chapter, you will have a solid foundation upon which to start writing your own classes. With a little effort, you'll find that writing your own classes is both worthwhile and kind of fun.

CONSTRUCTORS

You should think of *constructors* as methods designed to create, or instantiate, an object. The sole purpose of a constructor is to enable you to instantiate an object with a known state. The beauty of C# (and most other OOP languages) is that you get a default constructor automatically.

Default Constructors

To make the creation of a default constructor possible, a constructor always has the same name as its class. For example, if you want to create an object named `myDate` of the `clsDates` class, you would use the following statement:

```
clsDates myDate = new clsDate();
```

You've seen this syntax before, but now dig a little deeper.

First, notice that the leftmost reference to `clsDates` is simply the name of the class: No closing parentheses follow the class name. In effect, this reference to `clsDates` is simply telling you which cookie cutter to take from the thousands of them hanging on the wall.

Second, the purpose of the identifier `myDate` is to enable you to give a name to the *reference variable* that your code uses as a link to the data for the `clsDates` class. You learned in Chapter 5 that the rvalue of a reference variable is either `null` or the memory address of the location of the data for the object. For learning purposes, you can think of `myDate` as having the rvalue of `null` at this instant in time.

Third, the keyword `new` should always jog your memory and make you remember that there are going to be some messages exchanged between your program and the Windows Memory Manager. Specifically, `new` means that you are asking Windows for enough memory to store a `clsDates` object. Assuming that enough memory is found, the rvalue of `myDate` instantly changes from `null` to the memory address of where the object is stored.

Fourth, the final expression in the statement is `clsDates()`. Note that, unlike the first reference to the class at the beginning of the statement, this reference is followed by parentheses. This means that the code is calling a method. In this case `clsDates()` is a call to the constructor method. If you don't write your own constructor, C# still calls its own default class constructor. When the default constructor finishes executing, all the value type data in the class have the value 0, and all the reference variables have the value `null`. The default constructor places the object in a known state in which value types are 0 and references are `null` (unless the data is also initialized at its point of definition).

Nondefault Constructors

Okay, so when do you need to write a nondefault constructor? Under two basic circumstances: 1) when your class design is not happy with the default state of the object when it comes to life or 2) when a nondefault constructor makes life easier for the programmer who is using your class.

The first reason means that there is something about starting out with all the class data set to either 0 or `null` that just isn't the "right" state for the object. For example, in Chapter 9 the default constructor was changed to this:

```
public clsDates()
{
```

```
        current = DateTime.Now; // Sets DateTime to right now
    }
```

This constructor changes the `DataTime` data item named `current` from its uninitialized state to the present date and time. In other words, your design is such that you want to have `current` start out with its value set to the date and time at which the object was instantiated.

Creating a `clsDates` object with the present date and time already stored in `current` may make some aspect of the class easier to use. (Right now there's no code in the class that takes advantage of `current`, but that doesn't mean there won't be!)

Constructor Overloading

You've already studied method overloading in Chapter 5. Because a constructor is nothing more than a method that is always called when an object is instantiated, constructors may also be overloaded. For example, you can add the following constructor to the code shown in Listing 9-4:

```
public clsDates(int yr)
{
    year = yr;
}
```

Now you have two constructors. As mentioned in Chapter 5, method overloading is never a problem as long as the method signatures are different. Because this second constructor has an integer parameter (`yr`) passed to it, the signatures are different. However, you can now use the following statement to instantiate the `myDate` object:

```
clsDates myDate = new clsDate(year);
```

Now the instance variable named `year` in the `clsDates` object named `myDate` is initialized the moment the object is instantiated. Kinda neat, huh?

Well, not really.

Constructor Sloppiness

There's a problem with the way I've written the two constructors. Look at them side by side:

```
public clsDates()             // No-parameter constructor
{
    current = DateTime.Now; // Sets DateTime to right now
}

public clsDates(int yr)       // Constructor with parameter
{
    year = yr;
}
```

If I create the `myDate` object with the statement

```
clsDates myDate = new clsDate();
```

the no-parameter version means that `myDate` comes to life with the instance member named `current` initialized to the present date and time. However, if I use the statement

```
clsDates myDate = new clsDate(year);
```

then `current` is not initialized to its (assumed) default state! As a general rule, a nondefault constructor (that is, a constructor that has one or more arguments) should always subsume the default state of the object. What this means is that the parameterized version of the constructor should also initialize `current` to the present date and time. As the code stands right now, however, the default (parameterless) constructor initializes the member named `current`, but the overloaded constructor does not. Not good.

Fixing the Constructor Problem

The solution to the problem seems simple enough. Just call the default constructor from within the parameterized constructor:

```
public clsDates(int yr)      // Constructor with parameter
{
    clsDates();              // This won't work!
    year = yr;
}
```

This fix won't work because the compiler gets confused as to how `clsDates` is to be used in this context.

Now try the form in Listing 10-1 for the parameterized constructor.

LISTING 10-1: The correct way to call a parameterized contructor

```
public clsDates(int yr) : this()
{
    year = yr;
}
```

Note the (colon) operator (`:`) and the keyword `this` in the first statement. You've been using the colon operator in every program you've written but probably haven't thought much about it. For example, pick any program you've written and look at the first statement in the definition of `frmMain`:

```
public class frmMain : Form
```

You can verbalize the colon operator as the phrase "inherits from." In other words, your `frmMain` inherits the basic properties and methods of a common Windows form but is going to extend it with whatever objects and code you add to `frmMain`.

Now examine the following statement:

```
public clsDates(int yr) : this()
```

The `this` keyword is simply shorthand notation for a reference to the instance of the current object. In other words, `this` is a shorthand notation for the `clsDates` object that the program is in the process of constructing. However, because you have followed the `this` keyword with parentheses, the compiler knows that it must call the default (no-parameter) constructor for this class before it does anything else. (If you're ever at a cocktail party and someone mentions *constructor chaining*, this is exactly what that person is talking about.)

Add the code for the second constructor (refer to Listing 10-1) to the code presented in Listing 9-4. Now set a breakpoint on the first line of this new (parameterized) constructor, and then run and single-step through the program. You will find that, upon reaching the breakpoint in the second constructor, the program immediately jumps to the default constructor, initializes current to the proper value, and *then* executes the statement body for the second constructor. This is exactly what you want to happen because both flavors for creating the myDate object,

```
clsDates myDate = new clsDate();
```

and

```
clsDates myDate = new clsDate(year);
```

now leave current in the same state. The parameterized version of the constructor simply initializes an additional member (year) of the class to a known value.

Always Call the Default Constructor

You might be asking yourself: "Why bother calling the default constructor? If you never use the content of current, who cares?" Well, given the way clsDates is written presently, current isn't used, so it really doesn't matter. However, that does not mean you won't add code later on that does assume a default state for current.

More important, calling the default constructor gets you into the coding habit of establishing a "base state" for the object. Not starting all objects with the same base state may cause problems later. For example, you might be writing some form of a database class in which the default constructor creates a connection to the database. If an overloaded constructor didn't also establish that database connection, perhaps other methods in the class could not perform their functions properly.

If you do write a constructor that has parameters, you can no longer call the default constructor that has no parameters. The only way you can call a parameterless constructor once you have created a contructor with parameters is to explicitly write your own parameterless constructor. That is, the "no-code" default constructor no longer exists and you must supply your own.

Just as you've seen so many times before, the Initialization Step of the Five Program Steps creates the base environment in which the program code is to perform. Calling a constructor is similar to the Initialization Step for a program but viewed in the more narrowly defined context of a method. That is, the constructor establishes the environment in which a specific *object* is to exist and perform. Therefore, it is always a good idea for all overloaded constructors to call the default constructor so that the base state of the object can be safely assumed.

PROPERTY METHODS

So far you have designed and implemented the property members of the class, and you've also added two constructors to give the user some flexibility when he instantiates a clsDates object. Finally, you've written two General methods, getLeapYear() and getEaster(), that provide some functionality for the class. In the spirit of encapsulation, you defined all the property methods using the private access specifier. Using the private access specifier makes it difficult to inadvertently change the value of a class property. This protection for the class properties exists because the `private` access specifier limits the scope of the properties to the class in which they are defined. The class properties are invisible to the outside world!

Wait a minute....

If the properties are invisible to the outside world because of their scope, then there is no way to change them! If the class properties can't be changed, there is no way to change the state of the object. If you can't change the state of an object, you may as well have defined a boat anchor cast in concrete. It is the ability to use and change the state of an object that makes that object useful in a program. After all, how useful can an object be if its properties are always `null` or `0`?

Property Methods and Getters and Setters

Obviously, there's a method to this seeming madness. C# provides you with a program structure known as a *property method*, which is used to access private properties defined within a class. A class property method is built with *property getters* and *property setters*. These are special methods designed for use with class properties. As a rule, you define a set of getters and setters for each `private` property member.

The syntax for a property getter and setter is as follows:

```
AccessSpecifier   ReturnDataType   PropertyName
{
    get
    {
        return PropertyMember;
    }
    set
    {
        PropertyMember = value;
    }
}
```

An example using the `month` property of the `clsDates` class is shown in Listing 10-2. You should add the `month` property method to the code you wrote for Listing 9-4 as follows.

LISTING 10-2: Typical property method

```
public int Month
{
    get
    {
        return month;
    }
    set
    {
        if (value > 0 && value < 13)
        {
            month = value;
        }
    }
}
```

Property Method Rules

There are a number of things to notice about property methods. First, *all* property methods use the public access specifier. As you learned in Chapter 9, if a method uses the public access specifier, that method becomes part of the user, or public, interface (or API) of the class. Because property methods are public, they become the gateway into the class and provide a means to access the private property members of the class. If the property methods weren't defined with the public access specifier, they would be useless to the code that exists outside of the class because their scope would make them invisible.

Second, the return data type for the property method *must* match the data type of the property. If you defined the class property to be an int (as month is), then the property method must return an int. If the property member is a string data type, the return data type must also be a string.

Third, note that a *property method* is different from any other type of method because the name of the property method is *not* followed by a set of parentheses. A common programming convention is to make the name of the property method the same as that of the property, but to capitalize the first letter of the property name. In this example, the class property named month has a class property method named Month. (This is also consistent with making the first word of all class property names lowercase.) There will be no confusion between month and Month because C# is case-sensitive.

Fourth, the keyword get is used to mark the block of code within a property method that may be used to retrieve the value of a class property member. Usually, the statement within the get statement block is simply a return keyword followed by the property name, as shown in the example. You will often hear a get statement block referred to as a *getter*.

Finally, the keyword set is used to mark the block of code within a property method that may be used to assign a value to a class property member. The set statement block should be the only means by which the outside world can change the private property member of a class. (You could change it through a General class method, but that's an ugly way to do it and is discouraged.)

If you look at the set statement block in the Month property method, you can see that you validate that the value assigned into month is reasonable.

Wait a minute! Where did the variable named value come from?

The value Keyword

The keyword value is an implied variable used as part of the syntax of the set statement block. You can think of value as a *ghost variable* that holds the data that you want to assign into the property member. The data type of value always matches the return type specifier of the property method. For example, the Month property method returns an int, so value must be an int.

There is no formal definition of value in a property method or the class. The data type for value is implied by the context in which it is used. The type always matches the type specifier for the property method.

How the get Property Methods Work

Suppose you want to read the value of month as it is presently stored in a clsDates object. The following code fragment shows how to access the property member named month:

```
int myMonth;
clsDates myDate = new clsDates();

// Misc lines of code . . .

myMonth = myDate.Month;
```

The intent of the preceding code is to retrieve the value of month as it currently exists in the myDate object and assign that value into myMonth. When the last statement executes, program control executes the get statement block of the Month property method in clsDates and returns the value of the property named month.

Now that you understand the concepts for designing a class, let's see how everything fits together. In the next section you tie the class code to the end user interface to get a fully functional program.

TRY IT OUT   Using a Property Method (Chapter09ProgramClassDesign.zip)

In this case, you are actually reusing the code you wrote in the last chapter.

1. Load the code from the Class Design project discussed in Chapter 9.

2. Add the code from Listings 10-1 and 10-2 to the project.

3. Add the following code to frmMain.cs, after the Application.Run(main); statement:

```
int myMonth;
clsDates myDate = new clsDates();
myMonth = myDate.Month;
```

and set a breakpoint on the last statement in the code fragment, Now run the program and use the F11 key to single-step in the Month property method to see how program control works for such statements.

As the property method code in Listing 10-2 presently works, the value returned is 0 because no value has been assigned to the month property. You could modify Listing 10-2 to what is shown in Listing 10-3.

LISTING 10-3: Property method for the month property

```
public int Month
{
    get
    {
        if (month == 0)                 // New code
        {
            return current.Month;
        } else
        {
            return month;
        }
```

```
        }
        set
        {
            if (value > 0 && value < 13)
            {
                month = value;
            }
        }
    }
}
```

How It Works

With the property method code added to the class, you have a means by which to change the state of the month property. The code you just added to frmMain gives you a way to test how the month property's state can be changed. You also have the ability to validate any new value assigned into month by the use of the if statement block. Any attempt to change the state of month outside the class must pass the if statement block check before a new value for month can be accepted.

The modification in Listing 10-3 says that if the class member named month is unassigned (that is, if it has its default value of 0), return the Month value of the DateTime object named current. This returns a nonzero value because the constructor initializes current to the date and time at which the object is created. If you had defined the class member named current with the public access specifier, you could not do this kind of checking on current before it was used.

How the set Property Methods Work

Suppose you want to change the month property to 12. You can accomplish that with the following statements in frmMain:

```
int myMonth = 12;
clsDates myDate = new clsDates();

// Misc lines of code . . .

myDate.Month = myMonth;
```

If you set a breakpoint on the last statement of the preceding code and then use the F11 key to single-step into the Month property method, you can see that the set statement block is executed. The code in Listing 10-3 can check the ghost variable named value to see that an appropriate value is recorded for month in clsDates. If you use the debugger as suggested, you can see that the variable named value has the value of myMonth back in frmMain.

How Does Visual Studio Know Whether to Use the get or set Statement Block?

Visual Studio can determine what your intent is by the context in which you use the Month property method. For example, in the assignment statement,

```
myMonth = myDate.Month;        // A get operation
```

it's obvious that your intent is to fetch the current value of the month property of the myDate object and assign it into myMonth. The statement, therefore, must perform a get operation. (Because the Month property method as defined in the class does not use parentheses in its definition, you do not use parentheses when you call a property method.)

Conversely, in the assignment statement,

```
myDate.Month = myMonth;      // A set operation
```

your intent is to use the value stored in myMonth and assign it into the month property of the myDate object. Because you want to change the state of the month property of myDate, Visual Studio must perform a set operation. You can generalize these context behaviors into the following two rules for using class property methods:

➤ If the property method name appears on the right side of an assignment operator, a get statement is performed.

➤ If the property method name appears on the left side of an assignment operator, a set statement is performed.

Always keep in mind that a set operation has the potential to change the state of an object. Also, the set statement block is a good place to write any validation code you deem necessary to ensure that the property doesn't accept bogus or unwanted values.

If you see a property method used in an expression that does not involve the assignment or binary (i.e., ++ or --) operators, such as

```
for (j = 0; j < myDate.Days; j++)
```

the expression is performing a get operation. (Again, the property method appears on the right side of the relational operator (<), so it must be a get operation.)

WHAT TO DO IF AN ERROR OCCURS IN A PROPERTY METHOD

There will be times when a bogus value reaches a property method. However, the set statement block is used to change the state of the object and not to return a value to the caller. So how do you communicate to the user that your class code read a bad data value in a property method?

Your first approach might to be to use a MessageBox object to display a message to the user that a bad value for a property was read. The problem with this approach is that the data manipulation is going on in the class, not in frmMain where the end user is interacting. When you write code for a class, you should always keep in mind that *your* user is a programmer, not the end user running the program. Because of this, you need to let the person using your class know that something's amiss. (A general style convention is that property methods *never* use MessageBox objects.)

The main purpose of a set statement block is to change the value of the property associated with the method. Because a change in the value of a class property also means a change in the *state of the object*, the safest thing to do when an error is detected is to leave the state of the object unchanged. For example, if a bogus value for a month reaches the set statement block in Listing 10-3, the new value for month is ignored and the state of the object remains unchanged. It would be the responsibility of the programmer using your class to detect that the set operation failed, as shown by the unchanged state of the object.

Another possibility is to have a state flag as a property member of the class. You could have code similar to this:

```
private int errorStatus = 0;    // Assume no errors for object's state

            // more code for other class members . . .

public int getErrorStatus      // Property method for errorStatus member
{
    get
    {
        Return errorStatus;
    }
}
```

Notice that there is no set statement block for the getErrorStatus property method; it is a *read-only property method*. Because the property method is read-only, the user cannot change the state of errorStatus; only you can change it in your class code. Given that fact, you could modify Listing 10-3 to what is shown in Listing 10-4.

LISTING 10-4: A Property Method with Error Handling

```
public int Month
{
    get
    {
        if (month == 0)              // New code
        {
            return current.Month;
        } else
        {
            return month;
        }
    }
    set
    {
        if (value > 0 && value < 13)
        {
            month = value;
        } else
        {
            errorStatus = 1;        // Flag as error
        }
    }
}
```

Now any time the user of your class wants to see if a set operation worked properly, she could add code similar to this back in frmMain:

```
myDate.Month = myMonth;
if (myDate.getErrorStatus == 1)
{
    MessageBox.Show("The world is ending. Run for your lives!");
    return;
}
```

This would detect the occurrence of an error in the class. Other possibilities exist, but those shown here are the most direct.

Method Coupling and Cohesion

As you've learned in this chapter, property methods are used to read and write the values associated with the properties in a class. Because they are public, property methods form an important part of the user interface for the class. However, the purpose of a property method (either getting or setting) is correctly constrained to the property.

Helper and General methods, on the other hand, are designed to use or act upon the properties of the class. Because Helper methods always use the private access specifier, they do not form part of the user interface (API) for the class. Instead, they reduce the coding burden on you, the programmer of the class. Helper methods are often used for validation purposes. Checking and validating data, like the format of phone and Social Security numbers, is a task often given to Helper methods.

General methods, however, are often used to derive new data from the property data. For example, an inventory class might have a property that records the quantity of an item sold. There might be a General method that takes the quantity sold and multiplies it by a price per item to produce a total purchase amount. A General method for the class might be called getTotalCost(). Another General method named getShippingCost() might use the weight per unit and the quantity sold to calculate the shipping charges. Yet another method named getSalesTaxDue() might calculate the sales tax for the order, and so on.

Cohesion

The important thing to notice about each of these General methods is that each one is geared to a specific and narrowly defined task. These narrowly defined tasks illustrate the concept of *cohesion*. This term refers to the ability to describe what a method does in one or two sentences. If it takes more than a couple of sentences to define its purpose, chances are it is not a cohesive method. A cohesive method does a single task, and you should be able to describe its purpose crisply and concisely. If you can't, it's back to the drawing board to rethink the method's design.

Beginning programmers often try to create Swiss Army knives by designing a method that performs multiple tasks. This is usually a bad idea for two reasons. First, methods that attempt to multitask complicate the code. Several simple methods that perform one task each are simpler to write, test, debug, and maintain than one method that tries to multitask. Second, single-task methods have a higher chance of being reused than a complex method that attempts to solve multiple problems at once. The more tasks you try to pack into a single method, the less likely it is that the precise sequence of tasks can be reused in some other program.

Think about cohesion when you design your general methods. That is, keep your methods crisp, clean, short, and geared to a single task.

Coupling

Coupling refers to the degree of dependency between data elements in a program. *Method decoupling* refers to the ability to make code changes in one method without forcing changes in another. Methods that are coupled means that the behavior of one method is somehow dependent upon the behavior of another method. The goal is to have zero coupling between methods. That is, changing the code in one method should not force you to change code in another method. Obviously, the smaller the degree of method coupling, the greater the likelihood that you can reuse that method in another program because its functionality is less dependent on other methods.

Sometimes coupling introduces sequencing issues, too. For example, if you want to open a disk file for writing data, you must first make sure the file exists or create a new file if it doesn't. Clearly, you need to open the file, write the data to the file, and then close the file. The sequencing might seem to suggest that one method should be used to open, write, and close a disk file. Such a design is bad on two levels. First, the design is not cohesive because it is multitasking. Second, this is coupling to the highest degree because what should be three separate steps are instead rolled into a single method. A major reason for unrolling such a method is because errors can occur at each step along the way, it makes more sense to decouple these tasks and write three methods to attack all three. The code will be simpler and easier to maintain, plus you can pass back more meaningful error states to the user of the class if one of the methods fails to perform its specific task.

The goal is simple: Write simple methods geared to one task, and write them so they stand alone and operate independently.

CLASS DESIGN FOR DECK-OF-CARDS PROGRAM

Try your hand at a new program to incorporate some of the design elements discussed in the last two chapters. Suppose you want to write a program that models shuffling a deck of cards. In the following Try It Out, you will write a class that performs some basic card game tasks. If you design things correctly, the class should be usable in other games that involve a deck of cards.

TRY IT OUT   Shuffle Cards (Chapter10ProgramShuffleDeckClass.zip)

The program should simply display the shuffled deck of cards in a listbox object. Figure 10-1 shows a starting point of how you might construct the user interface for the program.

The figure shows what the output might look like after two clicks of the Shuffle button. Also note that a label object appears below the listbox to inform the user how many passes it took through the "shuffle loop" to produce a shuffled deck. (More on the shuffle loop in a minute.) Given that Figure 10-1 describes the way you want the user interface to look, how would you design and write the code? Equally important, where do you start the design process?

1. Create a new project in the usual manner. You may want to call it ShuffleDeck, but you can use whatever name you want.

2. Add the objects shown in Figure 10-1. Again, postpone the complete construction of the program until a little later. For now, just consider how you want it to work and be constructed.

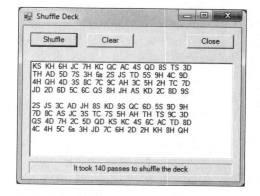

FIGURE 10-1: Program Shuffle

How It Works

As is almost always the case, you could write the code and stuff it all into `frmMain` and be done with it. However, is there a chance that at some time in the future you might write a game program that needs a deck of cards? A related question to ask is, "How difficult would writing the program be if you wrote a class to simulate a deck of cards instead of jamming all the code into `frmMain`?" The answer is that there is virtually no appreciable cost to separating the administration of the program from the simulation of the deck of cards.

The program is sufficiently simple so that you can keep all but the Process step (of the Five Program Steps) in `frmMain`. The Process step, however, should be the domain of a class that simulates the behavior of a deck of cards.

UML Class Diagram for Shuffle Deck Program

Figure 10-2 shows the first attempt in designing your card deck class. The UML notation discussed in Chapter 9 is used to construct the UML class diagram, as shown in Figure 10-2. You can examine the symbolic constants and properties of the class first.

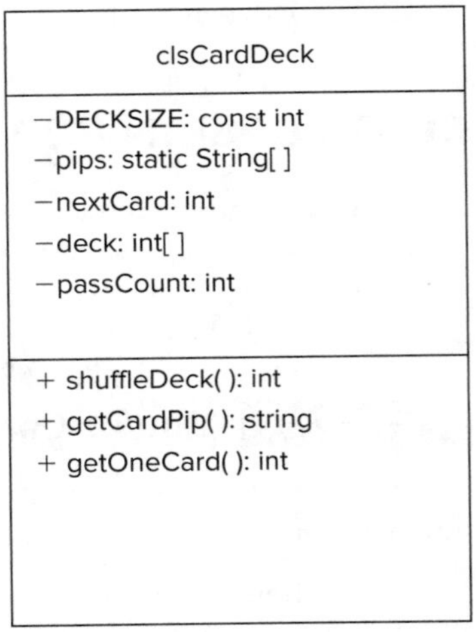

The first thing to note is that all the properties are prefixed by a minus sign, which means they use the `private` access specifier. Because the properties are not directly visible outside the class, they are not part of its user interface. The second thing to note is that all the methods use the `public` access specifier. (They are prefixed with the + sign.) Therefore, you know at a glance that all three methods are part of the user interface for the class.

As you can see in Figure 10-2, the property methods are not shown as part of the UML Light class depiction. Those methods are omitted for two reasons. First, property methods always use the `public` access specifier. This also means that *property methods* always form a part of the public user interface for the class. Second, because the property methods align one-to-one with the properties, it seems redundant to make them part of the UML class diagram.

FIGURE 10-2: UML Diagram for Shuffle Deck Program

Good class design almost always makes the properties of the class `private` but enables the outside world to have access to them through their associated property methods. Using this design approach gives you control over what values can be properly assigned into any given property.

Class Constants and Properties

In the UML class diagram shown in Figure 10-2, the symbolic constant `DECKSIZE` represents the number of cards in the deck. Although most games use 52 cards in a deck, there are games that don't (such as Euchre and Canasta). The `pips` variable is a `string` array that holds a nongraphic representation of each card. As you can see in Figure 10-1, the first entry, `KS`, represents the king of spades. The second shuffle begins with `2S`, or the two of spades, as so on.

You should know why the `pips` array is defined with the `static` storage class. The reason is that the contents of the array can be shared regardless of how many objects of `clsCardDeck` are instantiated.

The `nextCard` variable serves as an index into the card deck. If `DECKSIZE` is 52, when `nextCard` reaches the value 52, the interpretation is that all cards have been dealt from the deck. This allows the class to track where it is in the deck. Also, if `nextCard` has the value `DECKSIZE`, it's time to reshuffle the deck.

The variable `deck` is an integer array and represents the deck of cards. One of the design considerations discussed earlier is that you should design a class in a way that reflects how a user thinks about the properties and methods of the class. Again, most people do not think of a zero-based deck of cards. To a user, the first card in the deck is card number one, not card number zero. Therefore, you should set the dimension of the deck to `DECKSIZE + 1`. This allows the largest index for the `deck` array to match the user's ones-based perception of the deck of cards. That is, if the deck size is 52, making the dimension 53 lets you present the valid indexes for `deck` as the set 1 through 52. (It's that pesky N – 1 Rule again.)

You can make a valid argument that the user of this class is a programmer and they should be used to thinking of zero-based arrays. Very true, and if indexing from a non-zero base bothers you, you can easily modify the code to suit your needs.

Finally, `passCount` is an integer variable that stores the number of passes made through the loop that is used to shuffle the deck. Although this variable is probably not needed for any card game you might write, it does give you some information about the shuffling algorithm used to shuffle the deck and may be useful for debugging purposes.

Class Methods

Figure 10-2 shows that there are only three General methods in the class. (You know they are General methods because they are all defined with the `public` (+) access specifier. If they were Helper methods, they would must be defined with the `private` (–) access specifier. Although `Property` methods are also `public`, they are concerned only with getting or setting a property.) Because the methods are General methods, they become part of the user interface, or API, for the class.

As suggested in Chapter 9, method names should be action- or verb-based. If you have selected the method names well, they should reflect the tasks the methods are designed to accomplish. The methods `shuffleDeck()` and `getOneCard()` should be self-explanatory. The method `getCardPip()` is a little unusual and needs some explanation.

getCardPip( )

As mentioned earlier, the design uses two-letter abbreviations for the cards in the deck (3H, KS, and so on). These abbreviations are defined in the `static` array named `pip`. The definition of this array is:

```
    private static string[] pips = {"",
 "AS","2S","3S","4S","5S","6s","7S","8S","9S","TS","JS","QS","KS",
 "AH","2H","3H","4H","5H","6H","7H","8H","9H","TH","JH","QH","KH",
 "AD","2D","3D","4D","5D","6D","7D","8D","9D","TD","JD","QD","KD",
 "AC","2C","3C","4C","5C","6C","7C","8C","9C","TC","JC","QC","KC"
                                    };
```

Again, note that the first element in the initializer list is an empty string array element (`""`). This produces a valid (that is, non-null) array element, but one that contains no useful information. The element is nothing more than a placeholder to get away from the zero-based array configuration.

If you look at the organization of the array, you can see `pips[1]` is AS, `pips[14]` is AH; `pips[27]` is AD, and `pips[40]` is AC. What may be less obvious is that if you take the index into the `pips` array divided by the number of cards in each suit (13), the remainder is that suit's card. That is, 1 % 13 = 1, 14 % 13 = 1, 27 % 13 = 1, and 40 % 13 = 1. Therefore, anytime the index modulus 13 is 1, you know you are looking at the ace of some suit. You can determine which suit by looking at the quotient when the index is divided by 4 (the number of suits). For example, 2C has an index of 41. Dividing that index by 13 yields a quotient of 3, which you can interpret as the club's suit. It doesn't take too much thought to realize that values 2 through 10 represent those cards for each suit, and values 11 through 13 are the face cards. (The king of each suit has a modulus of 0 and forms a special case that needs to be checked.) Okay...so what?

Recall from the design discussion that you don't want to select a class method name that tells the user anything about the implementation details used in the method. However, suppose you want to use the `clsCardDeck` class to write a card game. Chances are, you're going to need to know the structure that produces the relationship between each card and its suit to make the card game work. Providing the `getCardPip()` method allows the user to "dump" the card deck and examine its structure. For example, the following loop helps to reveal to the user the organization of the data used to implement the deck:

```
clsCardDeck myDeck = new clsCardDeck();

for (int j = 0; j <= myDeck.DeckSize; j++)
{
    lstCard.Items.Add(myDeck.getCardPip(j));
}
```

In a real sense, therefore, the method named `getCardPip()` is a Helper method, but written for the user rather than yourself. Simply stated, this method is a debugging aid for the user of `clsCardDeck`.

Making the method part of the user interface allows the user to have access to data structure specifics that makes her coding tasks easier. This method is provided because the user may need this information to implement her card game. Also, with this structure and knowing that she needs the information it provides, you can ease her programming burden by doing away with a trial-and-error approach to figuring out the deck's organization.

Now that the design is finished, implement the code to see how all the pieces fit together. First, examine how the end-user interface is written.

The frmMain Code

Listing 10-5 presents the code that exercises `clsCardDeck`.

LISTING 10-5: Program Code to Exercise clsCardDeck. (frmMain.cs)

```
using System;
using System.Windows.Forms;
```

```
public class frmMain : Form
{
    const int CARDSPERLINE = 13;
    private Button btnShuffle;
    private Button btnClose;
    private Label lblPassCounter;
    private Button btnClear;
    private ListBox lstDeck;

    #region Windows code

    public frmMain()
    {
        InitializeComponent();
    }

    public static void Main()
    {
        frmMain main = new frmMain();
        Application.Run(main);
    }

    private void btnShuffle_Click(object sender, EventArgs e)
    {
        int j;
        int cardIndex;
        int deckSize;
        int passes;
        string buff;
        string temp;
        clsCardDeck myDeck = new clsCardDeck();

        passes = myDeck.ShuffleDeck();
        lblPassCounter.Text = "It took " + passes.ToString() +
                            " passes to shuffle the deck";
        deckSize = myDeck.DeckSize;

        for (cardIndex = 1; cardIndex < deckSize + 1; )
        {
            buff = "";
            for (j = 0; j < CARDSPERLINE ; j++)     // Show 13 cards per line
            {
                temp = myDeck.getOneCard(cardIndex);
                if (temp.Length == 0)
                {
                    MessageBox.Show("Error reading deck.", "Processing Error");
                    return;
                }
                buff += temp + " ";
                cardIndex++;
            }
            lstDeck.Items.Add(buff);
        }
        lstDeck.Items.Add(" ");       // Add an empty line
    }
```

(continues)

LISTING 10-5 *(continued)*

```
private void btnClose_Click(object sender, EventArgs e)
{
    Close();
}

private void btnClear_Click(object sender, EventArgs e)
{
    lstDeck.Items.Clear();
}
}
```

As usual, all the action takes place in the btnShuffle_Click() method. The code defines a cls-CardDeck object named myDeck and then calls the ShuffleDeck() method to shuffle the deck. The variable passCount is assigned the number of passes the code had to make to complete the shuffle. This information displays in the lblPassCounter object.

The statement

```
deckSize = myDeck.DeckSize;
```

uses the DeckSize property method to determine how many cards are in the deck. The return value from the property method is used to control the for loop that is responsible for displaying the deck.

A nested for loop actually displays the cards:

```
for (cardIndex = 1; cardIndex < deckSize + 1; )
{
    buff = "";
    for (j = 0; j < 13; j++)     // Show 13 cards per line
    {
        temp = myDeck.getOneCard(cardIndex);
        if (temp.Length == 0)
        {
            MessageBox.Show("Error reading deck.", "Processing Error");
            return;
        }
        buff += temp + " ";
        cardIndex++;
    }
    lstDeck.Items.Add(buff);
}
```

The outer for loop is controlled by the variable named cardIndex. Note how it is initialized to 1 in the first expression of the for loop. The second expression in the outer for loop simply suggests that all the cards in the deck are shown. The third expression in the outer for loop...doesn't exist! What?

Although you could have done away with the inner for loop, you elected to display the cards in a format that has 13 cards per row in the listbox object. Therefore, the code simply calls the getOneCard() method 13 times in the inner j loop, concatenating each card's pip representation to the string variable named buff. Note, however, that the code needs to increment cardIndex on each pass through the inner j loop to fetch the next card. Because the increment of cardIndex must be done within the inner j loop, the increment operation normally found in the third expression of the outer for loop is omitted.

After the inner j loop reads 13 cards from the deck, buff contains a string representation of those 13 cards. The last statement in the outer loop adds the row of cards to the listbox object using the Add() method. With a standard deck of cards, four rows display and the program run is complete.

The clsCardDeck Code

The code for clsCardDeck is shown in Listing 10-6.

LISTING 10-6: Source Code for clsCardDeck (clsCardDeck.cs)

```csharp
using System;

class clsCardDeck
{
    // =============== symbolic constants ==================
    private const int DECKSIZE = 52;  // The number of cards in the deck
    // =============== static members =====================
    private static string[] pips = {"",
 "AS","2S","3S","4S","5S","6s","7S","8S","9S","TS","JS","QS","KS",
 "AH","2H","3H","4H","5H","6H","7H","8H","9H","TH","JH","QH","KH",
 "AD","2D","3D","4D","5D","6D","7D","8D","9D","TD","JD","QD","KD",
 "AC","2C","3C","4C","5C","6C","7C","8C","9C","TC","JC","QC","KC"
                                     };

    // =============== instance members =====================
    private int nextCard;          // The next card to be dealt from deck
    private int[] deck = new int[DECKSIZE + 1];   // The deck of cards.
    private int passCount;         // To count loop passes to shuffle deck

    // =============== constructor(s) =====================
    public clsCardDeck()
    {
        nextCard = 1;
    }


    // =============== property methods =====================
    public int DeckSize
    {
        get
        {
            return DECKSIZE;  // How many cards in the deck
        }
        // No setter method since this is a read-only property
    }

    public int NextCard
    {
        get
        {
```

(continues)

LISTING 10-6 *(continued)*

```
                return nextCard;
        }
        set
        {
            if (value > 0 && value <= deck.Length)
            {
                nextCard = value;
            }
        }
    }

    public int PassCount
    {
        get
        {
            return passCount;
        }
    }
}
// =============== helper methods =======================

// =============== general methods =======================
/**
 * Purpose: Shuffle the deck
 *
 * Parameter list:
 *      N/A
 * Return value:
 *      int     number of passes to shuffle the deck
 */
public int ShuffleDeck()
{
    int index;
    int val;
    Random rnd = new Random();

    passCount = 0; // Count how many times through the while loop
    index = 1;
    Array.Clear(deck, 0, deck.Length);  // Initialize array to 0's

    while (index < deck.Length)
    {   // Add 1 to offset 0-based arrays
        val = rnd.Next(DECKSIZE) + 1;    // Generate values 1 thru 52
        if (deck[val] == 0)
        {               // Is this card place in the deck "unused"?
            deck[val] = index;       // Yep, so assign it a card place
            index++;                     // Get ready for next card
        }
        passCount++;
    }
    nextCard = 1;                       // Prepare to deal the first card
    return passCount;
}
```

```
/**
 * Purpose: Show a given card in the deck.
 *
 * Parameter list:
 *      int          the index of the position where the card is found
 * Return value:
 *      string       the pip for the card, or empty on error
 */
public string getOneCard(int index)
{
    if (index > 0 && index <= deck.Length && nextCard <= deck.Length)
    {
        nextCard++;
        return pips[deck[index]];
    }
    else
    {
        return "";       // Error
    }
}

/**
 * Purpose: Show the abbreviation used for a given card in the deck.
 *
 * Parameter list:
 *      index        an integer for the index position in the deck
 *
 * Return value:
 *      string       the pip for the card, or empty on error
 */
public string getCardPip(int index)
{
    if (index > 0 && index <= DECKSIZE)
    {
        return pips[index];
    }
    else
    {
        return "";       // Error
    }
}
}
```

Now examine each section of the class code. First, notice that when you created clsCardDeck, Visual Studio automatically enclosed the class within the project's namespace. The namespace is removed from the class, as in Chapter 9 and for the same reasons.

Class Properties, Constructor, and Property Methods

The properties are defined exactly as they were in Figure 10-2. The constructor doesn't do anything other than set the value of nextCard to 1. Do this because the first card in the deck is treated as deck[1] rather than deck[0]. Because the constructor initializes class properties to 0 or null, as dictated by the property's type, initialize nextCard explicitly to 1. Neither the DECKSIZE nor the passCount property method has a set statement block. In essence, this makes these read-only properties, which means that nothing outside of clsCardDeck can change the size of the deck of cards or the variable that counts the number of passes made to shuffle the deck. As you design other classes, you will find that read-only properties make sense in some situations. For example, if you create a clsCar to simulate an automobile, you might want to make the odometer a read-only property. (In some states, if you had a setter for the odometer property, you might find yourself a guest of the state in one of their jails!)

Class General Methods

As you gain more programming experience, you'll often find that a class design evolves as you get further into a project. Gone are the old days of BDUF (Big Design Up Front) program design whereby months were spent creating a design that went up in smoke about an hour after the project began. *Agile modeling*, whereby the program evolves through as a series of small design steps, seems to better capture the way software is developed today.

In clsCardDeck, your design provides for only three General methods. The codes for getOne-Card() and getCardPip() are straightforward, and you should have no difficulty explaining what they do and how they do it. The way ShuffleDeck() works, however, would benefit from some explanation.

The ShuffleDeck( ) General Method

There are likely dozens of different ways in which you can simulate the process to shuffle a deck of cards. The method implemented here is based on the following algorithm:

1. Initialize a card counter variable to 0.

2. Generate a random integer number that falls within the range of 1 to DECKSIZE, inclusively.

3. Use that random number as an index into the card deck array, and examine that element of the array.

4. If the indexed element of the deck array has the value 0, it is unassigned, so it is safe to assign the index number into that element of the array and increment the card counter by one.

5. If the indexed element of the deck array is not 0, that element of the array has already been used.

6. If the card counter is less than DECKSIZE, repeat step 2.

The implementation of the algorithm begins with the definition of a number of working variables. The statement

```
Random rnd = new Random();
```

uses Visual Studio's Random class to define an object named rnd. The Next() method of the Random class is used inside the while loop with the following syntax:

```
val = rnd.Next(DECKSIZE) + 1;   // Generate values 1 thru 52
```

The method Next() is design to generate a series of pseudo-random numbers that fall within the range of 0 to DECKSIZE. Assuming that DECKSIZE is 52, this means that Next() produces random numbers that fall within the range of 0 to 52. The set of values generated by Next() spans the domain from 0 to—but *not* including—52. However, because of the way that you have defined the `pips` array, you need the domain to be from 1 to 53, inclusively. You can generate that domain of values if you add 1 to each random number produced by the `Next()` method. In the preceding statement, `val` has the potential to store the values 1 through 53...exactly what you need.

In Chapter 8 you learned that the statement

```
Array.Clear(deck, 0, deck.Length);  // Initialize array to 0's
```

uses the `Clear()` method of the `Array` class to initialize all elements in the `deck` array to 0. Now see how your algorithm works.

The Implementation of the Shuffle Algorithm

The code for the program loop shown in Listing 10-6 is repeated here:

```
while (index < deck.Length)  // Add 1 to offset 0-based arrays
{
    val = rnd.Next(DECKSIZE) + 1;   // Generate values 1   52
    if (deck[val] == 0)
    {               // Is this card place in the deck is "unused"?
        deck[val] = index;        // Yep, so assign it a place
        index++;                  // Get ready for next card
    }
    passCount++;
}
```

At the start of the `while` loop, the deck array looks like Figure 10-3. The figure shows that none of the elements has been assigned a value. That is, each empty element shown in Figure 10-3 has the value 0 in it.

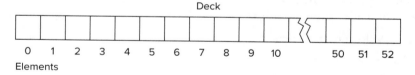

FIGURE 10-3: The state of the deck array before shuffling starts

To understand what is happening, assume that program control has entered the `while` loop and the first random number assigned into `val` is 5. The `if` statement checks to see if element `deck[5]` is 0. Because this is the first pass through the loop, `deck[5]` is "empty" (that is, its value is 0), so assign the value of `index` into the fifth element of the array. Because the variable `index` has been initialized to 1, the `deck` array now looks like Figure 10-4.

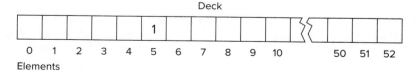

FIGURE 10-4: State after adding the first card

If you look at the `pips` array discussed earlier, you should figure out that the fifth card in the deck is now the ace of spades. (Think about it.) After the assignment of `index` into the `deck[val]` element of the array, `index` is incremented. Because `index`, with a value now equal to 2, is less than the size of the element count of the array (in this case 53), another pass is made through the loop.

On this second pass through the loop, assume the next random number is 51. Because element 51 is 0 (that is, "empty"), the `if` statement assigns the value 2 into `deck[51]`. You now know that the two of spades is the second-to-last card in the deck. The state of the card deck at this point is shown in Figure 10-5.

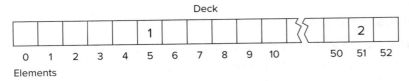

Deck

FIGURE 10-5: Adding the second card to the deck

On each pass through the loop, the code attempts to assign the current value of `index` into an empty element of the `deck` array using `val` as its index. If you think about it, as the arrays fill up, it gets harder and harder to find an empty array element. This is why it may take several hundred passes through the loop to fill up the array with the random card values. The variable `passCount` maintains a count of how many times the loop is executed before the `deck` array is filled. Usually the `deck` array is filled in less than 300 passes through the loop Although there are more efficient card shuffling algorithms out there, the simplicity of the code and its reasonable speed make this version acceptable for your purposes.

When the loop finishes filling the deck array, `nextCard` is assigned the value of 1, and the value of `passCount` is passed back to the caller in Listing 10-6.

If you set a breakpoint on the following statement

```
temp = myDeck.getOneCard(cardIndex);
```

in the nested `for` loops back in `frmMain` (Listing 10-5) and step into the `getOneCard()` method using the F11 key, you can see how the cards are added to the listbox object. Again, single-stepping through a program is a great way to understand how it actually works.

DESIGNING A CARD GAME USING CLSCARDDECK

Now that you have a class capable of shuffling a deck of cards and dealing them out one at a time, design a simple card game. The card game is a simplification of one called In Between.

The variation of this game begins with the dealer (the computer) giving you $100 to wager with a default wager of $10. The dealer then deals two cards face up. You may wager nothing on a game, or you may wager up to all the credit you have. If you don't want to bet, simply click the Deal button again to deal another set of cards. If you make a wager, the dealer deals the next card. If that card falls within the range formed by the other two cards, you win an amount equal to your wager. Your winnings are automatically added to your balance. If the third card falls outside the range of the first two cards, the dealer wins and your balance is reduced by the amount of your wager. If the third card equals either of the two first cards, the dealer wins. Aces are considered to have the lowest value (1) in the deck and the king the highest (13).

A sample run is shown in Figure 10-6.

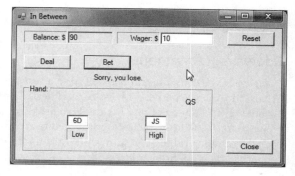

For example, if the first two cards are 6D and JS and the third card is QS, the player loses because the third card (a queen, or a 12 index) falls outside the range of 6 (a six) to 11 (a Jack) index. If the third card is an 11 or a Jack of any suit, the dealer wins because those cards form a tie, and the dealer wins ties. If the third card is 9H, the player wins because the 9 falls inside the range of 6 to 11.

Now that the rules have been stated, how would you design and implement the game?

FIGURE 10-6: In Between user interface

Aw, come on. Don't just continue reading. Take the time to draw up whatever class diagrams you think you need to make the game work. It's the only way you can learn this stuff. Come back and start reading again after you've given the program design some thought.

Again, you can defer the actual code and how it works until after you've read a few things about the game you may want to consider.

Design Considerations

If you think about it, games are actions governed by rules. Indeed, it is within the framework of rules that most games are played. Some require third parties to enforce the rules (such as a referee in football) whereas others may operate with self-enforcement (such as golf). The card game has rules, and it is your program that must enforce those rules. Given that viewpoint, where does your clsCardDeck come into the picture, and how do you enforce the rules of the game?

What Kind of Architecture?

If you step back and look at the forest rather than just the trees, your game is similar to a client-server architecture found in many database applications. The client is the player and the server is clsCardDeck, which "serves" cards to play the game. Simple client-server architectures are often called *two-tiered architectures* because the design contains two active elements: the client and the server. However, because there are rules to the game, you need to introduce an intermediary into the program to ensure that the rules of the game are enforced. You can draw this design for the game, as shown in Figure 10-7.

In Figure 10-7, a class named `clsInBetweenRules` is inserted between the client (`frmMain`) and the server (`clsCardDeck`). Because you have introduced another tier over the standard two-tier architecture, the design in Figure 10-7 is a *three-tier architecture*. (Sometimes programmers simply call anything above a two-tier architecture an *N-tier architecture*. Stick with the term *three-tier* because it is more descriptive.)

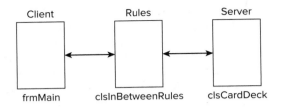

FIGURE 10-7: In Between architecture

Sideways Refinement

Using UML class diagrams to serve as a starting point in the program's design was previously discussed. An alternative and less formal design approach is what I call *Sideways Refinement*. With Sideways Refinement you list the Five Program Steps on the left side of a piece of paper. Then you write to the right of each Program Step those tasks that each element of the program must address. For example, Table 10-1 shows the various steps, the tasks to be performed, and where in the architecture they might be addressed:

TABLE 10-1: Sideways Refinement for In-Between Program

STEP	ACTION	RESPONSIBILITY
1. Initialization	Build and display the form (`frmMain`).	Set up form and all background data.
2. Input	Ask for new cards (`frmMain`).	
	Get amount of wager (`frmMain`).	
	Ask for bet (`frmMain`).	
3. Process	Deal a hand (`rules`).	Enough cards left in deck (`clsCardDeck`).
		Shuffle (`clsCardDeck`).
		Get three cards (`clsCardDeck`).
		Determine winner (`clsCardDeck`).
		Adjust player balance (`rules`).
4. Display	Show two cards (`frmMain`).	
	Show third card (`frmMain`).	
5. Terminate	Close.	

A Sideways Refinement is much less formal than a UML class diagram, but it serves as a good starting point for a program design. (You can always follow a Sideways Refinement with the more formal UML class diagrams.) As pointed out earlier, all but the Process step is normally performed as part of the program with which the user interacts. For the programs you've written thus far, frmMain is the class that presents the user interface for the program.

The class that sets the rules for the game assumes the processing responsibilities. That is, the game assumes that there are enough cards to deal a hand. If there aren't, the deck needs to be shuffled. The rules then ask for three cards. Although you could design the mechanics of the administration of the rules differently if you want, the author decided to determine the winner (or loser) when the first two cards are requested. That is, when the game displays the two cards and asks the player if she wants to bet, the third card is already waiting for display, and the rules class knows if the player is a winner or not before the third card is displayed. As soon as the user clicks the Bet button, the third card displays, and the player's game balance is adjusted accordingly.

Sideways Refinement does not necessarily show the sequencing of the program. Rather, it is meant to show the responsibilities each class has in the program relative to the Five Program Steps.

Now that you know how to design this game, in the following Try It Out you create the version available in the code provided for this chapter on wrox.com.

TRY IT OUT In Between Card Game (Chapter10ProgramInBetween.zip)

Now that you understand the design behind the game, you are ready to create it.

1. Create a new project in the normal manner.

2. Download Chapter10ProgramInBetween and copy it into the current project.

How It Works

The code for the frmMain class is shown in Listing 10-7. The nature of the code should be familiar to you now. The variable named position needs some explanation, however. The form shown in Figure 10-6 has five labels set across the top of the GroupBox object that I've labeled Hand. Because those labels have no border or text in them, they are not visible. However, when the rules class determines the winner of the hand, it also determines where the third card is to be displayed in the GroupBox object. In Figure 10-6, because the Queen of Hearts (QH) is greater than the high card that was dealt (9C), QH is assigned to the Text property of fifth label object. Therefore, the position variable is simply used to give a display of the third card relative to the range of the first two cards.

LISTING 10-7: In Between Card Program. (frmMain.cs)

```
using System;
using System.Windows.Forms;

public class frmMain : Form
{
    const int TIE = 0;
    const int PLAYERWINS = 1;
    const int DEALERWINS = 2;

    int betResult;
    int wager;
```

(continues)

LISTING 10-7 *(continued)*

```
    int balance;
    int position;

    clsInBetweenRules myRules = new clsInBetweenRules();
    string[] cards = new string[3];

    private Button btnDeal;
    private Button btnClose;
    private Label label1;
    private TextBox txtWager;
    private TextBox txtBalance;
    private Label label2;
    private GroupBox groupBox1;
    private Label lblLow;
    private Label label4;
    private Label label3;
    private TextBox txtHi;
    private TextBox txtLow;
    private Label lblMore;
    private Label lblLess;
    private Label lblHi;
    private Label lblMiddle;
    private Button btnBet;
    private Label lblOutcome;
    private Button btnReset;
    #region Windows code

    public frmMain()
    {
        bool flag;
        InitializeComponent();

        txtBalance.Text = myRules.Balance.ToString();   // Grub stake
        txtWager.Text = myRules.Wager.ToString();        // Default bet $10
        flag = int.TryParse(txtBalance.Text, out balance);
        flag = int.TryParse(txtWager.Text, out wager);

        myRules.Shuffle();                               // Shuffle deck
    }

    public static void Main()
    {
        frmMain main = new frmMain();
        Application.Run(main);
    }

    private void btnDeal_Click(object sender, EventArgs e)
    {
        int retval;

        ClearRanges();                  // Clear old data
        lblOutcome.Text = "";
```

```csharp
        retval = myRules.Balance;    // Money left to bet??
        if (retval == 0)
        {
            MessageBox.Show("You're broke. Game over.");
            return;
        }

        retval = myRules.getCardsLeft();    // Enough cards left??
        if (retval < 3)
        {
            lblOutcome.Text = "Deck was shuffled . . . ";
            myRules.Shuffle();
        }
        myRules.DealHand(cards, ref betResult, ref position);
        ShowHiLow();
    }

private void btnBet_Click(object sender, EventArgs e)
{
    bool flag = int.TryParse(txtWager.Text, out wager);
    if (flag == false)
    {
        MessageBox.Show("Dollar bets only. Re-enter.", "Input Error");
        txtWager.Focus();
        return;
    }

    switch (betResult)
    {
        case TIE:           // This is a tie
            lblOutcome.Text = "Tie. Dealer wins.";
            myRules.Balance = wager;
            break;

        case PLAYERWINS:
            lblOutcome.Text = "You win!";
            myRules.Balance +=  wager;
            break;

        case DEALERWINS:
            lblOutcome.Text = "Sorry, you lose.";
            myRules.Balance = wager;
            break;
    }
    txtBalance.Text = myRules.Balance.ToString();
    switch (position)
    {
        case 1:
            lblLess.Text = cards[2];
            break;
        case 2:
            lblLow.Text = cards[2];
            break;
        case 3:
```

(continues)

LISTING 10-7 *(continued)*

```csharp
                lblMiddle.Text = cards[2];
                break;
            case 4:
                lblHi.Text = cards[2];
                break;
            case 5:
                lblMore.Text = cards[2];
                break;
            default:
                MessageBox.Show("Results error.", "Processing Error");
                break;
        }
    }

    private void ShowHiLow()
    {
        txtLow.Text = cards[0];
        txtHi.Text = cards[1];
    }

    private void ClearRanges()
    {
        lblLess.Text ="";
        lblLow.Text = "";
        lblMiddle.Text = "";
        lblHi.Text = "";
        lblMore.Text = "";
    }

    private void btnReset_Click(object sender, EventArgs e)
    {
        myRules.Balance = 100;
        txtBalance.Text = "100";
        txtWager.Text = "10";
        ClearRanges();
    }
    private void btnClose_Click(object sender, EventArgs e)
    {
        Close();
    }
}
```

The code in the constructor simply initializes the textbox objects for play. When the user clicks the Deal button object, several method calls to the clsInBetweenRules class are made. The first checks to see if the player has any credit left with which to play the game. If the player is broke, the game cannot continue. The user can click the Reset button to reset her beginning balance. If the player has a balance, the program checks to see if there are enough cards left to play a hand. If not, the player sees a message stating that the deck was shuffled and the game continues. Finally, the hand is dealt and the two cards are shown to the dealer. If you look at the way the code works, the outcome of the bet is already known at this point. The outcome of the hand is simply a matter of whether the player clicks the Bet button.

Using the ref Keyword

If the player does decide to play, the `btnBet_Click()` code determines how things display to the user. When the hand was "dealt" by the call to

```
myRules.DealHand(cards, ref betResult, ref position);
```

the variable `betResult` determines who won the bet, and the variable `position` determines where among the five labels the third card displays, as explained earlier. The variable `cards` is an array filled in with the three cards for the hand being played.

Because C# methods can return only a single value, you cannot use a simple `return` statement within the method to return all the information you need from the call. Instead, you pass the `cards` array to the method along with the `betResult` and `position` variables. However, because the keyword `ref` appears before the two variables in the call, C# knows not to send each variable's rvalue to the method but sends the lvalue instead. Any time the `ref` keyword prefixes a variable name in a method call, the lvalue of the variable is passed to the method. Recall that arguments sent to methods pass a copy of the variable's rvalue to a method by default. However, when the `ref` keyword is used, the lvalue of the variable is sent to the method. Because an lvalue tells the method where the variable "lives" in memory, the method can permanently change the value of the variable. The code uses this mechanism to permanently change the values of `betResult` and `position`. The two `switch` statements in the `btnBet_Click()` method use these two variables to inform the player of the outcome of her bet.

Listing 10-8 shows the code for the `clsInBetweenRules` class.

LISTING 10-8: Source Code for Game Rules (clsInBetweenRules.cs)

```csharp
using System;
class clsInBetweenRules
{
    // =============== symbolic constants ==================
    const int TIE = 0;
    const int PLAYERWINS = 1;
    const int DEALERWINS = 2;

    // =============== static members ======================
    // =============== instance members ====================
    private int balance;        // The player's money balance
    private int wager;          // Amount of current bet
    private int lowCard;        // The low card value 1  13
    private int lowCardIndex;   // The position of this card in pips
    private int hiCard;         // The high card value 1  13
    private int hiCardIndex;    // The position of this card in pips
    private int dealtCard;      // The dealt card value 1  13
    private int dealtCardIndex; // The position of this card in pips

    private clsCardDeck myDeck; // A card deck object

    // =============== constructor(s) ======================
    public clsInBetweenRules()
    {
        balance = 100;
```

(continues)

LISTING 10-8 *(continued)*

```
        wager = 10;
        myDeck = new clsCardDeck();
    }
    // =============== property methods =====================
    public int Balance
    {
        get
        {
            return balance;
        }
        set
        {
            if (value >= 0)
            {
                balance = value;
            }
        }
    }

    public int Wager
    {
        get
        {
            return wager;
        }
        set
        {
            if (value > 0)
            {
                wager = value;
            }
        }
    }


    // =============== helper methods =======================

    /*****
     * Purpose: Deals out the next three cards and fills in the hand[]
     *          array that was passed in from frmMain. It always arranges
     *          cards so lower of first two cards is displayed on the
     *          left of frmMain.
     *
     * Parameter list:
     *   string[] hand        the three cards for a hand
     *
     * Return value:
     *   void
     *
     *   *****/
    private void SetCards(string[] hand)
    {
```

```
    int temp;

    hand[0] = myDeck.getCardPip(lowCardIndex);
    hand[1] = myDeck.getCardPip(hiCardIndex);
    hand[2] = myDeck.getCardPip(dealtCardIndex);

    if (lowCard == hiCard || lowCard < hiCard)        // A tie
    {
        hand[0] = myDeck.getCardPip(lowCardIndex);
        hand[1] = myDeck.getCardPip(hiCardIndex);
    }
    else
    {
        temp = hiCard;                // Swap hi and lo cards
        hiCard = lowCard;
        lowCard = temp;

        temp = hiCardIndex;           // Swap hi and lo indexes
        hiCardIndex = lowCardIndex;
        lowCardIndex = temp;

        hand[0] = myDeck.getCardPip(lowCardIndex);
        hand[1] = myDeck.getCardPip(hiCardIndex);
    }
}

/*****
 * Purpose: Sets the outcome of the bet and tells where to display the
 *          down card.
 *
 * Parameter list:
 *   ref int outCome        who won the game
 *   ref int position       where to display the down card
 *
 * Return value:
 *   void
 *
 * CAUTION: the two ints are passed in by reference, which means this
 *          method can permanently change their values.
 *   *****/
private void SetWinnerAndPosition(ref int outCome, ref int position)
{

    if (dealtCard == lowCard)    // Dealt and low card equal
    {
        outCome = DEALERWINS;
        position = 2;
        return;
    }
    if (dealtCard < lowCard)     // Dealt card less than low card
    {
        outCome = DEALERWINS;
        position = 1;
        return;
    }
```

(continues)

LISTING 10-8 *(continued)*

```
        if (dealtCard > lowCard && dealtCard < hiCard) // Card in range
        {
            outCome = PLAYERWINS;
            position = 3;
            return;
        }

        if (dealtCard == hiCard) // Dealt card equals hi card
        {
            outCome = DEALERWINS;
            position = 4;
            return;
        }
        if (dealtCard > hiCard) // Dealt card equals hi card
        {
            outCome = DEALERWINS;
            position = 5;
            return;
        }
    }


    // =============== general methods =====================

    /*****
     * Purpose: Gets the first card and treats it as first displayed card
     *
     * Parameter list:
     *   n/a
     *
     * Return value:
     *   void
     *
     * CAUTION: King is a special case since its modulus = 0
     *   *****/
    public void getFirstCard()
    {
        lowCardIndex = myDeck.getOneCard();
        lowCard = lowCardIndex % 13;
        if (lowCard == 0)                    // A King
            lowCard = 13;
    }

    /*****
     * Purpose: Gets second card and treats it as second displayed card
     *
     * Parameter list:
     *   n/a
     *
     * Return value:
     *   void
     *
     * CAUTION: King is a special case since its modulus = 0
```

```
 *   *****/
public void getSecondCard()
{
    hiCardIndex = myDeck.getOneCard();
    hiCard = hiCardIndex % 13;
    if (hiCard == 0)                 // A King
        hiCard = 13;
}
/*****
 * Purpose: Gets the last card and treats it as down card
 *
 * Parameter list:
 *  n/a
 *
 * Return value:
 *  void
 *
 * CAUTION: King is a special case since its modulus = 0
 *  *****/
public void getDealtCard()
{
    dealtCardIndex = myDeck.getOneCard();
    dealtCard = dealtCardIndex % 13;
    if (dealtCard == 0)              // A King
        dealtCard = 13;
}

/*****
 * Purpose: Shuffle the deck
 *
 * Parameter list:
 *  n/a
 *
 * Return value:
 *  void
 *
 *  *****/
public void Shuffle()
{
    myDeck.ShuffleDeck();
}

/*****
 * Purpose: Gets the number of cards left in the deck.
 *
 * Parameter list:
 *  n/a
 *
 * Return value:
 *  int              the number of cards left
 *
 * CAUTION: King is a special case since its modulus = 0
 *  *****/
public int getCardsLeft()
{
```

(continues)

LISTING 10-8 *(continued)*

```
            return myDeck.getCardsLeftInDeck();
    }

    /*****
     * Purpose: Deals out a hand. Note that all three cards are dealt at
     *          once, but the dealt card is not displayed until after the
     *          bet. The results are known before the bet, but not revealed
     *          now.
     *
     * Parameter list:
     *   string[] hand          the three cards for a hand
     *   ref int outCome        who won the game
     *   ref int position       where to display the down card
     *
     * Return value:
     *   void
     *
     * CAUTION: the two ints are passed in by reference, which means this
     *          method can permanently change their values.
     *   *****/
    public void DealHand(string[] hand, ref int outCome, ref int position)
    {
        getFirstCard();       // Get first two display cards
        getSecondCard();

        getDealtCard();       // Get down card

        SetCards(hand);       // Rearrange if necessary

                              // Who wins and where to display down card
        SetWinnerAndPosition(ref outCome, ref position);
    }

}
```

One thing to notice in the code presented in Listings 10-7 and 10-8 is that frmMain knows nothing about clsCardDeck. (That is, there is no coupling between the two classes.) All interaction with the deck of cards is managed by the clsInBetweenRules class. This is as it should be. If the game were not played with this enforced isolation between the card deck and the player, it would be like allowing gamblers in Vegas to deal their own hands of blackjack…not going to happen!

To accommodate the requirements of the game, you can add two new methods to the clsCardDeck class. These two methods are shown in Listing 10-9.

LISTING 10-9: Source Code for getOneCard() (clsCardDeck.cs)

```
    /**
     * Purpose: Get the index of a dealt card. This overloads the method
     *          that returns the string representation of the card.
     *
```

```
 * Parameter list:
 *      void
 *
 * Return value:
 *      int       the index into the pips array or 0 if no more cards
 *                left in deck.
 */
public int getOneCard()
{
    nextCard++;
    if (nextCard <= DECKSIZE)
    {
        return deck[nextCard];
    }
    else
    {
        return 0;
    }
}
/**
 * Purpose: Returns the number of cards left in the deck.
 *
 * Parameter list:
 *      void
 *
 * Return value:
 *      int       A count of card remaining in the deck.
 */
public int getCardsLeftInDeck()
{
    return DECKSIZE  nextCard;
}
```

The getOneCard() method is designed to return the index of a card rather than its string representation. The getCardsLeftInDeck() method simply returns the number of cards left in the deck. Note how easy it was to make this change for the game at hand. If you think about it, most card games will likely need these methods, too.

Although this program involves more code than others you've studied, you should follow what each method does. However, to make sure you do understand what's going on in the code, study it and describe in your own mind what happens as the game is played. When you feel you understand the program flow, rerun the program with breakpoints and single-step through the code to see if your expectations match what actually happens. If they don't, you need to figure out why. This kind of exercise can help you develop your debugging skills...the subject of the next chapter.

SUMMARY

In this chapter you learned the details of property methods and how they are part of the user interface for a class. It is the set statement blocks of the property methods that serve as your last line of defense against having a class object put into an unwanted state. You should also have a more complete appreciation of how the `private` access specifier for the class properties helps to safeguard the integrity of the data.

Someone once said, "Practice makes perfect." Well, not really. Perfect practice makes perfect. However, although perfection in writing classes may be your goal, a more reasonable objective right now is to get experience designing and writing classes for objects of your own creation. You are now familiar with the benefits of both UML class and Sideways Refinement design methods. Both are worthwhile tools to hang on your tool belt.

You should spend enough time to answer the exercises at the end of this chapter before moving on to Chapter 11. After completing the exercises, try to think up a few programming problems of your own design. Thinking about programming problems, designing a solution, and then implementing that solution is the *only* way to learn programming.

EXERCISES

You can find the answers to the following exercises in Appendix A.

1. Another game similar to the In Between game discussed in this chapter is called Acey-Deucey. This variant of the game is played exactly the same way, but the high card in the deck is an ace, and a two becomes the lowest card. What would you do to implement this variation of the game instead of In Between?

2. If you made the changes suggested in Exercise 1, can you see any improvements that might make the code easier to understand?

3. The game of Euchre uses a subset of a standard deck of cards. Specifically, only the nines, tens, jacks, queens, kings, and aces are used. If you want to write a program that plays Euchre, what problems does `clsCardDeck` pose?

4. Given the problem stated in Exercise 3, how would you resolve the problem?

5. Modify the program shown in Figure 10-1 to display only those cards that apply to the game of Euchre.

▶ **WHAT YOU LEARNED IN THIS CHAPTER**

TOPIC	KEY POINTS
Class constructors	How to write overloaded constructors.
Cohesion	Ability to state the purpose of a method in one or two sentences.
Coupling	Class methods should not be dependent on other class methods.
Property methods	Used to get or set the values of class properties. They form the class interface.
Getters	A property method used to fetch a property value.
Setters	A property method used to change the state of a property.
Class design	Design considerations that make a good, reusable class.
3-tier architecture	How classes can be used to augment N-tiered architectures.

11

Exception Handling and Debugging

- ➤ The differences among bugs, errors, and exceptions
- ➤ Syntax, semantic, and logic bugs
- ➤ Exception handling
- ➤ Throwing exceptions
- ➤ Using the debugger
- ➤ Debugging windows
- ➤ Bug detection, isolation, and correction

WROX.COM CODE DOWNLOADS FOR THIS CHAPTER

You can find the wrox.com code downloads for this chapter at `www.wrox.com/remtitle` `.cgi?isbn=9781118336922` on the Download Code tab. The code in the `Chapter11` folder is individually named according to the names throughout the chapter.

It would be wonderful if this chapter didn't need to be written. However, the truth is that problems do arise when programs are developed and run.

Most experienced programmers agree that approximately 20 percent of program development time consists of writing program code. The remaining 80 percent is used for testing, debugging, and maintenance of that code. Clearly, anything you can do to reduce that 80 percent figure can help keep you on time and on budget.

OVERVIEW

It's common for programmers to lump bugs, program errors, and program exceptions into a single concept. Technically, each of these types of errors is different. Now consider each in a little more detail.

Bugs

A *bug* is a specific type of error caused by the programmer. Bugs typically fall into one of three general categories:

➤ Syntax errors

➤ Semantic errors

➤ Logic errors

Syntax Errors

A *syntax error* occurs when a statement does not comply with the rules of the language. Just as English has specific rules, so do programming languages. A sentence in English, for example, is expected to have a noun and a verb. A programming statement is similar to a sentence, and if you don't obey the rules, syntax errors result. A program that has a syntax error cannot be compiled.

Visual Studio's IntelliSense does an excellent job of detecting syntax errors the instant you enter a program statement. The dreaded squiggly line tells you the nature of the syntax error that you've made. If you place the cursor over the squiggly line, Visual Studio presents a message informing you of the probable cause of the error. When you start writing programs, they probably have a ton of squiggly lines in them. However, as you gain experience with C#, the frequency of your syntax errors likely decreases. If you're like most programmers, however, you move to bigger, better, and more complex errors!

Semantic Errors

Semantic errors occur when you use the proper language syntax, but the context of the statement or expression is wrong. For example, you could say the following English sentence, "The dog meowed." The syntax is correct because the sentence has a noun and a verb, but the context of the noun and verb is wrong. A program with a semantic error can often be compiled, but the results are (usually) wrong.

Consider the following statements:

```
int j;
int answer;

j = 10;
answer = 1 / j;
```

The code generates no error messages from IntelliSense and does compile. However, answer is always 0 for any value of j that is greater than 1. (The code, for example, does produce the correct result if j equals 1.) In this context, you try to create a fractional value using integer math. If you write the last statement above as

```
answer = 1.0 / j;
```

IntelliSense issues an error message asking if you need to cast the expression. IntelliSense can ferret out the proper context now because it knows that 1.0 is a floating-point value. Semantic errors are a little harder to uncover than syntax errors because IntelliSense cannot always detect them.

Logic Errors

Logic errors exist when the program compiles but produces an incorrect result. This makes them sound a lot like semantic errors, but there is a distinction. Semantic errors reflect a bending of the syntax rules of the language. Logic errors, on the other hand, are the result of design errors the programmer makes when manipulating a program's data. The distinction is subtle, but real.

As you gain programming experience, syntax and semantic errors tend to become less and less frequent. Instead, you spend most of your time tracking down and correcting logic errors in the program. Every programmer makes logic errors, and you should expect to make your fair share. The attitude to take is that fixing any kind of bug is a learning experience. It is one of the oddities of programming that the more mistakes you make, the better you become as a programmer.

INPUT ERRORS

In a strict sense, a *input error* is an error made by the user. Sadly, end users are smart enough to know that they don't need to read the user's manual. It's sort of like refusing to ask for directions when you're lost. Users refuse to admit that they don't know how to run a program. As a result, strange things can happen when the program runs.

How can you reduce input errors? The following programming concepts can help.

Data Validation

Perhaps the most common type of input error occurs when the user provides input into the program but not input of the correct type. For example, the program might request the user to enter the number of units to purchase, and the user might mean to type 10 but because of a fat finger types 1o instead, pressing the "oh" key by mistake. However, a good programmer anticipates such mistakes by adding validation code to a program. If you want to validate that the user did correctly enter the quantity to be purchased, you can validate the input using the TryParse() method as you have done in the past:

```
bool flag;
int quantity;
flag = int.TryParse(txtQuantity.Text, out quantity);
if (flag == false)          // Things didn't go well
{
      MessageBox.Show("Expected digit characters only. Re-enter.",
                   "Input Error");
      txtQuantity.Focus();
      return;
}
```

This is a common validation routine you've seen in previous programs.

Invalid input data is probably the most common source of a program error. One reason this is true is that you cannot totally control what a user types into a textbox object. As a general rule, any time you ask for input from the user using a textbox object, you should validate the response. The general areas of validation include the following:

➤ **Type checking:** This is where you would use code such as `TryParse()` ensure the input characters are consistent with the wanted data type.

➤ **Consistency checking:** This type of check frequently compares two or more responses to ensure that the input data is consistent. For example, if users state their gender as male and later state they are 8 months pregnant, chances are they answered one of the input questions incorrectly.

➤ **Range checking:** This check attempts to verify that the input data is reasonable by checking the input to see if it falls within a reason range of values. For example, if you ask for someone's age and get a response of 422, it's likely that the user meant some other value. Your code should prompt the user to reenter the value.

➤ **Length checking:** Often a response requires a specific number of characters as input. Common examples are two-character state abbreviations, ZIP codes, and phone and Social Security numbers. Sometimes simply checking the length of the user's input can detect errors missed by other checks.

The rule is simple: Assume the user's input is *always* incorrect.

Limit User Input

You've doubtless run programs in which you've made a choice from a given list. Common input techniques are to present you with a list of options in the form of a listbox or combination box object. Although you may see this approach as a convenience provided by the programmer, the driving force was not your convenience, but rather a plan to restrict your choice to the options in the list.

Programmers know users can mess up program input. By presenting users with a limited list of options rather than letting them type something into a textbox, the programmer can limit users to input that is at least consistent with the expected data. True, users can still select the wrong option, but at least the answer is consistent with the processing that's to follow. For example, you could present a textbox with a label that reads, `Enter Gender (M, F)`. Clearly, you expect an M or an F to be entered by users. However, you've given users at least 24 chances to mess things up (and that's assuming that they select a letter character and get the case correct.)

Writing code designed to limit input errors by users is not very difficult. In the Try It Out that follows, you use radio buttons to constrain input choices.

TRY IT OUT **Restricting Input Choices (Chapter11ProgramRadioBu ttons.zip)**

In this Try It Out, you are presented with a program designed to restrict users' input choices by using radio buttons.

While you could use a listbox for the choices presented here, a better choice is to use radio buttons. Radio buttons let the user see all of the options without having to expand the listbox. Radio buttons are a good option when the number of options is relatively small. Figure 11-1 shows a simple program that exercises several input objects that can force users into more consistent program input.

1. Create a new project in the usual manner.

2. Add four radio buttons, as shown in Figure 11-1. If you download the code file, other objects are already placed on it (see Figure 11-3). However, you can still add a new set of radio buttons as shown here.

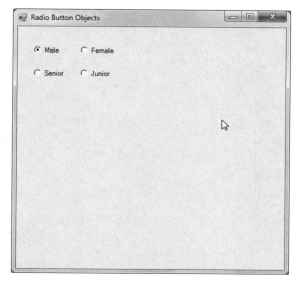

FIGURE 11-1: Using radio buttons

How it Works

The program shown suggests that the user should select either Male or Female and then select either Senior or Junior. Unfortunately, that's not the way the code works. As the form is currently laid out, if the user clicks the Male radio button, a small dot appears in that selection (refer to Figure 11-1). Having made that selection, the user then moves onto the next input and clicks Senior, which causes a small dot to appear in that selection. The bad news is that the selection of Male disappears, which is probably not what the programmer had in mind.

The problem is that radio buttons objects are associated with mutually exclusive choices. The program views all the radio buttons on the form as belonging to the same set of options. Therefore, selecting one option turns all the rest of the buttons off. This is precisely the behavior expected from radio button objects but not what the programmer expected. So how do you fix the problem?

Group Box

The solution is simple: Place each group of related radio button choices in its own GroupBox object. To add a GroupBox object to a form, select the Containers option in the Toolbox and drag a GroupBox object onto the form. Change the Text property of the object to Gender:. Now drag a second

GroupBox object onto the form and make its Text property read Membership group:. Now, while holding down the Shift key, click the Male and Female radio buttons. Now press Ctrl+X to cut those two radio buttons from the form. Click in the GroupBox to which you applied the Gender text and press Ctrl+V. The two radio buttons should now be copied inside the GroupBox with the Gender: heading. Repeat for the Membership radio buttons. Your form should now look like the one in Figure 11-2.

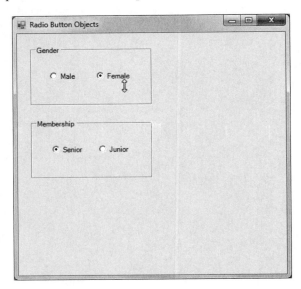

FIGURE 11-2: Correctly using radio buttons

As you can see in Figure 11-2, the GroupBox arranges the radio buttons in two groups, each of which can have its appropriate choice. (You can tell this is the case because both Female and Senior are selected.)

The code for processing radio button choices is essentially as follows:

```
int choice;
if (rbMale.Checked == true)
{
    choice = MALE;
}
else
{
    choice = FEMALE;
}
```

(I use rb as a prefix for radio buttons, which is a break from my normal three-character prefixes for Toolbox objects. The reason for a two-character prefix is...I don't have a reason. It just seems to make sense to me. If this bothers you, try rbt or rbn.) A radio button object has a Checked property that is logic true if the button is selected and logic false if it is not. (The program assumes that symbolic constants for MALE and FEMALE have been defined elsewhere in the program.) If the list of choices is greater than two, you can use nested if statements to process the selection.

Default Choices

Quite often you want to have a default choice for a series of radio buttons. It makes sense to have the default choice be the expected choice for most users. If you expect most users to be female, you can add the following code to the form's constructor:

```
public frmMain()
{
    InitializeComponent();
    rbFemale.Checked = true;
}
```

The `InitializeComponents()` method is used to build a memory image of the form. When control returns from that method call, the complete form object has been built in memory. If you want to change the default state of that form object, the constructor is the place to do it. When the form displays, it has the Female option selected. Note that placing the code inside the constructor means it falls within the Initialization step of the Five Program Steps.

Check Boxes

Another way to restrict the input from a user is to employ `CheckBox` objects, as shown in Figure 11-3.

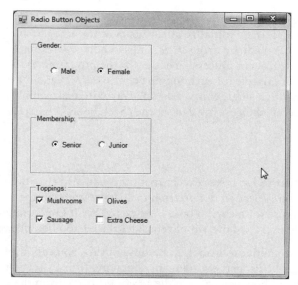

FIGURE 11-3: Using checkboxes to limit input

Unlike radio buttons, check box selections are not mutually exclusive. Users are free to check as many as they think are appropriate. The `GroupBox` object that holds the `CheckBox` objects in Figure 11-3 is not required. However, it is not uncommon for the range of options depicted by the check boxes to apply to some overriding choice. If that is the case, using a `GroupBox` helps to focus the users' attention on the choice of toppings.

Because each check box object can be selected, your code needs to examine the state of each one. One way to do this would be to use code similar to the following (I tend to use ckb as a prefix for check box objects):

```
Array.Clear(toppings, 0, toppings.Length);

if (ckbMushroom.Checked == true)
{
    toppings[MUSHROOMS] = 1;
}

if (ckbOlives.Checked == true)
{
    toppings[OLIVES] = 1;
}

if (ckbSausage.Checked == true)
{
    toppings[SAUSAGE] = 1;
}

if (ckbExtraCheese.Checked == true)
{
    toppings[EXTRACHEESE] = 1;
}
```

The code uses the Clear() method of the Array class to initialize all elements of the array to 0. Then a series of if statements records the choices made by the user. Again, symbolic constants are used to help document the choices and make subsequent processing easier for the programmer to understand. You could, of course, use a discrete variable for each topping choice. However, an array makes sense here because the choices all pertain to a single entity, and an array will likely simplify subsequent code. If you want to set a default set of choices, you can set the check boxes' Checked properties to true in the constructor.

Combination Boxes

Combination boxes, or *combo boxes*, are similar to list boxes except that users can also type in a response if they want. Normally, however, users select an option from the list presented in the combo box object. Figure 11-4 shows a typical use for a combo box. (The next "Try It Out" section also discusses the other objects shown in the figure. For now, simply consider the combo box object.)

As you can see in Figure 11-4, combo boxes are similar to listboxes. Because of this, you can initialize the list in the combo box either by using the Property window in design mode or by setting the list under program control. Figure 11-5 shows how you can use the Items property from the Property window to add items to the list.

Using the Items property in the Property window presumably means that you know the list of items that you want to place in the combo box before the program runs. However, in many cases you want to populate the combo with a list determined at run time rather than at compile time. For example, you might read a list of names from a database and want to place a subset of those names in a combo box from which the user can choose a specific name. To create the list shown in Figure 11-5, you can use the following code instead of the String Collection Editor:

```
cmbSize.Items.Add("Small");
cmbSize.Items.Add("Medium");
cmbSize.Items.Add("Large");
```

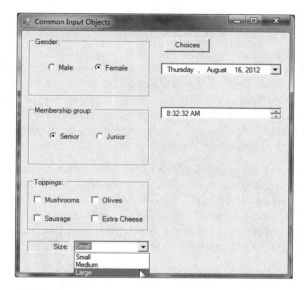

FIGURE 11-4: Using combo boxes

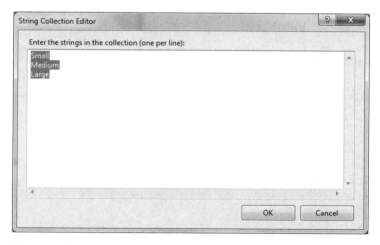

FIGURE 11-5: Using the String Editor of a combo box

If you have an array of names that you want to add to the combo box, you might use something like this:

```
int i;

// Assume names[] filled in here...
```

```
for (int i = 0; i < names.Length; i++)
{
    cmbPeople.Items.Add(names[i]);
}
cmbPeople.SelectedIndex = 0;
```

This code fragment simply adds the list of names stored in the `names` array to the combo box. (A simpler way to accomplish the same task is to use `cmbPeople.DataSource = names`.) The `SelectedIndex` property of the combo box determines which of the items added to the combo box displays as the default choice when the program runs. Because the list of items in the combo box is a zero-based list, the preceding code displays the first item in the list. You should set `SelectedIndex` to be the default item from the list. If you do not set the `SelectedIndex` property, the combo box is empty and looks similar to an empty textbox waiting for the user to type something into it. You can also retrieve the `SelectedIndex` property from the combo box.

You can also have the object sort the contents of the list of items added to the combo box. Often this makes it easier for the user to locate which item she wants to select from the list. Keep in mind, however, that sometimes the order in which the items are added to the combo box has an impact on subsequent code. For example, if the `names` array selection will be used later to index into the database for details about the person selected, that person's position in the `names` array may determine how to locate him in the database. In that case you would not want to set the `Sorted` property to true.

If you want to retrieve the text from a combo box, use something like this:

```
string buff = cmbPeople.Text;
```

Combo Boxes With or Without User Input

You can turn off the user's ability to type a value into the combo box by setting the `DropDownStyle` property to `DropDownList` in the Property window. This style makes the combo box a read-only object. This makes it easier to validate the data since your validation code does not need to worry about the differences if the user types "small," "Small," or "SMALL." If you do want to accept user input, then set the type to `DropDown`. This is the default style of behavior for a combo box.

Date and Time Input

Another common input is a date. Having the user enter a date is also a good way to get bogus input data because there are so many different date formats in use (military, French, and so on). The same confusion can arise for time, too, because time can be represented by a 12-hour or 24-hour clock.

You can standardize such information by using the `DateTimePicker` object. If you drag a `DateTimePicker` object onto a form and run the program, it looks similar to what is shown in Figure 11-6.

As you can see, the `DateTimePicker` object looks similar to a combo box but with a date in the `Text` property of the object. (The `DateTimePicker` is locale-aware, so it presents the proper format [e.g., US versus France].) However, if you click the down arrow on the object, the output changes to look like that shown in Figure 11-7.

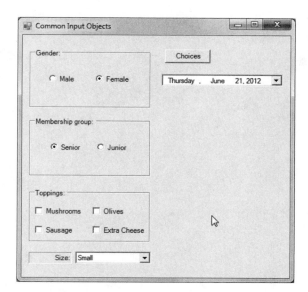

FIGURE 11-6: Date and time format

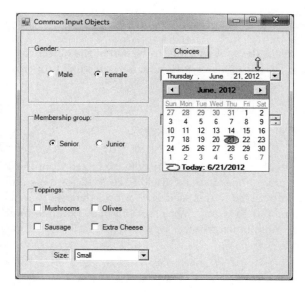

FIGURE 11-7: The DateTimePicker object

The Format and ShowUpDown Properties

The state of the object shown in Figure 11-7 assumes that the Format property of the object is set to Long and the ShowUpDown property is set to false. If you set the Format property to Short, the date would be shown as 6/21/2012.

Add a second `DateTimePicker` object to the form and set its `ShowUpDown` property to `true`. The form now looks like the one shown in Figure 11-8.

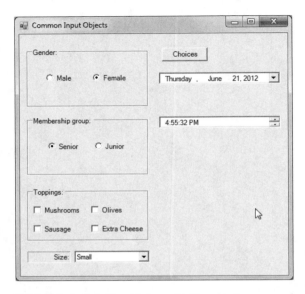

FIGURE 11-8: DateTimePicker with ShowUpDown

In the second `DateTimePicker` object, users can use the spin controls at the end of the object to change the hour displayed in the `Text` property. Users can also type a time into the `Text` property should they choose to do so.

To extract the information from a `DateTimePicker` object, use the following code:

```
string date = dtpDate.Value.ToShortDateString();
string time = dtpTime.Value.ToShortTimeString();
```

You can select different date and time methods to alter the format of the data extracted from the `DateTimePicker` object to suit your needs. The preceding statements yield 6/21/2012 for `date` and 4:55 PM for `time`. Although the various objects discussed in this section can force the user to input program data in a specific format, things can (and do) go wrong. With that in mind, examine some other techniques you can use to make your code more bulletproof.

EXCEPTION HANDLING

No matter how well you attempt to anticipate bad program input, the chance exists that something will be missed. When an error condition presents itself in a program, C# produces an exception. An *exception* is simply an unwanted program state. Note that an exception actually isn't a program bug. As pointed out earlier, a bug is a programmer mistake and you must correct that. Still, unexpected things can occur while the program runs even if there are no bugs in the program. For example, if you write a program that copies data to a DVD and the user forgot to load a blank DVD into the DVD drive, the program generates an exception. The simple program shown in Listing 11-1 illustrates an exception.

LISTING 11-1: Code to Generate an Exception

```
using System;
using System.Windows.Forms;

public class frmMain : Form
{
    private Button btnCalc;

    #region Windows code

    public frmMain()
    {
        InitializeComponent();
    }

    public static void Main()
    {
        frmMain main = new frmMain();
        Application.Run(main);
    }

    private void btnCalc_Click(object sender, EventArgs e)
    {
        int exp1 = 0;
        int exp2 = 5;
        int result;

        result = exp2 / exp1;

    }
}
```

The program is a standard C# form with a single button object on it. In the click event for the button object, exp1 is set to 0 and exp2 to 5. Dividing a value by zero produces a divide-by-zero exception. As it stands, if you run this program outside the Visual Studio environment, the program pops up the exception notification, as shown in Figure 11-9. (If you run the program within the Visual Studio environment, you get a similar message, but the precise statement where the exception occurred is highlighted.)

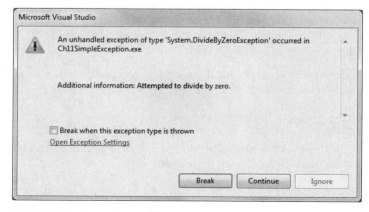

FIGURE 11-9: Exception notification

This is an ugly thing for the user to see! The message tells everyone who sees it that the programmer didn't expect the program to reach this (divide-by-zero) state, but let it happen anyway. Not good.

How can you prevent such ugliness?

try-catch Statement Blocks

You can use a try-catch statement block to "trap" program exceptions. The general syntax for a try-catch statement block is as follows:

```
try
{
    // try statement block
}
catch [(exception)]
{
    // catch statement block
}
[finally
{
    // finally statement block
}]
```

Although this looks rather intimidating, it isn't. The try block begins with the keyword try followed by an opening curly brace. Following the curly brace are the program statements that you think might cause an exception to be generated, or *thrown*, by the program. (Most programmers would say, "This code might *throw* an exception.") A closing curly brace for the try statement block appears after those program statements.

The catch block immediately follows the closing curly brace of the try block. The purpose of the catch block is to execute one or more statements if the exception is thrown. The brackets indicate that you can also follow the keyword catch with a specific exception if you want. (You see an example of this in a moment.) The closing curly brace marks the end of the catch statement block.

The optional finally statement block represents a block of code you want to have executed whether an exception is thrown or not. For example, you might have activated some resource in the try statement block (for example, you might have opened a file or database, or maybe a network or printer connection) that needs to be closed when you finish using it. By placing the required statements in the finally statement , you are ensured that, regardless of the exception or lack of one, those statements will be executed. Not all try-catch blocks use the (optional) finally block. However, a try block must have either a catch or a finally block.

The next section contains code that uses the try-catch block for exception handling. In the example, a specific exception is handled as well an unspecified exceptions.

TRY IT OUT An Exception Example

Modify the code in Listing 11-1 to include a try-catch block. All the code is presented here because it makes it easier to understand what the code does if you can see it all in one place.

1. Create a new project in the normal manner.

2. Add the code in Listing 11-2 or simply download its .zip file.

LISTING 11-2: Exception Handling Program (frmMain.cs)

```csharp
//#define DEBUG
#undef DEBUG
using System;
using System.Windows.Forms;

public class frmMain : Form
{
    private Button btnExit;

    private Button btnCalc;
    #region Windows code

    public frmMain()
    {
        InitializeComponent();
    }

    public static void Main()
    {
        frmMain main = new frmMain();
        Application.Run(main);
    }


    private void btnCalc_Click(object sender, EventArgs e)
    {
        int exp1 = 0;
        int exp2 = 5;
        int result;

#if DEBUG
        MessageBox.Show("exp1 = " + exp1.ToString());
#endif


        try
        {
            result = exp2 / exp1;
             MessageBox.Show("Never get here");
        }
        catch (DivideByZeroException)
        {
            MessageBox.Show("Divide by zero error.", "Exception Thrown");
            return;
        }
        catch (Exception ex)
        {
            MessageBox.Show("Error: " + ex.Message, "Exception Thrown");
        }
        finally
        {
            MessageBox.Show("In finally");
        }
```

(continues)

LISTING 11-2 *(continued)*

```
        }
        private void btnExit_Click(object sender, EventArgs e)
        {
            Close();
        }
    }
```

How It Works

Now, when you run the program and the click the Calculate button, the program looks like what is shown in Figure 11-10.

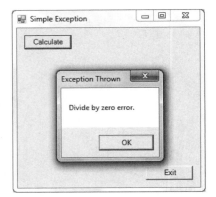

FIGURE 11-10: A divide-by-zero exception

Now, when the divide-by-zero exception occurs, the `catch` statement block is executed to present a message to the user.

The message box that appears in the `try` block after the divide-by-zero exception occurs is never executed. After the program control is passed to a `catch` block, the code path does *not* automatically return to the `try` block code.

Although the solution is less ugly than what happened with Listing 11-1, it's still not going to win any beauty contest. You can remove a few of the remaining warts by considering what the code is trying to do.

Anticipating a Specific Exception

One of the ways you can add improvements is to consider what exceptions might occur given what the `try` statement block does. It's obvious that one possible exception is the divide-by-zero exception with which you have been experimenting. So how can you find out what other possible exceptions might be thrown?

If you use the Debug ➪ Exceptions menu sequence (or Ctrl+D, E), expand the Common Language Runtime Exceptions heading, and finally expand the System heading, you see a list similar to that shown in Figure 11-11.

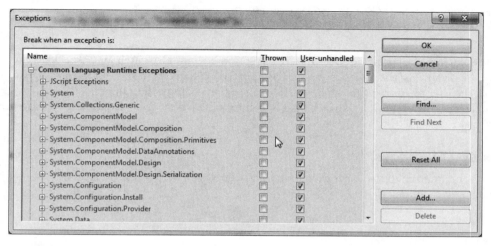

FIGURE 11-11: Exceptions list

Realizing that a certain type of error could occur, you can modify Listing 11-2 to include the following code fragment:

```
try
{
    result = exp2 / exp1;
    MessageBox.Show("Never get here");
}
catch (DivideByZeroException)
{
    MessageBox.Show("Divide by zero error.", "Exception Thrown");
}
```

The `catch` statement block is now prefaced by a parenthesized expression that uses the `DivideByZeroException` exception. Because you have anticipated the error with greater precision, you can give a more meaningful error message to the user.

For example, if the values for `exp1` and `exp2` come from other input sources, they could overflow the values allowed by an `int`. Or perhaps there's some kind of hardware failure that throws an exception. In those cases, you may want to provide multiple `catch` blocks, for example:

```
try
{
    result = exp2 / exp1;
    MessageBox.Show("Never get here");
}
catch (DivideByZeroException)
{
    MessageBox.Show("Expression 1 is zero. Please reenter.",
                    "Exception Thrown");
    txtExpression1.Focus();
    return;
}
catch
{
```

```
        MessageBox.Show("Something went terribly wrong.",
                        "Exception Thrown");
    }
```

The code now catches the specific divide-by-zero exception but can also catch an unspecified exception should one occur. For the divide-by-zero exception, you can give a more helpful error message and even ask the user to reenter the value, as shown in the preceding code snippet. The error message for the unspecified exception, however, is not helpful to the user. You need another way to get rid of a few more warts.

Fuzzy Exception Messages

Although you might not nail the exact exception that occurs, you can provide help to the user with the following modification:

```
    try
    {
        result = exp2 / exp1;
    }
    catch (DivideByZeroException)
    {
        MessageBox.Show("Expression 1 is zero. Please reenter.",
                        "Exception Thrown");
        txtExpression1.Focus();
        return;
    }
    catch (Exception ex)
    {
        MessageBox.Show("Error: " + ex.Message, "Exception Thrown");
    }
```

In this code you define an `Exception` object variable named ex. In the message box you use the `Message` property of the `Exception` object to provide a more precise message about the exception that occurred. These messages are *fuzzy exception messages* because they are better than no message, but often not precise enough to enable you to take some specific corrective action (as you did with the divide-by-zero exception). Although this may not resolve the problem for the user, at least the fuzzy message is better than the generic message you gave before.

Given that your code now handles fuzzy exceptions, how can you test it?

Testing Fuzzy Exceptions

You can test an exception by throwing that exception using the `throw` keyword. (catch…throw…get it?) To illustrate this, modify your click event code again as follows:

```
    try
    {
        throw new ArgumentOutOfRangeException(); // New statement
        result = exp2 / exp1;
    }
    catch (DivideByZeroException)
    {
        MessageBox.Show("Expression 1 is zero. Please reenter.",
```

```
                    "Exception Thrown");
    txtExpression1.Focus();
    return;
}
catch (Exception ex)
{
    MessageBox.Show("Error: " + ex.Message, "Exception Thrown");
}
```

The first statement in the try block uses a sample exception to try from the list of possibilities shown in Figure 11-11. As you probably expected, the parentheses at the end of the
ArgumentOutOfRangeException() expression mean that the program is going to "construct" an
ArgumentOutOfRangeException and then throw that exception. (The term *throw* simply means
that the program produces that exception at the moment the constructor executes.) Because the
exception is not a DivideByZeroException, the fuzzy exception handler is called. The message
actually displayed by the call to the Show() method is shown in Figure 11-12.

FIGURE 11-12: Throwing an exception

Clearly, this Exception object message is better than the generic message Something went terribly wrong. The ex.Message property is not the only useful property of the Exception object.
You can also use the StackTrace property (ex.StackTrace) to show the methods that you called
up to the point at which the exception occurred. (The methods display in reverse order, with the last
method called at the top of the list.) Although it probably is not a good idea to display stack trace
messages to the user, they can be useful for debugging complex programs.

The finally Statement Block

As I mentioned earlier, the finally statement block is used when you have a sequence of statements
that you want executed regardless of the presence or absence of an exception. Again, let's modify
the click event code for the button object, as follows:

```
try
{
    result = exp2 / exp1;
}
catch (DivideByZeroException)
{
    MessageBox.Show("Expression 1 is zero. Please reenter.",
                    "Exception Thrown");
    txtExpression1.Focus();
    return;
}
```

```
catch (Exception ex)
{
    MessageBox.Show("Error: " + ex.Message, "Exception Thrown");
}
finally
{
    MessageBox.Show("In finally");
}
```

The code throws a divide-by-zero exception and displays the appropriate message. The code then says to place the cursor in the `txtExpression1` textbox object and return from the subroutine. If you run the program, however, after the error message displays and you click the OK button, another message box displays with the `In finally` message.

Even though a `return` statement follows the divide-by-zero exception message box, control is passed to the `finally` statement block rather than returning from the click event. It should be clear that the `finally` block executes regardless of the intent of other code in the method block. Remember that a program control never returns to the `try` block after an exception is thrown.

Even though there are more than 100 defined exceptions, you can write code for custom exceptions. However, I am going to postpone that topic until after I've discussed inheritance.

PROGRAM DEBUGGING

The best way to solve program debugging is to never write a program with a bug in it. Because that's probably not going to happen anytime soon, your next best approach is to know how to use a program debugger effectively. Although you can write C# program code in other environments, you probably use Visual Studio; however, most of the debugging techniques discussed here apply to any programming environment.

The Nature of the Beast

You,ve already read about syntax and semantic errors and how they are different from one another. Logic errors are the third type of program error, or bug, and it is this type of error examined here. There are three steps in fixing a program error:

➤ Detection

➤ Isolation

➤ Correction

Detection

Strange as it sounds, detecting a program error isn't as easy as it might seem. If it were, no program would ever be released to the public with an error in it. As I mentioned before, my company produced a statistics package named Microstat, which sold for more than 20 years. After almost 7 years in the field with thousands of users, the Stepwise Multiple Regression component failed on one particular data set. The problem was caused when the U.S. Gross National Product (GNP) was entered *in dollars* and the program was calculating the sums of squares of cross products. The GNP data set was sufficiently large that the sums of squares overflowed the range of a floating-point number. (Floating-point values for the language back then had a smaller range than a C# `double` type does today.) After detecting the error that had lain hidden for 7 years, it took about 3 minutes to fix it. The real problem was producing a circumstance that caused the bug to manifest itself.

Most program bugs don't produce a numeric overflow exception the way the GNP data set did. More often, the program runs to completion and produces program output. Stated differently, the program manages to execute all Five Program Steps without fail. Given that the program runs to completion, how do you detect an error?

Test Data Sets

The key to bug detection is test data sets. To create these sets, take a known set of inputs (the Input step) and process that set of inputs by hand (the Process step). (Automated test sets can also be used, but that is beyond the scope of this book.) You then record the data from the Process step, the results of which become the Output step. These hand-generated test results serve as the yardstick by which you measure the output of your program.

How do you decide what data to test? In other words, how do you select the inputs by which to judge the output produced by the computer? First, select a "typical" data set that a user might be expected to use. For example, if you write a program that figures out the sales tax to apply to a purchase, you might test the method by supplying a purchase of 10 units at a price of $100 each to see if the computer produces the same sales tax figure as your hand-generated calculations. Such "typical" test data sets produce "typical" results. However, typical data rarely exercise those places where the bugs lurk.

Program bugs love to hide in what I call boundary conditions. *Boundary conditions* are those that lie at the extremes of the test data set. In the sales tax example, one test of a boundary condition is to determine what your method does if the sales tax rate is zero. Another boundary condition is when the quantity purchased is zero or the price is zero. Even if your sales tax method does properly handle a zero sales tax boundary condition, do subsequent methods called after this boundary condition handle the situation properly? A zero sales tax boundary is not as unusual as it sounds, especially when some purchases are exempt from sales tax. For example, some states exempt educational institutions from sales taxes, whereas other states exempt certain products (such as food).

Likewise, you should enter extremely large values that exercise the upper-boundary conditions of a test data set. A minimum test data set should target the smallest expected value (zero), some typical value(s), and the largest expected value. One upper-limit test is to have input values that run at or near the range limit for the data type being used in the test. For example, if `byte` data sets are used, try running an upper-limit test using an input value of `255`. Likewise, if textboxes are expecting numeric data to be entered, what does the program do if the user types in her first name? Good programs handle dumb data gracefully.

Simply stated, test data sets are the only means by which you can determine if your program properly processes its data. Whenever possible, make sure you include test data sets that exercise the program's boundary conditions as well as more typical values. If your program uses arrays, exercise data sets for the lowest and highest index values allowed for the arrays.

Your test data must exercise every code path. This means that programs with `if-else` code paths must have data sets that exercise both paths as part of the test suite. Too often programmers never test all their code paths: that's a train wreck just waiting to happen.

Other boundary situations can exist. For example, in the advanced OOP programming course I taught, one of the first things I did at the beginning of the semester was have the students write a program in which the computer tries to determine the number the user is thinking of. The program asks for the lower and upper values for the game and then proceeds to guess the number. The computer displays its guess, and the user clicks the appropriate button (Too High, Too Low, or Correct). If the limits are 0 and 100, even a nonbinary search algorithm using RDC can guess the number in 100 tries, right? Wrong. Because the limits are inclusive, it would take 101 guesses to be sure you include all values in the search. Indeed, when the students tell me they are ready for me to test their programs, the first numbers I try are 0 and 100. A disappointingly large number of their programs fail to function properly with these boundary numbers.

Another reason for having a suite of test data sets is to increase the chance that you can make the bug repeatable. Absolutely the most difficult bug to fix is one that cannot be repeated consistently. Some programming languages (such as C and C++) suffer from stray pointer problems that can make program bugs especially difficult to track down. (This is one reason C# discourages the use of the pointer data type.)

It's not uncommon for users to enter a set of input values, click a Calculate (or similar) button, and then have the program either crash or generate incorrect answers. When you ask what values produced the error, the user can't remember what he typed in. Sometimes only a particular value or sequence of values triggers a program state that produces output errors. It's frustrating when those values cannot be recalled by the user, especially when you cannot duplicate the error. (To aid program debugging, some programs have error-logging methods called in catch blocks to write to disk specific program values.)

Whatever test data sets you use, save them. They will likely come in handy later.

Isolation

Assuming you have a repeatable bug, the next step to removing it is to isolate it. In the bad ol' days before OOP techniques were used and global scope data prevailed, erroneous output values could be caused almost anywhere in the program. There was no such thing as "private" data or scope. Every variable was visible and globally available at all points in the program. Therefore, trying to pinpoint exactly where a particular variable was incorrect was extremely difficult.

With OOP designs, it's usually simple to figure out the class in which the program bug is hiding. Still, program classes can have a lot of code in them, so you can use any help you can find to simplify the discovery process. This is where a program debugger is invaluable.

Although this section discusses the Visual Studio program debugger specifically, most debuggers have the same general set of features. Therefore, although the mechanics of running debuggers may differ, their use and purpose are universally the same.

The Visual Studio Debugger

Perhaps the greatest benefit of a debugger is as an aid to isolate a program bug. The starting point for isolating a bug is the breakpoint. (Although you've read about the Visual Studio debugger in earlier chapters, I want to make a slightly more formal examination here.) A *breakpoint* is a place in the program's source code at which you want to force a pause in the execution of the program. By pausing program execution, you can examine the values of various data items that are in scope at that moment.

You already know that you can set a breakpoint by setting the cursor on the statement where you want the breakpoint to occur and then pressing the F9 key (or clicking the left margin of the Source window). The background color of the statement line immediately changes to red, and a red dot appears in the program margin, as shown in Figure 11-13.

FIGURE 11-13: Setting a breakpoint

When you run the program, it runs as usual until the breakpoint statement is reached. At that moment, the program pauses. The red background color is replaced with a yellow background color, and the program is ready to execute the breakpoint statement. Note that the breakpoint statement has not yet been processed.

At this point, you can move the cursor over different variables that are in scope and examine their values.

The Locals Window

You can see all the locally scoped variables by opening the Locals window. To do this, simply use the Debug ⇨ Windows Locals menu sequence (or Ctrl+D, L). The display changes to something similar to what is shown in Figure 11-14.

The Locals window shows all variables that have local scope, as discussed in Chapter 9. Generally it is easier to use the Locals window than to move the cursor to each variable to inspect its value. Notice that reference data types (such as `sender`) can be expanded if you want to inspect the properties associated with their objects.

Name	Value	Type
⊞ ● this	{frmMain, Text: Simple Exception}	frmMain
⊞ ● sender	{Text = "Ca&lculate"}	object {S
⊞ ● e	{X = 28 Y = 15 Button = Left}	System.E
● exp1	0	int
● exp2	5	int
● result	0	int

FIGURE 11-14: The Locals Debug window

The Immediate Window

You can activate the Immediate window by using the Debug ⇨ Windows ⇨ Immediate menu sequence (Ctrl+D, I). The purpose of the Immediate window is to enable you to type in an expression and examine its impact on the code. For example, Figure 11-15 shows exp1 = 2, thereby changing its coded value from 0 to a new value of 2. Therefore, the Immediate window enables you to immediately change the value of a local variable and assess its impact on the behavior of the code. This is much quicker than editing the source code to change the value of exp1, recompile, and run the program.

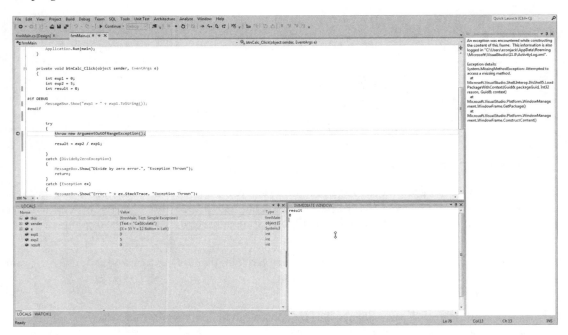

FIGURE 11-15: Immediate Debug window

Single-Stepping Through the Program

You already know how to single-step through a program. However, the debugger includes additional tools available to you. First, when you reach a breakpoint, you can press the F10 or F11 keys to advance to the next statement to be executed. When you advance to the next statement, the yellow arrow in the left margin moves to the next line to show you where program execution is at any moment.

Backing Up from a Breakpoint

What may not be obvious is that you can back up program execution, too. Figure 11-16 shows the yellow arrow in the left margin and a message stating that you can drag the (yellow arrow) cursor to a previous line to execute that line again. This enables you to execute a program statement without restarting the program and running it to the current breakpoint, which can be a real time-saver. You can see the cursor dragged to the second data definition, above a breakpoint.

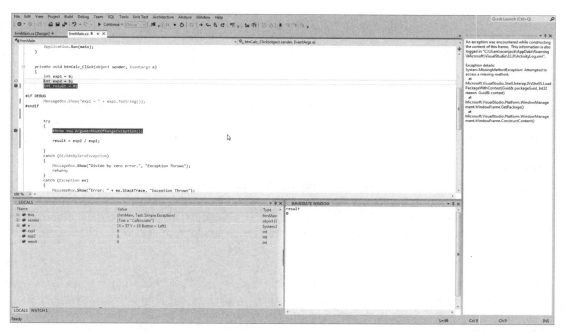

FIGURE 11-16: Drag a breakpoint

Although the message doesn't say so, you cannot advance the yellow arrow. To do so might mean bypassing needed statements to properly determine the values of the variables that are in scope. This is not a serious limitation because you can simply set a breakpoint further down in the source file and press F5 to execute "at full speed" to that breakpoint. (You can also right-click on a line and select Set Next Statement to set the breakpoint.)

The Debug Toolbar

The Debug toolbar is shown in Figure 11-17, along with callouts for the meaning of each icon on the toolbar. The Go icon simply causes the program to resume execution at normal speed from a breakpoint. The Break All icon provides a pause that enables you to enter the debug mode manually as the program executes. The Stop icon terminates the current run of the program. The Restart icon simply restarts the program. The Show Next icon shows the next statement to be executed. But perhaps the most interesting debugging features are associated with the Step icons, discussed in more detail now.

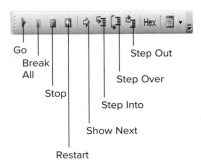

FIGURE 11-17: Debug toolbar

Step Into

With the Step Into icon, if the statement about to be executed is a method call for which the source code is available, program execution proceeds into that method's source code. This enables you to single-step through that method's source code.

Step Over

With the Step Over icon, if the statement about to be executed is a method call for which the source code is available, program execution skips over the method's source code and proceeds with the next statement after the current one. Stepping over a method is useful when you know the method about to be called works correctly and you don't want to waste time single-stepping through its source code.

Step Out

Finally, suppose you have single-stepped into a method's source code and you get halfway through and decide you want to return to the method's caller. By clicking the Step Out icon, you bypass the remaining source-code lines in the method and return to the point at which the method was called. This, too, can be a time-saver.

The Hex icon enables you to view the debugger information as hexadecimal values rather than their default base 10 representations. This could be useful for assembly language programmers. The final icon (Output) on the Debug toolbar presents additional information about the currently executing program. None of the information is terribly useful at this juncture.

Finding the Bug

The purpose of breakpoints and single-stepping through a program is to enable you to watch the values of the data change as the program executes. With the aid of your test data, you should see how you progress from good input values (assuming those values are correct) to bad output values. If you have sufficient granularity in your input test data (such as intermediate values for complex calculations), you should isolate exactly where the bug lies. (This is another argument for cohesive methods. If you write Swiss Army methods that try to do too many things, it makes debugging more difficult because multipurpose methods take longer to test and debug.)

Usually, fixing a bug is simple. You simply change the offending program statement(s) that generate the error. Sometimes you may need to change the way the calculation is done (that is, its algorithm).

Scaffold Code

In the days before symbolic debuggers existed, programmers were forced to print out the values of variables as the program ran. You would then look at those intermediate values and try to determine where things were going wrong. After you found the error, you had to go back and remove all the print statements that you used in the code. This was a error-prone process because it was easy to miss a print statement or two or to accidentally remove a line that should remain in the program.

Subsequent languages (such as C) enabled programmers to add preprocessor directives to the source code and enabled the compiler toggle debug statements into or out of the code. This debug code that was added or removed based on preprocessor directives was sometimes referred to as *scaffold code*. Letting the compiler toggle the code was much less likely to result in error.

C# enables you to use some preprocessor directives. You've already used the #region-#endregion directive in your programs. Now consider the following code:

```
#define MYDEBUG
// many lines of code.
// Now you're at a place where things often go amiss, so you add:
#if MYDEBUG
        MessageBox.Show("Value of exp1 = " + exp1.ToString());
#endif
```

The #define preprocessor directive must be the *first line* in the source code file. In this example, the #define MYDEBUG preprocessor directive causes MYDEBUG to be added to the symbol table. (You should not use DEBUG because Visual Studio already has that symbolic constant defined.) Because it is defined outside of any method, it has class scope. This also means that MYDEBUG is known throughout all elements of the program, including other source files.

You can place as many lines of code as you want between #if and #endif. You can also use the following variation:

```
#if MYDEBUG
        val = 3;
#else
        val = 0;
#endif
```

This enables you to toggle test values based upon the #define directive. A nice touch is that if you look at this code fragment using Visual Studio, the statement currently not compiled display in grayed out text. In other words, if MYDEBUG is defined, the statement val = 0; is grayed out.

Toggling Scaffold Code

The easiest way to toggle scaffold code into and out of a program is with the following two lines at the top of the source file:

```
#define MYDEBUG
//#undef MYDEBUG
```

By means of these two lines, the MYDEBUG symbol is defined for the program. If you uncomment the second line, the #undef preprocessor directive has the effect to remove the MYDEBUG symbol from the symbol table. (You should leave the #define MYDEBUG directive in the source file.) In the earlier code fragment, this would cause val to equal 0.

Using the preprocessor directives in this manner enables you to leave scaffold test code in the source files permanently, yet toggle them into and out of the program as needed.

Defensive Coding

Sometimes it's difficult to determine exactly which variable is responsible for generating an erroneous result. It's common to find complex expressions like the following:

```
delta = a * (b -1) + (h * math.pow(1+r, x) + 2 * d) / left + right;
```

All you know here is that something is wrong with delta. Such complex expressions make judging intermediate values difficult, even with a Watch window. Understanding and debugging this statement would be much easier if it were broken down into several smaller statements that generated intermediate values. It might take a few more lines of (less complex) code to arrange this, but the time you save testing and debugging can amply make up for it. Defensive coding simply means writing code in a manner that makes it easier to debug and maintain a program.

Earlier chapters presented other defensive coding techniques that should help make your debugging sessions more productive. You should define all your class properties using the private access specifier. If you do this, only your getter and setter property methods should change the state of a property. Use symbolic constants in your programs to make the code easier to read. Other stylistic suggestions throughout the text should help to either prevent bugs or make them easier to detect and isolate—use default in a switch even if it's not required; always use curly braces with if and for statements; don't rely on silent casts.

Other ideas about defensive coding techniques appear in later chapters. As you write your own programs, try to practice defensive coding techniques. Perhaps the easiest to implement is to write your code with the idea that someone else must fix it. Clever and obtuse code never wins in the long run. If you think a piece of clever code is warranted because it enhances performance enough to make it worthwhile, just make sure you comment the code so someone else can understand it—someone else may well be you 6 months from now.

SUMMARY

In this chapter you learned about the various types of errors and bugs that can creep into your programs. By now you have probably advanced to the point that you make relatively few syntax or semantic errors. You have moved up to the big time: logic errors. Some errors throw exceptions and you now know how to safeguard yourself against those using exception handlers. You also learned how to force an exception, which can be helpful to test your exception handlers.

Your biggest ally in correcting program errors is the program debugger. You should know how to set breakpoints, single-step through your programs, and use the various debugging windows to watch key variables as the program executes.

Finally, I mentioned how defensive programming can ease the burden of testing and debugging a program. Writing clear, concise code makes it much easier for you or anyone else to debug your code. Always write your code as though someone else will be responsible for maintaining it.

EXERCISES

You can find the answers to the following exercises in Appendix A.

1. The following code fragment generates a compile error. What's the problem with the code?

```
private int TestCode()
{
    int j;
    int x;

    j = 4;
    if (j == 4)
        x = 5;

    return x;
}
```

2. The present value of a future asset is determined by the number of years into the future at which the asset will be received and the current market rate of interest. For example, if Katie promises to pay you $100 a year from now and the current interest rate is 5%, the present value of the asset is $95.23. Stated differently, placing $95.23 in the bank today at 5% interest would yield you $100 a year from now. The equation is

$$p = \frac{a * 1}{(1+i)^y}$$

where p is the present value, a is the future amount, i is the interest rate, and y is the number of years into the future the asset is deferred. How would you code this formula and why?

3. C# enables you to use code like the following, in which several variables are defined with a single statement:

```
long number, val, len;
```

What are the pros and cons of this type of variable definition statement?

4. You've written a long and complex program that compiles and executes but produces an incorrect solution. You've tried to locate the error but so far without success. What would you do to fix the program bugs?

5. Most of my students are loath to place `try-catch` blocks in their code on their own. That is, unless I remind them to do so, I rarely see `try-catch` blocks in their assignments. If you were grading their assignments and were going to be dictatorial about it, where would you absolutely insist they use `try-catch` blocks or get a failing grade on the assignment?

▶ WHAT YOU LEARNED IN THIS CHAPTER

TOPIC	KEY POINTS
Difference between bugs, errors, and exceptions	A bug is a manifestation of an error, whereas exceptions are unwanted program states.
Syntax error	Not following the language rules.
Semantic error	Using a statement out of context.
Logic error	You messed up.
Exceptions and exception handling	How to cope with unexpected program states.
Exception throwing	How to force an exception.
Using the debugger	Program breakpoints and the various debug windows.
Bug detection, isolation, and correction	The proper sequence for fixing program bugs.

12

Generics

WROX.COM CODE DOWNLOADS FOR THIS CHAPTER

You can find the wrox.com code downloads for this chapter at `www.wrox.com/remtitle`
`.cgi?isbn=9781118336922` on the Download Code tab. The code in the `Chapter12` folder is
individually named according to the names throughout the chapter.

This chapter discusses generics, a feature that has been a part of C# since its 2005 release.
Generics have the potential to save you a ton of programming effort.

Generics offer you a way to stretch your programming time in ways that just make sense. In
this chapter you examine what this relatively new OOP feature has to offer.

WHAT ARE GENERICS?

The best way to appreciate what generics bring to the programming table is with an example.
Sorting data is a common programming problem. I once was interviewed for a consulting job
and part of the interview was a programming test in which I was expected to generate a series

of random numbers, display them in a listbox, sort them into ascending order, and redisplay them in a second listbox. The interviewers weren't happy when I bypassed writing my own sort routine and simply turned on the Sorted property in the second listbox. Moral: Know your toolkit. But suppose you have to sort a series of integer data into ascending order and you can't use the listbox trick. How would you write the solution?

As part of your introduction to generics, in the following Try It Out you write a short program that sorts a list of data into ascending order. The example is then modified to show you how generics can make such tasks much easier.

TRY IT OUT Quicksort (Chapter12ProgramQuickSort.zip)

Although volumes have been written on sorting algorithms, one of the fastest general-purpose sorts is the Quicksort. The algorithm uses a divide-and-conquer approach to partitioning the data and then calls itself recursively to perform the sorting task. A sample run of the program is shown in Figure 12-1 and may be used to lay out the user interface.

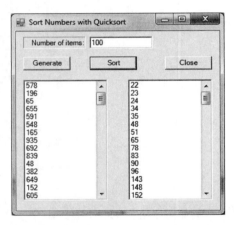

FIGURE 12-1: User Interface

To try this program:

1. Create a new project in the normal manner.

2. Create a user interface that looks something like that shown in Figure 12-1.

3. Download the code from the file: Chapter12ProgramQuickSort.zip.

The listbox object on the left shows the "raw" data produced by the generation of 10 integer values using the pseudo-random number class (Random). After the user clicks the Sort button, that same list of numbers is sorted and then displayed in the second listbox object. (No, I didn't take the shortcut and simply set the Sorted property to true.)

How It Works

As usual, frmMain performs four of the Five Program Steps, leaving the Process step for the code found in clsSort. The code for frmMain is shown in Listing 12-1.

LISTING 12-1: Program to Sort a List of Data. (frmMain.cs)

```csharp
#define MYDEBUG
//#undef MYDEBUG

using System;
using System.Windows.Forms;

public class frmMain : Form
{
    private const int MAXVAL = 1000;     // Max random number to generate

    private int[] data;                  // Data array to sort
    private int number;                  // Number of elements in array

    private TextBox txtNumber;
    private Button btnGen;
    private ListBox lstOutput;
    private Button btnClose;
    private Button btnSort;
    private ListBox lstSorted;
    private Label label1;

    #region Windows code

    public frmMain()
    {
        InitializeComponent();
    }

    public static void Main()
    {
        frmMain main = new frmMain();
        Application.Run(main);
    }

    private void btnGen_Click(object sender, EventArgs e)
    {
        bool flag;
        int i;

        flag = int.TryParse(txtNumber.Text, out number);
        if (flag == false)
        {
            MessageBox.Show("Enter whole digits only.", "Input Error");
            txtNumber.Focus();
            return;
        }
#if MYDEBUG
        Random rnd = new Random(number);     // For testing purposes
#else
        Random rnd = new Random();
#endif
```

(continues)

LISTING 12-1 *(continued)*

```csharp
        data = new int[number];

        lstOutput.Items.Clear();              // Clear listbox objects
        lstSorted.Items.Clear();

        for (i = 0; i < data.Length; i++)  // Set random values
        {
            data[i] = rnd.Next(MAXVAL);
            lstOutput.Items.Add(data[i].ToString());
        }
    }

    private void btnSort_Click(object sender, EventArgs e)
    {
        int i;
        clsSort mySort = new clsSort(data);

        mySort.quickSort(0, data.Length-1);   // Sort the data

        for (i = 0; i < data.Length; i++)     // Show it
        {
            lstSorted.Items.Add(data[i].ToString());
        }
    }

    private void btnClose_Click(object sender, EventArgs e)
    {
        Close();
    }
}
```

The listing takes advantage of the scaffold coding technique that was mentioned in Chapter 11. In particular, notice the lines at the top of the listing and the scaffolding that follows:

```csharp
#define DEBUG
#undef DEBUG

// Omitted lines of code. . .

#if DEBUG
    Random rnd = new Random(number);    // For testing purposes
#else
    Random rnd = new Random();
#endif
```

Because of the `#undef` preprocessor directive, the `#if` test later in the program is logic `False`, which means that the constructor for the `Random` class is called without an argument. This causes `rnd` to produce a differing set of pseudo-random numbers on each run of the program. (It's called *pseudo-random* because the distribution of numbers only approximates a true random distribution of numbers.) When you develop the code, it is often useful to have a repeatable series of numbers produced so that you have a stable test dataset while debugging and testing. To establish that testing environment, simply comment out the #undef DEBUG line that toggles in the parameterized constructor for the Random class. When you finish testing, remove comment characters for the #undef, as shown in Listing 12-1.

The line

```
data[i] = rnd.Next(MAXVAL);
```

simply generates a series of random numbers that fall within the domain of 0 to MAXVAL, which is a symbolic constant set to a value of 1000. The set of random values is then added to the listbox object.

The following statements define a clsSort object named mySort and then call the quickSort() method to sort the data:

```
clsSort mySort = new clsSort(data);

mySort.quickSort(data.Length  1);    // Sort the data
```

Notice that the constructor is passed the raw data as an argument. The code for clsSort is shown in Listing 12-2.

LISTING 12-2: Code for clsSort (clsSort.cs)

```
using System;
using System.Collections.Generic;
using System.Text;

class clsSort
{
    int[] data;

    public clsSort(int[] vals)
    {
        data = vals;     // Copies the rvalue
    }

    /*****
     * Purpose: This method sorts an array of integers values into
     *          ascending order via recursive calls to quickSort().
     *
     * Parameter list:
     *   int first        the first value to sort
     *   int last         the last value to sort
     *
     * Return value:
     *   void
     *****/
    public void quickSort(int first, int last)
    {
        int start;       // Index for left partition
        int end;         // Index for right partition

        start = first;   // Keep copy of first element of array...
        end = last;      // ...and the last one.

        if (last  first >= 1)    // Make sure there's enough data to sort
```

(continues)

LISTING 12-2 *(continued)*

```
    {
        int pivot = data[first];    // Set partitions

        while (end > start)          // While indexes don't match...
        {                            // Do left partition
            while (data[start] <= pivot && start <= last && end >
                                              start)
                start++;
                                    // Do right partition
            while (data[end] > pivot && end >= first && end >= start)
                end--;
            if (end > start)     // If right partition index smaller...
                swap(start, end); // ...do a swap
        }
        swap(first, end);      // Swap last element with pivot
        quickSort(first, end  1); // Sort around partitions
        quickSort(end + 1, last);
    }
    else
    {
        return;
    }

}

/*****
 * Purpose: This method performs the data swap for quickSort()
 *
 * Parameter list:
 *   int pos1          the array index to first value
 *   int pos2          the array index to second value
 *
 * Return value:
 *   void
 *****/
public void swap(int pos1, int pos2)
{
    int temp;

    temp = data[pos1];
    data[pos1] = data[pos2];
    data[pos2] = temp;
}
}
```

There are several things to notice about the class. First, in the constructor, the following statement does a normal rvalue-to-rvalue assignment:

```
data = vals;    // Copies the rvalue
```

However, if you recall, the rvalue of a reference variable is a memory address pointer to the memory location where the data resides, so the end result is that the variables data and vals now both refer to the same data. This also means, however, that the original sequence of random values will be lost after the data is sorted. If you need to preserve that sequence for some reason, you could define the data as an array of the same size and copy those values in the constructor's statement block:

```
public clsSort(int[] vals)
{
    int[] data = new int[vals.Length];
    Array.Copy(vals, data, vals.Length);
}
```

Recursion

The theory behind the Quicksort algorithm is to partition the set of numbers into two pieces around a *pivot point* in the data. The code looks at the data around the two partitions and calls a swap() method to exchange values to reorder the data. The code then calls the same quickSort() method from within itself. The process of a method calling itself is called *recursion*.

The good news about recursion is that you are, in effect, reducing the amount of code by reusing the same method call rather than by writing some form of loop to accomplish the same task. The bad news is that it's easy to get the code wrong, especially when determining that you've hit the last recursive call. Because a recursive method call creates a new set of local variables each time the method is called, a runaway recursion can eventually run out of memory and the program dies an ugly death. Also, because calling a method involves a certain amount of overhead each time the method is called (such as the overhead of pushing and popping data off the stack), recursion is often a little slower than a nonrecursive solution to the problem.

However, most Quicksort implementations use recursion so that's what's done here. You can see the two recursive calls toward the end of Listing 12-2. As mentioned earlier, the swap() method simply exchanges two values when the algorithm requires it.

Many sorting algorithms have performance factors dictated by *big-O notation* (for example, the notation $O(N^2)$). This type of notation suggests that if the number of values to sort increases tenfold, it takes a hundred times longer to sort the data. The Quicksort, on the other hand, is bound by the relationship $O(N * LogN)$ which can make the sort time almost linear. (That is, 10 times the data takes about 10 times as long.) A piece of trivia: Most programmers feel that the Bubble Sort is the slowest sorting algorithm on the planet. Actually, if the data is already in sorted order and a new item is added to the data set, the Bubble Sort can be one of the fastest algorithms to sort that new data set. (You can dazzle your friends at your next cocktail party when this topic comes up.) Conclusion: Few laws in programming are etched in stone.

Okay. Now you have a class that can sort data with good performance. You can save the code somewhere for later use. After all, one of the real benefits of OOP is code reuse, right? Well, it depends.

Data Problems

Fast-forward a few months: A client comes to you with a programming problem. Part of the solution requires that you sort the data prior to the final processing of the data. A few neurons fire and you remember the sorting code you wrote a while back. Cool! Time to drag out the `clsSort` code and integrate it into the solution. You read the rest of the client's specs for the program and....

Uh-oh.

The client's specs require sorting of the `double` data type, but your `clsSort` code works only with `int` data. Of course, you could rewrite the code, changing everything to use a `double` data type, but then you lose the ability to sort integer data. Or you could copy the code and have separate `int` and `double` sorting methods within the class. However, if you do that you have twice as much code to test, debug, and maintain. Wouldn't it be nice if one sorting method could be used to sort both types of data? This is exactly the type of problem that generics are designed to solve.

INTRODUCTION TO GENERICS

Simply stated, *generics* enable you to create "typeless" data structures in C#. In the Quicksort example presented earlier, you defined an instance of the `clsSort` object with the following syntax:

```
clsSort mySort = new clsSort(data);
```

As you saw, the problem is that the algorithm is based upon using an `int` data type for the processing. With a generic class, the definition becomes:

```
clsSort<T> mySort = new clsSort<T>(data);
```

The data type you want to use is substituted for the term `T` within the enclosing angle brackets. For example, if you want to sort the `int` data values stored in the `data` array, you would use this code:

```
clsSort<int> mySort = new clsSort<int>(data);
```

In some later project that uses the `double` data type, you would use this code:

```
clsSort<double> mySort = new clsSort<double>(data);
```

One of the key advantages of generics is that the same code can process different data types *without the source code being changed* for each data type! If you write a class using the generic model, that class can process different data types without your having to craft methods for each data type. The Visual Studio compiler generates the necessary code to handle the different data types for you.

Generics Versus ArrayLists

You might be saying, "Wait a minute! Can't `ArrayLists` do the same thing? After all, they come with a `Sort()` method." Well, not really. `ArrayLists` suffer from a few messy limitations. Consider the following code fragment:

```
ArrayList a = new ArrayList();
int i = 5;

a[0] = i;
a[1] = "t";
```

The preceding code compiles without complaint. So what's the problem? The problem is that it *doesn't* complain when it should. The good news about `ArrayLists` is that they are designed to hold anything. The bad news is that `ArrayLists` *can* hold anything. In the snippet you just saw, an integer is assigned into the `ArrayList` and that is followed with the assignment of a string literal into the same `ArrayList`.

Although sorting any data type in the array provides for a flexible means of storing things, it also means that no type checking is performed on the data. Further, how can you safely read back the data from the `ArrayList`? You give up the safety of data type checking with `ArrayLists`.

Now consider what happens if you add this statement for processing in the previously defined Arraylist:

```
i = a[0];
```

The compiler complains about this statement, saying:

```
Cannot implicitly convert type 'object' to 'int'. An explicit conversion exists
(are you missing a cast?)
```

The compiler removes the error message only if you change the statement to implement an explicit cast:

```
i = (int) a[0];
```

Casting everything from an `ArrayList` to its final destination type is tedious at best. Losing the benefits of data type checking is tantamount to writing code now that will produce a train wreck later. Finally, as mentioned in Chapter 8, there are some performance issues with the underlying way that `ArrayLists` work.

Boxing and Unboxing

Recall from Chapter 5 that C# surrounds all value types with object "wrappers" so that you can treat value types as though they were objects. Essentially, everything in C# derives from `System`.Object, and `ArrayLists` make use of this fact in performing their magic of allowing virtually any object to be stored in an `ArrayList`. However, anytime you use a value type as an object, C# must convert that value type into an object in a process called *boxing*. Likewise, the process to convert a boxed object back into its value type is called *unboxing*. It is this boxing/unboxing capability that enables you to use methods such as `ToString()` with a value type.

However, there is no such thing as a free lunch and the flexibility that wrappers bring to the party is paid for in performance. It has been estimated that there is approximately a 100 percent performance penalty associated with the boxing-unboxing process.

Generics overcome many of these limitations. Perhaps one of the greatest benefits of generics is that they provide strong type checking, yet enable you to avoid type casting every time you use a data item. To illustrate the use of generics, implement your Quicksort algorithm using them in the following "Try It Out."

TRY IT OUT **A Generic Quicksort (Chapter12ProgramGenericQuickSort.zip)**

The user interface for your generic version of the sort program is shown in Figure 12-2. The program asks the user to specify the data type she wants to use, and a click of the Show Unsorted button shows the raw data that is generated. In this example, the program has generated 10 random `double` data values. Clicking the Show Sorted button presents the same `double` data, but in sorted order. See Figure 12-2.

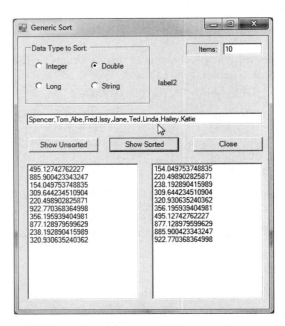

FIGURE 12-2: Generic Quicksort

If you select the String radio button, the program asks the user to enter a list of comma-separated strings in the textbox object. The `string` data is sorted using the same code used to sort the `double` data. A sample run for string data is shown in Figure 12-3.

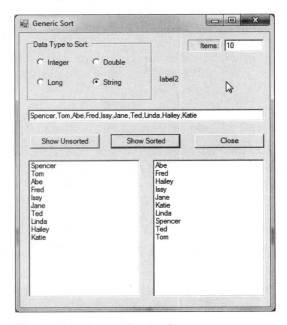

FIGURE 12-3: Generic Sort on Strings

Using Figure 12-2 as a model for the user interface:

1. Create a new project in the usual manner.

2. Fill in the source code from Listings 12-3 and 12-4 or download the file `Chapter12ProgramGenericQuickSort.zip`.

As you see in a moment, you can have such data sorting flexibility yet keep the strong data type checking protection without a heavy performance hit because of boxing and unboxing. You also don't need to mess around with type casts. Clearly, generics are a worthy addition to your programming toolkit.

How It Works

Examine the source code in `frmMain` that drives the sorting tests. This is shown in Listing 12-3.

LISTING 12-3: Using Generics to Sort Data (frmMain.cs)

```csharp
using System;
using System.Windows.Forms;

public class frmMain : Form
{
    const int INTEGER = 1;              // Symbolic constants
    const int LONG = 2;
    const int DOUBLE = 3;
    const int STRING = 4;

    const int UNSORTED = 1;
    const int SORTED = 2;

    const int MAXVALUE = 1000;

    int items;                          // Values to generate
    int choice;                         // Which data type selected
    int whichListbox;                   // Which listbox getting this data

    int[] iData;                        // Data arrays
    long[] lData;
    double[] dData;
    string[] sData;

    Random rnd = new Random();

    private GroupBox groupBox1;
    private RadioButton rbString;
    private RadioButton rbDouble;
    private RadioButton rbLong;
    private Label label1;
    private TextBox txtItems;
    private TextBox txtString;
    private ListBox lstUnsorted;
    private ListBox lstSorted;
    private Button btnRaw;
    private Button btnSort;
```

(continues)

LISTING 12-3 *(continued)*

```csharp
private Button btnClose;
private RadioButton rbInt;
#region Windows code

public frmMain()
{
    InitializeComponent();
    rbInt.Checked = true;       // Set defaults
    choice = INTEGER;
}

public static void Main()
{
    frmMain main = new frmMain();
    Application.Run(main);
}

private void btnClose_Click(object sender, EventArgs e)
{
    Close();
}

// Show the raw data first
private void btnRaw_Click(object sender, EventArgs e)
{
    bool flag;
    int i;

    flag = int.TryParse(txtItems.Text, out items);
    if (flag == false)
    {
        MessageBox.Show("Numeric only. Re-enter", "Input Error");
        txtItems.Focus();
        return;
    }

    lstUnsorted.Items.Clear();    // Clear old data
    lstSorted.Items.Clear();

    whichListbox = UNSORTED;

    switch (choice)                     // Select the data type
                                        //    in use
    {
        case INTEGER:                   // Integer

            iData = new int[items];
            for (i = 0; i < items; i++)
            {
                iData[i] = rnd.Next(MAXVALUE);
            }
            break;
```

```
            case LONG:                          // Long
                lData = new long[items];
                for (i = 0; i < items; i++)
                {
                    lData[i] = (long)rnd.Next(MAXVALUE);
                }
                break;
            case DOUBLE:                        // Double
                dData = new double[items];
                for (i = 0; i < items; i++)
                {
                    dData[i] = rnd.NextDouble() * MAXVALUE;
                }
                break;
            case STRING:                        // String
                sData = txtString.Text.Split(',');  // Split into
                                                        strings
                break;
        }
        ShowData();                             // Show data in listbox
                                                    object

    }

    private void btnSort_Click(object sender, EventArgs e)
    {
        whichListbox = SORTED;

        switch (choice)
        {
            case INTEGER:                       // Data types again. . .
             clsQuickSort<int> iSort = new clsQuickSort<int>(iData);
             iSort.Sort();
             break;
            case LONG:
             clsQuickSort<long> lSort = new clsQuickSort<long>
                                     (lData);
             lSort.Sort();
             break;
            case DOUBLE:
             clsQuickSort<double> dSort = new
                                    clsQuickSort<double>
                                    (dData);
             dSort.Sort();
             break;
            case STRING:
             clsQuickSort<string> sSort = new
                                    clsQuickSort<string>
                                    (sData);
             sSort.Sort();
             break;
        }
        ShowData();
    }
```

(continues)

LISTING 12-3 *(continued)*

```csharp
private void ShowData()        // Simply displays the data
{
    int i;

    switch (choice)
    {
        case INTEGER:                        // Data types again. . .
         for (i = 0; i < items; i++)
            {
                if (whichListbox == SORTED)
                    lstSorted.Items.Add(iData[i].ToString());
                else
                    lstUnsorted.Items.Add(iData[i].ToString());
            }
            break;
        case LONG:
            for (i = 0; i < items; i++)
            {
                if (whichListbox == SORTED)
                    lstSorted.Items.Add(lData[i].ToString());
                else
                    lstUnsorted.Items.Add(lData[i].ToString());
            }
            break;
        case DOUBLE:
            for (i = 0; i < items; i++)
            {
                if (whichListbox == SORTED)
                    lstSorted.Items.Add(dData[i].ToString());
                else
                    lstUnsorted.Items.Add(dData[i].ToString());
            }
            break;
        case STRING:
            for (i = 0; i < sData.Length; i++)
            {
                if (whichListbox == SORTED)
                    lstSorted.Items.Add(sData[i].ToString());
                else
                    lstUnsorted.Items.Add(sData[i].ToString());
            }
            break;
    }
}

private void rbInt_Click(object sender, EventArgs e)
{
    choice = INTEGER;
}

private void rbLong_Click(object sender, EventArgs e)
{
```

```
        choice = LONG;
    }

    private void rbDouble_Click(object sender, EventArgs e)
    {
        choice = DOUBLE;
    }

    private void rbString_Click(object sender, EventArgs e)
    {
        choice = STRING;
    }
}
```

The code starts with the definition of several symbolic constants, followed by a series of array reference objects. These arrays ultimately hold the data to be sorted. The frmMain constructor sets the default data type to be an integer for the radio button choices and the current choice (choice = INTEGER). The default number of values to generate for the numeric data types is 10, as shown in Figure 12-2.

Using the Split( ) Method for Strings

The count when string data types are selected is set by the number of comma-delimited string entries made in the txtString textbox object. This is accomplished with the statement:

```
sData = txtString.Text.Split(',');
```

The Split() method examines txtString looking for the comma character. Each time it finds a comma, it creates a new string for the characters leading up to (but not including) the comma. After all substrings have been read, the array of strings is assigned into sData. The Split() method can use multiple separator characters if you need them. You can find the details using the online help. (That is, double-click the word Split in the source code to highlight it, and then press the F1 key.)

If the user selects something other than the default INTEGER option, the variable choice is set in the appropriate radio button click event code. For example, if the user clicks the Double radio button, the following code executes, setting choice to the appropriate value:

```
private void rbDouble_Click(object sender, EventArgs e)
{
    choice = DOUBLE;
}
```

The variable choice selects the appropriate code via the various switch statements.

Generating the Data

Depending upon the value of choice, the appropriate array is filled with data. How this is done is shown in the following code fragment:

```
switch (choice)                 // Select the data type
                                    in use
{
    case INTEGER:               // Integer

        iData = new int[items];
```

```
            for (i = 0; i < items; i++)
            {
                iData[i] = rnd.Next(MAXVALUE);
            }
            break;
        case LONG:                      // Long
            lData = new long[items];
            for (i = 0; i < items; i++)
            {
                lData[i] = (long)rnd.Next(MAXVALUE);
            }
            break;

    case DOUBLE:                    // Double
            dData = new double[items];
            for (i = 0; i < items; i++)
            {
                dData[i] = rnd.NextDouble() * MAXVALUE;
            }
            break;

    case STRING:                      // String
            sData = txtString.Text.Split(',');  // Split into
                                                    strings
            break;
    }
```

For the INTEGER and LONG data types, the parameterized Next() method generates a pseudo-random number inside a for loop. The number of passes through the loop is determined by the items variable entered by the user. Passing in the value MAXVALUE means that the values generated fall within the range of 0 and MAXVALUE (exclusively). For the DOUBLE data type, the method NextDouble() returns a value between 0 and 1 (exclusively). Therefore, multiplying the fractional value returned from the NextDouble() method by MAXVALUE sets the same range for the double data type. For string data, the Split() method populates the sData array, as explained earlier.

After the values have been generated, the call to ShowData() moves the data into the listbox to show the values that were generated.

Using a Generic Class

After the raw data have been generated and displayed in the listbox object, you are ready to pass the unsorted data to the generic version of the Quicksort method. The following code fragment shows how the sort method is called for the differing data types:

```
private void btnSort_Click(object sender, EventArgs e)
{
    whichListbox = SORTED;

    switch (choice)
    {
        case INTEGER:                   // Integer
            clsQuickSort<int> iSort = new clsQuickSort<int>
                                        (iData);
            iSort.Sort();
```

```
        break;

    case LONG:
        clsQuickSort<long> lSort = new clsQuickSort<long>
                                        (lData);
        lSort.Sort();
        break;

    case DOUBLE:
        clsQuickSort<double> dSort = new
                                    clsQuickSort<double>
                                    (dData);
        dSort.Sort();
        break;

    case STRING:
        clsQuickSort<string> sSort = new
                                    clsQuickSort<string>
                                    (sData);
        sSort.Sort();
        break;
    }
    ShowData();
}
```

In each case, the code uses the generic syntax to create an object of the clsQuickSort class. That is, the statement to instantiate the object has the following form:

```
clsQuickSort<T> typeSort = new clsQuickSort<T>(typeData);
```

Therefore, depending upon the value of choice , the four objects are instantiated using one of the following four statements:

```
clsQuickSort<int> iSort = new clsQuickSort<int>(iData);
clsQuickSort<long> lSort = new clsQuickSort<long>(lData);
clsQuickSort<double> dSort = new clsQuickSort<double>(dData);
clsQuickSort<string> sSort = new clsQuickSort<string>(sData);
```

After the appropriate object has been instantiated, the code calls the object's Sort() method to sort the data (such as iSort.Sort()). After that, code has executed, the data has been sorted, and the sorted data is displayed in the second listbox object.

Now see what changes you have to make to the Quicksort code.

GENERIC QUICKSORT

The code for clsQuickSort is presented in Listing 12-4. Note the second using statement in the listing that makes generics possible in the clsQuickSort class. This Generic namespace contains generic classes, structures, and interfaces to support generic dictionaries, lists, queues, and stacks. In this section you draw upon generics only as they relate to the implementation of a generic class.

The third line in Listing 12-4,

```
public class clsQuickSort<T> where T : IComparable
```

uses the generic angle bracket notation that surrounds the data type (T) used by the object of the class. Recall that when you instantiated an object of a generic class, perhaps for the `double` data type, it took the following form:

```
clsQuickSort<double> dSort = new clsQuickSort<double>(dData);
```

Therefore, the `dSort` object is of type `double` and that becomes the `T` type in the opening statement of the class definition. In other words, instantiating object `dSort` makes the statement

```
public class clsQuickSort<T> where T : IComparable
```

appear as though the class is written as:

```
public class clsQuickSort<double> where double : IComparable
```

The compiler generates the necessary code to accommodate the data types that might be passed to the generic `clsQuickSort` class. For the moment ignore the expressions that follow the `where` keyword in the statement, which are discussed a little later in the chapter in the section titled "Using Generics with Constraints and Interfaces."

LISTING 12-4: Generic Quicksort Source Code (clsSort.cs)

```
using System;
using System.Collections.Generic;


public class clsQuickSort<T> where T : IComparable
{
    // ================ instance member ====================
    T[] data;

    // ================ constructor ====================
    public clsQuickSort(T[] values)
    {
        data = values;     // copy rvalue of unsorted data
    }
    // ================ Property methods ====================

    // ================ Helper methods ====================

    /*****
     * Purpose: This method gets the initial pivot point for the sort and then
     *          calls itself recursively until all values have been set.
     *
     * Parameter list:
     *   int first           index of first element of partition
     *   int last            index of last element of partition
     *
     * Return value:
     *   void
```

```
*****/
private void doSort(int first, int last)
{
    if (first == last)
    {
        return;    // Done
    }
    else
    {
        int pivot = getPivotPoint(first, last);

        if (pivot > first)
            doSort(first, pivot  1);
        if (pivot < last)
            doSort(pivot + 1, last);
    }
}

/*****
* Purpose: This method sets the pivot point for the sort.
*
* Parameter list:
*   int start           index to start of partition
*   int end             index to end of partition
*
* Return value:
*   void
*****/
private int getPivotPoint(int first, int last)
{
    int pivot = first;

    int start = first;  // Keep copies
    int end = last;

    if (last  first >= 1)
    {
        while (end > start)
        {
            while (data[pivot].CompareTo(data[start]) >= 0 &&
                             start <= last && end > start)
                start++;
            while (data[pivot].CompareTo(data[end]) <= 0 &&
                             end >= first && end >= start)
                end--;
            if (end > start)
                swap(start, end);
        }
        swap(first, end);
        doSort(first, end  1);
    }
    return end;
}
```

(continues)

LISTING 12-4 *(continued)*

```
/*****
 * Purpose: This method performs the data swap for quickSort()
 *
 * Parameter list:
 *   int pos1            index to first value to swap
 *   int pos2            index to second value to swap
 *
 * Return value:
 *   void
 *****/
private void swap(int pos1, int pos2)
{
    T temp;

    temp = data[pos1];
    data[pos1] = data[pos2];
    data[pos2] = temp;
}


// ================= General methods ====================
/*****
 * Purpose: This is the user interface entry point for the Quicksort
 *
 * Parameter list:
 *   n/a
 *
 * Return value:
 *   void
 *
 * CAUTION: This routine assumes constructor is passed unsort data
 *****/
public void Sort()
{
    int len = data.Length;
    if (len < 2)        // Enough to sort?
        return;
    doSort(0, data.Length  1);
}

}
```

You might think that it would be a fairly simple process to convert the code shown in Listing 12-2 to use generics. A complication, however, arises with statements like:

```
while (data[start] <= pivot && start <= last && end > start)
```

Unlike some other languages that support similar constructs (such as templates in C++), C# does not like the use of relational operators with a generic type T. Because of that limitation, the C# compiler complains about the expression,

```
data[start] <= pivot
```

in the `while` statement because you are trying to compare two operands of type `T`. Because the pivot point for the data array plays an important part in the Quicksort algorithm, you must modify the code to work around this limitation.

Fortunately, the points of complaint by the compiler center on the comparison of the pivot point with a particular element of the array. You can fix that.

Using Generics with Constraints and Interfaces

If you had written the first line of the class as:

```
public class clsQuickSort<T>
```

you would be saying that this class works with *any* data type you can think of. That is, you could use an object of this class with all value types and all reference types, including any custom objects you may have created. Such a class signature means that `clsQuickSort` is usable with any type of data on the planet. Such a generic class is known as an *unbounded generic class*. Unbounded generic classes are not limited, or constrained, to any particular type of data.

As you might imagine, however, there might be data types that don't lend themselves to the Quicksort algorithm. Indeed, I have chosen to limit the use of the class to those data types that support the `ICompare` interface. The following expression uses the `where` keyword to introduce a *constraint* for the class:

```
where T : IComparable
```

The expression begins with the `where` keyword followed by the generic data type indicator (`T`), a colon (`:`), and an interface name. You can verbalize the complete class signature,

```
public class clsQuickSort<T> where T : IComparable
```

as "The `clsQuickSort` may be used with any data type `T` subject to the constraint that data type `T` implements the `IComparable` interface." In other words, tight type checking on the types of data that may use this class is provided. If the data type supports the `ICompare` interface, that data type can be sorted by the implementation of the Quicksort algorithm. It should be clear, therefore, that the `where` keyword constrains the class to only those data types that support the `ICompare` interface. Therefore, `clsQuickSort` is known as a *constrained generic class*.

Interfaces

Okay, but what is an interface? An *interface* is a reference object that has no implementation, or code, associated with it. Recall from Chapter 4 that you made a strong distinction between the terms *define* and *declare*. Programmers use those two terms as if they are the same. They are not, and it's just plain sloppy to use them interchangeably. A data definition must have memory allocated for the data. This also means that an lvalue for that data exists in the symbol table. Conversely, it was pointed out that a data declaration does *not* cause memory to be allocated for the data. The purpose of a data declaration serves only to fill in an attribute list for the data item in the symbol table. Data declarations do not provide memory for the data. Interfaces may include declarations for method signatures, properties, and events. They do *not*, however, provide the code to implement those methods, properties, or events. As you can see, an interface is a declaration precisely because no code is associated with the interface.

The `IComparable` interface used in Listing 12-4 supports only one method in the interface. You can write this interface as follows:

```
public interface IComparable
{
    int CompareTo(Object obj);
}
```

Each of the value types supports the `IComparable` interface, which means that the wrapper class around each value type has a `CompareTo()` method that you can use to compare one data item of that type against another data item of the same type. If the `int` value returned from `CompareTo()` is less than `0`, it means that the current instance is less than `obj`. If the return value is `0`, the two instances are equal. If the return value is positive, the current instance is greater than `obj`.

For example, given an object named `obj`,

```
obj.CompareTo(obj)
```

is required to return `0` if the two objects are the same. Likewise, if a different object named `whatever` is different from `obj`, then,

```
obj.CompareTo(whatever)
```

must return a value other than 0 and,

```
whatever.CompareTo(obj)
```

must return a value of the opposite sign. That is, if `obj.CompareTo(whatever)` returns `1`, then `whatever.CompareTo(obj)` must return `1`.

An interface is a promise that you make as a programmer to anyone who uses the code in the class that implements the `IComparable` interface, including the C# compiler. If you want to use the `IComparable` interface with a class that you write that doesn't provide the `CompareTo()` method, your class must write the code for that method, ensuring that it obeys the return value rules for the interface.

Why Use an Interface?

Not too long ago, I flew in a private plane with a friend who has his private pilot's license. About 40 years ago I also had my pilot's license, but ran out of money as a broke graduate student and didn't fly a plane after that. What amazed me the most a while ago were the avionics (radar and other electronics) that I saw in my friend's plane. One of the questions that crossed my mind during the flight with my friend was, "Could I fly this plane with all these new electronic thingies?"

Actually, the basics of flying haven't changed much. You have a yoke and pedals that control the basic movements of the plane. Therefore, a basic plane class might have,

```
public clsPrivatePlane : IControls
```

and you might declare the `IControls` interface as:

```
public interface IControls
{
```

```
      int Yoke(int pitch, int yaw);
      int Pedals(int direction);
      int Throttle(int rateOfFuelFlow);
}
```

With these basic controls defined, a pilot could "fly" an object of the class, although the FAA might have dozens of citations for rules that might be broken along the way. Over the years, as new avionics were added, you could upgrade your private plane class to reflect the new stuff today's planes have. You might change the class to,

```
      public clsPrivatePlane : IControls, IAvionics
```

where `IAvionics` provides for the methods and members necessary to reflect today's avionics. If my friend later wants to do stunt flying, which may require certain devices to equip the plane, the class could again be expanded:

```
      public clsPrivatePlane : IControls, IAvionics, IStunts
```

(By convention, most interface declarations begin with the capital letter `I`.) The key thing to notice here is explained in the following Note.

> **NOTE** *Earlier versions of the* `plane` *class can still exist if classes are created that don't implement the newer interfaces or "empty" methods are used for the new interfaces.*

These empty interface methods simply mean the current plane object doesn't support these advanced features. Perhaps more important, an upgraded plane doesn't "break" the code for the earlier versions of the plane. This is the real strength of interfaces: If done correctly, *interfaces decouple the user interface from the underlying code.*

For example, consider the `IControls` that I used when I was flying. All the control surfaces for the plane were connected to the cockpit with steel cables. The `IControls` for many private planes today are based on a system of hydraulics for the control surfaces. The `IControls` for modern military aircraft are fly-by-wire, and the control surfaces are computer-controlled. However, as a pilot using an object of the class, I can view `IControls` as a black box because I don't care *how* the control surfaces are moved. That is, I don't care about the implementation of the controls. I care only that the controls *do* move the control surfaces when I touch them. (It's a big problem if the control surfaces stop moving while you're flying a plane!) Using an interface means that I can still use the same code to call the `Yoke()`, `Pedals()`, and `Throttle()` methods regardless of whether I'm flying a canvas-covered Piper J2 or the F/A-22 Raptor.

Using an Interface

If you look closely at the code in Listing 12-4, you find two statements,

```
      while (data[pivot].CompareTo(data[start]) >= 0 &&
                   start <= last && end > start)
```

and:

```
while (data[pivot].CompareTo(data[end]) <= 0 &&
                     end >= first && end >= start)
```

Each of these uses the `CompareTo()` method of the `IComparable` interface for examining the pivot values in the data arrays. Because the wrapper classes for value types implement the `CompareTo()` method, you don't need to write the code! Again, this is one of the nice features of OOP in general and interfaces in particular. The .NET Framework provides the code you need to use the `IComparable` interface.

If you want to compare objects of classes that you've written, you will probably need to write your own `CompareTo()` method. However, even if you do need to write the code to implement an interface, you still gain the flexibility provided by interfaces.

How Do You Know an Interface Is Implemented for a Data Type?

In Figure 12-3, the `btnSort_Click()` event uses a `switch` statement to determine which data object to create for the sort method. This means that only the four data types presented in the radio button objects can be selected. But how can you determine if a data type you use implements a specific interface? There are four ways to do this.

Implement the Interface Yourself

First, if the data type is an object that you created, you must specify the interface(s) it supports. This is what you did for the `clsQuickSort` class. You simply wrote the class stating as part of the class signature that the class is constrained for those data types that support the `IComparable` interface. You are free, of course, to add your own interfaces to a class. If you do that, then you must provide the interface declaration and its supporting code. (The `IControls` interface mentioned earlier in this chapter is an example of how to implement an interface with your code.)

Use the C# Documentation

The second way to determine if a data type supports a given interface is to examine its documentation. Using the C# documentation, you can look up the relevant data types to see if they support the `IComparable` interface.

For example, if you select Help Index from the C# main menu, you can search the `int` keyword. The search provides you with information about that data type. Figure 12-4 shows what you see when you index on the `int` keyword.

On the right side of the figure, in the middle, you can see the table heading .NET Framework Type. Immediately under that column heading is the link `System.Int32`. If you click that link, you see the information presented in Figure 12-5.

In the C# section, you can see that `System.Int32` supports the `IComparable` interface (along with several others).

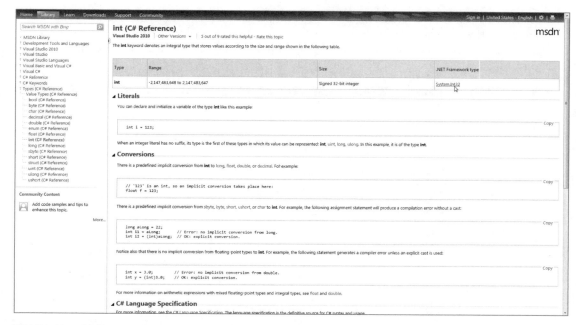

FIGURE 12-4: Help in int Keyword

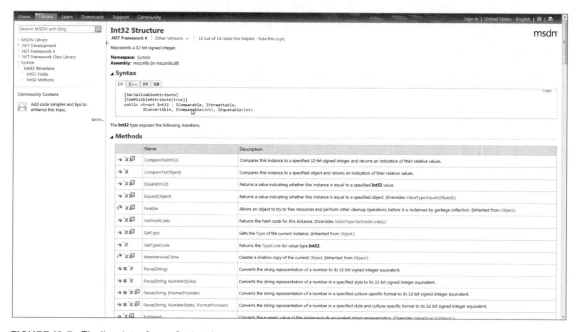

FIGURE 12-5: Finding interfaces for int data type

The process for the `string` data type is a little different because a `string` is a reference type to begin with. If you perform an index search on `string`, you are told that it is an alias name for `String` in the .NET Framework. Following that link, you find the information presented in Figure 12-6.

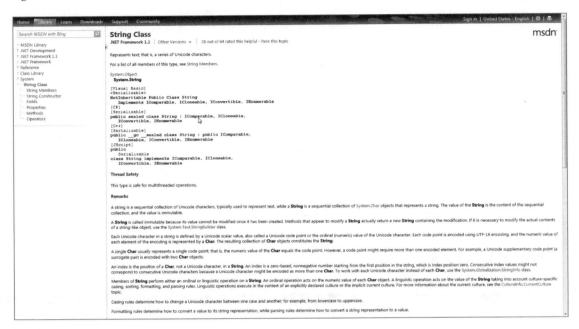

FIGURE 12.6: Finding the string interfaces

This confirms that the `string` data type also supports the `IComparable` interface. Using the C# documentation is an easy way to determine if a specific C# data type supports a specific interface. However, these two methods are not runtime ways to determine whether a data type supports a certain interface. How can you make the determination at run time?

Use the is Operator

The third way to determine if a data type supports a given interface is to use the `is` operator. The syntax for the `is` operator is as follows:

```
TypeInQuestion is InterfaceInQuestion
```

For example, if you want to see if a data type passed to the `clsQuickSort` constructor supports the `IComparable` interface, you can add the following test code to the constructor presented in Listing 12-4:

```
public clsQuickSort(T[] values)
{
    data = values;    // copy rvalue of unsorted data
    if (data[0] is IComparable)
    {
```

```
            Console.WriteLine("data[0] is IComparable");
        }
    }
```

Note the use of the `is` operator in the `if` statement. If you set a breakpoint on the `if` statement, you can check each data type passed to the class to see if it supports the `IComparable` interface. In the final version of the code, you would probably want to flag a data set that fails the `if` test and returns an error message to the caller.

Using the `IComparable` interface in `clsQuickSort` enables you to get around the fact that generics currently don't directly support the relational operators. If you take a little time, you can find that the code functions the same way it did in the nongeneric form of the class code.

Use the as Operator

Fourth, you can use the `as` operator to determine if an object supports a specific interface. The `as` operator has the following syntax form:

```
    expression as type
```

The `as` operator is actually used to perform conversions between compatible reference data types. However, if the conversion cannot be made, it produces `null` as the outcome of the expression. This is kind of nice because if the conversion fails, the result is `null` rather than an exception being thrown.

For example, `ArrayList` data types support only the `IList` interface. You could check this fact using code similar to that shown in the following code fragment:

```
    ArrayList val = new ArrayList();
    IComparable val1 = val as IComparable;
    if (val1 == null)
    {
        Console.WriteLine("val1 doesn't support IComparable");
    }
```

In this example, an `ArrayList` reference named `val` is defined and then used the `as` operator to see if you could convert `val` into an `IComparable` object named `val1`. If `ArrayList` objects don't support the `IComparable` interface, the conversion fails and `val1` is null. Because `ArrayLists` do not support the `IComparable` interface, the conversion fails, and the failure message is written to the console.

If you modify the code to define `val` using the following statement,

```
    int val = 5;
```

the conversion is made successfully, and the failure message is not displayed. (You must assign a value to `val` or the compiler issues an uninitialized local variable error message.)

Generics and interfaces can often team up to make a given class much more flexible for the data types it can process. Obviously, the time to think about generics is during the design phase of a project. Although the design time might increase slightly, you will be rewarded with a much more robust class for those that do implement generics.

SUMMARY

In this chapter you learned how generics can reduce the code burden to develop a new application. You concentrated on how generics enable you to write classes and methods in a way that makes them capable to process different data types. Not only do generics provide code flexibility, they also do it with strongly typed data yet without the hassles involved in having to cast every expression. You also learned how to use interfaces to simplify your code. Interfaces guarantee the user that specific functionality is provided by the code. Entire books have been written on interfaces and their related topics, which are worth your study.

EXERCISES

You can find the answers to the following exercises in Appendix A.

1. What are the major advantages of generics?

2. Listing 12-3 shows a method named `ShowData()` that you can use to fill the listbox objects with the appropriate data. How would you modify that method to take advantage of generics?

3. What are the major advantages of interfaces?

4. The `swap()` method in `clsQuickSort` is sloppy because you rely on class scope for the data swapped. Rewrite the `swap()` method so that it can still swap any type of data of the class, but without relying on class scope.

5. One of the major banes of writing commercial software is adding new features without breaking older versions. Do any of the topics discussed in this chapter cause you to rethink software versioning?

▶ WHAT YOU LEARNED IN THIS CHAPTER

TOPIC	KEY POINTS
Generics	A means to add code flexibility but retain strict type checking
Generic advantages	Enables one body of code to process what seems to be typeless code; enhances code reuse
Boxing, unboxing	The overhead processes associated with converting to-and-from value types to objects and back
Interfaces	A flexible means to add new class functionality without breaking old code

PART IV
Storing Data

13

Using Disk Data Files

WHAT YOU WILL LEARN IN THIS CHAPTER:

➤ Two basic file types: text and binary

➤ The advantages and disadvantages of each file type

➤ Computer streams

➤ Sequential files

➤ Random access files

➤ Serialization and deserialization

➤ Multiple document interface (MDI) programs

➤ Writing program menus

WROX.COM CODE DOWNLOADS FOR THIS CHAPTER

You can find the wrox.com code downloads for this chapter at `www.wrox.com/remtitle`
`.cgi?isbn=9781118336922` on the Download Code tab. The code in the `Chapter13` folder is
individually named according to the names throughout the chapter.

This chapter shows you how to use disk data files. If you think about it, computers would lose
much of their functionality if there weren't a way to permanently store, or *persist*, the data
generated by a computer. Things that you take for granted today, such as making an airline
reservation, must have been a nightmare before computers were in widespread use.

Up to this point you have written programs whose usefulness ended when the program ended.
After you master the contents of this chapter, you can write programs that can store data,
enabling you to recall that data at some later time. Programs take on a whole new light when
you know how to persist data.

Let's get started.

DIRECTORIES

Anytime I want to explore a new area in C#, the first thing I do is find out which namespaces are involved with that area. Because you're going to learn about file input and output (I/O), I simply typed in using System. at the top of the program and started looking for namespaces that may apply.

Sure enough, up popped System.IO. Just highlight IO and press the F1 key, and you'll get information about the IO namespace. All kinds of interesting things come up, but concentrate first on those classes that deal with directory and drive information.

The DriveInfo Class

Just as Ed McMahon used to say on the Johnny Carson show, "Everything you could ever possibly want to know....," about a disk drive is in the DriveInfo class. A few of the more useful methods and properties are presented in Table 13-1.

TABLE 13-1: The DriveInfo Class

METHOD OR PROPERTY	DESCRIPTION
GetDrives()	Returns an array with all the logical drives of the computer
AvailableFreeSpace	Gives the amount of free disk space (in bytes) on a drive
DriveFormat	Returns the format for the drive (such as NTFS or FAT32)
DriveType	Returns the type of drive (such as fixed, removable, RAM, and so on)
Name	Gives the name of the drive
TotalFreeSpace	Gives the amount of unused space on the drive
TotalSize	Gives the capacity of the drive

If you look in the IO namespace, you can also discover that there are classes named Directory and DirectoryInfo. These two classes present related, albeit different, information.

Directory Class

Table 13-2 presents a partial listing for methods found in the Directory class. (You can always get more complete information using the online help for the class.)

TABLE 13-2: The Directory Class

METHODS	DESCRIPTION
CreateDirectory()	Creates a directory for a given pathname
Delete()	Deletes a specified directory
Exists()	Determines if a specified directory exists

METHODS	DESCRIPTION
GetCreationTime()	Returns a `DateTime` type with the time a directory was created
GetCurrentDirectory()	Gets the current working directory of an application
GetFiles()	Returns the filenames in a given directory
GetLastAccessTime()	Returns the date and time the directory was last accessed
GetLastWriteTime()	Returns the data and time the directory was last written to
GetParent()	Returns the parent directory for a given path name
Move()	Moves a file or directory to a new location
SetCreationTime()	Sets the time for the creation of a file or directory
SetLastWriteTime()	Sets the date and time the file or directory was last written to

DirectoryInfo Class

Finally, Table 13-3 presents the methods and properties for the `DirectoryInfo` class. The `DirectoryInfo` class implements the `FileSystemInfo` interface. This means that you should also check the `FileSystemInfo` interface to see what properties and methods that interface requires.

TABLE 13-3: The DirectoryInfoClass

METHODS OR PROPERTY	DESCRIPTION
Create()	Creates a directory.
CreateSubdirectory()	Creates a subdirectory.
Delete()	Deletes a given directory.
Equals()	Compares directory objects.
GetDirectories()	Returns the subdirectories for the current directory.
GetFiles()	Returns the files in the current directory. This is overloaded so that you can do searches easily.
GetFileSystemInfos()	Returns strongly typed `FileSystemInfo` for files and subdirectories.
MoveTo()	Moves a `DirectoryInfo` object's contents to a specified path.
Exists	Returns a value to indicate if a directory exists.
Extension	Returns a string that represents the extension component of a filename.
FullName	Returns the full path of a directory or path.

With the properties and methods presented in the three preceding tables, you can obtain just about all the information you need to manipulate directories.

In the next Try It Out you write a program that exercises some of the methods presented in Tables 13-1, 13-2, and 13-3. You might try to work in a few other methods in the example just to see how they work.

Using Directories (Chapter13ProgramDirectories.zip)

The program shown in Figure 13-1 uses some of the directory methods and properties presented in the previous tables. The user types in a drive and directory (that is, a *pathname*) he is interested in and clicks the List button to show the directories in that directory. The program then presents a list of the directories and subdirectories. By the way, you may not want to type in just the drive name, like C:\. My C drive had 158,831 directories and subdirectories, and it took over one-half hour for the program to run to completion.

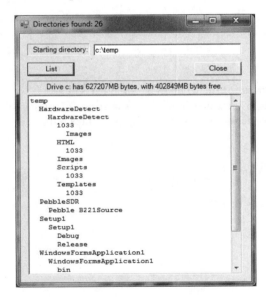

FIGURE 13-1: Sample run of directory program

To create the program:

1. Start a new project in the usual manner.

2. Add the form objects using Figure 13-1 as a guideline.

3. Add the code shown in Listing 13-1 to the project. The code may be downloaded from the Chapter13ProgramDirectories.zip file.

LISTING 13-1: Program to Present a Directory List (frmMain.cs)

```csharp
using System;
using System.IO;
using System.Collections;
using System.Windows.Forms;

public class frmMain : Form
{
    private ListBox lstDirectories;
    private Label label1;
    private TextBox txtStartingPath;
    private Button btnClose;
    private Label lblDriveInfo;
    private Button btnList;
    #region Windows code

    public frmMain()
    {
        InitializeComponent();
    }

    public static void Main()
    {
        frmMain main = new frmMain();
        Application.Run(main);
    }

    private void btnList_Click(object sender, EventArgs e)
    {
        string startingPath;
        int count;
        int i;
        ArrayList dirs = new ArrayList();
        // Where to start the listing
        startingPath = @txtStartingPath.Text;

        try
        {
            DirectoryInfo myDirInfo = new DirectoryInfo(startingPath);

            if (myDirInfo.Exists == false)
            {
                MessageBox.Show("Cannot find directory. Re-enter.", "Directory Not
                Found");
                txtStartingPath.Focus();
                return;
            }
            clsDirectory myDirs = new clsDirectory();

            ShowDriveInfo();

            lstDirectories.Items.Clear();
```

continues

LISTING 13-1 *(continued)*

```csharp
        count = myDirs.ShowDirectory(myDirInfo, 0, dirs);
        for (i = 0; i < dirs.Count; i++)
        {
            lstDirectories.Items.Add(dirs[i]);
        }
        this.Text = "Directories found: " + count.ToString();
    }
    catch (Exception ex) // Something went wrong?
    {
        MessageBox.Show("Error: " + ex.Message, "IO Error");
        return;
    }
}


/*****
 * Purpose: This shows some size info about the drive selected.
 *
 * Parameter list:
 *   n/a
 *
 * Return type:
 *   void
 *****/
private void ShowDriveInfo()
{
    int pos;
    long driveBytes;
    string buff;

    try
    {
        pos = txtStartingPath.Text.IndexOf('\\');// Get drive name
        buff = txtStartingPath.Text.Substring(0, pos);

        DriveInfo myDrive = new DriveInfo(@buff);  // Get its info

        driveBytes = myDrive.TotalSize / 1000000;
        lblDriveInfo.Text = "Drive " + buff + " has " +
                            driveBytes.ToString() + "MB bytes, with "
                            +  myDrive.TotalFreeSpace/1000000
                            + "MB bytes free.";
    }
    catch
    {
        txtStartingPath.Text = "";
    }
}
private void btnClose_Click(object sender, EventArgs e)
{
    Close();
}
}
```

How It Works

The program begins by including the Collections and IO namespaces. The real action, however, takes place in the btnList_Click() event code. The starting pathname entered by the user is assigned into the variable startingPath. The program instantiates a DirectoryInfo object named myDirInfo, passing the user's path information to the constructor.

If you want to get a list of all the drives currently available, you could use the following code:

```
DriveInfo[] listDrives = DriveInfo.GetDrives();
```

This statement creates a string array of all the drives on the system. You could use this information to check that the user typed in a valid drive name.

The code then calls the ShowDriveInfo() method. The ShowDriveInfo() method is simply a helper method that collects some statistics about the disk drive that the user entered. The code creates a DriveInfo object named myDrive, passing the drive name to its constructor. The code then gathers some statistics about the drive and displays them in a label object. The storage statistics are divided by one million simply to express the stats in terms of megabytes. (Remember that a megabyte is actually a thousand kilobytes, or 1,048,576 bytes = 1024 bytes × 1024 bytes.) You could also use

```
driveBytes = myDrive.AvailableFreeSpace;
```

to display the free space on the drive. This is the hard way just to show how to use those methods.

The program then creates a clsDirectory object named myDirs and calls the ShowDirectory() method. The code for the clsDirectory class is shown in Listing 13-2.

LISTING 13-2: Source Code for clsDirectory (clsDirectory.cs)

```csharp
using System;
using System.Collections;
using System.IO;


class clsDirectory
{
    const string TAB = " ";
    static private int visits;  // How many times here

    //=============== Instance variables ==================
    private int dirCounter;     // How many directories

    //=============== Constructor =======================
    public clsDirectory()
    {
        dirCounter = 1; // The directory passed in
    }
    //================= Property methods ====================

    public int DirectoryCount    // Make it read-only
    {
        get
```

continues

LISTING 13-2 *(continued)*

```
        {
            return dirCounter;
        }
    }

/*****
 * Purpose: This method creates a directory list at a given path
 *
 * Parameter list:
 *   DirectoryInfo curDir        the current directory info
 *   int inLevel                 how deep in list
 *   ArrayList dirs              array of directory strings
 *
 * Return value:
 *   int                         directory count or 1 on error
 *
 *****/
public int ShowDirectory(DirectoryInfo curDir, int inLevel,
                         ArrayList dirs)
{
    int i;
    string indent = "";

    try
    {
        for (i = 0; i < visits; i++)     // Indent subdirectories
        {
            indent += TAB;
        }

        dirs.Add(indent + curDir.Name); // Add it to list
        visits++;

        foreach (DirectoryInfo subDir in curDir.GetDirectories())
        {
            dirCounter++;
            ShowDirectory(subDir, visits, dirs);  // Recurse
                // FileInfo[] files = subDir.GetFiles();
        }
        visits--;   // Go back to previous directory level

        if (indent.Length > 0)  // Adjust the indent level accordingly
            indent.Substring(0, indent.Length - TAB.Length);
    }
    catch (Exception ex)
    {
        return 1;  // Could do something with ex.Message
    }
    return dirCounter;
    }
}
```

Most of the code in Listing 13-2 should look familiar by now. The `ShowDirectory()` method is passed three arguments: 1) A `DirectoryInfo` object. 2) An integer that keeps track of where you are in the directory structure. 3) An `ArrayList` variable to store the directory names. Note that `ShowDirectory()` is called recursively each time a directory is read. That way you can get a list of subdirectories and traverse those, too. The variable named `visits` keeps track of how far down the directory tree you are at any given moment. The `visits` variable is also used to indent the directory names for display in the `listbox` object. The recursive calls are performed by the loop:

```
foreach (DirectoryInfo subDir in curDir.GetDirectories())
{
    dirCounter++;
    ShowDirectory(subDir, visits, dirs);  // Recurse
        // FileInfo[] files = subDir.GetFiles();
}
```

You also keep a count of the directories read with the variable `dirCounter`. After all the directories have been read, this number displays in the title bar of the form. If you want to get a list of the files in a given subdirectory, uncomment the line in the `foreach` loop. You can then look at the files variable to see the files in each directory.

You should single-step through this program using the debugger to inspect each of the variables as the program is run. This gives you a better feel for how the `DirectoryInfo` class works.

FILE CLASS

The File class presents you with a number of useful methods that you will want to use in your programs. A partial list of the methods in the File class is presented in Table 13-4.

TABLE 13-4: The File Class

METHOD	DESCRIPTION
AppendAllText()	Appends a string of text to a specified file. The method is overloaded so that different encoding schemes may be used.
AppendText()	Uses a `StreamWriter` object to append UTF-8-encoded text to a specified file. UTF-8 is an 8-bit Unicode Transformation Format that is backward compatible with the ASCII character set.
Copy()	Copies a specified file.
Create()	Creates a specified file.
CreateText()	Creates or opens a file for UTF-8 encoded text.
Delete()	Deletes a specified file.
Exists()	Checks to see if a specified file exists.

continues

TABLE 13-4 *(continued)*

METHOD	DESCRIPTION
GetCreationTime()	Returns the date and time a file was created.
Move()	Moves a specified file to a specified location.
Open()	Uses a `FileStream` object to open a specified file.
OpenRead()	Opens an existing file for reading.
OpenText()	Opens a UTF-8 file for reading.
OpenWrite()	Opens an existing file for writing.
ReadAllBytes()	Opens a binary file and copies the contents into a byte array. (Each `ReadAll*()` method has a corresponding `WriteAll*()` method.)
ReadAllLines()	Opens a text file, reads all lines in the file into a string array, and closes it.
ReadAllText()	Opens a text file, reads the contents into a string, and closes it.
Replace()	Replaces the content of one file with that of another file, deleting the original file and making a backup of the replaced file.
SetAttributes()	Sets the attributes of a file.
WriteAllBytes()	Creates, writes, and then closes the file after an array of bytes has been written.
WriteAllLines()	Creates, writes, and then closes a file after writing an array of strings to the file.

The entries in Table 13-4 are just a partial listing of the methods available to you. If you want a specific File method, check the online help before writing the method.

FILEINFO CLASS

Listing 13-2 commented out a statement that uses the `FileInfo` class. This class provides a lot of details about the files you find on the system. Some of the more important properties and methods are presented in Table 13-5.

TABLE 13-5: The FileInfo Class

METHOD OR PROPERTY	DESCRIPTION
AppendText()	Appends text for the current `FileInfo` object using a `StreamWriter`
CopyTo()	Copies an existing file to a new file
Create()	Creates a new file

METHOD OR PROPERTY	DESCRIPTION
CreateText()	Creates a StreamWriter object that writes a new text file
Delete()	Deletes a file
Equals()	Determines if two FileInfo objects are equal
MoveTo()	Moves a file to a new location with the option to rename it
Open()	Opens a file with various read/write privileges
Replace()	Replaces a specified file with contents of current FileInfo file
Attributes	Gets the file attributes of a specified file
CreationTime	Gets or sets the creation time for a file
Directory	Gets an instance of the parent directory
DirectoryName	Returns the full pathname as a string
Exists	Determines if a file exists
Extension	Returns a string representation of a file's extension
FullName	Returns the complete path of a file or directory
LastAccessTime	Returns the last time the file was accessed
Length	Returns the number of bytes in a file
Name	Returns the name of the current file

The tables and their associated methods and properties should give you enough information about directories and files for you to manipulate them in your programs. You draw on several of these properties and methods later in this chapter. Before you do that, however, you need to understand the basic types of files that C# supports.

TYPES OF FILES

From a programming language point of view, there are two basic types of files: those that contain textual data and those that contain binary data. Often you can determine if a given file is a text or binary file by its name. Filenames are stored on disk using a primary and secondary filename. For example, a file named JaneAtParty.jpg has a *primary* name of JaneAtParty and a *secondary* filename of jpg. (Many people refer the primary filename as *the* filename and the secondary filename as the file's *extension*.) The secondary filename often gives a clue as to its type. For example, a file extension of txt is normally a textual data file, whereas those ending in jpg are binary image files. Although there is nothing that requires you to use common file extensions, it's usually a good idea to employ them in your programs.

Textual Versus Binary Data Files

Files that contain textual data are usually built from strings appended to the file. When a user types text into a textbox, that data is stored in memory as plain text in a string format. If you want to save that information permanently on disk, it means moving the strings from memory to a disk data file. If the user types a number into a textbox and that number is used numerically (for example, if the square root of that number is taken), the number is stored in memory in a binary format. For that number to be saved in a text file, it must be converted to a string and *then* written to disk. (You've done this conversion many times before when you used the ToString() method associated with a value type.) In other words, text files contain nothing but string data.

One of the nice things about text files is that it is easy to read the content of a text file. You can use a simple program like Notepad (which comes free with Windows) to read a text file. Because text files are so easy to read, programs that read and write text files are usually easier to debug. Figure 13-2 shows the output of a text file using Notepad to read it.

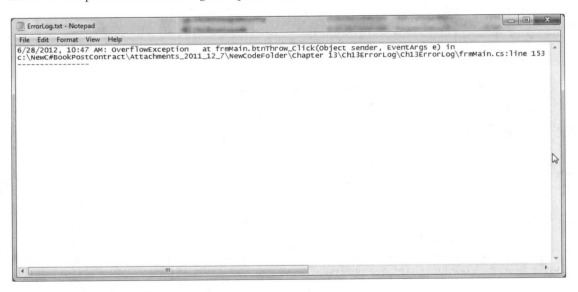

FIGURE 13-2: Sample text file

Binary files are a little different from text files. If a number is written to a binary file, no conversion of that number to a string occurs. If an int variable has the value 50, that value is written to the binary file as 4 bytes of data, even though it would only take 2 bytes if it were written as a string. (If Unicode is used, the string takes 4 bytes.) Because int value types are stored in memory as hexadecimal (base-16) values, the number 50 would be stored as 32 00 00 00 in a binary file. If that same value were a decimal data type, it would require 16 bytes to store that value in a binary file.

If some numbers (such as 50) take more bytes to store in memory than their string equivalents, why use binary files? First, if the value were 1 billion instead of 50, a string would require 10 bytes to store it as text but still would take only 4 bytes to store it as a binary value. Second, and more important, values stored as binary can be moved into memory and used without their values needing to be converted from the string format stored on disk to the hexadecimal format used in the program. Avoiding this conversion process makes binary files a little faster when reading numeric data from a disk file into a program.

If you take the same file shown in Figure 13-2 and read it using a program that displays that file in a binary format, the output looks like that shown in Figure 13-3.

> **NOTE** You can read a text file in binary from within Visual Studio. To read a text file in binary, use the menu sequence File ➪ Open ➪ File to navigate to the file you want to view. However, after you select the file and are ready to click the Open button to actually open and read the file, click the down arrow on the right side of the Open button; then select Open With and select Binary Editor. You then see the file presented in binary, as shown in Figure 13-3.

```
00000000   36 2F 32 38 2F 32 30 31   32 2C 20 31 30 3A 34 37   6/28/2012, 10:47
00000010   20 41 4D 3A 20 4F 76 65   72 66 6C 6F 77 45 78 63    AM: OverflowExc
00000020   65 70 74 69 6F 6E 20 20   20 61 74 20 66 72 6D 4D   eption    at frmM
00000030   61 69 6E 2E 62 74 6E 54   68 72 6F 77 5F 43 6C 69   ain.btnThrow_Cli
00000040   63 6B 28 4F 62 6A 65 63   74 20 73 65 6E 64 65 72   ck(Object sender
00000050   2C 20 45 76 65 6E 74 41   72 67 73 20 65 29 20 69   , EventArgs e) i
00000060   6E 20 63 3A 5C 4E 65 77   43 23 42 6F 6F 6B 50 6F   n c:\NewC#BookPo
00000070   73 74 43 6F 6E 74 72 61   63 74 5C 41 74 74 61 63   stContract\Attac
00000080   68 6D 65 6E 74 73 5F 32   30 31 31 5F 31 32 5F 37   hments_2011_12_7
00000090   5C 4E 65 77 43 6F 64 65   46 6F 6C 64 65 72 5C 43   \NewCodeFolder\C
000000a0   68 61 70 74 65 72 20 31   33 5C 43 68 31 33 45 72   hapter 13\Ch13Er
000000b0   72 6F 72 4C 6F 67 5C 43   68 31 33 45 72 72 6F 72   rorLog\Ch13Error
000000c0   4C 6F 67 5C 66 72 6D 4D   61 69 6E 2E 63 73 3A 6C   Log\frmMain.cs:l
000000d0   69 6E 65 20 31 35 33 0D   0A 2D 2D 2D 2D 2D 2D 2D   ine 153..-------
000000e0   2D 2D 2D 2D 2D 2D 2D 2D   2D 0D 0A                  ---------..
```

FIGURE 13-3: Viewing a text file in binaryx

This first column in Figure 13-3 begins with the value 00000000. This is the starting count of the number of bytes displayed in hexadecimal (often abbreviated to hex) format for the file. After that, you see the number 36. Because that number is expressed as a hex number, you need to convert it to the base-10 numbering system you are familiar with. Therefore, 2 × 16 + 4 = 32 + 4 = 36. If you look up the ASCII value for 36 (in hex), you find it represents the digit character 6. You can see this translated value in the first position of the last column. The next value in the row is 2F, so 2 × 16 + F = 47. If you look that ASCII value up, it is the slash character (/). (The hex numbering system counts the values 0 through 9 as standard numbers, but 10 through 15 are the letters A through F. Because 0 through F can represent 16 values, it is called a base-16, or hex, numbering system. Therefore, F has a numeric value of 15 in a hex numbering system.) Again, at the extreme right of the first row, you can see the hex values displayed as their ASCII character equivalents.

If you look closely at Figure 13-3, you can see the hex values 0D 0A are the last two characters in the file. These two characters form a carriage return-linefeed (CRLF) pair of characters. Think of a carriage return (CR) as moving the cursor to the extreme left of the screen. The linefeed (LF) moves the cursor down one line. Taken together, the CRLF combine to form the *newline* character, which is represented as \n in a string format. Simply stated, the CRLF sequence causes the subsequent text to appear on a new output line.

In the next Try It Out you create a program that displays the contents of a text file. Often, error log files are text files and may be used for phone-in software support.

Writing a Text File (Chapter13ErrorLog.zip)

In Chapter 11 you read about how using error log messages as part of exception handling can be a useful debugging technique. This section develops a program that you can easily modify to work as an error log class in your programs. A sample run of the program is shown in Figure 13-4.

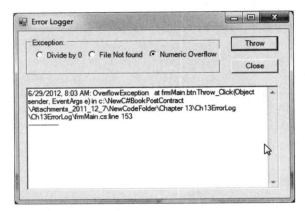

FIGURE 13-4: Error log program

The program lets the user select the type of error she wants to throw to test the error-logging feature. After the selection is made, the user clicks the Throw button, which throws the appropriate exception. That exception is then written to an error log file. The content of the error log file then displays in a `listbox` object, as shown in Figure 13-4. Because the error log file is a text file, you can use other programs, such as Notepad, to display its contents.

To create this program

1. Create a new project in the normal manner.

2. Add toolbox objects to a Windows form. You can use the code shown in Listings 13-3 and 13-4, or you can download the code file `Chapter13ProgramErrorLog.zip`.

How It Works

As usual, there are two parts to the program. `frmMain` provides the shell for testing the class that actually processes the error log file (`clsErrorLog`). The code for `frmMain` is presented in Listing 13-3.

LISTING 13-3: Program to Throw and Record an Exception (frmMain.cs)

```
using System;
using System.Windows.Forms;
using System.IO;

public class frmMain : Form
{
    string err;
```

```csharp
private RadioButton rbNumericOverflow;
private RadioButton rbFileNotFound;
private RadioButton rbDivideBy0;
private Button btnThrow;
private Button btnClose;
private TextBox txtErrorMsgs;
private GroupBox groupBox1;

#region Windows code

public frmMain()
{
    InitializeComponent();
    rbDivideBy0.Checked = true;
}

public static void Main()
{
    frmMain main = new frmMain();
    Application.Run(main);
}

private void btnThrow_Click(object sender, EventArgs e)
{
    try
    {
        // To use a general catch, uncomment the next line
        // throw new System.OutOfMemoryException();
        if (rbDivideBy0.Checked == true)
        {
            throw new System.DivideByZeroException();
        }
        else
        {
            if (rbFileNotFound.Checked == true)
            {
                throw new System.IO.FileNotFoundException();
            }
            else
            {
                throw new System.OverflowException();
            }
        }
    }
    catch (DivideByZeroException ex)
    {
        MessageBox.Show("DivideByZeroException thrown.",
                    "Exception Error");
        err = "DivideByZeroException: " + ex.StackTrace;
    }
    catch (FileNotFoundException ex)
    {
        MessageBox.Show("FileNotFoundException thrown.",
                    "Exception Error");
        err = "FileNotFoundException" + ex.StackTrace;
```

continues

LISTING 13-3 *(continued)*

```
        }
        catch (OverflowException ex)
        {
            MessageBox.Show("OverflowException thrown.",
                            "Exception Error");
            err = "OverflowException" + ex.StackTrace;
        }
        catch (Exception ex)
        {
            MessageBox.Show(ex.StackTrace, "Exception Error");
            err = ex.Message + " " + ex.StackTrace;
        }
        finally
        {
            clsErrorLog myErrLog = new clsErrorLog(err);
            myErrLog.PathName = Application.StartupPath;

            myErrLog.WriteErrorLog();
            txtErrorMsgs.Text = myErrLog.ReadErrorLog();
        }
    }

    private void btnClose_Click(object sender, EventArgs e)
    {
        Close();
    }
}
```

Most of the work is done in the `btnThrow_Click()` event code. Based upon the type of exception selected by the user, a series of nested `if` statements causes the appropriate exception to be thrown. The exception then triggers its associated `catch` block to be processed. For example, if the user selects the divide-by-zero exception, that exception is thrown, and the `catch` block is executed:

```
catch (DivideByZeroException ex)
{
    MessageBox.Show("DivideByZeroException thrown.",
                    "Exception Error");
    err = "DivideByZeroException: " + ex.StackTrace;
}
```

A message is shown to the user, and then the `string` variable `err` records the type of exception plus the `StackTrace` information from the `Exception` object `ex`.

The `finally` block instantiates an error log object named `myErrorLog`, passing in the error string (`err`) to the constructor. Finally, the `WriteErrorLog()` method appends the error string to the error log file. The `ReadErrorLog()` method simply displays the contents of the error log file in a multiline textbox object.

Managing the error log file is done through the `clsErrorLog` class. To see the code for the error log class, refer to Listing 13-4).

LISTING 13-4: Source Code for clsErrorLog (clsErrorLog.cs)

```csharp
using System;
using System.Collections.Generic;
using System.IO;

class clsErrorLog
{
    //=================== Instance members ====================
    private string fileName;
    private string pathName;
    private string errorMessage;
    private int errorFlag;

    StreamWriter sw = null;
    StreamReader sr = null;

    //=================== Constructor ========================
    public clsErrorLog(string msg)
    {
        errorMessage = msg;
        errorFlag = 0;
        fileName = "ErrorLog.txt";
    }
    //=================== Property Methods ===================
    public string FileName
    {
        get
        {
            return fileName;
        }
        set
        {
            if (value.Length > 0)
                fileName = value;
        }
    }
    public string Message
    {
        get
        {
            return errorMessage;
        }
        set
        {
            if (value.Length > 0)
                errorMessage = value;
        }
    }

    public string PathName        // Set the path name thingie
    {
        get
        {
```

continues

LISTING 13-4 *(continued)*

```
        return pathName;
      }

      set
      {
        if (value.Length > 0)
          pathName = value;
      }
  }
}
//=================== Helper Methods =====================
//=================== General Methods =====================

/*****
 * Purpose: This reads the error log file.
 *
 * Parameter list:
 *   n/a
 *
 * Return value
 *   string           the contents of the error log message file
 *****/
public string ReadErrorLog()
{
    string buff;
    try
    {
        string pfn = Path.Combine(pathName, fileName);
        if (File.Exists(pfn) == true)
        {
            sr = new StreamReader(pfn);

            buff = sr.ReadToEnd();
            sr.Close();
            return buff;
        }
    }
    catch
    {
        return "";
    }
    return "";
}
/*****
 * Purpose: This writes an error log message to the error log file.
 * The message has the date and time, the type of
 * error, and the stack trace for the error.
 *
 * Parameter list:
 *   n/a
 *
 * Return value
 *   int           0 = no errors, 1 otherwise
 *****/
```

```
public int WriteErrorLog()
{
    errorFlag = 0;
    DateTime currentDT = DateTime.Now;
    try
    {
      // Do we have all the stings need?
      if (errorMessage.Length != 0 && pathName.Length != 0 &&
                  fileName.Length != 0)
      {
        sw = new StreamWriter(Path.Combine(pathName,
                                      fileName), true);
        sw.WriteLine(currentDT.ToShortDateString() + ", " +
                  currentDT.ToShortTimeString() + ": " + errorMessage);
                  sw.WriteLine("---------------");
        sw.Close();
      }
      else
      {
        errorFlag = 1;   // Something bad happened
      }
    }
    catch (Exception ex)
    {
            errorMessage = ex.Message;
            errorFlag = 1; // Something bad happened
    }
      return errorFlag;
    }
    /*****
    * Purpose: This writes an error log message to the error log file.
    *
    * Parameter list:
    *   string msg        the error message to write
    *
    * Return value
    *   int               0 = no errors, 1 otherwise
    *****/
    public int WriteErrorLog(string msg)
    {
        errorMessage = msg;                   // Copy the message
        errorFlag = WriteErrorLog();   // Now call original one
        return errorFlag;
    }
}
```

The StreamWriter Object

The code makes use of a StreamWriter object to write the error message and related information to a disk file named ErrorLog.txt. (Refer to the constructor code in Listing 13-4.) The statement

```
sw = new StreamWriter(Path.Combine(pathName, fileName), true);
```

calls the StreamWriter constructor to instantiate the sw StreamWriter object. The constructor is overloaded, and the version you use here has two arguments.

The first argument, `Path.Combine(pathName, filename)`, combines the pathname and the filename to form a single argument. By default, if you do not supply a pathname for the file, C# assumes you want to place the file in the same directory as the executable file for the program. If you stored this program in a folder named `TestCode` on the `C` drive and named the project `ErrorLogger`, the default pathname supplied to the constructor would be

```
"C:\TestCode\ErrorLogger\bin\Debug\ErrorLog.txt"
```

The second argument is a boolean with the value `true`. If the second argument is `true`, all new text data is appended to the end of the file. If the file does not exist, the file is created. If the second argument is `false` and the file exists, any current data in the file is overwritten. If the file does not exist and the second argument is `false`, the file is created, and the new string data is written to the file.

You have overloaded the `WriteErrorLog()` method for the class. The signatures for the two methods are as follows:

```
public int WriteErrorLog()
public int WriteErrorLog(string msg)
```

In `frmMain`, you passed in the error message to the constructor. That error message is then assigned into a class member named `errorMessage`. However, if an object of `clsErrorLog` has already been instantiated and the user then wants to write another error message to the file, he can use the second `WriteErrorLog()` method that accepts a string as its argument. The code for this version shows that the error message passed in is assigned into `errorMessage` and then the no-parameter version of `WriteErrorLog()` is called. The appropriate return value is maintained in either call.

```
public int WriteErrorLog(string msg)
{
    errorMessage = msg;              // Copy the message
    errorFlag = WriteErrorLog();     // Now call original one
    return errorFlag;
}
```

The code for the `WriteErrorLog()` that does the real work is embodied within a `try-catch` block. This code block is always a good idea because electromechanical devices are the Achilles' heel of most computer systems. The `WriteLine()` method of the `StreamWriter` object is used to write the error message to the file. The `WriteLine()` method differs from the `Write()` method in that `WriteLine()` appends a newline character at the end of the string currently being saved to disk. The statements follow:

```
sw.WriteLine(currentDT.ToShortDateString() + ", " +
             currentDT.ToShortTimeString() + ": " + errorMessage);
sw.WriteLine("---------------");
sw.Close();
```

The first call to `WriteLine()` writes the current date and time to the file, followed by the error message that has been passed to the class. The second call to `WriteLine()` simply writes out a series of dashes to make the end of each error message entry easier to differentiate. The final statement closes the file by a call to the `Close()` method of the `StreamWriter` object.

Reading the Data

After the data has been written to the disk, control eventually returns to the statement:

```
txtErrorMsgs.Text = myErrLog.ReadErrorLog();
```

This statement uses the `ReadErrorLog()` method to read the contents of the error log file. (You could, of course, use Notepad or some equivalent program to read the file.) The code for reading the file is

```
public string ReadErrorLog()
{
    string buff;
    try
    {
        string pfn = Path.Combine(pathName, fileName);
        if (File.Exists(pfn) == true)
        {
            sr = new StreamReader(pfn);

            buff = sr.ReadToEnd();
            sr.Close();
            return buff;
        }
    }
    catch (Exception ex)
    {
        return ex.Message;
    }
    return "";
}
```

Again, the code is surrounded by a `try-catch` block to prevent an ungraceful death by the program. The program builds the path and filename and assigns them into the variable `pfn`. The code then uses a `File` object to determine if that file exists. (You can use `File.Exists(pfn)` directly without explicit instantiation because it is a `static` method.) Assuming the file does exist, you instantiate a `StreamReader` object named `sr`. The `ReadToEnd()` method of the `StreamReader` class reads all the string data in the file and assigns it into `buff`, which is returned to the caller. In the code, you simply copy the string to the `listbox` object.

Using clsErrorLog

Unlike most of your previous programs, the `clsErrorLog` class is actually useful in its own right. If you use `try-catch` blocks in your code or use `if` statements to sense error conditions other than exceptions, you can use this class to record what happened. Because you are free to pass in any string you want, its contents can vary according to your information needs when a given error occurs. If it is in a commercial product and someone calls for product support, you can have the caller read the `ErrorLog` `.txt` file with Notepad and at least have some idea of what went wrong.

True, the program's simple, but you can always add functionality if you need it. That's one of the nice things about OOP—you can always extend the class to suit your specific needs.

SEQUENTIAL VERSUS RANDOM ACCESS FILES

The error log program presented in Listings 13-3 and 13-4 writes textual data to a disk file named ErrorLog.txt. If the log file doesn't exist, it is created and the new data is written to the file. If the file exists and already has information stored in it, new data is appended to the end of the existing file. Over the years, this file could grow fairly large if errors continue to be added. Typically, when reading a text file, the reading program starts at the beginning of the file and reads the data in the file to the end.

Sequential Files

The process of continually adding new data to the end of an existing file creates a *sequential file*. With sequential files, new data is added on to the end of the file. There are no gaps in the data. Indeed, one of the advantages of sequential files is that they are dense. That is, every byte of storage space in a sequential file is filled with a piece of information.

Sequential files are like the old cassette music tapes. If you liked song number nine on the tape, you had to fast-forward the tape to that particular song to play it. If you were good at it, you could press the fast-forward button on the cassette player, count the required number of seconds in your head, and then press the play button. With practice, you could get close to your wanted song. The DVD players of today make this "timed search" seem archaic. You simply skip over the tracks you don't want to hear and immediately begin listening to the song of choice.

If you can visualize a disk file like a music tape, it would look something like Figure 13-5.

FIGURE 13-5: A sequential data file

The first thing to notice in the figure is that each song is free to be longer or shorter than any other song. The BOF in Figure 13-5 stands for *Beginning Of File*, whereas EOF stands for *End Of File*. You can think of the File Pointer as the ceramic read/write head of disk hardware. Sequential files are read sequentially from BOF to EOF. Therefore, to read the sequential file, the File Pointer is placed at the BOF when the file is opened, and it moves toward the EOF as the file is read. To get to song five, you must read through the first four songs. (Although the fast-forward button sped things up, you still had to read the intervening songs.) Sequential files have an EOF marker written at the end of the file, so the end of the file can be sensed by the program code. When the File Pointer has read through the file and reads the EOF marker, you know that the entire contents of the file have been read.

Advantages and Disadvantages of Sequential Files

For sequential files, the good news is that the files are dense: They waste no disk space. The bad news is that you are forced to read through unwanted data to get to the data you actually want to use. Also, editing the information in a sequential file is awkward at best. In most cases, editing some part of a sequential file means reading the old file into memory, rewriting the old file information up to the point of the edit to a new file, writing the new information to the new file, and then appending the remaining part of the old file onto the new file. Yep...it's as clumsy as described.

Sequential files are often used for information that rarely requires editing or updating. E-mail messages, error logs, documents, letters, and similar types of data are good candidates for sequential files because they store information that isn't often updated. However, the bulk of business transactions often employ information that needs to be updated frequently, so sequential files just aren't suited to the task. That's where random access files come in.

Random Access Files

Random access files are based upon the concept of a fixed record size. For example, when you open a credit account with a store, it records your name and home and work addresses, plus some credit information. Because people do move, change jobs, improve (or ruin) their credit history, get married, and do dozens of other things, such information needs to be updated fairly often. Because information of this nature does require frequent updating, software engineers make sure each record is the same size. This is shown in Figure 13-6.

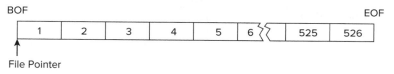

FIGURE 13-6: A random access data file

Whereas Figure 13-5 shows records of differing lengths, the byte length of each record in Figure 13-6 is identical. You can visualize a random access record as a line of bricks laid end to end, in which each brick represents the information about one customer. Because each brick has the same size, it's easy to pick up brick number five (perhaps the information about Ms. Smith) from the line, change the information written on the brick, and replace the brick at position number five in the line of bricks.

Fixed Record Sizes

So...big deal. What's the advantage of random access files? You can see the advantage by looking at a simple example. Suppose the information about each customer takes 300 bytes. This means the length of each "information brick" in Figure 13-6 is 300 bytes. Each information brick forms a *record* for one customer. The advantage of random access files is that you can pick up the File Pointer and *skip over* the four bricks (that is, records) you don't want to read and drop the File Pointer down at the exact beginning of brick five. By your not having to read the information contained in the first four bricks, physically getting to brick five is significantly faster.

C# provides you with a file method named Seek() that enables you to scoot the File Pointer to any point in the file you want. The Seek() method can move the File Pointer virtually instantaneously and significantly faster than you can move the File Pointer by reading the records between its current position and the record you want to read. The general syntax for the `Seek()` method is as follows:

```
Seek((desiredRecord - 1) * RECORDSIZE, SeekOrigin.Begin);
```

As with almost everything in computer programming, the first record in a random access file is actually record 0. Therefore, if each `RECORDSIZE` is 300 bytes and you want to read record number five, you need to position the File Pointer at a spot that is 1,200 bytes into the file, as measured from BOF. Because the wanted record is record number five, the actual position in the file must be calculated as follows:

```
Seek((desiredRecord - 1) * RECORDSIZE, SeekOrigin.Begin);
Seek((5 - 1) * 300, SeekOrigin.Begin);
Seek(4 * 300, BOF);
Seek(1200, BOF);
```

You can read this last statement as: "Use the `Seek()` Method to Position the File Pointer with a Byte Offset of 1,200 Bytes Relative to the Beginning of File." This position can be viewed, as shown in Figure 13-7.

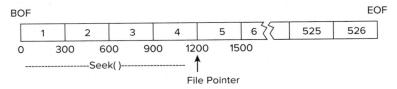

FIGURE 13-7: Using Seek( )

The first argument in the `Seek()` method is the *byte offset* that the File Pointer is to be moved expressed as a `long` data type. The second argument for `Seek()` is the *relative position* from which the File Pointer is to move. The second argument of the `Seek()` method provides three relative points for moving the File Pointer.

The first, `SeekOrigin.Begin`, positions the File Pointer with the byte offset relative to BOF. This is what is shown in Figure 13-7: The File Pointer is offset 1,200 bytes relative to BOF.

Second, `SeekOrigin.Current` moves the File Pointer relative to the current location of the File Pointer. For example, if you have read record number five, the File Pointer's current position would be at the start of record number six (byte offset 1,500 relative to BOF). If you want to now read record number four, you could use

```
Seek(-600, SeekOrigin.Current);
```

Because the byte offset is negative, the File Pointer is moved 600 bytes *back* from its current position, which would be at the start of record number four. (Byte offset = 900 in Figure 13-7.) A negative offset, therefore, means that you want to move the File Pointer toward the BOF.

The third relative point for the File Pointer is the end. The statement

```
Seek(0, SeekOrigin.End);
```

would place the File Pointer at the end of file (EOF). Where does Seek(-300, SeekOrigin.End) place the File Pointer? In terms of Figure 13-7, your code would be ready to read record number 526. If you think about it, it is an error to have a positive byte offset when SeekOrigin.End is used and you are reading the file. A positive byte offset would mean you are trying to read past the end of the file. Likewise, it is an error to have a negative byte offset when using SeekOrigin.Begin. This would imply placing the File Pointer at a location that is "in front of" the beginning of the file.

Advantages and Disadvantages of Random Access Files

The biggest advantage of random access files is that you can get to a particular record much faster than you can with sequential files. It's common to tie a customer's record location in the file to some unique piece of information associated with the customer. For example, imagine a customer's last name is Smith. The ASCII code for the letter S is 83. Therefore, you could write this customer at record position 83 in the file. If each record is 300 bytes, this person's information would be stored at byte offset 24,900 bytes relative to the BOF. The process to use one piece of information (an S) to derive a second piece of information (record 83) is called *hashing*. Using a hash code algorithm for record positions within a random access file makes locating an individual record fast. Obviously, if a second Smith is added to the file, this creates a *hash collision*, and the hash algorithm must accommodate such things. (If you're interested, C# provides a HashAlgorithm class that you can use in your own programs. Use the online help for further details.)

Not only are random access files better at finding a specific piece of information, random access files can update that information faster, too. Because each record in a random access file is exactly the same size, you can easily update a particular record and rewrite that record without needing to copy the entire file. Record updating is *much* faster with random access files because you must rewrite only the record that has been changed.

The bad news about random access files is that you must design the record size in terms of a worst-case scenario. Even though you know that most peoples' first names do not exceed 10 characters, you might need to design the number of bytes devoted to the customer's first name to be 15 bytes because of that one oddball whose parents thought it would be cute to name their son Guyfromtazmania. The same is true for all the information in the record. Street addresses, city names, e-mail addresses, and so on all must be designed for the largest possible size. Obviously, the trick to designing the byte size for each piece of string data is a balancing act between wasting bytes and recording the requisite information.

Because of this worst-case design philosophy, random access files are not dense like sequential files. If a customer has a short name and lives at an address like 1 Elm St., and has no e-mail address, that customer might use 100 bytes of the 300 bytes you've allowed for him in his record in the file. This means there are information "gaps" in the file where no data are stored. Such a random access file might look like that shown in Figure 13-8.

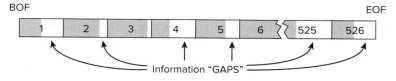

FIGURE 13-8: Random Access files are not dense

The shaded portion of each record in Figure 13-8 contains the actual data for a customer, whereas the unshaded portion is a gap where no useful information is present. However, if the person moves from 1 Elm St. to 657 White Oak Rd, you have enough room in the gap to update the customer's information with the longer street address.

Most programmers agree that the wasted bytes in the information "gaps" are a small price to pay for the increased performance and ease of updating that random access files bring to the table. Back in the early 1980s, I bought an IBM PC 5MB hard disk drive for $1,500. At that time, a megabyte of disk storage cost about $300. The price today is approaching 2 *cents* per megabyte! Although you still need to think about storage requirements, the cost constraints today are much less severe than in the past. As a result, random access rules for file may require frequent updating.

The next Try It Out presents the code for writing a random access file. As you examine the code, pay close attention to those points in the code where record sizes play a role. Notice how the code avoids magic numbers, too.

TRY IT OUT   **Random Access Files (Chapter13ProgramRandomAccess.zip)**

Now write an electronic phone book to maintain a record of your friends (or customers, or...whomever). The user interface for the program is shown in Figure 13-9.

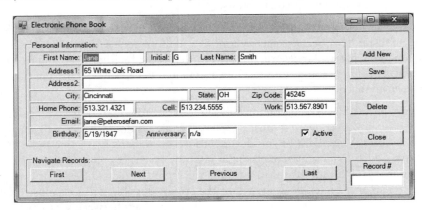

FIGURE 13-9: Phone book program

Two `groupbox` objects are present in the user interface. The first group is used to collect the personal information about the person via a collection of `textbox` objects. The second `groupbox` object contains several button objects that may be used to navigate through the records stored in the file.

To implement this program:

1. Create a new project in the usual manner.

2. Arrange the `groupbox`, `label`, `textbox`, and `button` objects on the form in a manner similar to that shown in Figure 13-9. Because there are a lot of form objects and code for this project, it makes a lot for sense to download the code from `Chatper13ProgramRandomAccess.zip`.

How It Works

Because this program is a more complex than earlier programs, the #region-#endregion preprocessor directives hide sections of code after they have been written, tested, and debugged. A picture of the source code window when finished is shown in Figure 13-10.

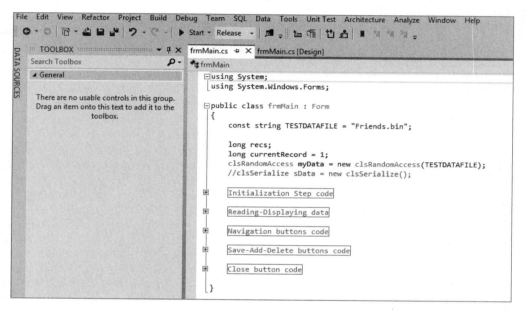

FIGURE 13-10: Hiding code with #region

By clicking the plus sign for any given #region, you can expand the code associated with that section. Using #regions can save you a lot of scrolling time for programs that have a lot of source code.

frmMain

The complete listing for frmMain is presented in Listing 13-5.

LISTING 13-5: Source Code for Writing Random Access Files (frmMain.cs)

```
using System;
using System.Windows.Forms;

public class frmMain : Form
{
    const string TESTDATAFILE = "Friends.bin";

    long recs;
    long currentRecord = 1;
    clsRandomAccess myData = new clsRandomAccess(TESTDATAFILE);
```

continues

LISTING 13-5 *(continued)*

```
#region Initialization Step code
private GroupBox groupBox1;
private Label label2;
private TextBox txtMI;
private Label label1;
private Label label6;
private TextBox txtZip;
private Label label7;
private TextBox txtState;
private Label label8;
private TextBox txtCity;
private Label label5;
private TextBox txtAddr2;
private Label label4;
private TextBox txtAddr1;
private Label label3;
private TextBox txtLastName;
private TextBox txtWork;
private Label label11;
private TextBox txtCell;
private Label label10;
private TextBox txtHome;
private Label label9;
private Label label13;
private Label label12;
private TextBox txtEmail;
private CheckBox chkStatus;
private TextBox txtAnniversary;
private Label label14;
private TextBox txtBirthday;
private Button btnAdd;
private Button btnSave;
private Button btnDelete;
private Button btnClose;
private GroupBox groupBox2;
private Button btnFirst;
private Button btnLast;
private Button btnPrevious;
private Button btnNext;
private Label label15;
private TextBox txtRecord;
private TextBox txtFirstName;

#region Windows code

public frmMain()
{
    InitializeComponent();
}

public static void Main()
{
```

```
        frmMain main = new frmMain();
        Application.Run(main);
    }
    #endregion

    #region Reading-Displaying data

    /*****
     * Purpose: Read a record and display the results
     *
     * Parameter list:
     *   n/a
     *
     * Return value:
     *   void
     ******/
    private int ReadAndShowRecord()
    {
        int flag = 1;

        try
        {
            myData.Open(myData.FileName);
            flag = myData.ReadOneRecord(currentRecord  1);
            if (flag == 1)
            {
                ShowOneRecord();
                txtRecord.Text = currentRecord.ToString();

            }
            else
            {
                MessageBox.Show("Record not available.", "Error Read");
                flag = 0;
            }
        }
        catch
        {
            flag = 0;
        }
        myData.Close();
        return flag;
    }

    /*****
     * Purpose: Move the record data into the textboxes
     *
     * Parameter list:
     *   n/a
     *
     * Return value:
     *   void
     ******/
    private void ShowOneRecord()
    {
```

continues

LISTING 13-5 *(continued)*

```csharp
            txtFirstName.Text = myData.FirstName;
            txtLastName.Text = myData.LastName;
            txtAddr1.Text = myData.Address1;
            txtAddr2.Text = myData.Address2;
            txtCity.Text = myData.City;
            txtState.Text = myData.State;
            txtZip.Text = myData.Zip;
            txtHome.Text = myData.HomePhone;
            txtCell.Text = myData.CellPhone;
            txtWork.Text = myData.WorkPhone;
            txtEmail.Text = myData.Email;
            txtBirthday.Text = myData.Birthday;
            txtAnniversary.Text = myData.Anniversary;
            if (myData.Status == 1)
                chkStatus.Checked = true;
            else
                chkStatus.Checked = false;
        }

        /*****
         * Purpose: Copies data from textboxes to class members.
         *
         * Parameter list:
         *   n/a
         *
         * Return value:
         *   void
         ******/

        private void CopyData()
        {
            myData.FirstName = txtFirstName.Text;
            myData.MiddleInitial = txtMI.Text;
            myData.LastName = txtLastName.Text;
            myData.Address1 = txtAddr1.Text;
            myData.Address2 = txtAddr2.Text;
            myData.City = txtCity.Text;
            myData.State = txtState.Text;
            myData.Zip = txtZip.Text;
            myData.HomePhone = txtHome.Text;
            myData.CellPhone = txtCell.Text;
            myData.WorkPhone = txtWork.Text;
            myData.Email = txtEmail.Text;
            myData.Birthday = txtBirthday.Text;
            myData.Anniversary = txtAnniversary.Text;
            if (chkStatus.Checked == true)
                myData.Status = 1;
            else
                myData.Status = 0;
        }
        #endregion
```

```csharp
#region Navigation buttons code

private void btnFirst_Click(object sender, EventArgs e)
{
    int flag;

    currentRecord = 1;
    flag = ReadAndShowRecord();
}

private void btnNext_Click(object sender, EventArgs e)
{
    int flag;

    currentRecord++;
    flag = ReadAndShowRecord();
    if (flag == 0)
    {
        currentRecord--;
    }
}

private void btnPrevious_Click(object sender, EventArgs e)
{
    int flag;

    currentRecord--;
    flag = ReadAndShowRecord();
    if (flag == 0)
    {
        currentRecord++;
    }
}

private void btnLast_Click(object sender, EventArgs e)
{
    int flag;

    myData.Open(myData.FileName);
    currentRecord = myData.getRecordCount();
    if (currentRecord > 1)
    {
        flag = ReadAndShowRecord();
    }
}
#endregion

#region Save-Add-Delete buttons code
/*****
 * Purpose: Save textbox info as a record.
 *
 * Parameter list:
 *  object sender    control that caused the event
 *  EventArgs e      details about the sender
```

continues

LISTING 13-5 *(continued)*

```
 *
 * Return value:
 *   void
 ******/
private void btnSave_Click(object sender, EventArgs e)
{
    CopyData();
    if (myData.Open(TESTDATAFILE) == 1)
    {
        recs = myData.getRecordCount();
        myData.Open(TESTDATAFILE);
        myData.WriteOneRecord(recs);
        myData.Close();
        MessageBox.Show("Data written successfully.");
    }
    else
    {
        MessageBox.Show("Could not open file " + TESTDATAFILE,
                        "File Error");
        return;
    }
}

/*****
 * Purpose: Clears out the textboxes and gets ready to accept new
 *          record
 *
 * Parameter list:
 *   object sender    control that caused the event
 *   EventArgs e      details about the sender
 *
 * Return value:
 *   void
 ******/
private void btnAdd_Click(object sender, EventArgs e)
{
    ClearTextboxes();
    if (myData.Status == 1)
        chkStatus.Checked = true;
    else
        chkStatus.Checked = false;

    txtFirstName.Focus();
}

/*****
 * Purpose: Clear textboxes.
 *
 * Parameter list:
 *   n/a
 *
```

```csharp
 *  Return value:
 *    void
 ******/
private void ClearTextboxes()
{
    txtFirstName.Text = "";
    txtMI.Text = "";
    txtLastName.Text = "";
    txtAddr1.Text = "";
    txtAddr2.Text = "";
    txtCity.Text = "";
    txtState.Text = "";
    txtZip.Text = "";
    txtHome.Text = "";
    txtCell.Text = "";
    txtWork.Text = "";
    txtEmail.Text = "";
    txtBirthday.Text = "";
    txtAnniversary.Text = "";
}
/*****
 * Purpose: Deletes a record by changing the status member
 *
 * Parameter list:
 *   object sender     control that caused the event
 *   EventArgs e       details about the sender
 *
 * Return value:
 *   void
 ******/
private void btnDelete_Click(object sender, EventArgs e)
{
    DialogResult ask;

    ask = MessageBox.Show("Are you sure you want to delete
         this record?", "Delete Record", MessageBoxButtons.YesNo);
    if (ask == DialogResult.Yes)
    {
        myData.Status = 0;
        myData.Open(myData.FileName);
        myData.WriteOneRecord(currentRecord  1);
        MessageBox.Show("Record deleted", "Delete Record");
    }
}
#endregion

#region Close button code

private void btnClose_Click(object sender, EventArgs e)
{
    Close();
}
#endregion
}
```

The program begins by defining a number of working variables and constants:

```
const string TESTDATAFILE = "Friends.bin";

long recs;
long currentRecord = 1;
clsRandomAccess myData = new clsRandomAccess(TESTDATAFILE);
```

These variables have class scope, so they are available to all methods within frmMain. As the TESTDATAFILE filename might suggest, a binary file is used to store the information about each friend. Although you know that file records begin with record 0, you initialize the currentRecord variable to 1 (the N − 1 Rule again) so the user can think of the first record as record number one. You administer the actual record number.

TESTING TIP

If you type in the code for this program, change the Text property of each textbox to give that variable a sample test value. This saves you from typing in data for each textbox each time you test the program. To add a new person, you can view the last person, add 01 to her last name, and then press the Save button. (Don't press the Add New button because it clears all the textbox objects.) On each run, just increment the value by one to differentiate it from the others.

You can use such test values anytime there is a lot of input information that you must enter to test the program.

Enter the requested information into the appropriate textbox objects, and then click the Save button. The btnSave_Click() event code calls the CopyData() method to copy the contents of the textboxes into the appropriate members of the clsRandomAccess object named myData:

```
private void btnSave_Click(object sender, EventArgs e)
{
    CopyData();
    if (myData.Open(TESTDATAFILE) == 1)
    {
        recs = myData.getRecordCount();
        myData.WriteOneRecord(recs);
        myData.Close();
    }
    else
    {
        MessageBox.Show("Could not open file " + TESTDATAFILE,
                        "File Error");
        return;
    }
}
```

The program then opens the data file and, if there is no error opening the file, calls the getRecord-Count() method of the clsRandomAccess class. This method simply determines where the new record should be placed in the file. The call to WriteOneRecord() writes the new data to the file, and the file is closed. (Instead of displaying the MessageBox.Show() message, you could use the error log program discussed earlier in this chapter to record the information about the error.)

Navigating the Records

The navigation buttons enable the user to roam around the records stored in the file. The code to provide this feature is simple. For example, if the user clicks the First button, the code sets the currentRecord variable to 1 and calls ReadAndShowRecord() to read and display the information in the appropriate textbox objects:

```
private void btnFirst_Click(object sender, EventArgs e)
{
    int flag;

    currentRecord = 1;
    flag = ReadAndShowRecord();
}

private void btnNext_Click(object sender, EventArgs e)
{
    int flag;

    currentRecord++;
    flag = ReadAndShowRecord();
    if (flag == 0)
    {
        currentRecord--;
    }
}
```

The Next button is similar, but it increments currentRecord before calling ReadAndShowRecord(). If the user tries to use the Next button on the last record in the file, an appropriate error message displays. Similar checks are made for the Previous button, too.

Delete a Record

To refer to "deleting" a record is misleading because the record isn't actually deleted. Instead, change the status member of the clsRandomAccess member to 0, thus marking it as an inactive record. Why not actually delete the record from the file?

There are several reasons for not deleting a record. First, ask yourself why you want to delete the record. Is this person no longer a friend? Was there a fight where all will be forgiven a few days later and you're just doing it now in a fit of pique? In other words, what is the reason for deleting the record? Most people would say it's to free up disk space. Aw, come on! At $.02/MB, are you *really* worried about 300 bytes? With a cost of $.0000006 per member, chances are you can afford to store a few inactive members.

Second, deleting any information is just not a good idea...period. For example, you might reuse the clsRandomAccess code as part of a membership program. Perhaps you have a second file that records membership dues payments, which uses a member club record number to tie the payments to the member. If you delete him from the membership file, you now have *an orphan record* in the membership dues file that can no longer be linked back to a member—active or not.

Also, you can bet that just as soon as you delete such a record, your luck might be such that the IRS comes in the next day and wants to audit your membership dues records. Now what do you do? If you use a status variable rather than physically deleting the record, such requests are easily fulfilled. Transactions-based programs rarely delete such information because without it, constructing a complete audit trail is difficult at best.

Finally, to completely delete the record would require rewriting the entire file after the deletion, bringing us back to a sequential file disadvantage. It's simply easier to mark the record as being deleted.

I would suggest you always use an `int` variable to record the status of a client. Don't make the status variable a `bool`. Often customer records appear to have either an active or inactive state, but other states are more common than you might think. For example, a golf club I've done some programming for has membership status states of 1) inactive, 2) active, 3) financial leave of absence, and 4) medical leave of absence. Had I elected to use a two-state `bool`, I would not have been able to record all data states for member status. As a general rule, a `bool` should not be used to record data; only a binary state (`true`, `false`).

If you delete a record in the program, you can still see the record displayed as you scroll through the file using the navigation buttons. However, the status flag check box object changes its state according to the status flag of the friend being reviewed. If you wanted to prevent the display of inactive friends, a minor change to the `ReadAndShowRecord()` method would do the trick. (See the exercises at the end of this chapter.)

clsRandomAccess

Now take a peek at the code for the `clsRandomAccess` class. The code is presented in Listing 13-6.

LISTING 13-6: Source Code for clsRandomAccess (clsRandomAccess.cs)

```
using System;
using System.IO;

class clsRandomAccess
{
    // --------------- Constants -----------------
    const int NAMESIZES = 20;
    const int ADDRESSSIZES = 30;
    const int PHONESIZES = 12;
    const int EMAILSIZE = 100;
    const int DATESIZES = 10;
    const int STRINGSINFILE = 14;

    const int RECORDSIZE = NAMESIZES          // First name
                      + 1                     // Middle Initial
                      + NAMESIZES             // Last name
                      + ADDRESSSIZES * 2      // Both addresses
                      + NAMESIZES             // City
                        2                     // Stateabbreviation
                      + 5                     // Zip
                      + PHONESIZES * 3        // Phone numbers
                      + EMAILSIZE             // Email address
```

```
                        DATESIZES * 2        // Birthday &
                        anniversary
                      + sizeof(int)          // Status
                        STRINGSINFILE;       // String's length
                        byte

    // -------------------- Instance variables ----------------
    private string firstName;        // Demographics
    private string middleInitial;
    private string lastName;
    private string address1;
    private string address2;
    private string city;
    private string state;
    private string zip;
    private string homePhone;
    private string cellPhone;
    private string workPhone;
    private string email;
    private string birthday;
    private string anniversary;

    private int status;              // Active = 1, inactive = 0

    private string errorMessage;
    private string fileName;

    private FileStream myFile;
    private BinaryReader br;
    private BinaryWriter bw;

    // -------------------- Constructor ------------------

    public clsRandomAccess()
    {
        // initialise instance variables
        myFile = null;
        errorMessage = "";
        fileName = "Friends.bin";              // Default file name
        status = 1;
    }
    public clsRandomAccess(string fn):this() // Call no-arg
                                             constructor first
    {
        fileName = fn;
    }
    #region Property Methods
    // ------------ Property Methods ------------------

    public string FirstName
    {
        get
        {
            return firstName;
        }
```

continues

LISTING 13-6 *(continued)*

```
        set
        {
            if (value.Length > 0)          // Do we have a string?
            {
                firstName = value;
                if (firstName.Length > NAMESIZES)  // Too long
                {                                  // Trim it.
                    firstName = firstName.Substring(0, NAMESIZES);
                }
            }
        }
    }

    public string MiddleInitial
    {
        get
        {
            return middleInitial;
        }
        set
        {
            if (value.Length > 0)         // Do we have a string?
            {
                middleInitial = value;
                if (middleInitial.Length != 1)    // Too long?
                {
                    middleInitial = "n/a";
                }
            }
        }
    }

    public string LastName
    {
        get
        {
            return lastName;
        }
        set
        {
            if (value.Length > 0)          // Do we have a string?
            {
                lastName = value;
                if (lastName.Length > NAMESIZES)    // Too long?
                {
                    lastName = lastName.Substring(0, NAMESIZES);
                }
            }
        }
    }

    public string Address1
```

```csharp
{
    get
    {
        return address1;
    }
    set
    {
        if (value.Length > 0)          // Do we have a string?
        {
            address1 = value;
            if (address1.Length > ADDRESSSIZES)   // Too long?
            {
                address1 = address1.Substring(0, ADDRESSSIZES);
            }
        }
        else
        {
            address1 = "n/a";
        }
    }
}
public string Address2
{
    get
    {
        return address2;
    }
    set
    {
        if (value.Length > 0)          // Do we have a string?
        {
            address2 = value;
            if (address2.Length > ADDRESSSIZES)   // Too long?
            {
                address2 = address2.Substring(0, ADDRESSSIZES);
            }
        }
        if (address2 == null)    // None given?
        {
            address2 = "n/a";
        }
    }
}
public string City
{
    get
    {
        return city;
    }
    set
    {
        if (value.Length > 0)          // Do we have a string?
        {
            city = value;
            if (city.Length > NAMESIZES)    // Too long?
```

continues

LISTING 13-6 *(continued)*

```csharp
                {
                    city = city.Substring(0, NAMESIZES);
                }
            }
        }
    }
    public string State
    {
        get
        {
            return state;
        }
        set
        {
            if (value.Length > 0)          // Do we have a string?
            {
                state = value;
                if (state.Length != 2)     // Must be 2
                {
                    state = "";   // Error
                }
            }
        }
    }
    public string Zip
    {
        get
        {
            return zip;
        }
        set
        {
            if (value.Length > 0)        // Do we have a string?
            {
                zip = value;
                if (zip.Length != 5)     // Must be 5
                {
                    zip = "";   // Error
                }
            }
        }
    }
    public string HomePhone
    {
        get
        {
            return homePhone;
        }
        set
        {
            if (value.Length > 0)        // Do we have a string?
            {
```

```
            homePhone = value;
            if (homePhone.Length > PHONESIZES)
            {
                homePhone = homePhone.Substring(0, PHONESIZES);
            }
        }
        if (homePhone == null)
        {
            homePhone = "n/a";
        }
    }
}

public string CellPhone
{
    get
    {
        return cellPhone;
    }
    set
    {
        if (value.Length > 0)        // Do we have a string?
        {
            cellPhone = value;
            if (cellPhone.Length > PHONESIZES)
            {
                cellPhone = cellPhone.Substring(0, PHONESIZES);
            }
        }
        if (cellPhone == null)
        {
            cellPhone = "n/a";
        }
    }
}

public string WorkPhone
{
    get
    {
        return workPhone;
    }
    set
    {
        if (value.Length > 0)        // Do we have a string?
        {
            workPhone = value;
            if (workPhone.Length > PHONESIZES)
            {
                workPhone = workPhone.Substring(0, PHONESIZES);
            }
        }
        if (workPhone == null)
        {
            workPhone = "n/a";
```

continues

LISTING 13-6 *(continued)*

```csharp
            }
        }
    }

    public string Email
    {
        get
        {
            return email;
        }
        set
        {
            if (value.Length > 0)        // Do we have a string?
            {
                email = value;
                if (email.Length > EMAILSIZE)
                {
                    email = email.Substring(0, EMAILSIZE);
                }
            }
            if (email == null)
            {
                email = "n/a";
            }
        }
    }

    public string Birthday
    {
        get
        {
            return birthday;
        }
        set
        {
            if (value.Length > 0)        // Do we have a string?
            {
                birthday = value;
                if (birthday.Length > DATESIZES)
                {
                    birthday = birthday.Substring(0, DATESIZES);
                }
            }
            if (birthday == null)
            {
                birthday = "n/a";
            }
        }
    }
    public string Anniversary
    {
        get
```

```csharp
            {
                return anniversary;
            }
            set
            {
                if (value.Length > 0)        // Do we have a string?
                {
                    anniversary = value;
                    if (anniversary.Length > DATESIZES)
                    {
                        anniversary = anniversary.Substring(0,
DATESIZES);
                    }
                }
                if (anniversary == null)
                {
                    anniversary = "n/a";
                }
            }
        }

        public int Status
        {
            get
            {
                return status;
            }
            set
            {
                if (value == 1)        // Active
                {
                    status = value;
                }
                else
                {
                    status = 0;        // Inactive
                }
            }
        }

        public string FileName
        {
            get
            {
                return fileName;
            }

            set
            {
                if (value.Length > 0)
                    fileName = value;
            }
        }

        public FileStream MyFile
```

continues

LISTING 13-6 *(continued)*

```
    {
        get
        {
            return myFile;
        }

        set
        {
            myFile = value;
        }
    }

    public BinaryReader BinReader
    {
        get
        {
            return br;
        }

        set
        {
            br = value;
        }
    }

    public BinaryWriter BinWriter
    {
        get
        {
            return bw;
        }

        set
        {
            bw = value;
        }
    }

    public String ErrorText
    {
        get
        {
            return errorMessage;
        }
    }
}
#endregion

// ------------ General Methods ------------------
/****
 * This creates a random access file.
 *
 * Parameter list:
```

```
 *      fn          a string that holds the file name to use
 *
 * Return value:
 *      int         0 if error, 1 otherwise
 ****/
public int Create(String fn)
{
    try
    {
        myFile = new FileStream(fn, FileMode.OpenOrCreate);
        bw = new BinaryWriter(myFile);
        fileName = fn;
    }
    catch
    {
        return 0;
    }
    return 1;
}

/****
 * This opens a file for reading
 *
 * Parameter list:
 *      fn          the file name
 *
 * Return value:
 *      int         0 if error, 1 otherwise
 ****/

public int Open(string fn)
{
    if (bw == null)
    {
        return Create(fn);
    }
    else
    {
        myFile = new FileStream(fn, FileMode.OpenOrCreate);
    }

    return 1;
}


/****
 * This closes the currently-open file.
 *
 * Parameter list:
 *      n/a
 *
 * Return value:
 *      void
 ****/

public void Close()
```

continues

LISTING 13-6 *(continued)*

```
    {
        if (myFile != null)
            myFile.Close();
        if (bw != null)
            bw.Close();
        if (br != null)
            br.Close();
    }

    /**
     * This writes one record to the currently-open file
     *
     * Parameter list:
     *    num              an integer that holds the record number
     *
     * Return value:
     *    int        0 if error, 1 otherwise
     *
     * CAUTION: this method assumes that the properties contain the
     * record to be written.
     */

    public int WriteOneRecord(long num)
    {
        int errorFlag = 1;

        try
        {
            if (myFile != null && bw != null)
            {   // Position the file pointer
                myFile.Seek(num * RECORDSIZE, SeekOrigin.Begin);
                bw = new BinaryWriter(myFile);

                bw.Write(firstName);           // Write the data
                bw.Write(middleInitial);
                bw.Write(lastName);
                bw.Write(address1);
                bw.Write(address2);
                bw.Write(city);
                bw.Write(state);
                bw.Write(zip);
                bw.Write(homePhone);
                bw.Write(cellPhone);
                bw.Write(workPhone);
                bw.Write(email);
                bw.Write(birthday);
                bw.Write(anniversary);
                bw.Write(status);
                bw.Close();
            }
        }
        catch (IOException ex)
        {
```

```csharp
                errorMessage = ex.Message;     // In case they want to
                                                     view it.
            errorFlag = 0;
        }
        return errorFlag;
    }

    /**
     * This reads one record and returns it as a string
     *
     * Parameter list:
     *   num              an integer that holds the record number
     *
     * Return value
     *   int              0 if error, 1 otherwise
     */

    public int ReadOneRecord(long num)
    {
        try
        {
            if (myFile != null)
                myFile.Close();

            myFile = new FileStream(fileName, FileMode.Open);
            br = new BinaryReader(myFile);

            if (myFile != null && br != null)
            {
                // Position the file pointer
                myFile.Seek(num * RECORDSIZE, SeekOrigin.Begin);
                firstName = br.ReadString();
                middleInitial = br.ReadString();
                lastName = br.ReadString();
                address1 = br.ReadString();
                address2 = br.ReadString();
                city = br.ReadString();
                state = br.ReadString();
                zip = br.ReadString();
                homePhone = br.ReadString();
                cellPhone = br.ReadString();
                workPhone = br.ReadString();
                email = br.ReadString();
                birthday = br.ReadString();
                anniversary = br.ReadString();
                status = br.ReadInt32();
                br.Close();

            }
        }
        catch (IOException ex)
        {
            errorMessage = ex.Message;
            return 0;
        }
```

continues

LISTING 13-6 *(continued)*

```
        return 1;
    }
    /**
     * Purpose: This determines the number of records currently in
     * the file
     *
     * Parameter list:
     *    void
     *
     * Return value
     *    long            the number of bytes in the file
     */
    public long getRecordCount()
    {
        long records = 0;
        long remainder;

        try
        {
            if (myFile != null)
            {
                // Position the file pointer
                records = myFile.Seek(0, SeekOrigin.End);
                Close();
            }
        }
        catch (IOException ex)
        {
            //MessageBox.Show("Error: " + ex.Message);
            return 1;
        }
        remainder = records % RECORDSIZE;      //  partial record?
        records = records / RECORDSIZE;        // Calc records
        if (remainder > 0)                     // Partial record...
            records++;                         // ...account for it.

        return records;
    }
}
```

The code listing seems quite long because...well...it is! However, a good part of its length is due to the Property methods' code, which is fairly repetitious.

Determining a Record Size

The first order of business is to determine the record size necessary to store your data. Near the top of Listing 13-6 you find this:

```
// --------------- Constants ------------------
const int NAMESIZES = 20;
const int ADDRESSSIZES = 30;
```

```
const int PHONESIZES = 12;
const int EMAILSIZE = 100;
const int DATESIZES = 10;
const int STRINGSINFILE = 14;

const int RECORDSIZE = NAMESIZES          // First name
                     + 1                  // Middle Initial
                     + NAMESIZES          // Last name
                     + ADDRESSSIZES * 2   // Both addresses
                     + NAMESIZES          // City
                     + 2                  // State abbrev
                     + 5                  // Zip
                     + PHONESIZES * 3     // Phone numbers
                     + EMAILSIZE          // Email address
                       DATESIZES * 2      // Birthday &
                       anniversary
                     + sizeof(int)        // Status
                       STRINGSINFILE;     // String's length
                                          // byte
```

The constants are used to set the maximum (worst-case) number of characters for various strings used to store the data. The property methods use these constants to truncate any string that exceeds the prescribed length. You can, of course, adjust these if you want, and the appropriate code reflects the changes after the program recompiles. The reason for using the constants is in case you need to change the size of a field in the data record, the new record size is automatically updated for you, as is all the code that needs to use that new record size. The constants also make it easier to read the code.

A couple of expressions need some explanation. The expression

```
sizeof(int)
```

uses the `sizeof()` operator to determine the number of bytes necessary to store an `int` value type. You can use the `sizeof()` operator with any value type. Simply place the value type within the enclosing parentheses.

Using the `sizeof()` operator makes your code more portable to other compilers and op systems. For example, I'm working on a programming book for microcontrollers where an `int` is only 2 bytes long instead of 4. Using the `sizeof()` operator takes care of this difference in data size automatically.

THE LENGTH OF A STRING IN A BINARY FILE

What's with the expression `STRINGSINFILE` near the end of the list of constants? The simple explanation is that there are 14 string variables stored in each record. To understand why this is necessary needs a little more detailed explanation.

The purpose to add all the constants together is to determine the number of bytes each record uses. This total is then stored in `RECORDSIZE` and is used at several places in the class when the File Pointer is moved around in the file. Figure 13-11 can help explain why the value 14 for `STRINGSINFILE` is necessary.

The first line in the figure has the following values:

```
000000   04 49 73 73 79 01 43 05    53 6D 69 74 68 0F 36 35
```

```
00000000  04 49 73 73 79 01 43 05  53 6D 69 74 68 0F 36 35  ⌐Issy.C.Smith.65
00000010  37 20 4D 61 69 6E 20 53  74 72 65 65 74 03 6E 2F  7 Main Street.n/
00000020  61 08 52 69 6E 67 67 6F  6C 64 02 47 41 05 33 30  a.Ringgold.GA.30
00000030  37 33 36 0C 37 30 36 2E  33 32 31 2E 34 33 32 31  736.706.321.4321
00000040  0C 37 30 36 2E 32 33 34  2E 35 35 35 35 0C 37 30  .706.234.5555.70
00000050  36 2E 35 36 37 2E 38 39  30 31 16 69 73 73 79 40  6.567.8901.issy@
00000060  72 6F 63 6B 79 74 6F 70  65 6D 61 69 6C 2E 63 6F  rockytopemail.co
00000070  6D 09 35 2F 31 30 2F 31  39 34 39 03 6E 2F 61 01  m.5/10/1949.n/a.
00000080  00 00 00 00 00 00 00 00  00 00 00 00 00 00 00 00  ................
00000090  00 00 00 00 00 00 00 00  00 00 00 00 00 00 00 00  ................
000000a0  00 00 00 00 00 00 00 00  00 00 00 00 00 00 00 00  ................
000000b0  00 00 00 00 00 00 00 00  00 00 00 00 00 00 00 00  ................
000000c0  00 00 00 00 00 00 00 00  00 00 00 00 00 00 00 00  ................
000000d0  00 00 00 00 00 00 00 00  00 00 00 00 00 00 00 00  ................
000000e0  00 00 00 00 00 00 00 00  00 00 00 00 00 00 00 00  ................
```

FIGURE 13-11: String Length Byte

If you decode these hex values into their appropriate ASCII values, you get

```
000000   04 49 73 73 79  01 43 05   53 6D 69 74 68 0F 36 35  (Hex)
          I  s  s  y   C      S  m  i  t  h     6  5   (ASCII)
         4             1     5                  15           (Decimal)
```

Notice the binary values that precede each string. The number 4 precedes `Issy`, 1 precedes `C`, 5 precedes `Smith`, and 15 precedes `657 Main Street`. Why...could it be? Does the number in front of each string tell how many bytes are necessary to store the string? Yep, it does.

When you store strings in a binary data file, the low-level file I/O code needs to know how many bytes are associated with each piece of string data. In some programming languages, the information necessary to store a string in a binary file is a little more complex and is called a *string descriptor block*. In C#, the string descriptor block is simply called the *length byte*. Because each string has one length byte and you have 14 strings in the file, you need to account for those length bytes in your total record size calculation—hence, the STRINGSINFILE (because of the 14 strings) at the end of the record size calculation.

If you add up all the byte requirements for all the data in a friend record, you find that RECORDSIZE equals 302 bytes. Therefore, after a few records are written to the file, the file is going to look similar to that shown in Figure 13-7.

Writing a Record

When the user wants to save a record, she clicks the Save button in `frmMain`. This causes the following methods to be called:

```
recs = myData.getRecordCount();
myData.Open(TESTDATAFILE);
myData.WriteOneRecord(recs);
```

The code in `getRecordCount()` uses the `Seek()` method to position the File Pointer at the end of the file (EOF). When the File Pointer has reached that position, it returns the number of bytes (as a `long`) that are in the file from its current position. If you divide the number of bytes in the file by its record size, you get the number of records that have already been written to the file. However, you need to refine the calculation to account for the fact that there could be an "information gap" in the last record. (Refer to Figure 13-8.) If that is the case, the record counter must be incremented by one.

Next, the data file is opened and the code calls `WriteOneRecord()`, passing in the record position (`recs`) that is used for the new file. The code for `WriteOneRecord()` is straightforward:

```
public int WriteOneRecord(long num)
{
    int errorFlag = 1;

    try
    {
        if (myFile != null && bw != null)
        {   // Position the file pointer
            myFile.Seek(num * RECORDSIZE, SeekOrigin.Begin);
            bw = new BinaryWriter(myFile);
            bw.Write(firstName);            // Write the data
            bw.Write(middleInitial);
            bw.Write(lastName);
            bw.Write(address1);
            bw.Write(address2);
            bw.Write(city);
            bw.Write(state);
            bw.Write(zip);
            bw.Write(homePhone);
            bw.Write(cellPhone);
            bw.Write(workPhone);
            bw.Write(email);
            bw.Write(birthday);
            bw.Write(anniversary);
            bw.Write(status);
            bw.Close();
        }
    }
    catch (IOException ex)
    {
        errorMessage = ex.Message;    //  view it.
        errorFlag = 0;
    }
    return errorFlag;
}
```

The code checks to make sure you have a valid `FileStream` object (`myFile`) and then positions the File Pointer at the spot in the file where the new record is to be written (that is, `num * RECORDSIZE` bytes into the file). The code then creates a `BinaryWriter` object (`bw`) and proceeds to write the data to the file. The file is then closed and you're done. (It's a good idea to close a file when you're done with it. In a networking environment, some files cannot be accessed if someone else is using them.) The code is encapsulated within a `try-catch` block just in case something goes wrong. You could work in the error-logging functionality in the `catch` block to make a more robust application.

Each string that is written by the `BinaryWriter` object `bw` automatically writes the length byte for each string. What about `status`? It's an `int`, not a string, so it has no length byte. How does `bw` know how many bytes to write? The Common Language Runtime knows how many bytes are associated with each value type, so `bw` writes four bytes for `status`.

Reading a Record

Reading a record is almost a mirror image of writing the record. The code for the ReadOneRecord() is shown here:

```
public int ReadOneRecord(long num)
{
    try
    {
        if (myFile != null)
            myFile.Close();

        myFile = new FileStream(fileName, FileMode.Open);
        br = new BinaryReader(myFile);

        if (myFile != null && br != null)
        {
            // Position the file pointer
            myFile.Seek(num * RECORDSIZE, SeekOrigin.Begin);
            firstName = br.ReadString();
            middleInitial = br.ReadString();
            lastName = br.ReadString();
            address1 = br.ReadString();
            address2 = br.ReadString();
            city = br.ReadString();
            state = br.ReadString();
            zip = br.ReadString();
            homePhone = br.ReadString();
            cellPhone = br.ReadString();
            workPhone = br.ReadString();
            email = br.ReadString();
            birthday = br.ReadString();
            anniversary = br.ReadString();
            status = br.ReadInt32();
            br.Close();

        }
    }
    catch (IOException ex)
    {
        errorMessage = ex.Message;
        return 0;
    }

    return 1;
}
```

Once again, a FileStream object named myFile is used to scoot the File Pointer to the location in the file from which you want to read the data. The code then creates a BinaryReader object (br) for use when reading the data. The BinaryReader class provides methods for reading each of the value types offered by C#. The last two statements show how a string is read followed by reading an int data type:

```
anniversary = br.ReadString();
status = br.ReadInt32();
```

Each read statement assigns its data into the appropriate member of the class. The order of the read statements *must* match the order used in the write statements. If you mess up the sequence of variables and their data types, don't be surprised that the data appears messed up as well. After the data is read, the file is immediately closed.

The best way for you to understand this program is to type it in and single-step through the writing and reading of the data. Make sure you use the Step Into (F11) feature of the debugger so you can see how each method works.

SERIALIZATION AND DESERIALIZATION

In OOP programs, reading and writing an object's data (like myData in the previous section) is so common that C# provides a simple mechanism for those tasks. In the previous program, each time you wrote a new friend's information to disk, you were actually saving the state of the clsRandomAccess object named myData to disk. Simply stated, *serialization* is the act to save, or persist, an object's state to disk. *Deserialization* is the act to reconstruct an object's state by reading the information stored on disk back into an object of that class. This process can reduce the burden of passing object data around in an application.

Because the primitive data types (byte, char, int, long, double, string, and so on) are not serializable by default, you must explicitly state that the object can be serialized using the [Serializable] attribute at the top of the class source file of the object to be serialized. This marks the object's data as serializable.

> **TIME-SAVING TIP**
>
> If you fail to mark a class as serializable using the [Serializable] attribute after you have already compiled the program, the program will fail. The error message tells you that one (or more) of the class members does not have the [Serializable] attribute set. If you see this error message, going back and adding [Serializable] to the class file does no good. Moral of the story: Don't forget to add the [Serializable] attribute to the class file before you compile it.

The next Try It Out shows how to serialize the data for an object and then read the data back into the object (deserialization).

TRY IT OUT   Serialization-Deserialization (Chapter13ProgramSerialization.zip)

Figure 13-12 shows a sample run of a program that uses serialization.

The program gathers the class information (such as name, e-mail address, and status) and serializes the data to a disk file named Test.bin when the user clicks the Serialize button. Clicking the Display button deserializes the data from the disk file and displays it in a listbox object.

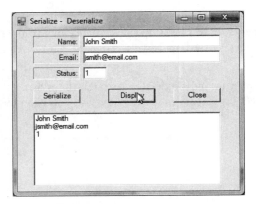

FIGURE 13-12: Serialize program

To implement this program:

1. Create a new project in the usual manner.

2. Create the user interface by adding the form objects (refer to Figure 13-12), or download the code file Chapter13ProgramSerialization.zip.

How It Works

The source code for frmMain is presented in Listing 13-7.

LISTING 13-7: Program Source Code to Serialize Data (frmMain.cs)

```csharp
using System;
using System.Windows.Forms;

public class frmMain : Form
{
    clsSerial myFriend = new clsSerial();      // Object to serialize

    private Label label1;
    private TextBox txtName;
    private TextBox txtEmail;
    private TextBox txtStatus;
    private Label label3;
    private Button btnSerial;
    private Button btnDisplay;
    private Button btnClose;
    private ListBox lstOutput;
    private Label label2;
    #region Windows code

    public frmMain()
    {
        InitializeComponent();
    }
}
```

```csharp
public static void Main()
{
    frmMain main = new frmMain();
    Application.Run(main);
}

private void btnSerial_Click(object sender, EventArgs e)
{
    int flag;

    MoveTextToClass(myFriend);      // Move from textboxes to data

    flag = myFriend.SerializeFriend(myFriend);
    if (flag == 1)
    {
        MessageBox.Show("Data Serialized successfully", "Data Write");
    }
    else
    {
        MessageBox.Show("Serialization failure", "Data Error");
    }
}

private void btnDisplay_Click(object sender, EventArgs e)
{
    clsSerial newFriend = new clsSerial();
    newFriend = newFriend.DeserializeFriend();
    lstOutput.Items.Clear();
    lstOutput.Items.Add(newFriend.Name);
    lstOutput.Items.Add(newFriend.Email);
    lstOutput.Items.Add(newFriend.Status.ToString());
}

private void MoveTextToClass(clsSerial obj)
{
    bool flag;
    int val;

    obj.Name = txtName.Text;
    obj.Email = txtEmail.Text;
    flag = int.TryParse(txtStatus.Text, out val);
    if (flag == false)
    {
        MessageBox.Show("Must be 1 or 0", "Input Error");
        txtStatus.Focus();
        return;
    }
    obj.Status = val;
}

private void btnClose_Click(object sender, EventArgs e)
{
    Close();
}
}
```

The user types in the data via the three textbox objects. (To keep the program short, no validation is done on the inputs, except for the variable status.) The method MoveTextToClass() simply copies the three properties to their associated members of the myFriend object. The SerializeFriend() method serializes the information to disk. (Listing 13-8 shows the clsSerial code.)

The Display button calls the DeserializeFriend() method to deserialize the data from the disk file. The members of the class are then displayed in the listbox object.

Listing 13-8 shows the source code for the clsSerial class.

LISTING 13-8: Source Code for clsSerial (clsSerial.cs)

```csharp
using System;
using System.IO;
using System.Runtime.Serialization;
using System.Runtime.Serialization.Formatters.Binary;

[Serializable]          // DON'T FORGET THIS
class clsSerial
{
    //------------------ Instance members ---------------
    private string name;
    private string email;
    private int status;

    //------------------ Property methods ---------------
    public string Name
    {
        get
        {
            return name;
        }
        set
        {
            name = value;
        }
    }
    public string Email
    {
        get
        {
            return email;
        }
        set
        {
            email = value;
        }
    }
    public int Status
    {
        get
        {
            return status;
```

```
        }
        set
        {
            status = value;
        }
    }
//------------------ Helper methods ----------------
//------------------ General methods ---------------

/*****
 * Purpose: To serialize the contents of this class
 *
 * Parameter list:
 *   clsSerial myFriend        Serialize an instance
 *
 * Return value:
 *   int                       0 on error, 1 otherwise
 *****/
public int SerializeFriend(clsSerial myFriend)
{
    try
    {
        BinaryFormatter format = new BinaryFormatter();
        FileStream myStream = new FileStream("Test.bin",
                                  FileMode.Create);
        format.Serialize(myStream, myFriend);
        myStream.Close();
    }
    catch (Exception ex)
    {
        string buff = ex.Message;
        return 0;
    }
    return 1;
}


/*****
 * Purpose: To deserialize an instance of this class from a file
 *
 * Parameter list:
 *   n/a
 *
 * Return value:
 *   clsSerial        an instance of the class with the data
 *****/
public clsSerial DeserializeFriend()
{
    clsSerial temp = new clsSerial();
    try
    {
        BinaryFormatter format = new BinaryFormatter();
        FileStream myStream = new FileStream("Test.bin",
                                  FileMode.Open);
        temp = (clsSerial)format.Deserialize(myStream);
        myStream.Close();
```

continues

LISTING 13-8 *(continued)*

```
        }
        catch (Exception ex)
        {
            string buff = ex.Message;
            return null;
        }
        return temp;
    }
}
```

Note the various elements include files that must be added to the top of the file. These make the various elements of the Serialization namespace available for use in the class. Again, you must add `[Serializable]` immediately before the class signature. Failure to do this is frustrating because you must start over if you compile the file without it.

Most of the code in the file should look familiar to you by now, so concentrate on the two methods that do most of the serialization work. In the following code fragment from Listing 13-8, it is the responsibility of the `BinaryFormatter` object `format` to convert the data held in the `myFriend` object into its required binary form:

```
public int SerializeFriend(clsSerial myFriend)
{
    try
    {
        BinaryFormatter format = new BinaryFormatter();
        FileStream myStream = new FileStream("Test.bin",
                                 FileMode.Create);
        format.Serialize(myStream, myFriend);
        myStream.Close();
    }
    catch (Exception ex)
    {
        string buff = ex.Message;
        return 0;
    }
    return 1;
}
```

A `Filestream` object (`myStream`) opens the test file named `Test.bin`. If the file does not exist, it is created automatically. (If you change `FileMode.Create` to `FileMode.Append`, you can append more than one object's state to the file.) The program then uses the `Serialize()` method of the `BinaryFormatter` class to store `myFriend`'s state to disk. Because exceptions can occur, you should enclose the code in a `try-catch` block.

Deserialization is little more than serialization in reverse:

```
public clsSerial DeserializeFriend()
{
    clsSerial temp = new clsSerial();
    try
    {
        BinaryFormatter format = new BinaryFormatter();
```

```
            FileStream myStream = new FileStream("Test.bin",
                                    FileMode.Open);
            temp = (clsSerial)format.Deserialize(myStream);
            myStream.Close();
        }
    catch (Exception ex)
    {
            string buff = ex.Message;
            return null;
    }
    return temp;
}
```

A `BinaryFormatter` object is instantiated and a `FileStream` object is also instantiated, but using the `Open` file mode. The `Deserialize()` method of the `BinaryFormatter` class reads the data from the disk file and formats into the `clsSerial` object. The explicit cast `(clsSerial)` is required because `Deserialize()` returns a plain object type. The `FileStream` is then closed and control returns to the caller. Back in `frmMain`, the returned object's data displays in the `listbox`.

To Serialize or Not to Serialize

Given how simple it is to serialize and deserialize an object, why wouldn't you use this kind of program rather than the random access program discussed earlier? After all, the random access program is also saving the state of an object to disk, but it requires quite a bit more code to do so.

First, the random access program is not specifically designed to simply serialize an object. Rather, it's intended to serve as a transactions-based structure where the object is permanently stored. Serialization of an object is more often used to temporarily store the state of an object so that it can be restored later. That object's state might be passed along to some other user of the object (such as a session state in a web app) or used to reestablish the state of an application when the application is reloaded.

Second, you may not want to have all the information in a class serialized. There could be sensitive information in the class that you don't want others to see. Even though the serialized file is in binary form, you can still read a good part of it with Notepad.

If you want to exclude a specific member of a class from being serialized as part of the object's state, you can use the following statement in the class definition:

```
[NonSerialized] string cellPhone;
```

This syntax marks the cell phone number as being excluded from the properties to be serialized to disk.

A third issue is that if your class includes other (nonprimitive) data types, like custom classes you've defined, those classes must also be compiled with the `[Serializable]` attribute set. This may not be a problem if you have access to the source code for these classes. However, if you use a class from a commercial product for which you don't have the source, you may not be able to mark that object as serializable.

MDI, MENUS, AND FILE DIALOGS

This section shows you how to use the Multiple Document Interface, the C# menu object, and the file dialog objects.

The next Try It Out expands on the basic single-form programs you've written thus far. In this program, you learn how to call a form within a form like most complex applications do.

MDI Interface (Chapter13ProgramMDI.zip)

Start by creating the project as you have all the others. With the `frmMain` form showing in the Design window, set the form's `IsMdiContainer` property to `true`. When you do this, the style of the form changes, and the client area of the form changes to a dark shade of gray. Scroll to the bottom of the form's property list, and set the `WindowState` property to `Maximized`.

How It Works

Adding a Menu

Now go to the Toolbox window, open up the Menu & Toolbars section, and double-click on the `MenuStrip` object. Your Design window should look like the one in Figure 13-13. Notice that the `MenuStrip` object (named `menuStrip1` by default) appears in the System Tray area at the bottom of the screen. (It is not viewable in Figure 13-13.) The object also causes a blank menu strip to appear just under the title bar of `frmMain`, as can be seen in Figure 13-13.

Place the cursor in the textbox on the menu strip where it says Type Here, type in `&File`, and press the Enter key. Your screen should look like Figure 13-14.

In Figure 13-14 there are two Type Here boxes. Although it may not be obvious, the lower textbox is tied to the File menu option you just entered. The second Type Here box is intended for additional menu options that you want to appear to the right of the File menu option. If you want the menu bar to look similar to that for Visual Studio, you would type `Edit` in that textbox. However, instead concentrate on submenus for the File menu option. In the textbox that is below File, type in `&Open` and press the Enter key. Move the cursor back into the `&Open` textbox, and change the `Name` property in the Properties window to `mnuOpen`.

Immediately below the Open menu option, type in `&Edit` and change its `Name` property to `mnuEdit`. Immediately below the Edit option, type in a dash. This serves as a menu separator. Finally, in the empty textbox below the menu separator line, type in `E&xit` and press the Enter key. Change its name to `mnuExit`. Your screen should look similar to what is shown in Figure 13-14.

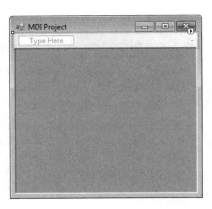

FIGURE 13-13: Adding an MDI menu

FIGURE 13-14: MDI menu change

Adding a File Open Dialog

Now examine the code for the program as it exists at this point. The code is shown in Listing 13-9.

LISTING 13-9: A Simple MDI Program (frmMain.cs)

```
using System;
using System.Windows.Forms;

public class frmMain : Form
{
    string selectFile;

    private ToolStripMenuItem mnuFile;
    private ToolStripMenuItem mnuOpen;
    private ToolStripMenuItem editToolStripMenuItem;
    private ToolStripSeparator toolStripMenuItem1;
    private ToolStripMenuItem mnuExit;
    private OpenFileDialog openFileDialog1;
    private MenuStrip menuStrip1;
    #region Windows code

    public frmMain()
    {
        InitializeComponent();
    }

    [STAThread]              // Something new
    public static void Main()
    {
        frmMain main = new frmMain();
        Application.Run(main);
    }

    private void mnuOpen_Click(object sender, EventArgs e)
    {
        OpenFileDialog fileOpen = new OpenFileDialog();

        fileOpen.Title = "Select file to open:";
        fileOpen.Filter = "(*.bin)|*.bin|(*.txt)|*.txt|All files
                          (*.*)|*.*";

        if (fileOpen.ShowDialog() == DialogResult.OK)
        {
            selectFile = fileOpen.FileName;
        }
    }
}
```

Notice the statement just before the `Main()` method:

```
[STAThread]                    // Something new
```

This statement is needed when the program is run with the debugger. It tells the compiler to generate the code using a *Single Thread Apartment*. Without going into details, C# enables you to have multiple threads, or processes, running simultaneously. Using this statement ensures that a single thread is used for communication with the `FileOpenDialog` object. If you want to use the debugger while working on this program, you need this attribute statement in the program. You can leave it out, but you need to run the program outside the debugger (that is, with Ctrl+F5 rather than F5). For now, leave it in.

In the `mnuOpen_Click()` event code, the first statement creates an instance of an `OpenFileDialog` object named `fileOpen`. The `Title` property for the object simply sets the text that appears in the title bar of the file dialog box. The `Filter` property sets the file types that you want to see when the dialog is run. The filter shown here establishes the default file type to `*.bin` files because that is the first file type that appears in the filter list. The user can opt to change this to a view-only text file (`*.txt`) or any file type, if she wants. These different file types appear in the familiar drop-down `listbox` object common to many Windows programs. A sample run of the code to this point is shown in Figure 13-15.

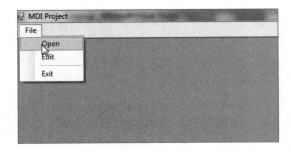

FIGURE 13-15: MDI program

When you run the program, click File ➤ Open. The result is the dialog you see in Figure 13-16. (When you run the program, notice that `frmMain` fills the entire display screen. This is because you set the `WindowState` property for `frmMain` to `Maximize`.)

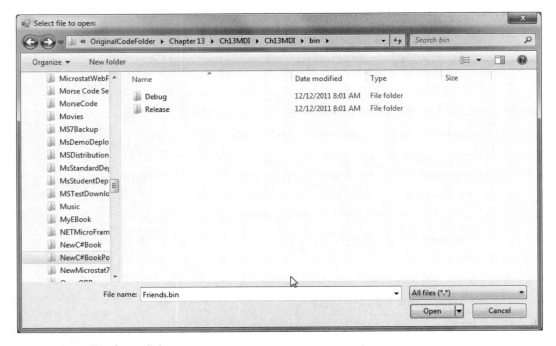

FIGURE 13-16: File Open dialog

Assuming the user clicks the Open button in Figure 13-16, the `selectFile` variable holds the name of the file, including its full pathname. That is, the string might be something like this:

```
"C:\C#Code\DataFiles\Friends.bin"
```

Obviously, this string can be used to open and read the file using the data held in `selectFile`. You can use the debugger to examine the filename returned by the `OpenFileDialog` object. You can test the return value (`DialogResult.OK`) to verify that the file operation was successful.

Calling Another Form

Now add another form to the project and name it `frmEditFriend`. Use Project ➤ Add New Item to add the new form. After the form is created and the stub code is visible in the Source window, delete *all* the stub code that appears in `frmEditFriend`. Now go to where you stored the random access program code shown in Listing 13-5. Using Notepad, open the `frmMain.cs` file and highlight and copy all the code in Listing 13-5 (Ctrl+A followed by Ctrl+C is the fastest way). Now paste that code (Ctrl+V) into the `frmEditFriend` source file in the Source window. Change the name of the class from `frmMain` to `frmEditFriend` and delete the following code:

```
public static void Main()
{
    frmMain main = new frmMain();
    Application.Run(main);
}
```

A program can have only one `Main()` method, and you already have one named `frmMain` in this project. Now make the `clsRandomAccess` code available to the project. You can do this either by using Project ➪ Add Exiting Item and selecting `clsRandomAccess` from the old project, or using Project ➪ Add Class and copying the code into the new file.

Add the following code to Listing 13-9:

```
private void mnuEdit_Click(object sender, EventArgs e)
{
    frmEditFriend frm = new frmEditFriend();
    frm.ShowDialog();
}
```

This code creates a `frmEditFriend` object named `frm` and then uses the `ShowDialog()` method to display that object on the screen, as shown in Figure 13-17.

Look familiar? It should because this was the main input form used in the random access file project.

Notice how simple it was to write this application. You "borrowed" (stole?) most of the work from an earlier project by simply copying the code. The result is a Multiple Document Interface program that could be used as the starting point to build a more robust electronic phone book application. Many Windows programs use the MDI interface to give a familiar look and feel to a suite of programs. Microsoft Office is but one example.

Try adding some additional menu options to the program, such as a form that displays the contents of a friend's data file.

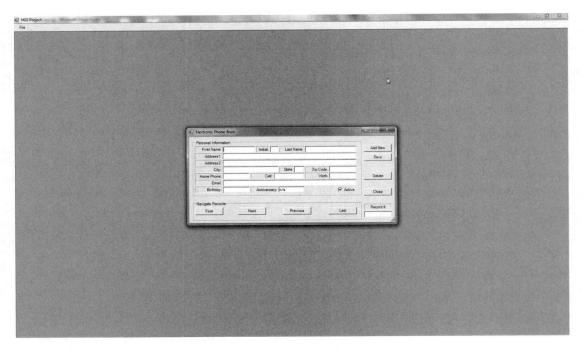

FIGURE 13-17: Child form

SUMMARY

We covered a lot of ground in this chapter. You should feel comfortable using both text and binary files in either a sequential or random access format. You also know how to serialize and deserialize an object to disk. You learned how to create an MDI program and a system of menus. Finally, you saw how easy it is to reuse a Windows form object in a different program. Indeed, you reused the `clsRandomAccess` class without modification! But then, that's what OOP is all about.

EXERCISES

1. How might you change the code in Listing 13-5 so that it would not show inactive records?

2. Looking at the information in Table 13-5, could you use any of the `FileInfo` class properties or methods in the `getRecordCount()` method shown in Listing 13-6?

3. If you design a program that must persist a specific set of information, how would you decide whether to use sequential or random access files?

4. Which approach would you use to persist the state of an object to disk: serialization or standard read/write methods of your own design?

5. Many program use an About box to convey information about the software (version number, company name, and so on) How would you add an About box to your programs?

▶ **WHAT YOU LEARNED IN THIS CHAPTER**

TOPIC	KEY POINTS
Text and binary file types	The two basic types of files used to store string and value type data.
Advantages and disadvantages of each file type	Text produces a dense file that is hard to update, whereas binary may use less space but is harder to read.
File streams	How C# organizes disk data files.
Sequential files	Data is written serially to the disk.
Random access files	Data is stored in easily updateable blocks.
Serialization	How objects can be persisted to disk.
MDI interface	Using the Multiple Document Interface.
Program menus	Using menus in an MDI program.

14

Using Databases

WHAT YOU WILL LEARN IN THIS CHAPTER:

➤ What a relational database is

➤ What tables, fields, records, and keys are

➤ What normalization is

➤ How to use the database Structured Query Language

➤ Implementing an MDI interface to a database

WROX.COM CODE DOWNLOADS FOR THIS CHAPTER

You can find the wrox.com code downloads for this chapter at `www.wrox.com/remtitle.cgi?isbn=9781118336922` on the Download Code tab. The code in the `Chapter14` folder is individually named according to the names throughout the chapter.

In Chapter 13 you learned how to persist data using several different types of data files. This chapter expands on that topic but persists the data using database techniques.

It's been said that of all the programs under development, more than 80 percent of them use a database in one form or another. Clearly, this is one tool that must hang from your tool belt.

WHAT IS A DATABASE?

A *database* is simply a grouping of data. If you wanted to, you could use the topics covered in Chapter 13 to construct your own database. However, if you value your time at more than 2 cents an hour, it's silly to reinvent the wheel. It is far wiser to use a commercially available database system than to attempt to write one yourself.

A *relational database* is a collection of information in which the data within the database is associated with one another in some way. Managing the interrelationships in a relational database can get rather complex. For that reason, most people prefer to use a commercially available *database management system (DBMS)* to manage a database. A DBMS is a suite of programs that simplifies the tasks associated with building and using a relational database. Many major software companies (such as Oracle, IBM, Microsoft, and others) market DBMS software for use with their databases.

Earlier versions of C# used the Microsoft Jet Engine and DBMS, which was designed to work directly with Microsoft Access database (*.mdb) files. However, Jet has been removed from Visual Studio and it doesn't appear that a 64-bit version is planned. For this chapter, you use Microsoft's SQL Server for your database work. SQL Server is an industrial-strength database system with numerous advantages over the Access Jet Engine. Indeed, the two database systems aren't even comparable in terms of performance and security issues. You only scratch the surface of SQL Server in this chapter. If you want to learn more about SQL Server, *Professional SQL Server 2008 Internals and Troubleshooting* by Christian Bolton, et al. (Wrox, 2010) and the *Microsoft SQL Server 2008 Bible* by Paul Nielsen, et al. (Wiley 2009)—a modest tome of 1,600+ pages—are both filled with useful information.

Starting with Visual Studio 2008 support is available for a new C# language feature named LINQ that provides some interesting features for manipulating data. The C# Express version directly supports the use of LINQ only with Microsoft's SQL Server databases. (The next chapter discusses LINQ in detail.) The Professional version of C# also supports other commercially available DBMS.

The Structure of a Database

A relational database is normally a collection of two or more database tables.

Database Tables, Fields, and Records

A database *table* is constructed of data arranged in rows and columns. Each row in a database table is called a *record*. Each column in a database table is called a *field*. A database table may have zero or more rows. If the table has zero rows, the database table is said to be *empty* and contains no useful information. Database tables almost always have at least two or more fields in them.

You can think of a database field as being similar to a property for a class. Each field is used to store values for a particular data item. For example, in Chapter 13 your electronic phone book program had properties for your friend's first name, middle initial, last name, addresses, city, state, ZIP code, and so on. Each of these properties could be used to construct a field in a database table. It follows, then, that each row in the database table would become a record for one of your friends in the phone book database. It should also be clear that each row in a table must have at least one field that is different than other rows in the table. If that were not the case, you would have two rows of identical information, which is redundant. Figure 14-1 summarizes these relationships.

In Figure 14-1, the database that you've named Cards is shown to hold two database tables named Friends and CardsExchanged. If the database is an SQL server DMBS database, it might be named `Cards.mdf`. If you created the same database with Microsoft's Access, it would be named `Cards .mdb`. (The secondary filename often suggests which DMBS was used to create the database.) You have assumed that the Friends table is constructed to hold the information similar to the `clsRandomAccess` class from Chapter 13 (Listing 13-6). As you might expect, each field in the Friends table can be thought of as a property in the `clsRandomAccess` class. (You have omitted some properties for the database example to keep the discussion a bit simpler.) You probably want the Friends data table to keep track of which friends sent you a card and when. You might also want to track their address in case you want to send them a card.

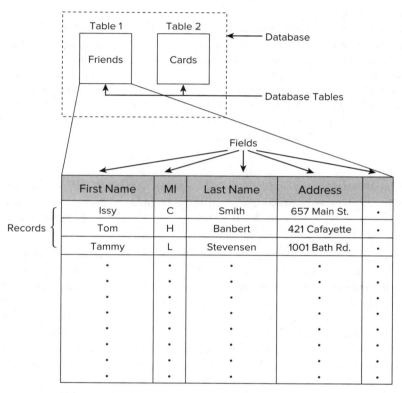

FIGURE 14-1: How a database is constructed

Designing Fields for a Database Table

The CardsExchanged table might be a database table you add to the database to keep track of which friends you sent a birthday card to and which friends sent you a birthday card. You think about the information that you need to store in the table and you come up with the following fields for the table:

➤ **firstName:** The first name of the friend

➤ **lastName:** The friend's last name

➤ **dateSent:** The date you sent the friend a birthday card

➤ **dateReceived:** The date you received a card from the friend

You sit back, admire your work for a moment, and then it hits you: This is an RDC approach to the problem. You now have two tables (Friends and CardsExchanged) that store the same information. That is, both tables store the first and last name of the friend under consideration. Not good.

Data Normalization

Data normalization is a process designed to remove duplicate or redundant data from a database. Because the current design has the friend's name stored in both tables, the database design is not normalized. There are rules that define the order in which a database is normalized. The current design doesn't even follow the first rule (that is, removing redundant data), so the current database design isn't even *first normal form*. Although there isn't space here for a complete discussion of the rules for database normalization, most programmers are happy if they fulfill "third normal form" for a database design. The higher the degree of normalization, the more time you must spend designing the database. (If you ever find yourself in jail with a lot of time on your hands, shoot for a seventh normal form in your design. It will help pass the time!)

Primary Key

You need to redesign your database to get rid of the duplicate data. You can do that if you can find a way to relate the information in the CardsExchanged table to the Friends table in a manner that forms a unique relationship. The easiest way to do this is to create a new field in the Friends table that ties it to a unique friend in the table.

Fields in a table that hold a unique value are called *primary key* fields. If a record has a unique value in one of its fields, you can say that each record in the table is unique because of the primary key field. You can use this primary key field value in a different table (such as the CardsExchanged table) to refer back to the information in another table (such as the Friends table). A Social Security number would do the trick, but your friends might be reluctant to give that to you. (They're not *that* good of friends.) Then…shazam! Lightning strikes and you have an epiphany. Why not just use the table row numbers as ID numbers? You add a new field to the Friends table named ID, which stores a number that corresponds to the friend's row number in the Friends table. This ID field would be simple to administer because its value is simply the previous record ID plus one.

With these changes in mind, you redesign the fields in the Friends and CardsExchanged table to be an identification number (ID) associated with each friend, and the last date that you exchanged a card with your friend. Table 14-1 shows your final design.

In the next section, you actually create the data tables. What you need to do here is provide a short discussion of what each of the columns mean in Table 14-1.

The field name is the name that you use to access any data associated with that particular field. Think of the field name as the variable name for the data associated with the field. In the first column, the field name *ID* can serve as a unique identifier tied to a particular friend. The ID is unique because each friend has a unique row number in the table that becomes the ID value. Because the ID value for each friend is unique, it ensures that all records in the table are also unique.

The second column in the Table 14-1 tells the type of data used to record the information for the field. Use the `int` type for the ID field. The value is simply an integer that equals the number of rows currently in the table, assuming that the first row is row 1. (That way, you don't need to think of the first entry in the table as being "friend zero".)

TABLE 14-1: Field Descriptions for the Friends and CardsExchanged Tables

FIELD NAME	DATA TYPE	NULL PERMITTED
ID	int	No
FirstName	nvarchar(15)	No
LastName	nvarchar(15)	No
Addr1	nvarchar(25)	No
Addr2	nvarchar(25)	Yes
City	nvarchar(15)	No
State	nvarchar(15)	No
ZIP	nvarchar(15)	Yes
LastContact	nvarchar(15)	Yes
----------------------	--------------------------	----------------------
ID	int	No
TypeOfCard	int	No
Sent	nvarchar(10)	Yes
Received	nvarchar(10)	Yes

The last column determines whether it's okay for a field not to be filled in with data. In other words, is it okay for that field to have a value of *null*. Note that field *Addr2* says Yes, which means it's okay to store this friend in the database table without a secondary address supplied.

The nvarchar() entries are the most common data type for the fields. The number in parentheses tells the maximum number of characters that can be stored in the field. SQL Server also enables you to use the varchar() data type. So what's the difference and which should you use? Well, obviously nvarchar() is the way to go because nvarchar() stores all character data in Unicode format, which can accommodate all character sets regardless of language. A varchar() data type can use only the ASCII character set, so it is a bit more restrictive. The cost of this flexibility is that with nvarchar(), each character takes 2 bytes for storage, whereas varchar() takes only 1 byte. Given that a megamunch of disk space costs about a penny, you can go big in this case.

Now assume that you received a card from Jane on April 30 and you sent her the same type of card on May 5. Assume that Jane's unique identifier in the Friends table is 1. (That is, she's the first person in the table.) If you record this information in the CardsExchanged table, the records might look similar to that shown in Table 14-2.

TABLE 14-2: Example of the CardsExchanged Data

ID	TYPEOFCARD	SENT	RECEIVED
1	4	null	04/30/12
1	4	05/05/2012	null

The first record details the card you received from Jane while the second record shows the type of card you sent to Jane and when you sent it. The ID field value in the CardsExchanged table tells you which friend in the Friends table exchanged cards with you. (Jane's data must reside in row 1 of the Friends table.) That is, the information in the CardsExchanged table now relates to the friends stored in the Friends table, but you are no longer duplicating that information in both tables. This is why such databases are called *relational databases*: Relationships usually exist between tables for the data stored in the database.

Over the years, you and Jane could exchange birthday cards many, many times. This forms a *one-to-many database* relationship between the Friends and CardsExchanged tables. That is, one friend (Jane in the Friends table) has sent many cards (as recorded in the CardsExchanged table) to you. There are a number of such potential database relationships possible (one-to-one, one-to-many, many-to-many, and so on).

Enhancing Functionality

Although the table design (refer to Table 14-1) fulfills your goal, what is the second field, TypeOfCard, in the CardsExchanged table all about? Think about it. What kind of cards do you get in the mail; just birthday cards? I don't think so. Because friends could exchange a variety of card types, why just limit this database to the exchange of birthday cards? If you add a third table to the database that stores information about the type of card that was received, you can significantly increase the usefulness of the database. The third table, CardTypes, needs just two fields: 1) the card type field stored as an *int* (*null* not allowed), and 2) an nvarchar(20) field that holds a description of this card type (*null* not allowed). Table 14-3 shows what the CardTypes table might look like after it's populated.

In Table 14-2, the TypeOfCard field shows that these two records exchanged a type 4 card to the friend associated with record 1 in the Friends table. If Jane is record 1 in the Friends table, you received a type 4 card from her on April 30 and then sent her a type 4 card on May 5. Looking in the CardTypes table, you can see that the type 4 card shown in Table 14-2 relates to a birthday card in the Table 14-3.

What do you gain by complicating your database design and adding the third (CardTypes) table? First, in your original design, you assumed you wanted to track only birthday cards. By adding the *TypeOfCard* field to the CardsExchanged table and relating it to the CardTypes table, you have enhanced the functionality of the database. Second, the current design enables you to extend the card types as you see fit, by simply adding another record to the CardTypes table (refer to

Table 14-3). For example, you might add a record for graduations, another for job promotions, or April Fools' Day. The CardTypes table gives you the flexibility to tailor the database to your own specific needs. Finally, by adding the two date fields to the CardsExchanged table, you can track whether you followed up on returning the card sent to you and vice versa.

TABLE 14-3: The CardTypes Data

CARDTYPE	DESCRIPTION
1	"Father's Day"
2	"Anniversary"
3	"Sympathy"
4	"Birthday"
5	"Mother's Day"
6	"Christmas"
7	"Arbor Day"
8	"Guy Fawkes' Day"
9	"Jack Purdum's birthday"

A reasonable question to ask is why use an `nvarchar()` data type for the dates when SQL Server does provide a date type? The reason is because the chances are that the data stored in that field is simply going to be either displayed on the screen or a printer, which would require changing it to a string anyway. If you want to use the date data type, by all means do so.

The primary key field in the CardTypes table would be the value in field CardType and would form a relationship to the CardsExchanged table that is a *many-to-one relationship*. (That is, the CardsExchanged table can have many different types of cards, but it must relate to one of the cards specified in the CardTypes table.)

Foreign Keys

In Figure 14-2, the field named ID serves as the primary key in the Friends table, but it also is used in the second table (CardsExchanged) to relate the information in the CardsExchanged table back to the friend in the Friends table. Therefore, the field named ID in the CardsExchanged table serves as a *foreign key* that tells you whom this card relates to in the Friends table. It follows that a field that serves as a foreign key in one table must have some established relationship with another table. The relationship between the Friends and CardsExchanged tables is one-to-many. This is simply a geeky way to say that a friend can send multiple cards.

Finally, there is a relationship between the CardsExchanged and CardTypes tables. Each row in the CardsExchanged table must have one card type defined in its row, but it can be any of the card types. Therefore, this relationship is shown in Figure 14-2 as a many-to-one relationship.

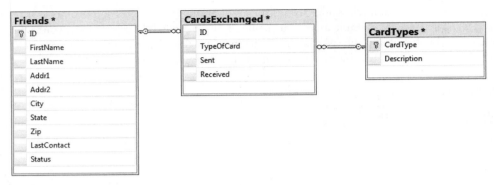

FIGURE 14-2: Relationships for the cards database

CREATING YOUR OWN DATABASES

Many different types of commercial databases are available. Some of the more popular include Microsoft's SQL Server, IBM's DB2, MySQL (which is open source), Oracle, and probably dozens of others. You can use C# to communicate with any of them. In this section, however, you use Microsoft's SQL Server database to illustrate how to use C# with commercial databases. There are several reasons for this choice. First (and foremost), you don't need to buy additional software to use the programs that follow in this chapter. If you followed the instructions in Chapter 1, you should have Microsoft's SQL Server installed. (This version is not the full version of the DBMS for SQL Server, but the Express version can serve all but the most demanding database needs.) Second, you can always upgrade to the full version of SQL Server if you need to, and the software written for the Express version can still work.

Although you can use C# with SQL to create and manage a database, it makes more sense to not reinvent the wheel and use SQL Server Management Studio instead. This tool makes it a snap to create new databases and tables within those databases.

Using SQL Server Management Studio

Start Microsoft's SQL Server Management Studio (SSMS). The exact location of your files depends upon where you installed SQL Server. However, it will likely look similar to the path:

```
C:\Program Files (x86)\Microsoft SQL Server\110\Tools\Binn\
    ManagementStudio\Ssms.exe
```

When SSMS first loads, you are asked which server you want to use. After answering that question, you see a screen similar to Figure 14-3.

To get to the screen shown in Figure 14-3, you will be asked to select the server name that you used when you installed SQL Server. Of course, that depends on your particular information for your computer. If you right-click the Database entry (refer to Figure 14-3), you are presented with the options, as shown in Figure 14-4.

Click the New Database option, which presents you with the screen shown in Figure 14-5. As you can see, you can fill in the Database name textbox with the name of your new database, Cards. The default values can be left as they are. Click OK and the `Cards.mdf` database is created. At this point, all you created is an empty database shell that is ready to have database tables added to it. Your screen reverts to that shown in Figure 14-3.

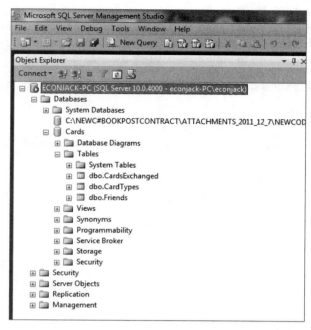

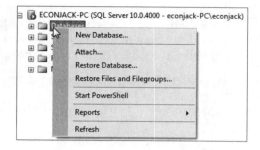

FIGURE 14-4: Right-click databases

FIGURE 14-3: SQL Server's Management Studio

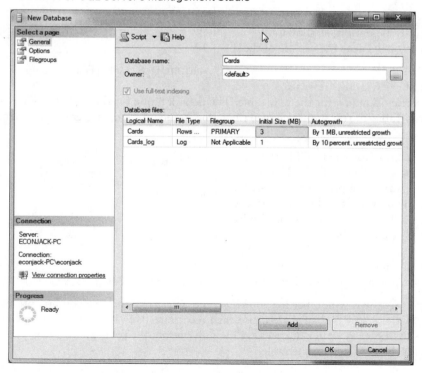

FIGURE 14-5: Creating a new database

To add a table to the new database, right-click the Database option. You are then presented with a list of all the databases currently available on your server. Click the Cards database, and the display expands to show you the possible objects that can be associated with the Cards database. Now, right-click the Tables option to see the options shown in Figure 14-6. Click the New Table option.

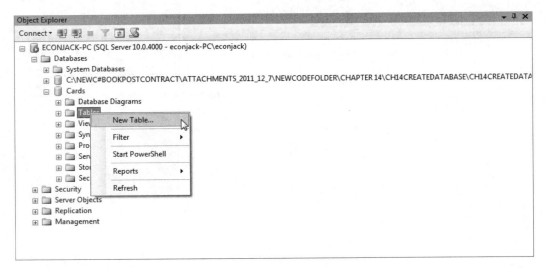

FIGURE 14-6: Adding a new table to database

When you click the New Table option, as shown in Figure 14-6, a new screen opens near the middle of the display and looks similar to Figure 14-7.

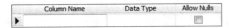

FIGURE 14-7: Adding column names

To the immediate right of the window (refer to Figure 14-7) is the Properties Window for the new table. The default name for the table shown in the Properties Window is Table-1. You should change the name to the table you are creating, Friends in this case.

The program should be waiting for you to fill in the Column Name textbox (refer to Figure 14-7). The column names are the names you want to apply to each of the fields in the table. The first field you want to add to the table is the ID field. Type in that field name and press the Tab key to advance to the Data Type combo box. SQL Server has a number of data types that you can assign to any given field. Clicking the drop-down arrow presents you with a list of the available data types, as shown in Figure 14-8.

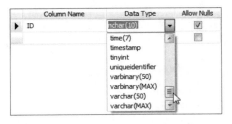

FIGURE 14-8: Setting the data type

Because you are simply using the row number for your ID value, select *int* from the combo options as the data type. Uncheck the Allow Nulls field because each record needs to have an ID associated with it. When you press the Enter key after unchecking the null option, the program presents you with another row to enter the next field in the table.

After entering the appropriate data, you screen looks something like Figure 14-9.

You can change the nvarchar() lengths to whatever you want, but the values shown in the table are the defaults. For example, you may want to increase the address fields to hold more than 15 charac-

ters. Right-click the header for the field entry window, and you are given the option to save the table. Save the table. When you do, the Tables field on the left side of the display (refer to Figure 14-5) now show the newly added Friends table.

You should repeat this process for the other two tables, following the design guidelines for those tables as discussed earlier. When you finish adding the tables, click the File ⇨ Save menu option to save the database. You now have a database named Cards.mdf, which contains the three tables you need to store your information. The next step is to start adding data to the tables.

Column Name	Data Type	Allow Nulls
ID	int	☐
FirstName	nvarchar(15)	☐
LastName	nvarchar(15)	☐
Addr1	nvarchar(15)	☐
Addr2	nvarchar(15)	☑
City	nvarchar(15)	☐
State	nvarchar(15)	☐
Zip	nvarchar(15)	☑
LastContact	nvarchar(15)	☑
Status	int	☐
		☐

FIGURE 14-9: A completed table definition

Before writing the code to manipulate the database you just created, it would be helpful to understand the language that databases use to create, retrieve, update, and delete (CRUD) information. That language is a standardized language called Structured Query Language, or SQL for short.

USING SQL

The Structured Query Language (SQL) was developed in the early 1970s by Donald Chamberlin and Ray Boyce of IBM. It was designed to be a universal database language that could create, manage, and maintain relational databases. Entire books have been written on various SQL topics, so full coverage isn't given here. Rather, concentrate on a useful subset of SQL that you can use in your programs. When you are comfortable with the basics, there are plenty of sources that you can use to expand your SQL prowess. Microsoft's SQL Server extends the normal SQL language into Transact SQL. However, because T-SQL extends the normal SQL language, SQL Server can process any standard SQL command.

The SELECT Statement

Perhaps the most used part of SQL is the query features that enable you to retrieve specific subsets of data from a database. Most queries are initiated with the SELECT statement. Its syntax is

```
SELECT fieldList FROM tableName
```

In this case, fieldList is a comma-separated list of the fields that you want to retrieve from the database. The SQL keywords SELECT and FROM do not need to be in uppercase letters, but convention typically writes SQL keywords in uppercase letters. Some feel it makes it easier to read the query statement.

Suppose you want to retrieve the first and last names from the phone book database using fields similar to those used in Chapter 13. Suppose the table that holds the relevant information is the Friends table. The SQL command would be written like this:

```
SELECT firstName,lastName FROM Friends
```

The sample SELECT statement generates a data set that contains the first and last names of everyone in the database.

You can also use the wildcard character in lieu of a fieldList:

```
SELECT * FROM Friends
```

This SQL query returns a data set that contains all the field data for every row in the Friends table… and that's the problem: The data set contains everyone in the database. Most of the time you want some subset of the database. Perhaps it's all the people with a specific last name. Or maybe everyone who lives in a certain ZIP code. Often what you want, therefore, is a way to filter the data set that comes back from a SELECT query.

The WHERE Predicate

You can use the WHERE predicate to filter the data set returned from a database. For example, the query

```
SELECT firstName,lastName FROM Friends WHERE Zip = 45245
```

returns a data set that contains all the first and last names for people who live in the 45245 ZIP code. You can also apply basic conditional operators to a WHERE predicate, for example:

```
SELECT firstName,lastName FROM Friends WHERE Zip > 46214 AND Zip < 46254
```

This enables somewhat less restrictive data sets to be formed. In this query, all people in the database who live in the 46215 to 46253 ZIP codes are shown.

The ORDER BY Clause

The ORDER BY clause enables you to reorganize the data sets into ascending or descending order. For example, the query

```
SELECT * FROM Friends WHERE Zip = 80120 ORDER BY lastName
```

returns the data set sorted in ascending order by the lastName field. If you want the same list, but in descending order, you would use

```
SELECT * FROM Friends WHERE Zip = 80120 ORDER BY lastName DESC
```

Note the SQL keyword DESC at the end of the SELECT statement. It should be clear that the default ordering using the ORDER BY clause is in ascending order. If you do not use the ORDER BY clause, the data set returns the data in the order in which it is read from the database.

Finally, as mentioned most programmers capitalize the SQL keywords in a query. Another popular style that's often used when formatting SQL queries is this:

```
SELECT *
FROM Friends
WHERE Zip = 80120
ORDER BY lastName
DESC
```

This format places all SQL operators on their own lines with the actual database arguments to the right of the appropriate SQL operators. Use whatever form makes sense to you...the choice is yours.

Aggregates

Some database operations are so common that SQL provides methods, called *aggregates*, to perform specific calculations on a database. Most databases, at a minimum, support the aggregates found in Table 14-4.

TABLE 14-4: Aggregate SQL Types

AGGREGATE NAME	DESCRIPTION
AVG	Returns the numeric average of a selected field: `SELECT AVG(Age) FROM Friend` Assuming field Age has each person's age, this returns the average age of the people.
COUNT	Returns the number of items found in a selected field: `SELECT COUNT(lastName) FROM Friend WHERE Status = 1` This tells how many active people are in the Friend table.
MIN	Finds the smallest value in a field: `SELECT MIN(Age) FROM Friend`
MAX	Finds the largest value in a field: `SELECT MAX(Age) FROM Friend`
SUM	Returns the sum of the values in a field: `SELECT SUM(Status) FROM Friend` If Status is 1 for active friends and 0 for inactive, this would return the number of active people in the table.

The aggregate methods don't give you anything you couldn't construct yourself from other (multiple) SQL queries. They do, however, make such information is easier to access.

There are SQL commands that you can use to create a new database, add new tables to the database, and the fields that populate those tables. In other words, you can use SQL to accomplish what you just did with SQL Server Management Studio. However, why reinvent the wheel if you don't have to. Again, there are dozens of online sites that can help you with all the SQL commands, if you want.

That's all you need for now! You will be surprised how much work you can do with databases building queries from these simple commands. In the following sections, you create a simple MDI program that allow you to manipulate the database and generate some simple reports about the content of the database.

A DBMS SYSTEM

In this section you use some of the SQL commands you learned to write a program that can manage the small database you just created. The program uses the MDI that you learned in the previous chapter to collect all the database activities into one program. As explained in the previous section, the general purpose of the program is to track various types of cards (for example, birthday, anniversary, Christmas, and so on) that you exchange with your friends. However, you could easily redesign the program to meet some need more to your liking. It would be a suitable starting point in any situation in which a list of people (for example, a membership list or a book club members) performs some task (that is, paying monthly dues or make the month's book selection). If you do decide on another program, read the rest of this chapter first, then design the objects you need for the program, and finally create the database and related tables that you need.

This program is the largest you've worked with in this book, so it will be a lot easier if you go to the Wrox website and download the code. Indeed, there is too much code to present all of it here. The narrative that follows highlights only those sections of code germane to the current discussion. The rest of the code is straightforward and you should have no trouble understanding it.

In the following Try It Out you develop a program that can create and maintain your own database. While you are free to design your own user interface, because of the complexity, you might want to get the code up and running and then make your modifications.

TRY IT OUT   A Mini Database Management System (MDMS)
(Chapter14ProgramCreateDatabase.zip)

Your MDMS program can use the Multiple Document Interface style with subforms invoked from the MDI menu system. The user interface can be modeled after that shown in Figure 14-10, but you can modify it if you want.

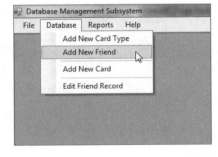

1.   Start a new project directory.

2.   Download the source code file, Chapter14ProgramCreateDatabase.zip, and add it to the project.

At this point, you should do nothing but read through all the code to get a feel for what everything does. Just because the

FIGURE 14-10: User interface for MDMS

Solution Explorer window shows a lot of source code files doesn't mean you should panic. As mentioned, this is your biggest project yet, but you have all the tools to make things work perfectly. You eat an elephant just like anything else: One bite at a time. The same is true for this program. After you take the time to study what each part does, you'll have a good understanding of how things work together.

How It Works

The first screen displayed to the user is an MDI menu of choices. As with most such applications, the first step is to select the database. That's a little more difficult here because the database could be on a remote server or at some other point on the network.

Gaining Access to the Database

When the program first starts, you need to identify the server where the database resides. This is actually a two-step process because there can be more than one server running, and that server can contain more than one database.

The MDI form is titled, as usual, `frmMain` and looks like that shown in Figure 14-10. As you progress through the program, you see what the menus and options look like.

The first task the user must do is select the server that holds the database. (Refer to Figure 14-10 to see this option.) Listing 14-1 shows the code associated with the Select Server menu option.

LISTING 14-1: Selecting the Server for the Database (frmMain.cs)

```
private void mnuSelectServer_Click(object sender, EventArgs e)
{
    // Debug code set here:
    /*
    whichServer = "ECONJACK-PC";
    dbName = "Cards";
    connectionString = "server=" + whichServer + ";integrated
                security=SSPI;database="  + dbName;'
    */

    frmServerSelect myServer = new frmServerSelect(this);
    myServer.ShowDialog();
    this.Text = "Database Management Subsystem:      Server:  " +
                whichServer + "      Database:  " + dbName;
    connectionString = "server=" + whichServer +
                ";integrated security=SSPI;database=" + dbName;
}
```

Some debug code that hardcodes the server and database names are in the listing. From those string literals, you can build a connection string used to tie into the database. When developing this database's software, I commented out the "real" code and used the debug literals instead. Why?

The reason to use the debug code is because each time you run the program to test something, Windows must do a lot of work to find out where the servers are located. On my system, this could take up to 10 seconds. Although that may not seem like a lot of time, when you run the program hundreds of times during development, the delay seems to take forever. By hard-coding the server and database names directly into the program, you can bypass this menu option and work directly on other program options. Clearly, the debug code should be commented out (refer to Listing 14-1) when you have the program stabilized.

The actual code in Listing 14-1 should look familiar. Note, however, that when you create an instance of the `frmServerSelect` form, you call the constructor using `this` as a parameter. As you can recall, `this` is a variable that holds the lvalue of where the data of the currently active form is stored. By passing that reference to the `frmServerSelect` form, that form has access to all the data associated with `frmMain`. Listing 14-2 presents the code for `frmServerSelect`. Also note that, upon return from the `mnuSelectServer_Click()` method, the title for `frmMain` changes to include the server and database names.

LISTING 14-2: Code for Selecting the Server for the Database (frmServerSelect.cs)

```csharp
using System;
using System.Data;
using System.Drawing;
using System.Windows.Forms;
using System.Data.Sql;
using System.Collections;
using System.Data.SqlClient;


public class frmServerSelect : Form
{

    private const int SYSTEMDBTYPES = 4;

  #region Windows stuff

   private frmMain mdiParent;
   string serverToUse;

   //============================ Constructor ===========================
   public frmServerSelect(frmMain me)
   {
       InitializeComponent();
       this.mdiParent = me;        // frmMain's lvalue
       string serverName;

        try
       {
          clsSqlServerList SqlSL = new clsSqlServerList();
          SqlDataSourceEnumerator instance = SqlDataSourceEnumerator.Instance;
          DataTable mySources = instance.GetDataSources();
          foreach (DataRow row in mySources.Rows)
           {
               SqlSL = new clsSqlServerList();
               serverName = row[0].ToString();
               cmbServer.Items.Add(serverName);
           }
          cmbServer.SelectedIndex = 0;
       } catch (Exception ex)
       {
          MessageBox.Show("Error: " + ex.Message);
       }
    }

    /*****
     * Purpose: List the available DB's
     *
     * Parameter list:
     *  object sender    control that caused the event
     *  EventArgs e      details about the sender
     *
```

```
 * Return value:
 *    void
 ******/
private void btnServer_Click(object sender, EventArgs e)
{
    short i;

    cmbServer.SelectedIndex = 0; // Server they selected to list databases
    serverToUse = cmbServer.SelectedItem.ToString();

    string conn = "Data Source=" + serverToUse +
            "; Integrated Security=True;";
    cmbDatabase.Visible = true;
    lblDb.Visible = true;

    try
    {
        using (SqlConnection sqlConn = new SqlConnection(conn))
        {
            sqlConn.Open();
            DataTable tblDbs = sqlConn.GetSchema("Databases");
            sqlConn.Close();
            foreach (DataRow row in tblDbs.Rows)
            {
                i = (short)row.ItemArray[1];
                if (i > SYSTEMDBTYPES)
                    cmbDatabase.Items.Add(row["database_name"].ToString());
            }
        }
        cmbDatabase.SelectedIndex = 0;
    } catch (SqlException ex)
    {
        MessageBox.Show("Error occurred while reading database data: "
                        + ex.Message);
    }
}

private void btnClose_Click(object sender, EventArgs e)
{
    // Now send the selections back to the parent.
    this.mdiParent.getServerName = cmbServer.SelectedItem.ToString();
    this.mdiParent.getDatabaseName = cmbDatabase.SelectedItem.ToString();
    Close();
}
}
```

If you look at the code in the constructor section of Listing 14-2, you can see the reference to frmMain is assigned into a variable named mdiParent using the statement:

```
this.mdiParent = me;
```

What this means is that mdiParent gives you a way to communicate with frmMain's data, even though you currently execute the code in frmSelectServer. This is a useful technique that you can use often. You see how this comes into play shortly.

The constructor code then tries to construct a list of the servers for the current machine. It is the `clsSqlServerList` code that causes the noticeable delay in the program and why you use the debug code during development. The delay is sufficiently annoying that you can add some additional code to the constructor after discussing threading in Chapter 18. (The code for the `clsSqlServerList` class is fairly simple but uses delegates; a topic we cover in Chapter 15.)

The `SqlDataSourceEnumerator` is a library class that enables you to iterate through a list of servers on the machine. The `foreach` loop adds the servers found to a combo box for display on the form. The `frmServerSelect` is shown in Figure 14-11.

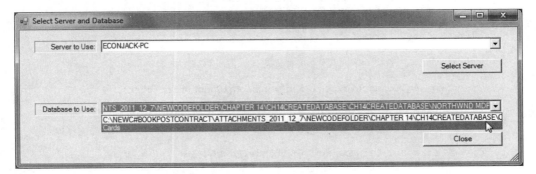

FIGURE 14-11: Selecting the database to use

If you follow the code in Listing 14-2, you can see that only the combo box that lists the servers is visible when the form first presents itself to the user. The reason is because you cannot list the databases available until after the user has told you the server they want to use. Presenting the database combo box would be confusing because there cannot be anything shown in the combo box until after the user selects the server. After the server is selected, you can set the `Visibilty` property of `cmbDatabase` to `true` after populating it with the databases found on that server. (Of course, this also means that `cmbDatabase.Visibilty` is `false` when the form first loads.)

The code that populates the database combo box has a syntax feature you have not used until now. Consider the following code snippet:

```
using (SqlConnection sqlConn = new SqlConnection(conn))
{
  sqlConn.Open();
  DataTable tblDbs = sqlConn.GetSchema("Databases");
    sqlConn.Close();
   foreach (DataRow row in tblDbs.Rows)
     {
        i = (short)row.ItemArray[1];
        if (i > SYSTEMDBTYPES)
           cmbDatabase.Items.Add(row["database_name"].ToString());
     }
}
cmbDatabase.SelectedIndex = 0;
```

Note the `using` statement at the start of the snippet. Up until this point, you have always used the `using` keyword to introduce a reference into the program. When `using` is implemented as shown in this snippet, it impacts the way the variables that are part of the `using` statement are treated by the operating system.

Recall that when a variable goes out of scope, the memory used by that variable can be reclaimed by Windows and reused for some other program data. This process, called *garbage collection*, is managed by Windows and you normally have no control over when Windows decides to take out the garbage. However, creating data (for example, `sqlConn`) with a `using` statement means that Windows can immediately free up the resources associated with the data as soon as the scope level containing that data is exited. Because the SQL resources are fairly heavy, it makes sense to use the `using` statement in this context. When the statement block terminates, the `cmbDatabase` combo box contains a list of all the databases registered on the selected server. This is why you didn't wrap the connection's `Close()` call in a `finally` statement block; the resources will be released even if there is an exception thrown. (The `using` statement can be used only this way when the `IDisposable` interface is present.

Adding Records to a Table (INSERT INTO)

You made life a little easier for adding data to the table by "borrowing" and slightly modifying the form shown in Figure 13-9 in Chapter 13. The modified form is shown in Figure 14-12. Most of the text boxes are self-explanatory. The Active check box simply indicates that this friend is still active (that is, not dead or mad at you). The Last Contact field is used to record the last time you exchanged some type of card with the friend.

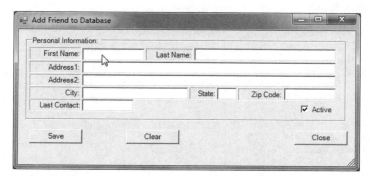

FIGURE 14-12: Friend input form

The user supplies the necessary information for the textboxes and, when finished, clicks the Save button. The code for the Save button appears in Listing 14-3.

LISTING 14-3: Saving a Record to the Database (frmAddFriend.cs)

```
/*****
Purpose: Save text
box info as a record.
*
* Parameter list:
*   object sender    control that caused the event
*   EventArgs e      details about the sender
```

continues

LISTING 14-3 *(continued)*

```
 *
 * Return value:
 *   void
 ******/
private void btnSave_Click(object sender, EventArgs e)
{
    int status;
    string sqlCommand;

    if (chkStatus.Checked == true)        // Status value
        status = 1;
    else
        status = 0;
    try
    {
        myDB = new clsDB(connectStr);
        records = myDB.ReadRecordCount(connectStr); // How many already in DB?
        records++;                                  // Going to add new record
    }
    catch (Exception ex)
    {
        MessageBox.Show("Database error: " + ex.Message);
        return;
    }

    // Build INSERT command
    sqlCommand = "INSERT INTO Friends" +
                "(ID,FirstName,LastName,Addr1,Addr2,City,State," +
            "Zip,LastContact,Status) VALUES (";
    // Now add the values
    sqlCommand += records + ",'" +
                txtFirstName.Text + "','" +
                txtLastName.Text + "','" +
                txtAddr1.Text + "','" +
                txtAddr2.Text + "','" +
                txtCity.Text + "','" +
                txtState.Text.ToUpper() + "','" +
                txtZip.Text + "','" +
                txtLastContact.Text + "'," +
                status + ")";
    try
    {
        using (SqlConnection myConnection = new SqlConnection(connectStr))
        {
            myConnection.Open();
            using (SqlCommand myCommand = new SqlCommand(sqlCommand,
                        myConnection))
            {
                myCommand.ExecuteNonQuery();
```

```
            }
            myConnection.Close();
            MessageBox.Show("Add new friend successful");
        }
    }
    catch (Exception ex)
    {
        MessageBox.Show("Database error: " + ex.Message);
        return;
    }
}
```

The code in Listing 14-3 sets up everything necessary to store the new friend in the database. To determine the ID value for the new friend, a call to `ReadRecordCount()` in `clsDB` is made. The method is simple and uses the COUNT aggregate to determine the record count:

```
SqlCommand cmd = new SqlCommand("SELECT COUNT(LastName) FROM Friends", conn);
```

The record count is returned and assigned into *records*, which is then incremented to reflect the addition of a new record to the Friends table.

Next, the `sqlCommand` string is built to move the textbox data for the new friends. Within the next `try` block, two `using` statements instantiate a connection object (`myConnection`) and command object (`myCommand`), which are then used to write the data to the Friends table. If all goes well, the user is given a message stating the friend was added to the database. Otherwise, the resources are cleaned up via the `using` statements and no success message appears.

The other database options (refer to Figure 14-10) enables the user to add a new type of greeting card and to add cards that have been exchanged between friends. The code for both options uses the SQL `INSERT` command much the same way that the code in Listing 14-3 does. Rather than killing a few more trees by repeating the code here, simply review the code at your leisure.

Data Binding to a Database Table

After you add a few friends and a few card types, and exchange a card or two, you want to see if the data actually was written to the database tables. The Reports option (refer to Figure 14-10) presents two different types of reports. The first option enables you dump the contents of a specified table. The second report type enables you to examine the CardsExchanged table in a variety of ways. Another reason, however, for presenting these two options is to show you two different ways to present the data to the user. The first option uses data binding to tie the table data to a `dataGridView` object. The second option simply uses a listbox without the overhead of data binding. Both techniques work, so both should be added to your programming toolbox. Now look at data binding first.

Figure 14-13 shows what the database report looks like at startup. A list of the tables in the database appears on the left, and a textbox pre-initialized with SELECT * FROM appears in the textbox. The user double-clicks the table they want to see, which copies that table name to the end of the textbox string to form a complete SQL query (that is, SELECT * FROM Friends). When the user clicks the Execute Query, the dgvFriends control is filled in with the data from the table.

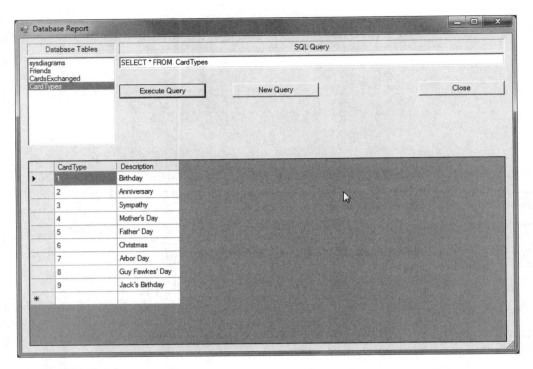

FIGURE 14-13: Database report

The code to do all this is amazingly simple, mainly because the `dataGridView` control is smart. The entire code for the report form appears in Listing 14-4.

LISTING 14-4: Report Display Code (frmReport.cs)

```csharp
using System;
using System.Configuration;
using System.Data;
using System.Data.Common;
using System.Data.SqlClient;
using System.Windows.Forms;

public class frmReport : Form
{
    private Label label1;
    private ListBox lstTables;
    private Label label2;
    private TextBox txtQuery;
    private Button btnExecute;
    private Button btnClose;
    private DataGridView dgvFriends;

    private frmMain mdiParent;
```

```csharp
    private string connectString;
    private string serverName;
    private string databaseName;
    private Button btnNew;
    private string sql;

    public frmReport(frmMain me)
    {
        InitializeComponent();
        this.mdiParent = me;
        serverName = me.getServerName;
        databaseName = me.getDatabaseName;
        connectString = me.getConnectString;

        sql = "SELECT * FROM " + databaseName + ".sys.tables";
        try
        {
            using (SqlConnection conn = new SqlConnection(connectString))
            {
                conn.Open();
                SqlDataReader myReader = null;
                SqlCommand myCommand = new SqlCommand(sql, conn);
                myReader = myCommand.ExecuteReader();
                while (myReader.Read())
                {
                    lstTables.Items.Add(myReader[0]);
                }
                myReader.Close();
                conn.Close();
            }
        }
        catch (Exception ex)
        {
            MessageBox.Show("Error: " + ex.Message);
        }

    }

    #region Windows code

    /*****
     * Purpose: Fills the data grid with the results of the query
     *
     * Parameter list:
     *  object sender    control that caused the event
     *  EventArgs e      details about the sender
     *
     * Return value:
     *  void
     *
     * CAUTION: This code has the ability to execute most queries, including DELETEs.
     ******/
    private void btnExecute_Click(object sender, EventArgs e)
    {
```

continues

LISTING 14-4 *(continued)*

```
            try
            {
                using (SqlConnection conn = new SqlConnection(connectString))
                {
                    DataSet myDataSet = new DataSet();
                    SqlDataAdapter myAdapter = new SqlDataAdapter(txtQuery.Text, conn);
                    myAdapter.Fill(myDataSet);
                    dgvFriends.AutoGenerateColumns = true;
                    dgvFriends.DataSource = myDataSet.Tables[0];
                    conn.Close();
                }
            }
            catch (Exception ex)
            {
                MessageBox.Show("Error: " + ex.Message);
            }
        }

        private void lstTables_DoubleClick(object sender, EventArgs e)
        {
          txtQuery.Text += " " + lstTables.SelectedItem;  // Space is for query string
        }

        private void btnClose_Click(object sender, EventArgs e)
        {
            Close();
        }

        private void btnNew_Click(object sender, EventArgs e)
        {
            txtQuery.Text = "SELECT * FROM ";
            dgvFriends.DataSource = null;
        }
    }
```

The constructor again accepts a parameter that references the parent form frmMain. The try block fills in the list box with the names of the data tables from the Cards database. An SqlDataReader object is used to read the database tables via the while loop. When the user sees the form, therefore, the listbox is filled in with the tables from the database.

When the user double-clicks a table name in the listbox, that selection is appended to the query string in the textbox. When the user clicks the Execute Query button, the click event codes execute.

In the click event code, an SqlConnection object is instantiated using the connection string passed in from the parent form. A DataSet object, myDataSet, is then instantiated. The myDataSet object is the real work horse and manages the data that ultimately appears in the dgvFriends object.

The SqlDataAdapter object, myAdapter, is used to fetch the data from the data source. (Each potential data source provides a data adapter, such as OleDataAdapter if you use an OLE data source.) The data adapter fills the myDataSet object with the data resulting from the query via the Fill() method. When the dataGridView's AutoGenerateColumns property is set to true, the grid control takes care of the column organization for you. Finally, the code sets the data source, and the data displays in the grid control, as shown in Figure 14-13.

The dataGridView control is a complex control and has many properties that you can set. Indeed, an entire chapter or a small book could cover the details of the properties that can be set on the control; However, only are cover here.

AUTOSIZECOLUMNMODE

By default, the column widths for the grid are fixed for all columns, regardless of data content. If you change this property to AllCells from the AutoSizeColumnMode drop-down combination box, the column widths automatically resize themselves to a width that accommodates the longest item in the data set for that field. Figure 14-14 shows what the Friends table might look like with AutoSizeColumnMode property set to AllCells. The shading you see in the table is explained in the next section.

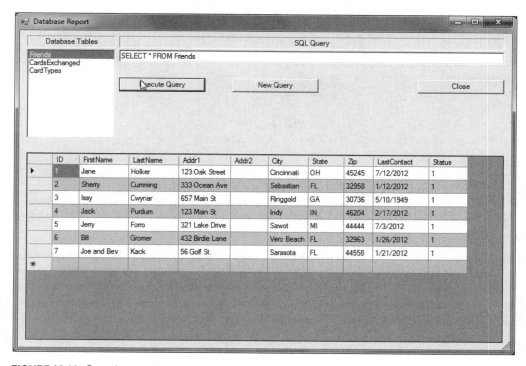

FIGURE 14-14: Sample report run

Although this does make some columns wider than you might prefer them, other columns (such as ZIP codes, state abbreviations, and so on) use much less display real estate than they would otherwise. Often this means seeing more data without needing to scroll the display horizontally.

ALTERNATINGROWSDEFAULTCELLSTYLE

If you select the AlternatingRowsDefaultCellStyle property for the grid object, you are presented with a dialog similar to that shown in Figure 14-15.

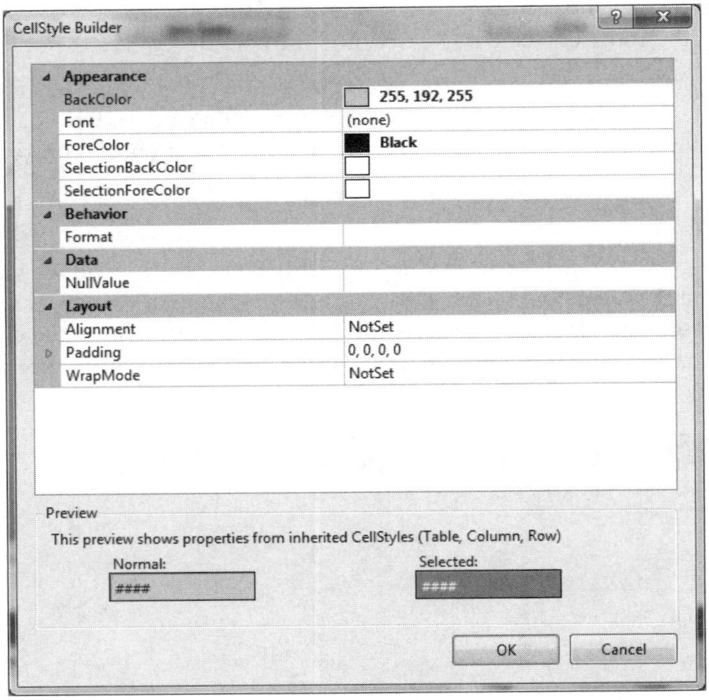

FIGURE 14-15: Cell shading

As you can see, there are a number of cell style attributes that you can set. At the top the background color is set to lavender (which is my favorite color). If you would like the display to look like the old IBM-style printout paper, click the `BackColor` box, click the down arrow, click the tab named Web, and select `PaleGreen`.

The `Behavior` attribute enables you to format the content of a cell in a manner that is consistent with the column type. For example, if you select `Numeric`, you can fix the number of decimal places that display. Commas are automatically inserted where appropriate. If you select `Currency`, a dollar sign appears before the numbers and negative amounts display using the accounting convention of surrounding the value with parentheses. Both of these attributes also allow you to sort the columns.

The `Data` attribute enables you to specify how null values display in the cell. If your data source enables null values, you might set this to n/a or some other value that makes sense for your application.

The `Layout` attribute has several properties that you can change. If you display currency values, you can right-justify the values

Of course, users can resize the columns widths by default if they want. (You can turn this ability off by changing `AllowUserToResizeColumns` to `false`.)

Of course, the `dataGridView` object subsumes many functions that you find with other Microsoft products. For example, double-clicking a column header sorts the grid data according to the values in the column selected. Experiment to see if your favorite "functionality" is implemented in the grid's default settings. If not, examine the properties for the grid object to see if that process can be adjusted.

> **WARNING** *There's a lot of stuff going on behind the scenes to end up displaying the data. Fortunately, prewritten Visual Studio classes do most of the heavy lifting for you. You should know, however, that the code used here is capable of executing almost any query you can think of, including SQL* DELETE *commands. If you think this might be a problem, you might want to parse the query to check for certain SQL commands before passing it off for execution.*

Displaying Database Data Without Data Binding

There are a number of Visual Studio controls that can be bound to a data source, including combo boxes and list boxes. In the previous section, you let the dataGridView control do most of the work for you. Yet, there may be times where you need greater control over the presentation than a bound source enables you to have. This section shows an example of how to read the database data and presents it without data binding.

The Windows form is shown in Figure 14-16.

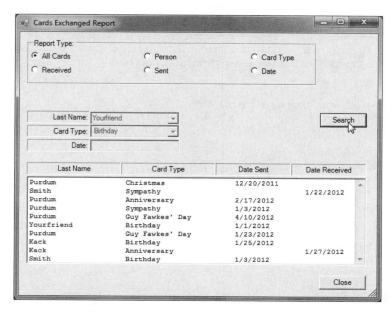

FIGURE 14-16: Cards Exchanged report

The radio button choices are probably self-explanatory. The Received and Sent buttons ask the user to supply a date, and the query then fetches the data for that receiving or sending date. The Date radio button searches both dates.

The use of the radio buttons complicates the code a little more than it may seem on the surface. The reason is because you can disable any controls that did not pertain the radio button selection. For example, if you select the Person radio button, the Card Type and Date input boxes should be disabled and the Last Name input enabled. However, if you select any of the date fields, the other two inputs should be turned off. As a result, most of the radio buttons react to a Change event, as suggested in the following code snippet:

```
private void rbType_CheckedChanged(object sender, System.EventArgs e)
{
    if (rbType.Checked == true)
    {
        cmbLastName.Enabled = false;
        txtDate.Enabled = false;
        cmbList.Enabled = true;
    }
}
```

In this snippet, if the card type radio button is checked, only the list of card types (that is, cmb-List) is available for input. This approach also means that, after one query is run, you can perform another run on the same type of query by simply selecting a different card type for the combo box.

Performing the Query

The code presented in Listing 14-5 details how each of the selected queries is processed. The query is passed to the method via the sql string argument.

LISTING 14-5: Code to Read the Content of the Database (frmCardReport.cs)

```
/*****
 * Purpose: A data dump of the exchanged cards table
 *
 * Parameter list:
 *   string sql
 *
 * Return value:
 *   void
 *****/
private void ReadAll(string sql)
{
    int nameIndex;
    int cardIndex;
    int count = 0;

    string result;
    string lastName;
    string whichCard;

    try
    {
        using (SqlConnection conn = new SqlConnection(connectStr))
        {
            conn.Open();
```

```
                SqlDataReader myReader = null;
                SqlCommand myCommand = new SqlCommand(sql, conn);
                myReader = myCommand.ExecuteReader();
                while (myReader.Read())
                {
                    nameIndex = (int) myReader[0];

                    // Need to subtract one because it's zero-based
                    lastName = myFriends[nameIndex - 1].ToString();

                    cardIndex = (int) myReader[1];
                    whichCard = myCardList[cardIndex].ToString();
                    result = string.Format("{0, -20} {1, -25} {2, -15} {3,
                            -15}",  lastName,
                                    whichCard, myReader[2],myReader[3]);
                    lstResult.Items.Add(result);
                    count++;
                }
                myReader.Close();
                conn.Close();
            }
        }
        catch (Exception ex)
        {
            MessageBox.Show("Error: " + ex.Message);
        }
        if (count == 0)
        {
            MessageBox.Show("No data found");
        }
```

The using statement establishes a connection to the database and that connection is opened. A data reader object, myReader, is defined followed by the definition of a command object, myCommand. After those two objects have been defined, the code executes the query and fills the data reader object via the call to Read(). Because the data reader reads the database one record at a time, the Read() call is placed in a while loop to walk through the records returned from the query. The reader object is indexed as though it were an array, as in myReader[0]. The index refers to the column position of the record returned. Because you are reading the CardsExchanged table, myReader[0] returns the ID of the friend who sent (or received) the card. Because you stored the last names of the friends in the myFriends array list, you can use the index returned by the query to retrieve the last name of the friend.

MyReader[1] in the CardsExchanged table is an index into the CardTypes table. Because myCardList holds the card types, you can use the index to display the string for the type of card that was sent (or received). The statement

```
    result = string.Format("{0, -20} {1, -25} {2, -15} {3, -15}", lastName,
                    whichCard, myReader[2],myReader[3]);
```

simply uses the string class Format() method to format the data before placing it into the listbox. Because you want the columns to align properly, you can change the font of lstResult to use a fixed font (Courier New) rather than a True Type font.

Edit a Record (UPDATE)

At some point in time, you will likely want to change an entry in the database. People move and change addresses and they get married and change names. When such events happen, you may need to change the data in one of the data tables. The UPDATE SQL command is used when you want to edit information already stored in the database. Figure 14-17 shows the form used to edit a friend in the Friends table.

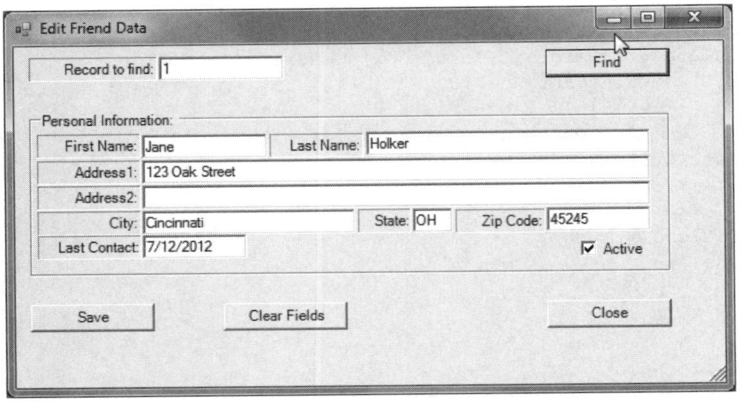

FIGURE 14-17: Edit a database record

When the form first displays, all fields are empty. If you know the record number of the friend you want to edit, you can enter that record number in the topmost textbox. (You can use the Report menu option to find the appropriate record number.) If you don't know the record number, the code also accepts the person's last name as the search criteria. If no data were present and you type in Yourfriend into the Last Name textbox and click the Find button, the rest of the data would display (refer to Figure 14-17). Although it may not be obvious, the Last Contact field is disabled, which means you cannot edit that field. That's as it should be because that data is determined by the exchange of cards.

Listing 14-6 shows the code associated with the Save button's click event.

LISTING 14-6: Editing a Database Record (frmEditFriend.cs)

```
/*****
 * Purpose: Save textbox info as a record in Friends table.
 *
 * Parameter list:
 *  object sender    control that caused the event
 *  EventArgs e      details about the sender
 *
 * Return value:
 *  void
 *****/
private void btnSave_Click(object sender, EventArgs e)
```

```
        {
            int status;
            int flag;
            string sqlCommand;

            if (chkStatus.Checked == true)
                status = 1;
            else
                status = 0;

            myData = new clsFriend(connectStr);

            // Build UPDATE command
            sqlCommand = "UPDATE Friends SET " +
                        "FirstName = '" + txtFirstName.Text + "'," +
                        "LastName = '" + txtLastName.Text + "'," +
                        "Addr1 = '" + txtAddr1.Text + "'," +
                        "Addr2 = '" + txtAddr2.Text + "'," +
                        "City = '" + txtCity.Text + "'," +
                        "State = '" + txtState.Text.ToUpper() + "'," +
                        "Zip = '" + txtZip.Text + "'," +
                        "LastContact = '" + txtLastContact.Text + "'," +
                        "Status = " + status.ToString() +
                        " WHERE ID = " + txtFindRecordNumber.Text;
            try
            {
                flag = myData.ProcessCommand(sqlCommand);
                if (flag > 0)
                {
                    MessageBox.Show("Record updated successfully.");
                }
                else
                {
                    MessageBox.Show("Failed to update data.", "Process Error");
                }
            }
            catch (Exception ex)
            {
                MessageBox.Show("Error: " + ex.Message);
            }
        }
```

Variable myData connects to the database, and the sqlCommand is built up from the content of the textboxes. The UPDATE command simply specifies the table to change followed by the SET keyword and then a list of the field names and the associated data. After the command is constructed, it is passed to the ProcessCommand() method of the clsFriend class. Listing 14-7 shows the code for the ProcessCommand() method.

LISTING 14-7: Process an SQL Query (clsFriend.cs)

```
/*****
 * Purpose: To process an SQL command on a database
 *
```

continues

LISTING 14-7 *(continued)*

```
 * Parameter list:
 *   string sqlCommand      a command string that holds the CREATE TABLE
 *                          directives
 *
 * Return value:
 *   int                    1 on success, 0 otherwise
 *
 * CAUTION: The method assumes the connect string is already set
 *****/
public int ProcessCommand(string sqlCommand)
{
    int flag = 1;
    try
    {
        using (SqlConnection conn = new SqlConnection(connectString))
        {
            conn.Open();
            SqlCommand command = new SqlCommand(sqlCommand, conn);
            flag = command.ExecuteNonQuery();            // Add new record
            conn.Close();
        }
    }
    catch
    {
        flag = 0;
    }
    return flag;
}
```

The code to process the command should look familiar to you by now. The command string, sql-Command, opens a connection and an ExecuteNonQuery() is called to process the UPDATE. Because the query string is passed into the ProcessCommand(), the method can process any SQL command on any table. Therefore, although the program discussed here does not provide for editing the type of cards or the exchange of cards, it would be fairly simple to do so, which is left as an exercise for you.

SUMMARY

You covered quite a bit of ground in this chapter. You should have a good idea of what a database is, how to create and expand one, and how otherwise to manipulate the data within the database. Now that you have discussed the major elements of the Cards database, you should spend some time single stepping through the code. Also experiment with the dataGridView control and changing some of its properties to see the impact it has on its behavior. It will be worth the effort.

You can find the answers to the following exercises in Appendix A.

EXERCISES

1. Suppose you define a Friends table using the data structure suggested in Chapter 13. Give two SQL commands that would return the number of active members of the Friends table.

2. Again using the Friends data structure from Chapter 13, construct an SQL statement that returns all the active members who live in Indiana (or whatever state you might use) and whose second address is not empty.

3. The code in `frmAddFriend` is a bit of a hack because it is tightly coupled with the user interface:

```
        // Build INSERT command
    sqlCommand = "INSERT INTO Friends" +
            "(ID,FirstName,LastName,Addr1,Addr2,City,State," +
            "Zip,LastContact,Status) VALUES (";

// Now add the values
sqlCommand += records + ",'" +
            txtFirstName.Text + "','" +
            txtLastName.Text + "','" +
            txtAddr1.Text + "','" +
            txtAddr2.Text + "','" +
            txtCity.Text + "','" +
            txtState.Text.ToUpper() + "','" +
            txtZip.Text + "','" +
            txtLastContact.Text + "'," +
            status + ")";
```

The reason it is tightly coupled is that the inputs are tied to the textbox objects used to gather the information from the user. Because you don't want end-user interface objects like textboxes in a non-UI class, the current code shouldn't be moved into class `clsDB`. However, it would be nice to move the database INSERT command out of the user-interface code in `frmAddFriend` and move it into the `clsDB` class where it belongs. How might you do that?

4. I'm not a big fan of nested *if* statements. In the `frmCardReport`'s search button's click event code, you see a six-level nested `if` statement. To me, this is SDC code (that is, Sorta Dumb Code). The reason is because in some cases you have to fall through five `if` tests to get to the proper statement block. If you had used a `switch` statement instead, the `switch` selection variable test results in a jump instruction that sends control immediately to the proper code block, thus avoiding the unnecessary `if` tests. Rewrite the code to use a `switch` statement.

▶ **WHAT YOU HAVE LEARNED IN THIS CHAPTER**

TOPIC	KEY POINTS
Database	A file that contains data organized in a row-column fashion. If the file has two or more tables related to one another, it is a relational database.
The elements of a database	Databases hold tables that hold fields and records.
Database keys	Primary and foreign keys are used to relate information between tables.
Normalization	How redundant data can be removed from a database.
SQL	Structure Query Language used to extract useful information from a database.
MDI for a database	How the MDI system can be used with a database.

15

Using LINQ

WHAT YOU WILL LEARN IN THIS CHAPTER:

➤ What LINQ is

➤ How to query data objects using LINQ

➤ The meaning of the var keyword

➤ The required LINQ namespaces

➤ The advantages of using LINQ to query data objects

WROX.COM CODE DOWNLOADS FOR THIS CHAPTER

You can find the wrox.com code downloads for this chapter at www.wrox.com/remtitle
.cgi?isbn=9781118336922 on the Download Code tab. The code in the Chapter15 folder is
individually named according to the names throughout the chapter.

SQL is so simple to use; wouldn't it be nice if you could apply its simplicity to data
structures other than databases? That's what Microsoft's LINQ is designed to do. LINQ
stands for *Language INtegrated Query* and is a feature that appeared with the debut of Visual
Studio 2008.

USING LINQ

Although you can use SQL with relational database objects, LINQ can also query object types
where the data source is not a database. You can use LINQ to query an object type, including
arrays, class objects, and XML, in addition to relational databases. Visual Studio incorporates the LINQ query engine directly but also has defined an extension definition that enables

third-party data sources to tie in to the engine via a translator. Just as SQL queries result in datasets stored in memory, LINQ returns a collection of memory-based objects.

Query Keywords

SQL has specific keywords used in query statements, and LINQ provides a similar set of keywords. Perhaps the easiest way to begin to understand LINQ is to try the following simple example.

TRY IT OUT   **A LINQ Program Example (Chapter15ProgramLINQTest.zip)**

In this example, the program generates MAXNUM (such as 100) random numbers and displays them in a listbox object. The program then uses LINQ to query that data list for values that fall within a specified range. Figure 15-1 shows a sample run of the program.

1.   Create a new project in the normal way.

2.   Download the code in the Chapter15ProgramLINQTest.zip file on this book's web page at wrox .com.

3.   Create a user interface with two listboxes, five labels, two textboxes, and two button objects using Figure 15-1 as a model.

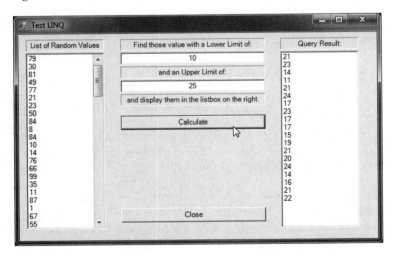

FIGURE 15-1: Sample run

The user enters an upper and lower (exclusive) boundary for the values to be extracted from the list of random values shown in the listbox on the left. The specified range is set by the values specified in the two textbox objects. The result of the query is shown in the right listbox object in Figure 15-1.

How It Works

The code for the program is shown in Listing 15-1.

LISTING 15-1: Program Using LINQ (frmMain.cs)

```csharp
using System;
using System.Collections.Generic;
using System.Linq;
using System.Windows.Forms;

public class frmMain : Form
{
    private const int MAXNUM = 100;                // Max random numbers
    static List<int> numbers = new List<int>(); // static list

    private Button btnClose;
    private ListBox lstOutput;
    private ListBox lstFull;
    private TextBox txtLow;
    private Label label1;
    private Label label2;
    private TextBox txtHi;
    private Label label3;
    private Label label4;
    private Label label5;
    private Button btnCalc;

    #region Windows code

    //========================== Constructor ===========================
    public frmMain()
    {
        InitializeComponent();
        GenerateRandomValues();
    }

    //=========================== Program Start ========================
    public static void Main()
    {
        frmMain main = new frmMain();
        Application.Run(main);
    }

    //========================= Helper Methods =========================
    private void btnCalc_Click(object sender, EventArgs e)
    {

        int lo;
        int hi;

        lstOutput.Items.Clear();

        SetTheLimits(out lo, out hi);
        DoLINQQuery(lo, hi);
    }

    /****
```

continues

LISTING 15-1 *(continued)*

```
 * Purpose: To generate a MAXNUM sequence of random integer values
 *
 * Parameter list:
 *  int lo          the lower limit for query
 *  int hi          the upper limit for query
 *
 * Return value:
 *  void
 *
 ****/
private void DoLINQQuery(int lo, int hi)
{
    var query = from p in numbers               // The "Query"
                where p > lo && p < hi
                select p;
    foreach (var val in query)                  // Display results
    {
        lstOutput.Items.Add(val.ToString());
    }

}


/****
 * Purpose: Set the upper and lower limits of the query
 *
 * Parameter list:
 *  out int lo          reference to the lower limit
 *  out int hi          reference to the upper limit
 *
 * Return value:
 *  void
 *
 ****/
private void SetTheLimits(out int lo, out int hi)
{
    bool flag = int.TryParse(txtLow.Text, out lo);   // Input validation
    if (flag == false)
    {
        MessageBox.Show("Numeric only, 0 to 100", "Input Error");
        txtLow.Focus();
    }
    flag = int.TryParse(txtHi.Text, out hi);
    if (flag == false)
    {
        MessageBox.Show("Numeric only, 0 to 100", "Input Error");
        txtHi.Focus();
    }
}

/****
 * Purpose: To generate a MAXNUM sequence of random integer values
 *
 * Parameter list:
```

```
    *   void
    *
    * Return value:
    *   void
    *
    ****/
    private void GenerateRandomValues()
    {
        int temp;
        DateTime current = DateTime.Now;
        Random rnd = new Random((int)current.Ticks);

        for (int i = 0; i < MAXNUM; i++)              // Random values
        {
            temp = rnd.Next(MAXNUM);
            numbers.Add(temp);                        // Copy into list
            lstFull.Items.Add(temp.ToString());
        }
    }

    private void btnClose_Click(object sender, EventArgs e)
    {
        Close();
    }

}
```

Namespaces and References for LINQ

In this example you use a generic `List` object, so you need to include the collections-generic namespace in the program. The necessary `using` statements for the sample program are as follows:

```
using System;
using System.Collections.Generic;
using System.Linq;
using System.Windows.Forms;
```

To have the proper references available, you need to add a few new references to the standard list. Your reference list should include these:

```
System
System.Core
System.Data
System.Data.DataSetExtensions
System.Data.Linq
System.Drawing
System.Windows.Forms
```

The new references provide the necessary libraries to use LINQ. (These references don't appear in the code listing but are in the Reference section of the project.)

The `btnCalc_Click()` event code does all the work. You begin by validating the upper and lower limits for the domain of random numbers generated by an object named `rnd` of the `Random` class. Recall that the statement,

```
List<int> numbers = new List<int>();
```

defines an object (numbers) that can store a list of int data. The first for loop simply defines a random number between 0 and MAXNUM and sets it into the numbers List object and copies the value to the lstFull listbox object. MAXNUM does double duty, controlling both the upper limit of the random number and the number of random values that are generated. This is SDC (Sorta Dumb Code) because it's rarely a good idea to have a symbolic constant to serve dual purposes. If this is nettlesome to you, add a new constant of your own choosing.

THE VAR KEYWORD

The following statement illustrates the syntax of a LINQ query. The query statement defines a variable named query, which is of type var:

```
var query = from p in numbers          // The "Query"
               where p > lo && p < hi
               select p;
```

A type var appears to enable you to define a variable without specifying what it is. You can, for example, have a definition like this:

```
var myVar = 61;
```

This leads some programmers to conclude that var is the same as the object data type. But var is truly different from object. You can prove this to yourself with the following statements:

```
var myVar = 61;
object myObj = 61;

myVar += 1;
myObj += 1;
```

The last line generates a compiler error stating that the += operator can't be applied to types object and int. You can further confirm that var is different from an object by attempting to assign myVar and myObj into a primitive value type, such as:

```
long big1 = myVar;
long big2 = myObj;
```

The first statement compiles without complaint, but the second draws a type mismatch error and suggests using a cast to fix the problem.

Finally, try to compile the statements:

```
myVar = "Lynne York";
myObj = "Tom Bangert";
```

Variable myObj sails through the compiler without causing complaint, but myVar draws an error message stating that it cannot convert a string to an int. This is the key difference between the var type and an object type: var *is strongly typed*. It also means that var infers its type from the context in which it is used.

So how does the compiler infer var's type? Its type is set at the time it is initialized. *You cannot define a* var *type without initializing it as part of its definition*. That is, the statement,

```
var myVar;                    // Causes compiler error!
```

draws a compiler error stating:

```
Implicitly-typed local variables must be initialized
```

Therefore, the actual type that var assumes is dictated by the expression that initializes it. Because the compiler must type the var variable when it is defined, any var type definitions must be initialized at the point of their definition.

USING VAR IN A QUERY

Consider this statement from Listing 15-1:

```
var query = from p in numbers            // The "Query"
              where p > lo && p < hi
              select p;
```

Because numbers is defined generically as a list of type int data, query assumes an int data type. The statement works like a FROM-WHERE clause in SQL to examine the numbers data set and extract those values that fall between lo and hi (exclusively). Think of the values that fall within the specified range as becoming part of a temporary data set named p, which is then assigned into query.

The statement,

```
foreach (var val in query)               // Display results
      lstOutput.Items.Add(val.ToString());
```

defines a second var type named val that, because of the initialization context in which it is defined, assumes the same data type that the query holds. The foreach loop simply iterates over the query collection and adds the values in query to the lstOutput listbox object.

Although LINQ doesn't give you anything that you couldn't write yourself without using it, LINQ sure makes it easier. The added bonus is that its syntax mimics SQL's, making it easier to use if you already know SQL.

In the following Try It Out, you recode the program to use LINQ and string data rather than integer data. The basics are much the same, as you can see in Listing 15-2.

TRY IT OUT | **Another LINQ Example Using String Data (Chapter15ProgramLINQExample02.zip)**

Now try another LINQ example. In this example, assume that the data are names followed by that person's state. The user types in a state abbreviation for the state she wants to examine from those shown in the left listbox object and then clicks the Calculate button. The right listbox object then displays those entries that match the selected state abbreviation. Figure 15-2 shows a sample run of the program.

The following steps detail how to set up the sample project.

1. Create a new project in the normal manner.

2. Download the project source code from file Chapter15ProgramLINQExample02.zip.

3. Create a user interface similar to that shown in Figure 15-2.

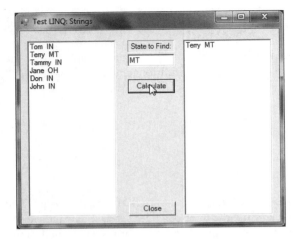

FIGURE 15-2: Sample run using LINQ with string data

How It Works

The code for the program is shown in Listing 15-2. The code is similar to that shown in Listing 15-10, so I limit my comments to those sections that are different. First, note that I define two static variables (passes and count) near the top of the listing. I use the static specifier because I want those variables available the instant the program loads. After the frmMain() constructor builds the form's image in memory and initializes its data, the left listbox object is filled in via a call to ShowAll().

LISTING 15-2: Using LINQ with String Data (frmMain.cs)

```
using System;
using System.Linq;
using System.Windows.Forms;

public class frmMain : Form
{
    static int passes = 0;
    static int count;

    private Button btnClose;
    private ListBox lstOutput;
    private ListBox lstFull;
    private Label label1;
    private TextBox txtState;
    private Button btnCalc;

    #region Windows code

    public frmMain()
    {
        InitializeComponent();
```

```csharp
        ShowAll();
    }

public static void Main()
{
    frmMain main = new frmMain();
    Application.Run(main);
}

private void btnCalc_Click(object sender, EventArgs e)
{
    ShowAll();
}

private void ShowAll()
{
    int i;
    var friends = new[] {
        new {name = "Tom", state = "IN"},
        new {name = "Terry", state = "MT"},
        new {name = "Tammy", state = "IN"},
        new {name = "Jane", state = "OH"},
        new {name = "Don", state = "IN"},
        new {name = "John", state = "IN"},
        new {name = "Linda", state = "FL"},
    };

    if (passes == 0)
    {
        count = friends.GetUpperBound(0);
        i = 0;
        for (i = 0; i <= count; i++)
        {
            lstFull.Items.Add(friends[i].name + "   " + friends[i].state);
        }
        passes++;
    }
    else
    {
        lstOutput.Items.Clear();

        var query = from p in friends            // The "Query"
                    where p.state == txtState.Text.ToUpper()
                    select p;

        foreach (var val in query)               // Display results
            lstOutput.Items.Add(val.name + "   " + val.state);
    }
}

private void btnClose_Click(object sender, EventArgs e)
{
    Close();
}
}
```

The `ShowAll()` method constructs a test data set using the `var` type and names it `friends`. (It would be nice to define `friends` as `static` data with class scope, but `var` types can assume only local scope, remember?) If `passes` is 0, the call was from the constructor, so the code moves the `friends` data to the left listbox object (`lstFull`) and increments `passes`. The next time `ShowAll()` is called after a button click event, filling in `lstFull` is bypassed because `passes` is no longer 0. In that case, the `else` statement block executes. The right listbox object (`lstOutput`) clears and the query processes.

The following query statement uses a LINQ `where` predicate to restrict the result of the query to the state selected by the user:

```
var query = from p in Friends      // The "Query"
                where p.state == txtState.Text.ToUpper()
                select p;

foreach (var val in query)          // Display results
    lstOutput.Items.Add(val.name + " " + val.state);
```

The `foreach` statement block then iterates through the result of the LINQ query (as stored in `query`) and displays the relevant information in the right listbox object (`lstOutput`).

Of course, the test data set can consist of more complex objects. For example, you could extend the set to something like

```
var friends = new[] {
    new {name = "Tom", state = "IN", age = 48},
    new {name = "Terry", state = "MT", age = 61},
    new {name = "Tammy", state = "IN", age = 46},
    new {name = "Jane", state = "OH", age = 65},
    new {name = "Don", state = "IN", age = 60},
    new {name = "John", state = "IN", age = 61},
    new {name = "Debbie", state = "IN", age = 58},
};
```

and change the query to

```
var query = from p in Friends                 // The "Query"
                where p.age < age
                select p;
```

where `age` is set from a textbox object and used as the `where` predicate in a search by age. Again, although you can accomplish the same results without using LINQ, the economy of expression with LINQ makes it the wise choice. Anytime you can accomplish the same task with less code, the less code route is almost always the way to go.

Other SQL-like keywords and operators are also available in LINQ. Although I am not prepared to discuss all of them given the limited look at SQL, Table 15-1 gives you a list of some of the more important keywords and operators. You can use the online help to explore further, if you want.

TABLE 15.1: Partial list of LINQ keywords

KEYWORD/OPERATOR	DESCRIPTION
`select, selectmany`	Like `SELECT` in SQL, `selectmany` may be used with another collection and enables the result set to return pairs.
`where`	Similar to the `WHERE` predicate in SQL.
`join, groupjoin`	Enables result sets to span multiple tables based upon matching keys in the tables.
`take, takewhile`	Selects the first N objects from a collection. `takewhile` uses a predicate to further refine the query.
`skip, skipwhile`	A complement of the `take` operator. The set skips the first N objects in the collection. `skipwhile` is the complement of `takewhile`.
`oftype`	Enables you to select elements of a certain type.
`concat`	Enables concatenation of two collections.
`orderby, thenby`	Specifies the primary sort order for a collection. The default is ascending order. You can use `orderbydescending` to reverse the default order. `thenby` enables subsequent orders after the primary sort key.
`reverse`	Reverses the current order of the collection.
`groupby`	Returns a collection of objects that supports the `IGrouping<key, values>` interface.
`distinct`	Removes all duplicates from the result set.
`union, intersect, except`	Used to perform specialized operations on two sequences.
`equalall`	Checks to see if all elements in two collections are equal.
`first, firstordefault, last, lastordefault`	Uses a predicate to return the first element for which the predicate is logic `True`. An exception is thrown if no match is found in the collection. `firstordefault` is like `first` but returns the first item in the collection if no match is found (that is, if no exception is thrown). `last` works in a similar fashion but looks for the last match in the collection.
`single`	Uses a predicate to find a match but throws an exception if none is found.

TABLE 15-1 *(continued)*

KEYWORD/OPERATOR	DESCRIPTION
elementat	Returns an element of the collection at the specified index.
any, all, contains	Uses a predicate to see if there are any matches (returns logic True or False), if they all match, or if the collection contains a match (returns logic True or False).
count, sum, min, max, average, aggregate	Like the aggregate functions in SQL.

Table 15-1 is not exhaustive, but it can help you start. (For more information, you can find a nice, short summary at: http://www.ezineasp.net/post/List-of-LINQ-Query-Keywords.aspx.) If you'd like to see some sample code using LINQ, check out http://code.msdn.microsoft .com/101-LINQ-Samples-3fb9811b.

LINQ is an important addition to C# and can make some programming tasks significantly easier to develop. You might try experimenting with some of the operators in Table 15-1, using the code in Listing 15-1 as a starting point.

SUMMARY

This chapter presented a brief introduction to LINQ, which brings a lot of SQL query functionality to data structures other than databases. I encourage you to experiment with the sample programs in this chapter and try to create a different array on your own. After you do that, add data to the tables so that they use LINQ instead of SQL to query the database. This should solidify your understanding of the database concepts in this chapter as well as LINQ.

EXERCISES

You can find the answers to the following exercises in Appendix A.

1. Using the Friends database table as an example, how could you use LINQ to process a database query?

2. Rewrite the query in Listing 15-1 so that the result of the query is presented in ascending order in the listbox.

3. If you're at a cocktail party and someone approaches you and asks, "Why should I use LINQ instead of SQL in my code?" what would you say? (What? This couldn't happen?)

▶ **WHAT YOU HAVE LEARNED IN THIS CHAPTER**

TOPIC	KEY POINTS
LINQ	Language Integrated Query.
LINQ query	How LINQ may be used to query data objects other than databases.
`var`	The data tied to LINQ whose type is determined by the context in which it is used.
LINQ namespaces	Certain namespaces must be available to programs that use LINQ.
LINQ advantages	The ability to apply SQL-like queries to objects other than databases.

PART V
Advanced Topics

16

Inheritance and Polymorphism

WHAT YOU WILL LEARN IN THIS CHAPTER:

➤ What inheritance is

➤ How inheritance simplifies program code

➤ What base classes and derived classes are

➤ What the `protected` access specifier is

➤ What polymorphism is

➤ How polymorphism can simplify your programs

➤ What extension methods are

WROX.COM CODE DOWNLOADS FOR THIS CHAPTER

You can find the wrox.com code downloads for this chapter at `www.wrox.com/remtitle`
`.cgi?isbn=9781118336922` on the Download Code tab. The code in the `Chapter16` folder is
individually named according to the names throughout the chapter.

This chapter expands the concept of inheritance. Although you have been using inheritance
since the first chapter, not much has been said about it. The reason for the delay is because
inheritance doesn't make much sense until you understand and appreciate OOP. My guess
is that you do see what OOP brings to the table and are ready to dig into the topic of inheritance. In this chapter you learn the details of inheritance necessary to use it properly in your
own programs.

As you read this chapter, keep in mind that inheritance was added to OOP languages to make
the programmer's life easier. Although the end user may not see any advantages to inheritance
and polymorphism, you can have a greater appreciation of how programmers can make program code simpler.

WHAT IS INHERITANCE?

Until now, inheritance has been a concept sitting in the background, making your life easier every time you designed a user interface for your programs. Indeed, you have probably glossed over that the program line

```
public class frmMain : Form
```

that appears in every program you've written has enabled you to inherit all the basic functionality of a Windows form without needing to write any of that code. The colon in the preceding statement could be verbalized as "inherits from."

The concept of inheritance is built upon the notion that many objects share similar properties. In the preceding statement, you state that you want to create a new class named frmMain that inherits all the functionality of a basic Windows form. Inheriting this functionality means that you don't need to write, test, debug, and maintain that inherited code. Therefore, the driving force behind inheritance is to simplify writing code. Inheritance makes it possible for your code to extend one class to suit your specific needs. Simply stated, *inheritance* is the ability to take one class and extend that class to suit a similar, albeit different, purpose. An example can help explain inheritance.

An Inheritance Example

Some time ago I was contracted to write a program for a real estate investor. The type of real estate the investor purchased could be classified as apartments, commercial properties (such as small strip malls), and residential homes. I sat down with the investor and asked her to describe the type of information that she needed to track with her investments. Table 16-1 is taken from my notes as she described her needs.

TABLE 16-1: Real Estate Types and Their Properties

APARTMENTS	COMMERCIAL	RESIDENTIAL
Purchase price	Purchase date	Address
Purchase date	Address	Purchase price
Address	Rent per month	Purchase date
Monthly mortgage payment	Purchase price	Square feet
Insurance	Property taxes	Number of bedrooms
Property taxes	Insurance	Number of bathrooms
Covered parking	Mortgage payment	Basement?
Storage units	Parking spaces	Fireplace(s)
Number of bedrooms	Restroom facilities	Garage size (cars)
Number of bathrooms	Handicap parking	Rent per month
Rent per month		Lot size

Given the data requirements presented in Table 16-1, I could design the three classes with properties that would track the information she required. Looking at the information she needed, you can simplify each property type by removing those pieces of information common to all investment types. Table 16-2 shows these common properties.

TABLE 16-2: Properties Common to All Types of Real Estate

INFORMATION COMMON TO ALL PROPERTIES
Purchase price
Purchase date
Address
Property taxes
Insurance
Mortgage payment
Rent per month

If you remove these common pieces of information from each investment type, you can simplify Table 16-1 to what is shown in Table 16-3. (This process to factor out duplicated data is similar to the normalization process discussed for databases.)

TABLE 16-3: Real Estate Types and Their Unique Properties

APARTMENTS	COMMERCIAL	RESIDENTIAL
Covered parking	Parking spaces	Square feet
Storage units	Restroom facilities	Number of bedrooms
Number of bedrooms	Handicap parking	Number of bathrooms
Number of bathrooms		Basement?
		Fireplace(s)
		Garage size (cars)
		Lot size

Less information is contained in Table 16-3 than in Table 16-1 because of the common information all three property types share in Table 16-2 is removed. You can express the relationships for the data as shown in the UML class diagrams in Figure 16-1. (You will learn about the `removeSnow()` method later in the section titled "The virtual Keyword.")

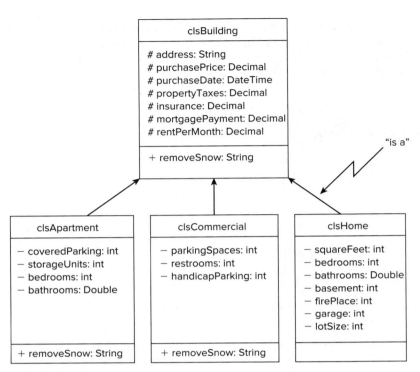

FIGURE 16-1: UML class diagrams

The Base and Derived Classes

As you can see in Figure 16-1, I used the UML notation to give a first approximation of how to organize the data for the investment types. At the top of the figure is clsBuilding. clsBuilding, which contains all the properties common to all the investment types and is called the *base class*. You can think of the base class as a common denominator of data for all the classes. (This is not a new concept; you've been inheriting all of a Windows form's properties using the :Form expression in frmMain in all your programs.)

Any classes that want to use the properties and methods of the base class are called a *derived class*. For Figure 16-1, clsBuilding is the base class, and classes clsApartment, clsCommercial, and clsHome are derived classes. You also hear the base class referred to as the *parent class* and a derived class as a *child class*. The interpretations are the same.

Referring to Figure 16-1 you can notice that three arrows point from the derived classes to the base class. Each of these arrows can be verbalized as "is a." That is, clsApartment "is a" clsBuilding. Using straight English, you can say, "An apartment object is a type of building object." Likewise, a commercial object is a type of building object. The arrows in the UML diagram indicate the nature of the inherited relationships that exist between classes.

The protected Access Specifier

Referring to Figure 16-1, you can see the seven common properties all investment types share in `clsBuilding` with the data type for each property indicated. However, unlike the `public` (+) and `private` (-) access specifiers you learned in Chapter 9, a new access specifier (#) is used. The sharp sign (#) denotes the `protected` access specifier. The `protected` access specifier is needed because of the symbiotic relationship ("is a") formed between the base class and the derived classes.

To understand why the `protected` class is used, consider how things would work if you were limited to either a `public` or a `private` access specifier. First, consider the `private` access specifier. If you use the `private` access specifier in `clsBuilding`, each method and property in `clsBuilding` has class scope. As you already know, this means that those properties and methods would not be visible outside the class. Stated another way, any private property or method in `clsBuilding` would not be available to any outside class, including the three derived classes. Therefore, nothing in the program would have access to the base properties and methods. If you can't access them, they are virtually worthless to the derived classes.

Now consider the other alternative: making all the properties and methods `public`. If you did that, you just threw away all the benefits that encapsulation brings to the party. Not only can the derived classes gain access to the properties and methods of the base class, but so can every other object in the program. As you learned in earlier chapters, encapsulation enables you to protect your data from evil agents who want to wreak havoc on your program.

Using either the `public` or `private` access specifier poses a dilemma: two choices, both bad. The *protected access specifier* solves this problem. The `protected` access specifier enables all derived classes to have access to those properties and methods defined with the `protected` access specifier in the base class. By your using the sharp sign in Figure 16-1 before the properties defined in `clsBuilding`, all three derived classes have access to those properties. However, any object in the program that is not derived from the base class does not have direct access to those protected properties. That is, `protected` properties and methods appear as `private` properties and methods to all but the derived class(es). The `protected` access specifier similar to a high school clique in that the base and derived classes can share information that people outside the clique don't know about. This enables the base and derived classes to encapsulate the data that they need without exposing it outside those symbiotic classes.

Just to drive the point home, given a line in `clsBuilding`,

```
protected decimal purchasePrice;
```

you could have the line,

```
purchasePrice = 150000M;
```

in `clsHome` and it would be perfectly acceptable. The reason is that the `protected` keyword for the definition of `purchasePrice` in `clsBuilding` is completely in scope within `clsHome`. Therefore, `protected` data definitions in the base class are within scope for any of its derived classes.

Advantages of Inherited Relationships

You might be asking what inheritance gets you. Well, to begin with, if you didn't have the inherited relationships shown in Figure 16-1, each of the derived classes would need its own copy of the data shown in Table 16-2. That would also mean that each of those properties would need its own `get` and `set` property methods. The same would be true for any methods that might be shared in the derived classes, such as `RemoveSnow()`, shown in Figure 16-1.

Inheritance enables you to write less code by sharing properties and methods between the base and derived classes. Writing less (duplicate) code means less testing, debugging, and maintenance. It also follows that if you need to change a `protected` property or method, you must change it in only one place, and all the derived classes can immediately take advantage of it.

The next step is to put everything that we've discussed thus far into a program. The next Try It Out provides the code to implement our investment property problem.

TRY IT OUT   **Inheritance Example (Chapter16ProgramInheritance.zip)**

Now write a simple version of the real estate investor program. Figure 16-2 shows a sample run of the program you write. Because this is a fairly large program, only parts of the code are shown here. You should use the download file for this project.

1. Create a new project in the usual manner.

2. Load the source files into the project from `Chapter16ProgramInheritance.zip`.

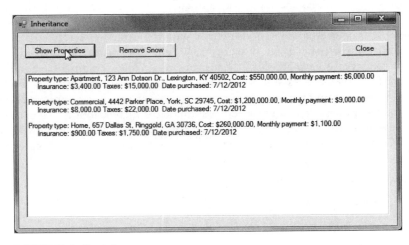

FIGURE 16-2: Sample program run

At the present time, all you want the program to do is display a description of each property type. You show the sample investment properties by clicking the Show Properties button.

How It Works

The program discussion began with the base `clsBuilding` class; Listing 16-1 shows the code.

LISTING 16-1: Source Code for clsBuilding (clsBuilding.cs)

```csharp
using System;
public class clsBuilding
{
    //-------------------- Symbolic constants ----------------
    public const int APARTMENT = 1;
    public const int COMMERCIAL = 2;
    public const int HOME = 3;

    //-------------------- Instance variables ----------------
    protected string address;
    protected decimal purchasePrice;
    protected decimal monthlyPayment;
    protected decimal taxes;
    protected decimal insurance;
    protected DateTime datePurchased;
    protected int buildingType;

    string[] whichType = {"", "Apartment", "Commercial", "Home" };

    //-------------------- Constructor -----------------------
    public clsBuilding()
    {
        address = "Not closed yet";
    }

    public clsBuilding(string addr, decimal price, decimal payment,
                    decimal tax, decimal insur, DateTime date,
                    int type):this()
    {
       if (addr.Equals("") == false)
           address = addr;
        purchasePrice = price;
        monthlyPayment = payment;
        taxes = tax;
        insurance = insur;
        datePurchased = date;
        buildingType = type;
    }
    //-------------------- Property Methods ------------------

    public string Address
    {
        get
        {
            return address;
        }
        set
        {
            if (value.Length != 0)
                address = value;
        }
    }
}
```

continues

LISTING 16-1 *(continued)*

```
public decimal PurchasePrice
{
    get
    {
        return purchasePrice;
    }
    set
    {
        if (value > 0M)
            purchasePrice = value;
    }
}

public decimal MonthlyPayment
{
    get
    {
        return monthlyPayment;
    }
    set
    {
        if (value > 0M)
            monthlyPayment = value;
    }
}

public decimal Taxes
{
    get
    {
        return taxes;
    }
    set
    {
        if (value > 0M)
            taxes = value;
    }
}

public decimal Insurance
{
    get
    {
        return insurance;
    }
    set
    {
        if (value > 0M)
            insurance = value;
    }
}

public DateTime DatePurchased
```

```
    {
        get
        {
            return datePurchased;
        }
        set
        {
            if (value.Year > 2008)
                datePurchased = value;
        }
    }

    public int BuildingType
    {
        get
        {
            return buildingType;
        }
        set
        {
            if (value >= APARTMENT && value <= HOME)
                buildingType = value;
        }
    }
    //-------------------- General Methods --------------------

    /*****
     * Purpose: Provide a basic description of the property
     *
     * Parameter list:
     *   string[] desc        a string array to hold description
     *
     * Return value:
     *   void
     *
     * CAUTION: Method assumes that there are 3 elements in array
     *****/
    public void PropertySummary(string[] desc)
    {
        desc[0] = "Property type: " + whichType[buildingType] +
                  ", " + address +
                  ", Cost: " + purchasePrice.ToString("C") +
                  ", Monthly payment: " + monthlyPayment.ToString("C");
        desc[1] = "    Insurance: " + insurance.ToString("C") +
                  " Taxes: " + taxes.ToString("C") +
                  "  Date purchased: "+ datePurchased.ToShortDateString();
        desc[2] = " ";
    }
}
```

The code begins by defining several symbolic constants followed by the property members of
`clsBuilding`. As specified in your design, each property method uses the `protected` access specifier.
The code also provides for the property `get` and `set` methods for each of the properties so that the user
can change the state of the object.

SYMBOLIC CONSTANTS VERSUS ENUMERATED TYPES

Symbolic constants are used in many programs throughout this text. If you think about it, however, you could also use enumerated types in the same way. For example, you could replace the symbolic constants shown in Listing 16-1 with this:

```
public enum bldgType {APARTMENT = 1, COMMERCIAL, HOME}
```

Then you could use the enum in the `BuildingType()` like this:

```
set
{
    if (value >= (int) bldgType.APARTMENT &&
        value <= (int) bldgType.HOME)
    {
        buildingType = value;
    }
}
```

The `int` cast is required in the `if` statement because `value` is defined as an `int` for the property. I find the syntax using the `enum` clumsy and prefers the use of symbolic constants. Select the style you prefer and use it consistently.

The method `PropertySummary()` is used to provide a summary of the building's description using the properties associated with each property. The method builds an array of strings, which are then returned to the caller in `frmMain` to display the property description in a listbox object. (Listing 16-2 presents the `frmMain` code.) The output generated by the `PropertySummary()` method looks like that shown in Figure 16-2.

There are two constructors in Listing 16-1. The first constructor assumes that you want to set the properties for the building by separate calls to the property methods:

```
public clsBuilding()
{
    address = "Not closed yet";
}
```

The constructor also sets the default address to a message that suggests you haven't actually purchased the property yet. The second constructor assumes that you want to initialize the properties when the building object is instantiated:

```
public clsBuilding(string addr, decimal price, decimal payment,
                   decimal tax, decimal insur, DateTime date,
                   int type):this()
{
    if (addr.Equals("") == false) {
        address = addr;
    }
    purchasePrice = price;
    monthlyPayment = payment;
    taxes = tax;
    insurance = insur;
    datePurchased = date;
```

```
        buildingType = type;
    }
```

Good coding practice of calling the first constructor via the this() call to the first (no-argument) constructor is followed. This also means that if you pass in a property address in addr, the second constructor overwrites the "Not closed yet" string with the address.

Listing 16-2 shows the frmMain code that drives the application.

LISTING 16-2: The frmMain Code for the Application

```
using System;
using System.Windows.Forms;

public class frmMain : Form
{
    DateTime myTime;                // instance members
    clsBuilding myBldg;
    clsApartment myApt;
    clsCommercial myComm;
    clsHome myHome;

    private ListBox lstMessages;
    private Button btnShow;
    private Button btnRemoveSnow;
    private Button btnClose;

    #region Windows code

    public frmMain()
    {
        InitializeComponent();     // Initialize the form

        myTime = DateTime.Now;
        myBldg = new clsBuilding();  // A base object

                                     // Derived objects
        myApt = new clsApartment("123 Jane Dr., Cincinnati, OH
                45245", 550000, 6000, 15000, 3400, myTime, 1);

        myComm = new clsCommercial("4442 Parker Place, York, SC
                  29745",1200000, 9000, 22000, 8000, myTime, 2);

        myHome = new clsHome("657 Dallas St, Ringgold, GA 30736",
                 260000, 1100, 1750, 900, myTime, 3);
    }

    public static void Main()
    {
        frmMain main = new frmMain();
        Application.Run(main);
    }
```

continues

LISTING 16-2 *(continued)*

```csharp
        // Show each of the properties...
        private void btnShow_Click(object sender, EventArgs e)
        {
            string[] desc = new string[3];

                myApt.PropertySummary(desc);
                ShowProperty(desc);

                myComm.PropertySummary(desc);
                ShowProperty(desc);

                myHome.PropertySummary(desc);
                ShowProperty(desc);
        }

        private void ShowProperty(string[] str)
        {
            int i;

            for (i = 0; i < str.Length; i++)
            {
                lstMessages.Items.Add(str[i]);
            }
        }

        private void btnClose_Click(object sender, EventArgs e)
        {
            Close();
        }
    }
```

In a "real" program you would likely have textbox objects that would fill in each of the properties for the different types of buildings. This code initializes the buildings using the parameterized constructors. You can see the data in the `frmMain()` constructor method.

Notice how the descriptions display in the listbox object, For example,

```csharp
    myApt.PropertySummary(desc);
    ShowProperty(desc);
```

calls the `PropertySummary()` method using the `myApt` object.

Listing 16-3 shows the code for the three derived classes. (The three class listings are separated with double-dashed lines to make it easier to see where one class ends and another begins.) If you look closely, you'll notice that `clsApartment` does not have a method named `PropertySummary()`, yet Figure 16-2 shows the correct information for the apartment property. The same is true for `clsCommercial` and `clsHome`: Neither has a `PropertySummary()` method. How does the program display the correct information for each building? Obviously, all three buildings use the `PropertySummary()` method from the base class to display their properties.

LISTING 16-3: Source for clsApartment (clsApartment.cs)

```csharp
using System;
class clsApartment : clsBuilding
{
    //-------------------- Instance variables ----------------
    private int units;
    private decimal rentPerUnit;
    private double occupancyRate;

    //-------------------- Constructor ----------------------
    public clsApartment():base()
    {
    }
    public clsApartment(string addr, decimal price, decimal payment,
                        decimal tax, decimal insur, DateTime date,
                        int type) :
                        base(addr, price, payment, tax,
                        insur, date, type)
    {
        buildingType = type;   // Apartment type from base
    }
    //-------------------- Property Methods ------------------
    public int Units
    {
        get
        {
            return units;
        }
        set
        {
            if (value > 0)
                units = value;
        }
    }
    public decimal RentPerUnit
    {
        get
        {
            return rentPerUnit;
        }
        set
        {
            if (value > 0M)
                rentPerUnit = value;
        }
    }
    public double OccupancyRate
    {
        get
        {
            return occupancyRate;
        }
```

continues

LISTING 16-3 *(continued)*

```
        set
        {
            if (value > 0.0)
                occupancyRate = value;
        }
    }

    //-------------------- General Methods --------------------
    public override string RemoveSnow()
    {
        return "Called John's Snow Removal: 859.444.7654";
    }
}
================================================================

using System;

class clsCommercial : clsBuilding
{
    //-------------------- Instance variables -----------------
    private int squareFeet;
    private int parkingSpaces;
    private decimal rentPerSquareFoot;

    //-------------------- Constructor -----------------------
    public clsCommercial(string addr, decimal price, decimal payment,
                         decimal tax, decimal insur, DateTime date,
                         int type) :
                         base(addr, price, payment, tax,
                              insur, date, type)
    {
        buildingType = type;    // Commercial type from base
    }
    //-------------------- Property Methods -------------------
    public int SquareFeet
    {
        get
        {
            return squareFeet;
        }
        set
        {
            if (value > 0)
                squareFeet = value;
        }
    }
    public int ParkingSpaces
    {
        get
        {
            return parkingSpaces;
```

```
        }
        set
        {
            parkingSpaces = value;
        }
    }
    public decimal RentPerSquareFoot
    {
        get
        {
            return rentPerSquareFoot;
        }
        set
        {
            if (value > 0M)
                rentPerSquareFoot = value;
        }
    }

    //-------------------- General Methods --------------------
    public override string RemoveSnow()
    {
        return "Called Acme Snow Plowing: 803.234.5566";
    }
}

=================================================================
using System;


class clsHome : clsBuilding
{
    //-------------------- Instance variables -----------------
    private int squareFeet;
    private int bedrooms;
    private double bathrooms;
    private decimal rentPerMonth;

    //-------------------- Constructor -----------------------
    public clsHome(string addr, decimal price, decimal payment,
                   decimal tax, decimal insur, DateTime date,
                   int type) :
                   base(addr, price, payment, tax,
                        insur, date, type)
    {
        buildingType = 3;      // Home type from base
    }
    //-------------------- Property Methods -------------------
    public int SquareFeet
    {
        get
        {
            return squareFeet;
        }
        set
```

continues

LISTING 16-3 *(continued)*

```
        {
            if (value > 0)
                squareFeet = value;
        }
    }
    public int BedRooms
    {
        get
        {
            return bedrooms;
        }
        set
        {
            bedrooms = value;
        }
    }
    public double BathRooms
    {
        get
        {
            return bathrooms;
        }
        set
        {
            bathrooms = value;
        }
    }
    public decimal RentPerMonth
    {
        get
        {
            return rentPerMonth;
        }
        set
        {
            if (value > 0M)
                rentPerMonth = value;
        }
    }

    //-------------------- General Methods --------------------

}
```

Each of the three building type begins with a line similar to

```
class clsApartment : clsBuilding
```

This is what establishes the "is a" relationship depicted in Figure 16-1. (This is no different than using the ": Form" that you've seen with virtually every form's class definition you've used throughout this text.) By tying each derived class to the base building class using this syntax, you can use the PropertySummary() found in clsBuilding in all the derived classes.

One more thing: Derived classes cannot inherit constructors. You must write a constructor for a derived class. If the base class doesn't have a default constructor, the constructor for the derived class must call the base constructor using the `base` keyword, as shown in `clsApartment`:

```
public clsApartment(string addr, decimal price, decimal payment,
                decimal tax, decimal insur, DateTime date,
                int type) :
                base(addr, price, payment, tax,
                    insur, date, type)
```

The keyword `base` is used here to pass parameters used to construct the `clsApartment` object on to the `clsBuilding` constructor. (The concept is similar to the `this` construct used with multiple constructors.)

Base Classes Are Not Derived Classes

The capability for a derived class to use a method in the base class is a one-way relationship. That is, the derived class can call a base class method, but the base class cannot directly call a derived class method. For example, suppose `clsCommercial` contains a public method named `HouseCleaning()`. If `myBldg` is a `clsBuilding` object, you cannot use

```
myBldg.HouseCleaning(); // Error!!
```

The compiler throws an error and informs you that it cannot find a definition for `HouseCleaning()`. This conclusion is true even if you use the `public` access specifier for the `HouseCleaning()` method. The reason you can't perform a base-to-derived method call is that the "is a" relationship shown in Figure 16-1 is a one-way street. That is, a `clsCommercial` object assumes all the property and methods of a `clsBuilding` object, but a `clsBuilding` object does not assume all the properties and methods of a `clsCommercial` object.

Abstract Classes

As I mentioned earlier, the base class is typically used to serve as a repository for all the properties shared among the derived classes. However, it is possible that the base class is so nondescript that instantiating an object of the base class doesn't make sense. For example, you might create a tree class called `clsDeciduous` that has the properties `leafColor`, `barkStyle`, `matureHeight`, and `ringCount`. The derived classes might be `clsOak`, `clsMaple`, `clsWillow` and so on. The problem is that even though all the derived classes have leaves, bark, a mature height, and a ring count, there are so many trees with these characteristics that it makes no sense to instantiate a `clsDeciduous` object. Only the details found in the derived classes, with the base class, have enough information to make an object useful.

To prevent instantiation of the base class, use the `abstract` keyword:

```
public abstract class clsDecidious
{
    // The class code...
}
```

If a class is defined by means of the abstract keyword, as shown here, you cannot instantiate an object of that class. This means that a statement like the following draws a compiler error telling you that you cannot instantiate an object of an abstract class:

```
clsDecidious myLeafyTree = new clsDecidious();
```

If you can't instantiate an object of the class, why use it?

By defining a class using the abstract keyword, you are telling the users of the class two things. First, they cannot instantiate an object of this class, which tips them off to the second reason. Second, and more important, the user must define derived classes to capture the functionality embodied in the base class. Indeed, there is no reason to use the base class in the absence of derived classes.

If you define a method using the abstract keyword, the derived classes *must* implement the method. There is no code in the base class for the method. In this way, abstract classes and methods are similar to interfaces in that interfaces contain no code either. However, interfaces cannot contain constructors.

POLYMORPHISM

Chapter 1 mentions that polymorphism is one of the three pillars of object-oriented programming. At that time I dismissed the topic, saying that the word *polymorphism* is derived from the Greek meaning "many shapes" and that was all that was said. Now that you understand what inheritance is, you are ready to more completely appreciate what polymorphism is.

Instead of sticking with the concept of "many shapes," perhaps the definition should be amended to mean "many messages." In essence, *polymorphism* means that you can send the same message to a group of different classes and that each class will know how to respond correctly to that message.

TRY IT OUT **Using Polymorphism**

Consider the following example. Where I live, if more than 2 inches of snow falls, you are supposed to get out and shovel your walkways. Let's further assume that our software should notify someone at each property location when our property manager sees that 2 or more inches of snow has fallen. (I will just pretend that there is an electrical hookup between the software and the phone system. I'll use things displayed in the listbox object as an indicator that the call(s) have been made.)

What you want to do is add a button that the manager can click when he sees that more than 2 inches of snow is on the ground. A sample run of the program is shown in Figure 16-3.

Notice that the apartment and commercial buildings are given a phone number to call for snow removal, but none is given for people who live in a rented home. The assumption is that, as part of their lease agreement, home renters are required to shovel the walks.

The code you downloaded already has the Remove Snow button and code in it. This exercise simply explains how polymorphism can be implemented.

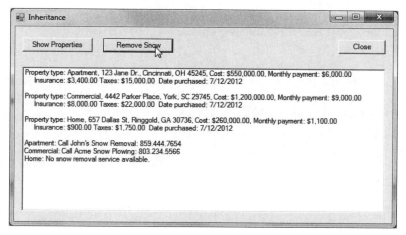

FIGURE 16-3: Snow removal output

How It Works

The first thing you need to do is modify the base class to process the snow-removal message. The code added to `clsBuilding` is as follows:

```
public virtual string RemoveSnow()
{
    return whichType[buildingType] +
            ": No snow removal service available.";
}
```

The virtual Keyword

The snow removal method in `clsBuilding`, `RemoveSnow()`, is defined via the keyword `virtual`. The word *virtual* is used to identify that the method may be overridden in a derived class. Stated differently, a `virtual` method can be replaced by a different definition of the method in any class derived from this base class.

If you refer to Figure 16-1, you can see that you provide `RemoveSnow()` methods for both `clsApartment` and `clsCommercial` objects. The code for these two methods is as follows:

```
public override string RemoveSnow()       // clsApartment
{
    return "Apartment: Call John's Snow Removal: 859.444.7654";
}

public override string RemoveSnow()       // clsCommerical
{
    return "Commercial: Call Acme Snow Plowing: 803.234.5566";
}
```

Figure 16-1 also shows that there is no `RemoveSnow()` method for `clsHome`. People who rent homes were informed when they signed their lease that they were responsible for snow removal.

The override Keyword

As you might guess, the `override` keyword goes hand in hand with the `virtual` keyword. Whereas `virtual` tells the reader of the code that the method may be overridden, the `override` keyword tells her that this method is overriding a method found in the class from which it inherits.

Normally, the derived class overrides a `virtual` method defined in the base class. However, you can define a new class from a derived class. For example, you could add `clsRecreational` to `clsHome`, perhaps with new properties for `lakeFrontage`, `boatRamp`, `availableFishingTackle`, and so on. The definition of that class might be as follows:

```
public class clsRecreational : clsHome
{
    // Class code
}
```

You can keep extending the class definitions as far as you think you need them. (If you want to prevent further inheritance from a class, you can use the `sealed` keyword as a modifier in the class definition, as in `public sealed clsLastClass`. Using the `sealed` keyword means that further derivations from this class are not permitted.)

Most of the time, however, you use `override` with a `virtual` method defined in the base class.

Sending the Snow-Removal Message

The new user interface for `frmMain` now contains a button that issues the snow-removal messages. It is the responsibility of each class to figure out what to do. The button click event code for the snow removal message is as follows:

```
private void btnRemoveSnow_Click(object sender, EventArgs e)
{
    lstMessages.Items.Add(myApt.RemoveSnow());
    lstMessages.Items.Add(myComm.RemoveSnow());
    lstMessages.Items.Add(myHome.RemoveSnow());
    lstMessages.Items.Add("");
}
```

Each derived class is sent the same message via the method call to `RemoveSnow()`. However, the message displayed is dictated by whatever process the derived class wants to attach to the method call.

Note that `clsHome` doesn't even *have* a `RemoveSnow()` method, yet it still displays the following message:

```
Home: No snow removal service available.
```

As you no doubt have already figured out, because `clsHome` has no `RemoveSnow()` method, the `RemoveSnow()` method in the base class is used. In other words, `clsHome` chose not to override the `RemoveSnow()` method but instead to use the "default" method as written in the base class.

The nice thing about using inheritance and polymorphic behavior is that each object knows the specifics of how it is supposed to react to whatever events or methods are called, even though the objects share a common method name.

At first blush, inheritance seems a little intimidating. However, if you run the program after setting a number of breakpoints at places where you feel you're unsure of what's going on, you can quickly understand what the code is doing. Single-stepping a program is a great way to get more depth of understanding of what a program is actually doing as it executes.

EXTENSION METHODS

Inheritance gives you a way to avoid duplicate code that could exist without the parent-child relationship. Of course, using inheritance requires that you have access to the source code for the class. Extension methods, however, allow you to extend the functionality of a class without the need for the source code.

You can think of extension methods as static methods that you can graft onto an existing class without having the source code for that class. The easiest way to understand what extension methods bring to the party is by example-like that in the next Try It Out.

Suppose you have a program that needs to verify that the user entered a valid Social Security number (SSN). A valid SSN is of the format ddd-dd-dddd, which means a field of three digits, a dash, two digits, another dash, and finally a four-digit sequence. What you want to do is extend the `String` class to add a method that checks for a valid SSN. Figure 16-4 shows a sample run of the program you are about to write. The next section presents an example of how you can use extension methods.

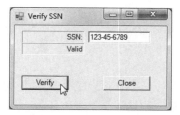

FIGURE 16-4: Using extension methods

TRY IT OUT Using Extension Methods (Chapter16ProgramInheritance.zip)

In the program shown in Figure 16-4, the user enters a SSN to be checked. The Verify button then calls code that determines whether the user entry forms a valid SSN or not and displays a message about the number entered. Although the format shown for the SSN in Figure 16-4 is the normal pattern for an SSN, sometimes you see SSN's entered as just a sequence of 9 digits with the dashes omitted. You should write your extension method to accept both forms.

To try out the extension program:

1. Create a new project in the normal way.

2. Create a user interface with two label, one textbox, and two button objects. You can also download the code from file `Chapter16ProgramInheritance.zip`.

3. Add the code from Listings 16-4 and 16-5.

How It WorksYou see the code for the extension method, as presented in Listing 16-4. You need to use the `System.Text.RegularExpression` reference because the code uses the regular expression parser library. In this example, you do use the `namespace` keyword to give the extension method its own identity (`StringExtensionMethods`).

LISTING 16-4: Source Code for clsExtension. (clsExtension.cs)

```
using System;
using System.Text.RegularExpressions;

namespace StringExtensionMethods
{
    public static class clsExtension
    {
        // For details on regualr expression pattern options, see:
        // http://www.regular-expressions.info/reference.html

        public static bool CheckValidSSN(this string str)
        {
            int len = str.Length;

            Regex pattern = null;
    // Is it xxx-xx-xxxx or xxxxxxxxx?
            if (len == 11 || len == 9)
            {
                if (len ==  9)
                {                   // Accept 9 digit characters
                    pattern = new Regex(@"\d{9}");
                } else {            // Accept ddd-dd-dddd
                    pattern =  new Regex(@"\d{3}-\d{2}-\d{4}");
                }
                return pattern.IsMatch(str);
            }
            else
            {
            return false;          // Not valid
            }
        }
    }
}
```

The regular expression parser provides an easy way for you to look for patterns in a string. For example, the pattern

```
\d{3}-\d{2}-\d{4}
```

says to look for three decimal digits (the \d {3} component) followed by a dash, then two decimal digits, another dash, and finally four more decimal digits. (Recall that the ampersand (@) before a string means that any dashes are not to be interpreted as an escape sequence but as part of the string itself.) The call to IsMatch() passes in the pattern to be checked and returns true of the string matches the pattern or false otherwise. The URL address that appears in Listing 16-4 provides a concise explanation of most of the pattern options you can use with the regular expression parser.

The signature for CheckValidSSN() begins with the keyword this. Because this always refers to the current object, CheckValidSSN() has a reference to the string being checked by the call. You can see what this means in Listing 16-5.

LISTING 16-5: Program to Use Extension Methods. (frmMain.cs)

```csharp
using System;
using System.Windows.Forms;
using StringExtensionMethods;

public class frmMain : Form
{
    private Label label1;
    private Label lblResult;
    private TextBox txtSSN;
    private Button btnVerify;
    private Button btnClose;

    #region Windows Code

    public frmMain()
    {
        InitializeComponent();
    }


    [STAThread]
    public static void Main()
    {
        frmMain main = new frmMain();
        Application.Run(main);
    }

    private void btnVerify_Click(object sender, EventArgs e)
    {
        string str = txtSSN.Text;

        if (str.CheckValidSSN())
            lblResult.Text = "Valid";
        else
            lblResult.Text = "Invalid";

    }

    private void btnClose_Click(object sender, EventArgs e)
    {
        Close();
    }
}
```

At the top of the listing you can see

```csharp
using StringExtensionMethods;
```

which makes the extension method available for use in the program. The rest of the code in the listing is nothing you haven't seen a dozen times before, except the call to the extension method:

```csharp
if (str.CheckValidSSN())
    lblResult.Text = "Valid";
```

```
else
    lblResult.Text = "Invalid";
```

You can call your validation method using the same syntax as any other other string method.

Wait a minute.

The signature for `CheckValidSSN()` says it expects a string to be passed to it. Ah, yes, but the keyword `this` in the signature tells the method that it is the current object that is being referenced by the call. Therefore, the extension method already has access to the string being tested and doesn't need the string to be passed. The call returns `true` or `false` depending on the content of the string and the appropriate label displays.

Extension methods give you a convenient way to extend the functionality of a class without using inheritance. If you ever say: "I wish this class could do....", you might consider writing an extension method. This is especially true if you write repetitive tests for string patterns or data values.

SUMMARY

This chapter completed your study of the three pillars of object-oriented programming: encapsulation, inheritance, and polymorphism. Throughout the importance of encapsulating your data inside a class or methods has been stressed. In this chapter you learned how the `protected` access specifier permits you to encapsulate data, yet share it with derived classes as needed. You learned how the base class serves as a common denominator for related, yet distinct, classes. You also learned how polymorphism enables you to have each derived class react to messages in a way that is appropriate for it. Finally, you saw how extension methods can extend the functionality of a class by "tacking on" new methods without having to use inheritance.

EXERCISES

You can find the answers to the following exercises in Appendix A.

1. A golf club wants to set up a membership program that can send mail, e-mails, and voting ballots to its members. The membership consists of junior, regular, and senior golfing members, plus a social membership, which excludes golf. The problem is that junior and social members are not allowed to vote on club issues. Also, social members should not receive mailings about golf tournaments because they are not allowed to use the course, only the pool and restaurant facilities. If you were to write the program, how would you organize it?

2. Suppose you see the following line of code in a program:

```
public clsJunior(string addr, int status, decimal minimum)
              : base(addr, status, minimum)
```

What can you tell me about the purpose of this line of code?

3. Some programmers don't like the `protected` access specifier. What do you think might be their reasons?

4. How would you prevent other programmers from extending one of your classes via inheritance?

5. Does inheritance bring anything to the party that you couldn't do without it?

▶ **WHAT YOU HAVE LEARNED IN THIS CHAPTER**

TOPIC	KEY POINTS
Inheritance	The ability to extend existing classes to accommodate the need for different properties and methods without duplicating code.
Why inheritance is useful	It enables you to reuse and simplify your code.
Base (parent) class	The class from which other classes are derived.
Derived (child) class	The class(es) that inherit the properties and methods from the base class.
`protected`	An access specifier that enables properties and methods to be shared between base and derived classes.
Polymorphism	The capability for each derived class to respond in its own way to program events.
Extension methods	How to extend class functionality without using inheritance.

17

Printing and Threading

WHAT YOU WILL LEARN IN THIS CHAPTER:

➤   How to initialize a printer object

➤   How to alter things such as fonts, page size, and margins

➤   How to create a printer class that can be used in other programs

➤   What threading is and how to use it with your printer class

➤   What reflection is

WROX.COM CODE DOWNLOADS FOR THIS CHAPTER

You can find the wrox.com code downloads for this chapter at www.wrox.com/remtitle
.cgi?isbn=9781118336922 on the Download Code tab. The code in the Chapter17 folder is
individually named according to the names throughout the chapter.

In this chapter you learn about using your printer and the resources associated with it. Some
of the topics learned here can be retrofitted to previous programs. For example, threading
might be useful in the database programs where there is a noticeable pause while network
information is updated.

USING A PRINTER

Often a program generates data that you don't necessarily want to persist on disk, but that you
might like to review at a later time without rerunning the program. Obviously, printed output of the data is one way to go. In this chapter, you examine some of the printer objects that
should prove useful in your programs.

In the following Try It Out you write a program that can read and print a simple text file.
Although a text file is used for the output to print, the methods used apply to almost any type
of data.

TRY IT OUT **Printing (Chapter17ProgramBasicPrint.zip)**

In this Try It Out, you write a program that simply opens a text file for printing. Rather than simply opening a file and dumping its contents to the printer, you can allow users to "preview" the content of the file before they print it. Often it's difficult to remember which files contain what. The content preview provides one way to do this. The user interface for your program is shown in Figure 17-1. The program uses a listbox, a label, and three button objects. Not visible is a PrintDialog object.

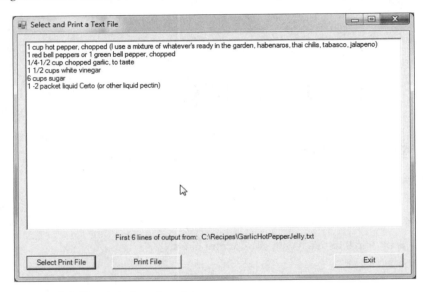

FIGURE 17-1: User interface for print program

Because this program is a little long, the easiest way to set things up is to create a new project and download the code found on this book's web page on Wrox.com, in `Chapter17ProgamBasicPrint.zip`. The steps for writing the program follow:

1. Create a new project in the usual manner.

2. Add the listbox, label, and button objects using Figure 17-1 as a model. Note that the label has its `Visibility` property set to `False` at program start.

3. Download the code for the project `Chapter17ProgamBasicPrint.zip`.

How It Works

Listing 17-1 shows the code associated with the `frmMain` code.

LISTING 17-1: Code to Print a Text File (frmMain.cs)

```
using System;
using System.Windows.Forms;
```

```
public class frmMain : Form
{
    private System.Windows.Forms.Button btnSelectPrintFile;
    private System.Windows.Forms.Button btnExit;
    private System.Windows.Forms.Button btnPrint;
    private System.Windows.Forms.TextBox txtSampleOutput;
    private PrintDialog prdMyPrintDialog;
    private Label lblSample;

    const int LINESTOPRINT = 6;     // Let them peek at this many lines
    string inFile = null;

    #region Windows Form Designer generated code

    public frmMain()
    {
        InitializeComponent();
    }

    [STAThread]
    public static void Main()
    {
        frmMain main = new frmMain();
        Application.Run(main);
    }

    private void btnSelectPrintFile_Click(object sender, EventArgs e)
    {
        clsSelectPrintFile myFile = new clsSelectPrintFile();
        myFile.SelectPrintFile();
        inFile = myFile.FileName;
        myFile.ReadSampleFromFile(inFile, LINESTOPRINT);
        txtSampleOutput.Text = myFile.GetBuffer;
        lblSample.Text = "First " + LINESTOPRINT.ToString() +
                         " lines of output from:  " + inFile;
        lblSample.Visible = true;
    }

    private void btnExit_Click(object sender, EventArgs e)
    {
        Close();
    }

    private void btnPrint_Click(object sender, EventArgs e)
    {
        try
        {
            if (inFile == null)
            {
                MessageBox.Show("Select a file to print first",
                                "Input File Name Error");
                return;
            }
            DialogResult result = prdMyPrintDialog.ShowDialog();
            clsPrint doPrint = new clsPrint(inFile);
```

continues

LISTING 17-1 *(continued)*

```
// If the result is OK then print the document.
            if (result == DialogResult.OK)
            {
                doPrint.Print();
            }
        }
        catch (Exception ex)
        {
            MessageBox.Show("Error: " + ex.Message);
            return;
        }
    }
}
```

After the form displays, the user must click the btnSelectPrintFile button to select the file to print. The first thing that happens in the click event is to instantiate a clsSelectPrintFile object named myFile. The code for the clsSelectPrintFile is shown in Listing 17-2.

LISTING 17-2: Source Code for clsSelectedPrintFile (clsSelectedPrintFile.cs)

```
using System;
using System.Windows.Forms;
using System.IO;

class clsSelectPrintFile
{
    const int SAMPLELINES = 6;

    private string fileName;
    private string buffer;

    //================================ Construcctor =================
    public clsSelectPrintFile()
    {
        buffer = null;
        fileName = null;
    }

    private StreamReader myReader;
    //================================ Property Methods =============
    public string FileName
    {
        get
        { return fileName;
        }
    }

    public string GetBuffer
    {
        get
        { return buffer;
```

```csharp
        }
    }

//================================ General Methods ===============
public string SelectPrintFile()
{
    try
    {
        OpenFileDialog myFile = new OpenFileDialog();
        myFile.Title = "Select File to Print";
        myFile.InitialDirectory = @"C:\ ";
        myFile.FilterIndex = 2;
        myFile.Filter = "Text files (*.txt | .txt | All files (*.*) | *.*";
        if (myFile.ShowDialog() == DialogResult.OK)
        {
            fileName = myFile.FileName;
            return myFile.FileName;
        }
        fileName = null;
        return null;
    }
    catch (Exception ex)
    {
        MessageBox.Show("File read error: " + ex.Message);
        return null;
    }
}

public void ReadSampleFromFile(string infile, int LINESTOPRINT)
{
    int lineCount = 0;
    string temp;

    try
    {
        myReader = new StreamReader(infile);

        while (true)
        {
            temp = myReader.ReadLine();
            if (temp == null)
                break;
            buffer += temp + Environment.NewLine;
            lineCount++;
            if (lineCount >= LINESTOPRINT)
                break;
        }
        myReader.Close();
    }
    catch
    {
        buffer = null;
    }
}
}
```

The method named `SelectPrintFile()` uses the `OpenFileDialog` object discussed in Chapter 13. (See Figure 17-2.)

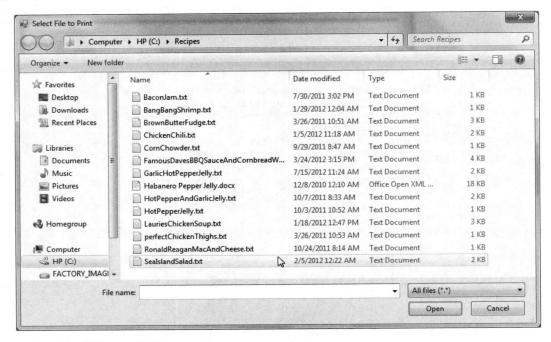

FIGURE 17-2: Selecting the file to print

Assuming all goes well (note the `try-catch` if things don't go well), the name of the file the user wants to use is passed back to `frmMain` and assigned into `inFile`. The statement:

```
myFile.ReadSampleFromFile(inFile, LINESTOPRINT);
```

calls the `ReadSampleFromFile()` method of the `clsSelectPrintFile` class, passing in the filename and the number of lines you want to display. The lines display in the listbox, as shown in Figure 17-1. By displaying a few lines in the listbox, users can confirm that the selected file contains the information they want to print.

If users are happy with the content of the file selected, they can click the Print File button to actually print the file. The code for `clsPrint` is shown in Listing 17-3.

LISTING 17-3: The clsPrint Print Code, (clsPrint.cs)

```csharp
using System;
using System.Drawing.Printing;
using System.Drawing;
using System.IO;

class clsPrint
```

```
{
    private string inFile;

    private Font myFont;
    private StreamReader myReader;

    public clsPrint(string file)
    {
        inFile = file;
    }

    public int Print()
    {
        try {

            myReader = new StreamReader (inFile);   // File to print
            myFont = new Font ("Arial", 10);        // Use this font and size

            PrintDocument myDocToPrint = new PrintDocument();
            // PrintPage event handler
            myDocToPrint.PrintPage += new
                        PrintPageEventHandler(this.PrintTextFileHandler);
            myDocToPrint.Print();
            if (myReader != null)   // If reader not closed already...
                myReader.Close();
            return 1;

        } catch {
            return -1;
        }
    }

    private void PrintTextFileHandler (object sender, PrintPageEventArgs printArgs)
    {
        int lineCount = 0;
        int index;

        float linesAllowed = 0.0f;
        const int CHARSPERLINE = 100;
        float yCoord = 0.0f;
        // The .5f below is kinda arbitrary, but it works
        float leftMargin = printArgs.MarginBounds.Left * .5f;
        float topMargin = printArgs.MarginBounds.Top;

        string buffer = null;
        string temp;
        Graphics g = printArgs.Graphics;

        // How many lines per page?
        linesAllowed = printArgs.MarginBounds.Height /
                    myFont.GetHeight (g);

        // Read the file
        while (lineCount < linesAllowed && ((buffer =
            myReader.ReadLine()) != null))
```

continues

LISTING 17-3 *(continued)*

```
        {
                        // Get the starting position
                        yCoord = topMargin + (lineCount * myFont.GetHeight(g));
                        // Wrap line if necessary
                        if (buffer.Length > CHARSPERLINE)
                        {
                            index = buffer.LastIndexOf(" ", (CHARSPERLINE - 10));
                            temp = buffer.Substring(0, index) +
                                        Environment.NewLine;
                            g.DrawString(temp, myFont, Brushes.Black, leftMargin,
                                        yCoord, new StringFormat());
                            lineCount++;      // Add for the extra line
                             // Set y coord for next line
                            yCoord = topMargin + (lineCount *
                                    myFont.GetHeight(g));

            // The rest of the line, with double-margin spacing added
                            g.DrawString(buffer.Substring(index + 1), myFont,
                                Brushes.Black, leftMargin + leftMargin, yCoord,
                                new StringFormat());
                            lineCount++;
                        }
                        else
                        {
                            g.DrawString(buffer, myFont, Brushes.Black,
                                        leftMargin, yCoord, new StringFormat());
                            lineCount++;
                        }
                    }

                    if (buffer == null)       // Are we done?
                    {
                        printArgs.HasMorePages = false; // yep
                    }
                    else
                    {
                        printArgs.HasMorePages = true;   // nope
                    }
                myReader = null;      // We're done with it
            }
        }
```

The Print() method in clsPrint class opens the selected file and sets the font and margins for the document. The rest of the code simply figures out how many lines have been printed (line-Count) and uses that information to set the print head for the document. The Environment.NewLine is appended to each line, so the next line begins on a new line. The actual printing is done using the graphics object, g, using its DrawString() method. The process continues as long as the StreamReader object (myReader) doesn't return null. When myReader reads null, all the characters in the file have been read.

THREADING

So far, so good. However, a problem often associated with printing a document is that it can take a long time. Depending on your printer and the size of the document, it could take several minutes for the document to print. While you are sitting there waiting for it to finish, perhaps you could use the program to look for the next file to print. Alas, that has to wait for the current file to finish printing. Not good.

You can solve this problem by making the program take advantage of a concept called *threading*. To keep things simple, when you design a program, perhaps using the Five Program Steps you learned about in Chapter 2, you can set the architecture for that application. Thus far, every program you have written has a single process that begins with the `Main()` method as typically found in the `frmMain` class. That single process is bound by whatever set of instructions your program feeds to it. Life is good...and simple.

When an application starts executing, the operating system dedicates a set of code instructions, memory, and other resources to that application. If there is but a single process running (for example, `Main()`), you can think of the application and its process as one and the same. Obviously, you can have multiple applications running under Windows.

As I write this, I am running a word processing application, an Internet browser, and the Task Manager application. Basically, I have three applications running. However, look at Figure 17-3, which shows that there are actually 28 processes running on my system. Further, if you look at the Internet browser application, you see that the browser is responsible for 12 of those 28 processes. If you look further, you can see that one of those 12 processes is running 27 threads.

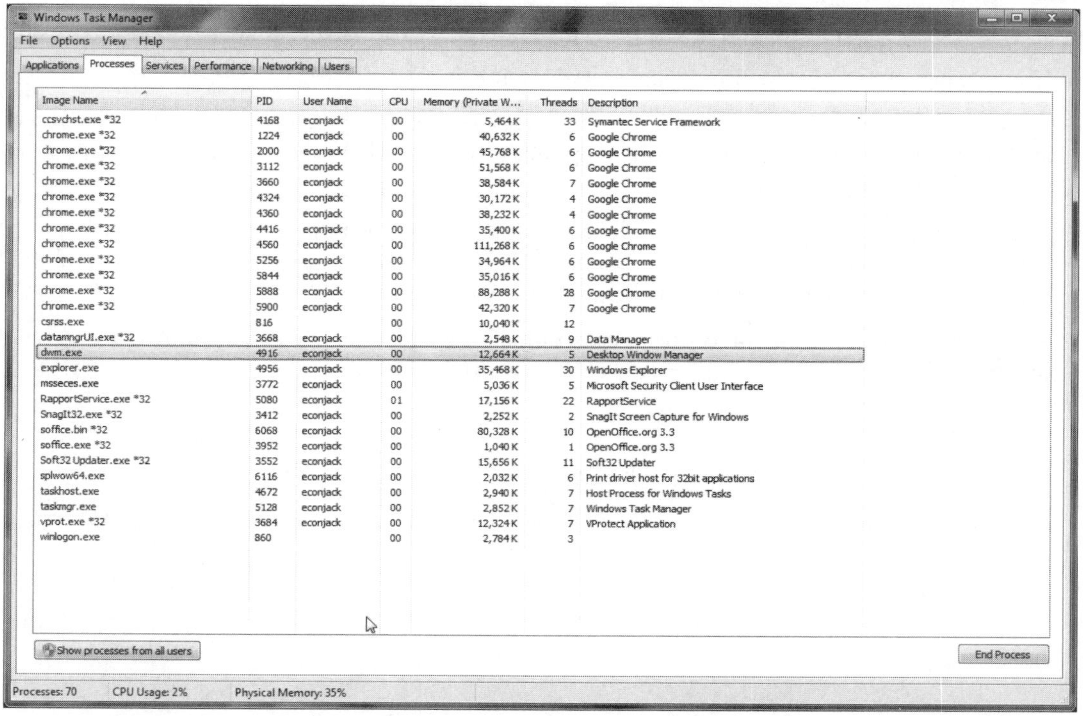

FIGURE 17-3: Using the Task Manager to show the Processes that are running

You can think of a thread as a separate set of instructions running within a process. Although each thread has its own stack (for temporary data), each thread shares its program memory and heap space with the process to which it belongs. Each application must have at least one process, and each process must have at least one thread. As Figure 17-3 shows, however, an application can have multiple processes, and those processes can have multiple threads. although it may appear that Windows is loafing along running three applications, which is true, all the processes and their threads keep Windows fairly busy.

A Threading Program

Although the print program functions as it should, it still leaves a little bit to be desired. The major shortcoming is that users have to sit there and wait for the print job to finish before they can do something else. Perhaps they have a second file to print. Users can't even look for the second file until after the first file is completely printed. Not good.

You can remove this limitation by implementing threading in your printer program. Although there are all kinds of problems that threading can conjure up (for example, deadlocks, race conditions, and so on), especially when accessing a database, your printing task is fairly simple, yet still gives you a chance to get your feet wet with threading.

In the following Try It Out you write a program that combines the printing and threading concepts into a single application.

> **TRY IT OUT**   Printing with Threading (Chapter17ProgramThreadingPrint.zip)

In this Try It Out, you want to modify the print program you wrote earlier to accommodate threading.

1. Create a new project in the usual manner, calling it **Print**.

2. Download the code from the book's website, `Chapter17ProgramThreadingPrint.zip`. (The code is almost identical to the previous print program, so you could also just move a copy of that program into this project's directory.)

3. Add a label object, `lblJobDone`, and place it somewhere between the Print File and Exit buttons. Set its `Text` property to `Print job finished`. Set its `Visibility` property to `false`. You don't want this button visible when the program starts executing.

4. Add a `BackgroundWorker` object from the Toolbox ⇨ Components menu option. You can see this in Figure 17-4.

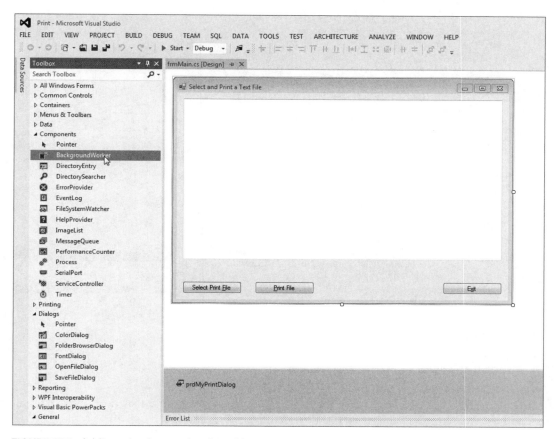

FIGURE 17-4: Adding a backgroundworker object to project.

5. Change the name of the `BackgroundWorker` object to `myBackgroundWorker`.

6. With the `myBackgroundWorker` object showing in the Properties Window, click the lightning bolt to switch to the object's events. The Properties Window now looks something like Figure 17-5.

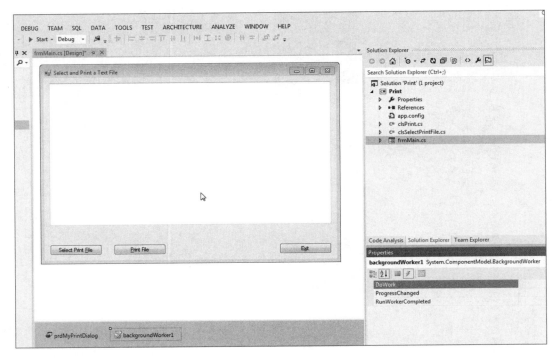

FIGURE 17-5: Adding event handlers to project

7. Double-click the `DoWork` and then the `RunWorkerCompleted` events. This causes Visual Studio to add the stub code for these events.

That's all you need to do in the design stage, but you do need to add some new code to the program.

The code for your threading program is presented in Listing 17-4.

LISTING 17-4: Print with Threading (frmMain.cs)

```csharp
using System;
using System.Windows.Forms;
using System.Threading;
using System.ComponentModel;


public class frmMain : Form
{
    private System.Windows.Forms.Button btnSelectPrintFile;
    private System.Windows.Forms.Button btnExit;
    private System.Windows.Forms.Button btnPrint;
    private System.Windows.Forms.TextBox txtSampleOutput;
    private PrintDialog prdMyPrintDialog;
    private Label lblSample;
```

```
const int LINESTOPRINT = 6;     // Let'em see this many lines

private System.ComponentModel.BackgroundWorker
                            myBackgroundWorker;
private Label lblJobDone;
string inFile = null;


public frmMain()
{
    InitializeComponent();
}


[STAThread]
public static void Main()
{
    frmMain main = new frmMain();
    Application.Run(main);
}

private void btnSelectPrintFile_Click(object sender,
                                     EventArgs e)
{
    clsSelectPrintFile myFile = new clsSelectPrintFile();
    myFile.SelectPrintFile();
    inFile = myFile.FileName;
    myFile.ReadSampleFromFile(inFile, LINESTOPRINT);
    txtSampleOutput.Text = myFile.GetBuffer;
    lblSample.Text = "First " + LINESTOPRINT.ToString() +
                     " lines of output from:  " + inFile;
    lblSample.Visible = true;
}

private void btnExit_Click(object sender, EventArgs e)
{
    Close();
}

private void btnPrint_Click(object sender, EventArgs e)
{
    try
    {    // Make sure "job done" message is hidden
        lblJobDone.Visible = false;
        if (inFile == null)
        {
            MessageBox.Show("Select a file to print first",
                      "Input File Name Error");
            return;
        }
        clsPrint doPrint = new clsPrint(inFile);
        DialogResult result = prdMyPrintDialog.ShowDialog();

        // If the result is OK then print the document.
```

continues

LISTING 17-4 *(continued)*

```
            if (result == DialogResult.OK)
            {
                myBackgroundWorker.RunWorkerAsync(doPrint);
            }
        }
        catch (Exception ex)
        {
            MessageBox.Show("Error: " + ex.Message);
            return;
        }
    }

    private void myBackgroundWorker_DoWork(object sender,
                System.ComponentModel.DoWorkEventArgs e)
    {
        try
        {
            clsPrint myPrinterJob = e.Argument as clsPrint;
// If you want to test this without wasting paper, uncomment the
// next line and comment out the call to myPrinterJob.Print();
            // Thread.Sleep(10000);
             // Comment out to avoid printing

            myPrinterJob.Print();
            e.Result = myPrinterJob;
        } catch (Exception ex) {
            MessageBox.Show("Error in DoWork: " + ex.Message);
        }
    }

    private void myBackgroundWorker_RunWorkerCompleted(object
                sender, RunWorkerCompletedEventArgs e)
    {
        // Let them know the job's done...
        lblJobDone.Visible = true;
    }
}
```

How It Works

Notice in the code that two new namespaces, `Threading` and `ComponentModel`, are added because the code references objects in those namespaces. Also near the top of the listing the statement

```
private System.ComponentModel.BackgroundWorker myBackgroundWorker;
```

is defined because of the `BackgroundWorker` object you need to use.

If you look closely at the code, virtually everything is the same, except in the `btnPrint` click event Instead of calling

```
doPrint.Print();
```

the code calls

```
myBackgroundWorker.RunWorkerAsync(doPrint);
```

The `RunWorkerAsync()` method causes the `DoWork()` threading event to be invoked. Note that the `doPrint` object is passed to the event handler so that the handler has access to any `clsPrint` data it may need. (Obviously, the event handler is going to need to know which file to print.)

Inside the event handler is the statement

```
clsPrint myPrinterJob = e.Argument as clsPrint;
```

In essence, the right side of the expression takes whatever was passed to the event handler as argument `e` and casts it as a `clsPrint` object using the `as` keyword. You've seen casts before, where you simply placed parentheses around the data type you want, as in

```
float val = (float) 12;
```

Knowing that, why not simply use the cast operator here? Well, the problem is that the cast operator works only with value types, not objects. The `as` keyword enables you to cast one object (for example, `e.Argument`) into another type of object (for example, `clsPrint`). In the code, this changes the event argument that was passed into the event handler (`doPrint`) into a `clsPrint` object. You do this so you can use your `Print()` method that's within `clsPrint`.

How does the thread know which file to print? This is not a problem because you already set the `inFile` property in `clsPrint` before you clicked the Print button. (If you didn't set it, `inFile` would be null and an error message would be issued.) When the print job finishes, the `myPrinterJob` object is set to `e.Result` and the event handler relinquishes control. This causes the last event handler, `myBackgroundWorker_RunWorkerCompleted()`, to fire. All this event does is change the Visibility property of `lblJobDone` to `true`, which causes the Print Job Finished message to display.

What Have You Gained with Threading?

The main benefit of adding threading to your program is that users don't need to sit in front of their monitor waiting for a print job to finish. If they have a second file to print, users can start looking for it by clicking the Select Print File button before the current file finishes printing.

If you want to test this "no-waiting" feature without wasting a lot of paper in the process, uncomment the line:

```
// Thread.Sleep(10000);
```

in the `DoWork()` event handler and comment out

```
myPrinterJob.Print();
```

These changes cause the program to pause for 10 seconds instead of printing the file, which is long enough for you to click the Select Print File button and verify that it works even as the printer is doing its thing.

Another benefit of adding threading to the basic print program is that you can see how simple it is to make your programs take advantage of threading if the need arises.

REFACTORING

Simply stated, refactoring is making changes to an existing program to either make it perform better or simplify the code. Figure 17-6 shows the different refactoring options as seen in the code editor's context menu.

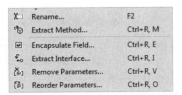

X⁻	Rename...	F2
⚙	Extract Method...	Ctrl+R, M
☑	Encapsulate Field...	Ctrl+R, E
ℒₒ	Extract Interface...	Ctrl+R, I
[ₐ]	Remove Parameters...	Ctrl+R, V
[ₐ]	Reorder Parameters...	Ctrl+R, O

FIGURE 17-6: Refactoring options

Rename

Simply stated, the Rename refactoring option enables you to rename a variable, method, class, or other program element. To use this option, simply move the cursor onto the element you want to change, double-click to highlight it, and then press F2. (You can also right-click the element to bring up the Refactor menu.) After you fill in the new name, Visual Studio makes the appropriate changes.

You may be thinking, "Why not just use the editor's search-and-replace functionality?" The reason is because Refactoring knows about the concept of scope and the editor doesn't. That is, if you have a variable named `flag` defined in one statement block and another variable with the same name in a different statement block, Refactoring changes only the occurrences of `flag` that have the same scope level. Using the editor for such changes makes the name change with no regard to scope... probably not what you have in mind.

Extract Method

The Extract Method refactoring option enables you to take duplicated code and easily integrate it into a method. For example, consider the RDC shown in Listing 17-5. Each textbox object has code tied to the object's Leave event (that is, the event that is fired when you press the Tab key to advance the cursor to the next field).

In the following Try It Out you use the code listing to see what the Extract Method refactoring brings to the party.

TRY IT OUT   Extract Method

To see how the Extract Method works, follow these steps:

1. Create a new project using the project name ExtractMethod.

2. Type in the code in Listing 17-5. (Or download it; it's in the `Chapter17ProgramRefactor.zip` file.)

3. Add three label and corresponding textbox objects plus an Exit button.

Your user interface might look similar to Figure 17-7.

FIGURE 17-7: Extract Method user interface

LISTING 17-5: Program Without Refactoring

```csharp
using System;
using System.Text.RegularExpressions;
using System.Windows.Forms;

public class frmMain : Form
{
    private Label label1;
    private Label label2;
    private Label label3;
    private TextBox txtHomePhone;
    private TextBox txtCellPhone;
    private TextBox txtWorkPhone;
    private Button btnCheck;
    private Button btnExit;

    // Regex myRegex = new Regex();

    #region Windows Code

    public frmMain()
    {
        InitializeComponent();
    }

    [STAThread]
    public static void Main()
    {
        frmMain main = new frmMain();
        Application.Run(main);
    }

    private void txtHomePhone_Leave(object sender,
                            EventArgs e)
    {
        Regex regexObj = new Regex("\\d{3}-\\d{4}");

        if (regexObj.IsMatch(txtHomePhone.Text) == false)
        {
            // Wrong format
            MessageBox.Show("Phone number must be in
                XXX-NNNN format.", "Format Error");
            txtHomePhone.Focus();
            return;
        }
    }

    private void txtWorkPhone_Leave(object sender,
                            EventArgs e)
    {
        Regex regexObj = new Regex("\\d{3}-\\d{4}");

        if (regexObj.IsMatch(txtWorkPhone.Text) == false)
```

continues

LISTING 17-5 *(continued)*

```
        {
            // Wrong format
            MessageBox.Show("Phone number must be in
                    XXX-NNNN format.", "Format Error");
            txtWorkPhone.Focus();
            return;
        }
    }

    private void txtCellPhone_Leave(object sender,
                EventArgs e)
    {
        Regex regexObj = new Regex("\\d{3}-\\d{4}");

        if (regexObj.IsMatch(txtCellPhone.Text) == false)
        {
            // Wrong format
            MessageBox.Show("Phone number must be in
                    XXX-NNNN format.", "Format Error");
            txtCellPhone.Focus();
            return;
        }
    }

    private void btnExit_Click(object sender, EventArgs e)
    {
        Close();
    }
}
```

How It Works

Looking closely at the code, you see that the code fragment

```
Regex regexObj = new Regex("\\d{3}-\\d{4}");
if (regexObj.IsMatch(txtWorkPhone.Text) == false)
{
    // Wrong format
    MessageBox.Show("Phone number must be in
            XXX-NNNN format.", "Format Error");
    txtWorkPhone.Focus();
    return;
}
```

is repeated for each textbox object. If you highlight the code shown in the preceding fragment and then select the Extract Method refactor option (Ctrl+R, M), Visual studio creates a new method with the name you supply to the rename dialog (see Figure 17-8).

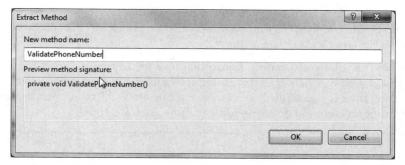

FIGURE 17-8: Extract method dialog

Clicking the OK button causes Visual Studio to create the following code:

```
private void ValidatePhoneNumber()
{
    Regex regexObj = new Regex("\\d{3}-\\d{4}");

    if (regexObj.IsMatch(txtHomePhone.Text) == false)
    {
        // Wrong format
        MessageBox.Show("Phone number must be in
            XXX-NNNN format.", "Format Error");
        txtHomePhone.Focus();
        return;
    }
}
```

To make this new method work for all textboxes, you still need to modify the code a little:

```
private void ValidatePhoneNumber(TextBox myTextbox)
{
    Regex regexObj = new Regex("\\d{3}-\\d{4}");

    if (regexObj.IsMatch(myTextbox.Text) == false)
    {
        // Wrong format
        MessageBox.Show("Phone number must be in
            XXX-NNNN format.", "Format Error");
        myTextbox.Focus();
        return;
    }
}
```

What you've done is add an argument to the method that allows you to pass in the textbox object to the method. Therefore, when you call the method

```
ValidatePhoneNumber(txtCellPhone);
```

the method knows to which object to send control that is the input is in error.

Although the code change in this example is fairly trivial, refactoring methods can save a huge amount of time when complex code is involved. The simplicity is enhanced when no arguments are passed to the refactored method. Still, it makes large scale changes simple.

The remaining refactoring options are what you'd expect. Encapsulating a field lets you change the access specifier for a specific field in a class, whereas Extract Interface enables you to convert one or more properties in a class to an interface if you want. The Remove Parameters and Reorder Parameters options simply go through the program code and delete or add a parameter to a method.

SUMMARY

This chapter ties together some of the less used features of C# and Visual Studio. Although threading is a technique common to many other languages, refactoring may be less pervasive. Still, these are more tools to hang on your belt.

EXERCISES

You can find the answers to the following exercises in Appendix A.

1. What would you guess is the most common mistake beginning programmers make when it comes to printing?

2. What is threading?

3. What does threading bring to the party?

4. What is a `BackgroundWorker`?

5. Are there any dangers to threading?

6. What is refactoring?

► **WHAT YOU HAVE LEARNED IN THIS CHAPTER**

TOPIC	KEY POINTS	
Printer object	What a printer object is and how it can be used in your programs.	
Printer properties and how they can be changed	How to change things such as fonts, margins, page margins, and related printer properties.	
Print class	How to write a printer class that wraps a lot of the printer details into a single class.	
Threading	A process in which a single program can have multiple processes.	
Reflection	The ability to make small improvements to your code with minimal effort.	

18

Web Programming

WHAT YOU WILL LEARN IN THIS CHAPTER:

➤ What a web page is and how it works

➤ The relationship between the client and web server

➤ The difference between static and dynamic web pages

➤ How to use C# with web pages

➤ How to write a simple dynamic web page

WROX.COM CODE DOWNLOADS FOR THIS CHAPTER

You can find the wrox.com code downloads for this chapter at `www.wrox.com/remtitle.cgi?isbn=9781118336922` on the Download Code tab. The code in the `Chapter17` folder is individually named according to the names throughout the chapter.

This chapter discusses how to use C# for programming web applications. There is no way that you can do justice to web programming in a single chapter. Indeed, there are hundreds of books devoted to just web programming. Instead, the goal here is to give you background information so that you understand the paradigm involved with programming for the web. After that, if you want to become more involved with web programming, there are a number of Wrox publications that can help you master the web.

Before you begin programming your first Internet web page, you need to understand the basics of how web pages are written and displayed on your browser.

STATIC WEB PAGES

Whenever you load your web browser and it displays an Internet page, whatever you see displayed on the monitor was constructed from a Hypertext Markup Language (HTML) script. A *static web page* is a page whose content never changes. Because the content never changes, the page always looks the same regardless of who visits the page or how they happened to land on that particular page. The view of the page is static and unchanging.

In the following Try It Out, you use Visual Studio to write a simple static web page. Assume you've loaded Visual Studio and are ready to make a project selection.

TRY IT OUT Static Web Page [Chapter18ProgramStaticWebPage.zip]

Writing a static Web page is not difficult—just follow these steps:

1. From the Visual Studio menu, select File ⇨ New ⇨ Web Site ⇨ ASP.NET Empty Web Site. This presents the dialog shown in Figure 18-1. The Web Location should be named **StaticWebPage**.

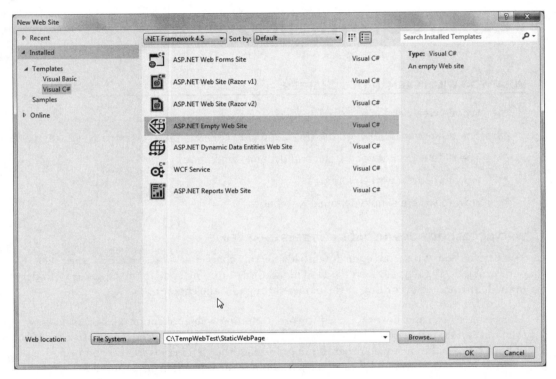

FIGURE 18-1: Web selection

2. Having made your selection, type in **StaticWebPage** for the project file and click OK. Visual Studio gets busy doing some background things and eventually presents you with the IDE that looks like Figure 18-2.

3. Move to the Solution Explorer Window, and right-click the project's name (StaticWebPage). Then select the Add ⇨ Web Form that calls up a dialog that asks you to enter the name of the form. This process is shown in Figure 18-3, whereas Figure 18-4 shows the dialog box.

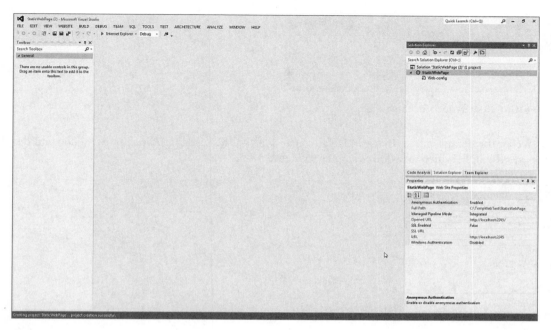

FIGURE 18-2: Visual studio environment

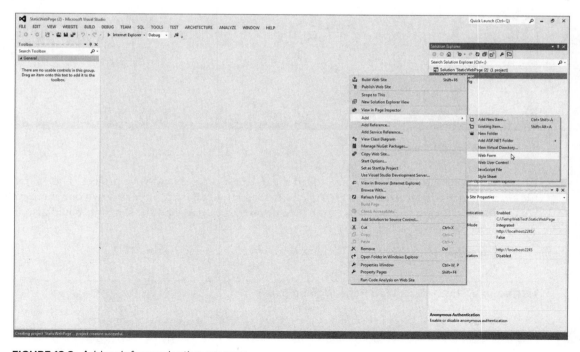

FIGURE 18-3: Add web form selection process

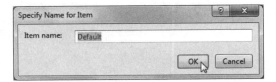

FIGURE 18-4: Web form name dialog

4. Accept the default name (that is, "Default") and click OK. Visual Studio creates the file and displays the IDE, which now looks similar to Figure 18-5.

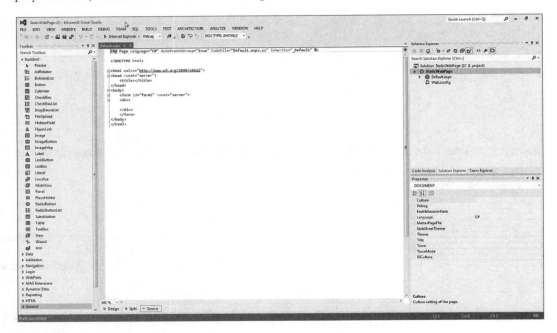

FIGURE 18-5: IDE after file selection

Notice that the Solution Explorer has added the Default.aspx file to your project. The .aspx file extension stands for Active Server Page Extended, and Default.aspx is now your static web page. (You could name the page **Default.htm** or **Default.html** and the same file could also be used as a web page.)

Replace that code you see in the Source Window with what you see in Listing 18-1.

LISTING 18-1: The Default Web Page (default.aspx)

```
<%@ Page Language="C#" AutoEventWireup="true" CodeFile="Default.aspx.cs"
              Inherits="_Default" %>

<!DOCTYPE html>
```

```html
<html xmlns="http://www.w3.org/1999/xhtml">
<head runat="server">
    <title>My First Web Page</title>
</head>
<body>
    <form id="form1" runat="server">
        <div>
            <h1>This is a static web page</h1>
            <br />
            Not much going on here...
        </div>
    </form>
</body>
</html>
```

Now run the program. Using whatever happens to be your default web browser, the output will look like that shown in Figure 18.6.

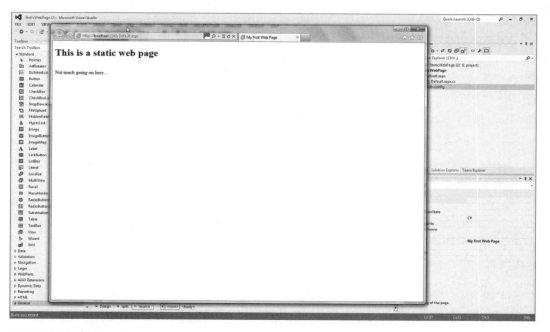

FIGURE 18-6: Static web page

Although this web page isn't much to look at, it can serve as a good starting point for a discussion about web pages.

How It Works

The first thing to notice is that the Source window has some new options presented at the bottom of the window, as shown in Figure 18-7.

FIGURE 18-7: Source Window options

The view you currently see on your display is the Source option, which displays the HTML code for the current web page. If you click on the Design option, the display changes and displays the current state of the page. In this example, the Design option looks like Figure 18-6. You can switch back and forth between these two windows to see the impact that your code changes in the Source window has on the way the page looks when it is displays. The Split option divides the Source window horizontally to enable you to see both the Source and Design windows at the same time. This saves you from having to click the option you want as you develop the page.

When you run the program (F5), the program looks like Figure 18.6. If you look closely, you can see that the URL address bar in the figure contains `http://localhost:2245/Default.aspx`.

The `http` means that you are using the Hypertext Transfer Protocol (HTTP) to exchange information between the server and the client. In this case, the term `localhost:2245` specifies that your computer is going to host the `Default.aspx` web page. The `.aspx` file extension stands for Active Server Page Extended and simply identifies the file as an extension of the older `.asp` file type. (Fortunately, these are details that Visual Studio uses in the background so you don't need to be concerned about them.) Stated differently, the line tells you the web page that is displayed on your computer. Using the `localhost` identifier makes it easier to develop, test, and debug a web application because you don't need to deploy the modified web page to some server each time you need to test the program.

Now that you know what the program looks like when it is run, examine the code for the web page. You can ignore the first two lines in Listing 18-1. Now consider the line

```
<!DOCTYPE html>
```

This line is an HTML comment line. The markup for a comment is

```
<! Comment >
```

where `<!` starts the comment and the `>` ends the comment. Technically, an HTML comment starts with `<!--` and ends with `-->`. If you change the comment to

```
<!-- DOCTYPE html -->
```

you can see that the font color changes to green to denote an HTML comment. If you run the program, there is no observable change in the program.

The next line

```
<html xmlns="http://www.w3.org/1999/xhtml">
<head runat="server">
```

defines the namespace for the HTML version used in the page. This reference tells you that Visual Studio uses Extended HTML. The next line simply says that the page is to be run at the server, in your case, the `localhost`.

The remainder of the program deals with displaying the page as you wrote it. You could simplify the page as shown here, and the output would still look the same.

```
<html>
    <head >
    <title>My First Web Page</title>
```

```
    </head>
    <body>
      <h1>This is a static web page</h1>
            <br />
            Not much going on here...
    </body>
  </html>
```

Although it may appear that much of the HTML in Listing 18-1 is unnecessary, that isn't the case when you develop more complex web pages.

Most of the HTML directives come in pairs. That is, an h1 header style is introduced with

```
<h1>
```

and terminates with

```
</h1>
```

These directives are often referred to as *HTML tags* or simply *tags*. The break tag, `<br />` doesn't require a pair of tags but still follows the convention of opening and closing brackets (`<>`).

The process to display a web page is shown in Figure 18-8. The user controlling the browser is called the *client*. (Technically, the browser is the client and it's the user who controls the browser. A browser is an application that can render HTML information on a display device.) The client requests a web page from the server (1). The system that stores the previously written HTML pages is called the *server*. When the client request comes in, the server locates the wanted web page (2) and then sends that page back to the browser (3). It is the responsibility of the browser to render the page on the browser for the client to view.

The server processing is limited to locating the proper page, and the processing on the client side is limited to the browser rendering the HTML page. The page does not change unless the client initiates some kind of request back to the server.

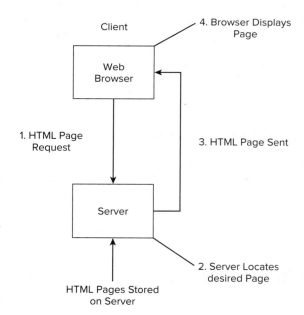

FIGURE 18-8: Process to display a web page

If you sit and watch the static web page for about one-half an hour, you can notice nothing changes. Static web pages are like that...they just sit there displaying the same content. Web browsing would be dull if all web pages were static. Fortunately, that's not the case. So now move on to see how dynamic web pages can liven things up a bit.

DYNAMIC WEB PAGES

Dynamic web pages have the capability to change their content. Visual Studio supports ASP.NET files that you can use on a dynamic web page. The web page you just created was a static web page but with the .aspx secondary file name. (As you learned earlier in this chapter, older ASP.NET files ended in. asp, whereas the extended pages have a secondary filename of. aspx. You use the .aspx files for the remainder of this chapter.)

ASP.NET files usually contain a blend of HTML script and ASP.NET tags. The ASP.NET tags enable you to mix in C# code with the HTML script to produce dynamic HTML pages. After the C# code executes, the results are reformatted into an HTML page that is then sent back to the browser for display.

Processing can be done on either the server or client side of the exchange. Most browsers, for example, have the capability to use JavaScript, Flash, and Silverlight code. Many servers can process code written in Java, Perl, ColdFusion, Python, Ruby, and ASP. If the server can process ASP.NET files, it has the capability to process pages with C#, Visual Basic, or C++ code. (They share a common intermediate language.) Although this duality exists, it seems clear that server-side processing wins the coin toss, especially in light of the advances in cloud computing. Sometimes this seems wasteful when I sit in front of my browser running on a computer with a quad-core CPU loafing along at 3Ghz, a megamunch of memory, a terabyte of storage but processing an HTML page that could be done in the blink of an eye by an 8080 CPU, not to mention the time wasted making the round trip to the server. Oh well....

In the next Try It Out, you develop a simple web application that calculates the monthly payment for a mortgage loan. Using the Five Program Steps from Chapter 2, the Initialization step doesn't require anything special other than the standard web setup information. The Input step requires the amount of the loan, the interest rate, and the number of months the mortgage is active. The Process step requires an algorithm that takes the data from the Input step and yields a monthly payment amount. The Output step simply involves formatting the payment amount as an HTML page and sending it back to the client. The Termination step doesn't require anything special. With this in mind, you can start.

TRY IT OUT **Mortgage Calculator [Chapter18ProgramMortgageCalculator.zip]**

The first thing you need to do is create a new project named MortgageCalculator. To do this, follow these steps:

1. Select new project using the File ⇨ New ⇨ Web Site and then select ASP.NET Empty Web Site (refer to Figure 18-1).

2. Give the new project the name **MortgageCalculator**.

3. In the Solution Explorer, right-click the project name, and use the Add ⇨ Add New and select Web Form from the dialog box, supplying the name Default.aspx (refer to Figure 18-4).

4. Select the Design tab at the bottom of the Source Window.

5. From the menu, select Format ⇨ Set Position ⇨ Absolute. This enables you to fix the location of the objects on the form.

6. Drag and drop four labels, four textboxes, and one button object onto the form. The user interface should look something like that shown in Figure 18-9.

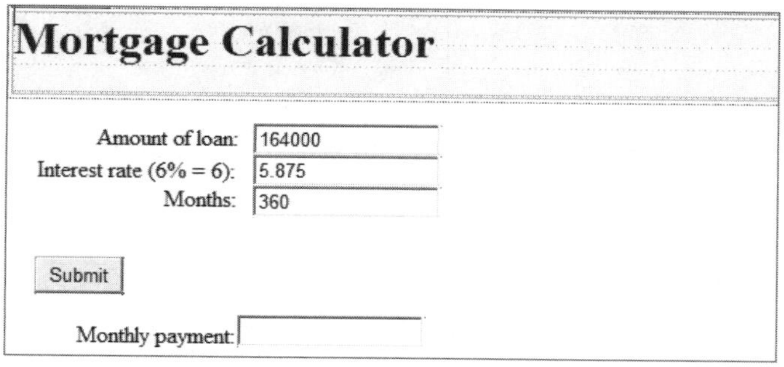

FIGURE 18-9: Mortgage calculator user interface

7. Apply the following attributes to the objects' properties, as shown in Table 18-1.

TABLE 18-1: Interface Objects and Their Settings

OBJECT TYPE	ID	PROPERTY	STATE
Textbox	txtAmount	Text	164000
Textbox	txtInterestRate	Text	5.88
Textbox	txtMonths	Text	360
Textbox	txtPayment	Visible	FALSE
Label*	lblPayment	Visible	FALSE
Button	btnSubmit	Text	Submit

* The first three labels can use their default name and values because they are not used in the program (That is, the default names are probably Label1 through Label3.)

The reason to write in values for the textbox objects is to make it easier when you run the program during testing and debugging. With the values shown, the monthly payment should be $970.12.

8. Click the Source tab at the bottom of the Source Window, and your code should look something like that shown in Listing 18-2.

LISTING 18-2: Mortgage Calculator Page (Default.aspx)

```
<%@ Page Language="C#" AutoEventWireup="true" CodeFile="Default.aspx.cs"
                 Inherits="_Default" %>
<!DOCTYPE html>
<html xmlns="http://www.w3.org/1999/xhtml">
<head runat="server">
```

continues

LISTING 18-2 *(continued)*

```
<title></title>
<style type="text/css">
    .auto-style1
    {
        width: 951px;
    }
    .auto-style2
    {
        width: 951px;
        height: 55px;
        position: absolute;
        left: 10px;
        top: 15px;
    }
    .auto-style3
    {
        height: 55px;
    }
    .auto-style4
    {
        position: absolute;
    }
    .auto-style5
    {
        left: 10px;
    }
    .auto-style6
    {
        top: 15px;
    }
</style>
</head>
<body>
    <form id="form1" runat="server" style="z-index: 1">
    <div class="auto-style2">
        <h1>Mortgage Calculator</h1>
        <asp:Label ID="Label1" runat="server" Font-Size="Medium"
                style="z-index: 1; left: 18px; top: 78px; position: absolute;
                 width: 136px; right: 797px; text-align: right;"
                Text="Amount of loan:"></asp:Label>
         <asp:TextBox ID="txtAmount" runat="server"
                style="z-index: 1; left: 165px; top: 77px; position:
                 absolute">164000</asp:TextBox>

        <asp:Label ID="Label2" runat="server" Font-Size="Medium"
          style="z-index: 1; left: 4px; top: 101px;
            position: absolute; width: 148px; right: 799px;
            text-align: right;" Text="Interest rate (6% = 6): ">
          </asp:Label>
         <asp:TextBox ID="txtInterestRate" runat="server"
            style="z-index: 1; left: 165px; top: 99px; position: absolute"
            TabIndex="1">5.875</asp:TextBox>
```

```
            <asp:TextBox ID="txtMonths" runat="server"
                style="z-index: 1; left: 165px; top: 121px; position: absolute"
                TabIndex="2">360</asp:TextBox>

            <asp:Button ID="btnSubmit" runat="server"
                style="z-index: 1; left: 16px; top: 172px; position: absolute"
                Text="Submit" TabIndex="3" OnClick="btnSubmit_Click" />    </div>

    <p>

            <asp:Label ID="lblPayment" runat="server" Font-Size="Medium"
                style="z-index: 1; left: 27px; top: 232px; position: absolute; width:
                  136px; right: 811px; height: 18px; text-align: right;"
                Text="Monthly payment:" Visible="False"></asp:Label>
    </p>

            <asp:Label ID="Label3" runat="server" Font-Size="Medium"
                style="z-index: 1; left: 27px; top: 136px; position: absolute; width:
                  136px; right: 808px; height: 18px; text-align: right;"
                Text="Months:"></asp:Label>
            <asp:TextBox ID="txtPayment" runat="server"
            style="z-index: 1; left: 165px; top: 227px; position: absolute"
            Visible="False"></asp:TextBox>
    </form>
</body>
</html>
```

If you have dragged and dropped the objects onto the web form, much of the code in Listing 18-2 has already been written for you by Visual Studio as you created the user interface. However, just cutting and pasting the code presented here is the easy way to do it.

9. Finally, double-click the Submit button, which opens the `Default.aspx.cs` and add the code shown in Listing 18-3. (Much of the stub code was automatically generated for you by Visual Studio.)

LISTING 18-3: The Code Behind Source Code for Mortgage Calculator (Default.aspx.cs)

```
using System;
using System.Text;


public partial class _Default : System.Web.UI.Page
{
    protected void Page_Load(object sender, EventArgs e)
    {

    }
    protected void btnSubmit_Click(object sender, EventArgs e)
    {
        bool flag;
        decimal amount;
```

continues

LISTING 18-3 *(continued)*

```csharp
        decimal interestRate;
        decimal months;
        decimal payment;
        decimal temp;

        flag = decimal.TryParse(txtAmount.Text, out amount);
        if (flag == false)
            payment = 0.0M;        // Bad input

        flag = decimal.TryParse(txtInterestRate.Text, out
                            interestRate);
        if (flag == false)
            payment = 0.0M;        // Bad input

        flag = decimal.TryParse(txtMonths.Text, out months);
        if (flag == false)
            payment = 0.0M;        // Bad input

        interestRate /= 1200;    // Need it as decimal fraction by month
        temp = (decimal) Math.Pow(1.0 + (double) interestRate,
                    (double)months);
        payment = interestRate * amount * (temp / (temp - 1.0M));

        StringBuilder myPayment = new StringBuilder();
        myPayment.AppendFormat("${0:F2}", payment);

        lblPayment.Visible = true;
        txtPayment.Visible = true;
        txtPayment.Text = myPayment.ToString();

    }
}
```

The code in Listing 18-3 is often called the code-behind file because it is the C# code that processes the information and, hence, is the work horse "behind" the web page.

You can now run the program.

How It Works

After you create the project and start to add objects to the web form in the Design mode, Visual Studio starts generating code in accordance to your interaction with the form. For example, consider the following line from Listing 18-2.

```
<asp:Label ID="Label2" runat="server" Font-Size="Medium"
  style="z-index: 1; left: 4px; top: 101px;
    position: absolute; width: 148px; right: 799px;
    text-align: right;" Text="Interest rate (6% = 6): ">
</asp:Label>
```

Because the name for this label object is not directly used in the code-behind file, the default name of Label2 is acceptable.

The `runat="server"` attribute means that the form and its related controls should be processed on the server and that the control can be accessed by server scripts. Most of the remainder of the line is concerned with the visible attributes of the object. In many cases, experienced programmers are so familiar with such code that they write the code faster themselves rather than dragging and dropping the objects.

In Listing 18-3, the `btnSubmit_Click()` event is triggered when the Submit button is clicked by the user of the web page. That method begins with several data definitions and then checks to see that the user supplied reasonable data via the `TryParse()` calls you've used before. Note how simple it is to add this code to the project. The information stored in the textboxes is actually on the client machine, but the processing is taking place on the server. The communication between the two is handled for you more or less automatically.

After the data is validated (this could be improved), the code calculates the appropriate monthly payment. Although you could use other means to format the answer, use a `StringBuilder` object to format the payment as a floating point number with two decimal points. (Notice the `using System.Text` reference.) The code then makes the result label and textbox visible and places the formatted result into the `txtPayment` textbox. The result is shown in Figure 18-10.

FIGURE 18-10: Web page with result

With the data supplied by the user, the monthly payment is $970.12.

Keep in mind what happened to make this simple program work when used on the web. First, the web page must be located when the user selects the page to use the mortgage calculator. That page is then sent back to users as an HTML document that displays on their browser.

Users then fill in the requested data and that data is sent back to the server. Because the page has ASP.NET tags in it, the server knows that the button click event in the code-behind file should be called for processing. This is known because of the

```
OnClick="btnSubmit_Click"
```

attribute in the Submit button's attribute list. This attribute tells the server which method to call when the user clicks the Submit button. After the C# code has done its job, the page is reformatted as an HTML page and returned to the user for viewing.

SUMMARY

Although fairly simple, this chapter showed how dynamic web pages can be constructed using Visual Studio. There are many ways to build more visually interesting web pages than what's presented here. As stated at the beginning of the chapter, web programming is worthy of a complete book. (You should consider the Wrox book *Beginning ASP.NET 4: in C# and VB* by Imar Spaanjaars (Wrox, 2010). This well-received book has more than 800 pages of how to write programs for the web.) The goal here, however, is simply to enable you to start investigating this popular element of C# programming.

EXERCISES

You can find the answers to the following exercises in Appendix A.

1. What is a web page?

2. What is the difference between static and dynamic web pages?

3. What is meant by the term code-behind file?

4. Look at the code in Listing 18-3 to find a reason why it is SDC.

5. Given that question 4 suggests that the program can crash, how would you fix this?

▶ **WHAT YOU HAVE LEARNED IN THIS CHAPTER**

TOPIC	KEY POINTS
Web page	An HTML document capable of being rendered in a web browser.
Web Client	The object that controls the web browser.
Web Server	The hardware that serves web pages to the client. It may or may not be responsible for page processing.
Static versus Dynamic Web pages	Static Web web pages have HTML content that does not change. Dynamic Web pages can respond to user (or other) input and alter the page rendering accordingly.
Code-behind file	The file that contains C# code that ASP.NET can process, thus affording the ability to alter the web page returned to the Client.

APPENDIX

Answers to Exercises

CHAPTER 2

Exercise 1 Solution

A class is a body of code that contains properties and methods that describe an object. An object is an instance of a class that can be used in a program. Classes and objects are related in that a class is a template from which an object is created. They are different in that a class is not directly used in a program, whereas an object is.

Exercise 2 Solution

The Five Program Steps:

➤   The Initialization step creates the environment in which the program is run.

➤   The Input step is responsible for collecting all the information necessary for the program to accomplish its given task.

➤   The Process step takes the data and acts on it in a way that accomplishes a given task.

➤   The Output step presents the results of the Process step in a way that is useful to the user.

➤   The Termination step is responsible for placing the program environment back to the state that prevailed before the program was run, updating any environment information that might be used the next time the program is run.

Exercise 3 Solution

The first statement defines a reference variable that you can use to access a `clsThingie` object. The second statement instantiates a `clsThingie` object and makes its properties and methods available through the reference variable named `myThingie`.

Exercise 4 Solution

A simple oven might have the following properties and methods:

```
// ================ Properties ===================
int ovenTemp;          // 0 is off, otherwise desired temperature
int ovenOnOff;
int ovenLight;         // 0 is off, 1 is on
int frontLeftBurner;   // 0 is off, otherwise its temperature
int frontRightBurner;
int backLeftBurner;
int backRightBurner;
int minutesToBake;     // Oven timer
// ================ Methods ===================
public int TurnOvenOn(int ovenTemp);
public int TurnOvenOff();
public int SetTimer(int minutes);
public int TurnFrontLeftBurnerOnOff(int front LeftBurner);
public int TurnFrontRightBurnerOnOff(int frontRightBurner);
public int TurnBackLeftBurnerOnOff(int backLeftBurner);
public int TurnBackRightBurnerOnOff(int backRightBurner);
public int OverLight(int ovenLight);
private int ReadTimer();
public int SelfClean(); // Set ovenTemp to MAX for 1 hour and shuts off
```

Exercise 5 Solution

A good interface is one that:

➤ Is intuitive to the user

➤ Gets the required information from the user easily

➤ Handles user input errors in a graceful manner

Exercise 6 Solution

There is no *correct* solution to the question of why you are making the effort to learn OOP, but you will probably find that answering this question is beneficial.

Exercise 7 Solution

For example, click `frmMain` in the Design view and change the form's `BackColor` to a color and see what happens.

CHAPTER 3

Exercise 1 Solution

The unsigned data types have the capability to essentially double the maximum positive number that a given unsigned data type can hold relative to its signed counterpart. The unsigned data attribute is only applicable to integral data types.

Exercise 2 Solution

All are legal except the following:

➤ 9WaysToSunday: Illegal because it starts with a number

➤ Ms.Mini: Illegal because it has a punctuation character (a period) in it

➤ Extern: Illegal because it is a keyword in C#

➤ My#Eye: Illegal because it has a reserved symbol (#) in it

Exercise 3 Solution

It appears that txtInput is a textbox object. The first dot operator gains you access to the Text object. Because Text is a String object, the next dot operator enables you to access the Length property of the Text object. Therefore, Length tells you how long the text string is in the textbox. That value is then assigned into len.

Exercise 4 Solution

First, the float data type uses 4 bytes of storage, whereas a double uses 8 bytes. Second, the range of numbers for a double is almost 10 times larger than for a float. Third, a float has only 7 digits of precision, whereas a double has 15.

Exercise 5 Solution

```
const int SNAKEEYES = 2;   // Minimum value for two die
const int BOXCARS = 12;    // Maximum value for two die

int ThrowDice()
{
    Random rnd = new Random();
            // Add 1 because it's exclusive
    return rnd.Next(SNAKEEYES, BOXCARS + 1);
}
```

Exercise 6 Solution

Use the decimal data type with its 28 digits of precision versus 15 for a double.

CHAPTER 4

Exercise 1 Solution

You can set a breakpoint at most points in the source code file. However, you cannot set a breakpoint on an empty line, on a line that uses the `using` keyword, or on a line that begins with a comment character. There may be other contexts in which a breakpoint cannot be set.

Exercise 2 Solution

The code for the button click event is:

```
private void btnCalc_Click(object sender, EventArgs e)
{
  bool flag;
  double operand1;
  double answer;

      //                        Input Step
      // Check first input...
  flag = double.TryParse(txtOperand1.Text, out operand1);
  if (flag == false)
  {
    MessageBox.Show("Enter Fahrenheit temperature", "Input Error");
    txtOperand1.Focus();
    return;
  }


      //                          Process Step

  answer = 5.0 / 9.0 * (operand1 - 32);

      //                         Display Step
  txtResult.Text = operand1.ToString() + " is " +
                   answer.ToString() + " Celsius";
  txtResult.Visible = true;

}
```

There are three magic numbers in this code, and you can replace them with:

```
const double RATIO5OVER9 = .555555555555555; // 5.0 / 9.0 in equation
const double FREEZEWATER = 32.0;
The equation then becomes:
    answer = RATIO5OVER9 * (operand1 - FREEZEWATER);
```

The only advantage of the first constant is that division is slow, and in a tight loop, the constant avoids the divide operation. Also, the constant makes it easier to read and understand than just a magic number. The second comment simply defines the freezing point of water.

Exercise 3 Solution

An lvalue is the memory address of a given variable that has been defined. The rvalue is what is stored at that memory address. If a variable has an lvalue that is `null`, that variable is not defined and therefore the entry is simply an attribute list for the data item. This is a data declaration. A non-`null` lvalue means the variable is defined. In this case, the data item has an attribute list, but exists in memory and is defined for use in the program.

Exercise 4 Solution

The size of the bucket depends upon the type of data that is defined. The bucket must be large enough to hold the number of bytes associated with the data item. The key elements of the Bucket Analogy are:

➤ The memory location of the bucket is the data item's lvalue.

➤ The contents of the bucket are the data item's rvalue.

➤ The size of the bucket equals the number of bytes necessary to store the data item in memory.

Exercise 5 Solution

The code could be written as:

```
using System;
using System.Windows.Forms;

public class frmMain : Form
{
    private TextBox txtOperand1;
    private TextBox txtOperand2;
    private Label label2;
    private Button btnCalc;
    private Button btnExit;
    private TextBox txtResult;
    private Label label1;
    #region Windows code
    private void InitializeComponent()
    {
        this.label1 = new System.Windows.Forms.Label();
        this.txtOperand1 = new System.Windows.Forms.TextBox();
        this.txtOperand2 = new System.Windows.Forms.TextBox();
        this.label2 = new System.Windows.Forms.Label();
        this.btnCalc = new System.Windows.Forms.Button();
        this.btnExit = new System.Windows.Forms.Button();
        this.txtResult = new System.Windows.Forms.TextBox();
        this.SuspendLayout();
        //
        // label1
        //
```

```
this.label1.BorderStyle = System.Windows.Forms.BorderStyle.Fixed3D;
this.label1.Location = new System.Drawing.Point(5, 22);
this.label1.Name = "label1";
this.label1.Size = new System.Drawing.Size(169, 20);
this.label1.TabIndex = 0;
this.label1.Text = "Item price:";
this.label1.TextAlign = System.Drawing.ContentAlignment.MiddleRight;
//
// txtOperand1
//
this.txtOperand1.Location = new System.Drawing.Point(180, 22);
this.txtOperand1.Name = "txtOperand1";
this.txtOperand1.Size = new System.Drawing.Size(100, 20);
this.txtOperand1.TabIndex = 1;
//
// txtOperand2
//
this.txtOperand2.Location = new System.Drawing.Point(180, 48);
this.txtOperand2.Name = "txtOperand2";
this.txtOperand2.Size = new System.Drawing.Size(100, 20);
this.txtOperand2.TabIndex = 3;
//
// label2
//
this.label2.BorderStyle = System.Windows.Forms.BorderStyle.Fixed3D;
this.label2.Location = new System.Drawing.Point(5, 47);
this.label2.Name = "label2";
this.label2.Size = new System.Drawing.Size(169, 20);
this.label2.TabIndex = 2;
this.label2.Text = "Number of units purchased:";
this.label2.TextAlign = System.Drawing.ContentAlignment.MiddleRight;
//
// btnCalc
//
this.btnCalc.Location = new System.Drawing.Point(5, 120);
this.btnCalc.Name = "btnCalc";
this.btnCalc.Size = new System.Drawing.Size(75, 23);
this.btnCalc.TabIndex = 4;
this.btnCalc.Text = "&Calculate";
this.btnCalc.UseVisualStyleBackColor = true;
this.btnCalc.Click += new System.EventHandler(this.btnCalc_Click);
//
// btnExit
//
this.btnExit.Location = new System.Drawing.Point(205, 120);
this.btnExit.Name = "btnExit";
this.btnExit.Size = new System.Drawing.Size(75, 23);
this.btnExit.TabIndex = 5;
this.btnExit.Text = "E&xit";
this.btnExit.UseVisualStyleBackColor = true;
this.btnExit.Click += new System.EventHandler(this.btnExit_Click);
//
// txtResult
//
this.txtResult.Location = new System.Drawing.Point(5, 82);
```

```
        this.txtResult.Name = "txtResult";
        this.txtResult.ReadOnly = true;
        this.txtResult.Size = new System.Drawing.Size(275, 20);
        this.txtResult.TabIndex = 6;
        this.txtResult.TextAlign = System.Windows.Forms.HorizontalAlignment.Center;
        this.txtResult.Visible = false;
        //
        // frmMain
        //
        this.ClientSize = new System.Drawing.Size(292, 165);
        this.Controls.Add(this.txtResult);
        this.Controls.Add(this.btnExit);
        this.Controls.Add(this.btnCalc);
        this.Controls.Add(this.txtOperand2);
        this.Controls.Add(this.label2);
        this.Controls.Add(this.txtOperand1);
        this.Controls.Add(this.label1);
        this.Name = "frmMain";
        this.StartPosition = System.Windows.Forms.FormStartPosition.CenterScreen;
        this.Text = "Figure Sales Tax Due";
        this.ResumeLayout(false);
        this.PerformLayout();

    }
    #endregion

    const decimal SALESTAXRATE = .06M;     // Sales tax rate for state

    public frmMain()
    {
        InitializeComponent();
        txtResult.Visible = false;
    }

    public static void Main()
    {
        frmMain main = new frmMain();
        Application.Run(main);
    }


    private void btnCalc_Click(object sender, EventArgs e)
    {

        bool flag;

        decimal operand1;
        decimal operand2;
        decimal answer;
        decimal salesTax;

        flag = decimal.TryParse(txtOperand1.Text, out operand1);
        if (flag == false) {
            MessageBox.Show("Enter a whole number", "Input Error");
            txtOperand1.Focus();
```

```
                return;
        }

        flag = decimal.TryParse(txtOperand2.Text, out operand2);
        if (flag == false) {
            MessageBox.Show("Enter a whole number", "Input Error");
            txtOperand2.Focus();
            return;
        }

        answer = operand1 * operand2;
        salesTax = answer * SALESTAXRATE;


        txtResult.Text = "Sales tax due on sale of " + answer.ToString() + " units
                                                is " + salesTax.ToString();

        txtResult.Visible = true;

    }

    private void btnExit_Click(object sender, EventArgs e)
    {
        Close();
    }

}
```

By using SALESTAXRATE as a symbolic constant, it makes it easier to adjust the rate for other states or if the current state's sales tax rate changes.

Exercise 6 Solution

```
using System;
using System.Windows.Forms;

public class frmMain : Form
{
    private TextBox txtAmount;
    private TextBox txtMonths;
    private Label label2;
    private Button btnCalc;
    private Button btnExit;
    private TextBox txtResult;
    private TextBox txtInterestRate;
    private Label label3;
    private Label label1;
    #region Windows code
    private void InitializeComponent()
    {
            this.label1 = new System.Windows.Forms.Label();
            this.txtAmount = new System.Windows.Forms.TextBox();
            this.txtMonths = new System.Windows.Forms.TextBox();
            this.label2 = new System.Windows.Forms.Label();
            this.btnCalc = new System.Windows.Forms.Button();
            this.btnExit = new System.Windows.Forms.Button();
```

```
this.txtResult = new System.Windows.Forms.TextBox();
this.txtInterestRate = new System.Windows.Forms.TextBox();
this.label3 = new System.Windows.Forms.Label();
this.SuspendLayout();
//
// label1
//
this.label1.BorderStyle = System.Windows.Forms.BorderStyle.Fixed3D;
this.label1.Location = new System.Drawing.Point(5, 22);
this.label1.Name = "label1";
this.label1.Size = new System.Drawing.Size(169, 20);
this.label1.TabIndex = 0;
this.label1.Text = "Loan amount:";
this.label1.TextAlign = System.Drawing.ContentAlignment.MiddleRight;
//
// txtAmount
//
this.txtAmount.Location = new System.Drawing.Point(180, 22);
this.txtAmount.Name = "txtAmount";
this.txtAmount.Size = new System.Drawing.Size(100, 20);
this.txtAmount.TabIndex = 1;
this.txtAmount.Text = "150000";
//
// txtMonths
//
this.txtMonths.Location = new System.Drawing.Point(180, 48);
this.txtMonths.Name = "txtMonths";
this.txtMonths.Size = new System.Drawing.Size(100, 20);
this.txtMonths.TabIndex = 3;
this.txtMonths.Text = "360";
//
// label2
//
this.label2.BorderStyle = System.Windows.Forms.BorderStyle.Fixed3D;
this.label2.Location = new System.Drawing.Point(5, 47);
this.label2.Name = "label2";
this.label2.Size = new System.Drawing.Size(169, 20);
this.label2.TabIndex = 2;
this.label2.Text = "Number of months for loan:";
this.label2.TextAlign = System.Drawing.ContentAlignment.MiddleRight;
//
// btnCalc
//
this.btnCalc.Location = new System.Drawing.Point(5, 167);
this.btnCalc.Name = "btnCalc";
this.btnCalc.Size = new System.Drawing.Size(75, 23);
this.btnCalc.TabIndex = 4;
this.btnCalc.Text = "&Calculate";
this.btnCalc.UseVisualStyleBackColor = true;
this.btnCalc.Click += new System.EventHandler(this.btnCalc_Click);
//
// btnExit
//
this.btnExit.Location = new System.Drawing.Point(205, 167);
this.btnExit.Name = "btnExit";
```

```
this.btnExit.Size = new System.Drawing.Size(75, 23);
this.btnExit.TabIndex = 5;
this.btnExit.Text = "E&xit";
this.btnExit.UseVisualStyleBackColor = true;
this.btnExit.Click += new System.EventHandler(this.btnExit_Click);
//
// txtResult
//
this.txtResult.Location = new System.Drawing.Point(5, 129);
this.txtResult.Name = "txtResult";
this.txtResult.ReadOnly = true;
this.txtResult.Size = new System.Drawing.Size(275, 20);
this.txtResult.TabIndex = 6;
this.txtResult.TextAlign = System.Windows.Forms.HorizontalAlignment.Center;
this.txtResult.Visible = false;
//
// txtInterestRate
//
this.txtInterestRate.Location = new System.Drawing.Point(180, 74);
this.txtInterestRate.Name = "txtInterestRate";
this.txtInterestRate.Size = new System.Drawing.Size(100, 20);
this.txtInterestRate.TabIndex = 8;
this.txtInterestRate.Text = "6";
//
// label3
//
this.label3.BorderStyle = System.Windows.Forms.BorderStyle.Fixed3D;
this.label3.Location = new System.Drawing.Point(5, 73);
this.label3.Name = "label3";
this.label3.Size = new System.Drawing.Size(169, 20);
this.label3.TabIndex = 7;
this.label3.Text = "interest rate (e.g., .06):";
this.label3.TextAlign = System.Drawing.ContentAlignment.MiddleRight;
//
// frmMain
//
this.ClientSize = new System.Drawing.Size(292, 222);
this.Controls.Add(this.txtInterestRate);
this.Controls.Add(this.label3);
this.Controls.Add(this.txtResult);
this.Controls.Add(this.btnExit);
this.Controls.Add(this.btnCalc);
this.Controls.Add(this.txtMonths);
this.Controls.Add(this.label2);
this.Controls.Add(this.txtAmount);
this.Controls.Add(this.label1);
this.Name = "frmMain";
this.StartPosition =
        System.Windows.Forms.FormStartPosition.CenterScreen;
this.Text = "Figure Sales Tax Due";
this.ResumeLayout(false);
this.PerformLayout();

    }
```

```
#endregion

const decimal INTERESTRATEASMONTHLYRATE = 1200.0M;
public frmMain()
{
    InitializeComponent();
    txtResult.Visible = false;
}

public static void Main()
{
    frmMain main = new frmMain();
    Application.Run(main);
}


private void btnCalc_Click(object sender, EventArgs e)
{

    bool flag;

    decimal amount;
    decimal months;
    decimal interest;
    decimal denominator;
    decimal payment;


    flag = decimal.TryParse(txtAmount.Text, out amount);
    if (flag == false) {
        MessageBox.Show("Enter a whole number", "Input Error");
        txtAmount.Focus();
        return;
    }

    flag = decimal.TryParse(txtMonths.Text, out months);
    if (flag == false) {
        MessageBox.Show("Enter a whole number", "Input Error");
        txtMonths.Focus();
        return;
    }
    flag = decimal.TryParse(txtInterestRate.Text, out interest);
    if (flag == false) {
        MessageBox.Show("Enter decimal number: 6 percent interest rate is 6",
                                                        "Input Error");
        txtInterestRate.Focus();
        return;
    }

    /*
     *    payment = (rate +  (interestRate / (1.0 + interestrate)^months - 1)
                                                            * amount

     */
```

```
        interest /= INTERESTRATEASMONTHLYRATE;
        denominator = (decimal) (Math.Pow((double) (1.0M + interest),
                                           (double) months) - 1.0D);
        payment = (interest + (interest / denominator)) * amount;


        txtResult.Text = "The monthly payment is: " + payment.ToString("C");
        txtResult.Visible = true;

    }

    private void btnExit_Click(object sender, EventArgs e)
    {
        Close();
    }
}
```

The statement,

```
denominator = (decimal) (Math.Pow((double) (1.0M + interest),
        (double) months) - 1.0D);
```

uses the cast operator to force the decimal data types to doubles for use in the Math.Pow() method because it expects its arguments to be double data types. However, because you assign the result into a decimal data type, you must cast the result from Pow() back to a decimal before the assignment can take place.

CHAPTER 5

Exercise 1 Solution

A value type variable is one whose rvalue is the variable's data. A reference variable has an rvalue that is the memory address of where the variable's data is to be found.

Exercise 2 Solution

```
message = message.Replace("Frday", "Friday");
```

Exercise 3 Solution

The easiest way would be to search the string for two blank spaces (" ") and use the Replace() method to replace those two blank spaces with one space (" ").

Exercise 4 Solution

Whenever you want to define a new object, that object's constructor is called to create the necessary memory space for the object and to set the properties of that object to its default values (that is, either 0 or *null*). If you want, you can write your own constructor to override the actions of the default constructor.

Exercise 5 Solution

```
public int CurrentAge(string txtBirthday)
{
    bool flag;
    int month;
    int day;
    int year;

    string temp = txtBirthday;
    flag = int.TryParse(temp.Substring(0, 2), out month);
    if (flag == false)
        return -1;
    flag = int.TryParse(temp.Substring(3, 2), out day);
    if (flag == false)
        return -1;
    flag = int.TryParse(temp.Substring(6, 4), out year);
    if (flag == false)
        return -1;
    DateTime birthdate = new DateTime(year, month, day);
    DateTime currentDate = DateTime.Now;

    int age = DateTime.Now.Year - birthdate.Year;
// subtract another year if we're before the
 // birth day in the current year
 if (DateTime.Now.Month < birthdate.Month ||
     (DateTime.Now.Month == birthdate.Month &&
     DateTime.Now.Day < birthdate.Day))
     age--;

    return age;
}
```

Exercise 6 Solution

```
clsMembers noviceMember = new clsMembers("Indianapolis", "IN");
```

In this case, you assume the club is in Indianapolis, IN. The constructor cost would then assign the two strings to the appropriate properties at the time the object is created by the constructor. The person who is then entering the club information would not need to type in the city and state data.

CHAPTER 6

Exercise 1 Solution

```
const int MAXIMUMDISCOUNTAGE = 12;
const int  MINIMUMDISCOUNTAGE = 65;
price = 6.00M;
if  (age <= MAXIMUMDISCOUNTAGE || age >= MINIMUMDISCOUNTAGE)
{
    price *= .5M;
}
```

Exercise 2 Solution

➤ Company style conventions for `if-else` statements.

➤ Placement of braces:

➤ Opening brace on `if` statement line or below it

➤ Closing `if` and opening `else` brace on same line as `else`

➤ Should single-line `if` or `else` blocks use braces at all?

➤ Is an `if-else` block the correct code choice or could some other structure (for example, a `switch`) be used.

Exercise 3 Solution

There aren't too many cases in which a cascading `if` statement is a good choice. Usually a `switch` block is clearer. However, there may be times when the `switch` value cannot be expressed as a constant. In that case, you are forced to use a cascading `if` statement.

Exercise 4 Solution

First, the test expression (`x = y`) actually uses the assignment operator rather than the (correct) relational operator (`==`). Second, the code probably should not have a trailing semicolon at the end of the first line. Third, the shorthand operator for multiply and assignment is `*=`. Finally, because the variable `price` is probably associated with money, the correct constant is `.06M`.

Exercise 5 Solution

```
const int SMALL = 1;       // Available sizes
const int MEDIUM = 2;
const int LARGE = 3;
const decimal COSTOFSMALL = 6.0M; // Cost for given size
const decimal COSTOFMEDIUM = COSTOFSMALL + 1.0M;
const decimal COSTOFLARGE = COSTOFMEDIUM + 1.0M;
switch (size)
{
   case SMALL:
     price = COSTOFSMALL;
     break;
   case MEDIUM:
     price = COSTOFMEDIUM;
     break;
   case LARGE:
     price = COSTOFLARGE;
     break;
   default:
     MessageBox.Show("No such size.);
     break;
}
```

The use of symbolic constants is not strictly necessary but can make it easier to account for any future price changes.

Exercise 6 Solution

The user interface code is left to the reader. One solution might be to call the following method:

```
public int ReturnDaysInMonth(int month, int year)
{
    int answer;
    // Assume January is month 1
    int[] days = new int[] {0, 31,28,31,30,31,30,31,31,30,31,30,31};

    answer = days[month];
    if (month == FEBRUARY)          // Assume this is defined earlier = 2
    {
          answer +=  IsLeapYear(year);
    }
    return answer;
{

public int IsLeapYear(int year)
{
    if (year % 4 == 0 & year % 100 != 0 || year % 400 == 0)
    {
          return 1;
    }
    return 0;
}
```

The `else` statement block is not needed in `IsLeapYear()` because when you know it's not a leap year, you can just `return 0`. If it were a leap year, the `return` statement prevents the `return 0` expression from being executed.

CHAPTER 7

Exercise 1 Solution

One possible solution is:

```
int factorial = 1;

for (i = num; i > 0; i--)
{
    factorial *= i;
}
lblAnswer.Text = factorial.ToString();
```

In the `for` loop, notice how the initial state of the loop is set to the number to factorial (`expression1`) and how the loop control expression (`expression3`) uses the post-decrement operator to walk "backward" through the loop.

Exercise 2 Solution

The solution shown for Exercise 1 produces the correct answers...provided you don't enter a large number to factorial. Because factorials can produce large numbers, one problem is using an int data type for variable factorial. Even a factorial as small as 13 overflows the range of an int. It would be better to use a double to extend its range.

A second, and more subtle problem, is that the test expression, i > 0, causes the loop to execute one more time than is necessary. The reason is because the last iteration of the loop ends up multiplying the current value of factorial by 1 which, of course, has no impact on the result. You can correct this inefficiency by changing the second expression of the for loop to:

```
i > 1
```

This does away with the unnecessary loop iteration that multiplies factorial by 1.

Exercise 3 Solution

```
const int FOURPOUNDS = 48;      // Ounces is 4 pounds
const double GRAMSPEROUNCE = 28.3495231;
int i;
double grams;
string buff;

for (i = 1; i <= FOURPOUNDS; i++)
{
   grams = (double) i * GRAMSPEROUNCE;
   buff = string.Format("{0, 4} {1, 15}", i, grams);
   lstResult.Items.Add(buff);
}
```

You can take this code and place it in the button click event.

Exercise 4 Solution

Because the table is constructed by increasing variable i by 1 on each pass through the loop, the expression,

```
grams = (double) i * GRAMSPEROUNCE;
```

could be replaced with the simpler,

```
grams += GRAMSPEROUNCE;
```

provided you change the definition of grams to,

```
double grams = GRAMSPEROUNCE;
```

so it is initialized as part of its definition. Now you have a simple addition taking place within the loop where there used to be a multiply and a cast.

Exercise 5 Solution

Your program should input the percent and year values in the manner you used for previous programs. Because you want to use monetary values, the `TryParse()` method is the one for the `decimal` data type.

```
int i;
int year = 10;
decimal percent = .06M;
decimal val = 100M;
string buff;
for (i = 1; i < year; i++)
{
    val *= (1.0M + percent);
    buff = string.Format("{0, 4} {1, 15:C}", i, val);
    lstResult.Items.Add(buff);
}
```

You used the `Format()` conversion for currency in the second formatting option. Of course, you wouldn't use constants in the code. The values would likely come from input textboxes.

CHAPTER 8

Exercise 1 Solution

The code has a user interface with two textboxes for getting the starting and ending heights for the table and a listbox or ListView object to present the results. The button click event code does most of the work, and one solution using a listbox is shown here.

```
const double MININCHES = 36;
const double MAXINCHES = 96;

private void btnCalc_Click(object sender, EventArgs e)
{
    bool flag;
    int i;
    int j;
    double start;
    double end;
    double male;
    double female;
    double[,] idealWeights;
    string buff;

    //=================== Input =========================
    flag = double.TryParse(txtStart.Text, out start); // Table start
    if (flag == false)
    {
```

```
      MessageBox.Show("Numeric only.");
      txtStart.Focus();
      return;
    }

    flag = double.TryParse(txtEnd.Text, out end);    // Table end
    if (flag == false)
    {
      MessageBox.Show("Numeric only.");
      txtEnd.Focus();
      return;
    }

    //=================== Validate Inputs ================
    if (start < MININCHES || start > MAXINCHES)    // Check table limits
    {
      MessageBox.Show("Table can only span " + MININCHES.ToString() +
                      " to " + MAXINCHES + " inches.");
      txtStart.Focus();
      return;
    }
    if (end < MININCHES || end > MAXINCHES)
    {
      MessageBox.Show("Table can only span " + MININCHES.ToString() +
                      " to " + MAXINCHES + " inches.");
      txtStart.Focus();
      return;
    }

    if (end <= start)         // Can we display anything?
    {
      MessageBox.Show("Starting value must be less than ending value");
      txtStart.Focus();
      return;
    }
    // Define the array for table data
    idealWeights = new double[2, (int) (end - start) + 1];


    //================== Process =====================
    female = 3.5 * start - 108;    // Set initial table values
    male = 4.0 * start - 128;

    for (i = (int)start, j = 0; i <= (int)end; i++, j++)
    {// Since linear relationships...
      idealWeights[0, j] = (female += 3.5);
      idealWeights[1, j] = (male += 4.0);
    }
    //================== Display =====================
    for (i = (int)start, j = 0; i <= (int)end; i++, j++)
    {
      buff = string.Format("{0,5}{1,15}{2,15}", i, idealWeights[0, j],
                           idealWeights[1, j]);
      lstResults.Items.Add(buff);
    }
}
```

The program validates the input values for the table. After the start and end values are determined, you can use those variables to set the array size:

```
idealWeights = new double[2, (int) (end - start) + 1];
```

Because start and end are double data types, you must cast those values to an `int` to use them to set the array size. The code then calculates the initial ideal weights for males and females. However, because the code increments the value by 1 on each pass through the loop, you can simply add 3.5 to the current female value and 4.0 to the current male value to derive the new table value. Because adding numbers is a little faster than multiplication, you get a small performance improvement. Also note how you can use the shorthand addition operators and the array reference to store the new values:

```
idealWeights[0, j] = (female += 3.5);
idealWeights[1, j] = (male += 4.0);
```

The second `for` loop simply displays the results in a listbox object. The code presented here is actually another RDC example because you would likely never write it this way in a production environment. Why? Because you could move everything into a single loop and even do away with the arrays if you wanted to. Think about it.

Exercise 2 Solution

Arrays of value types create a reference variable using the array name whose rvalue points to the starting memory address for the data array. Arrays of reference types, such as strings, create a reference variable using the array name whose rvalue points to an array of memory addresses, not the actual data. The memory addresses in the array point to the actual data for the reference object.

Exercise 3 Solution

One solution is:

```
using System;
using System.Windows.Forms;

public class frmMain : Form
{
  const int MAXVAL = 52;
  const int MAXELEMENTS = 100;

  int[] data = new int[MAXELEMENTS];
  private Button btnSort;
  private Button btnClose;
  private ListBox lstResult;
  private Button btnCalc;

  #region Windows code
  public frmMain()
  {
    InitializeComponent();
  }
```

```
public static void Main()
{
  frmMain main = new frmMain();
  Application.Run(main);
}

private void btnClose_Click(object sender, EventArgs e)
{
  Close();
}

private void btnCalc_Click(object sender, EventArgs e)
{
  int i;
  Random rd = new Random(5);      // Define a random object

  for (i = 0; i < data.Length; i++)
  {
    data[i] = rd.Next(MAXVAL);  // Get a random value
    lstResult.Items.Add(data[i].ToString());  // Put in listbox
  }
}

private void btnSort_Click(object sender, EventArgs e)
{
  int i;

  Array.Sort(data);                     // Sort the data

  lstResult.Items.Clear();              // Clear out old data

  for (i = 0; i < data.Length; i++)     // Show it
  {
    lstResult.Items.Add(data[i].ToString());
  }

}
}
```

Again, notice the use of symbolic constants. This makes it easy to change the number of items in the array. Also note that you should always use the Length property of an array to control walking through the array. That way, if you do change the array's size, the code controlling the loop does not need to be changed.

Finally, the statement,

```
data[i] = rd.Next(MAXVAL);
```

uses the Next() method of the Random class to generate a random number between 0 and MAXVAL. The set is exclusive of MAXVAL.

Exercise 4 Solution

This is actually easy to do. First, place the following definition at the top of the class:

```
static string stars = "********************************************************";
```

You can change the for loop code in the Calc event to:

```
int i;
int j;
string buff;
Random rd = new Random(5);    // Define a random object

for (i = 0; i < data.Length; i++)
{
  data[i] = rd.Next(MAXVAL);  // Get a random value
  buff = "";
  for (j = 0; j < data[i]; j++)
  {
    buff += "*";
  }
  lstResult.Items.Add(data[i].ToString() + " " + buff);
}
```

However, a better solution is:

```
for (i = 0; i < data.Length; i++)
{
  data[i] = rd.Next(MAXVAL);  // Get a random value
  buff = data[i].ToString() + " " + stars.Substring(0, data[i]);
  lstResult.Items.Add(buff);  // Put in listbox
}
```

You used the `Substring()` method of the stars string to display the proper number of stars. This is more efficient because you have done away with the inner for loop.

Exercise 5 Solution

Anytime you see an assignment statement, you should think in terms of rvalues. In this case, the rvalue of `str1` is assigned into `temp`. What this actually means is that you now have two reference variables that point to the same array of strings.

CHAPTER 9

Exercise 1 Solution

The definitions would be:

```
//============ static members ===============
private static string[] daysOfWeek = new string[] {"", "Monday",
    "Tuesday", "Wednesday","Thursday", "Friday", "Saturday",
    "Sunday"};

//============ instance members ===============
private string lastName;
private string zipCode;
```

You would want the daysOfWeek array to be static because all instances of the class could share this data. Also, we added an empty element at the front of the array because I tend to think of Monday as the first day of the week.

Exercise 2 Solution

One solution might be written as:

```
/*****
 * Purpose: Return the number of days in a given month.
 *
 * Parameter list:
 *    int month      the month   "        "
 *    int year       the year under consideration
 *
 * Return value:
 *    int            the number of days in the month or 0 on error
 *****/
public int getDaysInMonth(int month, int year)
{
    int days;

    if (month < 1 || month > 12 || year < 1 || year > 9999)
    {
        return 0;
    }
    if (month != 2)     // As long as it's not February
    {
        days = daysInMonth[month];
    }
    else
    {
        days = daysInMonth[2] + getLeapYear(year);
    }
    return days;
}
```

A discussion of this code appears in Chapter 10.

Exercise 3 Solution

I couldn't think of one, either.

Exercise 4 Solution

First, you need to define a temporary string:

```
string buff;
```

Now replace the statement with:

```
buff = year.ToString() + " is ";

if (leap == 1)     // leap is 1 for a leap year
{
    buff += "a leap year";
```

```
    } else
    {
        buff += "not a leap year";
    }
    lblLeapYearResult.Text = buff;
```

If I were writing the program, I would use the version shown here. Although the first version tests your knowledge of the ternary operator, that is not the goal for commercial code. You should design your code so that it is as easy to read as possible. Making code easy to read makes testing and debugging easier. About the only valid reason to use complex code is when you can demonstrate that the easy-to-read code executes noticeably slower than does more complex code. If that's the case, make sure you document clearly what the complex code is doing.

Exercise 5 Solution

You would create a new getLeapYear() method that overloads the existing getLeapYear() method. The new code would be:

```
public int getLeapYear()
{
    return getLeapYear(year);
}
```

Because the new constructor for clsDates can be called for the year under consideration, you can call the earlier version of getLeapYear() using the class property year as the argument. Because the two method signatures are different, Visual Studio knows which one to call based upon whether the year argument is passed.

Using a snippet of the code from Listing 9-5, you would use:

```
// clsDates myDate = new clsDates();

// Convert validate integer
flag = int.TryParse(txtYear.Text, out year);
if (flag == false)
{
    MessageBox.Show("Digit characters only in YYYY format.",
                    "Input Error");
    txtYear.Focus();
    return;
}
clsDates myDate = new clsDates(year); // Place it here!

leap = myDate.getLeapYear();          // Call overloaded method
lblLeapYearResult.Text = year.ToString() + " is " +
            ((leap == 1)? "":"not ") + "a leap year";
lblEasterResult.Text = myDate.getEaster(year);
```

With this approach, myDate is constructed passing the year variable to the constructor. You can then call the overloaded version of getLeapYear().

CHAPTER 10

Exercise 1 Solution

Because the only difference is in the range of cards, no changes are needed to either the client (frm-Main) or the server (clsCardDeck) objects. You do, however, need to change the way each card is viewed in the rules of the game. The change is quite simple: Force each ace to have a value greater than a king. This means modifying the code for getFirstCard(), getSecondCard(), and get-DealtCard() to reflect the following type of change:

```
public void getFirstCard()
{
    lowCardIndex = myDeck.getOneCard();
    lowCard = lowCardIndex % 13;
    if (lowCard == 0)                  // A King
        lowCard = 13;
    if (lowCard == 1)                  // View an Ace as high card
        lowCard = 14;
}
```

The last two lines of code must be added to each method, reflecting the card in question. This means that six new lines of code changes the way the game is played. No other changes are needed.

Exercise 2 Solution

The code shown in getFirstCard(), for example, has several magic numbers in it, which are usually not a good idea. Suppose you make the following changes to clsInBetweenRules:

```
// =============== symbolic constants ====================
const int CARDSINSUIT = 13;
const int ACE = 1;
const int KING = 13;
const int MAKEACEHIGH = 14;

// Other code in class…

public void getFirstCard()
{
    lowCardIndex = myDeck.getOneCard();
    lowCard = lowCardIndex % CARDSINSUIT;
    if (lowCard == 0)                  // A King
        lowCard = KING;
    if (lowCard == ACE)                // View an Ace as high card
        lowCard = MAKEACEHIGH;
}
```

The symbolic constants make it a little easier to read what the method is doing. Similar changes could be made to the other magic numbers in the clsInBetweenRules class code.

Exercise 3 Solution

The way clsCardDeck is presently designed, there is no way to prevent invalid cards (for example, 2 through 8) from being dealt. Also, the current state of the deck assumes that an ace is viewed as the lowest card in a suit rather than the highest as Euchre would require.

Exercise 4 Solution

Any time you face an issue like this, you need to ask where the problem lies. The way the question is phrased, it would appear that the issue is with clsCardDeck because it deals cards that should not be used in a game of Euchre. Indeed, when I pose this question to my students, one solution that is always offered is to add a method named getOneEuchreCard() to clsCardDeck. They suggest that the method can then be written so that only valid Euchre cards are returned. Although this might work, it detracts from clsCardDeck's purpose: to deal cards from a deck. Adding Euchre functionality to clsCardDeck adds a Swiss Army knife element to the class and reduces its cohesiveness.

For example, if there are one million card games in the world and each card game's quirkiness is added to clsCardDeck, how can you possibly hope to cope with its complexity?

A little thought reveals that it is the rules of Euchre that dictates which cards are valid. It is not the responsibility of clsCardDeck to determine what rules apply to each card. The tasks for clsCard-Deck remain the same: mainly, dealing a card from a shuffled deck of cards. A new class, clsEu-chreRules, should be written to enforce the valid cards returned from clsCardDeck.

Exercise 5 Solution

You could replace the shuffle button code in Listing 10-5 with the following code:

```csharp
private void btnShuffle_Click(object sender, EventArgs e)
{
    int j;
    int cardIndex;
    int cardsShown;
    int deckSize;
    int passes;
    int card;
    string buff;
    string temp;
    clsCardDeck myDeck = new clsCardDeck();

    passes = myDeck.ShuffleDeck();
    lblPassCounter.Text = "It took " + passes.ToString() +
                        " passes to shuffle the deck";

    deckSize = myDeck.DeckSize;

    cardIndex = 1;
    cardsShown = 0;
```

```
        buff = "";
        while (cardIndex < deckSize + 1)
        {
            card = myDeck.getCurrentCardIndex();
            if (card % 13 < 9 && card % 13 != 0 && card % 13 != 1)
            {
                cardIndex++;
                myDeck.IncrementCardIndex();
                continue;
            }
            temp = myDeck.getOneCard(cardIndex);
            buff += temp + "   ";
            cardIndex++;
            cardsShown++;
            if (cardsShown % 6 == 0 && cardsShown > 0)
            {
                lstDeck.Items.Add(buff);
                buff = "";
            }
        }
        lstDeck.Items.Add(" ");      // Add an empty line

}
```

You also need to add two new methods to clsCardDeck:

```
/**
* Purpose: Get the index of current card.
*
* Parameter list:
*       void
*
* Return value:
*       int      the index into the pips array
*/
public int getCurrentCardIndex()
{
    return deck[nextCard];
}
/**
* Purpose: Advance card index to next card
*
* Parameter list:
*       void
*
* Return value:
*       void
*/
public void IncrementCardIndex()
{
    nextCard++;
    if (nextCard > DECKSIZE + 1)
    {
        ShuffleDeck();
    }
}
```

CHAPTER 11

Exercise 1 Solution

The error message is:

```
Use of unassigned local variable 'x'
```

The problem is that C# doesn't want you to return a variable that has not been explicitly assigned a value. In the code, x is assigned a value only when the if statement is true. To fix the problem, you must explicitly assign x a value. The easiest fix is to change the definition of x:

```
int x = 0;
```

Exercise 2 Solution

The issue here is not that you can code the equation correctly, but rather that you make it readable for others. The first solution might be,

```
p = a  * 1 / (Math.Pow(1 + i, y));
```

and the code would compile and generate the correct values for p. However, which would you rather debug: the statement above or the following?

```
presentValue = futureAmount  * 1.0 / (Math.Pow(1.0 + interestRate,
                                       yearsIntoFuture));
```

The primary difference is the use of meaningful variable names. Another benefit is the use of numeric constants (1.0) that reflect that floating point values are used in the equation. Although you could make the argument that the decimal data type should be used because this is a financial calculation. However, the pow() method uses the double data type, so you would probably stuff this equation into a method that returned a double and let the user decide to cast it to a decimal if needed.

An alternative that makes debugging a bit easier would be:

```
discountFactor = 1.0 / (Math.Pow(1.0 + interestRate,
                                 yearsIntoFuture));
presentValue = futureAmount  * discountFactor;
```

This form uses an intermediate value (discountFactor) to simplify the code. This variation also enables you to generate a present value discount factor, the values for which can be found in published tables. This makes generating test data easier.

Exercise 3 Solution

You haven't used this style of variable definition because it discourages initialization and documentation of the variable. The pro is that is takes fewer keystrokes. That's not a strong enough argument to use that style. You should use:

```
long number = 2;    // The number of parameters
long val;           // The value of the solution
long len;           // The length of the steel bar
```

The single-statement definition discourages such comments. If you insist on using the short style, you could still comment the code using the following:

```
long number = 2,   // The number of parameters
     val,          // The value of the solution
     len;          // The length of the steel bar
```

Note the comma after the definition of number.

Exercise 4 Solution

This could be an example of the "forest-for-the-trees" problem. Hopefully you checked the obvious sources of error (for example, bogus input values) and those revealed nothing useful. It's not uncommon to look at the code so long that you are no longer actually reading the code closely enough to see what it does. That is, you've read the code so many times, your mind recognizes the patterns of the code, and you are convinced the bug is not in those familiar lines of code. Perhaps...perhaps not.

My first action for the "impossible bug" problem is to have someone else look at the code. It's not uncommon for another programmer to spot a program bug in minutes even though you've been staring at it for days. If you don't have another programmer you can call upon, simply take a long (at least 1 hour) break. Sometimes that gets your mind off the problem long enough so that when you come back, you're actually reading the code again.

Another technique is to force an exception just before you display the (erroneous) answer and have a catch block that does a stack trace. Because a stack trace shows the method calls that were made to generate the answer, you should use your test data set to examine each method in the order they are presented in the stack trace. (Remember, a stack trace shows the method calls in reverse order from last to first. This means you are working from the Output Step toward the Input Step for the Five Program Steps.) By hand calculating the value(s) that should be produced by each method call, you should isolate the method causing the error. Then just concentrate on what test values should be generated in each method until you isolate the bug. Correcting the bug is typically a simple process. It's the isolation process that eats up time.

Exercise 5 Solution

I've reached the point where I insist they use try-catch blocks in the Process Step of any program. That is the bare minimum. I also tell them that any method that does file or database I/O must be enclosed in a try-catch block. As a general rule, the two most dangerous places in a program where exceptions might lurk are in the Input and Process Steps of a program. I look for try-catch blocks in those two places.

I sometimes ask my students how they would rewrite their assignment if their code were going to be part of a mission-critical software package that manages the space shuttle. They almost always offer ideas of how they could have "tightened up" their code to make it less error prone in such circumstances. After they've presented all the improvements they could have made in their code, I ask them, "Which is more important to you: the next shuttle mission or your grade in this class?" They usually get the point.

There is no good reason not to sheathe each program you write in a protective coat of Kevlar whenever possible. It's just a good habit to get into.

CHAPTER 12

Exercise 1 Solution

The major advantage of generics is that they provide data flexibility without sacrificing strong type checking. Another advantage is that generics can avoid the overhead associated with boxing and unboxing the data. It's not uncommon for generics to provide a 100% performance increase over code that must exercise the boxing-unboxing process. Finally, the absence of generics almost always means that your code must use a lot of casts to accommodate more flexible coding practices. The "cast hassle" is avoided with generics.

Exercise 2 Solution

The first thing you would do is modify the ShowData() method along these lines:

```
private void ShowDataGeneric<T>(T[] val)
{
    int i;
    for (i = 0; i < val.Length; i++)
    {
        if (whichListbox == SORTED)
            lstSorted.Items.Add(val[i].ToString());
        else
            lstUnsorted.Items.Add(val[i].ToString());
    }
}
```

This allows you to pass in the data array that needs to be displayed. Note the use of the generic type specifier in the method's signature. Next, you would need to modify the code in the switch statements where ShowData() is used. For example, in btnSort_Click() event the code,

```
case INTEGER:                    // Integer
    clsQuickSort<int> iSort = new clsQuickSort<int>(iData);
    iSort.Sort();
    break;
```

needs to add a call to the new generic method and remove the old call to ShowData(). The next code for the integer data type would be:

```
case INTEGER:                    // Integer
    clsQuickSort<int> iSort = new clsQuickSort<int>(iData);
    iSort.Sort();
    ShowDataGeneric<int>(iData)
    break;
```

Exercise 3 Solution

This is kind of a trick question. As we have currently discussed interfaces, they indicate a guaranteed behavior or functionality as specified in the interface. You used the known behavior of the IComparable interface in your clsQuickSort code. You don't know how that functionality is implemented, only that you can rely on it being there. The trick part of the question comes into play because you discuss other advantages of interfaces when discussing inheritance in Chapter 16.

Exercise 4 Solution

The solution means that you must pass the data to be swapped into the method. One solution is

```
private void swap01<T>(T[] data, int pos1, int pos2)
{
    T temp;

    temp = data[pos1];
    data[pos1] = data[pos2];
    data[pos2] = temp;
}
```

Exercise 5 Solution

You would hope so. Just as you mentioned the role that interfaces could play in modernizing an aircraft (for example, IControls, IAvionics, and IStunts), the same concepts apply to software versioning. By encapsulating the new features inside interface declarations, you ensure that the older versions can still function, but they simply don't have the newer enhancements available to them. This approach is especially useful when enhancements alter the underlying data structures (for example, perhaps the members of a class that are persisted to disk).

CHAPTER 13

Exercise 1 Solution

There's probably a bazillion different ways to accomplish this task, of which the one here involves simple changes to the ReadAndShowRecord() method:

```
private int ReadAndShowRecord()
{
    int flag;

    try
    {
        myData.Open(myData.FileName);
        flag = myData.ReadOneRecord(currentRecord - 1);
        if (myData.Status == 0)
        {
            ClearTextboxes();
            txtRecord.Text = currentRecord.ToString() + " Not Active";
        }
        else
        {
            if (flag == 1)
            {
                ShowOneRecord();
                txtRecord.Text = currentRecord.ToString();

            }
            else
```

```
            {
                MessageBox.Show("Record not available.", "Error
                                Read");
                flag = 0;
            }
        }
    }
    catch
    {
        flag = 0;
    }

    myData.Close();
    return flag;
}
```

This solution displays the record position (currentRecord) in the txtRecord object but appends a Not Active message after clearing out all the textboxes. Presenting the information this way doesn't leave the user in the dark when an inactive record is read.

You could also put Read Active – Read All radio buttons on the form to give the user more control over reading the data.

Exercise 2 Solution

Obviously you can, or I wouldn't have asked the question. In the getRecordCount() method from Listing 13-6, delete the line,

```
records = myFile.Seek(0, SeekOrigin.End); // Position file pointer
```

and replace it with:

```
FileInfo myInfo = new FileInfo(fileName);
records = myInfo.Length;
```

This exercise simply confirms that there are almost always multiple ways to accomplish a given task. Part of the journey to becoming an experienced programmer is to learn what these alternatives are and which one offers the best solution for the task at hand.

Exercise 3 Solution

After people learn how to use random access files, they tend to throw away sequential files. You should never throw away a programming tool. Sequential files are often used for persisting non-transactions-based information. Nontransactions-based refers to those sets of data that do not require updating and editing. The density of sequential files makes them perfect correspondence types of data storage. However, when the data likely needs to be updated or otherwise edited, random access files are usually a better choice.

Exercise 4 Solution

This is sort of a trick question because there is no "right" answer. Without much conscious effort, I tend to use serialization techniques to pass an object's state to other applications that need it for their processing tasks. As such, it seems that I write one object to the file, pass it on to some other app, and that app hands it back to me with additional (or altered) information about the object's state. Perhaps it's just me and the type of programming I do, but most of the time I use serialization for temporary storage.

If I know that the object's information is going to hang around on a fairly permanent basis, like a client file, I tend to use standard read/write code. Therefore, the correct answer is, "It depends...."

Exercise 5 Solution

An About box is normally found under the rightmost menu option of MDI applications. Convention has Help as the rightmost menu option in MDI applications. Normally, the Help topic offers a means by which you can provide information about how to use the program. The last submenu item under Help is About. Therefore, the first thing you probably need to implement an About box is an application that implements the MDI interface.

Next, you need to create a new menu option, perhaps named mnuAbout. Finally, you need to add a new form to the project (frmAbout) and add labels that convey whatever information you deem desirable by the user. Finally, add the code,

```
private void mnuAbout_Click(object sender, EventArgs e)
{
    frmAbout frm = new frmAbout();
    frm.ShowDialog();
}
```

and recompile the program.

CHAPTER 14

Exercise 1 Solution

The two commands are

```
SELECT COUNT * FROM Friends WHERE status = 1
```

and

```
SELECT SUM(status) FROM Friends
```

The reason the aggregate SUM function works is because you assigned the value of 1 to an active member and 0 to inactive members. Therefore, SUM also produces a count of active members. This second form is less useful because it relies on the value of status.

Exercise 2 Solution

The SELECT statement might be written as:

```
SELECT * FROM Friends WHERE status = 1 AND ADDR2 <> '' AND State = 'IN'
```

Note that the middle expression of the WHERE predicate is two single-quotation marks, not a double-quotation mark.

Exercise 3 Solution

There are several ways to do this. First, you could create a new static class (for example, clsGlobalFriendData) and give it property members that match the data in the Friends data structure and use the property get and set methods to make the data available to clsDB. This would work because a static data item is instantiated at load time, so there is always one (and only one) instance of the class. You could then copy the data from frmAddFriend into the static class object and then let clsDB retrieve it. Although this works, it means that you always have a copy of that object hanging around chewing up resources when you may not need it. Also, there's just something about that approach that seems "messy"...sorta like using an H-bomb to kill an ant.

A less H-bombish approach would be to copy the contents of each textbox object into a string array and pass that string array to a new InsertFriend() method. A second parallel array would need to keep track of whether the string variable represented a string or numeric value. Assuming str holds the data and type holds the data type, you might have something in the InsertFriend() method that looks like:

```
public string InsertData(string[] str, int[] type, string sqlCommand)
{
    int i;

    for (i = 0; i < str.Length; i++)
    {
        switch (type[i])
        {
        case 0:                 // Numeric data
            sqlCommand += str[i] + ",";
            break;
        case 1:                 // String data
            sqlCommand += "'" + str[i] + "',";
            break;
        default:
            break;
        }
    }
    i = sqlCommand.LastIndexOf(',');    // Strip off last comma
    sqlCommand = sqlCommand.Substring(0, i) + ")";
    return str;
}
```

This assumes that the first part of the INSERT command has been built and only the textbox information needs to be added to the sqlCommand string.

Exercise 4 Solution

This is a short question with a fairly long answer. The necessary code is similar to the code found in frmQuery, which currently is:

```
private void DoQuery()
{
    try
    {
        ds = new DataSet();       // Instantiate DataSet object
```

```
        conn.Open();
        command.CommandText = txtQuery.Text;

        adapter = new OleDbDataAdapter(command);

        adapter.Fill(ds);
        dataGridView1.DataSource = ds.Tables[0];
        command.ExecuteNonQuery();
    }
    catch (Exception ex)
    {
        MessageBox.Show("Error: " + ex.Message);
    }
    finally
    {
        conn.Close();
    }
}
```

To modify the SQL query to use LINQ instead, change the code to something like

```
private void DoQuery()
{
    string buff;

    try
    {
        ds = new DataSet();       // Instantiate DataSet object
        conn.Open();
        command.CommandText = txtQuery.Text;

        adapter = new OleDbDataAdapter(command);

        adapter.Fill(ds);
        dataGridView1.DataSource = ds.Tables[0];

                                        // New stuff starts here...
        DataTable buddies = ds.Tables[0];

        IEnumerable<DataRow> query =
            from buddy in buddies.AsEnumerable()
            select buddy;
                                            // Sample output...
        foreach (DataRow myRow in query)
        {
            buff = myRow.Field<string>("LastName") + " " +
                myRow.Field<string>("Zip");
        }
    }
    catch (Exception ex)
    {
        MessageBox.Show("Error: " + ex.Message);
    }
    finally
    {
```

```
        conn.Close();
    }
}
```

The only major change is the inclusion of the `System.Collections.Generic` namespace. You must do this because in this example you did not use the `var` data type, but instead chose to use the `IEnumerable` interface using a `DataRow` object for the generic. The string variable `buff` then simply picks off two of the fields that result from the dataset using the Friends table.

CHAPTER 15

Exercise 1 Solution

To modify the SQL query to use LINQ instead, change the code to something like this:

```
private void DoQuery()
{
    string buff;

    try
    {
        ds = new DataSet();      // Instantiate DataSet object
        conn.Open();
        command.CommandText = txtQuery.Text;

        adapter = new OleDbDataAdapter(command);

        adapter.Fill(ds);
        dataGridView1.DataSource = ds.Tables[0];

                                      // New stuff starts here...
        DataTable buddies = ds.Tables[0];

        IEnumerable<DataRow> query =
            from buddy in buddies.AsEnumerable()
            select buddy;
                                      // Sample output...
        foreach (DataRow myRow in query)
        {
            buff = myRow.Field<string>("LastName") + " " +
                   myRow.Field<string>("Zip");
        }
    }
    catch (Exception ex)
    {
        MessageBox.Show("Error: " + ex.Message);
    }
    finally
    {
        conn.Close();
    }
}
```

Exercise 2 Solution

```
var query = from p in numbers          // The "Query"
            where p > lo && p < hi
            orderby p
            select p;
```

Exercise 3 Solution

Perhaps the simplest answer is that LINQ enables you to query across all object types whereas SQL is limited to databases. Therefore, programmers familiar with SQL can apply a good part of that knowledge directly to a LINQ implementation. Although there are ways to shoe-horn SQL queries to "fit" all object types, it would normally involve a lot of explicit casts to make things work. LINQ gives you the ability to work with various object types, yet retain strong typing of the data that comes from a query.

As you saw earlier in the chapter, var types that are often used with LINQ are not objects, but assume the type of the data used to instantiate the var variable.

CHAPTER 16

Exercise 1 Solution

Clearly this is a problem that begs for an inherited solution. The base class would be called clsMembers and would contain all the information that pertains to all members. That data would include name and mailing address, billing information, and the like. The derived classes would be clsSenior, clsRegular, clsJunior, and clsSocial. Each of these classes would have information that pertains to that class only (for example, dues rate, voting privileges, monthly food minimums, and so on.)

Exercise 2 Solution

You can tell that this line of code appears in the clsJunior class and is part of the constructor for the class. You can also tell that the base class has a similar constructor that the writer wants to call as part of setting the initial state of the object. As a general rule, the sequence displayed here is good because it shows that the writer is consistent with the initialization of new objects.

Exercise 3 Solution

Their concern is that the derived classes can directly change the value of a data item in the base class without having to be subject to any validation code that might be associated with that property's set method in the base class. This is a real concern. However, the concern, although real, is not serious. Users of the class will still go through the property's set method, and only the programmers of the derived classes can abuse this concern. If you can assume that your programming colleagues aren't out to sabotage your project, it's probably not going to be a serious problem.

Exercise 4 Solution

If you define a class using the sealed keyword, you are informing the compiler that it should not let this class be used as a base class for further inheritance. For example,

```
public sealed clsMyClass
```

prevents anyone from using clsMyClass as a base class for further inheritance.

Exercise 5 Solution

Most of the abilities of base-derived class behavior can be written without using inheritance. However, you do end up duplicating a lot of code by not using inheritance. Also, polymorphic behavior is not possible without using inheritance.

CHAPTER 17

Exercise 1 Solution

Students forget to use try-catch blocks in their code. This is especially bad for printers because they are largely electro-mechanical devices that have a lot of components that can fail. Also, running out of ink or paper is also a common issue.

Exercise 2 Solution

Threading is the ability to have more than one execution thread within the same process running in an application.

Exercise 3 Solution

It is not unusual for one process to take a fairly long period of time, such as printing. Without threading, the user is forced to sit there and wait for the process to finish. With threading, the user can do other activities while the threaded process completes its task.

Exercise 4 Solution

A BackgroundWorker is an object that enables you to easily start, control, and end a thread. BackgroundWorker objects make threading about as easy as it's going to get.

Exercise 5 Solution

Yes. There are synchronization issues to deal with, conditions that can lock up the system if done improperly (for example, deadlocks), plus other problems that can arise (that is, race conditions). These problems become more serious when the main thread is working with databases.

Exercise 6 Solution

Refactoring in Visual Studio is simply an easy way to implement changes to an existing body of code. Removing duplicate code (method extraction) and improving encapsulation are two of the most common uses of refactoring a program.

CHAPTER 18

Exercise 1 Solution

A web page is an HTML file capable of being rendered into a visual representation by a browser.

Exercise 2 Solution

Static web pages have HTML content that does not vary, whereas dynamic pages may vary their content in response to user (or other) inputs.

Exercise 3 Solution

Unlike pure HTML, ASP.NET enables special tags in the file that can be processed by the ASP engine for further processing. The instructions for this processing are located in the code-behind file. After the processing finishes, the results are then formatted as an HTML file and sent back to the client for rendering.

Exercise 4 Solution

Because of the statement,

```
interestRate /= 1200;
```

if the user does not enter a value for the interest rate (or an interest rate of zero), the program crashes.

Exercise 5 Solution

There are numerous ways to address the issue. First, it would make sense to surround all the statements in the `btnSubmit_Click()` event with a try-catch block. This would at least provide a means to prevent a program crash. Also, the content of each textbox could be examined if the `TryParse()` fails rather than just setting the payment to zero. Another possibility is to set the `txtPayment .Text` property to "interest rate error" and return from the `TryParse()` statement block. If you code in a commercial environment, there may be a company policy for such things. Otherwise, pick a method that prevents the crash yet still tells the user what went wrong.

INDEX

C

N

S